THE COLLECTED WORKS OF
ABRAHAM LINCOLN

THE COLLECTED WORKS OF

ABRAHAM LINCOLN

THE ABRAHAM LINCOLN ASSOCIATION
SPRINGFIELD, ILLINOIS

VIII

ROY P. BASLER, *EDITOR*

MARION DOLORES PRATT AND LLOYD A. DUNLAP

ASSISTANT EDITORS

RUTGERS UNIVERSITY PRESS

NEW BRUNSWICK, NEW JERSEY

SOURCES
AND LOCATION SYMBOLS

DESCRIPTION OF SOURCES

THE following symbols provide a description of sources as cited at the beginning of the first footnote to each item. In addition to the customary symbols for describing manuscripts, the editors have employed symbols or single words to identify other sources which have been cited repeatedly in the first footnote.

AD	Autograph Document
ADS	Autograph Document Signed
ADf	Autograph Draft
ADfS	Autograph Draft Signed
AE	Autograph Endorsement
AES	Autograph Endorsement Signed
AL	Autograph Letter
ALS	Autograph Letter Signed
ALS copy	Autograph Letter Signed, copied by Lincoln and preserved in his papers
Copy	Copy not by Lincoln
D	Document
DS	Document Signed
Df	Draft
DfS	Draft Signed
ES	Endorsement Signed
F	Facsimile—following any of the preceding symbols
LS	Letter Signed
P	Photostat—following any of the preceding symbols

Angle	*New Letters and Papers of Lincoln.* Compiled by Paul M. Angle. Boston and New York: Houghton Mifflin Company, 1930.
Herndon	*Herndon's Lincoln: The True Story of a Great Life.* By William H. Herndon and Jesse W. Weik. 3 volumes. Chicago, New York, and San Francisco: Belford, Clarke & Company, [1889].
Hertz	*Abraham Lincoln: A New Portrait.* By Emanuel Hertz. 2 volumes. New York: Horace Liveright, Inc., 1931.
Lapsley	*The Writings of Abraham Lincoln.* Edited by Arthur Brooks Lapsley. 8 volumes. New York: P. F. Collier and Son, 1905.

NH   *Complete Works of Abraham Lincoln.* Edited by John G. Nicolay and John Hay. 12 volumes. New York: Francis D. Tandy Company, 1905.

OR   *The War of the Rebellion: A Compilation of the Official Records of the Union and Confederate Armies.* 4 series; 70 "volumes"; 128 books. Washington: Government Printing Office, 1880-1901. Roman numerals are used for Series, Volume, and Part (if any); pages are in arabic.

Tarbell   *The Life of Abraham Lincoln.* . . . By Ida M. Tarbell. 2 volumes. New York: The Doubleday & McClure Company, 1900.

Tracy   *Uncollected Letters of Abraham Lincoln.* Edited by Gilbert A. Tracy. Boston and New York: Houghton Mifflin Company, 1917.

Wilson   *Uncollected Works of Abraham Lincoln.* Edited by Rufus Rockwell Wilson. 2 volumes. Elmira, New York: Primavera Press, 1947-1948.

LOCATION SYMBOLS

CCamStJ   St. John's Seminary Library, Camarillo, Calif.

CLCM   Los Angeles County Museum Library, Los Angeles, Calif.

CSmH   Henry E. Huntington Library, San Marino, Calif.

CoHi   State Historical Society of Colorado, Denver, Colo.

CoU   University of Colorado Library, Boulder, Colo.

Ct   Connecticut State Library, Hartford, Conn.

CtHi   Connecticut Historical Society, Hartford, Conn.

CtLHi   Litchfield Historical Society, Litchfield, Conn.

CtSoP   Pequot Library, Southport, Conn.

CtWat   Watertown Library Association, Watertown, Conn.

CtY   Yale University Library, New Haven, Conn.

DLC   Library of Congress, Washington, D. C.

DLC-HW   Herndon-Weik Collection, Library of Congress

DLC-RTL   The Robert Todd Lincoln Collection of the Papers of Abraham Lincoln, Library of Congress

DLM   Lincoln Museum, Ford's Theatre, National Park Service, Washington, D. C.

DNA   National Archives, Washington, D. C. All additional abbreviations and numbers given with this symbol are those employed by the National Archives at the time the manuscript was located.

DNM   National Museum Library, Washington, D. C.

DeHi	Historical Society of Delaware Library, Wilmington, Del.
DeWI	Wilmington Institute Free Library, Wilmington, Del.
I-Ar	Archives Division, Illinois State Library, Springfield, Ill.
IBloHi	McLean County Historical Society, Bloomington, Ill.
ICHi	Chicago Historical Society, Chicago, Ill.
ICU	University of Chicago Library, Chicago, Ill.
IDecJ	James Millikin University Library, Decatur, Ill.
IFre	Freeport Public Library, Freeport, Ill.
IHi	Illinois State Historical Library, Springfield, Ill.
IJI	Illinois College Library, Jacksonville, Ill.
ISLA	The Abraham Lincoln Association, Springfield, Ill.
IU	University of Illinois Library, Urbana, Ill.
IaCrM	Iowa Masonic Library, Cedar Rapids, Iowa
IaDaM	Davenport Public Museum, Davenport, Iowa
IaHA	Iowa State Department of History and Archives, Des Moines, Iowa
In	Indiana State Library, Indianapolis, Ind.
InFtwL	Lincoln National Life Foundation, Fort Wayne, Ind.
InHi	Indiana Historical Society, Indianapolis, Ind.
InLTHi	Tippecanoe County Historical Association, Lafayette, Ind.
InU	Indiana University Library, Bloomington, Ind.
KyBC	Berea College Library, Berea, Ky.
KyU	University of Kentucky Library, Lexington, Ky.
LU	Louisiana State University Library, Baton Rouge, La.
MB	Boston Public Library, Boston, Mass.
MCon	Free Public Library, Concord, Mass.
MFai	Millicent Library, Fairhaven, Mass.
MH	Harvard University Library, Cambridge, Mass.
MHi	Massachusetts Historical Society, Boston, Mass.
MS	Springfield Library Association, Springfield, Mass.
MSHi	Connecticut Valley Historical Society, Springfield, Mass.
MdAA	Hall of Records, State of Maryland, Annapolis, Md.
MdHi	Maryland Historical Society, Baltimore, Md.
MeHi	Maine Historical Society, Portland, Me.
MiD	Detroit Public Library, Detroit, Mich.
MiK-M	Kalamazoo Public Library Museum, Kalamazoo, Mich.
MiU-C	William L. Clements Library, University of Michigan, Ann Arbor, Mich.

MiU-Hi	Michigan Historical Collection, University of Michigan, Ann Arbor, Mich.
MnHi	Minnesota Historical Society, St. Paul, Minn.
MnSM	Macalester College Library, St. Paul, Minn.
MoHi	State Historical Society of Missouri, Columbia, Mo.
MoSHi	Missouri Historical Society, St. Louis, Mo.
N	New York State Library, Albany, N. Y.
NAuE	Fred L. Emerson Foundation, Auburn, N. Y.
NBLiHi	Long Island Historical Society, Brooklyn, N. Y.
NBuG	Grosvenor Library, Buffalo, New York
NBuHi	Buffalo Historical Society, Buffalo, N. Y.
NDry	Southworth Library, Dryden, N. Y.
NHi	New-York Historical Society, New York City
NIC	Cornell University Library, Ithaca, N. Y.
NN	New York Public Library, New York City
NNC	Columbia University Library, New York City
NNP	Pierpont Morgan Library, New York City
NRU	University of Rochester Library, Rochester, N. Y.
NSh	John Jermain Memorial Library, Sag Harbor, N. Y.
NSk	Skaneateles Library Association, Skaneateles, N. Y.
NWM	U. S. Military Academy Library, West Point, N. Y.
NbO	Omaha Public Library, Omaha, Nebr.
NcGu	Guilford College Library, Guilford, N. C.
NhExP	Phillips Exeter Academy, Exeter, N. H.
NjP	Princeton University Library, Princeton, N. J.
OCHP	Historical and Philosophical Society of Ohio, Cincinnati, Ohio
OClCS	Case Institute of Technology, Cleveland, Ohio
OClWHi	Western Reserve Historical Society, Cleveland, Ohio
OFH	Hayes Memorial Library, Fremont, Ohio
OMC	Marietta College Library, Marietta, Ohio
ORB	Oliver R. Barrett Collection, Chicago, Ill.*
OSHi	Clark County Historical Society, Springfield, Ohio
OrHi	Oregon Historical Society, Portland, Ore.
PHC	Haverford College Library, Haverford, Pa.
PHi	Historical Society of Pennsylvania, Philadelphia, Pa.

* After the *Collected Works* was in press, the collection of the late Oliver R. Barrett was sold at auction by Parke-Bernet Galleries (Catalog 1315) on February 19-20, 1952. It has been impossible to trace all new owners of the more than two hundred items, and impracticable to change the source citations for those which are known, but many of the more important items went to such well-known collections as those in the Library of Congress (Debates Scrapbook, purchased for the Alfred Whital Stern Collection) and Illinois State Historical Library (letters to Joshua F. Speed, etc.).

PMA	Allegheny College Library, Meadville, Pa.
PP	Free Library of Philadelphia, Philadelphia, Pa.
PPDrop	Dropsie College Library, Philadelphia, Pa.
PSt	Pennsylvania State College Library, State College, Pa.
PU	University of Pennsylvania Library, Philadelphia, Pa.
RPAB	Annmary Brown Memorial Library, Providence, R. I.
RPB	Brown University Library, Providence, R. I.
THaroL	Lincoln Memorial University, Harrogate, Tenn.
THi	Tennessee Historical Society, Nashville, Tenn.
ViU	University of Virginia Library, Charlottesville, Va.
VtU	University of Vermont Library, Burlington, Vt.
WBeloHi	Beloit Historical Society, Beloit, Wis.
WHi	State Historical Society of Wisconsin, Madison, Wis.
WvU	West Virginia University Library, Morgantown, W. Va.

APRIL 10, 1865
By Alexander Gardner

THE COLLECTED WORKS OF
ABRAHAM LINCOLN

———◀●▶———

To Isaac M. Schermerhorn[1]

Isaac M. Schemerhorn   Executive Mansion,
My dear Sir.   Washington, Sept. 12. 1864.

Yours inviting me to attend a Union Mass Meeting at Buffalo is received. Much is being said about peace; and no man desires peace more ardently than I. Still I am yet unprepared to give up the Union for a peace which, so achieved, could not be of much duration. The preservation of our Union was *not* the sole avowed object for which the war was commenced. It was commenced for precisely the reverse object—*to destroy our Union.* The insurgents commenced it by firing upon the Star of the West, and on Fort Sumpter, and by other similar acts. It is true, however, that the administration accepted the war thus commenced, for the sole avowed object of preserving our Union; and it is not true that it has since been, or will be, prossecuted by this administration, for any other object. In declaring this, I only declare what I can know, and do know to be true, and what no other man can know to be false.

In taking the various steps which have led to my present position in relation to the war, the public interest and my private interest, have been perfectly paralel, because in no other way could I serve myself so well, as by truly serving the Union. The whole field has been open to me, where to choose. No place-hunting necessity has been upon me urging me to seek a position of antagonism to some other man, irrespective of whether such position might be favorable or unfavorable to the Union.

Of course I may err in judgment, but my present position in reference to the rebellion is the result of my best judgment, and according to that best judgment, it is the only position upon which any Executive can or could save the Union. Any substantial departure from it insures the success of the rebellion. An armistice—a cessation of hostilities—is the end of the struggle, and the insurgents would be in peaceable possession of all that has been struggled for. Any different policy in regard to the colored man, deprives us of his help, and this is more than we can bear. We can not spare the hundred and forty or fifty thousand now serving us as soldiers, seamen, and laborers. This is not a question of sentiment or taste, but one of physical force which may be measured and estimated as horse-power and Steam-power are measured and estimated. Keep it and you can save the Union. Throw it away, and the Union goes with it. Nor is it possible for any Administration to retain the service of these people with the express or implied understanding that upon the first convenient occasion, they are to be re-inslaved. It *can* not be; and it *ought* not to be.

1 ADf, DLC-RTL. The draft is in pencil and unfinished. See Lincoln's telegram to Schermerhorn, September 9, *supra*, and letter, *infra*.

To Isaac M. Schermerhorn[1]

Private.   Executive Mansion,
Isaac M. Schemerhorn, Pres't &c.   Washington,
Buffalo, N.Y.   September 12th. 1864.

My dear Sir: Your letter, mentioned in your two telegrams, has not reached me; so that I am without knowledge of its particulars. I beg you to pardon me for having concluded that it is not best for me now to write a general letter to a political meeting. First, I believe it is not customary for one holding the office, and being a candidate for re-election, to do so; and secondly, a public letter must be written with some care, and at some expense of time, so that having begun with your meeting, I could not well refuse others, and yet could not get through with all having equal claims. Please tender to those you represent my sincere thanks for the invitation, and my appeal to their indulgence for having declined their request. Yours very truly.   A. LINCOLN.

1 Copy, DLC-RTL. See Lincoln's unfinished letter to Schermerhorn, *supra*.

To James G. Blaine[1]

                                 Office U.S. Military Telegraph,
Hon. J. G. Blaine   War Department,
Augusta, Maine   Washington, D.C., Sep. 13. 1864.

On behalf of the Union, thanks to Maine. Thanks to you personally for sending the news.   A LINCOLN

[2]

Send same to L. B. Smith and M. A. Blanchard, Portland, Maine.

A.L.

[1] ALS, DNA WR RG 107, Presidential Telegrams, I, 164. James G. Blaine, chairman of the Republican State Central Committee, sent two telegrams on September 12. The first was received at 8:40 P.M.: "The State Election today has resulted in a great victory for the Union Cause   Governor Cony re-elected by a large majority with the entire Cong ticket" (DLC-RTL). The second was received at 11 P.M.: "The Union majority in Maine will reach 20,000   We will give you thirty thousand (30,000) in November" (*ibid.*).

A telegram from Lewis B. Smith, chairman of the Union Committee of Cumberland County and M. A. Blanchard, secretary of the Union District Committee of Cumberland County, was received at 12 P.M.: "The First Congressional District of Maine endorses your administration. . . . The Star of the East fights it out on this line" (*ibid.*).

To Benjamin F. Butler[1]

"Cypher"
Major General Butler
Bermuda Hundred, Va.

Office U.S. Military Telegraph,
War Department,
Washington, D.C., Sept. 13. 1864.

The Ames guns I am under promise to pay, or rather to advise paying, a very high price for, provided they bear the test, and they are not yet tested, though I believe in process of being tested. I could not be justified to pay the extraordinary price without the testing. I shall be happy to let you have some of them so soon as I can. How comes on your canal?[2]   A LINCOLN

[1] ALS, DNA WR RG 107, Presidential Telegrams, I, 167. See Lincoln's order of August 21, 1864. Butler telegraphed on September 13, 1864: "I am informed that Mr Ames of Falls Village Conn has some wrought iron rifle guns of great strength & penetration which have commended themselves to your notes [notice] & that you have ordered some to be made. We need one (1) or two (2) guns of great power & penetration to use against the enemys iron clad on the James. Please permit me to order one (1) or two (2) to be rifled & forwarded here. . . ." (DLC-RTL).

[2] Lincoln probably refers to the Dutch Gap Canal being built on the James River. No reply to the question has been found.

Memorandum of Pre-election Poll[1]

Executive Mansion,
Washington, [c. September 13], 1864.
On train from Pittsburg to Harrisburg Sep. 13. 1864.

Lincoln	McClellan	Fremont
172.	66.	7.

[1] AD, DLC-Nicolay Papers.

[3]

Pass[1]

Let the Old Soldier pass according to his R.R. passes without hindrance.   A. LINCOLN.

Sept. 13, 1864.

[1] Anderson Galleries Catalog 1206, March 6, 1916, No. 388.

Pass for John Ehler[1]

September 13, 1864

Let this boy, John Ehler, have transportation, food, and whatever is necessary, to get him to his Uncle Dr. Ehler, at Cavalry Corps Hospital at City-Point, Va.   A. LINCOLN

Sep. 13. 1864.

[1] AES, DeWI. See Lincoln's endorsement of April 11, *supra*. Dr. Ehler has not been identified.

Response to Serenade[1]

September 13, 1864

Mr. Lincoln made a brief response, to the effect that he was not prepared to acknowledge the honor done him in a set speech. We had heard the right sort of speeches from Vermont and Maine lately, and previously from Mobile and Atlanta, and he was much in favor of hearing more of the same sort from the South.

He then thanked the assemblage and bade them farewell, upon which they took up the line of march for Mr. Seward's residence.

[1] Washington *Daily National Republican*, September 14, 1864. Following a Republican celebration at the Mount Vernon Hotel, where a banner forty feet long and twenty-six feet wide, bearing the names of Lincoln and Johnson, was run out from the hotel across Pennsylvania Avenue, the crowd paraded to the Executive Mansion and serenaded the president.

To William S. Rosecrans[1]

Major General Rosecrans   Executive Mansion,
St. Louis, Mo.   Washington, Sept 13, 1864.

Postpone the execution of S. H. Anderson for two weeks. Hear what his friends can say in mitigation and report to me.

A. LINCOLN

Maj. Eckert

Please send the above telegram.   JNO. G. NICOLAY   Priv. Sec.

[1] D, DNA WR RG 107, Presidential Telegrams, I, 165. The telegram, including Lincoln's signature, is in Nicolay's handwriting. Although the White House

ledger of court-martial cases lists the case of S. H. Anderson, citizen of Missouri, sentenced to death for being a guerrilla, as respited on February 9, 1865, to hard labor for the duration of the war, no record of the case has been found in the Judge Advocate General's files. (DNA WR RG 153).

To William S. Rosecrans[1]

Major General Rosecrans;   Executive Mansion,
St Louis   Washington, September 13th, 1864.
Postpone the execution of Joseph Johnson, for two weeks. Examine the case and report.   A. LINCOLN

Major Eckert:
Please send the above telegram.   JNO. G. NICOLAY   Priv: Sec

[1] D, DNA WR RG 107, Presidential Telegrams, I, 166. The telegram is in Edward D. Neill's handwriting, except the signatures which are in Nicolay's hand. The last entry on the case of Joseph Johnson, citizen of Missouri, sentenced to death for being a guerrilla, notes the respite of two weeks granted by Lincoln on September 13, 1864 (DNA WR RG 153, Judge Advocate General, NN 2126).

To Edward Bates[1]

Attorney General please make out a pardon in this case.
Sep. 14. 1864.   A. LINCOLN

[1] AES, DNA RG 204, U.S. Pardon Attorney, A 549. Lincoln's endorsement is written on a letter of Samuel S. Woods, Lewistown, Maine, September 12, 1864, introducing Mrs. Ellen Contner, who wished to ask a pardon for her son, Albert Contner, "convicted of manslaughter nearly three years since. . . . The young man volunteered among the first in the defence of Washington . . . & the offence was committed . . . under the influence of liquor. . . ."

Endorsements Concerning William Elmore[1]

September 14, 1864
If this man's Colonel will say in writing on this sheet that he is willing to receive him back into his regiment I will pardon and send him.   A LINCOLN
Sep. 14. 1864

According to the foregoing, this man is pardoned and ordered to his regiment.   A LINCOLN
Oct. 10. 1864

[1] AES, owned by Herman Smith, Grand Rapids, Michigan. Lincoln's endorsements are written on the back of a certificate signed by Justice of the Peace Frederick A. Boswell, Washington, D.C., September 14, 1864: "This is to certify that I know William Elmore, a private Soldier in Company D, Second District

of Columbia, who was convicted by Court Marshall and sentenced to be confined at fort-Delaware. he has a wife and one child who is perfectly destitute and any thing that can be done for her relief would be a charitable act."

Apparently William Elmore's wife could not get action from the commander of the regiment. Following Lincoln's first endorsement, she wrote, "Col will you Be so kind as to take William Elmore Back in the Regiment he is in prisen at fort Delaware Col the presdent sa if you would be willing to take him back in the Regiment he wold pardon him i have got a little Child an no one to help me look on this sheet you will see the president writing Col you must ancer me on this note and send it back as soon as you can to me

"Col will you be so kind to me as to take him back as I have no frends in Washinton no one to help me Mrs Frances C Elmore"

On October 11, Elmore was ordered to be released and returned to his regiment (AGO *Special Orders No. 342*).

To Herman H. Heath[1]

Major H. H. Heath   Executive Mansion
Baltimore, Md.   Washington, Sep. 15. 1864
  You are hereby authorized to visit Washington.

A. LINCOLN.

[1] ALS, DNA WR RG 107, Presidential Telegrams, I, 169. Major Herman H. Heath, Seventh Iowa Cavalry, was detailed to visit Baltimore and Washington on special business for Major General Samuel R. Curtis, commanding at Fort Leavenworth (Headquarters Department of Kansas, *Special Orders No. 191*, September 6, 1864, MS., RPB).

Memorandum:
Appointment of Wilbur R. Bacon[1]

[September 15, 1864]
Wilbur R. Bacon, born March 25. 1844, applies for West-Point— has two brothers in the Army, and is excellently well recommended. Resides in Conn.

[1] AE, DNA WR RG 94, U.S. Military Academy, 1863, No. 185. Lincoln's endorsement is written on an envelope with recommendations of Wilbur R. Bacon of New Haven, Connecticut. No record of his appointment has been found.

Reply to Eustorjio Salgar[1]

September 15, 1864
GEN. SALGAR: It is with very sincere satisfaction that I learn that peace and tranquillity have returned to the United States of Colombia. I fervently desire that your country may long continue to enjoy these great blessings, which are so essential to public happiness and to the progress of civilization, which is the great interest of all American States.

[6]

We have had the pleasure of knowing your respected President intimately at this capital, and thus we have been very well assured that whomsoever he should accredit as his representative here would be found not only a true patriot, but also a liberal friend to the United States and a firm supporter of republican institutions throughout the American Continent.

Your public character has preceded you here, sir, and I am happy in recognizing you, on this occasion, as such a Minister as this Government has so confidently expected. Be assured, sir, that no effort on my part will be spared to render your mission successful and satisfactory to yourself and to your enlightened countrymen.

1 Washington *Daily National Republican*, September 16, 1864. Substantially the same text appeared in other Washington papers. Lincoln replied to a brief speech made by General Eustorjio Salgar upon presenting his credentials as minister from Colombia.

To James B. Steedman[1]

Major General Steadman   Executive Mansion
Chattanooga, Tenn.   Washington, Sept 15. 1864

Mrs. McElrath, of East Tennessee is here saying she has been sent away by your order, and appealing to me to allow her to return to her home. I have told her I will if you say so. What say you?   A. LINCOLN

1 ALS, DNA WR RG 107, Presidential Telegrams, I, 168. No reply from General James B. Steedman has been discovered, and Mrs. McElrath has not been identified.

On October 27, however, Nathaniel G. Taylor wrote Lincoln of Mrs. McElrath's return to Knoxville: "Mrs McElrath (widow of Major McE. late of the rebel army) who recently had an interview with you at Washington, waited on . . . Brig Gen. S[amuel] P. Carter at Knoxville E.T. to take the oath of Amnesty, and speaking of yourself stated 'When Gen. Carters name was mentioned President Lincoln remarked "that he did not think Genl. C. was any better friend of his than she Mrs McE. was". . . .'" (DLC-RTL).

To William P. Fessenden[1]

September 16, 1864

If it is compatable for William M. [W.] Orme, to be appointed to the Vicksburg agency under the new rules, in addition to the appointment you have already given him, I shall be obliged to have it done.

1 Parke-Bernet Catalog 905, December 1-2, 1947, No. 278. According to the catalog description the text is from an autograph letter signed. The Treasury regulations referred to were those approved by Lincoln on July 30, *supra*. On September 6, 1864, Leonard Swett and others wrote:

"We . . . hereby recommend William W. Orme of Bloomington Illinois as a suitable man to be appointed an agent of the Government to get out cotton for the United States.

"We know him to be a man of strict integrity and honor.

"We would recommend that he be stationed at or near Vicksburgh Miss. . . ." (DLC-RTL).

Orme is listed in the U.S. *Official Register,* 1865, as "Supervising Special Agent" of the Treasury, at Memphis, Tennessee.

To James B. Fry[1]

Provost-Marshal-General: September 16, 1864

Please see and hear these gentlemen, who say that by an adjustment—settlement, so to speak—the aggregate quota for Illinois is 16,184 men, while by some result of sub-districting the draft is about to be enforced for 29,797.

Please look into this and correct the error if it exists, or make for me an intelligible statement; show no error to exist.

                                                                    A. LINCOLN.

[1] OR, III, IV, 702. Lincoln's endorsement was written on a petition presented by the Union State Central Committee of Illinois and the Grand Council of the Union League of Illinois, September 8, 1864, complaining of the draft quotas for the state. The petition is endorsed by Thomas J. Turner, chairman of the Central Committee, and Samuel H. Melvin, commissioner of the Union League: "If the Provost-Marshal-General will make a reduction of 50 per cent. upon the quotas of every sub-district where a draft has been ordered in Illinois, it will be satisfactory to the people of that State and settle difficulty in regard to the apportionment."

To Joseph Holt[1]

Judge Advocate General please examine & report on this case.

Sep. 16. 1864   A. LINCOLN

[1] AES, DNA WR RG 153, Judge Advocate General, NN 2393. Lincoln's endorsement is written on papers in the case of N. C. Trowbridge, convicted on charges of violating laws and customs of war and furnishing aid to the enemy, and sentenced to ten years' imprisonment. Holt opposed any mitigation of the sentence.

To Franz Sigel[1]

Major General Sigel   Executive Mansion,
Bethlehem, Pa.   Washington, Sep. 16, 1864.

You are authorized to visit Washington, on receipt of this.

                                                                    A. LINCOLN

[1] ALS, DNA WR RG 107, Presidential Telegrams, I, 172. Sigel replied on the same day: "I have the honor to acknowledge the receipt of your Telegram, saying that I am authorized to visit Washington. As I have made no application

[8]

to this effect I respectfully request you to inform me by letter or Telegraph, whether you wish or direct that I should come . . . in which case I would of course proceed there immediately. . . ." (DLC-RTL).

On September 19, Sigel telegraphed Nicolay: "Your dispatch recd today. I will leave for Washington tomorrow morning the twentieth. . . ." (*Ibid.*).

To John P. Slough[1]

Office U.S. Military Telegraph,
Gen. Slough,   War Department,
Alexandria, Va   Washington, D.C., Sep. 16, 1864.

On the 14th. I commuted the sentence of Conly, but fearing you may not have received notice I send this. Do not execute him.

A. LINCOLN

[1] ALS, DNA WR RG 107, Presidential Telegrams, I, 170. See Lincoln to Smith, September 8, *supra*. General Slough's telegram, dated September 15 and marked as received on September 15, 9:35 A.M., reads: "I recd in due time the notification that Conleys sentence had been commuted by you & will act accordingly" (DLC-RTL).

To William Sprague[1]

Office U.S. Military Telegraph,
Hon. William Sprague   War Department,
Providence, R.I.   Washington, D.C., Sep. 16. 1864.

I commuted the sentence of Conley two days ago.

A. LINCOLN

[1] ALS, DNA WR RG 107, Presidential Telegrams, I, 171. See Lincoln to Smith, September 8, *supra*. Sprague's telegram, received at 9:55 A.M., reads: "Circumstances indicate the innocence of Sergt Conley of R I sentenced to be shot today   Will you stay his sentence" (DLC-RTL).

To William T. Sherman[1]

Major General Sherman   Executive Mansion
Atlanta, Ga.   Washington, D.C. Sep. 17. 1864

I feel great interest in the subjects of your despatch mentioning corn and Sorghum, & a contemplated visit to you.

A LINCOLN

[1] ALS, DNA WR RG 107, Presidential Telegrams, I, 173. On September 15, 1864, Sherman had telegraphed Halleck: "My report is done, and will be forwarded as soon as I get a few more of the subordinate reports. I am awaiting a courier from General Grant. . . . Governor Brown has disbanded his militia, to gather the corn and sorghum of the State. I have reason to believe that he and Stephens want to visit me, and I have sent them a hearty invitation. I will exchange 2,000 prisoners with Hood, but no more." (OR, I, XXXIX, II, 381).

At 6 P.M. on September 17, he replied to Lincoln:

"I will keep the Department fully advised of all developements as connected with the subject in which you feel so interested. A Mr. [Augustus R.] Wright, former member of Congress from Rome Ga and a Mr. [William] King of Marietta are now going between Gov Brown and myself. I have said that some of the people of Georgia are now engaged in rebellion begun in error and per-petuated in pride; but that Georgia can now save herself from the devastation of war preparing for her, only by withdrawing her quota out of the confederate army, and aiding me to repel Hood from the border of the State; in which event instead of desolating the land, as we progress I will keep our men to the high roads and commons, and pay for the corn and meat we need and take. I am fully conscious of the delicate nature of such assertions, but it would be a magnificent stroke of policy, if I could without wasting a foot of ground or of principle arouse the latent enmity to Jeff Davis, of Georgia.

"The people do not hesitate to say, that Mr. Stevens was, and is, a Union man at heart, and they feel that Jeff Davis will not trust him, or let him have a share in his government." (DLC-RTL).

The visit of Governor Joseph E. Brown and Alexander H. Stephens did not materialize.

To Ethan A. Hitchcock[1]

September 19, 1864.

The writer of this, who appeals for his brother, is our minister to Ecuador, and whom, if at all compatible, I would like to have obliged by a special exchange of his brother. A. LINCOLN.

[1] OR, II, VIII, 30. Lincoln's endorsement is on a letter from Frederick Has-saurek, September 17, 1864, enclosing a letter from his half-brother, Lieutenant Leopold Markbreit, originally of the Twenty-eighth Ohio Volunteers and acting assistant adjutant general on General William W. Averell's staff when captured. Markbreit wrote from Libby Prison, July 10, 1864: "My situation could not be worse. I have become so weak and broken down from close confinement and want of food that I can hardly walk. Our daily ration consists of one-half pound of corn bread, one-half pound of boiled beans, and about two or three ounces of bacon. . . . I cannot say how long we shall be able to live on such rations. . . ." This same letter from Markbreit is printed elsewhere in the *Official Records* with the following endorsement by Charles A. Dana, October 10, 1864: "Respectfully referred to the Commissary-General of Prisoners, with directions to subject the officer held as hostage for the within-named prisoner to the same treatment." (OR, II, VII, 457). Not until January 5 was an exchange effected, on which date General Grant telegraphed Stanton, "Will you please say to the President that Lieutenant Markbreit has been released from prison and is now on his way North." (OR, II, VIII, 811).

To Joseph Holt[1]

This application being for the present denied I have allowed the applicant to withdraw the papers filed by him. A. LINCOLN

Sept. 19, 1864

[1] Copy, DNA WR RG 153, Judge Advocate General, LL 2292. The record in the case of First Lieutenant Edward P. McCreary, One Hundred Forty-third Pennsylvania Volunteers, dismissed from service, who had appealed for rein-statement, quotes the above endorsement as appearing on the application.

Memorandum[1]

[c. September 19, 1864]

A despatch of Gen. Sherman, dated Sep. 17, 1864 among other things, says

"The Secretary of War tells me the draft will be made on Monday next. If the President modifies it to the extent of one man, or waivers in it's execution he is gone ever. The Army would vote against him"

[1] AD, DLC-RTL. The telegram from which Lincoln inaccurately quotes is printed in OR, I, XXXIX, II, 396. See Stanton's correct quotation in the note to Lincoln's letter to Sherman, *infra.*

To William T. Sherman[1]

Executive Mansion, Washington, D.C.

Major General Sherman,   September 19th, 1864.

The State election of Indiana occurs on the 11th. of October, and the loss of it to the friends of the Government would go far towards losing the whole Union cause. The bad effect upon the November election, and especially the giving the State Government to those who will oppose the war in every possible way, are too much to risk, if it can possibly be avoided. The draft proceeds, notwithstanding its strong tendency to lose us the State. Indiana is the only important State, voting in October, whose soldiers cannot vote in the field. Any thing you can safely do to let her soldiers, or any part of them, go home and vote at the State election, will be greatly in point. They need not remain for the Presidential election, but may return to you at once. This is, in no sense, an order, but is merely intended to impress you with the importance, to the army itself, of your doing all you safely can, yourself being the judge of what you can safely do. Yours truly   A. LINCOLN

[1] LS, InFtwL; LS copy, DLC-RTL. See Lincoln's memorandum, *supra.* On September 12, 1864, Governor Morton, Indiana Republicans in congress, and others wrote Stanton:

". . . we express it as our profound conviction that upon the issue of the election that occurs within a month from this date may depend the question as to whether the secession element shall be effectually crushed or whether it shall acquire strength enough, we do not say to take the state out of the Union, but practically to sever her from the general government, so far as future military aid is concerned.

"We further express the gravest doubts as to whether it will be possible for us to secure success at the polls on the 11th of October unless we can receive aid—

"1. By delay of the draft until the election has passed.

"2. By the return, before election day, of fifteen thousand Indiana soldiers. . . ." (William Dudley Foulke, *Life of Oliver P. Morton,* I, 367).

On September 18 Stanton replied:

"It appears from a dispatch received from General Sherman last night that his army is jealously watching whether the draft will be suspended or enforced. The general says:

" 'If the President modifies it to the extent of one man, or wavers in its execution, he is gone. Even the army would vote against him.'

"You can judge from this what effect the recall of troops and delaying the draft is likely to have on your election." (OR, III, IV, 732).

See further Lincoln to Morton, October 13, *infra*.

To John C. Ten Eyck[1]

Hon. J. C. Ten Eyck   Executive Mansion,
My dear Sir.   Washington, Sep. 19, 1864.

Dr. J. R. Freese, now editor of a leading Union Journal in New-Jersey, resided, for a time, in Illinois, when & where I made his acquaintance, and since when I have enjoyed much of his friendship. He is somewhat wounded with me now, that I do not recognize him as he thinks I ought. I wish to appoint him a Provost-Marshal in your State. May I have your approval? Yours truly

A. LINCOLN

[1] ADfS, DLC-RTL. See Lincoln to James B. Fry, September 27, *infra*.

To Isachar Zacharie[1]

Dr. Zacharie   Executive Mansion,
Dear Sir   Washington, Sep. 19, 1864.

I thank you again for the deep interest you have constantly taken in the Union cause. The personal matter on behalf of your friend, which you mention, shall be fully and fairly considered when presented. Yours truly   A. LINCOLN.

[1] ADfS, DLC-RTL. Zacharie wrote Lincoln on September 21, 1864:

"Yours of the 19th came duly to hand. It has had the desiered effect, with the friends of the *parties*.

"I leave tomorrow for the interior of Pennsylvania. May go as far as Ohio. One thing is to be done. And that is for you to impress on the minds of your friends for them not to be so sure." (DLC-RTL). No satisfactory clues have been discovered to this cryptic letter.

To George G. Meade[1]

Majr Gen Meade   Executive Mansion
Hd Qurs Army Potomac.   Sept. 20th. 1864

If you have not executed the sentence in the case of private Peter Gilner Co. F. 62. Penn vols, let it be suspended until further orders. Report to me.   A. LINCOLN.

[1] LS, DNA WR RG 107, Presidential Telegrams, I, 175. See Lincoln to Meade, April 27, *supra.* Meade replied the same day: "Your dispatch relative to Peter Gelner [*sic*] . . . received. He is not now in this Army. His sentence was commuted by me to confinement at Dry Tortugas under your order. . . ." (DLC-RTL). See Lincoln to Moorhead, October 16, *infra.*

To Philip H. Sheridan[1]

"*Cyphcr*" Executive Mansion,
Major General Sheridan Washington,
Winchester, Va Sep. 20. 1864.

Have just heard of your great victory. God bless you all, officers and men. Strongly inclined to come up and see you.

A. LINCOLN

[1] ALS, DLC (on deposit). The original manuscript of this telegram was removed from the file of presidential telegrams and presented to General Sheridan on January 20, 1877, a certified copy replacing it (DNA WR RG 107, Presidential Telegrams, I, 174). Now on deposit in the Library of Congress, the autograph telegram is owned by the Sheridan heirs. On September 19 Sheridan had telegraphed Grant: "I have the honor to report that I attacked the forces of Genl Early over the Berryville Pike at the crossing of Opequan Creek, and after a most stubborn and sanguinary engagement . . . completely defeated him . . . driving him through Winchester, capturing about twenty five hundred (2500) prisoners—five (5) of artillery, nine (9) Army flags and most of their wounded. . . ." (DLC-RTL).

To Edwin M. Stanton[1]

Hon. Sec. of War Executive Mansion,
Dear Sir Washington, Sep. 20, 1864.

Let Mallison, the bogus proclamation man, be discharged. Yours truly A. LINCOLN

[1] ALS, DNA WR RG 94, Adjutant General, Letters Received, P 1064. Stanton endorsed on the bottom of the page "Adjt Genl will issue the order immediately to Gen Dix as directed by the Prest." Also endorsed on the bottom of the page is the telegram of Edward D. Townsend, September 22, directing General Dix to discharge Francis A. Mallison, who had collaborated with Joseph Howard, Jr., in producing the "bogus proclamation" of May 17, 1864 (see Lincoln to Dix, May 18, *supra*).
Among several letters in the Lincoln Papers suggesting the propriety of releasing Mallison is the following from Joseph Howard, Jr.:
"I have once intruded upon your cares to thank you for your kindness in granting an order for my release from . . . Fort Lafayette & to assure you of my sincere regret at my folly & its consequences; permit me to call your attention to the case once more in behalf of the young man who was placed there at the same time as myself, but who was not included in the order for release. . . .
"I regret to say that certain 'Democratic' stumpers are making a handle of his continued confinement, taking the absurd ground that he is held on account of his Democratic affiliations.
"Mr. Mallison has an aged Mother dependent upon him, was no deeper (nor

so deep) in the foolishness . . . than I, and has felt very keenly his position & its consequences. May I . . . urge you to direct his immediate discharge . . . ?" (DLC-RTL).

To Edwin M. Stanton[1]

September 20, 1864

The bearer will present the list of names contemplated within. The Provost Marshal General will please take the proper steps to have them examined, mustered in and discharged from prison, so as to be properly credited all according to the within.

Sept 20. 1864   A. LINCOLN

[1] Copy, IHi; OR, III, IV, 680. This endorsement was written on Lincoln's order to Huidekoper, September 1, *supra*. The date September 20, 1864, is given on the official copy, but the *Official Records* print it without date. On September 10, S. Newton Pettis had written Lincoln from Rock Island, Illinois, where he had gone with Lincoln's order of September 1. Colonel Huidekoper not being able to be there "for a day or two," Pettis had shown the order to the commandant:

"The first remark he made was, that he had often wondered why the Government had not allowed recruiting for the army before, as well as for the Navy. The second remark was that there would be a difficulty . . . for this reason. When the first body of men were recruited for the Navy, about a hundred who had *volunteered and taken the oath of allegiance* were rejected by the surgeon as unfit, and were at once discharged. The next party recruited for the Navy in the same way, about the same number rejected & the order for their discharge was revoked, consequently they were thrown back into prison and have been abused by the rabid and malicious secesh so that many are afraid to come out for . . . volunteering, lest they are rejected. . . .

"I read your order over again . . . and gave it as my opinion that you never intended to have a man *remanded* after he had volunteered and taken the oath even if he was rejected. . . . I also told him to say to those who feared that result if they took the oath and volunteered & were rejected by the Surgeon that they would be discharged. I have no doubt the letter & spirit of your order warranted such a request. . . ." (DLC-RTL).

On September 22, Captain Henry R. Rathbone of the Twelfth U.S. Infantry was ordered to Rock Island to make a "special inspection, under instructions to be given him by the Provost Marshal General" of the prisoners to be enlisted (AGO *Special Orders No. 315*), and on the same date Lincoln wrote Grant in explanation of his action (*vide infra*).

To Edward R. S. Canby[1]

Executive Mansion, Washington,

Major General Canby   Sep. 21. 1864.

Gen. Baily, of Rapides Parish, Louisiana, is vouched to me as entirely trustworthy, and appeals to me in behalf of the people in his region, who he says are mostly Union people, and are in great destitution—almost absolute starvation. He says their condition is greatly aggravated by Gen. Banks' expedition up Red-River, last

Spring, in reliance upon which they mostly took the oath of allegiance. Of course what Gen. Baily asks is permission to carry provisions to them. This I will not give without your consent; but I will thank you to hear and consider their case, and do for them the best you can, consistently with the interests of the public service.
Yours truly   A. LINCOLN

[1] ADfS, DLC-RTL. A letter of Crafts J. Wright, Willard's Hotel, to Thomas Corwin, September 20, 1864, explains Lincoln's letter:

"Gen Baily has explained to me his application to the President to allow him to collect in New Orleans and send to his empoverished friends in the Parish of Rapides La. food & raiment. Will you allow me to say to the President through you in regard to this mission.

"From many years intercourse in Louisiana I have a large acquaintance & this has been renewed the last nine months of being in N O. I have seen hundreds, who have been in the Red River country, since the withdrawal of Gen Banks and the vials of confederate wrath have been poured upon those who were *seduced* into open & manifest efforts of co operation, *believing* they would be protected. Hundreds & hundreds of the friends of the President . . . have been reduced to beggary. . . . The enemy have no supplies to give—and these people *must* starve if their friends in N O will not be allowed to send them food. You cannot *I know* carry on this . . . through officers of Government. . . . They will allow a responsible *citizen* . . . to go on such a mission & protect in the delivery to them it is designed for . . . but it cannot be done *officially*. . . .

"I know Gen B. he is entirely reliable & knows the wants of his neighbours. . . . Why not then allow him to collect gratuitously & take the donations of food & raiment. . . ." (DLC-RTL).

General Canby did not reply to Lincoln's letter until December 19:

"Genl Baily has just handed me your note of Sept. 24 [*sic*] in relation to the destitute union people in the neighborhood of Alexandria La. I would long since have sent supplies to them . . . if I could have had even a doubtful assurance that they would have reached their destination, or that they could have been applied to the benefit of those for whom they were intended, but my own convictions have been confirmed by the assurances of loyal persons living within the rebel lines, that any attempt of this kind would not be to their benefit and would only compromize them with the rebel authorities, and that any general system of supplying the inhabitants beyond the lines would have no other result than to prolong the war and their own suffering.

"The policy of the rebels in this respect is unrelenting. . . . I am satisfied that until we can break the armed power of the rebels we can do nothing that will not aid our enemies and injure our friends.

"My own sympathies have run strongly counter to my judgment and it has been with great pain that I have felt myself constrained to pursue a different course, not only as a question of policy, but (in the end) one of humanity. . . ." (*Ibid.*).

General Baily has not been further identified.

To Charles A. Dana[1]

Will Mr. Dana please see this young lady, and let her know the grounds on which her friends are detained at Fort-Warren.
Sep. 21. 1864   A. LINCOLN

[1] ALS, DLC-RTL. Dana endorsed, "These men are confined as bushwhackers, guerrillas, and persons who cannot be at large consistently with the public

safety. They were 50 committed on the recommendation of Gen. [John H.] Martindale." The young lady was Maggie K. Ryan, who wrote Lincoln on September 28, 1864:

"According to your orders I have atlass succeeded in getting the charges of my friends and have also had them disputed, as you will see which is all that I could posibly do and now my onely hopes is with you who I am in hopes will faivour thair release——in regard to my intercesion in thair behalf you will allow me to state that it is an intimacy from childhood and knowing them inocint of any crimes subjecting them to the misiries and sufferings they have undergone for the last twelve mounths

"Again I am bitroth of Geo. W Jamison the last act of my dieing Mother was to join our hand with a pray for our union which was to have been the thirtieth of Sept 1863 I am an orphand of poor but I am happy to say honerable ancestors I cam to this city a perfect stranger the 31 of March with the hope of affecting the release of my friend it was by the persuation of their Mother and sisters that I ever undertook sutch a task I am here now without . . . homer friends or money and I trust that you having the power you have to make One happy for life would not see them sink to misery and shame

"With the hopes that you may condesend to think your humble applicant worthy of your consideration I am with respect you most Obedient" (DLC-RTL).

George W. Jameson and David Jameson, imprisoned in Fort Warren, were citizens of Culpeper, Virginia.

To Ethan A. Hitchcock[1]

Executive Mansion Washington,

Gen. Hitchcock   Sep. 21, 1864

Please see the bearer Mr. Broadwell, on a question about a mutual supplying of clothes to prisoners   Yours truly

A. LINCOLN

[1] ALS-P, ISLA. On September 12, 1864, M. M. Broadwell of New York City wrote to Colonel William Hoffman, commissary general of prisoners: "I propose to effect an arrangement by which both the Federal and rebel prisoners shall be furnished with blankets and clothing. . . . My personal relations with most of the rebel officials, and my family connections with some, enable me to negotiate this matter with the rebel authorities. I propose, therefore, . . . to go to Richmond and get the consent of the rebel authorities to receive and distribute such blankets and clothing as the United States Government will furnish to the prisoners now held at the South. . . ." (OR, II, VII, 814-15).

On October 3, Charles A. Dana sent Broadwell a pass permitting him to go through the lines on his mission (ibid., p. 920).

To Joseph Holt[1]

September 21, 1864

Judge Advocate General please procure record and report on this case.   A. LINCOLN

Sep. 21. 1864

Pardon for unexecuted part of sentence   A. LINCOLN

Sept. 29. 1864

[16]

[1] AES, DNA WR RG 153, Judge Advocate General, NN 2094. Lincoln's endorsements are written on papers in the case of Private John (Jonas) Steed, Fifteenth West Virginia Volunteers, sentenced on charges of disobedience of orders and conduct prejudicial to good order, to serve the remainder of his enlistment at hard labor, forfeit all pay, etc. Holt recommended remitting remainder of punishment.

To Gustavus V. Fox[1]

Will Capt. Fox please see the bearer & examine the model he will present?   A. LINCOLN

Sep. 22. 1864

[1] ALS-P, ISLA. The bearer has not been identified.

To Ulysses S. Grant[1]

Executive Mansion, Washington,
Lieut. General Grant   Sep. 22, 1864.

I send this as an explanation to you, and to do justice to the Secretary of War. I was induced, upon pressing application, to authorize agents of one of the Districts of Pennsylvania to recruit in one of the prisoner depots in Illinois; and the thing went so far before it came to the knowledge of the Secretary of War that in my judgment it could not be abandoned without greater evil than would follow it's going through. I did not know, at the time, that you had protested against that class of thing being done; and I now say that while this particular job must be completed, no other of the sort, will be authorized, without an understanding with you, if at all. The Secretary of War is wholly free of any part in this blunder. Yours truly   A. LINCOLN

[1] ALS-P, ISLA; ADfS, DLC-RTL. See Lincoln's order to Huidekoper, September 1, and to Stanton, September 20, *supra*. On September 25 Stanton telegraphed Grant substantially the same information contained in Lincoln's letter of September 22, and Grant replied on the same day: "Your dispatch in relation to the organization of troops from prisoners of war is just received. I would advise that they be placed all in one regiment, and be put on duty either with Pope, or sent to New Mexico." (OR, III, IV, 744).

On September 26, S. Newton Pettis wrote Lincoln from Meadville, Pennsylvania:

"Nothing ever helped our cause here as your order, and the manner which you have so justly sustained it when assailed has quickened their efforts and renewed their energies. . . .

"I go to Rock Island by next train. I fear the War Department has sent a man out to embarrass our action, and if so shall telegraph you directly. . . . I asked when I left that nothing be said but there was no such thing as bridleing the tongues or pens of our people. Their gratitude will be mannifested at the Polls. . . .

"I pray you for the sake of our cause which is the cause of the country, allow no embarrassment to the execution of the order." (DLC-RTL).

See further Lincoln's order to Fry, October 8, *infra*.

To Joseph Holt[1]

September 22, 1864

Judge Advocate General please report on this case.

Sep. 22. 1864. A. LINCOLN

Pardon for unexecuted part of sentence upon party returning to his regiment and faithfully serving out his term.

Sep. 24. 1864 A. LINCOLN

[1] AES, DNA WR RG 153, Judge Advocate General, NN 1844. Lincoln's endorsements are written on papers in the case of Private Peter King, Company F, Ninth Veteran Reserve Corps, sentenced to two years at hard labor. Holt reported that King had served six months and had a previous good record.

To Montgomery Blair[1]

Hon. Montgomery Blair Executive Mansion,
My dear Sir. Washington, Sep. 23. 1864.

You have generously said to me more than once, that whenever your resignation could be a relief to me, it was at my disposal. The time has come. You very well know that this proceeds from no dissatisfaction of mine with you personally or officially. Your uniform kindness has been unsurpassed by that of any friend; and, while it is true that the war does not so greatly add to the difficulties of your Department, as to those of some others, it is yet much to say, as I most truly can, that in the three years and a half during which you have administered the General Post-Office, I remember no single complaint against you in connection therewith. Yours

A. LINCOLN

[1] ADfS, DLC-RTL. Blair replied on the same day:

"I have received your note of this date, referring to my offers to resign whenever you should deem it advisable for the public interests that I should do so and stating that in your judgment that time has now come.

"I now, therefore, formally tender my resignation of the Office of Postmaster General.

"I can not take leave of you without renewing the expressions of my gratitude for the uniform kindness which has marked your course towards, Yours very truly, M. BLAIR" (DLC-RTL).

Montgomery Blair's unpopularity with the radical Republicans, Frémont's supporters in particular, is borne out by numerous letters in the Lincoln Papers which recommend his removal. Undoubtedly Lincoln's action was prompted by his desire to consolidate Republican support in the forthcoming election. A letter of Francis P. Blair, Jr., to his father, September 30, 1864, reads: "I received yours and my sisters letter yesterday giving an account of late transactions in Washington. I feel in regard to the matter precisely as you do. Indeed before I received your letter my instincts told me that my brother had acted his part for the good of the country and for the re-election of Mr. Lincoln in which the safety of the country is involved I believe that a failure to re-elect Mr. Lincoln would be the greatest disaster that could befall the country and the sacrifice made by the Judge to avert this is so incomparably small that I felt it would not cost him a penny to make. Indeed the only sacrifice involved in it appears to be the triumph which it gives to our enemies & the enemies of the Presidents. It is somewhat mortifying to reflect that this triumph has been given to those who are equally the enemies of the President & 'the Blairs' but at the same time the Judge leaves the cabinet with an untarnished name and the reputation of having administered the Dept with the greatest ability & success and that as far as worldly considerations go, it is far better for him to go out than to remain in the cabinet. This is rather a contrast to the position of Chase, Fremont & all the rest of the enemies & persecutors of the 'Blairs'. . . ." (DLC-RTL).

Memorandum Concerning Alfred G. Lawrence[1]

September 23, 1864

I have said that if satisfactory evidence is brought to me, with this paper, that A. G. Lawrence, named within, is *non compos* mentis, I will discharge him   A. LINCOLN

Sep. 23. 1864

[1] AES, RPB. Lincoln's endorsement is written on the back of a telegram of Provost Marshal Alonzo D. Pratt, Harpers Ferry, September 22, to Provost Marshal Timothy Ingraham: "Private Alfred G. Lawrence alias Wright was forwarded to B Gen [Marsena R.] Patrick PM Gen A of P on the 19th Aug. I have forwarded papers containing endorsement &c concerning him this day." On October 12 John Hay telegraphed Major General Meade: "The President directs suspension of execution in case of Albert [*sic*] G. Lawrence 16th Mass. Vols until his further order."

To Frank W. Ballard[1]

Office U.S. Military Telegraph,
Frank W. Bollard   War Department,
New-York   Washington, D.C., Sep. 24 1864.

I shall be happy to receive the deputation you mention.

A. LINCOLN

[1] ALS, DNA WR RG 107, Presidential Telegrams, I, 177. A copy marked "repeated," received at New York on September 26, 4:55 P.M. is in the Lincoln Papers (DLC). Frank W. Ballard, whose name Lincoln misspelled because of an incorrect signature on the telegram received, was corresponding secretary of the Young Men's Republican Union of New York. His telegram of September 24 reads: "A deputation from the New York Young Mens republican union desires a brief interview on tuesday next will it be convenient & agreeable to you to grant it. Please reply by telegraph" (DLC-RTL).

To William Dennison[1]

"Cypher" Office U.S. Military Telegraph,
Gov. William Dennison War Department,
Columbus, Ohio Washington, D.C., Sep. 24 1864.

Mr. Blair has resigned, and I appoint you Post-Master General.
Come on immediately. A. LINCOLN

[1] ALS, DNA WR RG 107, Presidential Telegrams, I, 176. Noah H. Swayne
replied on the same day: "Mrs Dennison requests me to say that the Governor
is filling appointments in south eastern ohio away from any telegraph line &
that he will return on monday or tuesday He has been absent a week" (DLC-
RTL). William Dennison telegraphed on September 27: "I expect to leave for
Washington Thursday so as to reach there Friday to enter upon the duties of
the office with which you have honored me." (*Ibid.*).

Executive Order Relative to the Purchase of Products of Insurrectionary States[1]

Executive Mansion, September 24, 1864.

I. Congress having authorized the purchase for the United States
of the products of States declared in insurrection, and the Secretary
of the Treasury having designated New Orleans, Memphis, Nashville, Pensacola, Port Royal, Beaufort, North Carolina, and Norfolk,
as places of purchase, and, with my approval, appointed agents
and made regulations under which said products may be purchased: Therefore,

II. All persons, except such as may be in the civil, military, or
naval service of the government, having in their possession any
products of States declared in insurrection, which said agents are
authorized to purchase, and all persons owning or controlling such
products therein, are authorized to convey such products to either
of the places which have been hereby, or may hereafter be, designated, as places of purchase, and such products, so destined, shall
not be liable to detention, seizure, or forfeiture, while in transitu
or in store waiting transportation.

III. Any person having the certificate of a purchasing agent, as
prescribed by Treasury Regulation VIII, is authorized to pass, with
the necessary means of transportation to the points named in said
certificate, and to return therefrom with the products required for
the fulfilment of the stipulations set forth in said certificate.

IV. Any person having sold and delivered to a purchasing agent
any products of an insurrectionary State, in accordance with the
regulations in relation thereto, and having in his possession a certificate setting forth the fact of such purchase and sale, the charac-

[20]

ter and quantity of products, and the aggregate amount paid therefor, as prescribed by Regulation IX, shall be permitted by the military authority commanding at the place of sale to purchase from any authorized dealer at such place, or any other place in a loyal State, merchandise, and other articles not contraband of war, nor prohibited by order of the War Department, nor coin, bullion, or foreign exchange, to an amount not exceeding in value one third of the aggregate value of the products sold by him as certified by the agent purchasing; and the merchandise and other articles so purchased may be transported by the same route, and to the same place, from and by which the products sold and delivered reached the purchasing agent, as set forth in the certificate, and such merchandise and other articles shall have safe conduct, and shall not be subject to detention, seizure, or forfeiture while being transported to the places and by the routes set forth in the said certificate.

V. Generals commanding military districts, and commandants of military posts and detachments, and officers commanding fleets, flotillas, and gunboats, will give safe conduct to persons and products, merchandise, and other articles duly authorized as aforesaid, and not contraband of war, or prohibited by order of the War Department, or the orders of such generals commanding, or other duly authorized military or naval officer, made in pursuance hereof, and all persons hindering or preventing such safe conduct of persons or property will be deemed guilty of a military offense and punished accordingly.

VI. Any person transporting, or attempting to transport, any merchandise or other articles except in pursuance of regulations of the Secretary of the Treasury, dated July 29, 1864, or in pursuance of this order, or transporting or attempting to transport any merchandise or other articles contraband of war or forbidden by any order of the War Department, will be deemed guilty of a military offence and punished accordingly; and all products of insurrectionary States found in transitu to any other person or place, than a purchasing agent, and a designated place of purchase shall be seized and forfeited to the United States, except such as may be moving to a loyal State under duly authorized permits of a proper officer of the Treasury Department, as prescribed by Regulation XXXVIII, concerning "commercial intercourse," dated July 29, 1864, or such as may have been found abandoned, or have been captured, and are moving in pursuance of the act of March 12, 1864.

VII. No military or naval officer of the United States, or person in the military or naval service, nor any civil officer, except such as are appointed for that purpose, shall engage in trade or traffic in the products of insurrectionary States, or furnish transportation therefor under pain of being deemed guilty of unlawful trading with the enemy and punished accordingly.

VIII. The Secretary of War will make such general orders or regulations as will insure the proper observance and execution of this order, and the Secretary of the Navy will give instructions to officers commanding fleets, flotillas, and gunboats in conformity therewith.   ABRAHAM LINCOLN.

[1] Thirty-eighth Congress, Second Session, *House of Representatives Executive Document No. 3, Report of the Secretary of the Treasury*, pp. 348-49.

To William P. Fessenden[1]

Executive Mansion, September 24, 1864.
The foregoing rules and regulations of the Secretary of the Treasury, having been seen and considered by me, are hereby approved.
ABRAHAM LINCOLN.

[1] Thirty-eighth Congress, Second Session, *House of Representatives Executive Document No. 3*, p. 347. Lincoln's endorsement approved the Treasury's *General Regulations for the Purchase of Products of the Insurrectionary States on Government Account*, September 24, 1864.

To Joseph Holt[1]

Executive Mansion, Washington,
Judge Advocate General.   Sep. 24, 1864.
It is said that Simon Ready has recently been tried by one of our Military courts in this city. I can tell no more of the case; but his poor wife is bothering me & I will thank you, if practicable, to procure the record & report on the case. Yours truly

A. LINCOLN

[1] ALS, owned by Henry R. Benjamin, New York City. Simon Ready has not been identified, and no reply from Holt has been found.

To George H. Bragonier[1]

Geo. H. Bragonier,   Office U.S. Military Telegraph,
commanding at   War Department,
Cumberland, Md.   Washington, D.C. Sep. 25. 1864.
Postpone the execution of Private Joseph Provost until Friday the 30th. Instant.   A. LINCOLN.

[1] ALS, DNA WR RG 107, Presidential Telegrams, I, 178. Captain George H. Bragonier had telegraphed on September 23, 1864: "Gen [George] Crook by

order has fixed next Sabbath day twenty fifth (25) inst at twelve (12) o'clock in Cumberland for the execution of Joseph Provost private First (1) N York Cavy. Shall the order be carried into effect on Sunday?" (DLC-RTL).

To Henry W. Hoffman[1]

H. W. Hoffman.   Executive Mansion,
Baltimore, Md.   Washington, Sep 25, 1864.

Please come over and see me to-morrow, or as soon as convenient.

A. LINCOLN

[1] ALS, DNA WR RG 107, Presidential Telegrams, I, 179. See Lincoln to Hoffman, October 10, *infra*.

To Edward Bates[1]

I think this has been acted upon. Please file.

Sep. 26. 1864   A. LINCOLN

[1] AES, DNA RG 60, Papers of Attorney General, Appointments, Kentucky, Box 479. Lincoln's endorsement is written on a letter from Joshua Tevis, January 14, 1864, recommending appointment of William A. Merriwether as U.S. marshal for Kentucky. See Lincoln to Bates, January 23, *supra*.

To Edward Bates[1]

Let pardon issue in this case.   A. LINCOLN

Sep. 26. 1864

[1] AES, DNA WR RG 204, U.S. Pardon Attorney, A 553. Lincoln's endorsement is written on a petition of members of the jury, Washington, September 3, 1863, asking executive clemency for a Negro boy Nicholas Warner, whom they had sentenced at the May term of court to imprisonment for two years on charges of assault and battery. Marshal Ward H. Lamon endorsed the petition in concurrence on January 18, 1864.

To Stephen G. Burbridge[1]

Major General Burbridge   Executive Mansion,
Lexington, Ky.   Washington, Sep 26. 1864.

Terrible complaints are being made as to the discharge of Meade at Louisville. Please report the particulars of the case, including grounds of discharge.   A. LINCOLN

[1] ALS, DNA WR RG 107, Presidential Telegrams, I, 180. J. Bates Dickson, Burbridge's assistant adjutant general, telegraphed on September 27: "Gen Burbridge is absent with his command & cannot be communicated with at present No one here knows any thing in regard to the discharge of Mead. . . ." (DLC-RTL).

No further reference to Meade (or Mead) has been found.

[23]

To Joseph Holt[1]

Judge Advocate General please report.

Sep. 26. 1864.   A. LINCOLN

[1] AES, DNA WR RG 153, Judge Advocate General, NN 2273. Lincoln's endorsement is written on papers in the case of George W. Brown, citizen of Washington, fined $500 for running Negroes away to Baltimore to make them enlist. Holt reported in favor of clemency and Lincoln remitted the sentence on October 8, 1864.

Pass for Mrs. Defoe[1]

Allow this lady, Mrs. Defoe, to pass and have transportation from Washington to New-York.   A. LINCOLN

Sep. 26, 1864

[1] ADS; RPB. Mrs. Defoe has not been identified.

To William S. Rosecrans[1]

Executive Mansion,
Major General Rosecrans,   Washington, Sep. 26, 1864

One can not always safely disregard a report, even which one may not believe. I have a report that you incline to deny the soldiers the right of attending the election in Missouri, on the assumed ground that they will get drunk and make disturbance. Last year I sent Gen. Schofield a letter of instruction, dated October 1st, 1863, which I suppose you will find on the files of the Department, and which contains, among other things, the following:

"At elections see that those and only those, are allowed to vote, who are entitled to do so by the laws of Missouri, including as of those laws, the restrictions laid by the Missouri Convention upon those who may have participated in the rebellion."

This I thought right then, and think right now; and I may add I do not remember that either party complained after the election, of Gen. Schofield's action under it. Wherever the law allows soldiers to vote, their officers must also allow it. Please write me on this subject. Yours truly,   A. LINCOLN.

[1] Copy, DLC-RTL; copy, DNA WR RG 94, Adjutant General, Letters Received, P 1575. On October 3, 1864, Rosecrans wrote:

"In reply to your favor of the 26th ult. notwithstanding the reports you have received to the contrary, I have the honor to inform you that I have not nor ever had the slightest idea of preventing soldiers in my Department from attending the elections whenever and wherever they may have a legal right to vote, without neglecting paramount military duties. On the contrary I shall take such measures as . . . will most effectually secure to them and to every legal voter the right of voting according to the laws of the state. . . .

"I have have [sic] before me the orders and instructions to which you refer They seem good in principle and I shall prepare and publish one that will give satisfaction to all honest union men." (DLC-RTL).

To Edwin M. Stanton[1]

Hon. Sec. of War   Executive Mansion,
My dear Sir   Washington, Sep. 26. 1864.
    Have you, as yet definitely concluded whether the order prohibiting the exportation of arms shall be recinded?
    Please answer by bearer. Yours truly   A. LINCOLN

[1] ALS, NHi. No reply has been found.

To Benjamin F. Butler[1]

Major General Butler   Executive Mansion,
Bermuda Hd. Va.   Washington, Sep. 27, 1864.
    Assistant Surgeon Wm. Crouse is here complaining that you have dismissed him and ordered him out of the Department. Please telegraph me briefly the reasons.   A. LINCOLN

[1] ALS, DNA WR RG 107, Presidential Telegrams, I, 183. Butler replied the same day: "Asst Surg William Crouse has deceived the President. He has not been dismissed. He received an appointment as Asst Surge from me in writing he refused to accept the appointment which was thereupon revoked because of his refusal to accept it. Then finding that he was drinking & worthless & as some thought crazy I ordered him out of the Department. I will forward official copies of the papers tomorrow." (DLC-RTL).

To William Dennison[1]

                                        Office U.S. Military Telegraph,
Gov. Wm. Dennison   War Department,
Columbus, O.   Washington, D.C., Sep. 27 1864.
    Yours received. Come so soon as you can.   A. LINCOLN

[1] ALS, DNA WR RG 107, Presidential Telegrams, I, 182. See Lincoln to Dennison, September 24, *supra*. Dennison telegraphed from Steubenville, Ohio, on September 29: "Failed make railroad connection here will delay my arrival at Washington" (DLC-RTL).

To James B. Fry[1]

                                        Executive Mansion, Washington,
Provost-Marshal General   Sep. 27, 1864.
    Please let the appointment of Jacob R. Freese, as Commissioner of Board of Enrollment for 2nd. Dist. of New-Jersey, in place of

Mr. Wilson resigned, be made at once. Senator Ten Eyck is agreed to it. I have his letter to that effect, though I can not at this moment lay my hands on it. Yours truly   A. LINCOLN

¹ ALS-P, ISLA. See Lincoln to Ten Eyck, September 19, *supra*. James Wilson resigned as commissioner of enrollment for the Second District of New Jersey on September 2, and Freese, appointed on September 27, served until honorably discharged on April 30, 1865.

To Ulysses S. Grant¹

Executive Mansion   September 27. 1864
Respectfully referred to Lieutenant General Grant for his consideration and decision.   A. LINCOLN˙

¹ ES, DLC-RTL. Lincoln's endorsement is written on the following letter from William H. Kent, September 27, 1864: "In July last, my Pass as Army Correspondent of the N.Y. Tribune was revoked by order of Lt. Gen. Grant, at the request, I believe of Maj. Gen. Meade. I am not conscious of and certainly did not intend to write aught but what was true and proper for publication. Since that time the order relating to Mr. Wm. Swinton of the N.Y. Times who was sent from the Army at the same time has been rescinded by Gen. Meade. In behalf of the Tribune and myself I have respectfully to ask that similar action be taken in my case."
Endorsements by General George G. Meade and General Winfield S. Hancock (October 4 and 7) indicate that Kent had submitted false and injurious reports on Hancock's command, and Grant's endorsement of October 10 reads: "The most liberal facilities are afforded to newspaper correspondents, but they cannot be permitted to misrepresent facts to the injury of the service. When they so offend their pass . . . is withdrawn. . . . In this case there appears to have been a deliberate attempt to injure one of the best Generals and Corps in the service. I cannot therefore consent to Mr. Kent's return to this army."

To Andrew Johnson¹

Gov. Johnson   Executive Mansion
Nashville, Tenn.   Washington, Sep. 27. 1864
I am appealed to in behalf of Robert Bridges, who it is said is to be executed next Friday. Please satisfy yourself, and give me your opinion as to what ought to be done.   A. LINCOLN

¹ ALS, DNA WR RG 107, Presidential Telegrams, I, 184. See Lincoln to Johnson, September 7, *supra*. Governor Johnson telegraphed on September 28: "In reply to your despatch referring to Thos R Bridges who is to be executed on Friday the thirtieth inst I will say from all the information I have upon the subject that a commutation to confinement in the Penitentiary at hard labor during his natural life is the utmost extent that Executive Clemency should be extended at this time" (DLC-RTL).
See further Lincoln's communications to Miller, September 29, and to McClelland, December 24, *infra*.

Memorandum Concerning Edward Middleton[1]

September 27, 1864

When evidence shall be brought to me, with this paper, that the father has procured a substitute who shall have been duly mustered in, I will discharge the son.   A. LINCOLN

Sep. 27. 1864

[1] AES, OSHi. Lincoln's endorsement was written on a request from E. C. Middleton for exchange and discharge of his son Edward Middleton, Company I, Fourth Ohio Volunteers, age sixteen, who had enlisted as a bugler but had been assigned duties as a private before being captured. The father offered to furnish a substitute.

To William T. Sherman[1]

"Cypher"   Office U.S. Military Telegraph,
Major General Sherman   War Department,
Atlanta, Ga.   Washington, D.C., Sept. 27 1864.

You say Jeff. Davis is on a visit to Hood. I judge that Brown and Stephens are the objects of his visit.   A. LINCOLN

[1] ALS, DNA WR RG 107, Presidential Telegrams, I, 181. See Lincoln to Sherman, September 17, *supra.* Sherman had telegraphed Halleck on September 26: "I have re-enforced my line back as far as Chattanooga; but in Middle Tennessee we are weak. . . . I would like to have any regiments in Indiana or Ohio sent to Nashville. . . . Jeff. Davis is on a visit to [John B.] Hood at Palmetto." (OR, I, XXXIX, II, 479). On September 28, he replied to Lincoln:
"I have positive knowledge that Jeff Davis made a speech at Macon on the 22nd. . . . It was bitter against [Joseph E.] Johnston & Govr Brown. The militia is now on furlough. Brown is at Milledgeville trying to get a legislature to meet next month but he is afraid to act unless in concert with other Governors.
"Judge Wright of Rome has been here and Messrs [Joshua] Hill and [Thomas A. R.] Nelson former members of our Congress are also here now and will go to meet Wright at Rome and then go back to Madison and Milledgeville. Great efforts are being made to re-enforce Hood's army and to break up my Railroads, and I should have at once a good reserve force at Nashville. It would have a bad effect if I were to be forced to send back any material part of my army to guard roads so as to weaken me to an extent that I could not act offensively if the occasion calls for it." (DLC-RTL).

To Benjamin F. Butler[1]

Major General Butler   Executive Mansion,
Bermuda Hd. Va.   Washington, Sep. 28. 1864.

For what offence was the money of John H. Lester, confiscated. Please answer & if practicable send me the record of confiscation.

A. LINCOLN

[1] ALS, DNA WR RG 107, Presidential Telegrams, I, 187. Butler replied on September 29: "John H. Lesters property was confiscated to the use of the U.S. & is in the hands of the Pro Mar at Fortress Monroe. The record of Confiscation will be found in General Orders No. 50 published May 8th 1864 I will send for a copy & forward it as early as possible We did *not* confiscate *300,000* worth of cotton which Lester had at Wilmington & *60,000* in Gold which he had in Canada. The original record is in the Judge Advocates Office" (DLC-RTL).

To John R. Cannon[1]

<table>
<tr><td></td><td>Office U.S. Military Telegraph,</td></tr>
<tr><td>J. R. Cannon</td><td>War Department,</td></tr>
<tr><td>New-Albany, Ia.</td><td>Washington, D.C., Sept 28th. 1864.</td></tr>
</table>

It will be impossible for me to attend your ratification meeting. Thank you for the invitation   A. LINCOLN

[1] ALS, DNA WR RG 107, Presidential Telegrams, I, 186. "Sept 28th." in the date line is in Nicolay's handwriting. John R. Cannon telegraphed from New Albany, Indiana, on September 27, 1864: "We have announced your expected presence here at our grand ratification meeting on saturday next can you come answer by telegraph at length if you please" (DLC-RTL).

To Charles A. Dana[1]

Will Assistant Sec. of War, Dana please see & hear this lady?
Sep. 28. 1864   A LINCOLN

[1] ALS-F, ISLA. The lady has not been identified.

To John F. Miller[1]

<table>
<tr><td></td><td>Office U.S. Military Telegraph,</td></tr>
<tr><td>Officer in Command at</td><td>War Department,</td></tr>
<tr><td>Nashville, Tenn.</td><td>Washington, D.C., Sept. 28. 1864.</td></tr>
</table>

Execution of Jesse A. Broadway is hereby respited to Friday the 14th. day of October next.   A. LINCOLN

[1] ALS, DNA WR RG 107, Presidential Telegrams, I, 185. See Lincoln to Johnson, September 7, *supra*. On September 27, Jordan Stokes and T. A. Keicherd telegraphed Lincoln from Nashville: "We as the counsel for Jesse A Broadway who is sentenced to be hung at this city on next Friday the thirtieth inst would state that owing to the distance which the witnesses & friends live we have been unavoidably delayed in procuring the testimony which we desired to forward to you in his behalf. As the time is now too short for the papers in the case to reach you we therefore would most Respectfully ask . . . to extend the time for five or ten (10) days until the papers shall have reached you. We prove unconditionally that the said Jesse A Broadway was not present or in any way concerned with the crimes for which he stands charged. All of which your Excellency will see upon the arrival of the papers. . . ." (DLC-RTL).

On October 13 John Hay telegraphed Miller: "The sentence of Jesse Broad-way has been commuted by the President to imprisonment at hard labor for three years." (DNA WR RG 107, Presidential Telegrams, I, 203).

To John Cessna[1]

Hon. J. Cessna,   War Department
Harrisburg, Pa.   Washington City, Sep. 29. 1864
    Yours received. See McClure on the subject you speak of.
                                                A. LINCOLN

[1] ALS, DNA WR RG 107, Presidential Telegrams, I, 189. John Cessna, repre-sentative in the Pennsylvania legislature, wrote Lincoln on September 28, 1864: "The death of my father prevents my visiting you. If possible it would be just and fair & greatly to our advantage as well as your own could you construe the conscription law as to exempt for one (1) year all who paid commutation. Many of these are drawn & it operates very severely" (DLC-RTL).

To Ulysses S. Grant[1]

"Cypher"   Office U.S. Military Telegraph,
Lieut. Gen. Grant   War Department,
City-Point, Va   Washington, D.C., Sep. 29 1864.
    I hope it will lay no constraint on you, nor do harm any way, for me to say I am a little afraid lest Lee sends re-enforcements to Early, and thus enables him to turn upon Sheridan.
                                                A. LINCOLN.

[1] ALS, DNA WR RG 107, Presidential Telegrams, I, 188. Grant replied on the same day: "Your despatch just received. I am taking steps to prevent Lee sending reenforcements to Early by attacking him here. Our advance is now within six miles of Richmond and have captured some very strong enclosed forts, some fifteen or more pieces of artillery and several hundred prisoners. Although I have been at the front I can give no estimate of our losses, about 600 wounded men however have been brought in" (DLC-RTL).

To John F. Miller[1]

Officer in Command at   Executive Mansion
Nashville, Tenn.   Washington, Sept. 29. 1864
    Let the execution of Robert T. Bridges be suspended until further order from me.   A. LINCOLN

[1] ALS, DNA WR RG 107, Presidential Telegrams, I, 190. See Lincoln's com-munications to Johnson, September 7 and 27, *supra,* and to McClelland, Decem-ber 24, *infra.*

To Benjamin F. Butler[1]

Major General Butler   Executive Mansion,
Bermuda Hd. Va   Washington, Sep. 30, 1864.

Is there a man in your Department by the name of James Hallion, under sentence, and if so, what is the sentence,? and what for?

A. LINCOLN

[1] ALS, DNA WR RG 107, Presidential Telegrams, I, 191. Major Joseph L. Stackpole replied for Butler on October 1:
"There is no man named James Hallian [sic] under sentence in this Department.
"Private Jas Hallion Co 'K' 20th N.Y. Cavy was sentenced by Gen Court martial to be shot for rape & other offenses. Genl Butler has commuted this sentence to dishonorable discharge . . . & to three (3) years . . . at Hard Labor with ball & chain. The sentence will be published in a few days. I think this is the same man." (DLC-RTL). See Lincoln's telegram to Joseph Roberts, October 1, *infra*.

To William Hoffman[1]

                                              Executive Mansion
Col. Hoffman,   Washington, Sep. 30. 1864

Let John S. Conn, now a prisoner of war at Camp Douglas, Illinois, take the oath of Dec. 8. 1864 [sic], and be discharged.
Yours truly   A. LINCOLN

[1] ALS, IHi. No further reference has been found, and John S. Conn has not been further identified.

Order Concerning Lessees and Owners of Plantations Worked by Freedmen[1]

Executive Order   }
concerning Lessees and Owners of }   Executive Mansion,
Plantations worked by Freedmen. }   September [30?], 1864.

For the purpose of encouraging persons, formerly held as slaves, to labor as freedmen in insurrectionary States that they may become self-supporting, and that the products of their labor may benefit the country, and for the purpose of protecting all persons employing such labor under rules relating thereto, established under proper authority, it is hereby ordered:

I. All officers, commanding military Departments, Districts, Posts, Naval fleets and vessels, will at once suspend[2] all orders made by them or in force within their respective commands, so far as they[3] prohibit or in any manner interfere with the transportation of supplies to, or products from, any plantation worked by free labor under rules relating thereto, prescribed or approved by the Secretary of the Treasury: Provided such transportation is being made in pursuance of permits granted by duly authorized officers of the Treasury Department, and all persons hindering or interfering with transportation to or from such plantations so worked, which has been so permitted, will be deemed guilty of a military offence and punished accordingly.

II. Agreements have been made with owners of lands who have recognized the freedom of their former slaves, and leases have been made of abandoned plantations under authority of the Government, and good faith to such owners and lessees requires due observance of the terms of all such agreements and leases on the part of all civil and military officers of the Government; therefore all military and naval officers will aid in securing such observance by every means at their command which can be used for that purpose without interfering with active military or naval operations.

III. Such orders will be made by general and local military and naval commanders as will insure the fulfilment of the purposes of this order, and as will afford the greatest possible protection to the laborers and employers above named, consistent with the safety of their commands and the success of any military or naval movement being made by them.

[1] Df, DNA WR RG 94, Adjutant General, Letters Received, P 1589. Although corrected in Lincoln's autograph as indicated, this order was not signed or issued. See Lincoln to Stanton, *infra*.
[2] "Revoke" emended by Lincoln to "suspend."
[3] "Which" emended by Lincoln to "so far as they."

To Edwin M. Stanton[1]

Hon. Sec. of War   Executive Mansion
Dear Sir   Washington, Sep. 30. 1864

The accompanying is the draft of an order drawn up at the Treasury Department for me to sign. Please look over it, and say whether you perceive any objection. Yours truly

A. LINCOLN

[1] ALS, NHi. See Order, *supra*. Stanton replied on the same day: "Having examined the draft of the Treasury Order in relation to Freedmen and Plantations, referred to me by your note of this date, I cannot recommend its execution by you. It seems to me subject to very grave objections, which ought to be removed by satisfactory explanation, before the President would give such sweeping sanction and approval to the acts of Treasury Agents, in respect to which neither he nor this Department has any sufficient information. The specific objections will be stated to you at your convenience." (DLC-RTL).

To Edwin M. Stanton[1]

September 30, 1864.

I think the bearer of this, Second Lieutenant Albee, deserves a hearing. Will the Secretary of War please accord it to him?

A. LINCOLN.

[1] OR, I, XLII, III, 494. Lincoln's endorsement appears on a statement of Second Lieutenant George E. Albee, Thirty-sixth Wisconsin Volunteers, September 30, 1864, protesting against an order which disgraced his regiment and forbade it to carry colors as a result of the capture of the regimental colors at Ream's Station, Virginia, on August 25.

To Lorenzo Thomas[1]

September 30, 1864

I have seen this man, who seems to be an intelligent & manly man, and whose story I believe to be true. If it does not invol[v]e much inconvenience, let the transfer he asks, be made.

Sep. 30. 1864   A. LINCOLN

[1] AES-P, ISLA. Lincoln's endorsement is on a letter of David G. Lindsay, Company G, Ninetieth Pennsylvania Infantry, to Lorenzo Thomas, September 29, 1864: "I inlisted in the 17th. Regt Pa. Cavalry and through some missunderstanding I was Sent to the 90th. Pa Infantry. My reason for my inlisting in the 17th. Pa Cavalry was that I had a Brother in that Regiment, and wished to be along with Him. . . . I most respectfully & earnestly request you Sir to transfer me to my proper Regiment the one in which I inlisted. . . ." Private David Lindsay was ordered to be transferred to the Seventeenth Pennsylvania Cavalry on October 6, 1864 (AGO *Special Orders No. 336*).

To Edward Bates[1]

[October, 1864]

Attorney General please make out a pardon in this case.

A. LINCOLN

[1] AES, DNA RG 204, U.S. Pardon Attorney, A 554. Lincoln's endorsement is written on a petition signed by Robert M. Beale and others, Washington, October, 1864, asking pardon for Alfred More, convicted of larceny.

To Joseph Holt[1]

Executive Mansion   October 1, 1864

Will the Judge Advocate General please examine and report upon this case as soon as convenient.   A. LINCOLN

[1] ES, IHi. Lincoln's endorsement appears on a letter from Captain William Borrowe, Company H, Second Pennsylvania Artillery, October 1, 1864, sentenced by court-martial to loss of two months' pay, on charges of forgery and

making a false muster. Borrowe asked a "final decision . . . and that redress be granted me." Holt left the decision to the president, and on October 26, Lincoln endorsed the court-martial record "I decline to make any further order in this case. A. LINCOLN" (copy, DNA RG 130, U.S. Army Court-Martial Cases, White House Office). Borrowe was dismissed from service on March 8, 1865, but reinstated as first lieutenant in the Second Artillery, July 26, 1865.

Order for Pardon of John S. Ward[1]

Let this man, John S. Ward take the oath of Dec. 8 1863, be exchanged & report to Gov. Johnson at Nashville Tenn.

Oct 1 1864   A. LINCOLN

[1] AES, owned by Arthur Hansen, Milwaukee, Wisconsin. Lincoln's endorsement is written on a telegram of Andrew Johnson to W. C. Ward, September 28, 1864: "You will show this dispatch to the President. I should have no hesitancy in releasing your brother and permitting him to return home if I had the pardoning power providing he would take the oath of allegiance willingly and in good faith & report to the Executive of the State and enter into such bonds as may be required for the faithful observance of the same."

Order of Thanks to One Hundred Day Troops[1]

Executive Mansion,
Washington, October 1, 1864.

The term of 100 days, for which volunteers from the States of Indiana, Illinois, Iowa, and Wisconsin volunteered, under the call of their respective Governors, in the months of May and June, to aid in the recent campaign of General Sherman, having expired, the President directs an official acknowledgment to be made of their patriotic service. It was their good fortune to render effective service in the brilliant operations in the Southwest, and to contribute to the victories of the national arms over the rebel forces in Georgia under command of Johnston and Hood. On all occasions, and in every service to which they were assigned, their duty as patriotic volunteers was performed with alacrity and courage, for which they are entitled to and are hereby tendered the national thanks through the Governors of their respective States.

The Secretary of War is directed to transmit a copy of this order to the Governors of Indiana, Illinois, Iowa, and Wisconsin, and to cause a certificate[2] of their honorable services to be delivered to the officers and soldiers of the States above named, who recently served in the military force of the United States as volunteers for 100 days.

ABRAHAM LINCOLN.

1 OR, III, IV, 755-56. See Lincoln to Stanton, April 23, *supra*.

2 These printed certificates "of thanks" and "of honorable service," dated December 15, 1864, and signed by Lincoln and Stanton, incorporated Lincoln's order of October 1, 1864, in the body of their text.

To William T. Otto[1]

October 1, 1864

Understanding that persons giving credit in this case will have no strictly legal claim upon the government, yet the necessity for it is so great and urgent, that I shall most cheerfully urge upon Congress that such credit and claims fairly given and made, shall be recognized and paid.
A. LINCOLN

Oct. 1. 1864.

1 AES, DNA NR RG 48, Indian Division, Letters Received. Lincoln's endorsement appears on a letter of Acting Secretary of the Interior William T. Otto enclosing a letter of William P. Dole, October 1, 1864, suggesting that Cherokee Agent Justin Harlan be instructed to buy on credit in New York $30,000 worth of clothing and that Superintendent William G. Coffin at Leavenworth, Kansas, be instructed to buy $170,000 worth of food for relieving the refugee Indians in Kansas.

To Joseph Roberts[1]

Office U.S. Military Telegraph,
Officer in Command at War Department,
Fort-Monroe, Va. Washington, D.C., Oct. 1 1864.

Is there a man by the name of James Hallion (I think) under sentence? and what is his offence? what the sentence? and when to be executed?
A. LINCOLN

1 ALS, DNA WR RG 107, Presidential Telegrams, I, 192. See Lincoln to Butler, September 30, *supra*. Colonel Joseph Roberts replied on the same day: "Your telegram just received. The Provost Marshal of Dept . . . informs me that James Hallion twentieth (20th) N.Y. Cavalry was received at this office from Norfolk, sent here by order of Brig Genl Sheply [George F. Shepley] August ninth . . . as awaiting sentence of General Court Martial and is now at the Military Prison Camp Hamilton. I do not know what his offence is. Brig Genl Shepley at Norfolk can inform you no doubt as he was probably tried by a Court Martial convened by his orders. This man is not in my charge" (DLC-RTL).

To Edward Bates[1]

Let a pardon be made out in this case.
Oct. 3, 1864 A. LINCOLN

1 AES, DNA RG 204, U.S. Pardon Attorney, A 563. Lincoln's endorsement is written on a letter signed by Thomas D. Larner and others, Washington, October, 1864, asking pardon for William Trunnell, convicted of assault and battery.

To William P. Fessenden[1]

Executive Mansion, Washington,
Hon. Secretary of the Treasury: Oct. 3, 1864.

My dear Sir, Mr. Hallowell who brings this, has a very meritorious cotton-case & I hope it may be found that the same sort of thing can be done for him that was for Judge Johnson[2] of Cincinnati. Yours truly   A. LINCOLN

[1] Carnegie Book Shop Catalog 167, No. 266; Tracy, p. 245. On September 30, 1864, John W. Forney wrote Lincoln:

"I will have the honor to call upon you on Monday morning between ten and eleven o'clock in company with Morris L. Hallowell. He is one of the most upright and influential members of the Society of Friends in this city. . . . He was ruined by the Rebellion—all his trade South was cut off—his debtors refused to pay—and he was thus left almost bankrupt. He is a man of earnestness & integrity & to enable him to live he will lay before you the following. . . .

"One of his debtors in Arkansas who owes him . . . an immense sum has 3600 bales of cotton. If he could get these out of the State under the authority of the Government, it would be a source of great advantage to the common cause, & would also enable his party in Arkansas to pay him. Gen's Steele & Dana need only your permission to give protection to this cotton to get it out. . . ." (DLC-RTL).

[2] This case has not been identified, but Johnson was probably William Johnson an outstanding lawyer and jurist of Cincinnati.

Recommendation for Mrs. Charlotte Hough[1]

Executive Mansion
Washington, Oct. 3, 1864

I have but slight personal acquaintance with the bearer of this Mrs. Lotty Hough; but I have known something of her by reputation for several years and never heard aught against her. She is now struggling to support herself and her little boy, and I hope she may be afforded fair opportunities to succeed.   A. LINCOLN

[1] ADS, RPB. Concerning Mrs. Charlotte Hough, see Lincoln's order of March 7, 1865, *infra*, permitting her to bring products through the lines.

To Edwin M. Stanton[1]

If the service can be made useful, let Capt. Dewey be appointed an Assistant Quarter-Master   A. LINCOLN
Oct. 3. 1864

[1] AES, IHi. Lincoln's endorsement is written on a letter of Captain Lucien Eaton, district judge advocate at St. Louis, Missouri, to Captain William F. Dewey, Fifty-third Illinois Volunteers, January 27, 1864, commending him for his prior services as judge advocate at St. Louis. The letter is endorsed in concurrence by several other officers, including General John M. Schofield. Stanton endorsed "Applicant from Illinois to be filed and appointment [sic]." No further reference has been found.

Order for Discharge[1]

Let this boy be discharged, on refunding any bounty received.
Oct. 4. 1864   A. LINCOLN

[1] AES, InFtwL. Lincoln's letter is written on a letter of William D. Kelley, Philadelphia, October 3, 1864, to an unidentified person:

"My dear friend Will you look over the enclosed papers and get the subject fairly before the President soon as possible I know the parties, Miss Porters father & two uncles were lunatics, and from this trouble will send her to the asylum. Dr. Gardner is an eminent physician. I know all the parties & hope the President will grant the prayer if possible I am nearly worn out."

The papers are not with the letter and the case has not been identified.

Order for Pardon of Roswell McIntyre[1]

Executive Mansion,
Washington, Oct. 4. 1864.

Upon condition that Roswell McIntyre of Co. E. 6th. Regt. of New-York Cavalry returns to his Regiment and faithfully serves out his term, making up for lost time, or until otherwise lawfully discharged, he is fully pardoned for any supposed desertion heretofore committed; and this paper is his pass to go to his regiment.

ABRAHAM LINCOLN

[1] ADS-F, ISLA. An endorsement at the bottom of the page reads: "Taken from the body of R. McIntyre at the battle of Five Forks Va 1865." An endorsement across the face of the order indicates transportation furnished by the quartermaster's office from New York on October 22, 1864.

To Ulysses S. Grant[1]

Executive Mansion Washington
Lieut Gen Grant,   Oct. 5th. 1864.

I enclose you copy of a correspondence[2] in regard to a contemplated exchange of Naval prisoners through your lines and not very distant from your Head Quarters. It only came to the knowledge of the War Department and of myself yesterday, and it gives us some uneasiness. I therefore send it to you with the statement that as the numbers to be exchanged under it are small, and so much has already been done to effect the exchange, I hope you may find it consistent to let it go forward under the general supervision of Gen Butler, and particularly in reference to the points he holds vital in exchanges. Still you are at liberty to arrest the whole operation, if in your judgment the public good requires it. Yours Truly   A. LINCOLN

[1] Copy, DNA WR RG 108, HQA, Letters Received, P 459, Box 73. On October 11, 1864, Grant forwarded Lincoln's letter with the enclosures to General Benjamin F. Butler, turning "the whole matter over to you to conduct." (OR, II, VII, 965). Welles' *Diary* under dates of October 4 and 5 records at length the difficulty between the Navy and War departments, concluding as follows: "The President came to see me pretty early this morning in relation to the exchange of prisoners. It had troubled him through the night. . . . The President said he wanted the subject to be got along with harmoniously, that they were greatly ruffled at the War Department, and if I had no objection he would go and see Seward, tell him the facts, get him to come over, and bring the Secretary of War . . . to a consultation. . . .

"In less than an hour the President returned with Seward. We went briefly over the question. . . . After discussing the subject, went, by request of the President, with him to the War Department. General Hitchcock and General Halleck came in soon. Stanton was ill-mannered, as usual, where things did not please him. . . . The President said that the correspondence was a past transaction,—that we need not disturb that matter; the Navy arrangement must go forward, and the Navy have its men. He wrote and read a brief letter to General Grant proposing to turn over the prisoners we had sent to him. . . . Hitchcock . . . began a speech . . . intimating that the War Department should have exclusive control of the cartel. . . . I told him I was perfectly willing . . . if they would not obstruct the exchange but get back our men. All assented to the President's letter. Stanton and Seward preferred it should be addressed to General Butler. . . . But the President preferred addressing the General-in-Chief, and I commended his preference. We telegraphed Capt. Melancthon Smith, to turn the prisoners over to General Grant to be disposed of. . . ."

[2] See OR, II, VII, 661, for letter of Stephen R. Mallory to Gideon Welles, August 20, 1864, and Welles' reply, September 9, 1864 (*ibid.*, p. 790).

To William Hoffman[1]

Col. Hoffman please see & hear this lady & oblige her if it can be consistently done.   A. LINCOLN

Oct. 5, 1864

[1] Copy, ISLA. Lincoln's endorsement is on a letter from Anne Sweatman, Washington, October 5, 1864, asking release of her husband, First Lieutenant Robert Sweatman of Company E, Fifth U.S. Cavalry, taken prisoner at Beaver Dam Depot, Virginia, on May 10, 1864. Presumably Sweatman had been exchanged but was not yet returned to service.

To Joseph Holt[1]

October 5, 1864

Judge Advocate General please procure record & report on this case.

Oct. 5. 1864   A. LINCOLN

Pardon for unexecuted part of sentence.   A. LINCOLN

Jan. 23. 1865.

[1] AES, DNA WR RG 153, Judge Advocate General, NN 1187. Lincoln's endorsement is written on a letter asking clemency for Private Linden B. Esher, Company A, Seventy-second Pennsylvania Volunteers, sentenced to be shot for desertion. Holt reported on December 12, 1864, that sentence had already been commuted to imprisonment on Dry Tortugas.

[37]

To John F. Miller[1]

	Office U.S. Military Telegraph,
Officer in command at	War Department,
Nashville, Tenn.	Washington, D.C., Oct. 5 1864.

Suspend execution of Thomas K. Miller until further order from me.   A LINCOLN

[1] ALS, DNA WR RG 107, Presidential Telegrams, I, 193. On October 1, 1864, Andrew Johnson telegraphed Lincoln: "Thomas K Miller & Y[oung] C Edmondson are sentenced to be hanged on the seventh inst The friends of the Parties who are respectable & intelligent allege that they can present reasons & facts which will go a great way towards mitigating the sentence & desire an extension of time to enable them to do so. I hope that their request will be granted & the execution postponed a reasonable time" (DLC-RTL).

On October 4, Andrew Johnson's son Robert, acting as his secretary, telegraphed: "I would most respectfully call your attention to a telegraph of Gov Johnson of Oct first (1) in regard to Thos K Miller & Y C Edmondson sentenced to be hanged on the seventh inst & hope you will consider the case favorably Father is absent in Indiana." (*Ibid.*).

Lincoln endorsed the second telegram "Suspended till further order. Oct. 5, 1864. A.L." See Lincoln to Miller, October 25, *infra*.

To William P. Fessenden[1]

The bearer, Judge Peck, is my good friend, whom I hope the Sec. of Treasury will see & hear.   A. LINCOLN

Oct. 6. 1864

[1] ALS, N. Ebenezer Peck was associate justice of the U.S. Court of Claims.

To Edwin M. Stanton[1]

October 6, 1864

Hon. Sec. of War please see Mr. Wood, one of the Penn. agents, who has some fears that a misdescription of the functions of himself & colleagues in their passes, may create difficulty.

Oct. 6. 1864.   A. LINCOLN

[1] ALS, IHi. Mr. Wood has not been further identified, but may have been one of the agents named by the State Committee to obtain votes of Pennsylvania soldiers in the field.

Appointment of Directors of Union Pacific Railroad[1]

Executive Mansion, October 7th 1864.

By virtue of the authority conferred upon the President of the United States, by the thirteenth section of the act of Congress approved July 2, 1864, amending the act to aid in the construction of a Railroad and Telegraph line from the Missouri river to the Pacific Ocean &c.

Jesse L. Williams of Indiana
George Ashmun of Massachusetts
Charles T. Sherman of Ohio
Springer Harbaugh of Pennsylvania, and
Timothy J. Carter of Illinois

are hereby appointed directors on the part of the Government of the United States, for the Union Pacific Railroad and Telegraph Company, to serve until the next ensuing regular election of directors for said Company, and until their successors are qualified.

ABRAHAM LINCOLN

1 DS, DNA NR RG 48, Department of Interior, Union Pacific Railroad, Package 239. John A. Dix, president of the Union Pacific, wrote Lincoln on October 4, 1864: "I desire respectfully to call your attention to the fact that the term of service of the government Directors of this company expires tomorrow. As there will be a meeting of the Board of Directors at an early day, it is very desirable that the appointment of the five government Directors for the ensuing year should be made as soon as practicable." (DLC-RTL).

To Joseph Holt[1]

October 7, 1864

Believing there was technichal wrong in these cases, on a point which the government can not safely disregard, and yet having great doubt whether there was moral guilt in these particular cases, it is ordered that the fine in each case is reduced to one thousand dollars, the excess being remitted.   A. LINCOLN

Oct. 7. 1864

1 AES, DNA WR RG 153, Judge Advocate General, NN 2089. Lincoln's endorsement is written on the court-martial record of J. Paul Jones and William A. Jones. See Lincoln to Holt, September 9, *supra*.

To Henry J. Raymond[1]

October 7, 1864

I well remember the meetings herein narrated. See nothing for me to object to in the narrative as being made by General McDowell, except the phrase attributed to me *"of the Jacobinism of Congress,"* which phrase I do not remember using literally or in substance, and which I wish not to be published in any event.

October 7, 1864.   A. LINCOLN.

[1] Henry J. Raymond, *The Life and Public Services of Abraham Lincoln* (1865), p. 772. According to the source, Lincoln wrote this endorsement on a memorandum prepared by General Irvin McDowell of an interview with Lincoln on January 10, 1862. McDowell's lengthy memorandum may be consulted in the source. The passage to which Lincoln alludes is as follows: "The President was greatly disturbed at the state of affairs. Spoke of the exhausted condition of the Treasury; of the loss of public credit; of the Jacobinism in Congress; of the delicate condition of our foreign relations; of the bad news he had received from the West, particularly as contained in a letter from General Halleck on the state of affairs in Missouri; of the want of co-operation between General Halleck and General Buell; but, more than all, the sickness of General McClellan." (*Ibid.*, p. 773).

To James B. Fry[1]

War Department,
Washington, D.C., October 8, 1864.

It is now said that under present instructions in recruiting from prisoners at Rock Island the names of those willing to enlist have to be first ascertained and sent here, and then an order from here for their examination and muster of such as are found suitable.

It is proposed to change this so that the ascertainment of names, examination, and muster can all be gone through with there, under the supervision of Colonel Johnson and Captain Rathbone,[2] thus saving much time and trouble.

It is also proposed that the restriction in the President's order limiting the recruits to persons of foreign and Northern birth be removed, and that the question of good faith on the part of those offering to enlist be left to the judgment and discretion of Colonel Johnson and Colonel Caraher.[3] The limit of the whole not to exceed 1,750 men.

[1] OR, III, IV, 756-57. A footnote in the source identifies this memorandum as follows: "Unsigned memorandum made by President Lincoln and given to the Provost-Marshal-General with verbal instructions to conform thereto." See Lincoln's orders to Huidekoper, September 1, to Stanton, September 20, and letter to Grant, September 22, *supra*.
[2] Andrew J. Johnson, commanding at Rock Island, and Henry R. Rathbone.
[3] Andrew P. Caraher.

To Simon Cameron[1]

Office U.S. Military Telegraph,
Gen. Simon Cameron   War Department,
Philadelphia   Washington, D.C., Oct. 9. 1864.

There is absolutely no news here from the Army of the Potomac not published in Stantons bulletins of yesterday and before. The line is open, and mere business despatches are passing over it. Have no alarm, on bogus despatches. A. LINCOLN

[1] ALS, DNA WR RG 107, Presidential Telegrams, I, 195. No telegram from Cameron in regard to news from the Army of the Potomac has been found.

To Andrew G. Curtin[1]

Office U.S. Military Telegraph,

Gov. Curtin   War Department, Washington, D.C.,
Harrisburg Pa.   Oct. 10. 5. PM. 1864.

Yours of to-day just this moment received; & the Secretary having left it is impossible for me to answer to-day. I have not received your letter from Erie. A LINCOLN

[1] ALS, DNA WR RG 107, Presidential Telegrams, I, 194. Curtin's telegram or letter of October 10 has not been found. His letter from Erie, Pennsylvania, October 6, reads in part:

"Having . . . passed through the counties from Clinton west to Erie I fulfil my promise to write you.

"Whilst I anticipate our success on next Tuesday in this State our most reliable friends do not promise an increased vote in the counties mentioned. . . ."

"P.S. Will you not order the muster of Colonel [John H.] Stover of the 184th Reg P.V It is important and if he [Stanton] has any objections about him he can be disposed of after the election. . . ." (DLC-RTL).

See Lincoln's telegram to Curtin, October 11, *infra*.

To Henry W. Hoffman[1]

Hon. Henry W Hoffman   Executive Mansion, Washington,
My dear Sir: October 10, 1864.

A convention of Maryland has framed a new constitution for the State; a public meeting is called for this evening, at Baltimore, to aid in securing its ratification by the people; and you ask a word from me, for the occasion. I presume the only feature of the instrument, about which there is serious controversy, is that which provides for the extinction of slavery. It needs not to be a secret, and I presume it is no secret, that I wish success to this provision. I desire it on every consideration. I wish all men to be free. I wish the material prosperity of the already free which I feel sure the extinction of slavery would bring. I wish to see, in process of disappearing, that only thing which ever could bring this nation to civil war. I attempt no argument. Argument upon the question is already exhausted by the abler, better informed,[2] and more immediately interested sons of Maryland herself. I only add that I shall be gratified exceedingly if the good people of the State shall, by their votes, ratify the new constitution. Yours truly A. LINCOLN

[41]

[1] ALS, MdHi. This letter is incorrectly dated October 18, 1864, in Hertz (II, 952-53). Henry W. Hoffman, chairman of the Maryland Unconditional Union Central Committee, wrote Lincoln on October 3, 1864:

"Our grand Mass Meeting in favor of the 'Free Constitution' will be held in Monument Square on Monday evening October 10th.

"In consequence of local dissensions and with a view to general harmony and cordial fraternization upon the new Constitution, the Committee have resolved to rely exclusively upon speakers from other States at this meeting.

"We are convinced that your presence on the occasion would insure its success both as to harmony and point of numbers and that its influence upon the vote to be taken on the Following Wednesday would be to add hundreds and perhaps thousands of votes to the free State column. We therefore most cordially and earnestly invite your attendance. If however you should feel disinclined to comply with the urgent request of the Committee . . . we are well assured that a letter from you expressive of the deep interest which we know you feel in regard to its success would be productive of the greatest good. . . ." (DLC-RTL).

On October 12 Hoffman wrote: "Many thanks for your letter of Monday It was recd with the unbounded applause of the many thousands assembled The meeting was a great success in point of numbers Harmony & enthusiasm The new constitution will be adopted The majority in this city will not fall short of ten thousand from present indications. The voting is proceeding quietly. . . ." (*Ibid.*).

The new constitution was ratified by a vote of 30,174 to 29,799.

[2] Lincoln wrote "better posted," but John Hay erased "posted" and wrote "informed," as shown on the manuscript and recorded in Hay's *Diary* under date of October 9, 1864.

Recommendation for Josiah Shaw[1]

I shall be glad if Capt. Shaw, recently in our service, can get suitable employment in any of the Departments.

Oct. 10, 1864   A. LINCOLN

[1] American Art Association Anderson Galleries Catalog 3854, October 20, 1930, No. 159. According to the catalog description, this is the text of an autograph endorsement signed on the back of discharge papers of Captain Josiah Shaw, Company A, Fourth New Jersey Volunteers, mustered out on September 3, 1864.

Testimony Concerning Shelling of Houses Near Fort Stevens[1]

A.   Executive Mansion
                                          Washington Oct. 10. 1864

I was present at Fort Stevens (I think) on the afternoon of July 12th. 1864, when some houses in front were shelled by our guns, and understanding that the Military officers in command thought the shelling of the houses proper and necessary, I certainly gave my approbation to its being done   A. LINCOLN

[1] Copy, DNA RG 233, Forty-eighth Congress, House of Representatives Collection, Box 162. The copy of this communication is preserved in the record of

the proceedings of a board of officers convened by *Special Orders No. 228*, Headquarters, Department of Washington, September 13, 1864, upon the claim of Catharine Carberry for loss and damage to her property sustained during the raid of the Confederates on Washington in July, 1864. The proceedings refer to the communication as exhibit "A." These proceedings are filed in the Forty-eighth Congress collection presumably because the Committee on the Judiciary had under consideration the bill for claims of Catharine Carberry and Richard Lay (H.R. 5407). The committee reported the bill adversely:

"The claimants insist that these facts make a case of the taking of private property for public use, and entitle them to payment for their losses. Similar claims have been before Congress repeatedly since the close of the war of the rebellion, and have been discussed in many reports of committees, and on the floor of both houses.

"The committee think the law of this subject has become settled that such claims are for losses and damage by war, and not a taking of private property for public use. The subject was most exhaustively examined in a report of the Committee on War Claims in the Forty-seventh Congress. . . . We think their conclusions are sound, but they are fatal to this bill." (Forty-eighth Congress, First Session, *House of Representatives Report No. 1856*).

To Gideon Welles[1]

Executive Mansion,

My dear Sir   Oct. 10, 1864.

The bearer, Mr. Jones, calls on you to obtain facilities for taking the votes of Seamen & Sailors. Please do all for him in this respect which you consistently can. Mr. Jones is Chairman of the Union State Central Committee for the State of New York. Yours truly

A. LINCOLN

[1] Stan. V. Henkels Catalog 1342, January 4, 1924, No. 35. According to the catalog description this communication is an autograph letter signed. Welles' *Diary* under date of October 11 records the following: "The President and Seward called on me this forenoon relative to New York voters in the Navy. Wanted one of our boats to be placed at the disposal of the New York commission to gather votes in the Mississippi Squadron. A Mr. [Charles] Jones was referred to, who subsequently came to me with a line from the President, and wanted also to send to the blockading squadrons. Gave permission to go by the Circassian, and directed commanders to extend facilities to all voters. . . ."

To Simon Cameron[1]

Office U.S. Military Telegraph,

Gen. S. Cameron   War Department, Washington, D.C.,

Philadelphia Pa & Harrisburgh[2]   Oct. 11. 1864.

Am leaving office to go home. How does it stand now?

A. LINCOLN

[1] ALS, DNA WR RG 107, Presidential Telegrams, I, 198. No reply was received from Cameron until his telegram from Philadelphia was received at 9:05 P.M. on October 12: "Returns came in slowly but I still think we will have four

(4) additional Members of Congress & a large majority in the Legislature On the aggregate vote in thirty four counties we have lost . . . 6500 compared with Eighteen hundred Sixty three. . . . At the same ratio we will have more than three thousand majority on the home vote." (DLC-RTL).

2 "& Harrisburgh" is not in Lincoln's autograph.

To Andrew G. Curtin[1]

Office U.S. Military Telegraph,
Gov. Curtin   War Department, Washington, D.C.,
Harrisburg, Pa.   Oct. 11 1864.

On looking up the Col. Stover case this morning I find we could not, without further information, be at all justified in ordering him to be mustered. I hope it can be made straight; but the record as it stands is too bad. A copy will be immediately sent you by mail.

A. LINCOLN

1 ALS, DNA WR RG 107, Presidential Telegrams, I, 196. See Lincoln to Curtin, October 10, *supra*. Curtin wrote Lincoln again on November 2, asking action on Stover's case: "If the charges are true he is unfit for honorable position. . . . If they are not true he should command his regiment. . . ." (DLC-RTL). The roster of the One Hundred Eighty-fourth Pennsylvania Volunteers lists Colonel John H. Stover as mustered out with his regiment on July 14, 1865.

To Robert T. Lincoln[1]

Office U.S. Military Telegraph,
Robert T. Lincoln   War Department,
Cambridge, Mass.   Washington, D.C., Oct. 11 1864.

Your letter makes us a little uneasy about your health. Telegraph us how you are. If you think it would help you make us a visit.

A. LINCOLN

1 ALS, DNA WR RG 107, Presidential Telegrams, I, 197. No letter or telegram from Robert Lincoln has been found.

To Edwin M. Stanton[1]

October 11, 1864
I wish to appoint Ebenezer J. Bennett of St. Louis, Mo., an Assistant Quarter Master, or Commissary of Subsistence. If service can be found for him, let him be appointed.

1 *The Collector*, April-May, 1945, No. 2003. According to the catalog description this text is from an autograph letter signed. Captain Ebenezer J. Bennett, formerly of the Second Missouri Cavalry, was appointed commissary of subsistence on October 12, 1864.

To Ulysses S. Grant[1]

Office U.S. Military Telegraph,
Lieut. Genl. Grant   War Department,
City-Point, Va   Washington, D.C., Oct. 12. 1864.

Sec. of War not being in, I answer yours about election. Pennsylvania very close, and still in doubt on home vote. Ohio largely for us, with all the members of congress but two or three. Indiana largely for us. Governor, it is said by 15,000, and 8. of the eleven members of congress. Send us what you may know of your army vote.   A LINCOLN

[1] ALS, DNA WR RG 107, Presidential Telegrams, I, 199½. No communication from Grant in this connection has been found.

Order Concerning the *Fusigama*[1]

Executive Mansion,
Washington, 12th October, 1864.

The Japanese Government having caused the construction at New York of a vessel of war called the 'Fusigama,' and application having been made for the clearance of the same in order that it may proceed to Japan, it is ordered, in view of the state of affairs in that country and of its relations with the United States, that a compliance with the application be, for the present, suspended.

ABRAHAM LINCOLN.

[1] DS, DNA RG 56, General Records of the Treasury Department, AB Series, 1864, Letters from Executive Officers, State Department, Part 2, Volume II. This order was enclosed with a letter of Secretary Seward to William P. Fessenden, October 12, 1864: "I have the honor to enclose an order of the President of this date, suspending the granting of a clearance to the gunboat Fusigama, which has been built at New York for the Japanese, and which is represented to be ready to start for her destination."

Japan was in a state of semi-revolution led by the "Ronins," as a result of anti-foreign sentiment aroused by the efforts of England, France, and the Netherlands to get favorable commercial concessions similar to those granted by Japan to the United States. The *Fusigama* and the *Funayma Solace* (see Lincoln's order of December 3, *infra*) had been built under contracts arranged by Thurlow Weed and Charles B. Lansing (see Lincoln's communication to the Senate, February 6, 1863, *supra*).

To Edward Bates[1]

Attorney General please make out a pardon in this case.

Oct. 13, 1864   A. LINCOLN

[1] AES, DNA RG 204, U.S. Pardon Attorney, A 561. Lincoln's endorsement is written on a letter from William P. Fessenden, October 3, 1864, asking pardon for Franklin B. Furlong, convicted of stealing letters from the post office at Portland, Maine.

Estimated Electoral Vote[1]

Office U.S. Military Telegraph,
War Department,
Washington, D.C., October 13th. 1864.

Supposed Copperhead Vote.		*Union Vote, for President*	
New-York	33	New England States	39
Penn	26	Michigan	8
New Jersey	7	Wisconsin	8
Delaware	3	Minnesota	4
Maryland	7	Iowa	8
Missouri	11	Oregon	3
Kentucky	11	California	5
Illinois	16	Kansas	3
	—	Indiana	13
	114	Ohio	21
		W. Virginia	5
			117
		Nevada	3
			120

[1] AD, CSmH. Written on a printed telegraph blank, this document is in Lincoln's autograph except for the date, column headings, and "Nevada 3/ 120."

To Oliver P. Morton[1]

Cypher   Office U.S. Military Telegraph,
Gov. O. P. Morton   War Department, Washington, D.C.,
Indianapolis, Ind.   Oct. 13 1864.

In my letter borne by Mr. Mitchell to Gen. Sherman, I said that any soldiers he could spare for October need not to remain for November. I therefore can not press the General on this point. All that the Sec. of War and Gen. Sherman feel they can safely do, I however, shall be glad of.

Bravo, for Indiana, and for yourself personally.

A. LINCOLN.

[1] ALS, DNA WR RG 107, Presidential Telegrams, I, 200. William Mitchell, former representative from Indiana (1861-1863), who had carried Lincoln's letter of September 19 (*supra*), telegraphed Lincoln from Louisville, Kentucky, on October 7: "I have succeeded very well." (DLC-RTL).

Re-elected on October 11, Governor Morton telegraphed Lincoln and Stanton on October 12: "In consideration of the fact that nearly all of the Indiana sick & wounded soldiers furloughed from Hospitals under your late order did not reach their homes until within a few days past & many not until yesterday &

the day before leaving them little or no time to see their friends & families & secure the rest & recuperation they so much need on account of long & arduous Journey they have performed I most earnestly ask that their furloughs be extended by a special order until after the Presidential Election say Nov (10) tenth. If this is done I feel confident hundreds of them will return to the front able for active duty If sent on the fifteenth inst they will be worse off than ever For the best interests of the service and the sake of humanity I earnestly hope this request will be granted & the order telegraphed to me as soon as possible" (DLC-RTL).

Morton's reply to Lincoln's telegram was received October 13 at 1 P.M.: "I fear you misapprehend my dispatch of yesterday I only asked that the sick & wounded who are furloughed under Mr Stantons order to the Surgeon Genl be allowed to remain Genl Sherman had nothing to do with sending them home & would not be strengthened any by their return now as they would all have to go into Hospitals again It seems to me the order of extension asked for yesterday can be granted without consulting the Genl & without the least detriment, but rather benefit to the service Please let Mr Stanton see this & for God's sake let the order be made at once" (*ibid.*).

At 5 P.M. Morton telegraphed Lincoln and Stanton again: "It is my opinion that the vote of every soldiers in Indiana will be required to carry this state for Mr Lincoln in November. The most of them are sick and wounded and in no condition to render service and it is better to let them remain while they are here. "It is important that this be answered immediately." (*Ibid.*).

To Godlove S. Orth[1]

Office U.S. Military Telegraph,
Hon. G. S. Orth   War Department, Washington, D.C.,
LaFayette, Ind.   Oct. 13 1864.

I now incline to defer the appointment of Judge until the meeting of Congress.   A. LINCOLN

[1] ALS, DNA WR RG 107, Presidential Telegrams, I, 201. Godlove S. Orth telegraphed Lincoln on October 12: "Have you determined the question of Judge Whites successor If not will you defer appointment until meeting of congress Please answer by telegraph" (DLC-RTL). U.S. District Judge Albert S. White died on September 24, 1864. David McDonald of Indianapolis, his successor, took office on December 13, 1864.

To Benjamin F. Butler[1]

Major Gen. Butler   Executive Mansion,
Butlers Hd Qrs. Va.   Washington, Oct. 14, 1864.

It is said that Captain Joseph R. Findley of Co. F. 76. Penn. Vols. has been summarily dismissed the service for supposed skulking. Such representations are made to me of his good character, long service, and good behavior in many battles as to induce the wish that you would re-examine his case. At all events send me a statement of it as you have   A. LINCOLN

[1] ALS, DNA WR RG 107, Presidential Telegrams, I, 204. Butler replied the same day: "My order and a Report on the case of Capt Jos P Findley will be

sent by Mail. It has never been my misfortune to get so disgraceful a case of skulking" (DLC-RTL). The roster of the Seventy-sixth Pennsylvania Volunteers lists Captain Joseph R. Findley as discharged on October 4, 1864.

To James B. Fry[1]

Provost-Marshal-General.

Executive Mansion Washington,
Oct. 14, 1864

Hon. Charles O'Neill states that the 1st. Ward, in the 2nd. Congressional District in Philadelphia, is entitled to an additional credit on the draft of about 95 men, of Naval enlistments, which are only refused on a question of time—or, in other words, that they may have the credit on the *next*, but not on the *present* draft. If there be no mistake in this statement, let them have the credit *now*. Yours truly   A. LINCOLN

[1] John Heise Catalog 2487, No. 20. Charles O'Neill of Philadelphia was U.S. representative 1863-1871, 1873-1893.

To Edwin M. Stanton[1]

Please send the papers of Major Gansler, by the bearer, Mr. Long-necker.   A. LINCOLN

Oct. 14. 1864

[1] ALS, owned by John D. Lippy, Jr., Gettysburg, Pennsylvania. Mr. Long-necker was probably Henry C. Longnecker of Allentown, Pennsylvania. Major W. H. Gansler, Forty-seventh Pennsylvania Volunteers had been dismissed for cowardice at Sabine Cross Roads and Pleasant Hill on April 8 and 9, 1864 (AGO *Special Orders No. 169*, May 6, 1864). On October 17, "By direction of the President, so much of Special Orders, No. 169 . . . as relates to Major W. H. Gansler, 47th Pennsylvania Volunteers, is hereby revoked, and he is honorably discharged, on tender of resignation. . . ." (AGO *Special Orders No. 350*). Although the name appears as "Gansler" in *Special Orders*, it is "Gausler" on the roster of the regiment.

To Henry W. Hoffman[1]

Cypher
Hon. H. W. Hoffman
Baltimore, Md.

Office U.S. Military Telegraph,
War Department,
Washington, D.C., Oct 15. 1864.

Come over to-night and see me.   A. LINCOLN

[1] ALS, DNA WR RG 107, Presidential Telegrams, I, 205. Hoffman's telegram received at 11:20 A.M. on October 15 is as follows: "Returns from State come in slowly Probable maj. against the Constitution on the home vote of about one thousand It is believed that the soldiers vote may overcome this & give a small majority for the Constitution It is reported that in some of the rebel strongholds the oath was not administered & the Govr will consequently reject the returns" (DLC-RTL).
On October 17 Hoffman telegraphed again: "Allagheny official majority eight hundred and eighty five (885) for the Constitution Dorchester one thousand

and forty (1040) against. Worcester eleven hundred and ninety (1190) against Soldiers vote actually returned fourteen hundred and eighty (1480) majority for. Its estimated that at least one thousand further majority will be obtained from the soldiers. Our friends are still confident that the constitution will have a small majority on the total official vote" (*ibid.*).

On the back of the telegram appears the following tabulation in Lincoln's autograph:

"885	1092
7726	100
132	650
1	650
54	1040
992	120
1456	488
11.246	958
87	940
139	1237
172	1404
175	1650
94	978
660	590
250	1190
71	13087
12 894	12894
	193"

Endorsement[1]

More likely to abstain from *stopping* once they get at it, until they shall have voted several times each.   A.L.

Oct. 16. 1864

[1] AES, NAuE. Lincoln's endorsement (misdated October 16, 1863, in Lapsley, VI, 450) appears on a letter to Seward dated at New York on October 15, 1864, and signed with the unidentified initials "P.J.J.": "On the point of leaving I am told by a gentleman to whose statements I attach Credit, that the opposition Policy for the Presidential Campaign will be to '*abstain from voting.*'"

To James K. Moorhead[1]

Office U.S. Military Telegraph,
Hon. J. K. Moorehead   War Department,
Pittsburgh, Pa.   Washington, D.C., Oct. 16 1864.

I do not rem[em]ber about the Peter Gilner case, and must look it up before I can answer.   A. LINCOLN

[1] ALS, DNA WR RG 107, Presidential Telegrams, I, 206. See Lincoln to Meade, September 20, *supra*. James K. Moorhead telegraphed Lincoln on October 12: "Please stay the execution of Peter Gilner sixty second (62) Pa Letter by mail" (DLC-RTL). Moorhead's letter has not been found, but a second telegram on October 15 read: "Have you respited or pardoned Peter Gilner ans" (*ibid.*). AGO *Special Orders No. 355*, October 19, 1864, ordered that the unexecuted portion of Private Peter Gilner's sentence be remitted and that he be released from imprisonment and discharged the service.

Appointment of George Harrington[1]

Washington, October 17th. 1864.

George Harrington, is hereby appointed to discharge the duties of Secretary of the Treasury, during the absence of Wm. P. Fessenden, the Secretary. ABRAHAM LINCOLN

[1] DS, owned by J. G. Heyn, Minneapolis, Minnesota.

To Joseph K. Barnes[1]

Surgeon General please say in writing on this whether there is, & where, a vacant Hospital chaplaincy. A. LINCOLN

Oct. 17. 1864

[1] AES, OFH. Lincoln's endorsement is written on a letter from Thaddeus Stevens, October 15, 1864, recommending "the Revd. Mr. Bishop" for appointment as hospital chaplain. Acting Surgeon General Charles H. Crane endorsed, "Very respectfully returned to His Excellency the President. There is no vacancy at present in any hospital." The Reverend Mr. Bishop has not been further identified.

To Andrew G. Curtin[1]

Cypher   Office U.S. Military Telegraph,
Gov. A. G. Curtin   War Department,
Harrisburg, Pa.   Washington, D.C., Oct. 17 1864.

Your information is erroneous. No part of Sheridan's force has left him, except by expiration of terms of service. I think there is not much danger of a raid into Pennsylvania. A. LINCOLN

[1] ALS, DNA WR RG 107, Presidential Telegrams, I, 207. On October 17, Governor Curtin telegraphed Lincoln: "I have information . . . that the enemy has arranged for a raid into Pennsylvania about the end of this month. Part of my information is, that Sheridan's force has been reduced to 25,000, and that the Sixth and Nineteenth Corps are under orders to join General Grant. . . . I have little doubt a serious threat, much more a raid into Pennsylvania in this month, would be followed by serious disaster. . . . Will you please to telegraph me to-day on the subject. . . . In the meantime, if my information is at all correct, vigorous measures should at once be taken. . . ." (OR, I, XLIII, II, 392-93).

To Charles A. Dana[1]

Executive Mansion,
Washington, Oct. 17, 1864.

Will Mr. Dana please report to me on the case of Constantine Bowling? A. LINCOLN

[1] ALS, owned by Dale Carnegie, New York City. Constantine Bowling has not been identified, and no report from Dana has been found.

To Alfred B. Justice and Others[1]

Mr A. B. Justice & others;

Executive Mansion, Washington,
October 17th, 1864.

I have received at the hands of Hon. Wm. D. Kelley, a very beautiful and ingeniously constructed Pocket Knife, accompanied by your kind letter of presentation.

The gift is gratefully accepted and will be highly valued, not only as an extremely creditable specimen of American workmanship, but as a manifestation of your regard and esteem which I most cordially appreciate. Your ob't serv't   A. LINCOLN

[1] LS, owned by Mrs. Alfred R. Justice, Philadelphia, Pennsylvania. See the similar letter to Justice, September, *supra*.

To Horatio G. Wright[1]

Executive Mansion,
Washington, Oct. 17, 1864.

S. S. Bradford, whose residence is in Culpeper Co. Va, and who is a brother-in-law, of Gen. H. G. Wright, is now on parole not to go South of Philadelphia. If Gen. Wright will request it in writing on this sheet, I will allow Mr. Bradford to go home to Culpeper.

A. LINCOLN

[1] ALS, RPB. Major General Horatio G. Wright answered on the verso, from Headquarters, Sixth Army Corps, October 24, 1864:

"If my brother-in-law, Mr. S[laughter]. S. Bradford, shall give his parole of honor, in form satisfactory to the government, that he will remain entirely neutral, in word and act, as between the United States and the rebels, till regularly exchanged, I would ask that he be permitted to return to his home near Culpeper C. H. Va—otherwise not.

"Mr Bradford has never, as I believe, taken any active part in the present contest; and more over, I have such confidence in his integrity and sense of honor that I should unhesitatingly rely on his observing, strictly, any obligations he may take upon himself. Hence the above request."

See Lincoln's pass for Bradford, December 21, *infra*.

To Ethan A. Hitchcock[1]

Will Gen. Hitchcock, please see & hear the bearer, Mr. Leech.

Oct. 19. 1864   A. LINCOLN

[1] AES, DLC-RTL. Lincoln's endorsement is written on the envelope of a letter from Richard Yates, October 3, 1864, introducing "Mr. W. Leach, a loyal and praiseworthy citizen . . . who visits Washington to procure . . . the exchange of his Brother-in-Law Lt. A[braham]. Allee, of Co 'K' 16th Ills Cavly. . . . whose health has been impaired by exposure in the field and confinement in prison . . . at Savannah Ga. . . ." General Hitchcock wrote beneath Lincoln's endorsement, "The undersigned feels that it would be unjust to prisoners left in the South, to recommend a special exchange except upon grounds of a public character, and such grounds do not appear in this case." The address of W. Leech (or Leach) is noted on the envelope as "Lincoln, Ill."

AGO *Special Orders, No. 474,* December 30, 1864, ordered Second Lieutenant Allee and other officers "recently escaped Prisoners of War . . . to join their regiments in the field. Permission to delay reporting for thirty days, is hereby granted them."

Response to a Serenade[1]

Friends and Fellow-citizens:[2]   October 19, 1864

I am notified that this is a compliment paid me by the loyal Marylanders, resident in this District. I infer that the adoption of the new constitution for the State, furnishes the occasion; and that, in your view, the extirpation of slavery constitutes the chief merit of the new constitution. Most heartily do I congratulate you, and Maryland, and the nation, and the world, upon the event. I regret that it did not occur two years sooner, which I am sure would have saved to the nation more money than would have met all the private loss incident to the measure. But it has come at last, and I sincerely hope it's friends may fully realize all their anticipations of good from it; and that it's opponents may, by it's effects, be agreeably and profitably, disappointed.

A word upon another subject.

Something said by the Secretary of State in his recent speech at Auburn, has been construed by some into a threat that, if I shall be beaten at the election, I will, between then and the end of my constitutional term, do what I may be able, to ruin the government.

Others regard the fact that the Chicago Convention adjourned, not *sine die,* but to meet again, if called to do so by a particular individual, as the intimation of a purpose that if their nominee shall be elected, he will at once seize control of the government. I hope the good people will permit themselves to suffer no uneasiness on either point. I am struggling to maintain government, not to overthrow it. I am struggling especially to prevent others from overthrowing it. I therefore say, that if I shall live, I shall remain President until the fourth of next March; and that whoever shall be constitutionally elected therefor in November, shall be duly installed as President on the fourth of March; and that in the interval I shall do my utmost that whoever is to hold the helm for the next voyage, shall start with the best possible chance to save the ship.

This is due to the people both on principle, and under the constitution. Their will, constitutionally expressed, is the ultimate law for all. If they should deliberately resolve to have immediate peace even at the loss of their country, and their liberty, I know not the power or the right to resist them. It is their own business, and they must do as they please with their own. I believe, however, they are still resolved to preserve their country and their liberty; and in this, in office or out of it, I am resolved to stand by them.

I may add that in this purpose to save the country and it's liberties, no classes of people seem so nearly unanamous as the soldiers in the field and the seamen afloat. Do they not have the hardest of it? Who should quail while they do not?

God bless the soldiers and seamen, with all their brave commanders.

[1] AD, MH; New York *Tribune*, October 20, 1864. Henry Willis, chairman of the loyal citizens of Maryland resident in the District of Columbia, wrote Lincoln on October 19, that it was the intention of the group to "Serenade your Excellency this evening at 8 o'clock." (DLC-RTL).
[2] The salutation does not appear in the manuscript.

To Christopher C. Augur[1]

October 20, 1864

If not inconsistent with the service, will Gen. Augur please allow the furlough requested. The father of the boy is a domestic in my service.　　　　　　　　　　　　　　　　A. LINCOLN

Oct. 20, 1864

[1] ALS, NSh. The persons are unidentified.

To Isabel II[1]

October 20, 1864

Abraham Lincoln:
President of the United States of America.
To Her Majesty Doña Isabel II.
By the Grace of God and the Constitution of the Spanish Monarchy, Queen of Spain, &c. &c.

Great and Good Friend:—I have received the letter which Your Majesty was pleased to address to me on the 30th. of June last, announcing the marriage of your niece, Her Royal Highness, the Infante Doña Maria Isabel Francisca de Asis, to His Royal Highness the Count of Paris, Louis Phillippe of Orleans.

I participate in the satisfaction afforded by this happy event, and offer to Your Majesty my sincere congratulations on the occasion, and so recommend Your Majesty, and Your Majesty's Royal Family to the protection of the Almighty. Your Good Friend,

Washington, October 20th. 1864　　　　ABRAHAM LINCOLN.
By the President,
WILLIAM H. SEWARD, Secretary of State.

[1] Copy, DNA FS RG 59, Communications to Foreign Sovereigns and States, III, 242.

To Isabel II[1]

October 20, 1864

Abraham Lincoln:
President of the United States of America.

To Her Majesty Doña Isabel II.

By the Grace of God and the Constitution of the Spanish Monarchy, Queen of Spain, &c. &c.

Great and Good Friend: I have received the letter which Your Majesty was pleased to address to me on the 12th. of March last, conveying the melancholy tidings of the decease of His Royal Highness the Infante Don Felipe Ramon Marie, Your Majesty's beloved nephew.

I participate in the grief occasioned by this sad event and offer to Your Majesty and to Your Royal household my sincere condolence.

May God have Your Majesty always in His safe and holy keeping. Your Good Friend,   ABRAHAM LINCOLN.

Washington, October 20th. 1864.

By the President,

WILLIAM H. SEWARD, Secretary of State.

[1] Copy, DNA FS RG 59, Communications to Foreign Sovereigns and States, III, 243.

Memorandum Concerning James Hughes[1]

October 20, 1864

I am willing that any case, that of Judge Hughes as well as another, if coming within the precedent of what I call the Johnson case, may go as the Johnson case did. I really desire that Judge Hughes shall be obliged.   A. LINCOLN

Oct. 20, 1864.

[1] ADS, owned by Richard F. Lufkin, Boston, Massachusetts. See Lincoln's recommendation for Hughes, October 22, *infra*, and Lincoln to Fessenden, October 3, *supra*.

Order Concerning Mrs. Annie Wittenmyer[1]

October 20, 1864

Let this Lady have transportation to any of the Armies, and any previleges while there, not objected to by the commanders of the armies respectively.   A. LINCOLN.

Oct. 20. 1864

[54]

1 AES, owned by Don Knaur, Pottstown, Pennsylvania. Lincoln's endorsement is written on the back of a permit signed by Edwin M. Stanton, July 25, 1862:

"Permission is hereby given to Mrs. Annie Wittenmeyer, Special Agent of the Iowa Sanitary Association, to pass with such goods as she may have in charge, to and within the lines of any of the Armies of the Departments of Kansas and of the Mississippi, for the purpose of visiting the sick and wounded soldiers of the Iowa Regiments in either of those Armies.

"Quartermasters will furnish transportation for herself and stores, and Commissaries will provide her with subsistence. It is also specially enjoined upon all officers to afford her every facility in carrying out her charitable purpose, it being shown that she is worthy of great respect." Surgeon General Joseph K. Barnes also endorsed the document on October 20, 1864: "Mrs. A. Wittenmyer is specially commended to the attention and courtesy of all medical officers." Mrs. Wittenmyer inaugurated "diet kitchens" for the hospitals and organized aid for the widows and orphans of Union soldiers.

Proclamation of Thanksgiving[1]

October 20, 1864
By the President of the United States of America:

A Proclamation.

It has pleased Almighty God to prolong our national life another year, defending us with his guardian care against unfriendly designs from abroad, and vouchsafing to us in His mercy many and signal victories over the enemy, who is of our own household. It has also pleased our Heavenly Father to favor as well our citizens in their homes as our soldiers in their camps and our sailors on the rivers and seas with unusual health. He has largely augmented our free population by emancipation and by immigration, while he has opened to us new sources of wealth, and has crowned the labor of our working men in every department of industry with abundant rewards. Moreover, He has been pleased to animate and inspire our minds and hearts with fortitude, courage and resolution sufficient for the great trial of civil war into which we have been brought by our adherence as a nation to the cause of Freedom and Humanity, and to afford to us reasonable hopes of an ultimate and happy deliverance from all our dangers and afflictions.

Now, therefore, I, Abraham Lincoln, President of the United States, do, hereby, appoint and set apart the last Thursday in November next as a day, which I desire to be observed by all my fellow-citizens wherever they may then be as a day of Thanksgiving and Praise to Almighty God the beneficent Creator and Ruler of the Universe. And I do farther recommend to my fellow-citizens aforesaid that on that occasion they do reverently humble them-

[55]

selves in the dust and from thence offer up penitent and fervent prayers and supplications to the Great Disposer of events for a return of the inestimable blessings of Peace, Union and Harmony throughout the land, which it has pleased him to assign as a dwelling place for ourselves and for our posterity throughout all generations.

In testimony whereof, I have hereunto set my hand and caused the seal of the United States to be affixed.

Done at the city of Washington this twentieth day of October, in the year of our Lord one thousand eight hundred and [L.S.]   sixty four, and, of the Independence of the United States the eighty-ninth.   ABRAHAM LINCOLN

By the President:

WILLIAM H SEWARD Secretary of State.

[1] DS, DNA FS RG 11, Proclamations. On October 9, 1864, Sarah Josepha Hale wrote Seward to remind him of the approach of Thanksgiving:

"Enclosed is an article (or proof) on the National Thanksgiving. As you were, last year, kindly interested in this subject, I venture to request your good offices again.

"My article will appear in the *November* number of the "Lady's Book"; but before its publication I trust that *President Lincoln* will have issued his *proclamation appointing the last Thursday in November as the Day*.

"I send a copy of the *proof* for the President. You will greatly oblige me by handing this to him and acquainting him with the contents of this letter. I do not like to trouble him with a note. Should the president see fit to issue his proclamation at once, the important paper would have time to reach the knowledge of American citizens in Europe and Asia, as well as throughout our wide land. If the President should recommend that all American ministers and consuls etc– should observe the Day in their respective offices in Foreign countries would it not have a good effect on our citizens abroad? And if, on land and sea, wherever the American Flag floats over an American citizen all should be invited and unite in this National Thanksgiving, would it not be a glorious Festival?" (DLC-RTL).

To William I[1]

October 20, 1864

Abraham Lincoln:
President of the United States of America.

To His Majesty William I.
    King of Prussia, &c. &c.

Great and Good Friend: I have received the letter which Your Majesty was pleased to address to me on the 16th. ultimo, announcing the birth of a Prince to your well beloved daughter-in-law, the wife of the Prince Royal of Prussia, the Princess Victoria Adelaide Maria Louisa Princess Royal of Great Britain and Ireland and Duchess of Saxony.

I participate in the satisfaction which this happy event has afforded to Your Majesty, and to Your Majesty's Royal Family, and offer my sincere congratulations upon the occasion.

May God have Your Majesty, always in His safe and holy keeping. Your Good Friend, ABRAHAM LINCOLN.

Washington, October 20th. 1864.

By the President,

WILLIAM H. SEWARD, Secretary of State.

¹ Copy, DNA FS RG 59, Communications to Foreign Sovereigns and States, III, 244.

To John G. Nicolay[1]

"*Cypher*"   Office U.S. Military Telegraph,
J. G. Nicolay   War Department, Washington, D.C.,
St. Louis, Mo.   Oct. 21. 9/45 PM 1864.

While Curtis is fighting Price have you any idea where the force under Rosecrans is? or what it is doing?   A. LINCOLN

¹ ALS, DNA WR RG 107, Presidential Telegrams, I, 208. No reply from Nicolay has been found. General Curtis telegraphed Halleck from "Near Independence, Mo." on October 21: "I have been fighting Price three hours on the Little Blue with my cavalry. We have a strong position fifteen miles in the rear, where I intend to make a stand. . . ." (OR, I, XLI, IV, 163). On the same day Rosecrans was on the road to Lexington, Missouri, "Camp near Davis' Creek" (*ibid.*, p. 158). Nicolay had written Lincoln an eleven-page letter reporting on Missouri affairs, from Springfield, Illinois, October 18, which would indicate that he had already left St. Louis and hence probably never received Lincoln's telegram (DLC-RTL).

Pass for Mrs. J. R. Reid[1]

October 21, 1864

Allow Mrs. J. R. Reid, with her little daughter, to pass our lines at any convenient point on or near the James River, and come to Washington.   A. LINCOLN

Oct. 21. 1864.

¹ ADS-P, ISLA. Mrs. Reid has not been identified.

Response to a Serenade[1]

October 21, 1864

FELLOW-CITIZENS: I was promised not to be called upon for a speech to-night, nor do I propose to make one. But, as we have been

[57]

hearing some very good news for a day or two, I propose that you give three hearty cheers for Sheridan.

While we are at it we may as well consider how fortunate it was for the Secesh that Sheridan was a very little man. If he had been a large man, there is no knowing what he would have done with them.

I propose three cheers for General Grant, who knew to what use to put Sheridan; three cheers for all our noble commanders and the soldiers and sailors; three cheers for all people everywhere who cheer the soldiers and sailors of the Union—and now, good night.

1 Washington *Daily Morning Chronicle*, October 22, 1864. A torchlight parade "passed through the grounds in front of the Presidential Mansion, where a large crowd had gathered, and kept up a continual blaze of light with rockets, blue-lights, Roman-candles, &c., lighting up the upper windows under the portico, at which stood the President and 'little Thad,' . . . After the procession had left the grounds, the crowd called loudly for the President, and he responded as follows: [text as above]."

To William B. Campbell and Others[1]

Executive Mansion,
Washington, D.C., Oct. 22, 1864.

Messrs. Wm. B. Campbell, Thos. A. R. Nelson, James T. P. Carter, John Williams, A. Blizzard, Henry Cooper, Bailie Peyton, John Lellyett, Em. Etheridge, John D. Perryman:

Gentlemen: On the 15th day of this month, as I remember, a printed paper, with a few manuscript interlineations, called a protest, with your names appended thereto, and accompanied by another printed paper purporting to be a proclamation by Andrew Johnson, Military Governor of Tennessee, and also a manuscript

1 Washington *National Republican*, October 22, 1864. John Lellyett's account of the presentation of the protest is given in a letter to the editor of the New York *World*, October 15, 1864, which appeared in the *World* on October 18:

"I called upon the President to-day and presented and read to him the subjoined protest. Having concluded, Mr. Lincoln responded:

" 'May I inquire how long it took you and the New-York politicians to concoct that paper?'

"I replied, 'It was concocted in Nashville, without communication with any but Tennesseans. We communicated with citizens of Tennessee, outside of Nashville, but not with New-York politicians.'

" 'I will answer,' said Mr. Lincoln emphatically, 'that *I expect to let the friends of George B. McClellan manage their side of this contest in their own way; and I will manage my side of it in* MY *way.*'

" 'May we ask an answer in writing,' I suggested.

" 'Not now. Lay those papers down here. I will give no other answer now. I may or may not write something about this hereafter. I understand this. I know you intend to make a point of this. But go ahead, you have my answer.'

" 'Your answer then is that you expect to let General McClellan's friends manage their side of this contest in their own way, and you will manage your side of it in your way?'

" 'Yes.'

"I then thanked the President for his courtesy in giving us a hearing at all, and took my leave.

"Judge [Charles] Mason, of this city, was present at the interview, to whom I refer in regard to the correctness of this report. On stepping outside of the door of the executive mansion I immediately wrote down the President's emphatic response, and submitted it to Judge Mason and another gentleman who happened to be present, and they both pronounced it accurate.

"And now I have a word to say to the people of the United States, who are, or ought to be, the masters of Abraham Lincoln. The paper which I had the honor to present to the President is not the 'concoction of New-York politicians,' however that might affect its merits. It is the solemn voice of a once free and proud people, protesting against their own disfranchisement by the agent of Abraham Lincoln. It is the voice of those loyal men in Tennessee who have borne the reproach of a people they still loved, supporting the President in all lawful efforts to preserve the Union. The reward of our loyalty is disfranchisement. The cup of perjury is commended to our lips, because it is known that we will not touch its contents. Judge ye between the people of Tennessee and Abraham Lincoln. It may be meet that our solemn and respectful appeal should be thrown aside with a contemptuous sneer. Look to it. If you, the people of the Northern states, shall sustain this act of tyranny, your own time will soon come. If the President of the United States may 'manage his side of this contest' by setting aside the very letter of the Constitution, and altering the election laws of the state so as to disfranchise his opponents, liberty is already dead."

The reply to Lincoln's communication, signed by Campbell, Peyton, and Lellyett, appeared in the *World* on election day, November 8:

"To Abraham Lincoln, President of the United States.

SIR: Your letter in reply to the Tennessee protest has reached us, and has, no doubt, been read by the people. The argument on this subject is nearly exhausted, but we have some additional and most important *facts* to submit to the people, in further elucidation of the subject. Our wonder is not excited to learn that you had not seen the proclamation of Governor Johnson, and scarcely heard of it until presented by us. It is an evil of no small magnitude, connected with your administration, that military subordinates assume despotic powers without asking the sanction of their superiors—even presuming to give law to the people by proclamation and to repeal and modify our laws at will. The idea that the President himself can make, or repeal, or modify a law of the land, state or national, constitutional or statutory, though freely practiced upon by yourself, is a doctrine of despotism in 'irrepressible conflict' with the principles of public liberty. And when these things are done by subordinates, the evil becomes intolerably oppressive, and calls for the firmest and most active lawful resistance which a people deserving to be free can offer.

"You tell us that 'the movement set on foot by the convention and Governor Johnson does not, as seems to be assumed by you, emanate from the national executive.' What we did assume is, that the plan was promulgated by proclamation of the military governor, who has no authority but that derived directly from you, and it was given the force of law by his edict. It thus became indirectly your act; and now that you decline to order the edict to be recalled or modified, it becomes your own as fully as if it had *emanated* from you. 'In no proper sense,' you say, 'can it be considered other than an independent movement of at least a portion of the loyal people of Tennessee.' Independent of what? Manifestly independent of all lawful authority—independent of and at war with the federal Constitution, which you have both sworn to support, protect, and defend.

What right has a citizen or officer to favor an 'independent movement' at variance with the Constitution, and support the same by force of arms? What less is this than waging war against the Constitution of the United States, and the government established thereby? 'An *independent movement*' against the Constitution, supported by a military governor by force of arms, recommended by an assembly calling itself a convention. Such in principle were the 'independent movements' of governors and 'portions of the people' which set at first in motion the great rebellion in the South with which we are contending. The 'convention' calls upon a military governor to order an 'independent movement' to help your re-election, and to support it by force of arms, placing 'guards' around the ballot-box. And their recommendation is adopted by the military governor and 'made' by him 'part of his proclamation.' And yet you say, 'I do not perceive in the plan any menace of coercion or violence toward any one.' Just so with the earlier 'independent movement' of Governor [Isham G.] Harris in this state, which we opposed as we oppose this. There was no menace of coercion or violence toward any who should consent to see the Constitution violated and the 'political plan' carried out without opposition. But the bayonet was kept in view, as it is in this case. Public meetings were menaced, and perhaps broken up by armed force. And so it is now. Those opposed to the 'independent movement' were denounced as traitors, and so they are now. Troops from our own and from other states were used to overawe the people, and so they are now. We had vigilance committees and mob violence then. We have now secret leagues, and are liable at any time to arbitrary arrest, as well as to mob violence, which is now used in our midst.

"These are general facts, in support of which we add the following specifications: We have held a number of peaceable and loyal public meetings in this city, more than one of which has been 'menaced' by your partisans. On the 21st instant such a meeting was held at the court-house in this city. It was held 'peacefully' and conducted 'loyally,' the assembly consisting chiefly of the 'friends of George B. McClellan.' A number of provost guards were present, by request of those who conducted the meeting, to preserve order. The meeting had been addressed by a gentleman who is an exile from his home because of his loyalty, and who has spent much time in the military service of the government during the war. One of the undersigned, a McClellan elector (Hon. Balie Peyton), had taken the stand to address the meeting, when the hall was suddenly entered by a large party of soldiers, and the meeting violently broken up. These men rushed in with guns and drawn pistols, crying, 'disperse you d——d rebels and traitors,' extinguishing the lights and driving the people from the hall.

"We specify further that on the 25th instant the rioters, thirty in number, published a card in the Nashville *Times*, the organ in this city of Governor Johnson, to which they append their names, as 'all members of Company D, First Tennessee light artillery.' This company was raised and its officers appointed (as we understand) under the superintendence of Governor Johnson. The rioters speak thus in their card: 'Neither Governor Johnson, nor any other individual outside of the men who were active participants, knew anything of our intention till the affair was over. Some colored men may have followed us, but we knew nothing of them.' 'We do not fear a court-martial;' they defiantly add, 'and therefore cheerfully give our names as loyal and Union-loving soldiers.'

"We specify further that on the evening of the 24th instant, only three days after the McClellan meeting was broken up, our streets were paraded by an immense procession of negroes, bearing torches and transparencies, with such inscriptions on the latter as 'Lincoln and Johnson,' 'Liberty or Death.' Some disorders occurred in connection with this demonstration, and shots were freely fired by the negroes—some at a window where white persons were standing, and some at persons on the streets. One of the latter (an employe of the government) was dangerously, if not mortally, wounded, and it was thought others were hit.

In the course of these orgies the procession waited on Governor Andrew Johnson, at the Capitol, and he delivered to the negro assembly an address. A report of his speech was published and republished in his organ, the *Times*, and from that report we take the following extract. Governor Johnson says:

"'I speak to night as a citizen of Tennessee. I am here on my own soil, and mean to remain here, and fight this great battle of freedom through to the end. Loyal men, from this day forward, are to be the controllers of Tennessee's grand and sublime destiny, and rebels must be dumb. We will not listen to their counsels. Nashville is no longer the place for them to hold their meetings. Let them gather their treasonable conclaves elsewhere—among their friends in the confederacy. They shall not hold their conspiracies in Nashville.'

"The language of the rioters, 'Disperse rebels and traitors,' and the common application of such terms of abuse and terror to the friends of General McClellan here, do not admit of our ignoring the meaning of Governor Johnson in the language quoted. The allusion is evidently to the riotous dispersion of our meeting three evenings previous. He also seems to adopt your idea that, as a citizen of Tennessee, he 'has the right to favor any political plan he chooses.' And he unmistakably evinces his determination to 'manage' his 'side of this contest in his own way.'

"'Governor Johnson,' you say, 'like any other loyal citizen, has a right to favor any political plan he chooses.' We do not so read the duty of the citizen. Some of the political plans of our day are devised to overturn the Constitution and government of the United States—and this is one of them. The southern rebellion is another. Neither the citizens nor Governor Johnson has a right to favor such plans, unless it be upon the principle advanced by you as a member of Congress, that 'any people, any where, being inclined, and having the power, have the right' to revolutionize, their government; that 'this is a most valuable, a most *sacred* right.' We shall despair of the republic if these principles of anarchy, as embodied in you, shall be adopted by the people in your re-election.

"In the face of the reign of terror which has been established in Tennessee under the eyes of Governor Johnson, you say to us: 'Do as you please, on your own account, peacefully and loyally, and Governor Johnson will not molest you, but will protect you against violence so far as is in his power.' If you mean that Governor Johnson will allow us to stay away from the polls without molestation, we trust there is some truth in your assurance. But if you mean to suggest that we hold separate elections 'on our own account,' and to assure us that we shall not be molested but protected in such a 'movement,' we know by experience, and by the facts above set forth, that your assurance is a cruel mockery. We will not advise our citizens to put in jeopardy their lives in going through the farce you propose, of holding an election under the laws at one ballot-box, while Governor Johnson holds an election under his 'plan' at another. Too many unoffending citizens have already been murdered in our streets by negro soldiers—too many reputable women have been insulted by them. We do not wish to provoke further outrage. There will be no election for President in Tennessee in 1864. You and Governor Johnson may 'manage your side of it in your own way,' but it will be no *election*.

"After consultation with our friends, therefore, in different parts of the state, and having communicated with nearly all of our colleagues, we respectfully announce to the people of Tennessee that in view of what is set forth above—in view of the fact that our people are overawed by military power, the laws set aside and violated with impunity—and in view of the fact that we have appealed in vain to the President whose duty it is to 'see that the laws be faithfully executed,' and that those who act by his authority shall hold sacred the liberties of the people; in view of these things we announce that the McClellan electoral ticket in Tennessee is withdrawn.

"Nashville, October 29."

"W. B. CAMPBELL, of Wilson county,
"BAILIE PEYTON, of Sumner county,
"JOHN LELLYETT, of Davidson county."

paper purporting to be extracts from the Code of Tennessee, was laid before me. The Protest, Proclamation and Extracts are respectively as follows:

To his Excellency Abraham Lincoln, President of the United States:
SIR: The undersigned, loyal citizens of the United States and of the State of Tennessee, on our own behalf and on behalf of the loyal people of our State, ask leave to submit this Protest against the Proclamation of his Excellency Andrew Johnson, Military Governor, ordering an election to be held for President and Vice President, under certain regulations and restrictions therein set forth. A printed copy of said proclamation is herewith enclosed.

The Constitution of the United States provides that "Each State shall appoint, *in such manner as the Legislature thereof may direct,* a number of electors," &c. Under this provision of the Federal Constitution, the Legislature of Tennessee, years before the present rebellion, prescribed the mode of election to be observed, which will be found to differ essentially from the mode prescribed by the Military Governor. We herewith enclose a copy of the Law of Tennessee governing the holding of said election.

The Military Governor expressly assumes, by virtue of authority derived from the President, to so alter and amend the election law of Tennessee, (enacted under authority of the Constitution of the United States, as above set forth,) as to make the same conform to his own edict as set forth in the proclamation aforesaid.

He assumes so as to modify our law as to admit persons to vote at the said election who are not entitled to vote under the law and the Constitution of Tennessee. Instance this: our Constitution and Law require that each voter shall be "a citizen of the *county* wherein he may offer his vote, for six months next preceding the day of election;" while the Governor's order only requires that he shall (with other qualifications named) be a citizen of Tennessee for six months, &c. This provision would admit to vote many persons not entitled by law.

We will, for the sake of brevity, pass over some less important points of conflict between the proclamation and the law, but will instance in this place another. By our law it is provided that the polls shall be opened in every civil district in each county in the state; but the proclamation provides only for their being opened at one place in each county. This provision would put it out of the power of many legal voters to exercise the elective franchise.

We solemnly protest against these infringements of our law, conflicting as they do, with the very letter of the Federal Constitution, because they are without authority, and because they will prevent a free, fair, and true expression of the will of the loyal people of Tennessee.

But we protest still more emphatically against the most unusual and impracticable test oath which it is proposed to require of all citizen voters in Tennessee. A citizen qualified to vote, and whose loyalty cannot be "disproved by other testimony," is to be required to swear, first, that he "will henceforth support the Constitution of the United States, and defend it against all enemies." This obligation we are willing to renew daily; but this is not yet deemed a sufficient test of loyalty. He is required to make oath and subscribe to a mass of vain repetitions concerning his activity as a friend of the Union and the enemy of its enemies—concerning his desires his hopes and fears—and that he finds it in his heart to rejoice over the scenes of blood, and of wounds, of anguish and death, wherein his friends, his kindred, his loved ones are slain, or maimed, or made prisoners of war—whereby the land of his birth or adoption is made desolate, and lamentation and mourning are spread over the whole nation. While all the civilized world stands aghast in contemplation of the unequalled horrors of our tremendous strife, the citizen of Tennessee is called upon by her Military Governor, under your authority, to swear that in these things he finds occasion to *rejoice*! As if this were still not enough, the citizen is further required to swear to the indefinite prolongation of this war, as follows: "That I will cordially oppose all armistices or *negotiations for peace with rebels in arms*, until the Constitution of the United States and all laws and proclamations made in pursuance thereof shall be established over all the people of every State and Territory embraced within the National Union;" until (in brief) the war shall be at an end. Now, we freely avow to your Excellency, and to the world, that we earnestly desire the return of peace and good-will to our now unhappy country —that we seek neither pleasure, profit, nor honor in the perpetuation of war—that we should feel bound, as Christians, as patriots and as civilized men—that we are bound by the oaths we have taken—to countenance and encourage any negotiations which may be entered into by the proper authorities with the intent to restore peace and union under the Constitution we have sworn to support and defend. We should be traitors to our country, false to our oaths—false, indeed, to the primary clause of the oath we are now discussing, to oppose such negotiations. We cannot consent to swear at the ballot-box a war of extermination against our countrymen and kindred, or to prolong by our opposition, for a single day after it can be brought to an honorable and lawful conclusion, a contest the most sanguinary and ruinous that has scourged mankind.

You will not have forgotten, that in the month of July last, you issued the following proclamation:

"Executive Mansion,
"To whom it may concern: Washington, July 8 [18], 1864.
"Any proposition which embraces the restoration of peace, the integrity of the whole Union, and the abandonment of slavery, and which comes by and with an authority that can control the armies now at war against the United States, will be received and considered by the Executive Government of the United States, and will be met by liberal terms on other substantial and collateral points; and the bearer or bearers thereof shall have safe conduct both ways.

"ABRAHAM LINCOLN."

This is certainly a proposition to treat with rebels in arms—with their chiefs. Are we now to understand by this proclamation of one acting under your authority, and himself a candidate with you for the second office, that even the above proposition is withdrawn—that you will henceforth have no negotiations upon any terms, but unrelenting war to the bitter end? Or, are we to understand, that while you hold this proposition open, or yourself free to act as your judgment may dictate,

[63]

we, the citizens of Tennessee, shall *swear* to OPPOSE your negotiations?

In the next breath, the voter who has been thus *qualified,* is required to swear that he will "heartily aid and assist the loyal people *in whatever measures may be adopted* for the attainment of these ends." Adopted by whom? The oath does not say. We cannot tell what measures may be adopted. We cannot comment upon the absurdity of the obligation here imposed, without danger of departing from that respectful propriety of language which we desire to preserve in addressing the Chief Magistrate of the American people. But this is a clause of an oath which the candidate for the Vice Presidency requires at the lips of the loyal and qualified voters of Tennessee, before these citizens shall be allowed to vote for or against you and himself at the coming election!

For these reasons, and others, which, for the sake of brevity, we omit, we solemnly protest against the interference of the Military Governor with the freedom of the elective franchise in Tennessee. We deny his authority and yours, to alter, amend, or annul any law of Tennessee. We demand that Tennessee be allowed to appoint her Electors as expressly provided by the Federal Constitution, which you have sworn to support, protect, and defend, in the manner which the Legislature thereof has prescribed. And to that end we respectfully demand of you, as the principal under whose authority this order has been issued, that the same shall be revoked. We ask that all military interference shall be withdrawn so far as to allow the loyal men of Tennessee a full and free election. By the loyal men of Tennessee we mean those who have not participated in the rebellion, or given it aid and comfort; or who may have complied with such terms of amnesty as have been offered them under your authority.

On the 8th day of December, 1863, you, as President, issued a Proclamation, declaring that "a full pardon is hereby granted, with restoration of all rights of property," &c., to each of our citizens having participated, directly or by implication, in the existing rebellion, (with certain exceptions,) "upon the condition that every such person shall take and subscribe an oath, and thenceforward keep and maintain said oath inviolate." And it is further provided in the Proclamation aforesaid, that in the contingency of the reorganization of a State Government in Tennessee, or certain other States named, the persons having taken the oath referred to, being otherwise qualified by the election law of the State, shall be entitled to vote. The undersigned would state, that many of our citizens have complied in good faith with the terms of amnesty proposed in your Proclamation aforesaid; and are, therefore, by reason of the full pardon granted them, fully entitled to vote and exercise all other rights belonging to loyal citizens, without let or hindrance; and we respectfully appeal to you, as President of the United States, to make good your promise of pardon to these citizens, by the removal of all other and further hindrance to their exercise of the elective franchise.

But if it be claimed upon the plea of military necessity, that guards and restrictions shall be thrown around the ballot-box in Tennessee, we still ask the withdrawal of the Proclamation of the Military Governor, because the conditions thereby imposed upon the loyal men of Tennessee as a qualification for voting, are irrelevant, unreasonable, and not in any sense a test of loyalty. But they pledge the citizen to oppose the lawful authorities in the discharge of their duty. The oath required is only calculated to keep legal and rightful voters from the polls. We suggest that no oath be required but such as is prescribed by law. Our people will not hesitate, however, to take the usual oath of loyalty—for example, in the language of the primary clause of the oath in question: "That I will henceforth support the Constitution of the United States, and defend it against the assaults of its enemies." Denying your right to make any departure from the law in the case, we shall, however, feel no hardship in this.

The convention to which Governor Johnson refers was a mere partisan meeting, having no authority, and not representing the loyal men of Tennessee, in any sense.

The names of the signers of this protest have been placed before the people of Tennessee as candidates for Electors, who, if chosen, are expected to cast the electoral vote of Tennessee for George B. McClellan for President, and George H. Pendleton for Vice President. By virtue of such position, it becomes our province especially to appear before you in the attitude we do. We are aware that grave questions may arise, in any event, with regard to the regularity of the vote in Tennessee, in consequence of the partially disorganized condition of the State. The friends of your re-election, however, announced an electoral ticket; and the public became aware that preparations were being made for the holding of the election, leaving that matter no longer a question. Some time thereafter, our electoral ticket was placed before the public, and within a few days followed the proclamation complained of. We, for ourselves and those we represent, are willing to leave all questions involving the right of Tennessee to participate in the election to the decision of competent authority.

For the State at Large.
WM. B. CAMPBELL, of Wilson County.
THOS. A. R. NELSON, of Washington county.

For the Districts.
JAMES T. P. CARTER, of Carter county.
JOHN WILLIAMS, of Knox county.
A. BLIZARD, of McMinn county.
HENRY COOPER, of Bedford county.
BAILIE PEYTON, of Sumner county.
JOHN LELLYETT, of Davidson county.
EM. ETHERIDGE, of Weakley county.
JOHN D. PERRYMAN, of Shelby county.

PROCLAMATION.
BY THE GOVERNOR.

State of Tennessee,
Nashville, Tenn. Sept 30th, 1864.   Executive Department,
Whereas, a respectable portion of the loyal people of Tennessee, representing a large number of the counties of the State, and supposed to

reflect the will of the Union men in their respective counties, recently held a convention in the city of Nashville, in which, among other things touching the re-organization of the State, they with great unanimity adopted the following resolutions:

2. *Resolved*, That the people of Tennessee who are now and have been attached to the National Union, do hold an election for President and Vice President in the ensuing election in November.

3. That the electors shall be the following and no others; the same being free white men, twenty-one years of age, citizens of the United States, and for six months previous to the election, citizens of the State of Tennessee—

1st. All who have voluntarily borne arms in the service of the United States during the present war, and who are either in the service or have been honorably discharged.

2d. All the known active friends of the Government of the United States in each county.

4. *Resolved*, That the citizen electors designated in the foregoing resolutions shall, at least fifteen days before the election, register their names with an agent to be appointed for that purpose, and no citizen not thus registered shall be allowed to vote. Such registration shall be open to the public for inspection, and to be executed according to such regulations as may hereafter be prescribed: Provided that the officers of the election, in the discharge of their duty, may reject any party so registered on proof of disloyalty.

5. *Resolved*, That, as means for ascertaining the qualifications of the voters, the registers and officers holding the election may examine the parties on oath touching any matter of fact. And each voter, before depositing his vote, shall be required to take and subscribe the following oath, viz:

I solemnly swear that I will henceforth support the Constitution of the United States, and defend it against the assaults of all enemies; that I am an active friend of the Government of the United States, and the enemy of the so-called Confederate States; that I ardently desire the suppression of the present rebellion against the Government of the United States; that I sincerely rejoice in the triumph of the armies and navies of the United States, and in the defeat and overthrow of the armies, navies, and of all armed combinations in the interest of the so-called Confederate States; that I will cordially oppose all armistices or negotiations for peace with rebels in arms, until the Constitution of the United States and all laws and proclamations made in pursuance thereof, shall be established over all the people of every State and Territory embraced within the National Union, and that I will heartily aid and assist the loyal people in whatever measures may be adopted for the attainment of these ends; and further, that I take this oath freely and voluntarily, and without mental reservation. So help me God.

Said oath being *prima facie* evidence, subject to be disapproved by other testimony.

6. *Resolved*, That the polls be opened at the county seat, or some other suitable place in each county, and the ballot-box be so guarded and protected as to secure to electors a free, fair, and impartial election, and that polls also be opened for the convenience of the soldiers, at such places as may be accessible to them.

And whereas, it further appears from the proceedings of said Convention, "That the Military Governor of the State of Tennessee is requested to execute the foregoing resolutions in such manner as he may think best subserves the interests of the Government."

And whereas I, Andrew Johnson, Military Governor of the State of Tennessee, being anxious to co-operate with the loyal people of the State, and to encourage them in all laudable efforts to restore the State to law and order again, and to secure the ballot-box against the contamination of treason by every reasonable restraint that can be thrown around it, I do therefore order and direct that an election for President and Vice President of the United States of America be opened and held at the county seat, or other suitable place in every county in the State of Tennessee, upon the first Tuesday after the first Monday in the month of November next, at which all citizens and soldiers, being free white men, twenty-one years of age, citizens of the United States, and for six months prior to the election citizens of the State of Tennessee, who have qualified themselves by registration, and who take the oath prescribed in the foregoing resolutions, shall be entitled to vote, unless said oath shall be disproved by other testimony, for the candidates for President and Vice President of the United States.

And to the end that the foregoing resolutions, which are made part of this proclamation, may be faithfully executed, and the local citizens of the State, and none others, be permitted to exercise the right of suffrage I do hereby appoint the several gentlemen whose names are affixed to this proclamation, to aid in said election, and superintend the registration of the loyal voters in their respective counties, as provided by the fourth resolution above quoted.

But as the day of election is near at hand, and there may be a difficulty in completing the registration within the time limited, it is not intended that the registration be an indispensable prerequisite to the qualification of the voter; and in such cases, where it is impracticable, and where the voter is of known and established loyalty, he shall be entitled to vote, notwithstanding he may not have registered his name as required by the foregoing resolution.

The election shall be opened, conducted, returns made, &c., in all respects as provided by the 4th chapter of the "Code of Tennessee," except so far as the same is modified by this proclamation.

But in cases where the County Court fail or neglect to appoint inspectors or judges of election, and there is no sheriff or other civil officer in the county qualified by law to open and hold said election, the registrating agents, hereto appended, may act in his stead, and in all respects discharge the duties imposed in such cases upon sheriffs.

In like manner it is declared the duty of the military officers commanding Tennessee regiments, battalions, or detached squads, and surgeons in charge of the hospitals of Tennessee soldiers, to open and hold elections on the day aforesaid, under the same rules and regulations hereinbefore prescribed, and at such suitable places as will be convenient to the soldiers, who are hereby declared entitled to vote without oath or registration.

In testimony whereof, I, Andrew Johnson, Military Governor of the State of Tennessee, do hereunto set my hand, and have caused the Great

Seal of the State to be affixed at this Department, on the 30th day of September, A.D. 1864.

By the Governor: ANDREW JOHNSON. [L. S.]

Attest: EDWARD H. EAST, Secretary of State.

EAST TENNESSEE COUNTIES.

Anderson— John Leinart, Henry Hollaway, John Baker.

Bledsoe— William Foster, Frank Bridgeman.

Blount— Horace Foster, Stephen Mathis, James Henry, Jr.

Bradley— K. Clingam, W. R. Davis, John McPherson, A. J. McCaullie.

Campbell— John Preston, Reuben Rogers, Pryor Perkins.

Carter— Pleasant Williams, (of Stony Creek,) Elijah Simerly, Jones Smith.

Claiborne— Cannady Rodgers, Wm. D. Eppes, Ferney Jones.

Cocke— Jacob Reagan, Andrew Huff, Lt. Worthington, Sheriff Smith.

Cumberland— James Hamby, Thomas B. Swan, James H. Hamby.

Fentress— Henry Williams, Dr. J. D. Hale, David Baty, Rufus Dowdy.

Granger— John F. Nov, Anderson Acuff, M. Goldman.

Greene— R. C. Carter, Calvin Smith, Anderson W. Walker, James H. Reeves.

Hancock— Wm. Gilbert, Elbert Campbell, Isaac Campbell, Capt. Lewis Jarvis.

Hamilton— Col. C. C. McCaleb, Abe Pearson, Wash Evans.

Hawkins— Wm. D. Kanner, R. G. Wetherland, W. W. Willis.

Jefferson— J. Duffell Rankin, Press Swan, Wm. Harris, Duff G. Thornburgh.

Johnson— Col. R. R. Butler, Col. Sam Howard, Col. James Grayson.

Knox— Capt. Thos. Stephens, Andrew L. Knott, Wm. Hofner, Samuel McCammon.

Marion— Alexander Kelley, Robert Ralston, Pleasant Pryor, Wm. Pryor, Esq.

McMinn— James M. Henderson, John Mc———, G. W. Ross, F. B. McElwee.

Meigs— Wm. Adams, F. J. Mathis, Col. A. Cox, Robert Allen, James Gettys.

Monroe— Joseph Divine, Henry Duggan, Daniel Heiskell.

Morgan— James Langley, Sr., James Langley, Jr., S. C. Hunnycutt.

Overton— Rob't Smith, Anderson Winham, Geo. W. Bowman, Ellison Gussett.

Polk— Gen. James Gamble, Col. John Elliot, Charles McClary.

Rhea— Capt. J. B. Walker, Wm. H. Lowe, Samuel Lowe.

Roane— Joe D. Turner, Wm. Lowery, Wm. M. Alexander, J. Christopher Ables, Allen Robb, Sam. L. Childress.

Scott— Balie Putnam, Craven Duncan, James Lay.

Seviere— Col. Wm. Pickens, Reuben Hines, David McCroskey, Lemuel Dungan.

Sullivan— E. A. Millard, Wm. Mullenax, Esq., Enoch Shipley.

Union— James W. Turner, John Bayless, Calvin Monroe.

Washington— Calvin Hoes, John Mahoney, B. F. Swingle.

Sequatchie— Washington Hurd, Daniel McWilliams, B. F. Smith.

MIDDLE TENNESSEE COUNTIES,

Bedford— Joseph Thompson, Richard Phillips, Wm. T. Tune, Rob't T. Cannon.

Cannon— Hiram Morris, William Barten.

Cheatham— Warren Jordan.

Coffee— John F. Thomas.

Davidson— John Carper, Charles Sayers, Gen. J. Stubblefield, James Warren, T. J. Yarbrough, L. D. Wheeler, P. T. Phillips, J. B. Canfield, James Davis, W. W. Garrett.

DeKalb— William Hathaway, Wm. Blackburn, Andrew J. Garrison.

Dickson— Marsh Binkley.

Franklin—

Giles— J. C. Walker, Edward W. Rose, J. W. Alley, R. J. Gorden.

Grundy— William McCran, John Myers.

Hickman—

Humphreys— Wm. McKimmons, Wilkins Waggoner, David R. Owen, J. S. Spane, T. J. Winfrey, Mr. Thomas.

Jackson— James McKinney, John Gillem, Allen Davis.

Lawrence—

Lewis—

Lincoln— J. H. Fulgham, James T. Kirkpatrick.

Macon— Pleasant Chitwood, L. S. Clements, Geo. W. Clements.

Marshall— A. A. Steele

Maury— W. W. Jones, John D. Moore, John H. Campbell.

Montgomery— O. M. Blackman, Caleb Jones, D. S. Nye, Isaiah Barbee, Thomas F. Betters, Geo. Hampton.

Berry— W. O. Britt, F. M. Brasher, Jackson Taylor, J. S. Webb, A. H. Eathers.

Putnam— Joseph Rhea McColet.

Robertson— B. F. Aurt, Wiley Woodward, Jos. Starks.

Rutherford— Edward Jordan, Wm. Spence, Wm. C. Burt, James H. Carlton.

Smith— John W. Bowen, Asberry Griffin, Francis M. McKee.

Sumner—

Stewart—

Van Buren—

Warren— Samuel Henderson, Dr. J. B. Armstrong, Sam L. Colville, Miles Bonner.

White— Edward D. Pennington, Alex. Payne, James Coety

Williamson— A. W. Moss, Wm. P. Campbell, Franklin Hardeman, Wm. S. Campbell.

Wilson— Wm. Waters, Wm. J. Waters.

Wayne— Theodore H. Gibbs, Jas. Dougherty, F. Hall, Jasper Lypert, John Stamps.

WEST TENNESSEE COUNTIES

Benton— David Brewer, Allen Bearsons, David Little, Abraham Gussett, Sam. Tippett.

Carroll— Young W. Allen, John Wood, John Norman, Lucian Hawkins, Isaac Bouch.

Dyer— William Wesson.

[69]

Decatur— John Stegall, Simon Bonman, G. Menzies, James Roberts, W. H. Johnson.
Fayette—
Gibson—
Haywood—
Henderson— Robert Kizer, James Hart, James Smith.
Hardeman—
Henry— Anderson ———, Dr. J. W. Mathewson, Charles White, Temple Cowan.
Hardin— Thomas Maxwell, Michell Hood, Bailey Hinkell.
Lauderdale—
Madison— T. Skurlock.
McNairy— Wm. Scayne, John Barnes, ——— Gregg.
Obion— Dr. S. R. Chapin.
Shelby— J. B. Bingham, G. B. Ware, A. Gregg.
Tipton—
Weakley— J. W. Hays, Wm. Bell

EXTRACTS FROM CODE OF TENNESSEE. —

CHAPTER 4.

Of the Electors of President and Vice President

913. Each congressional district shall be an electoral district, and one Elector shall reside in each of said districts.

914. There shall be two Electors for the State who may reside in any part of the State.

915. Any citizen qualified by law to vote for members of the General Assembly, may vote for the whole number of Electors.

916. Said qualified voters shall meet at the places appointed by law for holding elections in every county, on the first Tuesday next after the first Monday in the month of November, in the years in which the President and Vice President are to be elected, and vote for a number of Electors equal to the whole number of Senators and Representatives to which the State is entitled in Congress.

917. The officer or person holding the election shall advertise at the court house in every county, and in every civil district of the county, the day on which said election shall take place, at least sixty days before the time of holding it.

918. The county court of every county shall appoint judges for every place of voting in the county, all of whom shall be sworn to conduct said election in the manner prescribed for electing members of the General Assembly.

919. If the county court neglect to appoint judges of the said elections, or those appointed refuse to act, the officer holding the election shall appoint judges out of the by-standers to hold the same.

920. [Of clerks and their qualifications.][2]

921. The election shall be conducted in the manner prescribed for electing members of the General Assembly.

[The other sections of this chapter prescribe rules concerning the

[2] Brackets are in the source.

comparison of polls, statements of same, returns, comparisons of returns, proceedings of Electors, vacancy, time of meeting to vote, certificate of voting, messenger, certificate by mail, lists of electors, and penalties on officers.][3]

Qualification of Voters for Members of the General Assembly
Referred to in Sec. 915 Above.

"Every free white man of the age of twenty-one years, being a citizen of the United States, and a citizen of the county where he may offer his vote, six months next preceding the day of election, shall be entitled to vote for members of the General Assembly."—*Code, Sec. 833, and Const. of Tenn., Art. 4, Sec. 1.*

Plans of Holding Elections, Referred to in Sec. 916, Above.

"The places of holding elections shall be in each civil district, at some convenient locality, to be designated by the county court at least six months before the election, and entered on record."—*Code 837.*

EXTRACTS FROM CODE.—ART. VI.
Officers of Popular Elections, Referred to in Sec. 917 Above.

839. The sheriff, or, if he is a candidate, the coroner, or if there be no coroner, some person appointed by the county court, shall hold all popular elections; and said officer or person shall appoint a sufficient number of deputies to hold said elections.

841. The county court, at the session next preceding the day of election, shall appoint three inspectors or judges for each voting place, to superintend the election.

842. If the county court fail to make the appointment, or any person appointed refuse to serve, the sheriff, with the advice of three justices, or, if none be present, three respectable freeholders, shall, before the beginning of the election, appoint said inspectors or judges.

843. If the sheriff, or other officer whose duty it is to attend at a particular place of voting under the foregoing provisions, fail to attend, any justice of the peace present, or, if no justice of the peace be present, any three freeholders may perform the duties prescribed by the preceding sections, or in case of necessity may act as officers or inspectors.

At the time these papers were presented as before stated, I had never seen either of them, nor heard of the subject to which they relate, except in a general way, only one day previously. Up to the present moment nothing whatever upon the subject has passed between Governor Johnson or anyone else connected with the proclamation and myself. Since receiving the papers as stated, I have given the subject such brief consideration as I have been able to do in the midst of so many pressing public duties. My conclusion is that I can have nothing to do with the matter, either to sustain the plan as the Convention and Governor Johnson have initiated it, or to revoke or modify it as you demand. By the Constitution and

[3] Brackets are in the source.

laws the President is charged with no duty in the conduct of a presidential election in any State; nor do I, in this case, perceive any military reason for his interference in the matter. The movement set on foot by the Convention and Governor Johnson does not, as seems to be assumed by you, emanate from the National Executive. In no proper sense can it be considered other than as an independent movement of at least a portion of the loyal people of Tennessee. I do not perceive in the plan any menace of violence or coercion towards any one. Governor Johnson, like any other loyal citizen of Tennessee, has the right to favor any political plan he chooses, and, as Military Governor, it is his duty to keep the peace among and for the loyal people of the State. I cannot discern that by this plan he purposes any more. But you object to the plan. Leaving it alone will be your perfect security against it. It is not proposed to force you into it. Do as you please on your own account peacefully and loyally, and Governor Johnson will not molest you; but will protect you against violence so far as in his power.

I presume that the conducting of a Presidential election in Tennessee in strict accordance with the old code of the State is not now a possibility. It is scarcely necessary to add that if any election shall be held, and any votes shall be cast in the State of Tennessee for President and Vice President of the United States, it will belong, not to the military agents, nor yet to the Executive Department, but exclusively to another department of the Government, to determine whether they are entitled to be counted, in conformity with the Constitution and laws of the United States. Except it be to give protection against violence, I decline to interfere in any way with any presidential election. ABRAHAM LINCOLN.

To James B. Fry[1]

Will the Provost-Marshal General, please see & hear, Capt. Muzzy, for whom it seems is sought a place in the Veteran Reserve Corps.

Oct. 22, 1864   A. LINCOLN

[1] AES, owned by R. E. Burdick, New York City. Lincoln's endorsement is written on a letter of Governor Oliver P. Morton to Fry, October 17, 1864, introducing "L[eonard]. F. Muzzy, late Captain in the 114th Ohio Vols." No record has been found of Muzzy's appointment to the Veteran Reserve Corps.

Pass for Joseph J. Neave and William Norton[1]

October 22, 1864

These Friends, Joseph J. Neave and William Norton, reside in England and wish to visit the Friends in North Carolina. Allow

them to pass, with ordinary baggage, to Gen. Grant's Head Quarters, and by his consent through our lines.   A. LINCOLN.
    Oct. 22, 1864.

[1] American Art Association Catalog, December 3, 1923, No. 557. See Lincoln's pass for King, October 25, *infra*.

To William Price[1]

William Price   Office U.S. Military Telegraph,
District Attorney   War Department,
Baltimore, Md   Washington, D.C., Oct. 22 1864.
    Yours received. Will see you any time when you present yourself.   A. LINCOLN

[1] ALS, DNA WR RG 107, Presidential Telegrams, I, 209. William Price telegraphed Lincoln on October 22, 1864: "Information has this moment come into my possession which I think ought to be communicated at once to the Govt. I will leave Baltimore in the three thirty (3 30) PM train for Washington & be accompanied by three (3) persons Can we have an interview with the Prest in the evening & what hour" (DLC-RTL).

Recommendation for James Hughes[1]

Executive Mansion,
Washington, Oct 22, 1864.
    James Hughes of Indiana is a worthy gentleman and a friend, whom I wish to oblige.
    He desires to trade in southern products, and all officers of the Army and Navy and other agents of the government will afford him such protection and such facilities of transportation, and otherwise in such business as can be consistently done with the regulations of trade and with the public service.

ABRAHAM LINCOLN

[1] Copy, DLC-RTL. See also Lincoln's memorandum concerning Hughes, October 20, *supra*. Two drafts of orders to Treasury agents and to Army and Navy officers, dated October 21, 1864, which give substantially the same directions contained in this copy, were apparently never issued (*ibid.*), but were discarded in favor of the less peremptory recommendation.

To Philip H. Sheridan[1]

Executive Mansion Washington,
Major General Sheridan   Oct. 22. 1864
    With great pleasure I tender to you and your brave army, the thanks of the Nation, and my own personal admiration and grati-

[73]

tude, for the month's operations in the Shenandoah Valley; and especially for the splendid work of October 19, 1864. Your Obt. Servt.   ABRAHAM LINCOLN.

[1] ALS, DLC; ADfS, DLC-RTL. On October 19, following Sheridan's famous "ride" from Winchester, Virginia, to rally his defeated army, the Union forces routed the Confederates at Cedar Creek to conclude the Shenandoah Valley campaign.

To Edwin M. Stanton[1]

October 22, 1864

Judge Hughes leaves these letters with me, requesting me to lay them before the Sec. of War, and to state that he Judge Hughes is opposed, *in toto* to the proposition contained in Davis letters.

Oct. 22, 1864   A. LINCOLN

[1] AES, IHi. Lincoln's endorsement appears on a letter of Edwin A. Davis of Indianapolis to Judge James Hughes, October 14, 1864, asking attention to an enclosed letter of Andrew Humphreys to Stanton: "Humphreys has an idea that you would give the matter personal attention as a favor to him." Humphreys' letter is not present but probably referred to his arrest and trial by a military commission at Indianapolis in September, 1864, on charges of disloyalty and conspiracy against the government. Found guilty and sentenced to confinement at hard labor during the war, Humphreys' sentence was remitted by General Alvin P. Hovey: ". . . as the evidence does not show that . . . Andrew Humphreys took any active part or committed any overt acts which were calculated to incite an insurrection or aid the conspiracy. . . ." (Headquarters District of Indiana, January 2, 1865, *General Orders No. 1*, OR, II, VIII, 11). See further Lincoln's telegram to Hooker, January 11, 1865, *infra*.

To George H. Thomas[1]

"Cypher"   Office U.S. Military Telegraph,
Major General Thomas   War Department,
Nashville, Tenn.   Washington, D.C., Oct. 23. 1864.

I received information to-day, having great appearance of authenticity, that there is to be rebel raid into Western Kentucky—that it is to consist of four thousand Infantry, and three thousand Cavalry, and is to start from Corinth, Mississippi on the fourth day of November.   A. LINCOLN

Send copy to Gen. Washburne[2] at Memphis.   A.L.

[1] ALS, DNA WR RG 107, Presidential Telegrams, I, 210. General Thomas telegraphed Halleck at 9:30 P.M.: "The dispatch of the President of to-day, concerning the threatened raid into Western Kentucky, has been received. I will gain all the information I can about the rumor, and prepare to prevent its being carried into execution. . . ." (OR, I, XXXIX, III, 408).

[2] Cadwallader C. Washburn was in command of the District of West Tennessee, Department of the Tennessee.

Pass for Mr. Livingston[1]

Allow the bearer, Mr. Livingston, to have transportation, and pass to Gen. Grant's Head Quarters and return.

Oct. 24. 1864   A. LINCOLN

[1] AES, CSmH. Lincoln's endorsement is written on the back of an envelope addressed to Brigadier General Daniel H. Rucker. Mr. Livingston was probably H. P. Livingston. See Lincoln to Seward, November 17, 1864.

Speech to One Hundred Eighty-Ninth New York Volunteers[1]

October 24, 1864

SOLDIERS: I am exceedingly obliged to you for this mark of respect. It is said that we have the best Government the world ever knew, and I am glad to meet you, the supporters of that Government. To you who render the hardest work in its support should be given the greatest credit. Others who are connected with it, and who occupy higher positions, their duties can be dispensed with, but we cannot get along without your aid. While others differ with the Administration, and, perhaps, honestly, the soldiers generally have sustained it; they have not only fought right, but, so far as could be judged from their actions, they have voted right, and I for one thank you for it. I know you are en route for the front, and therefore do not expect me to detain you long, and will therefore bid you good morning.

[1] New York *Times*, October 25, 1864. "The One Hundred and Eighty-ninth Regiment New-York Volunteers, organized under the late call for 500,000 men, . . . passed through this city [Washington] to-day, on their way to the front. Prior to their departure by transport, the regiment was paraded in front of the White House, and presented to the President. . . ." (*Ibid.*).

To John F. Miller[1]

Executive Mansion
Officer in Command at   Washington D.C.
Nashville, Tenn.   Oct. 25, 1864.

Suspend execution of Young C. Edmonson, until further order from me. Answer if you receive this.   A. LINCOLN

[1] ALS, DNA WR RG 107, Presidential Telegrams, I, 211. See Lincoln to Miller, October 5, *supra*. Brigadier General John F. Miller replied the same day: "Your order suspending execution of Young C. Edmonton [*sic*] received" (DLC-RTL).

Pass for Francis T. King[1]

Allow Francis T. King of Baltimore, to pass with the English Friends, through our lines to North Carolina.   A. LINCOLN

Oct. 25. 1864

[1] ADS, NcGu. See Lincoln's pass for Neave and Norton, October 22, *supra*.

To Gilbert P. Robinson[1]

Lieut. Col. Robinson   Executive Mansion
of 3rd. Maryland Battallion   Washington,
Near Petersburg, Va.   Oct. 25. 1864

Please inform me what is the condition of, and what is being done with, Leut. Charles Saumenig, in your command.

A. LINCOLN

[1] ALS, DNA WR RG 107, Presidential Telegrams, I, 212. No reply from Lieutenant Colonel Gilbert P. Robinson has been found. The roster of Company A of the Third Maryland Infantry lists First Lieutenant Charles Saumenig as discharged on December 29, 1864.

To Edwin M. Stanton[1]

October 25, 1864

The bearer, Mr. Alderson, says he has good recommendations, among others, from Senator Henderson, on file at the War Department. If so, I shall be glad for him to get some suitable situation.

Oct. 25, 1864   A. LINCOLN

[1] ALS, owned by Miss Nellie W. Donley, Morgantown, West Virginia. Alderson has not been identified.

To Joseph Holt[1]

Judge Advocate General please examine and report

Oct. 26. 1864   A. LINCOLN

[1] AES, DNA WR RG 153, Judge Advocate General, MM 1421. Lincoln's endorsement is written on an envelope filed with the record of John Scally, citizen of Maryland, convicted on charges of recruiting for the rebel army and sentenced to imprisonment for two years. The record shows Holt's recommendation of rigid enforcement on April 24, and affirmation of his recommendation on October 31, 1864.

Order for Discharge of Big Eagle[1]

Let the Indian "Big Eagle" now confined at Davenport, Iowa, be discharged at once.   A. LINCOLN

Oct. 26. 1864

[1] ADS-P, ISLA. See further Lincoln's telegram to Alfred Sully, November 19, *infra*.

To Mrs. George W. Swift[1]

Mrs. George W. Swift   Executive Mansion,
My dear Madam   Washington, Oct. 26, 1864.

Your complimentary little poem, asking for my autograph was duly received. I thank you for it, and cheerfully comply with your request   Yours truly   A. LINCOLN.

[1] ALS, CCamStJ; ADfS, DLC-RTL. The autograph draft is written on a letter from John Perkins, Jr., Quartermaster General's Office, October 4, 1864:
"The writer of the inclosed lines is a poetess of some reputation in Massachusetts and a lady who truly honors her President.
"Will you at a leisure moment deign to look at them, and comply with her request by presenting her your autograph.
"Mr Bates who hands you this will receive and forward it" (DLC-RTL).
The poem by Mrs. Swift of Falmouth, Massachusetts, has not been found in the Lincoln Papers, but a copy is preserved with Lincoln's letter in St. John's Seminary.

To John R. Underwood and Henry Grider[1]

Hon. J. R Underwood,   Executive Mansion
Hon. Henry Grider   Washington, Oct. 26. 1864

Gentlemen   A petition has been presented to me on behalf of certain citizens of Allen and Barren counties in the State of Kentucky assuming that certain sums of money have been assessed and collected from them by the United States Military authorities, to compensate certain Union citizens of the same vicinage, for losses by rebel depredations, and praying that I will order the money to be refunded. The petition is accompanied by a letter of yours, which so presents the case as to induce me to make a brief response. You distinctly admit that the petitioners "sympathize with the Confederate States & regard them as warring to preserve their Constitutional & legal rights." This admitted, it is scarcely possible to believe that they do not help the cause they thus love whenever they conveniently can. Their sons and relatives go into the rebel, but we may not be able to distinctly prove that they out-fitted, and sent them. When armed rebels come among them, their houses and other property are spared; while Union men's houses are burned, and their property pillaged. Still we may not be able to specifically prove that the sympathizers, protected and supplied the raiders in turn, or designated their Union nei[g]hbors for plunder and devastation. Yet we know all this exists even better than we could know an isolated fact upon the sworn testimony of one or two witnesses, just as we better know there is fire whence we see much smoke rising than could know it by one or two witnesses swearing to it. The witnesses may commit perjury, but the smoke

[77]

can not. Now, experience has already taught us in this war that holding these smoky localities responsible for the conflagrations within them has a very salutary effect. It was obviously so in and about St. Louis, and on Eastern Shore of Virginia.

[1] ADf, DLC-RTL. The draft is in pencil and appears to be incomplete. No further record of the letter has been found, and it seems probable that Lincoln abandoned the idea of writing Underwood and Grider, and wrote instead to Stephen G. Burbridge, October 27, *infra*. The petition and the letter from Underwood and Grider to which Lincoln refers, have not been found.

To Stephen G. Burbridge[1]

Executive Mansion
Major General Burbridge   Washington, Oct. 27. 1864
It is represented to me that an officer has, by your authority, assessed and collected considerable sums of money from citizens of Allen and Barren counties, Kentucky, to compensate Union men for depredations committed upon them in the vicinity by rebels; and I am petitioned to order the money to be refunded. At most I could not do this without hearing both sides, which, as yet, I have not. I write now to say, that, in my opinion, in some extreme cases, this class of proceedings becomes a necessity; but that it is liable to —almost inseparable from—great abuses, and therefore should only be sparingly resorted to, and be conducted with great caution; that you, in your department, must be the judge of the proper localities and occasions for applying it; and that it will be well for you to see that your subordinates be at all times ready to account for every dollar, as to why collected, of whom, and how applied. Without this, you will soon find some of them making assessments and collections merely to put money in their own pockets, and it will also be impossible to correct errors in future and better times.

In the case I have mentioned, such good men as Hon. J. R. Underwood & Hon. Henry Grider though not personally interested, have appealed to me in behalf of others. So soon as you can, consistently with your other duties, I will thank you to acquaint yourself with the particulars of this case, and make any correction which may seem to be proper. Yours truly   A LINCOLN

[1] ADfS, DLC-RTL. See Lincoln to Underwood and Grider, October 26, *supra*. No reply from General Burbridge or further reference has been found.

To Edwin M. Stanton[1]

If the services of this applicant can be made useful, I shall be glad for him to be appointed.   A. LINCOLN
Oct. 27. 1864

¹ AES, Herman Blum, Blumhaven Library, Philadelphia, Pennsylvania. Lincoln's endorsement is written on a letter signed by twenty-six citizens of Columbus, Ohio, October, 1864, recommending "George E Hutchinson, late Captain in the 10th. Ohio Cavalry, for appointment of Commissary [of] Subsistan[ce] with the rank of Captain in the Army." No record of Hutchinson's appointment has been found.

To Albert G. Hodges¹

Hon. A G. Hodges   Executive Mansion
Frankfort, Ky.   Washington, Oct. 28. 1864

Mrs. Margaret C. Price, is here asking that her son, Philemon B. Price, now a prisoner of war at Camp Chase, may be discharged, and I have told [her] I will do it if you say so. What say you?

                               A. LINCOLN

¹ ALS, DNA WR RG 107, Presidential Telegrams, I, 213. Hodges telegraphed Lincoln in reply on October 29, but the telegram has not been found. In a postscript to his letter of November 1, however, Hodges commented: "I do not know young Price, whom you telegraphed me about. He grew from childhood to manhood in this community without my having any recollection of him. I could not, from inquiries made of his antecedents, recommend him, unconditionally, to executive clemency, and hence the form of the dispatch sent you Oct. 29th." (DLC-RTL).

To John A. Prall¹

J. A. Prall,   Executive Mansion
Paris, Ky   Washington, Oct. 28. 1864

Mrs. George W. Bowen, is here asking for the discharge of her husband, now a prisoner of war, at Camp Chase, and I have told her I will do it if you say so. What say you?   A. LINCOLN

¹ ALS, DNA WR RG 107, Presidential Telegrams, I, 214. No reply has been found. John A. Prall was a member of the Kentucky Senate and a delegate to the Baltimore Convention in 1864. George W. Bowen has not been further identified.

To S. Austin Allibone¹

                 Executive Mansion, Washington,
Dear Sir,   October 29th, 1864.

Mr Everetts address of 19th. inst. which you so kindly sent, has been received, and you will please accept my thanks. Your ob't. serv't   A. LINCOLN.

S. Austin Allibone Esq
Philadelphia, Pa

1 LS, CSmH. On October 26, 1864, S. Austin Allibone enclosed the Boston *Advertiser* of October 22, containing Edward Everett's speech of October 19 on "The Duty of Supporting the Government in the Present Crisis of Affairs." (DLC-RTL).

To Edward Bates[1]

Will the Attorney General please have a report made on this case.
Oct. 29. 1864   A. LINCOLN

1 AES, DLC-RTL. Lincoln's endorsement is written on a copy of the court record in the case of the U.S. *vs.* Charles Randall and Edward Scott, on trial for counterfeiting Treasury notes. On November 21, 1864, Bates wrote Lincoln:

"I have considered the Petition, herewith returned, addressed to you by H[ugh]. B. McCracken of Jefferson County, Pennsylvania.

"It appears that Mr. McCracken became surety for the appearance at the May Sessions, 1864, of the United States District Court for the Western District of Pennsylvania of one Charles Randall, indicted in that Court for the offence of passing an altered United States Treasury Note; that the said defendant, Randall, having failed to appear, according to the condition of the obligation, the recognizance executed by Mr. McCracken was forfeited, and that an action . . . was . . . brought . . . in which judgment for $3000 was obtained by the United States against Mr. McCracken on the 15th of August 1864.

"Mr. McCracken, appealing 'to the Executive Clemency' now prays, 'that upon the payment of costs and the sum of thirty dollars . . . the said judgment may be remitted.' . . . The question, I presume, which you desire me to answer . . . is, whether you have any Constitutional or statutory power to grant the relief which is prayed? I am of opinion that you have none. . . ." (DLC-RTL).

Endorsement Concerning Thomas Berington[1]

October 29, 1864

I do not think a man offering himself a volunteer when he could receive a bounty & being rejected for disability should afterwards be compelled to serve without bounty as a drafted man. Let this man be discharged.   A. LINCOLN
Oct. 29. 1864

1 AES, IHi. Lincoln's endorsement is written on a letter from Robert B. Carnahan, U.S. attorney for the Western District of Pennsylvania, Pittsburgh, October 28, 1864:

"Mrs Berington, who will hand you this note, is about to visit Washington for the purpose of having an interview with you, and to request the discharge of her husband Thomas Berington, recently drafted and now in service in the Army of the Potomac

"The case of Berington is a hard one. In August last he offered himself as a volunteer, and could have then obtained about $550.00 as bounty, but was rejected by physical disability. In September he was drafted and was accepted. He wished to volunteer to avoid the draft, but could not get into the service, and now he is drafted and cannot receive any bounty I am a near neighbor of the family. They are highly respectable people, and the family is entirely dependent upon the fathers exertions for support. A wife and three young children the oldest not more than 13 years old are left at home without support. Mr Berington is an excellent man of good habits. If consistent with the public service I would be much pleased if your Excellency would either discharge Mr Berington from the army or permit him to enlist and receive bounty. I cannot but think the case a very hard one."

To Edwin M. Stanton[1]

October 29, 1864

As the resignation of officers is not likely to become a great evil, let this resignation be accepted on the usual condition of settling accounts.　　　　　　　　　　　　　　　　　　A. LINCOLN

Oct. 29. 1864

[1] AES, IHi. Lincoln's endorsement appears on a letter from Captain Henry C. Holloway, October 28, 1864, tendering his resignation as commissary of subsistence of Volunteers. Holloway's resignation was promulgated in AGO *Special Orders No. 422*, November 28, 1864.

To Isaac S. Burrell[1]

I shall be pleased to see Col. Burrell and his Regiment, at the time and place within indicated.　　　　　　　　　　　A. LINCOLN

Oct. 30. 1864.

[1] AES, owned by Mrs. Olin J. Cochran, Windham, New Hampshire. Lincoln's endorsement is written on a letter from Colonel Isaac S. Burrell, Forty-second Massachusetts Volunteers, a one hundred days' regiment: "My Regt. will start for Boston on Monday; and it would give me great pleasure to present it to you at the White House, on Monday AM at 9 o'clock if agreeable to you." See Lincoln's speech to the Forty-second Massachusetts, October 31, *infra*.

To Alexander K. McClure[1]

"Cypher"　　　　　　　　　　　　　　　　　Executive Mansion
Hon. A. K. McClure　　　　　　　　　　　　　　Washington,
Harrisburg, Pa.　　　　　　　　　　　　　　　Oct. 30. 1864

I would like to hear from you.　　A. LINCOLN

[1] ALS, DNA WR RG 107, Presidential Telegrams, I, 215. No reply from McClure has been found prior to the following letter, dated November 5, 1864:
"The work is as well done as it can be done, & well enough I have no doubt. We shall carry the State by from 5,000 to 10,000 on the home vote, & it may be more, unless all signs are deceptive.
"We should have had much more, but it is too late for complaint, & we shall have enough.
"I go home to-morrow greatly encouraged by the conviction that your Election will be by a *decisive* vote, & give you all the moral power necessary for your high & holy trust. . . ." (DLC-RTL).

To Edward Bates[1]

Please file & remind me, at next Territorial Judge appointment.
Oct. 31. 1864   A. LINCOLN

[1] AES, CSmH. Lincoln's endorsement is written on an envelope on which appears a further endorsement not Lincoln's: "Refiled Oct. 2. '69 for 5th. Circuit under late act of congress." On the other side of the envelope appears an endorsement of Henry Sherman of Hartford, Connecticut: "Recd from Atty Gen's office July 1865. Enclosed herein was an original letter reminding him of his promise to give me a Judicial appointment, which has been mislaid." Sherman was employed in the Treasury Department 1861-1868.

To Thomas T. Davis[1]

Hon. Thos. T. Davis   Executive Mansion
Syracuse, N.Y.   Washington, D.C. Oct. 31. 1864
   I have ordered that Milton D. Norton be discharged on taking the oath. Please notify his mother.   A. LINCOLN

[1] ALS, DNA WR RG 107, Presidential Telegrams, I, 216. No communication from U.S. Representative Thomas T. Davis nor further reference to Milton D. Norton has been found.

To Thomas H. Hicks or Francis S. Corkran[1]

If Gov Hicks or Francis Corcoran, will request it in writing, I will allow this lady and family to return home.   A. LINCOLN
   Oct. 31. 1864

[1] AES, THaroL. Lincoln's endorsement is written on a letter from Major John I. Yellott, First Potomac Home Brigade, Maryland Infantry, who was provost marshal at Frederick, Maryland, October 27, 1864:
   "About the 20th. day of July 1864, I received an order from Maj Genl. Hunter then commander Department of West Virginia requiring me to send South of the Lines of the Military Forces of the United States all secessionists & their families resident in Frederick City, Md. A number of occurrences combined delayed the full execution of this order during which delay its execution was suspended by order of the President of the United States.
   "Before the order of suspension reached me one or two families had been sent South and among them the family of John W Baughman consisting of Mrs Baughman & three children.
   "Mrs Baughman with her family are now in the Shenandoah Valley of Virginia alone, entirely isolated from her friends the order sending other families South never having gone into effect.
   "I think if consistent with the Policy & opinions of the Government permission granted on the part of the same for this family to return, would be regarded by the loyal community of Frederick as but an act of Justice & humanity."
   No reply from Thomas H. Hicks or Francis S. Corkran has been found.

To William Nast[1]

Executive Mansion, Washington,

Reverend & Dear Sir: October 31st, 1864..

It is with feelings of cordial gratification, that I acknowledge the reception of your communication of the 20th. of October, covering the Resolutions of the Central German Conference of the Methodist Episcopal Church, adopted at their recent session.

I have not been unprepared for this definite and unequivocal statement of the continued loyalty and devotion of the Church you represent, to the free institutions of the country of your adoption. The conduct of your people since the outbreak of this desolating rebellion, has been the best proof of the sincerity of your present professions.

I trust it is not too early for us to rejoice together over the promise of the speedy removal of that blot upon our civilization, always heretofore a standing menace to our peace and liberties, whose destruction, so long desired by all friends of impartial freedom, has at last been rendered possible by the crimes of its own reckless friends   I am very truly, Your obedient servant,

Reverend William Nast   A. LINCOLN

1 LS-P, ISLA. Reverend William Nast's letter of October 20 is not in the Lincoln Papers. The Central German Methodist Conference had met in Cincinnati August 24-30. Nast was editor of *Der Christliche Apologete,* the organ of the German Methodists published at Cincinnati, Ohio.

Proclamation Admitting Nevada into the Union[1]

October 31, 1864

By the President of the United States of America

A Proclamation:

Whereas the Congress of the United States passed an Act which was approved on the 21st. day of March, last, entitled, "An Act to enable the people of Nevada to form a Constitution and State Government, and for the admission of such State into the Union on an equal Footing with the original States";

And whereas, the said Constitution and State Government have been formed pursuant to the conditions prescribed by the fifth section of the Act of Congress aforesaid, and the certificate required by the said act, and also a copy of the Constitution and ordinances have been submitted to the President of the United States;

Now, therefore, be it known that I, Abraham Lincoln, President of the United States, in accordance with the duty imposed upon me by the Act of Congress aforesaid, do, hereby, declare and proclaim that the said State of Nevada is admitted into the Union on an equal footing with the original States.

In witness whereof, I have hereunto set my hand, and caused the seal of the United States to be affixed.

Done at the City of Washington this Thirty first day of October, in the year of our Lord one thousand eight hundred and [L.S.] sixty four, and of the Independence of the United States the Eighty ninth.   ABRAHAM LINCOLN

By the President:
WILLIAM H. SEWARD   Secretary of State.

[1] DS, DNA FS RG 11, Proclamations.

Speech to Forty-second Massachusetts Regiment[1]

October 31, 1864

You have completed a term of service in the cause of your country, and on behalf of the nation and myself I thank you. You are going home; I hope you will find all your friends well. I never see a Massachusetts regiment but it reminds me of the difficulty a regiment from that State met with on its passage through Baltimore; but the world has moved since then, and I congratulate you upon having a better time to-day in Baltimore than that regiment had.

To-night, midnight, slavery ceases in Maryland, and this state of things in Maryland is due greatly to the soldiers. Again I thank you for the services you have rendered the country.

[1] Washington *Daily National Republican*, November 1, 1864. See Lincoln to Burrell, October 30, *supra*.

To Edwin M. Stanton[1]

Hon. Sec. of War   Executive Mansion,
Sir: Washington, Oct. 31, 1864.

Herewith is a letter of Gov. Curtin which speaks for itself. I suggest, for your consideration, whether, to the extent of, say, five thousand, we might not exempt from the draft, upon the men being put in good shape to defend & give assurance to the border. I have not said even this much to the bearer, Gen. Todd,[2] whom I hope you will see & hear. Yours truly   A. LINCOLN

¹ ALS, owned by Edward C. Stone, Boston, Massachusetts. Governor Curtin's letter has not been found.
² Probably Lemuel Todd, formerly major in the Thirtieth Pennsylvania Volunteers.

To Edward Bates¹

Atty General, please make out a pardon in this case.
Nov. 1. 1864   A. LINCOLN

¹ AES, DNA RG 204, U.S. Pardon Attorney, A 565. Lincoln's endorsement is written on a petition of citizens of the District of Columbia, October 17, 1864, asking pardon for Annie M. Branson, convicted on charges of larceny.

To John A. Dix¹

Major General Dix   Executive Mansion
New-York.   Washington, Nov. 1. 1864
   Please suspend execution of private P. Carroll until further order.
Acknowledge receipt.   A. LINCOLN

¹ ALS, DNA WR RG 107, Presidential Telegrams, I, 217. See Lincoln's telegram to Raymond and Strong, November 2, *infra*. General Dix acknowledged receipt of Lincoln's telegram on November 2 (DLC-RTL).

Endorsement Concerning H. Warren Stimson¹
West-Point.

I wish this "soldier boy" to have a chance.   A. LINCOLN
   Nov. 1. 1864

¹ AES, DNA WR RG 94, U.S. Military Academy, 1864, No. 388. Lincoln's endorsement is written on a letter of Sergeant H. Warren Stimson, Company A, One Hundred Forty-second Pennsylvania Volunteers, to John Hay, October 25, 1864:
   "I have taken the liberty of addressing you, for the purpose of asking your opinion in respect to the matter of obtaining one of the appointments as cadet at West Point, annually made by the President.
   "I hardly expect that you will pay any attention to me; but I thought there would be no harm in writing to you.
   "I am 19 years of age. I have carried my musket nearly thirty months, and am willing to carry it, thirty more if by so doing the Rebellion may be crushed. I have had plenty of chances to be detailed: but have refused, because I believe that when a man enlists, it is his duty to *fight* & not to '*bum.*' I have been in every action since the '2d. Bull Run,' and have been wounded twice. I expect to go into another one tomorrow, as we are ordered to march at 5 A.M. Perhaps by tomorrow night I may be beyond the need of any cadetship, but I hope not.
   "As far as regards education I think I am fully competent to pass a creditable examination. I was in the Sophomore class of Columbia college, and ran away from there 'to go for a soldier.' I am an orphan. Hoping that my communication may meet with your favorable consideration, and trusting soon to hear from you I have the honor to remain."
   There is no record of Stimson's appointment.

[85]

To Albert Hobbs[1]

Hon. A. Hobbs.   Executive Mansion
Malone, N.Y.   Washington, Nov. 1. 1864
 Where is Nathan Wilcox, of whom you telegraph, to be found?
              A LINCOLN

 [1] ALS, DNA WR RG 107, Presidential Telegrams, I, 218. Albert Hobbs, senator in the New York legislature, had telegraphed on November 1: "Mr Nathan Wilcox who is under sentence of death for desertion . . . is my relative & for the sake of his . . . large circle of loyal relatives I humbly pray . . . his life may be spared He was a member of the twenty second . . . Massachusetts Volunteers" (DLC-RTL).
 He replied to Lincoln's telegram on November 2: "Nathan Wilcox is in the 22d Mass Regt fifth Corps now at the repair Depot City Point." (*Ibid.*).
 Nathaniel M. Wilcox, Company C, Twenty-second Massachusetts Volunteers, had been sentenced for desertion to be shot on November 4, 1864 (Army of the Potomac, *General Court Martial Orders No. 41*, October 25, 1864). See further Lincoln's telegram to Grant November 2, *infra*.

Order for Discharge of Kentuckians[1]

            [c. November 1, 1864]
 Let the following named prisoners of war, take the oath of Dec. 8, 1863, and be discharged.
Josiah Gentry—   at Camp Douglas,
Archibald W. Kavanaugh, "   "
John W. Mitchell,   "   "
Jonathan D. Jones.   "   "
Roger X. Quisenberry Camp. Chase.
William T. Simmons. Camp. Douglas.

              A. LINCOLN

 [1] AES, owned by William H. Townsend, Lexington, Kentucky. Lincoln's order is written on a letter from General Stephen G. Burbridge, Lexington, Kentucky, November 1, 1864: "Hon C. F Burmond speaks of going to the City of Washington in a few weeks to see you on some personal [business] connected with the release of several person[s] confined in our Millitary Camps I can say to you that he will make no statement that you may not rely upon and I am satisfied that the public service in this department will suffer no detriment from granting his request I hope you will do so."

To Gideon Welles[1]

           November 1, 1864
If the Sec. of the Navy can find employment for this gentleman in the capacity stated, I will discharge [him] from the service under the draft, so that he may go into the other service.
Nov. 1. 1864   A. LINCOLN

[1] AES, RPB. Lincoln's endorsement is written on a letter from John W. Forney, October 31, 1864, recommending that Thomas C. Curry of Danville, Pennsylvania, "who has been drafted, should be permitted to enter as a Machinist in the Navy Yard." G. R. Wilson, master machinist at the Navy Yard, endorsed on November 2, "We are in want of 1st. 2d & 3d Class Machinists and Pattern Makers"; and Welles forwarded the letter to Commodore John B. Montgomery who endorsed, "Approved."

To Ulysses S. Grant[1]

Lieut. Genl. Grant   Executive Mansion
City-Point   Washington, Nov. 2. 1864

Suspend until further [order][2] the execution of Nathan Wilcox, of 22nd. Mass. Regt. Fifth Corps, said to be at Repair Depot.

A LINCOLN

[1] ALS, DNA WR RG 107, Presidential Telegrams, I, 219. See Lincoln to Hobbs, November 1, *supra*. Grant replied the same day: "The following despatch from Gen Meade in reply to your telegram of three forty is forwarded for your consideration. . . .

"'Hd Qrs A of P. Nov. 2nd. Lieut Genl U S Grant   The despatch of the President . . . has been received. There is no soldier of that name given under sentence of death in this Army & the Presidents order was no doubt intended to apply to the case of Private Nathaniel M. Wilcox Company C twenty second (22d) Mass Volunteers who was to have been executed on friday next. The suspension of his execution will at once be ordered'. . . ." (DLC-RTL).
[2] "Order" was omitted by Lincoln and inserted in the manuscript by a clerk.

To Joseph Holt[1]

If a report is made in the case of Wm. Stretch, please send the papers to me.   A. LINCOLN
   Nov. 2, 1864

[1] ALS, PHi. William Stretch's case has not been found.

To Henry J. Raymond and William K. Strong[1]

Hon. H. J. Raymond &   Office U.S. Military Telegraph,
Gen. W. K. Strong   War Department,
New-York   Washington, D.C., Nov. 2. 1864.

Telegraphed Gen. Dix last night to suspend execution of P. Carroll, and have his answer that the order is received by him.

A. LINCOLN.

[1] ALS, DNA WR RG 107, Presidential Telegrams, I, 220. See Lincoln's telegram to Dix, November 1, *supra*. William K. Strong had telegraphed on November 1: "I recommend that you telegraph Maj General Dix to postpone

execution of sentence of death upon Private P. Carroll for two (2) weeks from 4th November" (DLC-RTL).

On November 2, Henry J. Raymond and Thurlow Weed telegraphed: "If possible please telegraph Genl Dix to postpone execution of Patrick Carroll fixed for friday for ten or fifteen days." (*Ibid.*).

No further reference has been found.

To Stephen G. Burbridge[1]

Officer in command at   Executive Mansion
Lexington, Ky   Washington, Nov. 3. 1864

Suspend execution of Vance Mason until further order. Acknowledge receipt.   A LINCOLN

[1] ALS, DNA WR RG 107, Presidential Telegrams, I, 221. Lieutenant Colonel Benjamin J. Spaulding, Thirty-seventh Kentucky Volunteer Mounted Infantry, had telegraphed Lincoln on November 3: "Vance Mason Co C thirty seventh Ky Vols mounted Infy on the charge of desertion is condemned to be shot on the sixth of this month. I pray you that you reprieve him or grant a respite until I can bring the matter before you in form There are mitigatory circumstances about his case which I am sure will recommend him to your clemency" (DLC-RTL).

General Burbridge replied on the same day: "Your dispatch recd. Generals Orders from . . . Dept of the Ohio direct the execution of five soldiers for desertion at Louisville on Sunday next. Vance Mason is one of the number I am charged with the execution of the orders & have asked that the sentences may not be carried out on Sunday but could obtain no change of the order." (*Ibid.*).

See further Lincoln's telegram to Burbridge, November 4, *infra*.

To William P. Fessenden[1]

Will the Sec. of the Treasury & Mr. Risley please give Dr. Roe a hearing. His object is certainly a worthy one.   A. LINCOLN
Nov. 3. 1864

[1] ALS, IHi. Hanson A. Risley was a special agent of the Treasury Department. Dr. Edward R. Roe, physician and editor, formerly of Jacksonville, at this time of Bloomington, Illinois.

To George G. Meade[1]

         Executive Mansion Washington,
Major General Meade   Nov. 3, 1864

Suspend execution of Samuel J. Smith, and George Brown, alias George Rock, until further order & send record.   A. LINCOLN

[1] ALS, DNA WR RG 107, Presidential Telegrams, I, 222. George Brown, alias George Rock, Company A, Fifteenth New York Engineers, and Samuel J. Smith alias William Jones, Sixty-eighth Pennsylvania Volunteers, had been sentenced for desertion. General Meade replied on the same day: "Your dis-

patch of this date directing that execution of the sentence in the cases of Samuel J Smith and George Brown alias George Rock be suspended until further orders has been received The records in these cases were forwarded to the Judge Advocate General some days ago." (DLC-RTL). No reference has been found to the final disposal of Smith's case, but AGO *Special Orders No. 52,* February 1, 1865, cancelled the suspension of sentence for George Rock (George Rock Brown) and ordered that "the sentence will be executed at such time and place as the Commanding General may direct."

To Edwin M. Stanton[1]

This man wants to go home to vote. Sec. of War please see him

Nov. 3. 1864   A. LINCOLN

[1] ALS-P, ISLA.

Approval of First Hundred Miles of Union Pacific Railroad[1]

Executive Mansion
November 4th 1864.

The permanent location of the Union Pacific Railroad, for one hundred miles west from Omaha, Nebraska, as shown by the map thereof certified by the President and Secretary of said Company, Oct. 19, 1864, is hereby approved.   ABRAHAM LINCOLN.

[1] ES, DNA NR RG 48, Department of Interior, Lands and Railroad Divisions, Union Pacific Railroad Company, Package 239. Lincoln's endorsement is written on the back of a letter from Thomas C. Durant, vice-president of the Union Pacific, November 3, 1864: "I have the honor to ask your approval of the permanent location of the first one hundred miles of the Union Pacific RailRoad as indicated by the map forwarded to the Department of the Interior on the 24th. ulto."

To Stephen G. Burbridge[1]

Major General Burbridge   Executive Mansion,
Lexington, Ky   Washington, Nov. 4, 1864.

Suspend execution of all the deserters ordered to be executed on Sunday at Louisville, until further order, and send me the records in the cases. Acknowledge receipt.   A. LINCOLN

[1] ALS, DNA WR RG 107, Presidential Telegrams, I, 223. See Lincoln to Burbridge, November 3, *supra*. Burbridge replied on the same day: "Your dispatch received and orders issued in conformity thereto. The record will be forwarded at once" (DLC-RTL). AGO *Special Orders No. 64,* February 9, 1865, directed remission of the sentence of Vance Mason, "on condition that he returns to and serves out the remainder of his term of enlistment. . . ."

To Joseph Holt[1]

Judge Advocate General please procure record & papers & report on this case.   A. LINCOLN

Nov. 4. 1864

[1] AES, DNA WR RG 153, Judge Advocate General, LL 2237. Lincoln's endorsement is written on a petition in behalf of Captain Frank B. Holt, First New Jersey Volunteers, dismissed for disobedience of orders. Judge Holt reported that there was room for executive clemency, and Lincoln directed that "so much of Special Orders, No. 280, August 25th, 1864, as dismissed Captain F. B. Holt, 1st New Jersey Volunteers, is hereby revoked, and he is honorably discharged the service. . . ." (AGO *Special Orders No. 409*, November 21, 1864).

Memorandum[1]

[c. November 4, 1864]

For the Message

Mrs. Hutter suggests that there be four Assylums in each State, aid by the General Government, for the orphans & perhaps the other destitute of the war.

[1] AD, DLC-RTL. Since Mrs. Elizabeth E. Hutter called on Lincoln on November 4 (see Lincoln to Stanton, *infra*), this undated memorandum has been assigned this date. Lincoln made no use of her suggestion in his annual message of December 6, *infra*.

Order Concerning Prisoners from Coles County, Illinois[1]

November 4, 1864.

Let these prisoners be sent back to Coles County, Ill., those indicted be surrendered to the sheriff of said county, and the others be discharged.   A. LINCOLN.

[1] OR, I, XXXII, I, 643. Lincoln's order is endorsed on a report of Addison A. Hosmer, acting judge advocate general, July 26, 1864. See Lincoln's communications to Davis and to Treat, July 2, and to Ficklin, July 22, *supra*.

To Edwin M. Stanton[1]

November 4, 1864

I really wish Mrs. Hutter to be obliged in this case.

She is one of the very best friends of the soldiers. Honorable Secretary of War please see her.   A. LINCOLN.

Nov. 4, 1864.

[1] Lebanon, Pennsylvania, *Reporter*, February 10, 1909. According to the article in the *Reporter* in which the above item appears, Mrs. Hutter was the wife of Dr. E. W. Hutter of Philadelphia, the same Elizabeth E. Hutter to whom Lincoln wrote on August 10, 1863, *supra*.

To Caleb H. Carlton[1]

Officer in command at   Executive Mansion
Chattanooga, Tenn.   Washington, Nov. 5, 1864

Suspend execution of Robert W. Reed until further order & send
record. Answer.   A. LINCOLN

[1] ALS, DNA WR RG 107, Presidential Telegrams, I, 224. Colonel Caleb H.
Carlton, Eighty-ninth Ohio Volunteers, was in command of post at Chattanooga,
but no reply from him or any officer has been found. Lincoln's action was
prompted by a telegram from John Boyle, Louisville, Kentucky, November
3, 1864: "Robert W Reed Company A fourth Ky Cavalry at Chattanooga is
sentenced to die November twentieth for killing John Arterburris his messmate
& friend Arterburris brother witnessed the killing & represents it as committed in momentary passion wantonly provoked by deceased & repented as
soon as done. . . . Officers & others think it a proper case for executive clemency
& beseech you to commute the sentence to imprisonment for term of years or
life. grant reprieve until the case can be laid before you. . . ." (DLC-RTL).

To William H. Seward[1]

Hon. W. H. Seward   Executive Mansion
Auburn, New-York   Washington, Nov. 5. 1864

No news of consequence this morning.   A LINCOLN

[1] ALS, DNA WR RG 107, Presidential Telegrams, I, 225.

To Edwin M. Stanton[1]

Capt. Shindel will report to Gen. W. T. Sherman instead of to
Gen. Canby as within directed.   A. LINCOLN.

Nov. 5, 1864.

[1] Lebanon, Pennsylvania, *Reporter*, February 10, 1909. According to the
source, Lincoln's order overruled an order directing Captain Jacob A. Shindel,
assistant quartermaster, to report to Major General Edward R. S. Canby at
New Orleans.

To Edwin M. Stanton[1]

November 5, 1864

I think this might lie over till morning. The tendency of the order,
it seems to me, is to bring on a collision with the State authority,
which I would rather avoid, at least until the necessity for it is
more apparant than it yet is.   A. LINCOLN

Nov. 5. 1864

[1] AES, DLC-Stanton Papers. Lincoln's endorsement is written on a telegram
to Stanton received on November 5 from General Benjamin F. Butler, who
had been sent to New York with troops to maintain order until after the election:

"I desire to issue the following portion of an order about Brig Genl John A. Green as commander of the District of New York.

"Gen Dix objects not on account of any difference as to jurisdiction between us but because he thinks we have no power to touch Green & desires me to ask you.

"Will you sanction it?

" 'There can be no military organization in any state known to the laws save the militia & armies of the United States. The president is the constitutional Comdr in chief of the militia & army of the U.S. therefore where in any portion of the U.S. an officer of superior rank is detailed to command all other military officers in that district must report to & be subordinate to him therefore all persons exercising any military authority in this District will at once report to these HdQuarters for orders A military order purporting to be issued by Br Genl John A Green is countermanded & revoked & Brig Genl Green if exercising any military command will forthwith report to these Hd Qurs & any attempt to exercise military authority without so reporting will be summarily punished as wilful disobedience of orders.'

"I will wait for answer at the telegraph office Troops are beginning to arrive." (Telegram, DLC-Stanton Papers; OR, I, XLIII, II, 549-50).

Stanton replied on the same day: "Your telegram has been submitted to the consideration of the President, and all action upon the subject-matter will be suspended until his instructions are received." (OR, I, XLIII, II, 550).

On November 7 Stanton telegraphed Butler: "The President thinks it expedient to avoid precipitating any military collision between the United States forces and the militia of the State of New York; and as General Dix, the commanding officer of the department, does not approve of the order proposed by you to be issued, in reference to the militia of the State and Brigadier-General Green, the President is of the opinion that it had better not be issued. If Green, under any color of pretense, should undertake to resist the military authority of the United States, he may then be dealt with as circumstances require, without any general order that may become the subject of abstract discussion." (*Ibid.*, p. 568).

This exchange of telegrams grew out of an order issued on October 29 by Brigadier General John A. Green, Jr., commanding the New York State Militia, which reads in part as follows: "The General-Commanding recognizes danger to the public peace in the proposed attempt of a Major-General holding a commission under the Federal Government to take under his care and supervision within the . . . district, the election to be held as aforesaid. For this contemplated interference there is no necessity, authority or excuse. The Federal Government is charged with no duty or responsibility whatever relating to an election to be held in the State of New-York. . . ." (New York *Times,* November 1, 1864).

To Charlotte B. Wise[1]

Executive Mansion, Washington,
My dear Mrs. Wise   Nov. 5. 1864.
It gives me pleasure to comply with your request. Yours truly
A LINCOLN

[1] ALS, IHi. On November 2, 1864, Charlotte B. (Mrs. H. A.) Wise wrote Lincoln from Boston:

"I am getting up a Navy Photograph Book for our Sailors' Fair, which opens on the 9th.

"I want your likeness to begin the book, as head of the Navy.
"Will you write your name on one of your Photographic Cards & sent [*sic*] it to me? . . ." (DLC-RTL).

To Edward R. S. Canby[1]

"*Cypher*"   Executive Mansion
Major General Canby   Washington,
New-Orleans, La.   Nov. 6. 1864

Please forward, with all possible despatch, to the Naval-Officer commanding at Mobile Bay, the following order.

A. LINCOLN.

"Naval Officer in command at   Executive Mansion
Mobile Bay.   Washington, Nov. 6. 1864

Do not, on any account, or on any showing of authority whatever, from whomsoever purporting to come, allow the blockade to be violated.   A. LINCOLN"

[1] ALS, DNA WR RG 107, Presidential Telegrams, I, 227. See Lincoln to David G. Farragut, *infra*.

To David G. Farragut[1]

Naval Officer in command at   Executive Mansion,
Mobile Bay   Washington, Nov. 6. 1864.

Do not, on any account, or on any showing of authority whatever, from whomsoever purporting to come, allow the blockade to be violated.   A. LINCOLN.

[1] ALS, DNA WR RG 107, Presidential Telegrams, I, 228. The following endorsement by a telegraph clerk appears on the bottom of the telegram: "Send this to Care of Capt [George D.] Sheldon/Hilton Head/to be forwarded from there to Mobile by first opportunity." See Lincoln's order to General Edward R. S. Canby, August 9, *supra*, which was also issued to Farragut on the same day. Welles' *Diary* under date of October 3, 1864, records: "Had an interview with Seward, agreeable to the wishes of the President, concerning the order to A. J. Hamilton for bringing out cotton. . . . He said that the scheme was one by which certain important persons in the Rebel cause were to be converted. Had himself not much faith that it would amount to anything, and yet it might. The President believed there would be results; but had been very confidential and secret in all that was done. He (S.) had drawn up the order carefully by special request of the President, but had never communicated to any one but Stanton what had been done. . . . I remarked that the subject was of a character which seemed to deserve general consultation in the Cabinet . . . that I was especially so, it being my special duty to prevent intercourse with the Rebels and enforce the blockade. But this order conflicted with that duty, was not in good faith, I apprehended, with others of our people, or with foreign powers. I told him I had made inquiries of Fessenden, for the order expressly referred to the Treasury agents, and they would of course report to him. Seward

said there was no interference with the blockade. He had prepared the order with great care and sent one copy to General Canby, and one to Admiral Farragut, and proposed to send and get it for my perusal. I told him I already had a copy, which seemed to surprise him. . . . He appeared not to be aware that . . . all the three Departments must come into possession of this confidential circular, and not unlikely it would go into the courts. He is not yet dispossessed of his early error that the government can be carried on by executive order regardless of Department or laws."

See further Lincoln's order to Farragut, November 11, *infra*.

To William H. Seward[1]

	Office U.S. Military Telegraph,
Hon. W. H. Seward	War Department,
Auburn, N. Y.	Washington, D.C., Nov. 6. 1864.

Nothing of much importance. Day-before-yesterday rebels destroyed two more of our wooden gun-boats, at Johnsonville, on Tennessee River. Curtis, on the 4th., was at Fayetteville, Ark. still pursuing and damaging Price. Richmond papers say Yankees landed at Escambia Bay, below Hilton[2] (not far from Mobile) captured fifty men, and destroyed all camp equipage, wagons Saltworks, &c and every thing in and about Hilton. Richmond papers also confirm the destruction of the Albemarle & the consequent evacuation of Plymouth N.C.   A. LINCOLN

[1] ALS, DNA WR RG 107, Presidential Telegrams, I, 226.
[2] Either the Richmond papers or Lincoln was in error. The U.S. naval expedition of October 25-28 landed below Milton, Florida, near Pensacola.

Endorsement[1]

Let this appointment be made if there is a vacancy.
Nov 7, 1864.   A. LINCOLN

[1] Tracy, p. 246. No identification is given in the source.

Endorsement Concerning James W. Hughlett[1]

Treat him with mercy as he makes the disclosure himself.
Nov. 7. 1864   A. LINCOLN

[1] AES, IHi. Lincoln's endorsement is written on a letter from Private James W. W. Hughlett, First Maryland Veteran Volunteers, November 1, 1864: "I being A Member of Company G, 1st Regt Md Vet Vols I was wouned in action, at Front Royal Virginia and I was taken Prisoner also and I was Paroled and ordered to report to Camp Parole Annapolis Md During wich time I received all the Pay was Due me From the Goverment and I then stayed at Camp Parole untill their was two months Pay Due me and wen I came to Draw my Pay their was eight months Pay Due me on the Muster Role and

I Did Not Rectify the mistake wich I have of often bin sorry For and you would raleive my mind greatly by Leting me No My sentence I am wiling to suffer what ever sentence you May Pass I am willing to make the money good by having my Pay stoped I Drew $104.75 cents where i should only have Drew 22 the odd cents was clothing money Due me but I had received the amount Due me for clothing before that time I was A Drummer at the time I was wouned I should have writen Long ago but I had not courage enough, and I was ashamed." The regimental roster lists James Hughlett as discharged with his regiment on July 2, 1865.

Order Concerning A. W. White[1]

November 7, 1864

Lieut. A. W. White is allowed a leave of absence of five days from date, with pass & transportation to Philadelphia & back to Washington   A. LINCOLN

Nov. 7. 1864

[1] ADS, owned by Charles W. Olsen, Chicago, Illinois. Lieutenant A. W. White has not been identified.

To Ethan A. Hitchcock[1]

Will Gen. Hitchcock please see & hear this lady about a special exchange   A. LINCOLN

Nov. 8. 1864

[1] ALS, IHi. According to a note preserved with this communication, signed by Mary Emmons Collins, Lincoln's note was given to "Aunt Mary about special exchange of W. A. Collins . . . my grandfather." William A. Collins was captain of Company D, Tenth Wisconsin Infantry.

To the Managing Committee of the Sailors' Fair[1]

The Managing Committee   Executive Mansion,
of the Sailor's Fair: Washington,
Boston, Mass.   Nov. 8, 1864.

Allow me to wish you a great success. With the old fame of the Navy, made brighter in the present war, you can not fail. I name none, lest I wrong others by omission. To all, from Rear Admiral, to honest Jack I tender the Nation's admiration and gratitude

A. LINCOLN

[1] ALS, MCon. On October 15, 1864, Alexander H. Rice, chairman of the Managing Committee of the National Sailors' Fair to be held at Boston, November 9-21, had written asking Lincoln to be present (DLC-RTL). See also Lincoln to Rice, *infra*.

Response to a Serenade[1]

November 8, 1864

FRIENDS AND FELLOW-CITIZENS: Even before I had been informed by you that this compliment was paid me by loyal citizens of Pennsylvania friendly to me, I had inferred that you were of that portion of my countrymen who think that the best interests of the nation are to be subserved by the support of the present Administration. I do not pretend to say that you who think so embrace all the patriotism and loyalty of the country. But I do believe, and I trust, without personal interest, that the welfare of the country does require that such support and indorsement be given. I earnestly believe that the consequences of this day's work, if it be as you assure me and as now seems probable, will be to the lasting advantage, if not to the very salvation, of the country. I cannot at this hour say what has been the result of the election; but, whatever it may be, I have no desire to modify this opinion—that all who have labored to-day in behalf of the Union organization, have wrought for the best interests of their country and the world, not only for the present, but for all future ages. I am thankful to God for this approval of the people. But while deeply grateful for this mark of their confidence in me, if I know my heart, my gratitude is free from any taint of personal triumph. I do not impugn the motives of any one opposed to me. It is no pleasure to me to triumph over any one; but I give thanks to the Almighty for this evidence of the people's resolution to stand by free government and the rights of humanity.

[1] New York *Times*, November 10, 1864. This speech is misdated November 9, 1864, in Nicolay and Hay (X, 261-62). Concerning John Hay's transcription of this speech, see the note to Lincoln's response to a serenade on November 10, *infra*.

To Alexander H. Rice[1]

Hon. A. H. Rice   Executive Mansion,
Boston, Mass   Washington, Nov. 8, 1864.

Yours received. I have no other notice that the ox is mine. If it be really so I present it to the Sailors Fair, as a contribution.

A LINCOLN

[1] ALS, DNA WR RG 107, Presidential Telegrams, I, 229. Alexander H. Rice telegraphed Lincoln on November 8, 1864: "The mammoth Ox, Genl Grant is presented to you today Will you pass him over to the sailors fair as a contribution" (DLC-RTL). On November 22 Rice telegraphed: "I have the pleasure of informing you that the Mammoth Ox, General Grant, which was presented to you on the 8th of the present month, by Carlos Pierce Esq, of this city, and by

you donated to the National Sailors' Fair on the ninth inst, has yielded upwards of Three Thousand two hundred dollars to its treasury, and that sum is held as your contribution. . . ." (*Ibid.*).

To William H. Seward[1]

	Office U.S. Military Telegraph,
Hon. W. H. Seward	War Department,
Auburn, N.Y.	Washington, D.C., Nov. 8. 1864.

News from Grant, Sherman, Thomas and Rosecrans, satisfactory, but not important. Pirate Florida captured by the Wauchusetts [*Wachusett*] Oct. 7th. on coast of Brazil. The information is certain. A. LINCOLN

[1] ALS, DNA WR RG 107, Presidential Telegrams, I, 230.

To Timothy P. Andrews[1]

November 9, 1864

This poor soldier is in distress because he can get no pay. Will Pay Master-General, please have him put on the right track to get his pay. A. LINCOLN

Nov. 9, 1864

[1] American Art Association Anderson Galleries Catalog 4150, February 7-8, 1935, No. 363. According to the catalog description this item is an autograph note signed.

To Charles Butler[1]

| | Executive Mansion, |
| My dear Sir: | Washington, Nov. 9, 1864. |

I have received your letter of the 5th November, and beg to express my regret that it will not be possible to avail myself of your courteous invitation.

Praying that you will present to your distinguished guest the assurance of my high regard, I am, very truly, Your obedient servant, A. LINCOLN.

Charles Butler, Esq.,
13 East 14th St., N.Y.

[1] New York Citizens: *Welcome to Goldwin Smith* (1864), p. 14; Df, DLC-RTL. The draft is in John Hay's autograph. On November 5, 1864, Charles Butler and others of New York wrote Lincoln:

"On behalf of a number of our fellow citizens, we have the honour to invite your attendance at an entertainment, which they propose to give to Prof. Goldwin Smith, of Oxford, at the Rooms of the Union League Club, on Saturday, the 12th of November inst. at Ten oclock.

"In this distinguished Gentleman is recognized a judicious and eloquent representative of that large and right minded class of Englishmen, who, from the beginning of this rebellion, have extended to the Rebels neither moral sympathy nor material aid; and one who . . . has steadily protested against the violations of British neutrality, to aid the establishment of a Slave Empire upon the ruins alike of American Nationality and of Republican Government. . . ." (DLC-RTL).

To Benjamin B. French[1]

If Commissioner of Public Buildings chooses to give laborers at White House a holiday I have no objections.   A. LINCOLN. November 9, 1864.

[1] Hertz, II, 954. According to the source, this communication was received "following the reelection of Lincoln," on November 8.

To Anson G. Henry[1]

November 9, 1864

With returns and States of which we are confident, the re-election of the President is considered certain, while it is not certain that McClellan has carried any State, though the chances are that he has carried New Jersey and Kentucky.

[1] Noah Brooks, "Lincoln's Re-election," *The Century Magazine*, XLIX (April, 1895), 866. According to Brooks, "Dr. A. G. Henry . . . had been promised that he should receive a despatch from Mr. Lincoln when the result of the presidential election . . . should be definitely ascertained. Accordingly, on . . . November 9, President Lincoln dictated a despatch, the terms of which were as follows [text as above]. When I had written the despatch at the President's dictation, I passed it to him for his signature; but he declined to 'blow his own horn,' as he expressed it, and said: 'You sign the message, and I will send it.' "

To Edward Bates[1]

Attorney General please comply with this request.   A. LINCOLN Nov. 10. 1864

[1] AES, DNA GE RG 60, Papers of Attorney General, Segregated Lincoln material. Lincoln's endorsement is written on a letter from Mrs. Agnes Mary Grant of Toronto, Canada, November 10, 1864, enclosing her petition to the U.S. Supreme Court (not then in session) for redress in the matter of a mortgage on "The Saratoga Water Cure," which she claimed should rightfully be paid to her in gold rather than paper.

To Thomas E. Bramlette[1]

Office U.S. Military Telegraph,
Gov. Bramlette   War Department,
Frankfort, Ky.   Washington, D.C., Nov. 10 1864.

Yours of yesterday received. I can scarcely believe that Gen. Jno. B. Houston has been arrested "for no other offence than opposition to my re-election" for if that had been deemed sufficient cause of arrest, I should have heard of more than one arrest in Kentucky on election day. If however, Gen. Houston has been arrested for no other cause than opposition to my re-election Gen. Burbridge will discharge him at once, I sending him a copy of this as an order to that effect.   A. LINCOLN.

[1] ALS, DNA WR RG 107, Presidential Telegrams, I, 233 Governor Bramlette telegraphed Lincoln on November 9, 1864: "Genl Jno B. Houston, a loyal man and prominent citizen was arrested and yesterday started off by Genl Burbridge to be sent beyond our lines by way of Catlettsburg for no other offence than opposition to your reelection. . . . You are doubtless reelected, but surely it cannot sanction this ostracising of loyal men who honestly opposed you" (DLC-RTL). See Lincoln to Burbridge, infra.

To Stephen G. Burbridge[1]

                                        Office U.S. Military Telegraph,
Major General Burbridge   War Department,
Lexington, Ky.   Washington, D.C., Nov. 10. 1864.

I have just received a telegram from Gov. Bramlette saying "Genl. Jno. B. Houston, a loyal man and prominent citizen was arrested and yesterday started off by Gen. Burbridge to be sent beyond our lines by way of Catlettsburg for no other offence than opposition to your re-election" and I have answered him as follows below, of which please take notice and report to me.

                                                                A LINCOLN

[1] ALS, DNA WR RG 107, Presidential Telegrams, I, 232. See Lincoln to Bramlette, supra. Burbridge replied on November 11: "Gov Bramlette is wrong in saying that Jno B Huston was arrested for no other offence than opposition to your reelection. Hustons influence & speeches have been of a treasonable character & he persisted in making the latter after several warnings of what the consequences would be   He has been allowed however to return from Covington under oath & bond not again to oppose his Govt.   A vigorous policy against rebel sympathizers in this State must be pursued & if I have erred I fear I have made too few arrests instead of too many" (DLC-RTL).

To William Dennison[1]

Will the Post-Master General please see the bearer, Miss. Brady, daughter of and [sic] old friend and oblige her, if possible.
Nov. 10. 1864   A. LINCOLN

[1] ALS-F, Des Moines, Iowa, Capital, February 12, 1922. According to the source Miss Brady was the daughter of Jasper E. Brady, former U.S. congressman from Chambersburg, Pennsylvania (1847-1849), who served as clerk in the office of the paymaster general (1861-1869).

[99]

To Henry W. Hoffman[1]

	Office U.S. Military Telegraph,
H. W. Hoffman	War Department,
Baltimore, Md.	Washington, D.C., Nov. 10 1864.

The Maryland soldiers in the Army of the Potomac cast a total vote of 1428, out of which we get 1160 majority. This is directly from Gen. Meade and Gen. Grant.   A LINCOLN

[1] ALS, DNA WR RG 107, Presidential Telegrams, I, 235. On November 9 General Grant had telegraphed Stanton: "The following official statement of the vote polled in the Army of the Potomac yesterday has just been received from General Meade: Maine, total vote, 1677; Lincoln's majority, 1,143. New Hampshire, 515; Lincoln's majority, 279. Vermont, 102; Lincoln's majority, 42. Rhode Island, 190; Lincoln's majority, 134. Pennsylvania (seven counties to hear from), 11,122; Lincoln's majority, 3,494. West Virginia, 82; Lincoln's majority, 70. Ohio, 684; Lincoln's majority, 306. Wisconsin, 1,065; Lincoln's majority, 633. Michigan, 1,917; Lincoln's majority, 745. Maryland, 1,428; Lincoln's majority, 1,160. U.S. Sharpshooters, 124; Lincoln's majority, 89. New York, 305; Lincoln's majority, 113. Majority for Lincoln, 8,208." (OR, I, XLII, III, 570).

Hoffman replied to Lincoln's telegram on the same day: "I am much obliged for your dispatch giving soldiers vote in Army of Potomac. . . . The soldiers are quite as dangerous to Rebels in the rear as in front." (DLC-RTL).

To Timothy Ingraham[1]

Suspend execution of the order in the case of Brintnall, until the Judge Advocate General shall have reported to the President.

Nov. 10, 1864.   A. LINCOLN

[1] William D. Morley, Inc., Kolb Sale Catalog, November 17, 1941, No. 217. According to the catalog description, this item is an autograph card signed. Colonel Timothy Ingraham was provost marshal in the military governor's office in Washington. Sewall Brintnall, a government contractor was convicted on charges of attempting to bribe a government official and sentenced to pay a fine of $1,000 and remain in prison until the fine was paid. On January 25, 1865, Lincoln denied his application for pardon (DNA U.S. Army Court Martial Cases, RG 130, White House Office).

Response to a Serenade[1]

November 10, 1864

It has long been a grave question whether any government, not *too* strong for the liberties of its people, can be strong *enough* to maintain its own existence, in great emergencies.

On this point the present rebellion brought our republic to a severe test; and a presidential election occurring in regular course during the rebellion added not a little to the strain. If the loyal people, *united*, were put to the utmost of their strength by the rebellion, must they not fail when *divided*, and partially paralized, by a political war among themselves?

But the election was a necessity.

We can not have free government without elections; and if the rebellion could force us to forego, or postpone a national election, it might fairly claim to have already conquered and ruined us. The strife of the election is but human-nature practically applied to the facts of the case. What has occurred in this case, must ever recur in similar cases. Human-nature will not change. In any future great national trial, compared with the men of this, we shall have as weak, and as strong; as silly and as wise; as bad and good. Let us, therefore, study the incidents of this, as philosophy to learn wisdom from, and none of them as wrongs to be revenged.

But the election, along with its incidental, and undesirable strife, has done good too. It has demonstrated that a people's government can sustain a national election, in the midst of a great civil war. Until now it has not been known to the world that this was a possibility. It shows also how *sound*, and how *strong* we still are. It shows that, even among candidates of the same party, he who is most devoted to the Union, and most opposed to treason, can receive most of the people's votes. It shows also, to the extent yet known, that we have more men now, than we had when the war began. Gold is good in its place; but living, brave, patriotic men, are better than gold.

But the rebellion continues; and now that the election is over, may not all, having a common interest, re-unite in a common effort, to save our common country? For my own part I have striven, and shall strive to avoid placing any obstacle in the way. So long as I have been here I have not willingly planted a thorn in any man's bosom.

While I am deeply sensible to the high compliment of a re-election; and duly grateful, as I trust, to Almighty God for having directed my countrymen to a right conclusion, as I think, for their own good, it adds nothing to my satisfaction that any other man may be disappointed or pained by the result.

May I ask those who have not differed with me, to join with me, in this same spirit towards those who have?

And now, let me close by asking three hearty cheers for our brave soldiers and seamen and their gallant and skilful commanders.

1 AD, NDry. Concerning this speech and Lincoln's response to a serenade on November 8 (*supra*), John Hay's *Diary* records under date of November 11: "The speeches of the President at the two last serenades are very highly spoken of. The first I wrote after the fact to prevent the 'loyal Pennsylvanians' getting a swing at it themselves. The second one, last night, the President himself

wrote late in the evening and read it from the window. 'Not very graceful,' he said, 'but I am growing old enough not to care much for the manner of doing things.' "

To William S. Rosecrans[1]

Office U.S. Military Telegraph,

Major General Rosecrans   War Department,

St. Louis, Mo.   Washington, D.C., Nov. 10 1864.

Suspend execution of Major Wolf until further order, & meanwhile, report to me on the case.   A. LINCOLN

[1] ALS, DNA WR RG 107, Presidential Telegrams, I, 234. On November 10, 1864, Lincoln received telegrams from James E. Yeatman, Able Barton, and P. L. Terry, of St. Louis, Missouri, asking clemency in the case of Major Enoch O. Wolf (DLC-RTL). Wolf was one of seven Confederates held as hostages to be shot in retaliation for the murder by Confederate guerrilla Colonel Timothy Reeves of Major James Wilson and six Union soldiers, all of the Third Missouri State Cavalry. Six Confederate soldiers had already been shot on October 29 in retaliation for the Union men murdered with Wilson. On November 7, Department of the Missouri, *Special Orders No. 287*, ordered that Wolf be shot on November 11, in retaliation for the murder of Major Wilson. On November 10, Rosecrans acknowledged receipt of Lincoln's telegram, and on November 11 wrote a detailed report covering the essential facts as given above (DLC-RTL). See further Lincoln to Rosecrans, November 19, *infra*.

To William H. Seward[1]

[November 10, 1864]

I have a despatch from Chicago as follows:

"Arnold, Farnsworth, Washburne, Lovejoy & Norton, republicans elected. 4th. & 7th. Districts in doubt. In 8th. Swett probably defeated. Other five Districts Democrats elected. Ingersoll, Republican candidate at large probably elected, but vote close."

LINCOLN

[1] ALS, NAuE. Since Seward did not return to Washington until November 10, it seems likely that Lincoln's undated note was written on that day. The telegram from which Lincoln quotes has not been found.

To Edwin M. Stanton[1]

November 10, 1864

This lady would be appointed Chaplain of the First Wisconsin Heavy Artillery, only that she is a woman. The President has not legally anything to do with such a question, but has no objection to her appointment.   A. LINCOLN.

[1] DeRobigne Mortimer Bennett, *The World's Sages, Infidels, and Thinkers* (New York, 1876), p. 951. According to the source, Lincoln gave this communication to Ella E. Gibson (Mrs. Ella E. G. Hobart), "ordained as a minister

by the Religio-Philosophical Society of St. Charles, Ill." Although she was "unanimously elected Chaplain and the Colonel confirmed the election," Secretary Stanton "declined to recognize the mustering on account of her sex, not wishing to establish a precedent."

Discharge for Richard H. Lee[1]

Executive Mansion,
Washington, [November 11], 186[4].
Richard Henry Lee   Private 1st. Rebel Maryland Artillery
Prisoner at Fort Delaware   Division 20. (said to be sick)

Let this man take the oath of Dec. 8. 1863. and be discharged.
Nov. 11. 1864   A. LINCOLN

[1] AES-P, ISLA. John Hay wrote this note on Executive Mansion stationery, and Lincoln endorsed it with his order for discharge.

Endorsement Concerning Furlough for H. P. Morley[1]

If consistent I would be glad for this to be done   A. LINCOLN
Nov. 11. 1864

[1] AES, RPB. Lincoln's endorsement is written on a letter from S. Newton Pettis, asking a furlough for H. P. Morley (Marley?) of Crawford County, Pennsylvania. H. P. Morley has not been further identified, but Hiram P. Manly, Company F, One Hundred Eleventh Pennsylvania Volunteers, was discharged on a surgeon's certificate.

To David G. Farragut[1]

Executive Mansion,
Washington, November 11, 1864.
An Executive order to Rear-Admiral David G. Farragut having been issued on the 9th of August last, directing that, if Andrew J. Hamilton, or any person authorized in writing by him, should come out of either of the ports of Galveston or Sabine Pass with any vessel or vessels freighted with cotton shipped to the agent of the Treasury Department at New Orleans, the passage of such person, vessels, and cargoes should not be molested or hindered, but should be permitted to pass to the hands of such consignee, the said order is from this date to be considered as revoked.
ABRAHAM LINCOLN.

[1] Naval Records, I, XXI, 727. See Lincoln to Farragut, November 6, *supra.* The above order was enclosed by Gideon Welles to Farragut on November 14 following receipt of Farragut's report No. 511, October 30, 1864. Farragut reported that upon receiving on October 8 a copy of Lincoln's order of August 9

he had not felt authorized to permit ships to enter the ports mentioned, and that on October 9 he had instructed Commander William E. LeRoy to escort any qualified vessels from the ports, but to allow none to enter (*ibid.*, pp. 706-707). On November 16 Farragut wrote Lincoln: "I have the honor to acknowledge the receipt of a telegram from New Orleans forwarded by General Canby from Your Excellency and beg to state that I have never allowed the Blockade to be violated—but as I understand the Regulations of Trade dated Jany 26th 1864 articles are permitted to come out into our lines but nothing to go into the Rebel lines. . . ." (DLC-RTL). On November 18, Farragut reported to Welles that he had issued orders to Captain John B. Marchand, senior officer of the ships blockading the coast of Texas, in part as follows: "You will therefore consider the instructions given to Commander LeRoy of noneffect and be governed by the orders of the President as contained in the above telegram of the 6th instant, and you will at once instruct the commanding officers of the vessels of your division to the same effect. . . ." (Naval Records, I, XXI, 730).

Endorsement[1]

[c. November 12, 1864]

Hon. John A. Bingham brings this to me.

[1] AE, DLC-RTL. Lincoln's endorsement is written on the envelope of Green Clay Smith's letter to John A. Bingham, asking him to intercede for a pass for Mrs. E. M. Bradley of Georgetown, Kentucky, November 12, 1864. No further reference has been found.

To Joseph Holt[1]

Executive Mansion, Washington,

Judge Advocate General   Nov. 12. 1864.

Please procure record, & examine and report, upon the case of ——— Stettler, convicted & sent to Auburn Penitentiary for five years. His home was in Philadelphia, and his trial was here in Washington, on some charge about adulterated coffee. Yours truly

A LINCOLN

[1] ALS, DNA WR RG 153, Judge Advocate General, MM 1107. This letter is filed with papers in the case of John K. Stetler, citizen of Philadelphia, sentenced to five years' imprisonment on charges of wilful neglect of duty as a contractor furnishing coffee to the government. Holt had recommended enforcement of sentence in order to make an example of Stetler, and Lincoln had approved the sentence on November 20, 1863. No record of Lincoln's further action has been found.

To Joseph Holt[1]

Judge Advocate General please report on this case.   A. LINCOLN

Nov. 12. 1864

[1] AES, DNA WR RG 153, Judge Advocate General, NN 1774. Lincoln's endorsement is written on an application for remission of fine in the case of James Judge, citizen of Missouri, sentenced for disloyalty and violation of oath. Holt reported unfavorably and Lincoln denied the application on January 25, 1865.

To John A. Logan[1]

Major Genl. John A. Logan
Carbondale, Ills.

Executive Mansion
Washington,
Nov. 12. 1864

Yours of to-day just received. Some days ago I forwarded to the care of Mr. Washburne, a leave for you to visit Washington, subject only to be countermanded by General Sherman. This qualification I thought was a necessary prudence for all concerned. Subject to it, you may remain at home thirty days, or come here, at your own option. If, in view of maintaining your good relations with Gen. Sherman, and of probable movements of his army, you can safely come here, I shall be very glad to see you.

A. Lincoln

[1] ALS, DNA WR RG 107, Presidential Telegrams, I, 236. General Logan, who had been making campaign speeches in Illinois, telegraphed Lincoln on November 12: "I am suffering very much with inflammation in the throat & not able to do duty at present will start to my command as soon as able Can I be permitted to remain a few days for rest & improvement of health before starting" (DLC-RTL). Elihu B. Washburne had telegraphed Lincoln on October 27: "Genl. Jack Logan sends word to me that he wants to go to Washington after the election to see you about certain matters that he does not wish to write about. He wishes me to obtain the permission, which I know you will most gladly grant. Please send to me such permission and I will see it reaches him. . . ." (*Ibid.*).

Memorandum Concerning John C. Lewis[1]

Executive Mansion,
Washington, Nov 12. 1864.

Whenever proper evidence shall be brought to me along with this paper that a substitute has been procured, received and duly mustered in, in place of John C. Lewis, private in Company B. 188th. Regt. N.Y. Vols. I will will [*sic*] discharge the latter.

Nov. 12. 1864   A. Lincoln

[1] ADS, IHi. No further reference has been found.

To Marsena R. Patrick[1]

Gen. Patrick

Executive Mansion,
Washington, Nov. 12. 1864.

Please oblige me by seeing and hearing the bearer, Lt. Col. Kretschmar, who is well vouched to me as a most worthy gentleman, and who wishes to see you on business. Yours truly

A. Lincoln

[1] ALS, CSmH. General Marsena R. Patrick was provost marshal general of the Army of the Potomac. Julius C. Kretchmar was lieutenant colonel of the One Hundred Third New York Volunteers.

To Edward Bates[1]

Attorney General
Sir

Executive Mansion,
Washington, Nov. 14, 1864.

Please allow Hon. Mr. Corwin to have a copy of your legal opinion, given me, in the case of Col. Gates. Yours truly

A. LINCOLN

[1] ALS, DNA GE RG 60, Papers of Attorney General, Segregated Lincoln Material. The case in which Thomas Corwin was interested was probably that of Colonel William Gates. See Lincoln to Cameron, September 5, 1861, *supra*.

Endorsement[1]

Charge of desertion removed, restoring such rights, if any, as were thereby cut off.   A. LINCOLN

Nov. 14, 1864

[1] Stan. V. Henkels Catalog, October 21, 1936, No. 110. According to the catalog description Lincoln's autograph endorsement appears on an envelope. Another catalog listing of this endorsement describes the envelope as being of "the U.S. Sanitary Commission addressed to Gen. [George?] C. Jones, Washington." (J. C. Morgenthau & Company, Inc., Catalog, May 8, 1934, No. 163).

Extension of Leave for Nathaniel P. Banks[1]

This leave of absence is extended indefinitely, and until further order.   A. LINCOLN

Nov. 14. 1864

[1] AES, IHi. Lincoln's endorsement is written on a copy of AGO *Special Orders No. 341*, October 11, 1864: "The leave of absence heretofore granted Major General N. P. Banks, U.S. Volunteers, is hereby extended thirty days."

To Stephen A. Hurlbut[1]

Private
Major General Hurlbut

Executive Mansion
Washington, Nov. 14. 1864

Few things, since I have been here, have impressed me more painfully than what, for four or five months past, has appeared as bitter military opposition to the new State Government of Louisiana. I still indulged some hope that I was mistaken in the fact; but copies of a correspondence on the subject, between Gen. Canby and yourself, and shown me to-day, dispel that hope. A very fair proportion of the people of Louisiana have inaugerated a new State Government, making an excellent new constitution—better for the poor black man than we have in Illinois. This was done under military protection, directed by me, in the belief, still sincerely entertained, that with such a nucleous around which to build, we could get the State into position again sooner than otherwise. In this belief a general promise of protection and support, applicable alike to Louisiana and other states, was given in the last annual message. During the formation of the new government and constitution, they were supported by nearly every loyal person and opposed by every secessionist. And this support, and this opposition, from the respective stand points of the parties, was perfectly consistent and logical. Every Unionist ought to wish the new government to succeed; and every disunionist must desire it to fail. It's failure would gladden the heart of Slidell in Europe, and of every enemy of the old flag in the world. Every advocate of slavery naturally desires to see blasted, and crushed, the liberty promised the black man by the new constitution. But why Gen. Canby and Gen. Hurlbut should join on the same side is to me incomprehensible.

Of course, in the condition of things at New-Orleans, the military must not be thwarted by the civil authority; but when the constitutional convention, for what it deems a breach of previlege, arrests an editor, in no way connected with the military, the military necessity for insulting the Convention, and forcibly discharging the editor, is difficult to perceive.[2] Neither is the military necessity for protecting the people against paying large salaries, fixed by a Legislature of their own choosing, very apparant. Equally difficult to perceive is the military necessity for forcibly interposing to prevent a bank from loaning it's own money to the State. These things, if they have occurred, are, at the best, no better than gratuitous hostility. I wish I could hope that they may be shown to not have occurred. To make assurance against misunderstanding, I repeat that in the existing condition of things in Louisiana, the military must not be thwarted by the civil authority; and I add that on points of difference the commanding general must be judge and master. But I also add that in the exercise of this judgment and control, a purpose, obvious, and scarcely unavowed, to transcend all military necessity, in order to crush out the civil government, will not be overlooked. Yours truly   A. LINCOLN

[1] ADfS, DLC-RTL; LS, DLC. The correspondence between General Edward R. S. Canby and Hurlbut may be found in OR, I, XLI, IV, 412-13. In reply to

Hurlbut's question "to what extent am I compelled . . . to recognize the acts and proceedings of the State of Louisiana in its several branches. . . ." Canby replied on October 29, "It is scarcely necessary for me to say that until the President . . . revokes his proclamation of December 8, 1863, or until Congress has acted definitely upon the subject, all attempts at civil government, within the territory declared to be in insurrection, are the creation of military power, and, of course, subject to military revision and control. . . ."

On November 29, Hurlbut replied to Lincoln's letter:

"I am this day in receipt of your letter of November 14th. I confess myself much surprised at the tenor and spirit of its contents and am well assured that correct information has not been furnished you of the position either of Genl Canby or myself.

"I recognize as thoroughly as any man the advance toward the right made by the adoption of the Free Constitution of Louisiana, and have done and shall do all in my power to vindicate its declaration of freedom, and to protect and prepare the emancipated Bondsmen for their new status & condition. The fact has been withheld from you, Mr President, but it still exists that nothing has been done for this purpose since the adoption of the Constitution—*except by military authority.* . . ." (DLC-RTL).

For Canby's reply to Lincoln's letter to Hurlbut, see the note to Lincoln's letter to Canby, December 12, *infra*.

2 Thomas P. May, the radical editor of the New Orleans *Times*, had been arrested for publishing a description of the convention in which delegates were described as being drunk.

Pass for Mrs. Mary A. Stevens[1]

Allow this lady, Mrs. Stevenss,[2] to pass our lines, with ordinary baggage only, and go to Houston, Texas.   A. LINCOLN

Nov. 14. 1864.

1 ADS, The Rosenbach Company, Philadelphia and New York. A letter from Andrew Johnson, October 31, 1864, accompanies this pass, and introduces Mrs. Mary A. Stevens: "I am fully satisfied of her loyalty to the Gov't, and personally know that, when residing at Lexington, Ky., she manifested the same in the kindness and hospitality she was pleased to extend to Union Refugees of East Tennessee driven over the mountains into the state of Kentucky."

2 Lincoln first wrote "Stevenson," then erased the last two letters and added "s," making the name inaccurate as "Stevenss."

To Samuel A. Cony and Others[1]

Office U.S. Military Telegraph,
The Governor of Maine   War Department,
Augusta, Me.   Washington, D.C., Nov. 15 1864.

Please send, as soon as practicable, exactly, or approximately, the aggregate of votes cast in your State at the late election. It is desired with reference to the forthcoming Message.

A. LINCOLN

Saml Cony
Gov of Maine
Augusta Me

Jos. A. Gilmore
Gov of N.H.
Concord NH.

Jno Gregory Smith
Govr of Vermont
Montpelier Vt.

John A. Andrew
Govr of Massachusetts
Boston Mass

Jas Y. Smith
Gov of Rhode Island
Providence R I.

Wm. A. Buckingham
Govr of Connecticut
Hartford Conn.

Horatio Seymour
Govr of New York
Albany N.Y.

Joel Parker
Gov of New Jersey
Trenton N.J.

A. G. Curtin
Gov. of Penna
Harrisburg Pa.

Wm. Cannon
Gov of Delaware
Dover Del

A. W. Bradford
Govr of Maryland
Annapolis

A. I. Boreman
Govr West Va.
Wheeling Va

Andrew Johnson
Mil Govr of Tenn
Nashville Tenn

Thos. E. Bramlette
Gov of Kentucky
Lexington Ky.

John Brough
Govr of Ohio
Columbus O.

Austin Blair
Gov of Michigan
Lansing Mich

O. P. Morton
Gov of Indiana
Indianapolis Ind

Richard Yates
Govr of Illinois
Springfield Ill

Willard P Hall
Lt Govr of Missouri
Jefferson City Mo

Wm. M. Stone
Gov of Iowa
Des Moines Iowa

James T. Lewis
Govr of Wisconsin
Madison Wis

Stephen Miller
Govr of Minnesota
St Paul Minn

Thomas Carney
Govr of Kansas
Leavenworth Kan

Frederick F. Low
Govr of California
Sacramento Cal

Jas W. Nye
Govr of Nevada
Carson City
Nevada

Maj Gen J. E. Steele[2]
Little Rock
Ark

Michael Hahn
Govr of Louisiana
New Orleans   via Cairo

[1] ALS, DNA WR RG 107, Presidential Telegrams, I, 240-42. The names of the governors to whom the telegram was sent are listed on two separate telegraph blanks (241-42), not in Lincoln's autograph. The telegrams from the governors in reply (DLC-RTL) were utilized by Lincoln in compiling his tabulation of votes (December 1, *infra*), which furnished the basis for his analysis of the election in his annual message to congress on December 6. See also Lincoln's second telegram to Stone and others, November 29, *infra*.

[2] Clerk's error for Major General Frederick Steele.

To Jesse K. Dubois[1]

Hon J K. Dubois,   Washn., Nov. 15, 1864.
Springfield Ills.

Yours of today asking that (530) five hundred and thirty men may be assigned to the 32d. Illinois shall be attended to.

You say "State gone twenty five thousand." Which way did it go? How stand the members of congress and the other officers

A. LINCOLN.

[1] Copy, DNA WR RG 107, Presidential Telegrams, I, 237. Lincoln's original autograph telegram has been removed from the file and a copy substituted. The date as given by the copy is open to question. No telegram of November 15 from Dubois has been found, but a telegram from Dubois, marked as received at 11 P.M. on November 14, reported "State carried for Lincoln & the Union by upwards of thirty thousand for Congress," and named the successful candidates (DLC-RTL). In view of the implication of Lincoln's telegram, it would seem either that the date of the copy is in error or that Lincoln had not seen Dubois' telegram of November 14.

To William P. Fessenden and Hanson A. Risley[1]

Will the secretary of the Treasury and Mr. Risley please see & hear the bearer, Mr McBernie   A LINCOLN
    Nov. 15. 1864

[1] Copy, ISLA. McBernie has not been identified.

To Ethan A. Hitchcock[1]

Will Gen. Hitchcock please see the bearer, Mrs. Gimber.
    Nov. 15, 1864.   A. LINCOLN

[1] Thomas F. Madigan, *A Catalogue of Lincolniana* (1929), p. 32. Mrs. Gimber has not been identified.

[110]

Order Concerning Alfred Everson[1]

Executive Mansion,
Washington, 15th November, 1864.

It is hereby ordered that the sentence of Acting Master Alfred Everson, of the Navy of the United States, convicted by Court Martial of assault with intent to kill James O'Neill, a fireman on board the captured blockade runner, Nicholas 1st, be so far mitigated as to allow him the freedom of the prison where he is confined, on condition of good behaviour on his part, as a prisoner.

ABRAHAM LINCOLN

[1] DS, DNA FS RG 59, Miscellaneous Letters, Part I. The Navy register lists Alfred Everson as resigning on April 6, 1865.

To William H. Purnell[1]

Office U.S. Military Telegraph,
W. H. Purnell,   War Department,
Baltimore, Md.   Washington, D.C., Nov. 15 1864.

I shall be happy to receive the committee on Thursday morning (17th.) as you propose.   A. LINCOLN

[1] ALS, DNA WR RG 107, Presidential Telegrams, I, 239. William H. Purnell of Baltimore, chairman of the Maryland State Central Committee, telegraphed Lincoln on November 15: "The State Central Com of the Union party of Md propose to visit the President for the purpose of tendering their congratulations on the result of the recent election particularly in their own State Will it be convenient for the Prest receive the Committee on the morning of Thursday the seventeenth . . . inst" (DLC-RTL). See Lincoln's reply to the Maryland committee, November 17, *infra*.

To George H. Thomas[1]

Cypher   Office U.S. Military Telegraph,
Major General Thomas   War Department,
Nashville. Tenn.   Washington, D.C., Nov. 15. 1864.

How much force and Artillery had Gillem?   A LINCOLN

[1] AL, DNA WR RG 107, Presidential Telegrams, I, 238. The penciled signature is in the handwriting of a clerk. General Thomas had telegraphed Halleck on November 14, 1864, concerning the action near Russellville, Tennessee:

"The following despatch received from General [Jacob] Ammen, Knoxville, via Chattanooga:

" 'General [Alvan C.] Gillem was attacked above Morristown at 12 o'clock last night, routed, and lost his artillery, and is reported captured. Nearly 1,000 of his troops have arrived at Strawberry Plains. I sent some infantry to Morristown yesterday to support General Gillem; they were in the fight, and reported captured. . . . [John C.] Breckinridge is reported in command, with his force

variously estimated at from 2,000 to 8,000 men'. . . ." (OR, I, XLV, I, 876).
    Thomas replied to Lincoln's telegram on the same day:
    "Gen Gillems force consisted of three regiments of Tennessee Cavalry, and one battery of six guns belonging to the Governors Guard, about fifteen hundred men." (DLC-RTL).

Pardon[1]

November 16, 1864

Upon rejoining his regiment as soon as practicable & faithfully serving out his term, this man is pardoned for any overstaying of time or desertion heretofore committed.   A. LINCOLN
    Nov. 16. 1864

[1] ADS, owned by Richard F. Lufkin, Boston, Massachusetts. The soldier has not been identified.

To Edwin M. Stanton[1]

November 16, 1864

Hon. Sec. of War please see Mr. Gear, on the question of furnishing some small arm amunition to loyal people in Northern Alabama.   A. LINCOLN
    Nov. 16. 1864

[1] ALS, owned by Frederic F. Van de Water, Brattleboro, Vermont. On September 28, 1864, Andrew Johnson wrote Lincoln, introducing Jean Joseph Giers, a refugee from Morgan County, Alabama (DLC-RTL).

To Edward Bates[1]

Pardon, for unexecuted part of sentence.
    Nov. 17, 1864   A. LINCOLN

[1] AES, DNA RG 204, U.S. Pardon Attorney, A 570. Lincoln's endorsement is written on a certificate of good behavior from the deputy warden of the U.S. jail in favor of James Welch, sentenced for assault and battery.

Endorsement Concerning Arthur Taylor[1]

Let this man be paroled for sixty days from this date.
    Nov. 17, 1864.   A. LINCOLN.

[1] Stan. V. Henkels Catalog, May 19, 1925, No. 155. According to the catalog description Lincoln's endorsement is written on a letter from Assistant Surgeon T. E. Mitchell, asking release of Arthur Taylor, Eighth Louisiana Regiment (CSA), in the hospital at Frederick, Maryland, and not likely to recover from his wounds.

To William P. Fessenden[1]

In addition to what is within said, I know Mr. Scovel to be one of our best friends. Will the Sec. of Treasury please see him.

Nov. 17, 1864   A. LINCOLN.

[1] AES, ORB. "Scovel" was probably James M. Scovel of Camden, New Jersey.

Reply to Maryland Union Committee[1]

November 17, 1864

The President, in reply, said: "He had to confess that he was fully notified of the intention thus kindly to call upon him, and by that means he had a fair opportunity offered to be ready with a set speech; but he had not prepared one, having been very busy with his public duties; therefore, he could only speak as the thoughts might occur to him. He would not attempt to conceal from them the fact that he was gratified at the results of the Presidential election, and he would assure them that he had kept as near as he could to the exercise of his best judgment, for the promotion of the interests of the whole country; and now, to have the seal of approbation marked on the course he had pursued was exceedingly gratifying to his feelings. He might go further and say that, in as large proportion as any other man, his pleasure consisted in the belief that the policy he had pursued would be the best and the only one that could save the country. He had said before, and would now repeat, that he indulged in no feeling of triumph over any one who thought or acted differently from himself. He had no such feeling towards any living man.

"When he thought of Maryland in particular, it was that the people had more than double their share in what had occurred in the elections. He thought the adoption of their free State constitution was a bigger thing than their part in the Presidential election. He could, any day, have stipulated to lose Maryland in the Presidential election to save its free constitution, because the Presidential election comes every four years and the adoption of the constitution, being a good thing, could not be undone. He therefore thought in that they had a victory for the right worth a great deal more than their part in the Presidential election, although he thought well of that. He once before said, and would now say again, that those who had differed from us and opposed us would see that it was better for their own good that they had been defeated, rather than to have been successful. Thanking them for

[113]

their compliment, he said he would bring to a close that short speech."

¹ Washington *Daily Morning Chronicle* and *Daily National Republican*, November 18, 1864. See Lincoln to Purnell, November 15, *supra*. As chairman of the committee, William H. Purnell "delivered an eloquent address, in which he said:

"They rejoiced that the people, by an almost unanimous and unprecedented majority, had again elevated the President to the proudest and most honorable position on earth, and had endorsed his course of action. They felt under deep obligations to him, because he had appreciated their condition as a slave State. It was not too much to say that, by means of the exercise of a rare discretion on his part, Maryland occupies a position in favor of freedom, having forever abolished slavery by the sovereign decree of her own people. They desired that his Administration in the future, as in the past, would result in the restoration of the Union, with freedom as its immutable basis. After further remarks of a like appropriate character, Mr. Purnell expressed the hope that the President, on retiring from his high and important position, would receive the universal approval of mankind; and 'may Heaven,' he said, 'crown your days with loving kindness and tender mercy.'"

To William H. Seward¹

Livingston

What says the Sec. of State to within?   A. LINCOLN

Nov. 17, 1864

¹ AES, DLC-RTL. Lincoln's endorsement is written on a letter from H. P. Livingston, Willard's Hotel, November 14, 1864:

"Allow me to present to you a plan, whearby the Union sentiment at the South, would be strengthened, The dissatisfaction of the people with their Government, increased and their Armey demoralized.

"Their are now but (36) newspapers printed in the Confederacy. they are poor few of them makeing money.

"I would suggest that the controle of many and nearley all of them may be had by purchase of the controleing interest. The amount of funds required would be small in comparison to the advantages that would result to our cause from the control of the Southern Press.

"Their are in the South a large number of inteligent Union men who are able writers, and would hail with joy an opertunity to assist in puting down the rebellion."

Seward endorsed in reply:

"It seems to me very judicious and wise. But I have no adequate fund. Will the President submit the plan to Sec. War. I do not know that he has the funds necessary, and of course he must judge of the propriety of the application if he has.

"If not T. W. [Thurlow Weed]—might find money by contribution."

Endorsement Concerning John T. Cox¹

[c. November 18, 1864]

No particular controversy

1 AE, DNA NR RG 48, Department of Interior, Indian Agents, Box 66. Lincoln's endorsement is written on the envelope containing a letter of Samuel J. Crawford and others, Leavenworth, Kansas, to Senator James H. Lane, November 18, 1864, recommending appointment of John T. Cox as agent for the Osage Indians. No record of the appointment has been found.

Proclamation Concerning Blockade[1]

November 19, 1864

By the President of the United States of America:

A Proclamation.

Whereas, by my Proclamation of the nineteenth of April, one thousand eight hundred and sixty one, it was declared that the ports of certain States including those of Norfolk, in the State of Virginia, Fernandina and Pensacola, in the State of Florida, were, for reasons therein set forth, intended to be placed under blockade; and whereas the said ports were subsequently blockaded accordingly, but having, for some time past, been in the military possession of the United States, it is deemed advisable that they should be opened to domestic and foreign commerce:

Now, therefore, be it known that I, Abraham Lincoln, President of the United States, pursuant to the authority in me vested by the fifth section of the act of Congress, approved on the 13th. of July 1861, entitled "An act further to provide for the collection of duties on imports and for other purposes," do hereby declare that the blockade of the said ports of Norfolk, Fernandina and Pensacola, shall so far cease and determine from and after the first day of December next that commercial intercourse with those ports, except as to persons, things and information contraband of war, may, from that time, be carried on, subject to the laws of the United States, to the limitations and in pursuance of the regulations which may be prescribed by the Secretary of the Treasury, and to such military and naval regulations as are now in force or may hereafter be found necessary.

In witness whereof, I have hereunto set my hand, and caused the seal of the United States to be affixed.

Done at the city of Washington, this nineteenth day of November, in the year of our Lord one thousand eight hundred and sixty four, and of the Independence of the United States the eighty-ninth.

[L.S.]

By the President: ABRAHAM LINCOLN

WILLIAM H. SEWARD, Secretary of State.

1 DS, DNA FS RG 11, Proclamations.

To William S. Rosecrans[1]

Executive Mansion, Washington,
Major General Rosecrans.   Nov. 19, 1864.

A Major Wolf, as it seems, was under sentence, in your Department, to be executed in retaliation for the murder of a Major
Wilson; and I, without any particular knowledge of the facts, was
induced by appeals for mercy, to order the suspension of his execution until further order. Understanding that you so desire, this letter places the case again within your control, with the remark only
that I wish you to do nothing merely for revenge, but that what
you may do, shall be solely done with reference to the security of
the future. Yours truly   A. LINCOLN

[1] ADfS, DLC-RTL; LS, ORB. See Lincoln to Rosecrans, November 10, *supra.*
On February 24, 1865, Major Enoch O. Wolf was sent to City Point and ex-
changed. For a detailed narrative of the case, see Oliver R. Barrett, "Lincoln and
Retaliation," *Lincoln Herald,* December, 1947, pp. 2-23.

To Alfred Sully[1]

Officer in command at   Executive Mansion,
Davenport, Iowa.   Washington, Nov. 19. 1864.

Let the Indian "Big Eagle" be discharged. I ordered this some
time ago.   A. LINCOLN

[1] ALS, DNA WR RG 107, Presidential Telegrams, I, 243. See Lincoln's order
of October 26, *supra.* On November 14, 1864, George S. C. Dow, a lawyer and
banker of Davenport, Iowa, wrote Lincoln:

"You will remember me as the person to whom you were kind enough to give
an order for the release of the Indian 'Big Eagle.'

"This order failed to effect his release. The person in charge and to whom I
presented it, treated me very rudely. I may as well say that he insulted me most
grossly. He treated also the order and yourself with great contempt because as
he said, you ought to know better than to write an order in pencil, or give it to
a civilian.

"I did not intend to trouble you again, but for reasons not necessary to be
stated, I think I should report the facts to you, and request of you, that you will
be kind enough to direct a note to the proper military officer, requesting him to
issue the proper order for 'Big Eagle's' discharge. . . ." (DLC-RTL).

General Alfred Sully was in command of the District of Iowa with headquarters at Davenport, from August, 1864, through April, 1865, but no reply from
any officer at Davenport has been found. On December 3, 1864, AGO *Special
Orders No. 430,* directed that " 'Big Eagle,' an Indian, now in confinement at
Davenport, Iowa, will, upon the receipt of this Order, be immediately released
from confinement and set at liberty."

To Mrs. Lydia Bixby[1]

Executive Mansion,
Washington, Nov. 21, 1864.

Dear Madam,—I have been shown in the files of the War Department a statement of the Adjutant General of Massachusetts,

that you are the mother of five sons who have died gloriously on the field of battle.

I feel how weak and fruitless must be any words of mine which should attempt to beguile you from the grief of a loss so overwhelming. But I cannot refrain from tendering to you the consolation that may be found in the thanks of the Republic they died to save.

I pray that our Heavenly Father may assuage the anguish of your bereavement, and leave you only the cherished memory of the loved and lost, and the solemn pride that must be yours, to have laid so costly a sacrifice upon the altar of Freedom. Yours, very sincerely and respectfully,   A. LINCOLN.

Mrs. Bixby.

[1] Boston *Transcript*, November 25, 1864. The purported facsimiles of this letter have long been adjudged to be forgeries, but there is no reason to question the authenticity of the text of the letter which appeared in the *Transcript* and other contemporary sources. Controversy over the claim that John Hay composed this letter has somewhat abated, with the claim remaining unproved. Lincoln was in error as to Mrs. Bixby's five sons because her case had been inaccurately presented to him by the Adjutant General's Office. Later investigations have revealed that only two sons were killed: Sergeant Charles N. Bixby, Twentieth Massachusetts Infantry, killed May 3, 1863, and Private Oliver C. Bixby, Fifty-eighth Massachusetts Infantry, killed July 30, 1864. Private George W. (A.?) Way (Bixby), Fifty-sixth Massachusetts Infantry, who had enlisted under an assumed name, was captured July 30, 1864. Imprisoned first at Richmond and later at Salisbury, North Carolina, George Way was reported (1) to have deserted to the enemy and (2) to have died in prison at Salisbury. Neither of these reports has been established beyond doubt. Corporal Henry C. Bixby, Thirty-second Massachusetts Infantry, was honorably discharged at Boston on December 17, 1864. Private Edward (Arthur Edward) Bixby, First Massachusetts Heavy Artillery, deserted May 28 or 29, 1862. The most complete single source of information among the several books and pamphlets, as well as the numerous articles on the subject, is F. Lauriston Bullard, *Abraham Lincoln and the Widow Bixby* (1946).

To William P. Fessenden[1]

November 21, 1864

Hon. Secretary of the Treasury please see & hear Hon. Mr. Allen who will present this. Mr. Allen's representations may be safely relied on; and if the removal he seeks shall be made, I personally know that a better man can not be found for the vacancy than Joseph G. Bowman. In fact I should dislike to appoint any other, he being an applicant   A. LINCOLN

Nov. 21. 1864

[1] ALS, IHi. Cyrus M. Allen of Vincennes, Indiana, was recommending his fellow townsman, Joseph G. Bowman, who had formerly resided in Wabash County, Illinois, and served with Lincoln in the Illinois legislature in 1839. Bowman was appointed assessor of Internal Revenue, First District, Indiana, 1865.

To John Phillips[1]

Executive Mansion. Washington,
My dear Sir   21st. November, 1864

I have heard of the incident at the polls in your town, in which you bore so honored a part, and I take the liberty of writing to you to express my personal gratitude for the compliment paid me by the suffrage of a citizen so venerable.

The example of such devotion to civic duties in one whose days have already extended an average life time beyond the Psalmist's limit, cannot but be valuable and fruitful. It is not for myself only, but for the country which you have in your sphere served so long and so well, that I thank you. Your friend and Servant

A. LINCOLN.

[1] Copy, DLC-Nicolay Papers; New York *Tribune*, December 9; 1864. The draft or copy in the Nicolay Papers is on Executive Mansion stationery in an unidentified handwriting. On November 9, 1864, F. W. Emmons of Sturbridge, Massachusetts, wrote Lincoln:

"I send you with this, a pamphlet of 'The Centenarian Deacon John Phillips[']—of the celebration of his one Hundreth birth day and am happy to inform you that he still lives, now in his 105th year.

"He is a Democrat, of the Jeffersonian School: voted for Washington, as President of the United States; and, yesterday, voted for your re-election to this honorable and responsible place.

"He rode from home, two miles, to our Town Hall, with his son, Col. Edwd Phillips, aged 79 yrs, to cast this vote. He entered it between two unfurled flags of his country, bearing on them the Stars and Stripes; all within, at the time rising, with uncovered heads, to do him homage. And when offered two votes, to take his choice, he said: '*I vote for Abraham Lincoln.*'

"He has been, for several years, the oldest citizen of this town; and is now, probably, the oldest man in the commonwealth. . . ." (DLC-RTL).

On January 16, 1865, Phillips replied to Lincoln's letter:

"I trust you will pardon me in trying to answer the kind letter you sent me for which I would return my thanks.

"It was an honor I never expected to receive and feel that your goodness of heart with respect for my *extreme age* alone prompted the act—while your mind and time must be occupied by so many national cares and anxieties.

"I feel that I have no desire to live but to see the conclusion of this wicked rebellion, and the power of God displayed in the conversion of the nation.

"I beleive by the help of God you will accomplish the first—and also be the means of establishing universal freedom and restoring peace to the Union.

"That the God of mercy will bless you in this great work and through life is the prayer of your unworthy servant." (LS, IHi-Nicolay and Hay Papers).

To Edwin M. Stanton[1]

If the service can be useful let the appointment be made.
Nov. 21, 1864   A. LINCOLN

[1] The Morris Book Shop (Chicago) Catalog 56, December, 1912, No. 147. According to the source, Lincoln's endorsement was written on an envelope

"addressed to Hon. Cyrus M. Allen," enclosing five letters recommending appointment of Theodore R. McFerson, as assistant quartermaster. McFerson has not been identified.

To Edwin M. Stanton[1]

Executive Mansion,
November 21, 1864.

My dear Sir: I now propose that Smithson and Yocum, respectively, be enlarged, allowing their sentences to stand as security for their good behavior—that is, not pardon them, but if they misbehave, re-arrest and imprison them on the old score.

Also, I think if Waring's premises down in Maryland are [not][2] in use by the government, he and his family might be allowed to re-occupy them. Yours truly,   A. LINCOLN.

[1] NH, X, 275. Stanton replied on the same day: "The Adjutant General has been instructed to issue orders in the cases of Yokum Smithson & Waring in conformity with the views expressed in your note of this date. . . ." (DLC-RTL). On November 25, 1864, AGO *Special Orders No. 417* directed:
"I. That William T. Smithson and William Yokum, now confined in the Penitentiary at Albany, New York, under sentences published in General Orders, No. 371, of November 18th, 1863, and No. 31, of January 25th, 1864, be enlarged, until further orders, on condition of future good behavior towards the Government of the United States.
"II. That John H. Waring be allowed to re-occupy his premises in Maryland, with his family, and that he be put in possession accordingly, on condition that he shall neither hold intercourse with rebels, nor give them aid or comfort."
[2] Brackets in source.

To Edwin M. Stanton[1]

If another Commissary is needed, let this gentleman be appointed.   A. LINCOLN.
Nov. 21, 1864.

[1] Tracy, p. 247. According to the source this endorsement was written on a "letter of A. Johnson to Secretary of War in favor of James H. Woodward." No record has been found of Woodward's appointment.

To Augustus R. Wright[1]

Hon. A. R. Wright   Executive Mansion,
Louisville, Ky.   Washington, Nov. 21, 1864.

Admitting that your cotton was destroyed by the Federal Army, I do not suppose any-thing could be done for you now. Congress has appropriated no money for that class of claims, and will not, I expect, while the active war lasts.   A. LINCOLN

[1] ALS, DNA WR RG 107, Presidential Telegrams, I, 244. Augustus R. Wright, former U.S. congressman from Georgia (1857-1859), telegraphed Lincoln from

Louisville, Kentucky, on November 21, 1864: "My cotton was burned by the Federal Army If I return with proof can you do anything for me. I find my brother here in want. Reply." (DLC-RTL).

On November 24 Wright telegraphed from Nashville, Tennessee: "At Louisville, I met with my brother & a Mr Stewart, refugees from Rome Ga. They told me the cotton at Rome was burnt. This was the cause of my telegram. On arriving at this place, I meet others from Rome who tell me all the cotton [in] the *ware houses* was burnt but none other, & that my 220 bales which was over the river in a gin house, was still safe. . . ." (*Ibid.*).

To Thomas E. Bramlette[1]

Gov. Bramlette
Frankfort, Ky.

Office U.S. Military Telegraph,
War Department,
Washington, D.C., Nov. 22 1864.

Yours of to-day received. It seems that Lt. Gov. Jacobs & Col. Wolford are stationary now. Gen. Sudarth & Mr. Hodges are here & the Secretary of War, and myself are trying to devise means of pacification and harmony for Kentucky, which we hope to effect soon, now that the *passion-exciting* subject of the election is past.

A. LINCOLN.

[1] ALS, DNA WR RG 107, Presidential Telegrams, I, 245. On November 22 Governor Bramlette telegraphed Lincoln:

"Lt Gov [Richard T.] Jacob is at Catlettsburg & Col [Frank L.] Wolford at Covington both are under arrest & by order of the Secret Inquisition ordered into the rebel lines Will you either order their release at once or a suspension of the order until you receive my communication of this date" (DLC-RTL).

Bramlette's letter of the same date forwarded a petition for the release of Jacob and Wolford, signed by Joshua F. Speed and others. The arrangements which Lincoln hoped to work out with Albert G. Hodges and General Samuel G. Suddarth of the Kentucky State Militia seem not to have materialized. See Lincoln to Dickson, December 27, *infra*.

A communication from General Stephen G. Burbridge to Colonel Norton P. Chipman, November 23, 1864, gives the reasons for Jacob's arrest: "Lieutenant-Governor Jacob was arrested for making speeches in Kentucky, in which he advised armed resistance to the enrollment and enlistment of slaves; advised citizens to arm to resist military interference at the polls; and generally his whole conduct and speeches have been wholly disloyal. . . ." (OR, I, XLV, I, 1010).

To Robert N. McLaren[1]

Officer in command at
Fort-Snelling, Minn.

War Department
Washington City,
Nov. 24, 1864

Suspend execution of Patrick Kelly, John Lennor [*sic*], Joel H. Eastwood, Thomas J. Murray, and Hoffman until further order from here. A. LINCOLN

[1] ALS, DNA WR RG 107, Presidential Telegrams, I, 247. Colonel Robert N. McLaren was in command at Fort Snelling. Concerning the prisoners named, see Lincoln's telegram to Rice, *infra*.

To Henry M. Rice[1]

	War Department
Hon. Henry M. Rice	Washington City,
St. Paul, Minn.	Nov. 24. 1864

Have suspended execution of deserters named in your despatch, until further order from here.   A. LINCOLN

[1] ALS, DNA WR RG 107, Presidential Telegrams, I, 246. Henry M. Rice, former U.S. senator from Minnesota, and Governor Stephen A. Miller telegraphed on November 23, 1864: "We respectfully apply for postponement of execution for thirty (30) days of Patrick Kelly   John Lennon   Joel H Eastwood   Thomas J Murray & John Hoffman five (5) deserters now under sentence of death at Fort Snelling" (DLC-RTL).

To Andrew G. Curtin[1]

| Gov. Curtin | War Department Washington City, |
| Harrisburg, Pa. | Nov. 25. 1864 |

I have no knowledge, information, or belief, that three States, or any state, offer to resume allegiance.   A. LINCOLN

[1] ALS, DNA WR RG 107, Presidential Telegrams, I, 248. Governor Curtin had telegraphed on November 25, 1864: "Our people are excited by a rumor that three States have offered to return to their allegiance. Is it true?" (OR, III, IV, 942).

To Nathaniel P. Banks[1]

| | Executive Mansion, Washington, |
| Major General Banks. | Nov. 26. 1864. |

I had a full conferrence this morning with the Secretary of War in relation to yourself. The conclusion is that it will be best for all if you proceed to New-Orleans, and act there in obedience to your order; and, in doing which, having continued, say, one month, if it shall then, as now, be your wish to resign, your resignation will be accepted. Please take this course. Yours truly

A. LINCOLN.

[1] ALS, IHi; ADfS, DLC-RTL. Although ordered to return to his command of the Department of the Gulf on November 23 (AGO *Special Orders No. 413*), Banks remained in Washington for four months, with Lincoln's consent, to help in Lincoln's effort to have the Louisiana state government recognized by congress. See further Lincoln to Banks, December 2, *infra*.

To Edward Bates[1]

Let this appointment be made.   A. LINCOLN
Nov. 26. 1864

¹ AES, DNA RG 60, Papers of Attorney General, Appointments. Lincoln's endorsement is written on a letter from John H. Hubbard and others, Litchfield, Connecticut, October 4, 1864, recommending John Gould for U.S. marshal in case Henry Hammond resigned. See Lincoln's communication to the Senate, January 27, 1865, *infra*.

Order Concerning Joseph M. Locke¹

November 26, 1864

Report approved. Let Captain Locke be re-instated according to the recommendation of the Lieutenant General & the Judge Advocate General.   A. LINCOLN

Nov. 26, 1864

¹ Copy, DNA RG 130, U.S. Army Court Martial Cases, White House Office. Captain Joseph M. Locke, Fourteenth Regiment, U.S. Army, had been dismissed for failure to render account of goods furnished him by the U.S. Sanitary Commission.

To William S. Rosecrans¹

Major General Rosecrans   Executive Mansion,
St Louis   Washington, Nov. 26. 1864.

Please telegraph me briefly on what charge and evidence Mrs. Anna B. Martin has been sent to the Penitentiary at Alton.

A LINCOLN

¹ ALS, DNA WR RG 107, Presidential Telegrams, I, 249. General Rosecrans telegraphed on November 30, 1864: "Annie B. Martin on her written request & in accordance with instructions from War Dept date of April twenty fourth eighteen sixty three sent beyond the lines not to return during the war under pain of imprisonment during the war she returned without authority was tried by Military Commission & sentenced to imprisonment during the war in her examination she states she is disloyal & if released would return south" (DLC-RTL).   ² "St Louis" is not in Lincoln's handwriting.

To Henry F. Harrington and Others¹

Executive Mansion,
Gentlemen   Washington, 28 November, 1864.

I have received with gratification your letter of the 12th November, and beg that you will accept my cordial thanks for your kind and generous words.

I am very truly Your friend and Servant   A. LINCOLN

Revd. Henry F. Harrington
&c   &c

¹ LS, InFtwl. The body of the letter is in John Hay's handwriting. Harrington's letter of November 14 has not been found, and Harrington has not been further identified.

To Heads of Departments and Bureaus[1]

I shall be very glad if the Head of any Department or Bureau, can find for, and give this young lady suitable employment.

Nov. 29. 1864   A. LINCOLN

[1] AES, DLC-Hitchcock Papers. Lincoln's endorsement is written on the back of a note of the same date from General Ethan A. Hitchcock: "Gen. Hitchcock presents his respects to the President in behalf of Miss Eliot, the young lady who (accompanied by Miss Williams) presented a request this morning asking his assistance in obtaining some employment, and begs to recommend her to his kindness." Miss Eliot and Miss Williams have not been identified.

To Alvin P. Hovey[1]

Major General Hovey, or   Executive Mansion,
whoever may have charge   Washington,
at the proper time.   Nov. 29. 1864.

Whenever John B. Castleman shall be tried, if convicted and sentenced, suspend execution until further order from me, and send me the record.   A. LINCOLN.

[1] ALS-F, Louisville, Kentucky, *Post*, September 4, 1916. Captain John B. Castleman of General John H. Morgan's command was one of a group of rebels who went to Chicago during the Democratic Convention, with plans, it was charged, to release prisoners of war and to assist the Sons of Liberty in a "Northwestern Insurrection." (OR, I, XLV, I, 1077, Colonel Benjamin J. Sweet to James B. Fry, November 26, 1864). He was captured and held in close confinement as a spy at Camp Morton. After being transferred to Point Lookout and later to the Old Capitol Prison in Washington, Castleman was returned on April 28, 1865, to Hovey's command at Indianapolis, where he was to be tried (OR, II, VIII, 87, 477, 511, 519). He was released without trial, however, on condition that he leave the United States.

According to an article accompanying the facsimile published in the Louisville *Post*, Lincoln gave his order of November 29 to Judge Samuel M. Breckinridge, of St. Louis, Missouri, whose wife was Virginia Castleman, sister of John B. Castleman, with the comment, "Sam, this is for you and Virginia, entrusted in confidence, with the condition that its existence shall not be known unless the emergency arises for which this letter provides." Castleman's banishment lasted for eighteen months, and he never knew of Lincoln's order until the original was given to him by his brother-in-law fifteen years later.

To Ward H. Lamon[1]

Executive Mansion   Nov 29th [1864?]

Will Col Lamon please say, what at present prices, the feed for two horses & two ponies, would cost, per month.   A. LINCOLN

[1] LS, CSmH. No reply or further reference has been found.

To William M. Stone and Others[1]

Executive Mansion Washington,

Governor of Iowa. DesMoines[2]　　　　　　　Nov. 29. 1864

May I renew my request for the exact aggregate vote of your State cast at the late election? My object fails if I do not receive it before Congress meets.　　　　　　　　　　　A. Lincoln

Michigan	Oregon
Wisconsin	Penn.
Missouri	Kansas
Ohio	West-Virginia.

[1] ALS, DNA WR RG 107, Presidential Telegrams, I, 250. Following the name of each state listed by Lincoln, the number of the despatch and the capital city, written in by clerks in the telegraph office, have been omitted. See Lincoln's telegram to Cony and others, November 15, *supra.*

[2] "DesMoines" is not in Lincoln's handwriting.

Endorsement[1]

November 30, 1864

I think this is a meritories application, and I shall be glad if the Head of any Bureau or Department can and will give the lady suitable employment　　　　　　　　　　　A. Lincoln

Nov. 30. 1864

[1] AES, CSmH. The endorsement has been removed from the application, and the lady has not been identified.

Endorsement Concerning John W. and Joseph Tatum[1]

November 30, 1864

This paper is presented to me by Friends John W. Tatum, of Del. and Joseph Tatum of New-Jersey, who are satisfied that the statement is correct. Let the men within named, be discharged on affirming according to the oath of Dec. 8. 1863, and that they will remain North.　　　　　　　　　　　A. Lincoln

Nov. 30. 1864

[1] AES, IHi. Lincoln's endorsement is written on the back of an unsigned memorandum, written on Department of Agriculture stationery, November 29, 1864: "Three Friends confined amongst the Confederate Prisoners at 'Point-Look-out'

"Noah Nickols from Yadkin County N.C aged about 45.
"Isaac Davis　　"　Randolph　"　　"　　"　　"　50.
"Thomas E Davis "　　　"　　　"　　"　　"　　"

"These 3 Friends, were pressed into the confederate army against their will, and conscience; one of them was butted, and gagged, for not help[ing] in the confederate service;—they are willing, and desirous, to take an affirmation of

[124]

allegiance to the United States—to testify to the Truth of the above, and exhibit some documents in confirmation thereof;—they wish to go, to their friends in Grant County Indiana."

To Edwin M. Stanton[1]

[c. November 30, 1864]

Ought not there to be an examination in the case of these men.

[1] Copy, DNA WR RG 107, Secretary of War, Letters Received, P 1115, Register. A copy of Lincoln's endorsement is preserved in a register notation concerning the cases of Cyrus H. Carver and James H. Stagg, confined to Central Guard House for receiving stolen money. The original papers are missing and no further reference has been found.

To Charles A. Dana[1]

Will Mr. Dana, Asst. Sec. of War, please see and hear, Hon. S. F. Headley, of New-Jersey. A. LINCOLN

Dec. 1. 1864

[1] ALS, DLC.

To Andrew Johnson[1]

Gov. Johnson
Nashville, Tenn.

Executive Mansion, Washington,
Dec. 1, 1864.

I am applied to for the release of Alexander B. Kinney, John P. Carter, and Samuel A. Owens. Your name, commending their application to favorable consideration, is on the papers. If you will say directly that you think they ought to be discharged I will discharge them. Answer. A. LINCOLN

[1] ALS, DNA WR RG 107, Presidential Telegrams, I, 251. The telegram is marked by the telegraph clerk "sent 12.35 pm." Governor Johnson replied on December 3, 1864: "From Representation made to me by persons of reliability & loyalty I should have no hesitancy in releasing Alex B Ramsay [sic], John B [sic] Carter & Saml A Owen the Prisoners named in your dispatch" (DLC-RTL).

To Andrew Johnson[1]

His Excellency Andrew Johnson
Nashville
Tennessee

Executive Mansion,
Washington,
1 December, 1864.

In the cases of Alexander B. Kinney, John P. Carter, and Samuel A. Owens, Col. Wm B. Stokes has recommended the release of all three. His recommendation is on file here. A. LINCOLN

Send above
John Hay AAG

[125]

[1] D, DNA WR RG 107, Presidential Telegrams, I, 252. The telegram is in John Hay's autograph, "A. Lincoln" appearing to have been signed by Hay also. The telegraph clerk endorsed "sent 215." Colonel William B. Stokes commanded the Fifth Tennessee Cavalry. No further reference to these cases has been found.

Recommendation[1]

Executive Mansion. Dec. 1, 1864.

I do not personally know these ladies, but very cheerfully endorse Judge Wylie and Mayor Wallach, and shall be glad if the ladies can find employment in any Department or Bureau.

A. LINCOLN.

[1] Tracy, p. 249. Andrew Wylie was associate justice of the Supreme Court of the District of Columbia. Richard Wallach was mayor of Washington. The ladies have not been identified.

To James Speed[1]

Hon. James Speed
Louisville, Ky

Executive Mansion
Washington, Dec. 1. 1864

I appoint you to be Attorney General. Please come on at once.

A LINCOLN

[1] ALS, DNA WR RG 107, Presidential Telegrams, I, 253. James Speed replied on the same day: "Will leave tomorrow for Washington" (DLC-RTL). On November 24, 1864, Edward Bates submitted his letter of resignation as attorney general:

"For some months past, you have been aware of my desire to withdraw from the active labors & constant cares of the office which I hold by your favor.

"Heretofore, it has not been compatible with my ideas of duty to the public & fidelity to you, to leave my post of service for any private consideration, however urgent. Then, the fate of the nation hung, in doubt & gloom. Even your own fate, as identified with the nation, was a source of much anxiety. Now, on the contrary, the affairs of the Government display a brighter aspect; and to you, as head & leader of the Government, all the honor & good fortune that we hoped for, has come. And it seems to me, under these altered circumstances, that the time has come, when I may, without dereliction of duty, ask leave to retire to private life.

"In tendering the resignation of my office of Attorney General of the United States (which I now do) I gladly sieze the occasion to repeat the expression of my gratitude, not only for your good opinion which led to my appointment, but also for your uniform & unvarying courtesy & kindness during the whole time in which we have been associated in the public service. The memory of that kindness & personal favor, I shall bear with me into private life, and hope to retain it in my heart, as long as I live.

"Pray let my resignation take effect on the last day of November

"With heartfelt respect I remain your friend & servant" (ibid.).

On November 30, Judge Advocate General Joseph Holt declined to accept appointment as Bates' successor: "I have with your permission, held under consideration until this moment, the offer of the office of Attorney General of the U.States, so kindly made to me a few days since. The result is that after the most careful reflection, I have not been able to overcome the embarrassments referred to in our last interview, & which then disinclined me to accept, as they must now determine me respectfully to decline the appointment. . . . In view of all the circumstances, I am satisfied that I can serve you better in the position which I now hold at your hands. . . ." (*Ibid.*).

On December 1, Holt recommended the appointment of James Speed: "Referring to our conversation of yesterday, I beg to say that the opinion there expressed in regard to Mr S. remains unchanged. I can recall no public man in the State, of *uncompromising loyalty*, who unites in the same degree, the qualifications of professional attainments, fervent devotion to the union, & to the principles of your administration & spotless points of personal character. To these he adds—what I should deem indispensable—a warm & hearty friendship for yourself, personally & officially." (*Ibid.*).

To James Speed and Joshua F. Speed[1]

Executive Mansion,
Washington, Dec. 1. 1864.

I have stated that if either Mr. James Speed, or Joshua F. Speed, will say in writing on this sheet that he has inquired into the cases of John H. Schramm, and C. T. Smith, and that he believes they or either of them ought to be discharged, on return of the paper I will order the discharge accordingly on the taking of the oath.

A. LINCOLN

Let these two men Smith & Schramm be discharged on taking the oath of December 8. 1863.   A. LINCOLN

Dec. 10. 1864

[1] ALS, and ES, owned by Foreman M. Lebold, Chicago, Illinois. Joshua F. Speed endorsed Lincoln's note on December 5, 1864: "I have enquired into the character of the signers to the two petitions in favor of the discharge of the two men C. T. Smith & John H. Schramme—now confined at Rock Island Illinois.

"I know some of the gentlemen and all of them from enquiry to be good Union men.

"The prisoners are also men of heretofore good character—are truly penitent and would from all the information I can get—give willing obedience to the law—and whatever influence they may have in favor of the Government.

"I would not ask their release if I did not believe that they would observe their promises."

To Edwin M. Stanton[1]

Hon. Sec. of War   Executive Mansion,
Sir: Washington, Dec. 1, 1864.

Hon. George F. Miller, M.C. elect for the Harrisburg District, has a son—Daniel B. Miller—who for a long time has been acting Commissary of Subsistence, now wishes the appointment for him, with rank of Captain. He is now with the Army of the James. Let him be appointed. Yours truly   A. LINCOLN

[1] ALS F, ISLA. Daniel B. Miller was appointed captain and commissary of subsistence of Volunteers on December 12, 1864.

Tabulation and Comparison of Election Returns—1860 and 1864[1]

[Total]		Lincoln	Douglas	Breckinridge	Bell]	[Lincoln	McClellan	Total]
118.840	California	39.173	38.516.	34.334.	6.817.	44.511.	42.105	86.616
77.246	Connecticut	43.792	15.522.	14.641.	3.291.	8 162.	8 762	16.924
16.039	Delaware [sic]	3.815	1.025	7.337.	3.864			
339.693	Illinois	172.161.	160.215	2.404	4.913.	189.505.	158.730	348.235
272.143	Indiana	139.033.	115.509	12.295	5.306.	150.422.	130.223.	280.645
128.331	Iowa	70.409	55.111	1.048	1.763			143.331
146.216	Kentucky	1.364	25.651	53.143	66.058			80.000
50.510	Louisiana		7.625	22.681	20.204.			
97.918	Maine	62.811	26.693	6.368	2.046			111.000
92.502	Maryland	2.294	5.966	42.482	41.760	40.007.	32.726.	72.733.
169.175	Massachusetts	106.533	34.372	5.939	22.331	126.742.	48.745.	175.487.
154.747	Michigan	88.480	65.057	805	405			162.413.
34.799	Minnesota	22.069	11.920	748	62			42.500.
165.538	Missouri	17.028	58.821	31.317	58.372			
65.953	New-Hampshire	37.519	25.881	2.112	.441	34.486. 1.998. 36.484.	32.048. 679. 32.727	66.434 2.677 69.111
121.125	New-Jersey.	58.324	62.801					128.630.
675.156	New-York.	362.646	312.510			368.730.	361.934.	730.664.
442.441	Ohio	231.610	187.232	11.405	12.194			

[1] AD, IHi-Nicolay and Hay Papers. Prepared on the basis of the figures received from the governors of the Union states (see Lincoln to Cony, November 15, and to Stone, November 29, *supra*), these tables furnished the basis for Lincoln's comparison of the popular vote of 1860 and 1864 in his Annual Message, December 6, *infra*.

	[Total]	Lincoln	Douglas	Breckinridge	Bell]	[Lincoln	McClellan	Total]
Oregon	14.410	5.270	3.951	5.006.	183			
Pennsylvania	476.442	268.030	16.765	178.871	12.776			556.382
Rhode Island	19.931	12.224.	7.707			13.624.	8 563	22.187
Tennessee	145.333		11.350	64.709	69.274			
Vermont	42.844	33.808	6.849	218	1.969.	42.490.	13.321.	55.811
West-Virginia	46.195	1.302	5.196.	19.075.	20.622	23.437	10.437	33.874
Wisconsin [sic].	152.180	86.110	65.021	888	161			
Nevada.								16.528
Kansas	15.454					14.000.	4.000	18.000

	1860	1864
California	118.840	110.000
Connecticut.	77.246	86.616
Delaware	16.039	16.924
Illinois	339.693	348.235
Indiana	272.143	280.645
Iowa	128.331	143.331
Kentucky	146.216	90.000
Maine	97.918	111.000
Maryland	92.502	72.703
Massachusetts	169.533	175.487
Michigan	154.747	162.413
Minnesota	34.799	42.500
Missouri	165.538	90.000
New-Hampshire	65.953	69.111
New-Jersey	121.125	128.680

Tabulation and Comparison of Election Returns—1860 and 1864—*Continued*

[Total]	Lincoln	Douglas	Breckinridge	Bell]	[Lincoln	McClellan	Total]
New-York.	675.156		730.664			457.102	
Ohio	442.441		470.558				
Oregon	14.410		14.410				
Pennsylvania	476.442		571.000				
Rhode Island	19.931		22.187				
Vermont	42.844		55.811				
West-Virginia	46.195		33.874				
Wisconsin	152.180		146.000				
	3.870.222		3.958.693				
			3.870.222				
Increase—			88.471				
Add Kansas.			23.000		really 17.234		
" Nevada.			16.528		16.528		
			127.999		33.762		
			16.500		3.982.011		
					4.015.773		
Soldiers vote in Mass.			3.000		3.870.222		
" R.I.					145.551		
" N.J.			7.500				
" Del.			1.500				
" Ia.			16.500				
" Ills.			21.000				
			193.999				
Cal.			4.500				

Soldiers vote not in

[130]

To Nathaniel P. Banks[1]

Major General Banks.

Executive Mansion, Washington,
Dec. 2. 1864.

I know you are dissatisfied, which pains me very much; but I wish not to be argued with further. I entertain no abatement of confidence, or friendship for you. I have told you why I can not order Gen. Canby from the Department of the Gulf—that he whom I must hold responsible for military results, is not agreed. Yet I do believe that you, of all men, can best perform the part of advancing the new State government of Louisiana; and therefore I have wished you to go and try, leaving it to yourself to give up the trial at the end of a month, if you find it impracticable, or personally too disagreeable. This is certainly meant in no unkindness; but I wish to avoid further struggle about it. Yours truly

A LINCOLN

[1] ALS, CSmH. See Lincoln to Banks, November 26, *supra*. Banks answered Lincoln on the same day: "You are under some misapprehension as to my views of the command assigned to me at New Orleans. I am not at all dissatisfied. It is my wish on the contrary to do every thing in my power to aid you and your administration, whether or not it comports with my wishes or interests. The Secretary of War has said to me that in civil matters you had generally given directions yourself—with which, while he had known what was done—he did not interfere. My wish is to know from you what should be done by me in the execution of orders, that I have received. In accordance with your suggestion conveyed to me by Mr Nicolay I will call at the Executive Mansion at 7 o clock this evening." (DLC-RTL).

To Ethan A. Hitchcock[1]

Gen. Hitchcock

Executive Mansion, Washington,
Dec. 2. 1864.

If you can oblige Mrs. Welles, by effecting a special exchange of Lieut. or Capt. Richard Dinsmore, now in the Poor-House prison at Charleston, I will be greatly obliged   Yours truly

A. LINCOLN

[1] ALS-P, ISLA. Richard Dinsmore, captain of Company E, Thirty-fourth Pennsylvania Volunteers, may have been a relative or friend of Mrs. Gideon Welles (Mary Jane Hale) who was originally from Lewistown, Pennsylvania, the vicinity in which Dinsmore's regiment was recruited.

Order Concerning the Steamer *Funayma Solace*[1]

Executive Mansion,
Washington, 3d December, 1864.

A war steamer called the 'Funayma Solace,' having been built in this country for the Japanese government and at the instance of that government, it is deemed to comport with the public interest, in view of the unsettled condition of the relations of the United States with that Empire, that the steamer should not be allowed to proceed to Japan. If, however, the Secretary of the Navy should ascertain that the steamer is adapted to our service, he is authorized to purchase her, but the purchase money will be held in trust towards satisfying any valid claims which may be presented by the Japanese on account of the construction of the steamer and the failure to deliver the same as above set forth.

ABRAHAM LINCOLN

[1] DS, DNA FS RG 59, General Records of the Department of State, Notes from the Japanese Legation, Volume I. See Lincoln's similar order of October 12, 1864. Gideon Welles' *Diary* under dates November 30 and December 3, 1864, gives an account of the conferences leading up to Lincoln's issuance of this order of December 3. Under date of December 5 Welles wrote: "Mr. Seward sent for my perusal a draught of an executive order forbidding the Japanese vessel from leaving, and authorizing the Navy Department to purchase. I dislike this thing in every aspect. . . . Some weeks since application was made for a survey and appraisal of this vessel. This was ordered . . . and without any connection with the government or the Japanese. The Board valued her at $392,000, and at this price we, under direction of the President at the solicitation of Seward, agreed to take her. These late government movements make it embarrassing. I declined to give any opinion or make any suggestion in regard to the executive order, but said orally to the clerk that our offer was still considered as good. . . . Two hundred thousand dollars in gold would purchase this vessel. It is easy to perceive that Mr. [Thurlow] Weed and Mr. [Robert H.] Pruyn will realize a clever sum for their labors. They have had for one or two years the use of $800,000 in gold. This vessel has not cost them over $200,000 in gold. The government takes it at $392,000 and must pay that sum in gold to Japan. Who pockets the $192,000? It cannot be otherwise than that this subject will be inquired into. It ought to be."

Order for Discharge[1]

I suppose there is some charge against this man; but if there is none, let him be discharged.   A. LINCOLN

Dec. 4, 1864

[1] Stan. V. Henkels Catalog 1470, November 22, 1932, No. 47. According to the catalog description this item is an autograph note signed.

Endorsement[1]

I perceive the within is about business, and not about pictures.

Dec. 5. 1864   A. LINCOLN

[1] AES, DNA FS RG 59, Appointments, Box 223. Lincoln's endorsement is written on a letter from James McBride, consul at Honolulu, September 22, 1864, recommending John L. Barnard as consular student at Honolulu.

To Joseph Holt[1]

Let execution be suspended until the record can be examined.
Dec. 5. 1864   A. LINCOLN

[1] ES, DNA WR RG 153, Judge Advocate General, NN 3012. Lincoln's endorsement appears on the court-martial record of Private William Stevenson, Co. K, Second Pennsylvania Heavy Artillery, sentenced to be shot for attempting to shoot his captain. The roster of Battery K shows Stevenson to have been discharged with the battery on January 29, 1866.

To Andrew Johnson[1]

December 5, 1864

If Gov. Johnson will say in writing on this sheet that in his opinion this man should be discharged, I will discharge him.
Dec. 5. 1864.   A. LINCOLN

Let this man take the oath of Dec. 8. 1863 & be discharged as recommended by Gov. Johnson.   A. LINCOLN
Dec. 22. 1864

[1] AES, owned by James W. Smith, New York City. Lincoln's endorsements are written on the back of a fragment of a petition for the discharge of a Tennesseean who was held a prisoner of war. The man is not identified, and Johnson's reply is not given.

To the Senate[1]

To the Senate of the United States: December 5, 1864

By virtue of the authority contained in the 6th section of the act of 21 April, 1864, which enacts "that any officer in the Naval service, by and with the advice and consent of the Senate, may be advanced not exceeding thirty numbers in his own grade, for distinguished conduct in battle or extraordinary heroism,"

I recommend that Commander Wm. H. Macomb, U.S. Navy, for advancement in his grade ten numbers, to take rank next after Commander Wm. Ronckendorff, for distinguished conduct in the capture of the town of Plymouth, N.C., with its batteries, ordnance stores, &c., on the 31 October, 1864, by a portion of the naval division under his command. The affair was executed in a most creditable manner.   ABRAHAM LINCOLN.

Washington City, 5 December, 1864.

[1] *Executive Journal*, XIV, 9. Macomb's advancement was confirmed by the Senate on December 21, 1864.

To the Senate[1]

To the Senate of the United States: December 5, 1864

By virtue of the authority contained in the 6th section of the act of 21 April, 1864, which enacts "That any officer in the naval service, by and with the advice and consent of the Senate, may be advanced not exceeding thirty numbers in his own grade, for distinguished conduct in battle or extraordinary heroism," I recommend that Lieutenant Commander James S. Thornton, U.S. Navy, the executive officer of the U.S. steamer Kearsarge, for advancement in his grade ten numbers, to take rank next after Lieutenant Commander Wm. D. Whiting, for his good conduct and faithful discharge of his duties in the brilliant action with the rebel steamer Alabama which led to the destruction of that vessel on the 19 June, 1864.   ABRAHAM LINCOLN.

Washington City,
5 December, 1864.

[1] *Executive Journal*, XIV, 3. Thornton's advancement was confirmed by the Senate on December 21, 1864.

To the Senate and House of Representatives[1]

To the Senate and   December 5, 1864
House of Representatives.

In conformity to the Law of 11 July 1862, I most cordially recommend that Lieutenant Wm. B. Cushing, U.S. Navy, receive a vote of Thanks from Congress, for his important, gallant and perilous achievement in destroying the Rebel iron-clad Steamer "Albemarle," on the night of the 27 October 1864, at Plymouth, N.C. The destruction of so formidable a vessel, which had resisted the continued attacks of a number of our vessels on former occasions, is an important event touching our future Naval and Military operations and would reflect honor on any Officer and redounds to the credit of this young officer and the few brave comrades who assisted in this successful and daring undertaking.

This recommendation is specially made in order to comply with the requirements of the 9th. Section of the aforesaid Act, which is in the following words, viz:—

"That any line officer of the Navy or Marine Corps may be advanced one grade, if upon recommendation of the President by name, he receives the thanks of Congress for highly distinguished conduct in conflict with the enemy, or, for extraordinary heroism in the line of his profession."   ABRAHAM LINCOLN

Washington City,
5 December 1864.

[1] DS, DNA RG 46, Senate 38A F2; DS, DNA RG 233, House Executive Document No. 7. A resolution of thanks was approved on December 20, 1864. Cushing was nominated lieutenant commander on January 9 and the nomination was approved by the Senate on February 6, 1865.

To the Senate and House of Representatives[1]

To the Senate and   December 5, 1864
House of Representatives:—

In conformity to the Law of 16 July 1862, I most cordially recommend that Captain John A. Winslow, U.S. Navy, receive a vote of Thanks from Congress, for the skill and gallantry exhibited by him in the brilliant action, whilst in command of the U.S. Steamer Kearsarge, which led to the total destruction of the Piratical craft "Alabama," on the 19 June 1864,—a vessel superior in tonnage, superior in number of guns, and superior in number of crew.

This recommendation is specially made in order to comply with the requirements of the 9th. Section of the aforesaid Act, which is in the following words, viz:—

"That any line officer of the Navy or Marine Corps may bo ad vanced one grade, if upon recommendation by the President by name, he receives the thanks of Congress for highly distinguished conduct in conflict with the enemy, or for extraordinary heroism in the line of his profession."   ABRAHAM LINCOLN

Washington City,
5 December 1864.

[1] DS, DNA RG 46, Senate 38A F2; DS, DNA RG 233, House Executive Document No. 6. A resolution of thanks was approved on December 20, 1864. Winslow was nominated commodore on January 9, and his promotion was approved by the Senate on February 6, 1865.

To George H. Thomas[1]

Major General Thomas
Nashville, Tennessee.

Executive Mansion,
Washington,
December 5th. 1864.

Let execution in the case of Oliver B. Wheeler, Sergeant in the 6th Regiment Missouri Vol's, under sentence of death for desertion at Chattanooga, on the 15th. inst, be suspended until further order, and forward record for examination.   A. LINCOLN

Major Eckert
Please forward the above   JNO. G. NICOLAY

[1] D, DNA WR RG 107, Presidential Telegrams, I, 254. The telegram is in Edward D. Neill's handwriting. Lincoln's signature as well as Nicolay's is in Nicolay's handwriting. Brigadier General Henry B. Carrington wrote Lincoln from Indianapolis, Indiana, on November 30, 1864:

"Oliver B. Wheeler, who entered the service at the age of seventeen, is under sentence of death for desertion, after twelve months of service.

"His friends who are honorable persons, and of character, believe there are circumstances . . . softening his offence, and appealing to just clemency. They hope to obtain a suspension of the sentence, beyond Dec. 15 prox. day fixed for the execution, that they may do what they can in way of proof of tenuating circumstances. . . ." (DLC-RTL).

On December 1 Oliver P. Morton wrote, introducing George Lawe of Indianapolis and George A. Wheeler of Chicago, in quest of clemency for Oliver B. Wheeler, and enclosed an undated petition signed by "Thomas à Becket" and fifty-one members of the theatrical profession asking clemency for Oliver B. Wheeler "a member of the Theatrical profession . . . . naturally a good natured, unreflecting, foolish boy. . . ." (Ibid.).

On December 8 General Thomas replied to Lincoln's telegram: "There is no record at these Hd Qrs of Oliver B Wheeler Sergt 6th Missouri Vols under sentence of death." (Ibid.).

The Sixth Missouri Volunteers were not in General Thomas' Department, but were in the Fifteenth Army Corps commanded by Major General Peter J. Osterhaus in the Department of the Tennessee under Major General Oliver O. Howard. No further reference to the case has been found.

Annual Message to Congress[1]

Fellow-citizens of the Senate   December 6, 1864
and House of Representatives:

Again the blessings of health and abundant harvests claim our profoundest gratitude to Almighty God.

The condition of our foreign affairs is reasonably satisfactory.[2]

[1] DS, DNA RG 46, Senate 38A F1; DS, The Rosenbach Company, Philadelphia and New York. The two almost identical manuscripts of this message were copied by three different clerks, the respective portions appearing in the same handwriting in each copy. The figures on the vote in the November election (see note 39 infra) appear to have been inserted in both copies by Lincoln himself. Several fragments of Lincoln's original autograph draft have been preserved as indicated below in the notes to the respective passages. Endorsements by John D. Defrees on some of these fragments indicate that Defrees cut up the autograph draft and distributed the fragments among his friends. Other fragments may exist, but if so, they have escaped the editors.

[2] The Report of the Secretary of State, upon which Lincoln's summary is based, may be found in Thirty-eighth Congress, Second Session, House Executive Document No. 1, Volumes I-IV.

Mexico continues to be a theatre of civil war. While our political relations with that country have undergone no change, we have, at the same time, strictly maintained neutrality between the belligerents.[3]

At the request of the states of Costa Rica and Nicaragua, a competent engineer has been authorized to make a survey of the river San Juan and the port of San Juan. It is a source of much satisfaction that the difficulties which for a moment excited some political apprehensions, and caused a closing of the inter-oceanic transit route, have been amicably adjusted, and that there is a good prospect that the route will soon be reopened with an increase of capacity and adaptation.[4] We could not exaggerate either the commercial or the political importance of that great improvement.

It would be doing injustice to an important South American state not to acknowledge the directness, frankness, and cordiality with which the United States of Colombia have entered into intimate relations with this government. A claims convention has been constituted to complete the unfinished work of the one which closed its session in 1861.[5]

The new liberal constitution of Venezuela having gone into effect with the universal acquiescence of the people, the government under it has been recognized, and diplomatic intercourse with it has opened in a cordial and friendly spirit. The long-deferred Aves Island claim has been satisfactorily paid and discharged.[6]

Mutual payments have been made of the claims awarded by the late joint commission for the settlement of claims between the United States and Peru.[7] An earnest and cordial friendship continues to exist between the two countries, and such efforts as were

[3] Crowned in June, 1864, Emperor Maximilian was captured and executed in June, 1867, by the Mexican forces of President Benito P. Juarez.

[4] The revolt of 1863 led by Maximo Jerez against the government of Tomas Martinez had been suppressed in 1864.

[5] The convention signed on February 10, 1864, and ratified on July 9, 1864, provided for completion of the work of the convention signed on September 10, 1857, and ratified in November, 1860, to adjust claims arising out of a riot in Panama during April, 1856. Five claims had been denied by the United States of Colombia, which government had succeeded the United States of New Granada in 1863.

[6] In September, 1864, the reorganized United States of Venezuela under Juan José Falcon completed payment of a claim of $130,000, in favor of Lemvis W. Tappan, Philo S. Shelton and George R. Sampson, shipowners and merchants of Boston, who had been forced to abandon their Aves Island (West Indies) development of guano deposits.

[7] The convention meeting at Lima, Peru, from July 17 to November 27, 1863, awarded $57,196.23 to the United States, and $25,300 to Peru.

in my power have been used to remove misunderstanding and avert a threatened war between Peru and Spain.[8]

Our relations are of the most friendly nature with Chile, the Argentine Republic, Bolivia, Costa Rica, Paraguay, San Salvador, and Hayti.

During the past year no differences of any kind have arisen with any of those republics, and, on the other hand, their sympathies with the United States are constantly expressed with cordiality and earnestness.

The claim arising from the seizure of the cargo of the brig Macedonian in 1821 has been paid in full by the government of Chile.[9]

Civil war continues in the Spanish part of San Domingo, apparently without prospect of an early close.

Official correspondence has been freely opened with Liberia, and it gives us a pleasing view of social and political progress in that Republic. It may be expected to derive new vigor from American influence, improved by the rapid disappearance of slavery in the United States.

I solicit your authority to furnish to the republic a gunboat at moderate cost, to be reimbursed to the United States by instalments.[10] Such a vessel is needed for the safety of that state against the native African races; and in Liberian hands it would be more effective in arresting the African slave trade than a squadron in our own hands. The possession of the least organized naval force would stimulate a generous ambition in the republic, and the confidence which we should manifest by furnishing it would win forbearance and favor towards the colony from all civilized nations.

The proposed overland telegraph between America and Europe,[11] by the way of Behring's Straits and Asiatic Russia, which was sanctioned by Congress at the last session, has been undertaken, under very favorable circumstances, by an association of American citizens, with the cordial good-will and support as well of this government as of those of Great Britain and Russia. Assur-

[8] The difficulties growing out of a Peruvian attack in 1863 on the Spanish settlement of Talambo and the subsequent seizure by Spain of the Chincha Islands was settled by treaty in January, 1865. The U.S. minister to Spain, Gustave Koerner, had promoted the arbitration. The peace was broken, however, by Peru's declaration of war on Spain in January, 1866.

[9] See Lincoln's letter to King Leopold of Belgium, June 13, 1863, *supra*. Payment of the award was made in April, 1864.

[10] A bill (S. 356) authorizing the president to transfer a gunboat to the government of Liberia was introduced in the Senate by Charles Sumner on December 13, 1864. The bill passed the Senate but died in the House. A similar act was finally passed and approved on April 17, 1866.

[11] See Lincoln's Annual Message of December 8, 1863.

ances have been received from most of the South American States of their high appreciation of the enterprise, and their readiness to co-operate in constructing lines tributary to that world-encircling communication. I learn, with much satisfaction, that the noble design of a telegraphic communication between the eastern coast of America and Great Britain has been renewed with full expectation of its early accomplishment.

Thus it is hoped that with the return of domestic peace the country will be able to resume with energy and advantage its former high career of commerce and civilization.

Our very popular and estimable representative in Egypt died in April last.[12] An unpleasant altercation which arose between the temporary incumbent of the office and the government of the Pacha resulted in a suspension of intercourse. The evil was promptly corrected on the arrival of the successor in the consulate, and our relations with Egypt, as well as our relations with the Barbary powers, are entirely satisfactory.

The rebellion which has so long been flagrant in China, has at last been suppressed, with the co-operating good offices of this government, and of the other western commercial states.[13] The judicial consular establishment there has become very difficult and onerous, and it will need legislative revision to adapt it to the extension of our commerce, and to the more intimate intercourse which has been instituted with the government and people of that vast empire. China seems to be accepting with hearty good-will the conventional laws which regulate commercial and social intercourse among the western nations.

Owing to the peculiar situation of Japan, and the anomalous form of its government, the action of that empire in performing treaty stipulations is inconstant and capricious.[14] Nevertheless, good progress has been effected by the western powers, moving with enlightened concert. Our own pecuniary claims have been allowed, or put in course of settlement, and the inland sea has been reopened to commerce. There is reason also to believe that these proceedings have increased rather than diminished the friendship of Japan towards the United States.

[12] Following the death of William S. Thayer, Charles Hale of Massachusetts was appointed consul and presented his credentials in October, 1864. During the intervening time an acting vice-consul named (Francis?) Dainese, who had been acting since the death of Vice-consul Charles Marsh in January, 1864, had become *persona non grata* to the Egyptian government (Hale to Seward, October 22, 1864, *House Executive Document No. 1*, IV, 406 ff.).

[13] The Taiping rebellion ended with the fall of Nanking, the rebel capital, in the summer of 1864 (Anson Burlingame to Seward, August 15, 1864, *ibid.*, III, 438).　　[14] See notes to Lincoln's orders of October 12 and December 3, *supra*.

The ports of Norfolk, Fernandina, and Pensacola have been opened by proclamation.[15] It is hoped that foreign merchants will now consider whether it is not safer and more profitable to themselves, as well as just to the United States, to resort to these and other open ports, than it is to pursue, through many hazards, and at vast cost, a contraband trade with other ports which are closed, if not by actual military occupation, at least by a lawful and effective blockade.

For myself, I have no doubt of the power and duty of the Executive, under the law of nations, to exclude enemies of the human race from an asylum in the United States. If Congress should think that proceedings in such cases lack the authority of law, or ought to be further regulated by it, I recommend that provision be made for effectually preventing foreign slave traders from acquiring domicile and facilities for their criminal occupation in our country.

It is possible that, if it were a new and open question, the maritime powers, with the lights they now enjoy, would not concede the privileges of a naval belligerent to the insurgents of the United States, destitute, as they are, and always have been, equally of ships-of-war and of ports and harbors. Disloyal emissaries have been neither less assiduous nor more successful during the last year than they were before that time in their efforts, under favor of that privilege, to embroil our country in foreign wars. The desire and determination of the governments of the maritime states to defeat that design are believed to be as sincere as, and cannot be more earnest than our own. Nevertheless, unforeseen political difficulties have arisen, especially in Brazilian and British ports,[16] and on the northern boundary of the United States, which have required, and are likely to continue to require, the practice of constant vigilance, and a just and conciliatory spirit on the part of the United States as well as of the nations concerned and their governments.

Commissioners have been appointed under the treaty with Great Britain on the adjustment of the claims of the Hudson's Bay and Puget's Sound Agricultural Companies, in Oregon, and are now proceeding to the execution of the trust assigned to them.[17]

[15] See proclamation of November 19, *supra.*

[16] In October, 1864, the U.S.S. *Wachusett* had rammed and captured the Confederate *Florida* in port at Bahia, Brazil. British complaints concerned a violation of neutrality by the U.S. gunboat *Tioga*, reported to have anchored without permission at Bimini Roadstead, in the Bahamas (Charles F. Adams to Seward, June 16, 1864, *House Executive Document No. 1*, II, 120).

[17] See Lincoln's communication to the Senate and House of Representatives, March 14, *supra.* The U.S. settled the claims of the British companies by two payments of $325,000 on September 26, 1870, and September 15, 1871.

In view of the insecurity of life and property in the region adjacent to the Canadian border,[18] by reason of recent assaults and depredations committed by inimical and desperate persons, who are harbored there, it has been thought proper to give notice that after the expiration of six months, the period conditionally stipulated in the existing arrangement with Great Britain, the United States must hold themselves at liberty to increase their naval armament upon the lakes, if they shall find that proceeding necessary. The condition of the border will necessarily come into consideration in connection with the question of continuing or modifying the rights of transit from Canada through the United States, as well as the regulation of imposts, which were temporarily established by the reciprocity treaty of the 5th of June, 1854.

I desire, however, to be understood, while making this statement, that the Colonial authorities of Canada are not deemed to be intentionally unjust or unfriendly towards the United States; but, on the contrary, there is every reason to expect that, with the approval of the imperial government, they will take the necessary measures to prevent new incursions across the border.

The act passed at the last session for the encouragement of emigration has, so far as was possible, been put into operation. It seems to need amendment which will enable the officers of the government to prevent the practice of frauds against the immigrants while on their way and on their arrival in the ports, so as to secure them here a free choice of avocations and places of settlement.[19] A liberal disposition towards this great national policy is manifested by most of the European States, and ought to be reciprocated on our part by giving the immigrants effective national protection. I regard our emigrants as one of the principal replenishing streams which are appointed by Providence to repair the ravages of internal war, and its wastes of national strength and health. All that is necessary is to secure the flow of that stream in its present fullness, and to that end the government must, in every way, make it manifest that it neither needs nor designs to impose involuntary military service upon those who come from other lands to cast their lot in our country.

18 On October 19, 1864, a band of Confederate raiders led by Lieutenant Bennett H. Young had crossed the Canadian border and robbed a bank in St. Albans, Vermont. One U.S. citizen was killed and several were wounded in the raid.
19 On February 7, 1865, Representative Elihu B. Washburne introduced a bill to amend the act to encourage immigration approved July 4, 1864, and the act to regulate carriage of passengers in steamships approved March 3, 1855. Although the bill passed the House on February 24, 1865, it died in the Senate.

The financial affairs of the government have been successfully administered during the last year.[20] The legislation of the last session of Congress has beneficially affected the revenues, although sufficient time has not yet elapsed to experience the full effect of several of the provisions of the acts of Congress imposing increased taxation.

The receipts during the year, from all sources, upon the basis of warrants signed by the Secretary of the Treasury, including loans and the balance in the treasury on the first day of July, 1863, were $1,394,796,007 62; and the aggregate disbursements, upon the same basis, were $1,298,056,101 89, leaving a balance in the treasury, as shown by warrants, of $96,739,905 73.

Deduct from these amounts the amount of the principal of the public debt redeemed, and the amount of issues in substitution therefor, and the actual cash operations of the treasury were: receipts, $884,076,646 57; disbursements $865,234,087 86; which leaves a cash balance in the treasury of $18,842,558 71.

Of the receipts, there were derived from customs, $102,316,-152 99; from lands, $588,333 29; from direct taxes, $475,648 96; from internal revenue, $109,741,134 10; from miscellaneous sources, $47,511,448 10; and from loans applied to actual expenditures, including former balance, $623,443,929 13.

There were disbursed, for the civil service, $27,505,599 46; for pensions and Indians, $7,517,930 97; for the War Department $690,791,842 97; for the Navy Department $85,733,292 77; for interest of the public debt $53,685,421 69;—making an aggregate of $865,234,087.86, and leaving a balance in the treasury of $18,842,-558.71, as before stated.

For the actual receipts and disbursements for the first quarter, and the estimated receipts and disbursements for the three remaining quarters of the current fiscal year, and the general operations of the treasury in detail, I refer you to the report of the Secretary of the Treasury. I concur with him in the opinion that the proportion of moneys required to meet the expenses consequent upon the war derived from taxation should be still further increased; and I earnestly invite your attention to this subject, to the end that there may be such additional legislation as shall be required to meet the just expectations of the Secretary.

The public debt on the first day of July last, as appears by the books of the treasury, amounted to $1,740,690 489 49. Probably, should the war continue for another year, that amount may be in-

[20] The Report of the Secretary of the Treasury may be found in Thirty-eighth Congress, Second Session, *House Executive Document No. 3.*

[142]

creased by not far from five hundred millions. Held as it is, for the most part, by our own people, it has become a substantial branch of national, though private, property. For obvious reasons, the more nearly this property can be distributed among all the people the better. To favor such general distribution, greater inducements to become owners might, perhaps, with good effect, and without injury, be presented to persons of limited means. With this view, I suggest whether it might not be both competent and expedient for Congress to provide that a limited amount of some future issue of public securities might be held by any bona fide purchaser exempt from taxation, and from seizure for debt, under such restrictions and limitations as might be necessary to guard against abuse of so important a privilege. This would enable every prudent person to set aside a small annuity against a possible day of want.

Privileges like these would render the possession of such securities, to the amount limited, most desirable to every person of small means who might be able to save enough for the purpose. The great advantage of citizens being creditors as well as debtors, with relation to the public debt, is obvious. Men readily perceive that they cannot be much oppressed by a debt which they owe to themselves.

The public debt on the first day of July last, although somewhat exceeding the estimate of the Secretary of the Treasury made to Congress at the commencement of the last session, falls short of the estimate of that officer made in the preceding December, as to its probable amount at the beginning of this year, by the sum of $3,995,097 31. This fact exhibits a satisfactory condition and conduct of the operations of the Treasury.

The national banking system is proving to be acceptable to capitalists and to the people. On the twenty-fifth day of November five hundred and eighty-four national banks had been organized, a considerable number of which were conversions from State banks. Changes from State systems to the national system are rapidly taking place, and it is hoped that, very soon, there will be in the United States, no banks of issue not authorized by Congress, and no bank-note circulation not secured by the government. That the government and the people will derive great benefit from this change in the banking systems of the country can hardly be questioned. The national system will create a reliable and permanent influence in support of the national credit, and protect the people against losses in the use of paper money. Whether or not any further legislation is advisable for the suppression of State bank issues, it will be for Congress to determine. It seems quite clear that the treasury cannot be satisfactorily conducted unless the government can exercise a restraining power over the bank-note circulation of the country.

The report of the Secretary of War[21] and the accompanying documents will detail the campaigns of the armies in the field since the date of the last annual message, and also the operations of the several administrative bureaus of the War Department during the last year. It will also specify the measures deemed essential for the national defence, and to keep up and supply the requisite military force.

The report of the Secretary of the Navy presents a comprehensive and satisfactory exhibit of the affairs of that Department and of the naval service.[22] It is a subject of congratulation and laudable pride to our countrymen that a navy of such vast proportions has been organized in so brief a period, and conducted with so much efficiency and success.

The general exhibit of the navy, including vessels under construction on the 1st. of December, 1864, shows a total of 671 vessels, carrying 4,610 guns, and of 510,396 tons, being an actual increase during the year, over and above all losses by shipwreck or in battle, of 83 vessels, 167 guns, and 42,427 tons.

The total number of men at this time in the naval service, including officers, is about 51,000.

There have been captured by the navy during the year 324 vessels, and the whole number of naval captures since hostilities commenced is 1,379, of which 267 are steamers.

The gross proceeds arising from the sale of condemned prize property, thus far reported, amount to $14,396,250 51. A large amount of such proceeds is still under adjudication and yet to be reported.

The total expenditures of the Navy Department of every description, including the cost of the immense squadrons that have been called into existence from the 4th of March, 1861, to the 1st. of November, 1864, are $238,647,262 35.

Your favorable consideration is invited to the various recommendations of the Secretary of the Navy, especially in regard to a navy yard and suitable establishment for the construction and repair of iron vessels, and the machinery and armature for our ships, to which reference was made in my last annual message.[23]

[21] The Report of the Secretary of War may be found in Thirty-eighth Congress, Second Session, *House Executive Document No. 83*.

[22] The Report of the Secretary of the Navy may be found in Thirty-eighth Congress, Second Session, *House Executive Document No. 1*, Volume VI.

[23] Secretary Welles recommended that a navy yard be built on League Island near Philadelphia. Several bills were introduced in the House authorizing establishment of yards at other places, but none passed.

Your attention is also invited to the views expressed in the report in relation to the legislation of Congress at its last session in respect to prize on our inland waters.

I cordially concur in the recommendation of the Secretary as to the propriety of creating the new rank of vice-admiral in our naval service.[24]

Your attention is invited to the report of the Postmaster General for a detailed account of the operations and financial condition of the Post Office Department.[25]

The postal revenues for the year ending June 30, 1864, amounted to $12,438,253.78 and the expenditures to $12,644,786.20; the excess of expenditures over receipts being $206,652.42 [$206,532.42].

The views presented by the Postmaster General on the subject of special grants by the government in aid of the establishment of new lines of ocean mail steamships and the policy he recommends for the development of increased commercial intercourse with adjacent and neighboring countries, should receive the careful consideration of Congress.[26]

It is of noteworthy interest that the steady expansion of population, improvement and governmental institutions over the new and unoccupied portions of our country have scarcely been checked, much less impeded or destroyed, by our great civil war, which at first glance would seem to have absorbed almost the entire energies of the nation.

The organization and admission of the State of Nevada has been completed in conformity with law,[27] and thus our excellent system is firmly established in the mountains, which once seemed a barren and uninhabitable waste between the Atlantic States and those which have grown up on the coast of the Pacific ocean.

The territories of the Union are generally in a condition of prosperity and rapid growth.[28] Idaho and Montana, by reason of their great distance and the interruption of communication with them by Indian hostilities, have been only partially organized; but it is understood that these difficulties are about to disappear, which will permit their governments, like those of the others, to go into speedy and full operation.

[24] An act to establish the grade of vice-admiral was approved on December 21, 1864.

[25] The Report of the Postmaster General may be found in *House Executive Document No. 1*, Volume V.

[26] An act to authorize establishment of ocean mail service between the United States and China was approved on February 17, 1865.

[27] See Lincoln's proclamation of October 31, *supra*.

[28] The Report of the Secretary of the Interior may be found in Thirty-eighth Congress, Second Session, *House Executive Document No. 1*, Volume V.

As intimately connected with, and promotive of, this material growth of the nation, I ask the attention of Congress to the valuable information and important recommendations relating to the public lands, Indian affairs, the Pacific railroad, and mineral discoveries contained in the report of the Secretary of the Interior, which is herewith transmitted, and which report also embraces the subjects of patents, pensions and other topics of public interest pertaining to his department.

The quantity of public land disposed of during the five quarters ending on the 30th of September last was 4,221,342 acres, of which 1,538,614 acres were entered under the homestead law. The remainder was located with military land warrants, agricultural scrip certified to States for railroads, and sold for cash. The cash received from sales and location fees was $1,019,446.

The income from sales during the fiscal year, ending June 30, 1864, was $678,007,21, against $136,077,95 received during the preceding year. The aggregate number of acres surveyed during the year has been equal to the quantity disposed of; and there is open to settlement about 133,000,000 acres of surveyed land.

The great enterprise of connecting the Atlantic with the Pacific States by railways and telegraph lines has been entered upon with a vigor that gives assurance of success, notwithstanding the embarrassments arising from the prevailing high prices of materials and labor. The route of the main line of the road has been definitely located for one hundred miles westward from the initial point at Omaha City, Nebraska, and a preliminary location of the Pacific railroad of California has been made from Sacramento eastward to the great bend of the Truckee river in Nevada.

Numerous discoveries of gold, silver and cinnabar mines have been added to the many heretofore known and the country occupied by the Sierra Nevada and Rocky mountains, and the subordinate ranges, now teems with enterprising labor, which is richly remunerative. It is believed that the product of the mines of precious metals in that region has, during the year, reached, if not exceeded, one hundred millions in value.

It was recommended in my last annual message that our Indian system be remodelled. Congress, at its last session, acting upon the recommendation, did provide for reorganizing the system in California,[29] and it is believed that under the present organization the management of the Indians there will be attended with reasonable

29 The act was approved on April 8, 1864. An amendment to the act was approved on March 3, 1865, but no legislation for improving the Indian system generally was passed.

success. Much yet remains to be done to provide for the proper government of the Indians in other parts of the country to render it secure for the advancing settler, and to provide for the welfare of the Indian. The Secretary reiterates his recommendations, and to them the attention of Congress is invited.

The liberal provisions made by Congress for paying pensions to invalid soldiers and sailors of the republic, and to the widows, orphans, and dependent mothers of those who have fallen in battle, or died of disease contracted, or of wounds received in the service of their country, have been diligently administered. There have been added to the pension, rolls, during the year ending the 30th day of June last, the names of 16,770 invalid soldiers, and of 271 disabled seamen, making the present number of army invalid pensioners 22,767, and of navy invalid pensioners 712.

Of widows, orphans and mothers, 22 198 have been placed on the army pension rolls, and 248 on the navy rolls. The present number of army pensioners of this class is 25,433, and of navy pensioners 793. At the beginning of the year the number of revolutionary pensioners was 1,430; only twelve of them were soldiers, of whom seven have since died. The remainder are those who, under the law, receive pensions because of relationship to revolutionary soldiers. During the year ending the 30th of June, 1864, $4,504,616,92 have been paid to pensioners of all classes.

I cheerfully commend to your continued patronage the benevolent institutions of the District of Columbia which have hitherto been established or fostered by Congress, and respectfully refer, for information concerning them, and in relation to the Washington aqueduct, the Capitol and other matters of local interest, to the report of the Secretary.

The Agricultural Department,[30] under the supervision of its present energetic and faithful head, is rapidly commending itself to the great and vital interest it was created to advance. It is pe-

[30] The Report of the Secretary of Agriculture may be found in Thirty-eighth Congress, Second Session, *House Executive Document No. 68.* Lincoln's brief paragraph on the Department of Agriculture is a revision of the shortest of three tentative drafts prepared by the department:

"The Agricultural Department under the management of its present experienced and efficient head, is giving daily proofs of valuable benefits that enure to the agriculture of the country by the judicious application of the means appropriated by government. It is encouraging a more vigorous prosecution of industry, by its taking hold of the information that is imparted, and is opening new fields of enterprise, and new channels of wealth.

"So fully am I convinced of the capabilities and advantages of the agricultural Department to the objects of its institution, and to the benefits it is dispensing, that I respectfully commend it to your favorable consideration, and liberal encouragement." (DLC-RTL, 39059).

culiarly the people's department, in which they feel more directly concerned than in any other. I commend it to the continued attention and fostering care of Congress.

The[31] war continues. Since the last annual message all the important lines and positions then occupied by our forces have been maintained, and our arms have steadily advanced;[32] thus liberating the regions left in rear, so that Missouri, Kentucky, Tennessee and parts of other States have again produced reasonably fair crops.

The[33] most remarkable feature in the military operations of the year is General Sherman's attempted march of three hundred miles directly through the insurgent region. It tends to show a great increase of our relative strength that our General-in-Chief should feel able to confront and hold in check every active force of the enemy, and yet to detach a well-appointed large army to move on such an expedition.[34] The result not yet being known, conjecture in regard to it is not here indulged.

Important movements have also occurred during the year to the effect of moulding society for durability in the Union. Although short of complete success, it is much in the right direction, that twelve thousand citizens in each of the States of Arkansas and Louisiana have organized loyal State governments with free constitutions, and are earnestly struggling to maintain and administer them. The movements in the same direction, more extensive, though less definite in Missouri, Kentucky and Tennessee, should not be overlooked. But Maryland presents[35] the example of complete success. Maryland is secure to Liberty and Union for all the future. The genius of rebellion will no more claim Maryland. Like

[31] A fragment of Lincoln's autograph draft of this message comprising this paragraph and owned by Mrs. George E. Mack of New York City, bears the following endorsements:

"Washington, June 1 1866
"This is a portion of Mr. Lincoln's last annual message in his own hand writing.
"Jno. D. Defrees
"Govt Pub Printer
"This is to be given to Morris W Defrees.   J.D.D."

[32] The autograph fragment reads "steadily incroached upon the insurgent borders; thus liberating. . . ."

[33] The autograph fragment comprising this paragraph is in the Oliver R. Barrett Collection.

[34] The autograph fragment contains a sentence which Lincoln deleted: "We must conclude that he feels our cause could, if need be, survive the loss of the whole detached force; while, by the risk, he takes a chance for the great advantages which would follow success."

[35] The autograph fragment beginning with "presents" and continuing to the end of the paragraph is owned by Justin G. Turner of Los Angeles, California. The fragment bears on the verso a certification by John D. Defrees dated June 1, 1866.

another foul[36] spirit, being driven out, it may seek to tear her, but it will woo her no more.

At[37] the last session of Congress a proposed amendment of the Constitution abolishing slavery throughout the United States, passed the Senate, but failed for lack of the requisite two-thirds vote in the House of Representatives. Although the present is the same Congress, and nearly the same members, and without questioning the wisdom or patriotism of those who stood in opposition, I venture to recommend the reconsideration and passage of the measure at the present session. Of course the abstract question is not changed; but an intervening election shows, almost certainly, that the next Congress will pass the measure if this does not. Hence there is only a question of *time* as to when the proposed amendment will go to the States for their action. And as it is to so go, at all events, may we not agree that the sooner the better? It is not claimed that the election has imposed a duty on members to change their views or their votes, any further than, as an additional element to be considered, their judgment may be affected by it. It is the voice of the people now, for the first time, heard upon the question. In a great national crisis, like ours, unanimity of action among those seeking a common end is very desirable—almost indispensable. And yet no approach to such unanimity is attainable, unless some deference shall be paid to the will of the majority, simply because it is the will of the majority. In this case the common end is the maintenance of the Union; and, among the means to secure that end, such will, through the election, is most clearly declared in favor of such constitutional amendment.

The most reliable indication of public purpose in this country is derived through our popular elections. Judging by the recent canvass and its result, the purpose of the people, within the loyal States, to maintain the integrity of the Union, was never more firm, nor more nearly unanimous, than now. The extraordinary calmness and good order with which the millions of voters met and mingled at the polls, give strong assurance of this. Not only all those who supported the Union ticket, so called, but a great majority of the opposing party also, may be fairly claimed to entertain, and to be actuated by, the same purpose. It is an unanswerable argument to this effect, that no candidate for any office whatever, high or low, has ventured to seek votes on the avowal that

36 The autograph fragment has "unclean" instead of "foul."
37 The autograph fragment comprising the first two sentences of this paragraph is owned by Frank L. Pleadwell of Honolulu, Hawaii. On the verso appears an undated certification by John D. Defrees.

he was for giving up the Union. There have been much impugning of motives, and much heated controversy as to the proper means and best mode of advancing the Union cause; but on the distinct issue of Union or no Union, the politicians have shown their instinctive knowledge that there is no diversity among the people. In affording the people the fair opportunity of showing, one to another and to the world, this firmness and unanimity of purpose, the election has been of vast value to the national cause.

The[38] election has exhibited another fact not less valuable to be known—the fact that we do not approach exhaustion in the most important branch of national resources—that of living men. While it is melancholy to reflect that the war has filled so many graves, and carried mourning to so many hearts, it is some relief to know that, compared with the surviving, the fallen have been so few. While corps, and divisions, and brigades, and regiments have formed, and fought, and dwindled, and gone out of existence, a great majority of the men who composed them are still living. The same is true of the naval service. The election returns prove this. So many voters could not else be found. The States regularly holding elections, both now and four years ago, to[39] wit, California, Connecticut, Delaware, Illinois, Indiana, Iowa, Kentucky, Maine, Maryland, Massachusetts, Michigan, Minnesota, Missouri, New Hampshire, New Jersey, New York, Ohio, Oregon, Pennsylvania, Rhode Island, Vermont, West Virginia, and Wisconsin cast 3.982.-011 votes now, against 3.870.222 cast then, showing an aggregate now of 3.982.011. To this is to be added 33.762 cast now in the new States of Kansas and Nevada, which States did not vote in 1860, thus swelling the aggregate to 4.015.773 and the net increase during the three years and a half of war to 145.551. A table is appended showing particulars. To[40] this again should be added the number of all soldiers in the field from Massachusetts, Rhode Island, New Jersey, Delaware, Indiana, Illinois, and California, who, by the laws of those States, could not vote away from their

[38] The autograph single page comprising this paragraph down to and including the phrase "during the three years and a half of war" is owned by Mrs. W. R. Gordon, Beloit, Wisconsin.

[39] The autograph fragments (notes 38 and 40) do not contain the names of the states as listed in the signed copies. Blank spaces also are left in these two fragments where the figures for votes appear. Lincoln's tabulation of election returns (see December 1, *supra*) was not completed until after the Annual Message had been prepared, and the signed copies show these figures to have been inserted.

[40] The autograph single page comprising the remainder of this paragraph is in the Beloit Historical Society, Beloit, Wisconsin.

homes, and which number cannot be less than 90.000. Nor yet is this all. The number in organized Territories is triple now what it was four years ago, while thousands, white and black, join us as the national arms press back the insurgent lines. So much is shown, affirmatively and negatively, by the election. It is not material to inquire *how* the increase has been produced, or to show that it would have been *greater* but for the war, which is probably true. The important fact remains demonstrated, that we have *more* men *now* than we had when the war *began;* that we are not exhausted, nor in process of exhaustion; that we are *gaining* strength, and may, if need be, maintain the contest indefinitely. This as to men. Material resources are now more complete and abundant than ever.

The national resources, then, are unexhausted, and, as we believe, inexhaustible. The public purpose to re-establish and maintain the national authority is unchanged, and, as we believe, unchangeable. The manner of continuing the effort remains to choose. On careful consideration of all the evidence accessible it seems to me that no attempt at negotiation with the insurgent leader could result in any good. He would accept nothing short of severance of the Union—precisely what we will not and cannot give. His declarations to this effect are explicit and oft-repeated. He does not attempt to deceive us. He affords us no excuse to deceive ourselves. He cannot voluntarily reaccept the Union; we cannot voluntarily yield it. Between him and us the issue is distinct, simple, and inflexible. It is an issue which can only be tried by war, and decided by victory. If we yield, we are beaten; if the Southern people fail him, he is beaten. Either way, it would be the victory and defeat following war. What is true, however, of him who heads the insurgent cause, is not[41] necessarily true of those who follow. Although he cannot reaccept the Union, they can. Some of them, we know, already desire peace and reunion. The number of such may increase. They can, at any moment, have peace simply by laying down their arms and submitting to[42] the national authority under the Constitution. After so much, the government could not, if it would, maintain war against them. The loyal people would not sustain or allow it. If questions should remain, we would adjust them by the peaceful means of legislation, conference, courts, and votes, operating only in constitutional and lawful channels. Some certain,

---

[41] The autograph single page comprising the remainder of this paragraph is in the Oliver R. Barrett Collection.

[42] The autograph page had "re-accepting" instead of "submitting to."

and other possible, questions are, and would be, beyond the Executive power to adjust; as, for instance, the admission of members into Congress, and whatever might require the appropriation of money. The Executive power itself would be greatly diminished by the cessation of actual war. Pardons and remissions of forfeitures, however, would still be within Executive control. In what spirit and temper this control would be exercised can be fairly judged of by the past.

A year ago general pardon and amnesty, upon specified terms, were offered to all, except certain designated classes; and, it was, at the same time, made known that the excepted classes were still within contemplation of special clemency. During the year many availed themselves of the general provision, and many more would, only that the signs of bad faith in some led to such precautionary measures as rendered the practical process less easy and certain. During the same time also special pardons have been granted to individuals of the excepted classes, and no voluntary application has been denied. Thus, practically, the door has been, for a full year, open to all, except such as were not in condition to make free choice—that is, such as were in custody or under constraint. It is still so open to all. But the time may come—probably will come—when public duty shall demand that it be closed; and that, in lieu, more rigorous measures than heretofore shall be adopted.

In[43] presenting the abandonment of armed resistance to the national authority on the part of the insurgents, as the only indispensable condition to ending the war on the part of the government, I retract nothing heretofore said as to slavery. I repeat the declaration made a year ago, that "while I remain in my present position I shall not attempt to retract or modify the emancipation proclamation, nor shall I return to slavery any person who is free by the terms of that proclamation, or by any of the Acts of Congress." If[44] the people should, by whatever mode or means, make it an Executive duty to re-enslave such persons, another, and not I, must be their instrument to perform it.

In stating a single condition of peace, I mean simply to say that the war will cease on the part of the government, whenever it shall have ceased on the part of those who began it.

December 6. 1864.   ABRAHAM LINCOLN

[43] The autograph fragment comprising all but the last sentence of this paragraph is in the Oliver R. Barrett Collection.

[44] The autograph fragment beginning with this sentence and including the final paragraph is in The Library of Congress. It is accompanied by a letter of John D. Defrees, April 19, 1866, presenting the fragment to "Mrs. Perry" of Auburn, New York.

Table showing the aggregate votes in the States named, at the presidential election respectively in 1860 and 1864.[45]

	1860.	1864.
California	118,840	*110,000
Connecticut	77,246	86,616
Delaware	16,039	16,924
Illinois	339,693	348,235
Indiana	272,143	280,645
Iowa	128,331	143,331
Kentucky	146,216	*91,300
Maine	97,918	115,141
Maryland	92,502	72,703
Massachusetts	169,533	175,487
Michigan	154,747	162,413
Minnesota	34,799	42,534
Missouri	165,538	*90,000
New Hampshire	65,953	69,111
New Jersey	121,125	128,680
New York	675,156	730,664
Ohio	442,441	470,745
Oregon	14,410	†14,410
Pennsylvania	476,442	572,697
Rhode Island	19,931	22,187
Vermont	42,844	55,811
West Virginia	46,195	33,874
Wisconsin	152,180	148,513
	3,870,222	3,982,011
Kansas		17,234
Nevada		16,528
		33,762
		3,982,011
Total		4,015,773
		3,870,222
Net increase		145,551

*Nearly   †Estimated.

[45] No manuscript of this table is with the manuscript of the Message in the National Archives. The table is reproduced here as printed in the *Senate Journal*, page 15, immediately following the Message. A similar text appears in the *House Journal* and in *House Executive Document* No. 1.

Response to a Serenade[1]

December 6, 1864

FRIENDS AND FELLOW-CITIZENS: I believe I shall never be old enough to speak without embarrassment when I have anything [nothing?] to talk about. [Laughter and cheering.] I have no good news to tell you, and yet I have no bad news to tell. We have talked of elections until there is nothing more to say about them. The most interesting news we now have is from Sherman. We all know where he went in at, but I can't tell where he will come out at. [Cheers and cries, "He'll come out all right."] I will now close by proposing three cheers for Gen. Sherman and the army.

[1] New York *Tribune*, December 8, 1864. Brackets are in the source except in the case of the single emendation.

To the Senate[1]

Executive Mansion Washington, D.C.

To the Senate of the United States   Dec. 6. 1864

I nominate Salmon P. Chase of Ohio, to be Chief Justice of the Supreme Court of the United States vice Roger B. Taney, deceased.

ABRAHAM LINCOLN

[1] ALS-P, ISLA. On the bottom of Lincoln's letter appears the following endorsement:

"United States Senate
"In Executive Session
"Decr. 6. 1864.

"Read; considered by unanimous consent, and nomination unanimously confirmed.

"Attest: D.W.C. CLARKE

"Principal Executive Clerk."

Chase wrote Lincoln on the same day: "On reaching home tonight I was saluted with the intelligence that you this day nominated me to the Senate for the office of Chief Justice. I cannot sleep before I thank [you] for this mark of your confidence, & especially for the manner in which the nomination was made. I shall never forget either and trust that you will never regret either Be assured that I prize your confidence & goodwill more than nomination or office" (DLC-RTL).

Story Written for Noah Brooks[1]

[December 6, 1864]

THE PRESIDENT'S LAST, SHORTEST, AND BEST SPEECH.

On thursday of last week two ladies from Tennessee came before the President asking the release of their husbands held as prisoners of war at Johnson's Island. They were put off till friday, when they came again; and were again put off to saturday. At each of the interviews one of the ladies urged that her husband was a religious man. On saturday the President ordered the release of the prisoners, and then said to this lady "You say your husband is a religious man; tell him when you meet him, that I say I am not much of a judge of religion, but that, in my opinion, the re ligion that sets men to rebel and fight against their government, because, as they think, that government does not sufficiently help *some* men to eat their bread on the sweat of *other* men's faces, is not the sort of religion upon which people can get to heaven!"

A. LINCOLN.

1 ADS, MeHi. Nicolay and Hay date this item "December 3, 1864." (X, 279), while Tracy dates it "Nov. ——, 1864." (pp. 248-49.) December 3 was on Saturday, which would seem from Lincoln's narrative to have been in the past at the time of writing. December 6 has been assigned because the item appeared in the Washington *Daily Chronicle* on December 7, 1864. Noah Brooks records the circumstances under which it was written:

". . . Upon another occasion, hearing that I was in the parlor, he sent for me to come up into the library, where I found him writing on a piece of common stiff box-board with a pencil. Said he, after he had finished, 'Here is one speech of mine which has never been printed, and I think it worth printing. Just see what you think.' He then read the following, which is copied *verbatim* from the familiar handwriting before me: [text as above]

"To this the President signed his name at my request, by way of joke, and added for a caption, 'The President's Last, Shortest, and Best Speech,' under which title it was duly published in one of the Washington newspapers. . . ." ("Personal Recollections of Abraham Lincoln," *Harper's New Monthly Magazine*, July, 1865, p. 230).

Endorsement[1]

On the strength of Gen. Dix' indorsement, I approve.

Dec. 7. 1864   A. LINCOLN

1 AES, owned by Arthur Hanson, Charleston, West Virginia. Lincoln's endorsement has been removed from the attendant documents.

To James B. Fry[1]

December 7, 1864

I know nothing of this gentleman or his case, except as presented by these papers. I merely submit to the Provost Marshal General whether an inquiry is not due him.   A. LINCOLN

Dec. 7, 1864.

[1] AES, owned by R. E. Burdick, New York City. Lincoln's endorsement is written on a letter from John Foster, December 6, 1864, asking reinstatement as clerk in the office of the provost marshal general. Relating that he had been dismissed on charges of having made speeches in favor of McClellan's election, Foster submitted letters disproving the charges. No record has been found of his reinstatement.

To Willard P. Hall[1]

Gov. Hall   Executive Mansion, Washington,
Jefferson City   Mo.   Dec. 7, 1864.
Complaint is made to me of the doings of a man at Hannibal, Mo. by the name of Haywood, who, as I am told, has charge of some militia force, and is not in the U.S. service. Please inquire into the matter & correct anything you may find amiss if in your power.   A LINCOLN

[1] ALS, DNA WR RG 107, Presidential Telegrams, I, 255. Governor Hall forwarded a copy of Lincoln's telegram to General Rosecrans at St. Louis (OR, I, XLI, IV, 799). No further reference to the complaint has been found. Colonel John T. K. Hayward, Thirty-eighth Regiment Enrolled Missouri Militia, operated against guerrillas in the area around Hannibal, Missouri.

To John B. Henderson[1]

December 7, 1864
Will Senator Henderson please see and hear this Missouri lady, and report to me on the case she shall present.   A. LINCOLN
Dec. 7, 1864

Let this man be discharged on taking the oath of Dec. 8, 1863.
Dec. 8, 1864   A. LINCOLN

[1] Anderson Galleries Catalog 2193, November 15, 1927, No. 343. According to the catalog description, Senator Henderson's recommendation for the discharge appears between Lincoln's endorsements, but no names are given in the source.

Memorandum:
Appointment of Daniel H. Brush, Jr.[1]

File & remember.   A. LINCOLN
Dec. 7. 1864

[1] AES, DNA WR RG 94, U.S. Military Academy, 1864, No. 297. Lincoln's endorsement is written on a letter from Daniel H. Brush, Carbondale, Illinois, November 3, 1864, asking his son's appointment to West Point. Daniel H. Brush, Jr., did not enter West Point until June, 1867, and graduated in 1871.

Memorandum
Concerning Benjamin F. Flanders[1]

[December 7? 1864]

Gen. Banks thinks Mr. Montague, while a good man would scarcely be active enough for Flander's place. He thinks Col. Frank W. Howe would be better.

[1] AD, DLC-RTL. The supplied date is that given to the memorandum by The Library of Congress. On the verso of the manuscript Lincoln merely endorsed "Flanders." Neither Montague nor Frank W. Howe have been further identified. Benjamin F. Flanders had been defeated for governor of Louisiana in 1864, but remained special agent of the Treasury Department at New Orleans (*U.S. Official Register*, 1865).

Memorandum
Concerning William W. Ketchum[1]

If there should be a change of Governor of New-Mexico, I wish to be reminded of this paper. A. LINCOLN

Dec. 7. 1864.

[1] AES, DNA FS RG 59, Appointments, Box 323. Lincoln's endorsement is written on a letter from Simon Cameron, December 2, 1864, recommending William W. Ketchum for "Governor of New Mexico, or Gov. of some other Territory." Henry Connelly remained governor of New Mexico.

Memorandum
Concerning New Mexico Appointments[1]

Executive Mansion,
Washington, Dec. 7, 1864.

To-day Mr. Perea, Delegate from New-Mexico, asks that Arny, Secretary of the Territory be removed, and Charles P. Clever be appointed in his stead. Also Dr. Steck, Sup. Ind. Affairs, be removed, & Philip P. Delgado. Also John Greiner, Receiver of Public-Monies & James L. Collins appointed [in] his place.

[1] AD, DLC-RTL. William F. M. Arny remained in office. Felipe Delgado, nominated to replace Michael Steck on February 21, 1865, was confirmed by the Senate on March 3, 1865. John Greiner remained in office.

To the Senate[1]

To the Senate of the United States: December 7, 1864

In answer to the Senate's Resolution of yesterday, requesting information in regard to aid furnished to the rebellion by British subjects, I transmit a Report from the Secretary of State and the documents by which it was accompanied.   ABRAHAM LINCOLN

Washington,
7 December, 1864.

[1] DS, DNA RG 46, Senate 38A F2. The report of Secretary Seward transmitted by Lincoln is printed in Thirty-eighth Congress, Second Session, *Senate Executive Document No. 2.*

To James Speed[1]

Attorney General please have a Brief made of these and all other papers on file in relation to Indiana vacant Judgeship.

Dec. 7. 1864   A. LINCOLN

[1] AES, DNA RG 60, Papers of Attorney General, Appointments, Indiana, Box 406. Lincoln's endorsement is written on an envelope containing testimonials in favor of John D. Howland for judge of the U.S. District Court to succeed Albert S. White, who died on September 24, 1864. David McDonald received the nomination and was confirmed by the Senate on December 13, 1864.

To Edwin M. Stanton[1]

Hon. Sec. of War   Executive Mansion, Washington,
Sir: Dec. 7. 1864.

Senator Hicks again calls on me in relation to the Commission sitting in Maryland, constituted of Rogers, Timmons & Straughn. Please have it looked after, so as to know whether anything, and if any thing, what, is wrong. Yours truly   A. LINCOLN

[1] ALS, NHi. See footnote to Lincoln to Bowman, August 6, *supra.* A letter of Thomas H. Hicks to Thomas Timmons, December 15, 1864, enclosed by Timmons to Lincoln on December 19, sets forth the charges as follows:

"I learn that you have been somewhat disturbed at hearing that I had preferred charges agt yourself & colleagues in the commission or court to investigate character, decide loyalty and issue certificates &c. I preferred no charge, but spoke of universal rumors in regard to tardiness in discharge of duty, I said nothing that was not true, to wit—that the Court had affected but little by way of satisfying the loyal people of our State, and that you had told me that the trouble grew out of yr inability to get the detective list. . . .

"I made no specific charge, I spoke of general and believed reports, but did not know of my own knowledge, but did know that true or false, these reports was injuring us Politically in the state and that the Prest was held responsible for all that is being done by his appointees, and I felt it to be my duty to put him in possession of the fact that the reports indicated above was damaging his administration. . . . I urged an investigation, and the Secretary had heard this report before I said anything of it. . . ." (DLC-RTL).

Endorsement[1]

If this is consistent, I shall be glad for it to be done.

Dec. 8, 1864   A. LINCOLN.

1 Estate of Gabriel Wells Catalog 4, May, 1950, No. 126. According to the catalog description, Lincoln's endorsement is written on a short note addressed to the Senate Chamber regarding the promotion of an officer. No names are given.

To Thomas B. Fairleigh[1]

Col. Farleigh   Executive Mansion Washington D.C
Louisville, Ky   Dec. 8. 1864

I am appealed to in behalf of a man by the name of Frank Fairbairn, said to have been for a long time, & still in prison, without any definite ground stated. How is it?   A LINCOLN

1 ALS, DNA WR RG 107, Presidential Telegrams, I, 256. Lieutenant Colonel Thomas B. Fairleigh, Twenty-sixth Regiment, Veteran Reserve Corps, replied on the same day: "Farbai[r]n was arrested & sent here & there being no proof against him I released him He was again arrested by order from District Hd Qrs but again released yesterday by orders from the same source" (DLC-RTL).

Recommendation for John C. Hutton[1]

If this gentleman could find, in any Department or Bureau, employment suitable to him I should be glad.   A LINCOLN
     Dec. 8. 1864

1 AES, DNA FI RG 56, General Records of Treasury Department, Personnel File, John C. Hutton. Lincoln's endorsement is written on a petition signed by officers of the Third Regiment, Delaware Volunteers, October 16, 1864, recommending Dr. John C. Hutton, hospital steward, who had been forced to resign from the service because of ill health. Hutton is listed in the *U.S. Official Register*, 1865, as clerk in the office of the Sixth Auditor.

To William S. Rosecrans[1]

Major General Rosecrans comdg   Executive Mansion
St. Louis Mo   Dec. 8. 1864

Let execution in case of John Berry & James Berry be suspended until further order.   A. LINCOLN

Major Eckert
Will you please hurry off the above   Tomorrow is the day of execution.   JOHN HAY A.A.G.

1 LS, DNA WR RG 107, Presidential Telegrams, I, 257. This telegram is in John Hay's handwriting except for Lincoln's signature. An article in *The Missouri Republican* (St. Louis) for November 16, 1864, announced the court-martial sentence of Second Lieutenant James Berry, Company D, Fourteenth Kansas Cavalry, "that he be shot to death with musketry, in St. Louis, on the 9th proximo. The charges   were that he deserted . . . at Fort Smith in January last, and took away a horse and equipments. . . . John W. Berry, a brother

. . . Sergeant of the same company, on similar charges . . . was also sentenced to be shot; but . . . the sentence has been mitigated to imprisonment and hard labor. . . ."

Order Concerning Elijah Morgan[1]

Executive Mansion,
Washington, Dec. 9, 1864.

Today, on the application of Hon. Mr. Whaley, of West Virginia, I direct that Elijah Morgan a prisoner of war at Fort-Delaware, be discharged on taking the oath of Dec. 8, 1864.   A. LINCOLN.

[1] American Autograph Shop Catalog, January, 1937, No. 154. According to the catalog description this is an autograph order signed. If the source is correct, Lincoln erred in referring to the oath of December 8, 1864, instead of December 8, 1863.

Pass[1]

Allow this Soldier's wife to pass free from Washington to New-York.   A. LINCOLN

Dec. 9. 1864

[1] ADS, CSmH.

Recommendation for Discharged Soldiers[1]

I shall be glad if any Department or Bureau can give employment to the discharged soldiers.   A. LINCOLN

Dec. 9, 1864

[1] American Art Association Catalog, March 12, 1920, No. 538. According to the catalog description this communication is an autograph note signed.

To James Speed[1]

December 9, 1864

Induced by the within, and by other representations, to believe there may have been [a] mistake, and consequent injustice in the removal of Justice Miller, let him be re-appointed.   A. LINCOLN

Dec. 9. 1864.

[1] AES, DNA RG 60, Papers of Attorney General, 1864, Box 117. Lincoln's endorsement is written on a letter from David K. Cartter, chief justice, and Andrew Wylie, associate justice of the Supreme Court of the District of Columbia, December 5, 1864, stating that their decision to remove Justice of Peace Nehemiah H. Miller from office would have been different if they had seen evidence produced by Miller after his trial.

To Robert K. Stone[1]

December 9, 1864

If Dr. Stone pleases to call & see me at 9. A.M. to-morrow, I will talk with him about trying to oblige his family in regard to Mrs. Ritchie at Richmond.   A. LINCOLN.

Dec. 9, 1864

[1] ALS-P, ISLA. Dr. Robert K. Stone's wife was Margaret Ritchie whose family lived in Richmond. Lincoln gave an order "to pass *Mourning Garments* &c. . . . This was gratefully accepted & the box, got as far, as *Fortress Monroe*, on its way, to her sisters, in Richmond. . . ." (Stone to Lincoln, April 11, 1865, DLC-RTL).

Introduction[1]

Introducing Col. Jason March.   A. LINCOLN.

Dec. 10, 1864.

[1] American Autograph Shop Catalog, September, 1942, No. 103. According to the catalog description, this is an autograph note signed. Jason Marsh (not "March") was colonel of the Seventy-fourth Illinois Infantry.

Order Appointing Commissioners
to Investigate the Military Division
Bordering upon and West of the Mississippi[1]

Executive Mansion, December 10, 1864.

Ordered, First. That Maj. Gen. William F. Smith and the Hon. Henry Stanbery be, and they are hereby, appointed special commissioners to investigate and report, for the information of the President, upon the civil and military administration in the military division bordering upon and west of the Mississippi, under such instructions as shall be issued by authority of the President and the War Department.

Second. Said commissioners shall have power to examine witnesses upon oath, and to take such proofs, orally or in writing, upon the subject-matters of investigation as they may deem expedient, and return the same together with their report.

Third. All officers and persons in the military, naval, and revenue services, or in any branch of the public service under the authority of the United States Government, are required, upon subpoena issued by direction of the said commissioners, to appear before them at such time and place as may be designated in said subpoena and to give testimony on oath touching such matters as may be inquired of by the commissioners, and to produce such books, papers, writings, and documents as they may be notified or required to produce by the commissioners, and as may be in their possession.

Fourth. Said special commissioners shall also investigate and report upon any other matters that may hereafter be directed by the Secretary of War, and shall, with all convenient dispatch, make report to him in writing of their investigation, and shall also from time to time make special reports to the Secretary of War upon such matters as they may deem of importance to the public interests.

Fifth. The Secretary of War shall assign to the said commissioners such aid and assistance as may be required for the performance of their duties, and make such just and reasonable allowances and compensation for the said commissioners and for the persons employed by them as he may deem proper.   ABRAHAM LINCOLN.

[1] OR, I, XLI, IV, 817. Lincoln's order is printed in the source as an enclosure with Stanton's communication to General Edward R. S. Canby, December 10, 1864, notifying Canby that the commissioners "are directed to report to you and to commence their investigations at New Orleans. . . ." See Lincoln to Canby, December 12, *infra*.

To Joseph Roberts[1]

[c. December 10, 1864.]

It is confessed in this case that Samuels when arrested, had on his person a paper *prima facie* showing that he was going North to obtain medical supplies for the rebels. Will the officer in command at Fort-Monroe[2] please give him an opportunity of trying to prove that this was not his real object, and report the evidence, with his opinion on it, to me?   A. LINCOLN

Let the Prisoner Samuels be discharged.   A. LINCOLN
Dec. 10. 1864

[1] AES, owned by Max Thorek, Chicago, Illinois. Lincoln's endorsements are written on a letter of General Benjamin F. Butler to C. C. Callam of Baltimore, September 15, 1864:

"I suppose yours is the fiftieth communication I have received about [Abraham] Samuels, some asking that he be tried, and some asking one thing, and some another; and this is the last communication I shall answer about Samuels from any source, except under orders from the President.

"Samuels' case is this: He left Richmond with a list of Medical supplies in his pocket under an agreement to procure those supplies for the Rebel Medical Department.

"He was detected, arrested, examined, and confined, and he will be confined during the War, so far as any act of mine can aid that desirable result."

Lincoln's first undated endorsement was presumably written between September 15 and December 10, probably closer to the later date. On January 8, 1865, General Butler wrote Lincoln:

"Abraham Samuels was arrested in January, 1864, when endeavoring to make his way through my lines across the Potomac. Upon examination he confessed that the paragraph in the Richmond *Examiner*, December 28th, 1863, herewith furnished, was furnished to that paper by himself in answer to a paragraph in a former issue saying . . . that Samuels had endeavored to escape to the Yankees. He farther confessed that when he left Richmond he had the list of medical stores which is mentioned in the *Examiner*, which he recovered from the medical purveyor of the Confederate Army, and that he had engaged to run the blockade and bring back the stores: that he had destroyed this paper. From all the surroundings and his story I was satisfied that he was in the interest of the Confederates, and I caused him to be held as a dangerous and disloyal person, and confiscated the money he had with him . . . and placed it to the credit of the United States where it remains.

"A great number of applications were made for his release, to all of which I would not listen until after we had so constructed our lines about Richmond that I was satisfied that Samuels' vocation as blockade runner was gone, and then upon an intimation from the President I released him, not because of his innocence . . . but because he was no longer dangerous. . . ." (*Private and Official Correspondence of General Benjamin F. Butler*, V, 474-75).

2 Lincoln first wrote "Gen. Wallace," and changed to "the officer in command at Fort-Monroe." Colonel Joseph Roberts, Third Pennsylvania Heavy Artillery was in command through December, 1864.

To Edward R. S. Canby[1]

Executive Mansion, Washington,

Major General Canby: Dec 12, 1864.

I think it is probable that you are laboring under some misapprehension as to the purpose, or rather the motive of the government on two points—*Cotton*, and the new *Louisiana State* Government. It is conceded that the military operations are the *first* in importance; and as to what is indispensable to these operations, the Department Commander must be judge and master. But the other matters mentioned, I suppose to be of public importance also; and what I have attempted in regard to them, is not merely a concession to private interest and pecuniary greed.

As to cotton. By the external blockade, the price is made certainly six times as great as it was. And yet the enemy gets through at least one sixth part as much in a given period, say a year, as if there were no blockade, and receives as much for it, as he would for a full crop in time of peace. The effect in substance is, that we give him six ordinary crops, without the trouble of producing any but the first; and at the same time leave his fields and his laborers free to produce provisions. You know how this keeps up his armies at home, and procures supplies from abroad. For other reasons we cannot give up the blockade, and hence it becomes immensely important to us to get the cotton away from him. Better give him *guns* for it, than let him, as now, get both guns and ammunition for it. But even this only presents part of the public interest to get out cotton. Our finances are greatly involved in the matter. The way cotton goes now carries so much gold out of the country as to leave us paper currency only, and that so far depreciated, as that for every hard dollar's worth of supplies we obtain, we contract to pay two and a half hard dollars hereafter. This is much to be regretted; and while I believe we can live through it at all events, it demands an earnest effort on the part of all to correct it. And if pecuniary greed can be made to aid us in such effort, let us be thankful that so much good can be got out of pecuniary greed.

As to the new State Government of Louisiana. Most certainly there is no worthy object in getting up a piece of machinery merely to pay salaries, and give political consideration to certain men. But it is a worthy object to again get Louisiana into proper practical relations with the nation; and we can never finish this, if we never begin it. Much good work is already done, and surely nothing can be gained by throwing it away.

I do not wish either cotton or the new State Government to take precedence of the military, while the necessity for the military remains; but there is a strong public reason for treating each with so much favor as may not be substantially detrimental to the military.

Allow me a word of explanation in regard to the telegram which you kindly forwarded to Admiral Faragut for me.[2] That telegram was prompted by a piece of secret information inducing me to suspect that the use of a forged paper might be attempted on the Admiral, in order to base a claim that we had raised our own blockade.

I am happy in the hope that you are almost well of your late and severe wound   Yours very truly,

[1] Copy, DLC-RTL. The copy is on Executive Mansion stationery. On December 2, apropos of Lincoln's communication to Hurlbut of November 14, *supra*, General Canby had written Lincoln:

"Major General Hurlbut has shown me your communication of the 14th inst., in which that officer and myself are charged with bitter animosity to the new State Government of Louisiana.

"I have had very little official connection with the convention, and none at all with the State Government, or the State Legislature. Matters connected with these bodies, being under the supervision of the Department Commander, do not reach me, except by way of appeal, and my own duties have been sufficiently engrossing, to prevent any disposition to interfere, unless the subject was submitted to me for decision. Of the three instances cited in evidence of this bitter animosity, the first is the only one of which I have any knowledge, either official or personal. The others I had never heard of until I read your letter. In the case of Mr. [Thomas P.] May I *did* interfere upon an appeal, and for the reason simply, that the power claimed by the Convention to punish for contempt not committed in its presence, could not be admitted without establishing, in the military circumstances of the community, a very dangerous precedent. *That opinion* I still entertain. I saw then, and I see now, no reason why the usual limit of legislative power, and which the convention had, a few days previous, (Act 30, of the Convention,) defined for the Legislature, and, by implication, for itself, should have been transcended. There was no necessity for it, for the convention was under military protection, and that protection would have been given to it under any circumstances, and to any extent.

"Of the details of the insult offered to the convention in the release of Mr. May, I know nothing. My decision was communicated to General Banks, and the orders were given by him; but I *do* know, that, while we differed on some points, we concurred in the opinion, that the convention had no legitimate power to arrest, or try, or punish any one, for a contempt, not committed in its presence.

"I think it only necessary to add to this, that it has been, and is my purpose, not only as a question of duty, but of feeling, to give whatever support and aid I can, to the State Government; but it is proper that your Excellency should be advised, that matters that will, ultimately, come under the control of the State Government, are now so complicated with questions of military administration, that, in the changes to be made, differences of opinion may arise, which should not subject officers of the army to the imputation of opposition or animosity. . . ." (DLC-RTL).   [2] See Lincoln to Canby, November 6, *supra*.

To Henry S. Lane[1]

Will Senator H. S. Lane please call and see me at once.

Dec. 12, 1864   A. LINCOLN

[1] American Art Association Anderson Galleries Catalog 3995, November 10, 1932, No. 66. According to the catalog description this item is an autograph note signed.

Order for Discharge of Thomas Rice and Reuben Turner[1]

December 12, 1864

At the request of Hon. Mr. Randall of Ky, it is ordered that Thomas Rice prisoner of War at Rock-Island, and Reuben Turner, prisoner of war at Johnson's Island, be discharged, on taking the oath of Dec. 8. 1863.   A. LINCOLN

Dec. 12. 1864

[1] AES, owned by R. E. Burdick, New York City. Although written at the request of Representative William H. Randall, Lincoln's endorsement appears on a letter from Daniel Breck, December 5, 1864, introducing "my friend, Mr. Billingsley" of Richmond, Kentucky.

[165]

To Cyrus Wick[1]

Executive Mansion Washington

My Dear Sir   12 De[ce]mber 1864

I take pleasure in acknowledgeing the receipt of your letter and poem and in thanking you for your kindness   Yours very truly

A. LINCOLN

[1] Copy, DLC-HW. The copy of Lincoln's letter was enclosed by Cyrus Wick to Herndon, January 23, 1867. Wick's poem, "inspired by a sentiment expressed in one of his [Lincoln's] messages early in 1861 and by the scenery where his childhood was passed" was written after Wick's regiment (Seventeenth Indiana Volunteers) had been "encamped for several weeks on Nolin Creek one mile and a quarter from Hodgenville La Rue County Kentucky" in November, 1862. A printed copy which Wick sent to Lincoln in November, 1864, brought Lincoln's brief acknowledgment.

To Grenville M. Dodge[1]

Major Gen. Dodge   Executive Mansion
St. Louis, Mo.   Washington, Dec. 13. 1864

Please suspend the sending South of Mrs. Nancy H. Thompson, wife of Gideon H. Thompson, of Platte Co. Mo. but now in rebel army, until further order, & in mean time, ascertain and report to me whether there is any thing, & what, against her, except that her husband is a rebel.   A. LINCOLN

[1] ALS, DNA WR RG 107, Presidential Telegrams, I, 259. Major General Grenville M. Dodge relieved Rosecrans as commander of the Department of the Missouri (AGO *General Orders No. 294*, December 2, 1864). No further reference to Mrs. Nancy Thompson has been found. There are references in the *Official Records* to Colonel Gideon W. (not H.) Thompson of the Confederate Army.

To Ira Goodnow[1]

I shall be glad if Capt. Goodenow can & will find a suitable position for this fine little boy.   A. LINCOLN
Dec. 13, 1864

[1] Parke-Bernet Catalog 1352, May 27, 1952, No. 181. According to the catalog description, this item is an autograph note signed. Ira Goodnow was doorkeeper of the House of Representatives.

•

To the Senate[1]

To the Senate of the United States: December 13, 1864

I transmit to the Senate, for consideration with a view to ratification, "a treaty of amity, commerce, and navigation, and for the

extradition of fugitive criminals, between the United States of America and the Republic of Hayti, signed by their respective plenipotentiaries at Port-au-Prince on the 3d of November" last.

Washington, December 13, 1864.   ABRAHAM LINCOLN.

[1] *Executive Journal*, XIV, 8. The treaty was ratified by the Senate on January 17, 1865.

To the Senate[1]

To the Senate of the United States: December 13, 1864

I transmit to the Senate, for consideration with a view to ratification, "a treaty of friendship, commerce, and navigation between the United States of America and the Republic of Honduras," signed by their respective plenipotentiaries, at Comayagua, on the 4th of July (1864) last.   ABRAHAM LINCOLN.

Washington, December 13, 1864.

[1] *Executive Journal*, XIV, 8. The treaty was ratified by the Senate on February 20, 1865.

To Lewis Wallace[1]

Major General Wallace   Executive Mansion
Baltimore, Md.   Washington, Dec. 13. 1864

Do not send Levin L. Waters and the judges away, until further order; and send me at once a statement of the cause or causes for which they are dealt with.   A. LINCOLN

[1] ALS, DNA WR RG 107, Presidential Telegrams, I, 258. On December 2, 1864, Samuel B. Lawrence, assistant adjutant general to General Wallace, ordered Brigadier General Henry H. Lockwood to "arrest Daniel Jones and Joseph Bralton of Somerset County, and Levin D. [L.] Waters, of Princess Anne, and send them, as disaffected and dangerous men, by steamer to Fortress Monroe, to be sent across the lines into Confederate jurisdiction. . . ." (OR, I, XLIII, II, 729).

See further, Lincoln to Wallace, December 19, *infra*.

To Ulysses S. Grant[1]

Lieut. General Grant.   Executive Mansion,
City-Point, Va.   Washington, Dec. 14. 1864.

Please have execution of John McNulty, *alias* Joseph Riley, Co. E. 6. N.H. Vols. suspended, and record sent to me.

A. LINCOLN

[1] ALS, DNA WR RG 107, Presidential Telegrams, I, 260. General Grant replied on the same day, forwarding the following despatch from General Meade: "I yesterday remitted the sentence in the case of John McNulty alias Joseph

Riley Company E 6th New Hampshire Vols and beg leave to refer to my letter to you in the case. The record will be forwarded to the President as directed." (DLC-RTL).

The roster of the Sixth New Hampshire Volunteers lists John McNulty as having deserted on October 15, 1864. Returned to his regiment, he was reported on the muster roll of July 17, 1865, as absent without leave since July 4, 1865.

To William H. Seward[1]

Will the Sec. of State please call at once? A. LINCOLN
Dec. 14. 1864

[1] ALS, ORB.

To James Speed[1]

Send me a nomination for Gooding. A. LINCOLN
Dec. 14. 1864.

[1] AES, DNA RG 60, Papers of Attorney General, Appointments, New Mexico, Box 660. Lincoln's endorsement is written on an envelope containing recommendations of David S. Gooding for associate justice in New Mexico. Gooding's nomination was tabled by the Senate on January 10, 1865.

To Edwin M. Stanton[1]

December 14, 1864

I think a man who offers to volunteer and is rejected, should not afterwards be drafted and forced to serve. This lady alleges that such is the case of her husband. Please have the case investigated and reported on.

[1] Copy, DNA WR RG 107, Secretary of War, Letters Received, P 1165, Register. Although the original documents are missing from the file, Lincoln's endorsement referring the case of William Richardson, Company F, Second District of Columbia Volunteers, is preserved as a notation in the Register. No further reference has been found.

To William P. Fessenden[1]

Will the Secretary of the Treasury please see & hear Mr. Gumpert, so well vouched within? A. LINCOLN
Dec. 15, 1864

[1] Anderson Galleries Catalog, November 13-14, 1916, No. 213. According to the catalog description, this item is an autograph endorsement signed on a recommendation by William D. Kelley of Gustave Gumpert for appointment as special agent in the Treasury Department.

To Caleb H. Carlton[1]

Officer in command at   Executive Mansion,
Chattanooga Tenn.   Washington, Dec. 16. 1864.

It is said that Harry Walters private in the Anderson Cavalry is now, and for a long time has been in prison at Chattanooga. Please report to me what is his condition, and for what he is imprisoned.   A. LINCOLN

[1] ALS, DNA WR RG 107, Presidential Telegrams, I, 262. Colonel Caleb H. Carlton, Eighty-ninth Ohio Volunteers, was in command at Chattanooga, but no reply to Lincoln's telegram has been found. Harry Walters of the Fifteenth Pennsylvania Cavalry (known as "Anderson Cavalry" because recruited to serve as bodyguard to General Robert Anderson) is listed as discharged on a surgeon's certificate in February, 1865.

Pass for William Y. Dulin[1]

Allow this gentleman to pass to Fairfax Co. Virginia.
Dec. 16, 1864   A. LINCOLN

[1] American Art Association Anderson Galleries Catalog 3927, November 19-20, 1931, No. 141. According to the catalog description, Lincoln's note is written on a card, on the back of which is endorsed: "Mr. Dulon, give pass to Fairfax Co & Alexandria for one month. C.C.A." Mayor Richard Wallach of Washington wrote Lincoln on December 16, 1864: "Mr William Y. Dulin who bears this once resided in Fairfax County Virginia where he had large possessions. . . . He desires your permission to go there & attend to some matters of personal interest.

"I have known him for many years & have the most implicit confidence in his integrity. . . ." (DLC-RTL).

To George H. Thomas[1]

                                          Office U.S. Military Telegraph,
Major General Thomas   War Department,
Nashville, Tenn.   Washington, D.C., Dec. 16. 1864.

Please accept for yourself, officers, and men, the nation's thanks for your good work of yesterday. You made a magnificent beginning. A grand consummation is within your easy reach. Do not let it slip.   A. LINCOLN

[1] ALS, DNA WR RG 107, Presidential Telegrams, I, 261. On December 15, General Thomas telegraphed General Halleck from Nashville: "I attacked the enemy's left this morning and drove it from the river, below the city, very nearly to the Franklin pike, a distance about eight miles. Have captured General [James R.] Chalmers' headquarters and train, and a second train of about 20 wagons, with between 800 and 1,000 prisoners and 16 pieces of artillery. The troops behaved splendidly. . . . I shall attack the enemy again to-morrow, if he stands to fight, and, if he retreats during the night, will pursue him, throwing a heavy cavalry force in his rear, to destroy his trains, if possible." (OR, I, XLV, II, 194).

To Gideon Welles[1]

Allow the bearer to bring me the record containing the evidence in the case of Capt. Reynolds.   A. LINCOLN

    Dec. 17. 1864

[1] ALS, CtHi. Lincoln's note probably referred to the case of Captain Edward M. Reynolds of the Marine Corps, dismissed as morally unfit. (Navy Department, *General Orders No. 43*, December 7, 1864).

To Joseph K. Barnes[1]

Executive Mansion Washington

Surgeon General,   Dec. 19, 1864

    Please have an examination made of Corporal Charles H. Thompson of Co. B. 11th N.H. Vols. in the 9th Corps, with reference to discharge for physical disability   Yours truly

     A. LINCOLN

[1] ALS, owned by Sigurd S. Storm, Chicago, Illinois. Corporal Charles H. Thompson, wounded at Spotsylvania on May 16, 1864, was discharged for disability on January 19, 1865.

To Joseph H. Choate[1]

Executive Mansion,

Washington, Dec. 19, 1864.

My Dear Sir— I have the honor to acknowledge the reception of your kind invitation to be present at the annual festival of the New England Society to commemorate the landing of the Pilgrims, on Thursday, the 22d of this month.

My duties will not allow me to avail myself of your kindness. I cannot but congratulate you and the country, however, upon the spectacle of devoted unanimity presented by the people at home, the citizens that form our marching columns, and the citizens that fill our squadrons on the sea—all animated by the same determination to complete and perpetuate the work our fathers began and transmitted.

The work of the Plymouth emigrants was the glory of their age. While we reverence their memory, let us not forget how vastly greater is our opportunity. I am very truly, your obedient servant,

    Joseph H. Choate, Esq.   A. LINCOLN.

[1] New York *Herald*, December 23, 1864. On November 28, 1864, Joseph H. Choate, chairman, wrote Lincoln: "On behalf of The New England Society in the City of New York, I have the honor to invite you to be present, as the guest of the Society, at its Annual Festival in commemoration of the Landing of the Pilgrims, to be held at the Astor House on Thursday the 22nd day of December next at 6 oclock P.M. . . ." (DLC-RTL).

To Ladies Managing the Soldiers' Fair at Springfield, Massachusetts[1]

The ladies managing the Soldier's Fair at Springfield, Massachusetts.

Executive Mansion, Washington, Dec. 19, 1864.

Your kind invitation to be present at the opening of your Fair is duly received by the hand of Mr. Ashmun. Grateful for the compliment, and ever anxious to aid the good cause in which you are engaged, I yet am compelled by public duties here, to decline. The recent good news from Generals Sherman, Thomas, and indeed from nearly all quarters, will be far better than my presence, and will afford all the impulse, and enthusiasm, you will need. Your Obt. Servt   A. LINCOLN

[1] ALS, owned by E. H. Brewer, Chicago, Illinois. Charles Marsh, secretary of committee, Springfield, Massachusetts, wrote Lincoln on December 10:

"The object of this communication which will be presented to you by our distinguished fellow citizen, Hon. Geo. Ashmun, is to invite you to be present at the opening of a 'Soldiers Fair' to be held in this City, on the 19th, 20th, 21st, & 22d days of the present month

"While we appreciate the laborious and harassing duties, incident to your high position, we venture to suggest that the respite afforded by the acceptance of this invitation would prove most welcome to you.

"You need no other assurance, than that given by the recent vote of the Old Bay State, that, here, you would be among your *friends*. . . ." (DLC-RTL).

Proclamation Calling for 300,000 Volunteers[1]

December 19, 1864

By the President of the United States:

A Proclamation.

Whereas, by the act approved July 4, 1864, entitled "An Act further to regulate and provide for the enrolling and calling out the national forces, and for other purposes," it is provided that the President of the United States may, "at his discretion, at any time hereafter, call for any number of men, as volunteers, for the respective terms of one, two, and three years, for military service," and "that in case the quota, or any part thereof, of any town, township, ward of a city, precinct, or election district, or of any county not so sub-divided, shall not be filled within the space of fifty days after such call, then the President shall immediately order a draft for one year, to fill such quota, or any part thereof, which may be unfilled:"

And whereas by the credits allowed in accordance with the act of Congress on the call for five hundred thousand men made July 18th. 1864, the number of men to be obtained under that call was reduced to two hundred and eighty thousand; and whereas the operations of the enemy in certain States have rendered it impracticable to procure from them their full quotas of troops under said call; and whereas, from the foregoing causes, but two hundred and forty thousand men have been put into the Army, Navy, and Marine Corps under the said call of July 18, 1864, leaving a deficiency on that call of two hundred and sixty thousand: (260,000):

Now, therefore, I, Abraham Lincoln, President of the United States of America, in order to supply the aforesaid deficiency, and to provide for casualties in the military and naval service of the United States, do issue this my call for three hundred thousand (300,000) volunteers to serve for one, two, or three years. The quotas of the States, districts, and sub-districts under this call will be assigned by the War Department through the Bureau of the Provost Marshal General of the United States, and, "in case the quota or any part thereof of any town, township, ward of a city, precinct or election district, or of any county not so sub-divided, shall not be filled" before the fifteenth day of February, eighteen hundred and sixty-five, then a draft shall be made to fill such quota, or any part thereof, under this call, which may be unfilled on said fifteenth day of February 1865.

In testimony whereof, I have hereunto set my hand, and caused the seal of the United States to be affixed.

Done at the city of Washington, this nineteenth day of December, in the year of our Lord one thousand eight hundred and [L.S.] sixty-four; and of the Independence of the United States the eighty-ninth. ABRAHAM LINCOLN

By the President:

WILLIAM H. SEWARD Secretary of State.

[1] DS, DNA FS RG 11, Proclamations.

To Lewis Wallace[1]

Executive Mansion
Major General Wallace   Washington, Dec. 19. 1864

Several days ago I sent you a despatch directing that one Waters and two others should not be sent away immediately, and asking you to send me a statement of the cause or causes of your action in regard to them. I have received nothing from you on the subject. May I against [*sic*] ask for such statement? and also where the men now are?   A LINCOLN

[1] ALS, DNA WR RG 107, Presidential Telegrams, I, 263. Lincoln's telegram is marked by the telegraph operator as sent at 3:10 P.M. Wallace replied on the same day:

"The telegram of your Excellency of this date relative to the cases of Levin S Walters [Levin L. Waters] and two (2) others has been received. The reports called by your Excellency in a previous telegram December thirteenth were forwarded to Washington on the fifteenth inst & were full & explicit & were accompanied by all the papers in their cases.

"They are in charge of the Provost Marshal of this Department. . . ." See Lincoln to Wallace, *infra*.

To Lewis Wallace[1]

Major General Wallace   Executive Mansion,
Baltimore, Md.   Washington, Dec. 19, 1864.
   To whom were the reports sent? I have not received them
                                A. LINCOLN

[1] ALS, DNA WR RG 107, Presidential Telegrams, I, 264. See Lincoln's telegram, *supra*. On December 31, 1864, Nicolay or Hay referred the papers to Stanton, but they are missing from the file (DNA WR RG 107, Secretary of War Letters Received, P 1256). See further, Lincoln to Stanton, January 4, 1865, *infra*.

To Benjamin W. Brice[1]

                                December 20, 1864
Will the Pay-Master-General please inform Hon. Mr. Eckley what is the trouble about Col. Fyffe's pay, & whether there is any thing the President can lawfully do about it.   A. LINCOLN
   Dec. 20, 1864

[1] ALS, owned by Verne Miners, Chicago, Illinois. Benjamin W. Brice was appointed paymaster general as of November 29, 1864. Lincoln's note was enclosed in a letter of U.S. Representative Ephraim R. Eckley to Brice of the same date, asking why Colonel Edward P. Fyffe, Twenty-sixth Ohio, Veteran Reserve Corps, could not get his pay. Brice endorsed the letter on December 21, 1864, that there appeared to be "no difficulty on the part of Col. Fyffe drawing his pay, except the want of funds. . . . Major H. A. Hutchins, is now in funds, and Col. Fyffe can be paid. . . ."

To Edwin M. Stanton[1]

   Hon. Secretary of War please see & hear this man.
   Dec. 20, 1864   A. LINCOLN

[1] Anderson Galleries Catalog 2193, November 15, 1927, No. 284. According to the catalog description this item is an autograph endorsement signed on a portion of an envelope.

[173]

To Lewis Wallace[1]

Major General Wallace   Executive Mansion
Baltimore, Md.   Washington, Dec. 20. 1864
    Suspend execution of James P. Boileau, until further order from
here.   A LINCOLN

[1] ALS, DNA WR RG 107, Presidential Telegrams, I, 265. No reply or further
reference to Boileau has been found.

To Benjamin F. Butler[1]

                                  Executive Mansion, Washington,
Major General Butler   Dec. 21, 1864.
    On the 9th. of August last I began to write you a letter, the in-
closed being a copy of so much as I then wrote. So far as it goes, it
embraces the views I then entertained, and still entertain. A little
relaxation of complaints made to me on the subject, occurring about
that time, the letter was not finished and sent. I now learn, correctly I suppose, that you have ordered an election, similar to the one
mentioned, to take place on the Eastern Shore of Virginia. Let this
be suspended, at least until conference with me, and obtaining my
approval. Yours truly   A. LINCOLN.

[1] ADfS, DLC-RTL; LS, RPB. The letter sent is in Hay's handwriting signed
by Lincoln. The enclosed copy of Lincoln's communication of August 9 (*supra*),
is also in Hay's handwriting.
    Butler telegraphed his reply on December 27:
    "I have just received your note relating to the Election on the Eastern Shore.
The President is incorrectly informed. I have not, nor has any officer under my
command ordered an election on that Shore.
    "The inhabitants asked of me, leave to hold a meeting to take into considera-
tion their relations to the state Government of Virginia. I replied that I would
not order such a meeting, but that if the people chose to assemble . . . to petition for a redress of supposed grievances, or to consider any question of civil
order I could see no military objection. . . .
    "I have heard nothing on the subject since, and do not know even when
the meeting is to be
    "Shall I issue an order to prevent their assembling to vote on civil affairs?"
(DLC-RTL. As published in *Private and Official Correspondence of General
Benjamin F. Butler*, V, 443, this telegram is misdated December 29.)
    See further Lincoln's telegram to Butler on December 28, *infra*.

To Mary Todd Lincoln[1]

Mrs A Lincoln   Washington
Continental Hotel   Dec. 21. 1864
    Do not come on the night train. It is too cold. Come in the morn-
ing.   A. LINCOLN

Please send above and oblige the President. JOHN HAY
A.P.S.

¹ D, RPB. This telegram is entirely in John Hay's handwriting. As printed both by Nicolay and Hay (VIII, 148) and Tarbell (Appendix, p. 357), it is misdated "1862." No reply has been found.

Pass for Slaughter S. Bradford¹

December 21, 1864

Allow the bearer, S. S. Bradford, to pass by any route to his home in Culpeper Co. Va, and there to remain so long as he does not misbehave. A. LINCOLN

Dec. 21. 1864.

¹ ADS-F, ISLA. See Lincoln to Wright, October 17, *supra*.

To Edwin M. Stanton¹

December 21, 1864

Submitted to the Secretary of War. The recommendations are excellent, & it is said that Col. Post was wounded, perhaps mortally at the late battles in front of Nashville. I commend the case to the special attention of the Secretary A. LINCOLN

Dec. 21. 1864

¹ AES, owned by Milton H. Shutes, Oakland, California. Lincoln's endorsement is written on a letter signed by Governor Richard Yates and other state officials of Illinois, November 29, 1864, recommending promotion of Colonel Philip Sidney Post, Fifty-ninth Illinois Volunteers, to brigadier general. Post was brevetted brigadier general of Volunteers as of December 16, 1864, the date of his citation for gallant and distinguished service in the battles before Nashville, Tennessee. In 1893 he was awarded the Congressional Medal of Honor.

Approval of Treasury Regulation No. 55¹

Executive Mansion
December 22. 1864.

I, Abraham Lincoln, President of the United States, having seen and considered the within amended Regulation numbered LV. prescribed by the Secretary of the Treasury, do hereby approve of the same, and I further declare and order that products moving in compliance with the said Regulation shall be exempt from seizure and from confiscation and forfeiture to the United States.

ABRAHAM LINCOLN.

¹ Copy, DNA RG 56, General Records of the Treasury Department, Copies of Letters from the Secretary of the Treasury, Volume VIII, Set BE, Restricted Commercial Intercourse. The original order has not been found. A copy of the amended Regulation, December 22, 1864, is as follows:

"Regulation LV. concerning Commercial Intercourse series of July 29. 1864, is hereby amended as follows:

"LV. All existing authorities to purchase products in insurrectionary States are hereby revoked; except that products purchased in good faith under such authorities, and paid for, in whole or in part, prior to the 29th. day of July 1864, may be transported to market as before the passage of the Act of July 2. 1864, subject to the following limitations and conditions; and included in the following classes:

"1st. Those which have been wholly paid for.

"2d. Those upon which part payment has been made, coupled with a legal obligation to pay the residue, so that the articles purchased are at the risk of that purchaser, and such payment is in no wise dependent upon their delivery.

"3d. Where part payment has been made, without such obligations as to the balance, so much of the products alleged to have been purchased as the amount actually advanced will pay for at the stipulated price.

"The original permits must be produced in each case, and proof furnished to the satisfaction of a proper permit officer and a Supervising or Assistant Special Agent, for the Agency or district in which proof is to be made that the property desired to be moved comes within one of the classes named above, and that the privilege conferred by the original permit has been in no way violated or abused,—a certificate of which facts must be endorsed upon the permit over their official signature, which permit, so endorsed, will then be considered as revived and in full force, to the extent specified in the endorsement, in accordance with this rule. W. P. FESSENDEN Sec. Treas." (*Ibid.*).

To John B. Majors[1]

Officer in command at   Executive Mansion,
St. Joseph, Mo.   Washington, Dec. 22, 1864.

Postpone the execution of Higswith, Holland & Way, for twenty days.   A. LINCOLN

[1] ALS, DNA WR RG 107, Presidential Telegrams, I, 266. Captain John B. Majors of the Forty-third Missouri Regiment was senior officer at St. Joseph. On December 22, Brigadier General James Craig of the Enrolled Missouri Militia, telegraphed Lincoln from St. Joseph: "I respectfully & earnestly recommend that the execution of Higswith Holland & Utz sentenced to be hung tomorrow in this city be postponed for twenty (20) days" (DLC-RTL). Lincoln misread "Utz" as "Way." A further error seems to have been made in transmitting the telegram, for the name "Higswith" is an error for "Highsmith." Concerning the cases of James P. Holland, John H. Utz, and Henry W. Highsmith, see Lincoln's further telegram to Majors, January 9, and his endorsement to Joseph Holt, January 11, 1865, *infra*.

Order Concerning John Bliss[1]

Executive Mansion Dec. 22, 1864

To-day John Bliss, of Co. L in 1st Vermont Cavalry, comes to me voluntarily, under apprehension of being treated as a deserter. Now on condition that he returns to his regiment at once and faithfully serves out his term . . . he is fully pardoned.   A. LINCOLN

[1] Anderson Galleries Catalog 1179, December 6, 1915, No. 233. According to the catalog description this item is an autograph note signed. The ellipsis is in the source. Lincoln's order was promulgated by AGO *Special Orders No. 465,* December 23, 1864.

Pass for James Harrison[1]

Executive Mansion,
Washington, Dec. 22, 1864.

Allow Mr. James Harrison, of St. Louis, Mo. at such point as he may choose, to pass our military lines, once and return, at his pleasure.   A. LINCOLN

[1] ADS, MoSHi; ADf, DLC-RTL. Letters from Edward Bates, December 12, and Samuel T. Glover and others, December 15, 1864, recommended Harrison to Lincoln (DLC-RTL). On December 17 at Washington, Harrison wrote Lincoln:

"Believing that I can command the influence and credit necessary to bring out a large amount of cotton from Red River and its tributaries, say from 10,000 bales upwards . . . and supposing that it would be an object of importance to the Government to get out cotton in large quantities; I have determined to ask permission to pass through our lines to go up Red River to the head quarters of the rebel commander to negotiate arrangements for his permission to trade. . . .

"When I shall have made arrangements with the Confederate authorities to bring out cotton, and for their protection to my Boats and property against seizure; I want your permission to take steam Boats through our lines to within the Confederate lines and return with their cargoes

"To accomplish this object . . . I respectfully ask an order from the President, or from the Secretaries of both the army and Navy to their respective commanders in that department. . . ." (*Ibid.*).

See further Lincoln's order of December 23, *infra.*

To James Speed[1]

Attorney General please make out a pardon in this case.

Dec. 22, 1864   A. LINCOLN

[1] AES, DNA RG 204, U.S. Pardon Attorney, A 537. Lincoln's endorsement is written on a letter from A. Q. Keasbey, Newark, New Jersey, October 3, 1864, asking pardon for Charles Donnelly, convicted of counterfeiting.

To Adoniram J. Warner[1]

Officer in command at   Executive Mansion
Indianapolis, Ia.   Washington, Dec. 22. 1864

Postpone, the execution of John Doyle Lennan *alias* Thomas Doyle, for ten days.   A. LINCOLN

[1] ALS, DNA WR RG 107, Presidential Telegrams, I, 267. On December 22, 1864, Felix Lennan of Indianapolis telegraphed Lincoln: "My brother John Doyle Lennan alias Thomas Doyle is under sentence of death for desertion and ordered to be shot tomorrow at Indianapolis Ind. I humbly petition you for the postponement of the execution for ten days. please give me an answer" (DLC-RTL). See further Lincoln to Warner, December 30, *infra.*

Endorsement[1]

If the facts within stated be shown to be true, let the transfer be
made.   A. Lincoln
    Dec. 23. 1864

[1] AES-P, ISLA. This endorsement has been removed from attendant papers.

Order Concerning James Harrison[1]

Executive Mansion,
Washington, December 23, 1864.

All Military and Naval commanders will please give to James
Harrison, Esq. of St. Louis, Missouri, (with any number of[2] Steam-
Boats not exceeding three, taking in tow any number of barges,
scows, flats, and the like, not having steam power, which they may
be able to so take, with[3] such goods & money, as the Treasury
agents may grant permits for under the rules of the Dept. and none
other, and only with crews to navigate the whole, and necessary
provisions for himself and said crews,) protection and safe conduct
from New-Orleans[4] or Memphis to Red River, and up said river
and its tributaries, till he shall pass beyond our Military lines, and
also give him such protection and safe conduct on his return to
our lines, back to New-Orleans[5] or Memphis, with any cargoes he
may bring; and on his safe return from beyond our lines, with said
boats and tows, allow him to repeat once or twice if he shall desire.
                                                ABRAHAM LINCOLN.

[1] DfS, DLC-RTL. The signed draft includes corrections in Lincoln's autograph as noted. Accompanying the draft is Harrison's signed pledge, also with
corrections by Lincoln:

"Washington, D.C. December 23, 1864.
"In consideration that the President of the United States today delivers to me
a paper of which the within is a copy, I pledge him my word of honor that whatever I may do thereunder shall be at my own expense and risk of person and
property, with no claim upon him or upon the government in any contingency
whatever; that I will take absolutely nothing into the insurgent lines, which
could be of value to them, except the boats, tows, goods money and provisions as
stated; and that I will not take said boats, tows, and other matters stated, [Lin-
coln amended "provisions" to "other matters stated"] or any of them, into said
insurgent lines, unless I shall first have the personal pledge of Gen. Kirby
Smith, or the officer in chief command, given directly by him to me, that said
boats and tows shall without condition, safely return to our Military lines.
                                                        "JAS HARRISON"

[2] Lincoln deleted "inferior" at this point.
[3] Lincoln revised to the present reading from "without money, and without
cargoes outgoing, and only with crews. . . ."
[4] Lincoln deleted "Cairo" and inserted "New-Orleans or Memphis."
[5] See note 4.

[178]

To Robert K. Stone[1]

Will Dr. Stone please make me a prescription for a ring worm?
Dec. 23, 1864.   A. LINCOLN.

[1] Copy, ISLA.

To Thomas J. Durant[1]

My Dear Sir
Executive Mansion, Washington,
December 24, 1864.

I have received the elegantly-mounted volume, commemorative
of the celebration in honor of the passage of the Ordinance of
Emancipation of the State of Louisiana, held on the 11th of June,
in New Orleans, which you, in behalf of the following citizens of
that State: Henry Raymond, Francois Boisdoré, John Smith, Peter
Hillud [Hillard?], Robert Smith, A. L. Young, Henry Chevanne
[Chevunne? Chevarre?], Lawrence Quanders, Rev. Geo. W. Steptoe, Rev. R. H. Steptoe, and Rev. S. W. Rogers, have had the goodness to transmit to me.[2]

I beg that you will express to the donors the assurance of my
grateful appreciation of their kindness, and that you will accept
my personal acknowledgements for the manner in which you have
conveyed this manifestation of their regard.

I am very truly Your Obedient Servant
Thomas J Durant Esq

[1] Df, DLC-Nicolay Papers. The draft is in John Hay's handwriting on Executive Mansion stationery. The letter was printed in the Washington *Daily Morning Chronicle* on January 31, 1865, with the following note: "On the passage of
the act of emancipation, an elegantly bound volume was sent to President Lincoln by the colored people of Louisiana in commemoration of the event. The
following letter of the President, after receiving the gift, was read by Thomas
J. Durant, Esq. on Wednesday [January 25], before a large assemblage of ladies,
gentlemen, and colored people."
[2] The book and the letter from Durant, December 8, 1864, accompanying it,
are in the Oliver R. Barrett Collection.

Endorsement
Concerning Samuel D. Lockwood[1]

Judge Lockwood, the writer, is one of the best men in the world.
File.   A.L.

Dec. 24, 1864.

[1] American Autograph Shop Catalog, March, 1939, No. 101. According to
the catalog description, Lincoln's endorsement was written on a letter from
Samuel D. Lockwood, Batavia, Kane County, Illinois, December 6, 1864. The
conclusion of Lockwood's letter is reproduced as follows:
". . . I feel fully conscious that heavier burden's & responsibilities never

rested on the mind and heart of any man, but I sincerely hope & believe, that you will come out of them all with an untarnished reputation & the complete establishment for our Country of the Glorious principle enunciated in the Declaration of Independence, 'That all men are created equal.' If such shall be the result of your sacrifices & labours, no man need ever aspire to a more glorious or a more benificent reputation. May God grant it.

"Please excuse this hasty scrawl. Ill health & cramp in my hand forbid my revising or copying it."

To Joseph Holt[1]

December 24, 1864

Judge Advocate General please report to me on this case.

Dec. 24, 1864   A. LINCOLN

Pardon for unexecuted part of sentence.   A. LINCOLN

Jan. 26, 1865

[1] AES, DNA WR RG 153, Judge Advocate General, NN 2740. Lincoln's endorsements are written on the court-martial record of August P. Dumont, contractor of Philadelphia, sentenced, November 3, 1864, on charges of willful neglect of duty, to $1,000 fine and imprisonment until the fine was paid or not to exceed one year.

To John McClelland[1]

John McClelland   Executive Mansion
Nashville, Tenn.   Washington, Dec. 24. 1864

A letter of yours is laid before me, in which you seek to have John S. Young, James Mallory & R. T. Bridges released, adding "My word for it they are innocent." It is fair to presume that you would not say this without *knowing* what you say to be true. But a telegraphic despatch of Gov. Johnson, now before me, says of this very man Mallory "has been guilty of the most outrageous and atrocious murders known to civilization" and that "the punishment of death is not half atonement for the crimes he has committed on the defenceless & unoffending Union-men of the country" As I know Gov. Johnson would not purposely misle[a]d me, I think it be well for you to communicate the particulars of your information to him.   A LINCOLN

[1] ALS, DNA WR RG 107, Presidential Telegrams, I, 268. This telegram as printed by Nicolay and Hay is incorrectly addressed to "John McClernand." John McClelland was assessor of internal revenue at Nashville (*U.S. Official Register*, 1865). His letter referred to by Lincoln has not been found. Andrew Johnson's telegram of December 3, 1864, reads in part as follows: "James R Mallory who was convicted of violation of the Laws & usages of civilized warfare of murder & two robberies sentenced to be hung on the second instant has been respited by Genl Thomas for a short time so that his friends can have an opportunity as they say to present circumstances which will mitigate his sentence. Two young ladies, one assuming to be his sister & the other his cousin asked & obtained a simple letter of introduction to the President & will be presented by

them in a few days. This man Mallory . . . has been a terror to the whole surrounding country and has been guilty of the most outrageous and atrocious murders known to civilization. . . . I told the two young ladies who will apply for the pardon that I could not even recommend a commutation of his punishment to imprisonment for life . . . & that the punishment of death was not half atonement for the crimes he had committed on the defenceless & unoffending Union men of the country. Duty & conscience required me to say as much to the President in this case." (DLC-RTL).

James R. Mallory, citizen of Tennessee, was sentenced to death by hanging, on charges of murder and violation of the laws and customs of war. On April 21, 1864, Lincoln approved the sentence, and on August 9, 1864, endorsed a second application for clemency, "Second application denied. August 9. 1864. A. LINCOLN" (DNA WR RG 153, Judge Advocate General, MM 1375). See further Lincoln to Miller, December 28, infra.

To William H. Seward[1]

December 24, 1864

Gen. C. S. Todd, once much of a man, is now superannuated, and would be an incumbrance upon the Commander in New-Orleans, unjustifiable in me to impose upon him.   A. LINCOLN

Dec. 24. 1864.

[1] AES, NAuE. Lincoln's endorsement is written on Seward's letter of December 23, 1864, to Representative George H. Yeaman: "I have had the honor to receive and have commended to the consideration of the President, your note of the 21st instant and the accompanying letter addressed to me by C. S. Todd, Esqr."

A letter from Charles S. Todd to Francis P. Blair, Sr., November 29, 1864, sets forth Todd's wish to live in New Orleans, the inadequacy of his current salary as assessor of internal revenue at Owensboro, Kentucky, and his belief that "as a pupil of [William Henry] Harrison and Minister to Military Governments guided by [Simon] Bolivar and [Czar] Nicholas" he would be valuable to General Nathaniel P. Banks in a military appointment (DLC-RTL).

To William T. Sherman[1]

Executive Mansion, Washington,

My dear General Sherman.   Dec. 26, 1864.

Many, many, thanks for your Christmas-gift—the capture of Savannah.

When you were about leaving Atlanta for the Atlantic coast, I was *anxious*, if not fearful; but feeling that you were the better judge, and remembering that "nothing risked, nothing gained" I did not interfere. Now, the undertaking being a success, the honor is all yours; for I believe none of us went farther than to acquiesce. And, taking the work of Gen. Thomas into the count, as it should be taken, it is indeed a great success. Not only does it afford the obvious and immediate military advantages; but, in showing to the world that your army could be divided, putting the stronger part to an important new service, and yet leaving enough to vanquish the old opposing force of the whole—Hood's army—it brings those who sat in darkness, to see a great light. But what next? I suppose it will be safer if I leave Gen. Grant and yourself to decide.

Please make my grateful acknowledgments to your whole army, officers and men. Yours very truly   A. LINCOLN.

[1] ALS, DLC; LS copy, DLC-Stanton Papers. The signed copy in the Stanton Papers is in John Hay's handwriting and is endorsed by Lincoln at the top of the first page "(Original sent by Gen. Logan)." General Sherman's despatch to Lincoln from Savannah, Georgia, via Fort Monroe, Virginia, December 22, 1864, was received on December 25: "I beg to present you as a Christmas gift the city of Savannah with 150 heavy guns & plenty of ammunition & also about 25000 bales of cotton." (DLC-RTL).

Sherman replied on January 6, 1865: "I am gratified at the receipt of your letter of Dec 26, at the hand of General Logan. Especially to observe that you appreciate the division I made of my army, and that each part was duly proportioned to its work. The motto, 'Nothing ventured Nothing won' which you refer to is most appropriate, and should I venture too much and happen to lose I shall bespeak your charitable influence. I am ready for the Great Next as soon as I can complete certain preliminaries, and learn of Genl Grant his and your preference of intermediate 'objectives.' " (DLC-RTL).

To Gideon Welles[1]

Hon. Secretary of the Navy.   Executive Mansion,
Sir: Washington, Dec. 26. 1864.

The unexecuted part of the sentence of the General Court-Martial in the case of Com. Charles Wilkes, U.S.N. is hereby remitted, this remission to take effect at the end of one year from the day on which the sentence took effect.   ABRAHAM LINCOLN

[1] ALS, DNA WR NB RG 45, Executive Letters, No. 178. Commodore Charles Wilkes had been sentenced by court-martial, April 27, 1864, to be reprimanded and suspended from duty for three years, for publication of official correspondence. See Lincoln's communications to Browning and to Ewing, May 16, *supra*.

To J. Bates Dickson[1]

Officer in Command at   Executive Mansion
Lexington, Ky: Washington, Dec. 27. 1864

If within your power, send me the particulars of the causes for which Lieut. Govr. Jacobs was arrested and sent away.

                                                    A. LINCOLN

[1] ALS, DNA WR RG 107, Presidential Telegrams, I, 269. See Lincoln to Bramlette, November 22, *supra*. On December 26, 1864, Richard T. Jacob wrote Lincoln from Richmond, Virginia: "On the night of the 11th of November last, I was arrested by the order of . . . General Burbridge at my country home. . . . I was carried to Lexington, and kept at General McLeans head quarters some two hours. I courted [?] and confidently expected to have had an interview with General Burbridge. I was by his orders carried under strict guard, and expelled through the Federal lines under the penalty of death if I returned

during the war. I was thus forced by necessity into the Confederate lines, to accept the hospitality and protection of a people that I had fought against. . . . A poor return for wounds received, and hard service rendered to ones country. Even a thief has the boon of being condemned before he is punished. . . . It is difficult to defend ones self, when no charges are preferred. I have not even a conjecture to go on except a telegram that I had cut out of the Cincinnatti Commercial. Which is as follows, 'The Post's Washington letter says the arrest of Lieutenant Governor Jacob will lead to important disclosures. There are rumors of a wide spread conspiracy existing in that State, not to take it over to a rebel confederacy, but to inaugurate a second revolution, the object of which is to make Kentucky independent of the General Government.' If my arrest would lead to important disclosures would not common sense have suggested that I should have been detained and examined. If there was a wide spread conspiracy I knew not of it, nor do I believe for one moment there was any such. I never was connected with a conspiracy. . . . True Mr. President I was opposed to your re-election, and it is the only charge that can with truth be brought against me. . . . Three days after the election I was seized. I find this in the Richmond Sentinel of the first of December taken from the Louisville Journal. [']We are happy to announce that President Lincoln has consented to the release of Lieutenant Governor Jacob and Col. Frank Wolford. We sincerely hope that this may be the commencement of a new policy. . . .' Now Sir, I wish to find out whether this is true or not, and if so whether you will not order that I be passed through the lines to return to my duties as Lieutenant Governor of Kentucky. . . . As I have committed no crime, I ask not for pardon, but merely simple justice. . . ."

Captain J. Bates Dickson, assistant adjutant general in command in the absence of General Stephen G. Burbridge, answered Lincoln's telegram on December 28, 1864: "So far as I am informed, . . . Jacob's offense was making treasonable and seditious speeches, calculated and intended to weaken the power of the Government. . . . His arrest was advised by Doctor [Robert J.] Breckinridge and other prominent loyal men of Kentucky. General Burbridge will address you fully on the subject upon his return. I have had no communication with him since the 14th instant, and do not know his present location" (OR, I, XLV, II, 402).

See further Lincoln to Grant, January 5, 1865, *infra*.

To Haidie M. Jones[1]

Executive Mansion Washington,

Miss Haidie M. Jones. Dec 27. 1864

I have received your pretty present by the hand of Hon. Mr Ashley, and for which please accept my thanks Yours truly

A. LINCOLN

1 Copy, ISLA. James M. Ashley was U.S. representative from Toledo, Ohio. No further identification of Miss Jones or her present has been found.

To John Maclean[1]

Executive Mansion, Washington,

My Dear Sir December 27, 1864.

I have the honour to acknowledge the reception of your note of the 20th of December, conveying the announcement that the Trustees of the College of New Jersey have conferred upon me the Degree of Doctor of Laws.

The assurance conveyed by this high compliment, that the course of the government which I represent has received the approval of a body of gentlemen of such character and intelligence in this time of public trial, is most grateful to me.

Thoughtful men must feel that the fate of civilization upon this continent is involved in the issue of our contest. Among the most gratifying proofs of this conviction is the hearty devotion everywhere exhibited by our schools and colleges to the national cause.

I am most thankful if my labors have seemed to conduce to the preservation of those institutions under which alone we can expect good government and in its train sound learning and the progress of the liberal arts.

I am sir very truly   Your Obedient Servant   A. LINCOLN
Dr. John MacLean

[1] LS, NjP. President John Maclean of the College of New Jersey, Princeton, wrote Lincoln on December 20, 1864:

"I have the honour to inform you, that, at the semi-annual meeting of the Trustees of this College this day, the Degree of *Doctor of Laws* was conferred upon you, by the unanimous consent of the Board.

"Hoping that this expression of their respect for you both personally, and as the Head of our Nation will not be unacceptable to you, I am most sincerely and with the highest respect. . . ." (DLC-RTL).

Knox College at Galesburg, Illinois, was first to honor Lincoln with an LL.D., on July 4, 1860, and Columbia College, New York City, came next with an LL.D. conferred on June 26, 1861.

Memorandum: Appointment of William H. Lee[1]

[c. December 27, 1864]
West-Point. Mr. Lee, the father, was in the Ills. Leg. 1854-5.

[1] AE, DNA WR RG 94, U.S. Military Academy, 1864, No. 362. Lincoln's endorsement is written on a letter of William L. Lee, Rock Island, Illinois, December 27, 1864, to Edwin M. Stanton, submitting the application of his son William H. Lee for appointment to West Point. No record of Lee's appointment has been found.

Memorandum: Appointment of Franklin Yeaton[1]

Executive Mansion,
Washington, Dec. 27, 1864.
I this morning promise Mr. Fessenden that when I shall appoint the ten cadets at large for the now incoming year, Franklin Yeaton shall be one.   A. LINCOLN

[184]

[1] ADS, DNA WR RG 94, U.S. Military Academy, 1864, No. 225. Franklin Yeaton of New Brunswick, Maine, entered West Point in July 1865 and graduated in 1869.

Order Concerning William N. Symington[1]

Allow William Symington, now a prisoner at Fort Warren to leave there and report to me now at Washington.   A. LINCOLN.

December 27, 1864.

[1] Copy, ISLA. Orville H. Browning's *Diary* records on December 27: "President sent for me. . . . He wished to talk . . . about releasing Mrs Symingtons Son who is a prisoner at Fort Lafayette [*sic*]. . . ." Under date of January 11, 1865, Browning records: "At 9 O'clock this morning went with Wm N Symington to the Presidents and got a pass for him to go to Richmond & report himself to his uncle Andrew Johnston to be exchanged for any prisoner of ours, either civil or military. If no exchange can be effected he is to return here and report to me. . . ."

Order for Hanson A. Risley[1]

December 27. 1864

I, H A Risley agent for the purchase of products of insurrectionary states on behalf of the Government of the United States at Norfolk Va. do hereby certify that I have agreed to purchase from I. Seymour ten thousand bales of Cotton and one million feet of Lumber, which products it is represented are or will be at points on or near the lines of the United States forces in the State of Florida on or before the first day of May 1865 and which he stipulates shall be delivered to me unless prevented from so doing by the authority of the United States.

I therefore request safe conduct for the said Seymour and his agents and his means of transportation and said products from the points on or near the lines of the United States forces in Florida aforesaid to Fernindena when the products so transported are to be sold and delivered to me under the stipulations referred to above and pursuant to regulations prescribed by the Secretary of the Treasury   H A RISLEY

Sup. Spl Agt &

Executive Mansion Dec 27. 1864

An authorised agent of the Treasury Department having with the approval of the secretary of the Treasury contracted for the products above mentioned and the party having agreed to sell and deliver the same to such agent, it is ordered, that products moving in compliance with and for fulfilment of said contract and being transported to such agent or under his direction shall be free from seizure or detention by any officer of the Government: and commandants of military departments, districts, posts and detachments, naval stations, gun boats, flotillas and fleets, will observe this order and give the said Seymour his agents and means of transportation free and unmolested passage for the purpose of getting said products through the lines, other than blockaded lines, and safe conduct within our lines, while the same are moving in compliance with Regulations of the secretary of the Treasury and for fulfilment of said contract with the agent of the Government.

ABRAHAM LINCOLN

[1] DS, RPB.

To Benjamin F. Butler[1]

Office U.S. Military Telegraph,
War Department,
Major General Butler
Fort-Monroe, Va   Washington, D.C., Dec. 28. 1864.

I think you will find that the Provost-Marshal on the Eastern Shore has, as by your authority, issued an order, not for a *meeting*, but for an *election*. The order printed in due form was shown to me, but as I did not retain it I can not give you a copy. If the people on their own motion wish to hold a peaceful meeting I suppose you need not to hinder them.   A LINCOLN

[1] ALS, DNA WR RG 107, Presidential Telegrams, I, 271. See note to Lincoln's communication to Butler on December 21, *supra*. Colonel Frank J. White wrote Butler on December 30 from Eastville, Virginia: "In obedience to your telegram, received this morning, I have the honor to enclose the only order issued by me concerning an election upon this shore. This order was issued by me in obedience to what I supposed to be your instructions. . . ." (*Private and Official Correspondence of General Benjamin F. Butler*, V, 444). The order has not been found.

To John G. Foster[1]

Executive Mansion,
General: Washington, 28 December, 1864.
The bearer, Mr. Charles D. Chase, visits your Department on business. He is a gentleman with whom I am personally acquainted and whom I can commend to your courteous consideration. Yours very truly   A LINCOLN
Major General Foster

[1] LS, IHi. Except for Lincoln's signature this letter on Executive Mansion stationery is in John Hay's handwriting. On the verso is an undated note written to Foster by Charles D. Chase: "Being unable to attend to my business South

[186]

in person, I beg to introduce Mr W C Churchill, for whom I ask any facilities which might have been extended me from the letter of the President."

Chase and Churchill have not been further identified. General Foster was in command of the Department of the South at Hilton Head, South Carolina.

To Ulysses S. Grant[1]

"Cyphar"   Office U.S. Military Telegraph,
Lieut. Genl. Grant   War Department, Washington, D.C.,
City-Point, Va.   Dec. 28. 5/30. P.M. 1864.

If there be no objection, please tell me what you now under-stand of the Wilmington expedition, present & prospective.

A. LINCOLN

[1] ALS, DNA WR RG 107, Presidential Telegrams, I, 270. Grant replied on the same day: "The Wilmington expedition has proven a gross and culpable failure. Many of the troops are now back here. Delays and free talk of the object of the expedition enabled the enemy to move troops to Wilmington to defeat it. After the expedition sailed from Fort Monroe three days of fine weather was squandered, during which the enemy was without a force to protect himself. Who is to blame I hope will be known." (OR, I, XLII, III, 1087).

The joint expedition under Admiral David D. Porter and General Benjamin F. Butler was abandoned on December 25 when Butler and General Godfrey Weitzel decided that Fort Fisher at Wilmington, North Carolina, could not be carried by assault.

To Joseph Holt[1]

Let this man, Louis A. Welton be enlarged, the sentence against him standing as a security for his good behavior.   A. LINCOLN

Dec. 28. 1864.

[1] AES, DNA WR RG 153, Judge Advocate General, NN 2120. See Lincoln's communication to Morgan, Weed, and Raymond, August 31, *supra*. A letter from Welton dated October 23, 1864, undertakes to defend his action on the ground that although a contract to supply the rebels was found on his person, his intention was to use his connections in the South to obtain large amounts of cotton for the United States (DLC-RTL). On December 20, Henry T. Blow wrote Lincoln:

"From the conversation with you to day, I am encouraged to hope that you will bear with me while I say something in regard to the release of Mr. L A Welton.

"I never learned the circumstances which proved his guilt . . . until you informed me of them, but concluded of course that our Government had acted justly. . . .

"I do not hesitate to say also, that to ask the pardon of any man who has been tried and found guilty of so grave a crime . . . is a hard task, and only under-taken for the following reasons.

"Mr. Welton is the brother in law of Wm. M. Fishback one of the Editors & proprietors of the Missouri Democrat. Mr. F. is deeply attached to his wife's brother, and believes that however circumstances may have been against him, that he is *innocent*. . . . Mr. Fishback is loyal to the core, he has for years been . . . the proprietor . . . of a paper which has done as much to further the cause of freedom & patriotism as any printed in the West. . . .

"Such a man *deserves*, I am sure *enjoys* your sympathy & respect, he prays you to pardon Welton. . . .

"I knew Welton before he acted so badly . . . and . . . if I thought for a moment, that he would ever again dishonor himself & be faithless to his . . . country, I would be the last one to appeal to you in his behalf. . . ." (*Ibid.*).

Lincoln's order for Welton's release was promulgated on December 30, 1864, in AGO *Special Orders No. 475.*

To John F. Miller[1]

Officer in command at	Executive Mansion,
Nashville, Tenn.	Washington, Dec. 28. 1864.

Suspend execution of James R. Mallory, for six weeks from Friday the 30th. of this month, which time I have given his friends, to make proof, if they can, upon certain points.　　A. LINCOLN

[1] ALS, DNA WR RG 107, Presidential Telegrams, I, 272. See Lincoln to McClelland, December 24, *supra.* Brigadier General John F. Miller replied on the same day: "Your dispatch granting respite to James R. Mallory for six (6) weeks from thirtieth (30) received" (DLC-RTL).

See further Lincoln's telegram to Miller, February 4, 1865, *infra.*

Pass for Francis P. Blair, Sr.[1]

Allow the bearer, F. P. Blair, Senr. to pass our lines, go South and return　　　　　　　　　　　　　　　　　　A. LINCOLN

Dec. 28. 1864

[1] ADS, DLC-RTL. This card pass is preserved with the autograph document addressed to the House of Representatives, February 10, 1865, *infra.*

On December 30, 1864, Blair wrote Jefferson Davis two letters, copies of which are among the Lincoln Papers. The covering letter is as follows:

"The loss of some papers of importance . . . which I suppose may have been taken by some persons who had access to my house when Genl Earlys army was in possession of my place induces me to ask the privilege of visiting Richmond & beg the favor of you to facilitate my inquiries in regard to them."

The second letter sets forth Blair's real purpose:

"The fact stated in the enclosed note may seem to answer inquiries as to the object of my visit, which if allowed by you I would not communicate fully to any one but yourself. The main purpose I have in seeing you is to explain the views I entertain in reference to the state of the affairs of our country & to submit to your consideration ideas which in my opinion you may turn to good & possibly bring to practical results that may not only repair all the ruin the war has brought upon the Nation but contribute to . . . the welfare of other nations that have suffered from it

"In candor I must say to you in advance that I come to you wholly unaccredited except in so far as I may be by having permission to pass our lines & to offer to you my own suggestions—suggestions which I have submitted to no one in authority on this side & will not without my conversation with you may lead me to suppose they may lead to something practicable. With the hope of such result, if allowed I will confidentially unbosom my heart frankly & without reserve. You will of course hold in reserve all that is not proper to be said to one coming as I do merely as a private citizen and addressing one clothed with the highest responsibilities

"Unless the great interests now at stake induce you to attribute more importance to my application than it would otherwise command I would not expect that you would invite the intrusion. I venture however to submit the matter to your judgment."

For Lincoln's report on Blair's mission, see the communication to the House of Representatives, February 10, 1865, *infra*.

To Edwin M. Stanton[1]

The writer of this is Gen. Grant's father. Let Mr. McKenezie be appointed if his services are needed.   A. LINCOLN
     Dec. 28. 1864

[1] AES-P, ISLA. Lincoln's endorsement is written on a letter from Jesse R. Grant, Covington, Kentucky, November 10, 1864, recommending appointment of Alexander McKenzie of Kentucky as quartermaster. McKenzie was appointed captain and assistant quartermaster of Volunteers as of January 28, 1865.

To Edwin M. Stanton[1]

I specially request that the Secretary of War give a hearing to these men—representatives of Co. F of 4. Mass. Heavy Artillery.
     Dec. 28. 1864   A. LINCOLN

[1] ALS-P, ISLA. Twelve unattached companies of heavy artillery raised in the summer of 1864 for coastal defense in Massachusetts were sent to Washington in September to garrison forts around the District of Columbia. On November 12, 1864, these companies were consolidated into the Fourth Massachusetts Heavy Artillery (AGO *Special Orders No. 395*), and continued in the defenses of the capital until mustered out on June 17, 1865.

To Benjamin F. Butler[1]

                        Executive Mansion, Washington,
Major General Butler   Dec. 29, 1864.
     There is a man in Co I. 11th. Conn. Vols. 1 Brigade 3. Division 24th. Army Corps, at Chapins Farm, Va, under the assumed name of Wm. Stanley, but whose real name is Frank R. Judd; and who is under arrest, and probably about to be tried for desertion. He is the son of our present Minister to Prussia, who is a close personal friend of Senator Trumbull and myself. We are not willing for the boy to be shot, but we think it as well that his trial go regularly on, suspending execution until further order from me & reporting to me   A. LINCOLN

[189]

[1] ALS, DNA WR RG 107, Presidential Telegrams, I, 273. See Lincoln to Stanton, November 21, 1863. The case of Frank R. Judd is tangled. Following his enlistment in the Eighth Illinois Cavalry on February 6, 1864, he was appointed to West Point, where he reported on June 4, 1864, but left without taking his entrance examination. He enlisted as Frank Judson in the Third Massachusetts Cavalry on July 15, 1864, and was listed as a deserter on September 30, 1864. He enlisted in the Eleventh Connecticut Volunteers under the name of William Stanley on November 26, 1864. See further Lincoln to Ord, January 19, 1865.

To Thomas B. Fairleigh[1]

Officer in command at   Executive Mansion,
Louisville Kentucky   Washington, Dec. 29th, 1864.

Suspend execution of death sentence of George S. Owen until further orders, and forward record of trial for examination

                           A. LINCOLN
Maj. Eckert

Please send the above telegram   Yours   JNO G NICOLAY

[1] D, DNA WR RG 107, Presidential Telegrams, I, 274. This telegram, in the hand of Nicolay, bears his autograph signature but not Lincoln's. Thomas B. Fairleigh replied on December 30: "No such man here as Geo S Owen under sentence your despatch has been forwarded to Division District & Dept Head Quarters" (DLC-RTL). George S. Owen has not been further identified.

To James Speed[1]

            Executive Mansion, Washington,
Hon. Attorney General   Dec. 29, 1864.

Please give me your opinion in writing whether the Secretary of the Navy, or any of his subordinates, is bound in law, on application of individuals, to furnish exemplified copies of records, or parts of records, of Naval Courts-Martial, on file in the Navy Department.

Also, whether the Secretary of the Navy, or any of his subordinates is bound in law to answer to a Commission of a State court, directing the taking of his or their testimony, as to the contents of records of Naval Courts-Martial on file in the Navy Department.

                           ABRAHAM LINCOLN

[1] ALS copy (ADfS?), DLC-RTL; LS, DNA RG 60, Papers of Attorney General, 1864, Box 117. Attorney General Speed replied in a twelve-page opinion on January 3, 1865. His conclusions were: ". . . the written record of the proceedings before a naval Court martial becomes, when the proceedings are consummated by the action of the proper revisory authority, the record of an adjudicated case tried and determined by a legally constituted court of justice; and . . . any limitation to an exemplified copy of such a record on file in the

Navy Department, when properly applied for by an individual, would be contrary to law. . . .

"With respect to the *second* point submitted to me, I am of opinion, that the Secretary of the Navy, and any of his subordinates, having knowledge of the contents of records of naval courts martial on file . . . after the proceedings have been consummated . . . are bound in law to answer to a commission of a State Court directing the taking of his and their testimony as to the contents of such records. . . ." (DLC-RTL).

To Edwin M. Stanton[1]

If the services are needed let this appointment be made.

Dec. 29, 1864   A. LINCOLN

[1] Retz & Storm Catalog, No. 110. According to the catalog description, Lincoln's endorsement appears on the verso of a petition signed by Richard Yates and others, October 10, 1864, for appointment of Orlu C. Richardson as commissary. Richardson had resigned as captain in the Thirtieth Illinois Infantry on August 12, 1864. He was appointed captain and commissary as of March 2, 1865.

Endorsement[1]

Send some papers in these cases.   A. LINCOLN.

Dec. 30, 1864

[1] American Art Association Catalog, December 3, 1923, No. 558. According to the catalog description, this clipped endorsement has on the verso, "John B. Hibbitt, Private Co. A 9th Cavalry Confined at Rock Island—Papers on file at Commissary General Wm. R. Neblett Co. C." No further reference has been found.

Endorsement[1]

Send me papers in this case.   A. LINCOLN

Dec. 30, 1864

[1] Stan. V. Henkels Catalog, October 9, 1914, No. 1194. According to the catalog description, on the back of this clipped endorsement appear part of four lines in Lincoln's autograph.

To Elijah C. Middleton[1]

Mr. E. C. Middleton   Executive Mansion,
Dear Sir.   Washington, Dec. 30, 1864.

Your picture presented by Mr. Lutz is, in the main, very good. From a line across immediately above the eye-brows, downward it appears to me perfect. Above such line I think it is not so good,— that is, while it gives perhaps a better fore-head, it is not quite true to the original. If you were present I could tell you wherein, but I can not well do so on paper. The next best thing I suppose would be to carefully study a photograph   Yours truly   A LINCOLN

[1] ALS, NN. No communication from Elijah C. Middleton has been found, but his firm (Middleton, [Hines] Strabridge & [D. C.] Fabronius) were lithographers at Cincinnati, Ohio, who published a chromolithograph of Lincoln in the autumn of 1864. Mr. Lutz has not been identified.

To Adoniram J. Warner[1]

Executive Mansion Washington
Col. Warner– Indianapolis, Ia.   Dec. 30. 1864

It is said that you were on the Court-Martial that tried John Lennan, and that you are disposed to advise his being pardoned and sent to his regiment. If this be true, telegraph me to that effect at once.   A. LINCOLN

[1] ALS, DNA WR RG 107, Presidential Telegrams, I, 275. See Lincoln to Warner, December 22, *supra*. Colonel Adoniram J. Warner replied on the same day: "I do not advise that Jno Lenon be pardoned and sent to his regt   he enlisted under a false name & I believe with the intention of deserting after drawing his bounty. In consideration however of his age & his conduct since his trial I could recommend that his sentence be commuted to hard labor for life" (DLC-RTL).

To Ethan A. Hitchcock[1]

Gen. Hitchcock, please see & hear this lady.
Dec. 31. 1864.   A. LINCOLN

[1] AES, IHi. Lincoln's endorsement is written on a letter from James Pollock, director of the United States Mint at Philadelphia, December 29, 1864, introducing Mrs. G. J. Laurence: "She desires to have her nephew Lt. G. L. Brown of the 101st P.V. now a prisoner at Columbia S.C. released or exchanged. . . ."

Order Designating Offices to Receive Subscriptions to Union Pacific Railroad[1]

December 31, 1864

By the authority conferred upon the President of the United States by the 2d. section of the act of Congress, approved July 2d., 1864, entitled "An act to amend an act to aid in the construction of a Railroad and Telegraph line from the Missouri River to the Pacific Ocean," &c. &c.

I, Abraham Lincoln, President of the United States, do hereby designate the Merchants' National Bank, Boston; the Chicago and

Rock Island Railroad Company's Office, Chicago; the First National Bank at ——— Philadelphia; the First National Bank at Baltimore; the First National Bank at ——— Cincinnati; and the Third National Bank at St. Louis, in addition to the General Office of the Union Pacific Railroad Company, in the city of New York, as the places at which the said Union Pacific Railroad Company shall cause books to be kept open to receive subscriptions to the capital stock of said Company.   ABRAHAM LINCOLN

Washington, D.C.

December 31st., 1864.

[1] DS, DNA NR RG 48, Department of Interior, Union Pacific Railroad, Package 239.

To James Speed[1]

Attorney General please make out pardons in these two cases.

Dec. 31. 1864   A. LINCOLN

[1] AES, CSmH. Lincoln's endorsement is written on a letter from Representative Austin A. King, December 31, 1864, asking pardon for Levi Brashear and William A. Guthrie, both of Platte County, Missouri, indicted for conspiracy in April, 1862.

To Edwin M. Stanton[1]

Executive Mansion, Washington,

Hon. Secretary of War.   Dec. 31, 1864.

You may remember that some time in June last (I think) an Assistant Inspector General on Col. Speer's[2] staff, in Gen. Butler's army, by name Andrew J. Smith, was convicted of a rape upon a colored girl. Gen. Butler, Mr. Holt, and yourself, each in turn, on examination of the evidence, thought there was no doubt of his guilt, while I thought there was some slight room for doubt on the question of personal indentification [sic]. I concluded however, to let him suffer a while, and then discharge him. Twice within two or three weeks I made a short order for his pardon for the unexecuted part of the sentence, which, however it seems has not yet been done. Let it be done now. Yours truly   A. LINCOLN

[1] ALS, DNA WR RG 94, Adjutant General, Letters Received, P 1567 (with V-31-VS-1865). On November 28 Lincoln had endorsed the record in the case of Lieutenant Andrew J. Smith, Eleventh Pennsylvania Cavalry, sentenced to prison for ten years for rape: "Pardon for unexecuted part of sentence Nov. 28. 1864, A. LINCOLN." Again on December 12, he endorsed the record "Pardon Dec. 12, 1864 A. LINCOLN" (DNA WR RG 153, Judge Advocate General, NN 2099). No record of the promulgation of Lincoln's order has been found.

[2] Colonel Samuel P. Spear.

To Edwin M. Stanton[1]

Please send me the papers within refered to.
Dec. 31. 1864   A. LINCOLN

[1] AES, owned by Dale Carnegie, New York City. Lincoln's endorsement appears on a letter of E. A. Manning, "Pastor D st. M.E. Church, So. Boston," to Senator Charles Sumner, May 30, 1864, setting forth his physical disability for which local authorities had refused to exempt him from the draft. Sumner endorsed on June 1, 1864: "I hope you will be able to grant the within request. It seems strange that the local officers have failed to do it." No further reference has been found.

To Adoniram J. Warner[1]

Col. A. J. Warner   Executive Mansion, Washington,
Indianapolis, Ia.   Decr. 31. 1864.

Suspend execution of John Lennan until further order from me & in the mean time send me the record of his trial.

A. LINCOLN

[1] ALS, DNA WR RG 107, Presidential Telegrams, I, 276. See Lincoln to Warner, December 30, *supra*.

Endorsement[1]

[1865]

This application is made on the idea that the incumbent is to go out at the end of four years.   A.L.

[1] AES, DNA NR RG 48, Indian Agencies, Applications, Choctaw, Box 1271. Lincoln's undated endorsement is written on an envelope marked "D. W. Houston/Garnett Kansas/Application for the office of Agent of the Choctaw Indians." No record has been found of Houston's appointment.

Endorsement[1]

Will Sec. of Treasury and Comr. of Int. Revenue, please file & preserve.   A LINCOLN
    21. 1865.

[1] AES, MS. Lincoln's endorsement, with the name of the month cut off, has been clipped from an envelope.

Endorsement Concerning Robert H. Hendershot[1]

[c. January 1, 1865]

I know something of this boy, and believe he is very brave, manly and worthy.   A. LINCOLN.

1 William S. Dodge, *Robert Henry Hendershot; or, The Brave Drummer Boy of the Rappahannock* (Chicago, 1867), p. vi. According to the source, Lincoln's endorsement appears on a letter of Francis E. Spinner, January 1, 1865, recommending Hendershot for appointment to West Point. See Lincoln's letter to Stanton, March 15, 1864, *supra.*

To Salmon P. Chase[1]

Chief Justice Chase   Executive Mansion
My dear Sir: Washington, Jan. 2. 1865.

Without your note of to-day, I should have felt assured that some sufficient reason had detained you. Allow me to condole with you in the sad bereavement you mention   Yours truly   A. LINCOLN

1 ADfS, DLC-RTL. On January 2, 1865, Chase wrote Lincoln: "The death of my only surviving sister prevented me from joining personally in the congratulations of this morning. But let me assure you that no one more earnestly wishes every blessing of the New Year to you and yours. . . ." (DLC-RTL). Chase referred to the customary call of government officers to pay their New Year's respect.

Reply to a Delegation of Kentuckians[1]

January 2, 1865

You howled when Butler went to New-Orleans. Others howled when he was removed from that command. Somebody has been howling ever since at his assignment to military command. How long will it be before you, who are howling for his assignment to rule Kentucky, will be howling to me to remove him?

1 New York *Tribune*, January 4, 1865. Lincoln's reply was made to a delegation of Kentuckians who applied "to have Gen. Butler assigned to a command that should embrace their State." The account notes further, that the Kentuckians in reply persisted in their demand for Butler.

To William H. Seward[1]

Executive Mansion Washington,
Hon. Sec. of State   Jan. 3. 1865

A hungarian by the name of Foegelmeisy, was on Gen. Stahl's staff, and by his going out of active service is thrown out. Some of our Pennsylvania friends are desirous to get him a Consulship. Can you find one for him? If you can, I will ascertain the Christian name. Yours truly   A. LINCOLN.

1 ALS, NAuE. Frederick W. Seward endorsed this letter, "Appoint." The resignation of Colonel Philip Figyelmesy (Figyelmessy), additional aide-de-camp on the staff of General Julius H. Stahel, was accepted as of December

20, 1864 (AGO *Special Orders No. 45*, January 28, 1865), and his appointment as consul at Demerara, British Guiana, was confirmed by the Senate on January 30, 1865.

To James Speed[1]

Attorney General please make out a pardon in this case.

Jan. 3, 1865.   A. LINCOLN

[1] AES, DNA RG 204, U.S. Pardon Attorney, A 577. Lincoln's endorsement appears on a copy of the conviction of Edward Tichenor (Tichnor), July 13, 1864, in the U.S. District Court of Oregon on charges of cutting timber from public lands.

Cotton Permit for Fergus Peniston[1]

Executive Mansion,
Washington, January 4th. 1865.

Whereas satisfactory evidence, has been furnished to me by Fergus Peniston, that he is now and was prior to April 1864 the legitimate owner of large amounts of cotton and naval stores situated in Louisiana and Southern Mississippi and reposing special trust and confidence in said Peniston, I do by these presents, authorize him to proceed with steamboats barges and other conveyances, at his own risk, up and down the Mississippi river and land at any points on said river between Natchez & Port Hudson, also up and down Red river and its tributaries and navigate the waters of Lakes Pontchartrain & Borgne to and from East & West Pascagoula and mouth of Pearl River and up and down Pearl & Pascagoula Rivers for the purpose of bringing out Twenty three Thousand Six Hundred & Forty Bales of Cotton and Seventeen Thousand Two Hundred Barrels of naval stores and continue said voyages until this stated amount of cotton & naval stores shall have been brought by him to new orleans. And in order to secure the products specified in this permit, I do furthermore authorize said Peniston to take on his boats or conveyances outside the Military lines of the United States and carry to any of the above designated localities, plantation supplies to the extent of Thirty per cent of the value of the cotton or naval stores brought to new orleans by his vessels.

Nothing in this permit is to be so construed as to prevent said Peniston from disposing of said cotton or naval stores in new orleans or new york at his option, after payment of the Internal Revenue & other taxes, fixed by Congress, not including however the Twenty five per cent tax.

All officers of the army or navy of the United States & civil officers of the Government are hereby particularly required not only to not obstruct but to extend to said Peniston all facilities that may be required to carry out the design of this permit which is the introduction of cotton and naval stores within the Military lines of the United States.

[1] Df (copy), DLC-RTL. The unsigned draft or copy is written on Executive Mansion stationery. On January 3 Hannibal Hamlin wrote Lincoln: "I have confered with Mr Peniston in relation to the action you have so kindly taken in his case, and the Permit you have given him to obtain the cotton contracted for. The permit meets that case fully, but does not meet the case of the cotton owned and paid for. If you will allow him to explain the matter to you, I am sure you will see it is as I state. May I not ask that you will see him, and also that you will give your permit to him to get the cotton he has paid for. *I will regard it as a favor to me.*" (DLC-RTL).
See also Lincoln's order concerning Peniston, January 28, *infra*.

To Edwin M. Stanton[1]

January 4, 1865

I did promise Gen. Logan that this appointment should be made *if it consistently could,* and I personally carried the paper to Col. Hardie who will inform the Secretary of War all about it.

Jan. 4. 1865. A. LINCOLN

[1] AES, IHi. Lincoln's endorsement has been removed from attendant papers, and the appointment has not been identified.

To Edwin M. Stanton[1]

January 4, 1865

I think this order should be so modified as to allow unrestricted trade *from* Kentucky across the Ohio river. Will the Secretary of War, please see Mr. Marshall, the bearer, & consider the matter?

Jan. 4. 1865. A. LINCOLN

[1] AES, IHi. Lincoln's endorsement is written on a letter from Green Clay Smith, Covington, Kentucky, December 28, 1864, introducing Thornton F. Marshall, who "calls on you in regard to the trade regulations in our portion of Ky." On January 5, Marshall wrote Lincoln: "I submitted the order of Genl Burbridge upon the subject of trade between Kentucky & Ohio to the Secretary of War together with your note to him upon the same subject. I cannot get to see him today & . . . I shall leave for Kentucky this evening. I therefore *much* regret I can't return you the Secretarys decision upon the subject as *you* requested. I will leave the matter with Col Pennabaker [Charles D. Pennebaker] agent for the State of Kentucky, with the request that if the Secretary's action is not in accordance with your suggestion, he will inform you. . . ." (DLC-RTL).

To Edwin M. Stanton[1]

Hon. Sec. of War   Executive Mansion,
My dear Sir   Washington, Jan. 4, 1865.

You remember that upon consultation with me you ordered two men arrested by Gen. Wallace to be discharged, and the third, a Mr. Waters, to be held for trial. As Waters is a State Senator elect, I think extra effort to give him a speedy trial should be made, so as to avoid injurious inferrences arising. Please attend to this. Yours truly   A LINCOLN

[1] ALS, owned by Charles C. Harris, New York City. See Lincoln's communications to Wallace, December 19, 1864. On January 5, 1865, a petition signed by Daniel Clarke, Sprigg Harwood, and others, was submitted to Lincoln:
"The undersigned a committee of Democratic Senators from Maryland, respectfully represent . . . that Levin L. Waters the Senator Elect from Somerset County, is now in confinement in the jail of Baltimore City under the orders of Major General Wallace upon the charge that he 'flew the rebel flag from his office for months after the 19th of April 1861'
"This charge . . . we are authorized to deny and we are prepared to disprove. . . .
"The undersigned therefore respectfully ask . . . the release of the said Levin L. Waters. . . ." (DLC-RTL).
No reply from Stanton has been found. See further Lincoln's telegram to Wallace, January 21, *infra.*

To John Williams[1]

John Williams   Executive Mansion
Springfield, Ills.   Washington Jan. 4. 1865

Let Trumbo's substitute be regularly mustered in, send me the evidence that it is done and I will then discharge Trumbo.

                                A. LINCOLN

[1] ALS, DNA WR RG 107, Presidential Telegrams, I, 277. On January 4, John Williams telegraphed Lincoln: "Chas A Trumbo Co K one hundred fourteenth (114) Ills only stay of his widowed mother wishes to put an acceptable substitute in his place Can you grant permission" (DLC-RTL). AGO *Special Orders No. 36,* January 23, 1865, directed the discharge of Private Charles A. Trumbo "upon the receipt of this order."

To Ulysses S. Grant[1]

Lieut. Genl. Grant   Executive Mansion,
City-Point, Va   Washington, Jan. 5, 1864.

Richard T. Jacob, Lieutenant Governor of Kentucky, is at the Spotswood-House in Richmond under an order of Gen. Burbridge not to return to Kentucky. Please communicate leave to him to pass your lines, and come to me here at Washington.   A. LINCOLN

[1] ALS, DNA WR RG 107, Presidential Telegrams, I, 278. See Lincoln to Dickson, December 27, 1864, *supra,* and Lincoln to Jacob, January 18, *infra.*

To the House of Representatives[1]

January 5, 1865

To the House of Representatives of the United States.

I herewith return to your honorable body, in which it originated, a "Joint Resolution to correct certain clerical errors in the Internal Revenue Act" without my approval.

My reason for so doing is, that I am informed that this Joint Resolution was prepared during the last moments of the last session of Congress, for the purpose of correcting certain errors of reference in the Internal Revenue Act, which were discovered on an examination of an official copy procured from the State Department, a few hours only before the adjournment. It passed the House and went to the Senate, where a vote was taken upon it, but by some accident it was not presented to the President of the Senate for his Signature.

Since the adjournment of the last session of Congress, other errors of a kind similar to those, which this resolution was designed to correct, have been discovered in the law, and it is now thought most expedient to include all the necessary corrections in one Act or Resolution.

The attention of the proper Committee of the House, has I am informed, been already directed to the preparation of a bill for this purpose.   ABRAHAM LINCOLN

Executive Mansion,
January 5, 1865.

[1] DS, DNA RG 233, House Executive Document No. 123. The joint resolution (H.R. 123) introduced and passed on July 2, 1864, was presented to Lincoln on December 21. The act to amend the act of June 30, 1864, was approved by Lincoln on March 3, 1865.

Order Permitting Robert E. Coxe to Bring Products through the Lines[1]

Executive Mansion,
January 5, 1865

An authorized agent of the Treasury Department having, with the approval of the Secretary of the Treasury, contracted for the cotton and other products above mentioned,[2] and the party having agreed to sell and deliver the same to such agent.

It is ordered that the cotton and other products, moving in compliance with, and for fulfilment of said contract, and being transported to said agent, or under his direction, shall be free from seizure or detention by any officer of the government, and, commandants of military Departments, districts, posts and detachments, naval stations, gun boats, flotilla's and floats [fleets] will observe this order, and give the said Robert E Coxe, his agents and transports, free and unmolested passage for the purpose of getting the said cotton or any part thereof through the lines, other than blockaded lines, and safe conduct within our lines while the same is moving in strict compliance with the regulations of the Secretary of the Treasury, and for fulfilment of said contract with the agent of the government   ABRAHAM LINCOLN

[1] Copy, ORB. The original order has not been located. The copy along with other documents in the case was submitted by Hanson A. Risley to General Grant on April 21, 1865, with a request for another pass for Robert E. Coxe to pass through the lines. Although Lincoln's order is dated January 5, Risley's request to Grant explained that it was not signed by the President until March 16, at which time Lincoln gave him also a pass for Robert E. Coxe dated March 15 (*infra*). In the meantime, according to Risley, "Mr. Coxe not yet having gone through the lines, and the President being dead, I went this morning to Genl Grant, and got another pass. . . ." (*Ibid.*). See also the note to Lincoln's passes for James W. Singleton, *infra*.

[2] Hanson A. Risley's request for safe conduct for Coxe, upon which Lincoln's permit was written as an endorsement, enumerates "Fifty Thousand bales of cotton, Ten Thousand boxes of manufactured tobacco, Ten Thousand barrels turpentine, and Ten Thousand barrels rosin. . . ." (*Ibid.*).

Passes for James W. Singleton[1]

Allow the bearer James W Singleton, to pass our lines with ordinary baggage, and go South   A LINCOLN
Jany 5. 1865

Allow the bearer James W Singleton to pass our lines, with any Southern products, and go to any of our trading posts, there to be subject to the Regulations of the Treasury Department
Jany 5. 1865   A LINCOLN

[1] Copies, DLC-RTL. See Lincoln's order issued to Robert E. Coxe, *supra.* Orville H. Browning's *Diary* records under date of December 24, 1864, a conference with Lincoln "about letting Genl Singleton go to Richmond for the purpose of purchasing Cotton &c. . . . If it succeeds quite a number of gentlemen, including Senator [Edwin D.] Morgan of N.Y.—Mr [Robert E.] Coxe now of Canada, Judge [James] Hughes of the court of claims, and myself." The entry stops thus abruptly, but on January 5, 1865, Browning writes again: "The President sent me word last night that he wished to see me this morning I had previously talked with him about permitting Singleton to go South . . . a scheme out of which he, Singleton, Judge Hughes of the Court of Claims, Senator Morgan myself and some others, hope to make some money. . . ." The Richmond *Examiner* for January 16, 1865, announced Singleton's arrival in that city. A note from Browning to Lincoln, undated but January 30, 1865 (incorrectly catalogued as 1864 in the Lincoln Papers) is as follows:

"Singleton has returned. Has letters & messages for you, and much to tell that it will be interesting to hear.

"We will call at 7 o'clock this evening, or any other time that may suit your convenience." (DLC-RTL).

To Edwin M. Stanton[1]

Hon. Sec. of War   Executive Mansion,
Dear Sir,   Washington, Jan. 5, 1865.

Since parting with you, it has occurred to me to say that while Gen. Sherman's *"get a good ready"* is appreciated, and is not to be overlooked, *time,* now that the enemy is wavering, is more important than ever before. Being on the down-hill, & some what confused, keeping him going. Please say so much to Genl. S. Yours truly   A LINCOLN

[1] ALS, IHi. On December 31, General Sherman had written General Halleck from Savannah, Georgia: ". . . I write only to say that since my last . . . there is nothing of importance. . . . The city is perfectly quiet. . . . As soon as I can accumulate a sufficient surplus of forage and provisions to load my wagons, I shall be ready to start. . . . I propose . . . to make lodgments in South Carolina, about Port Royal, opposite this city, and up about Sister's Ferry. When all is ready I can feign at one or more places and cross at the other, after which my movements will be governed by those of the enemy, and such instructions as I may receive from Lieutenant-General Grant before starting. I do not think I can employ better strategy than I have hitherto done, namely, make a good ready and then move rapidly to my objective, avoiding a battle at points where I would be encumbered by wounded, but striking boldly and quickly when my objective is reached. I will give due heed and encouragement to all peace movements, but conduct war as though it could only terminate with the destruction of the enemy. . . . I should like to receive, before starting, the detachments left behind in Tennessee. . . ." (OR, I, XLIV, 842).

To Napoleon J. T. Dana[1]

Executive Mansion Washington
Major General Dana   Jany 6 1865

The attached document perporting to be an order issued by your authority, is sent you with the request that you will inform me whether such order has been issued by you, and if it has, please inform me by what authority it is that you undertake to impose terms in the premises not imposed by the government and which in effect, entirely thwart and defeat the object of the government

It is suggested that if executing in good faith the order of the government in the matter in question, or any other matter, operates injuriously to the Military Service, it would be proper for you to report to the government fully upon it, and that would be the only proper course   Yours &c   A. LINCOLN

1 LS (copy?), DLC-RTL. Filed with this letter is a newspaper clipping of General Dana's order to Lieutenant Colonel J. P. Harper, permit officer at Memphis, Tennessee, December 26, 1864:

"The very great latitude allowed to persons in procuring 'applications' from the Purchasing Agent of the Treasury Department, and the facility with which they are issued, appears to render it imperative, on the part of the military authorities, that all applicants be required to set aside doubts as to their actually and 'bona fide' *owning or controlling* the products named in their application; and that they are not mere speculators and adventurers, who have procured papers merely to furnish them the opportunity of going around to hunt up products for purchase; nor persons who have gotten them merely for the object of passing through the lines.

"Of the class of applicants who *own* products there may be two descriptions, viz: those who have raised them, and those who have purchased them.

"Of the first division of this class, prior to issuing a safe conduct or permit, you will require an affidavit of themselves, and one other loyal, disinterested respectable person, showing when and where the products were raised, the quantity, where they are at the time of making the affidavit, and in whose possession, in case they have been moved from the place where they were raised, the time of removal, etc.

"Of the second division of this class, you will require affidavit as above, of who was the last preceding owner—the time and place of purchase, the price paid, or to be paid, and the description of money or property in which payment was made, or is to be made, the place where the products were when purchased, the quantity, and the place where they are at the time of making the affidavit, and in whose possession.

"Of the persons *controlling* products you will require a similar affidavit, showing precisely where the products were raised or were stored at the time they obtained *control* of them; the quantity and to whom belonging; the means and circumstances by which they obtained control; the place where they are at the time of making affidavit and in whose possession.

"In all instances where persons are unable to make the above proofs, or when you are satisfied of any fraudulent intent, you are forbidden to issue safe guard or permit, and you will note that fact on the application.

"You will keep exact record of all rejected applications."

On January 17, General Dana replied to Lincoln's letter:

"I have the honor to reply to the letter of your Excellency dated the 6th instant, and, whilst I express my unfeigned regret . . . that any misconception of mine, arising from a misunderstanding of the policy of the government, under the requirements of orders from my immediate superior, should subject me to your Excellency's disapprobation, I have no hesitancy in believing that I shall henceforth, in the matter, have no fear of censure, as I believe I now fully understand your wishes. . . .

"It was hardly to be expected that, in the inauguration of a system so new to us and so entirely contrary to our previous instructions, that Commanders would not find many difficulties to encounter; but I expected to obviate these in a very short time. When my first safeguards were issued . . . certain persons who held them were arrested by Naval Commanders who desired to know by what proofs I was satisfied they 'owned or controlled' the products and stated that they knew the contrary. Thereupon I issued the letter of instructions and supposed, so far from thwarting and defeating the objects of the government, that I was carrying them out in good faith. . . . On the 5th of January Genl. Canby . . . disapproved my action . . . and I immediately discontinued the requirement. . . .

"I am persuaded that however much many persons, who had not fully informed themselves at the inauguration of a new set of regulations, were disposed to complain and make trouble, they are now convinced that they were more impatient than injured, and that the people of this Department [of the Mississippi] are, at present, well satisfied that the Executive Order and Treasury Regulations of Sept 24 are being carried out with the least possible obstruction. . . ." (DLC-RTL).

To Ulysses S. Grant[1]

Lieut. Gen. Grant   Executive Mansion, Washington,
City Point   Jan. 6, 1865

If there is a man at City-Point, by the name of Waterman Thornton who is in trouble about desertion, please have his case briefly stated to me & do not let him be executed meantime

A LINCOLN

[1] ALS, DNA WR RG 107, Presidential Telegrams, I, 279. Grant replied on January 7: "In reply to your dispatch of this morning I have to state that Genl Griffin commanding 2nd Division 9th Army Corps telegraphs me that private Waterman Thornton one hundred seventy ninth (179) New York Volunteers was executed yesterday . . . for desertion to the enemy" (DLC-RTL).

Endorsement[1]

This boy having served faithfully since is pardoned for the old desertion   A. LINCOLN
Jan. 7. 1865

[1] AES, IHi. Lincoln's endorsement has been clipped from attendant papers.

To Richard L. Ferguson[1]

R. L. Ferguson   Executive Mansion
Provost-Marshal   Washington,
Warrensburg, Mo   Jan. 7. 1865.

Suspend, until further order, proceedings to enforce a bong[2] given by Hicklin, Hicklin & Spratt. It is not my view of the law that Provost-Marshals are to decide whether bonds are or are not forfeited.   A LINCOLN

[1] ALS, DNA WR RG 107, Presidential Telegrams, I, 280. No reply or further reference has been found.
[2] In appearance this word cannot well be anything but "bong," but Lincoln probably intended to write "bond."

To the Senate and House of Representatives[1]

January 7, 1865

To the Senate and House of Representatives.

I transmit to Congress a copy of two Treaties between the United States and Belgium, for the extinguishment of the Scheldt dues, &c,

[203]

concluded on the 20th of May, 1863, and 20th of July, 1863, respectively, the ratifications of which were exchanged at Brussels on the 24th of June last, and I recommend an appropriation to carry into effect the provisions thereof relative to the payment of the proportion of the United States towards the capitalization of the said dues. ABRAHAM LINCOLN

Washington, January 7th 1865.

[1] DS, DNA RG 46, Senate 38A F2. The treaties transmitted are printed in *House Executive Document No. 19*. The appropriations act approved on March 2, 1865, appropriated $55,584 and interest for the first installment due under the treaties.

To Schuyler Colfax[1]

Hon. Schuyler Colfax,   Executive Mansion,
Speaker, House of Representatives,   Washington,
Sir,   January 9 1865.

I transmit herewith the letter of the Secretary of War with accompanying report of the Adjutant General, in reply to the Resolution of the House of Representatives, dated December 7, 1864, requesting me "to communicate to the House the Report made by Colonel Thomas M. Key, of an interview between himself and General Howell Cobb on the 14th day of June, 1862, on the bank of the Chickahominy, on the subject of the exchange of prisoners of war." I am, Sir, Very Respectfully, Your obdt. servant,

ABRAHAM LINCOLN

[1] LS, DNA RG 233, House Executive Document No. 20. Stanton's letter of January 5 and accompanying report were printed in Thirty-eighth Congress, Second Session, *House Executive Document No. 20*, in spite of Stanton's opinion that "As the discourse with Howell Cobb on the subject of the existing contest was improper, it is believed that its publication would also be improper."

To Mrs. Milton C. Egbert[1]

                     Executive Mansion Washington,
Mrs. Milton C. Egbert.   Jan. 9. 1865

Col. Forney assures me that you will not be displeased if I tender, as I most heartily do, my sincere thanks for your munificient Christmas donation of five thousand dollars to the sick and wounded soldiers in the Philadelphia hospitals. Your Obt. Servt.

A. LINCOLN

[1] ALS-P, ISLA. On January 7, 1865, John W. Forney wrote Lincoln: "About a month ago Mrs. M. C. Egbert, through her husband, Dr. Milton C. Egbert, of Venango Co. Penna. sent Five thousand dollars for a Christmas dinner for

the sick and wounded soldiers in the hospitals in Philadelphia. This was the result of benevolence and patriotism. . . . The husband of Mrs. Egbert is an immensely wealthy man, having amassed a very large fortune out of the oil trade. . . . Mrs Egbert is a young and accomplished woman much beloved by a large circle of friends in Philadelphia. These friends are now exceedingly anxious that you should address Mrs. Egbert a line . . . alluding to the noble donation she has made. . . . Her address is Mrs. Milton C. Egbert, Egbert Farm, Venango Co. Penna. If you will write the lines . . . and send the note to me I will forward it to her friends in Philadelphia. . . ." (DLC-RTL).

To Mrs. Charles J. Faulkner[1]

Mrs. Faulkner:[2]   Executive Mansion,
Madam   Washington, Jany. 9. 1865.

It was with regret I learned that your brother, whom I had ordered to be discharged on taking the oath, under the impression that he was a *private,* is a *captain.* By an understanding the Commissary of prisoners detains such cases until a further hearing from me. I now distinctly say that if your Father shall come within our lines and take the oath of Dec. 8. 1863, I will give him a full pardon, and will, at the same time, discharge your brother on his taking the oath, notwithstanding he is a captain. Respectfully

A. LINCOLN.

[1] ALS, owned by Louis H. Max, Wilmington, Illinois; ADfS, DLC-RTL. On the back of the letter appear two endorsements, the first certifying that Charles James Faulkner took the oath of allegiance on May 30, 1865, and the second, by James Speed, ordering: "Pardon & file this paper." On the bottom of the letter, however, appears the following unsigned note in pencil: "My Father *never* took the oath of allegiance after the War and did not return until *after* the surrender." It would appear that Lincoln's letter was written to Mary Boyd Faulkner, who was the wife of the Charles James Faulkner, Sr. (see note to Lincoln's order to Martindale, July 17, 1864, *supra*). But this seems improbable, since her father was not living at the time and no brother has been identified who would fit the description in Lincoln's letter. Another possibility is that Lincoln's letter was intended for "Miss" rather than "Mrs." Faulkner. In this case the father would be Charles James Faulkner, Sr., and the brother would be Captain Elisha Boyd Faulkner, captured in June, 1864, and confined on Johnson's Island at the time of Lincoln's letter. Which one of Charles James Faulkner's six daughters may have received Lincoln's letter has not been ascertained.
[2] "Mrs. Faulkner:" is not in the autograph draft.

To John B. Majors[1]

Officer in command   Executive Mansion, Washington,
at St. Joseph, Missouri.   January 9, 1865.

Postpone the execution of the death sentence of Holland, Highsmith and Utz ten days longer unless you receive orders from me to the contrary   A. LINCOLN.

[205]

Maj. Eckert
Please send the above telegram   JNO. G. NICOLAY
Jan'y 9th 1865.

[1] D, DNA WR RG 107, Presidential Telegrams, I, 281. This is in the handwriting of Nicolay, including Lincoln's signature. See Lincoln's telegram to Majors, December 22, 1864, *supra*, and his endorsement concerning Holland, Highsmith, and Utz, January 11, 1865, *infra*.

Order Concerning Solomon Young[1]

Executive Mansion,
Washington, Jan 9, 1865

Let Solomon Young be examined to ascertain whether he possesses the physical qualifications for a soldier, in which case he will be discharged from confinement in jail and enrolled as a substitute for William D McMahon drafted in the first Ward of this city.

A. LINCOLN

[1] DS, owned by R. E. Burdick, New York City.

To the Senate[1]

To the Senate of the United States   January 9, 1865

In compliance with the Resolution of the Senate of the 15th. ultimo, requesting information concerning an arrangement limiting the Naval Armament on the Lakes, I transmit a Report of this date from the Secretary of State, to whom the Resolution was referred.   ABRAHAM LINCOLN

Washingon 9th. January 1865

[1] DS, DNA RG 46, Senate 38A F3. Seward's report of January 9, which Lincoln transmitted, referred the Senate to President Monroe's message of April 6, 1818, "with the accompanying papers . . . found in the series of American State papers published by Messrs. Gales & Seaton under the authority of Congress, Class I, Foreign Relations, volume IV, pages 202 to 207 inclusive."

To Lyman Trumbull[1]

Hon. Lyman Trumbull,   Executive Mansion,
My dear Sir: Washington, January 9, 1865.

The paper, relating to Louisiana, submitted to the Judiciary Committee of the Senate, by Gen. Banks, is herewith returned. The whole of it is in accordance with my general impression, and I *believe* it to be true; but much the larger part is beyond my absolute *knowledge*, as in it's nature it must be. All the statements which lie within the range of my knowledge are strictly true; and I think of nothing material which has been omitted. Even before Gen. Banks went to Louisiana I was anxious for the loyal people there to move for re-organization and restoration of proper practical relations with the Union; and when he, at last, expressed his decided conviction that the thing was practicable, I directed him to give his official co-operation to effect it. On the subject, I have sent and received many letters to and from Gen. Banks and many other persons. These letters, as you remember, were shown to you yesterday, as they will be again, if you desire.

If I shall neither take sides nor argue, will it be out of place for me to make what I think is the true statement of your question as to the proposed Louisiana Senators?

"Can Louisiana be brought into proper practical relations with the Union, sooner, by *admitting* or by *rejecting* the proposed Senators?"[2] Yours truly   A LINCOLN

[1] ALS, VtU; ADfS, DLC-RTL. On January 9, Senator Trumbull wrote Lincoln:

"Agreeably to our verbal understanding, I enclose you the statement of Maj. Gen. Banks made to the Judiciary Com. of the Senate. The committee meets Wednesday, before which please return it, if convenient.

"In my statement as to what constitutes 'enemy property' I may have been in error in supposing that the domicil & character of the owner was immaterial. As to some property this would be true but not in all cases." (DLC-RTL).

The lengthy statement of General Nathaniel P. Banks may be found in Thirty-eighth Congress, Second Session, *Senate Miscellaneous Document No. 7.*

[2] Charles Smith and R. King Cutler, senators-elect from Louisiana, were not seated.

To Benjamin F. Butler[1]

Major General Butler   Executive Mansion,
Fort-Monroe, Va.   Washington, Jan. 10. 1865

No principal report of yours on the Wilmington expedition has ever reached the War Department, as I am informed there. A preliminary report did reach here, but was returned to Gen. Grant at his request. Of course, leave to publish, can not be given, without inspection of the paper, and not then, if it should be deemed to be detrimental to the public service.   A. LINCOLN

[1] ALS, DNA WR RG 107, Presidential Telegrams, I, 282. On January 8, General Butler was relieved from command of the Department of Virginia and North Carolina and replaced by General Edward O. C. Ord. On January 9, he telegraphed Lincoln: "I have telegraphed to the Secretary of War for leave to publish my report of the Wilmington affair. I have received no answer. He is absent; in his absence I respectfully ask your leave to publish it. It is but justice. . . ." (DLC-RTL).

On January 11, Butler telegraphed Grant: "I have asked the President for

permission to publish my report of the Wilmington affair. He answers that no report has ever been received at the War Department. You told me you had forwarded it. Has it been lost again? If so, I have a copy." (OR, I, XLVI, II, 97).

General John A. Rawlins replied the same day: "General Grant telegraphed to Captain [George K.] Leet to return your report to enable him to revise his endorsement on it. It will arrive here probably to-day, and will be returned by special messenger to-morrow. He has requested its publication." (*Ibid.*, p. 98).

To John W. Garrett[1]

Mr. J. W. Garrett   Executive Mansion
My dear Sir.   Washington, Jan. 10. 1865

It is said we shall soon all be in the dark here, unless *you can* bring coal to make gas. I suppose you would do this, without my interference, if you could; and I only write now to say, *it is very important to us;* and not to say that you must *stop* supplying the army to make room to carry coal. Do all you can for us in *both matters.* Yours truly   A. LINCOLN

[1] ALS, DLC-Garrett Papers. President John W. Garrett of the Baltimore and Ohio Railroad replied on January 13:

"I have the pleasure of acknowledging the receipt of your valued favor of the 10th inst.

"The pressure upon our Company for supplies for army purposes, and for the immense variety of interests which depend upon the route . . . is exceedingly great. . . .

"The demand for coal for the manufacture of gas, as well as the Bituminous coals for the Navy, and other purposes . . . is much beyond our present capacity. . . .

"I have . . . repeatedly advised the Gas Light Company of Washington, that our capacity on the Road betwixt Baltimore and Washington, is much greater than the entire demands upon us, and that any coal brought to Baltimore by other routes, can be transferred, without delay or difficulty, to Washington. It is true, that by . . . proper foresight, the Managers . . . should have obtained a portion of their supplies elsewhere . . . but I am especially determined that our friends at the White House, as well as in the City of Washington, shall not suffer by being 'placed in the dark'. . . .

"I have instructed that, until the Gas Light Company can improve its position, a sufficient quantity of gas coal shall be forwarded to them daily, to the partial exclusion of much other very urgent business. . . ." (DLC-RTL).

Proclamation Concerning Commerce[1]

January 10, 1865
By the President of the United States of America.

A Proclamation.

Whereas, the Act of Congress of the 28th. of September 1850, entitled "An act to create additional collection districts in the State of California and to change the existing districts therein, and to modify the existing collection districts in the United States," extends to merchandise warehoused under bond the privilege of being exported to the British North American Provinces, adjoining the United States, in the manner prescribed in the Act of Congress of the 3d. of March 1845, which designates certain frontier ports through which merchandise may be exported, and further provides "that such other ports situated on the frontiers of the United States adjoining the British North American Provinces, as may hereafter be found expedient may have extended to them the like privileges on the recommendation of the Secretary of the Treasury, and proclamation duly made by the President of the United States, specially designating the ports to which the aforesaid privileges are to be extended."

Now, therefore, I, Abraham Lincoln, President of the United States of America, in accordance with the recommendation of the Secretary of the Treasury, do hereby declare and proclaim that the port of St. Albans, in the State of Vermont, is and shall be entitled to all the privileges in regard to the exportation of merchandise in bond to the British North American Provinces adjoining the United States, which are extended to the ports enumerated in the 7th. Section of the Act of Congress of the 3d of March 1845, aforesaid, from and after the date of this proclamation.

In witness whereof, I have hereunto set my hand and caused the Seal of the United States to be affixed.

Done at the City of Washington, this Tenth day of January, in the year of our Lord, one thousand eight hundred and [L.S.] sixty-five, and of the Independence of the United States of America the Eighty-ninth.   ABRAHAM LINCOLN

By the President:

WILLIAM H. SEWARD, Secretary of State.

1 DS, DNA FS RG 11, Proclamations.

Cotton Permit for Henry J. Eager[1]

Executive Mansion
January 11, 1865.

An authorized agent of the Treasury Department having with the approval of the Secretary of the Treasury, contracted for the cotton above mentioned and the party having agreed to sell and deliverer [sic] the same to such agent.

It is ordered that the Cotton moving in compliance with and for fulfilment of said contract and being transported to said agent, or under his direction, shall be free from seizure or detention by any officer of the Government and commanders of military departments, districts posts and detachments, naval stations gunboats flotillas and fleets will observe this order and give the said Henry J. Eager his agents and transports free and unmolested passage for the purpose of getting the said cotton or any part thereof through the lines other than blockaded lines, and safe conduct within our lines while the same is moving in strict compliance with the regulations of the Secretary of the Treasury and for fulfilment of said contract with the agent of the Government.

ABRAHAM LINCOLN

[1] DS, DNA RG 56, Cotton and Captured Property Records, No. 17500. An accompanying certificate of the same date signed by Hanson A. Risley agrees to purchase from Henry J. Eager 10,000 bales of cotton.

Endorsement Concerning Winston Somers[1]

I personally know Dr. Somers & suppose his appointment will be proper if the vacancy exists.   A. LINCOLN

Jan. 11. 1865.

[1] AES, owned by Dale Carnegie, New York City. Lincoln's endorsement is written on a petition of Thompson R. Webber and other citizens of Champaign County, Illinois, recommending Dr. Winston Somers for surgeon of the Board of Enrollment for the Seventh District in Illinois. Dr. Somers was appointed January 13, 1865, to replace Dr. Joseph T. Miller, resigned.

To Joseph Holt[1]

Sentences in these three cases commuted to imprisonment in the penitentiary at hard labor during the war.   A. LINCOLN

Jan. 11, 1865

[1] AES, DNA WR RG 153, Judge Advocate General, LL 2944. Lincoln's endorsement is written on the court-martial record in the cases of James P. Holland, John H. Utz, and Henry W. Highsmith. See Lincoln's telegram to Majors, January 9, *supra*. On January 13, General Grenville M. Dodge telegraphed Lincoln from St. Louis: "Utz, Highsmith & Holland whose execution you have ordered delayed until further orders attempted to kill the Jailer at St Joseph and escape last night. They were however defeated   They are bad men & their sentence should be carried into effect" (DLC-RTL).

To Joseph Hooker[1]

Major General Hooker   Executive Mansion
Cincinnati, O   Washington, Jan. 11. 1865

It is said that you have ordered Andrew Humphreys to imprisonment at hard labor, in accordance with his original sentence, on the ground that it was not legally competent for Gen. Hovey, having approved the sentence to afterwards modify it. While I incline to the belief that you are technically right, please let Gen. Hovey's modification be acted upon until further order from me.

A LINCOLN

[1] ALS, DNA WR RG 107, Presidential Telegrams, I, 284. See Lincoln to Stanton, October 22, 1864, *supra*. General Alvin P. Hovey in command at Indianapolis, Indiana, answered Lincoln's telegram by letter on the same day:

"In answer to your telegram . . . 'Duplicate of Message sent to Maj. Genl. Hooker' I have the honor herewith to transmit a copy of my communication to Genl. Hooker dated January 10th 1865."

[Enclosure]

"I have just received your letter of the 6th Inst. requesting me to carry into effect the sentence of the Military Commission in the case of Andrew Humphreys. I herewith send you a copy of the order promulgated, and most respectfully ask your attention to the following points: First, your letter doubts my authority to organize a military commission.

"Now if my letter of instructions from the Secretary of War does not give me that power, *the trial is void and the sentence cannot be legally carried into effect.* If I had the right to convene the court, then by the acts of Congress, Approved July 2nd 1864, I am clothed with the full power to pardon the convicted or mitigate his punishment. . . .

"In my opinion there are two errors committed by the commission, on the trial of Humphreys, which would, before a civil court reverse his case. . . .

"With a defective record, with the light testimony, and with a strong feeling in the public mind in his favor, I deemed it prudent and politic to release him.

"He resides in Green County, an inaccessible part of the State, and his re-arrest would be attended, at this time, with considerable feeling.

"Believing, as I do, that my action has been entirely lawful, and for the good of the country, I most earnestly request, that you will not order his arrest, until the president shall have acted. . . .

"The record . . . has been sent to the President more than ten days since. . . ." (DLC-RTL).

To John F. Miller[1]

Office U.S. Military Telegraph,
War Department,
Officer in command at
Nashville, Tenn. Washington, D.C., January 11 1865

Postpone the execution of S. W. Elliott and C. E. Peacher until the third day of February 1865. A. LINCOLN

[1] ALS, DNA WR RG 107, Presidential Telegrams, I, 283. On January 10, Andrew Johnson telegraphed Lincoln for a respite of fifteen days for Cornelius E. Peacher, and John S. Brien telegraphed a request for twenty days respite for Captain S. W. Elliott (DLC-RTL). General Miller replied on January 11: "Your order postponing execution of S. W. Elliott & C. E. Peacher to thirtieth [*sic*] of February next is received" (*ibid.*). Elliott's first initial, given incorrectly as "S" in this correspondence, appears as "J" later on. See Lincoln's telegrams to Miller, January 25 and 27, *infra*.

To James Speed[1]

January 11, 1865

Submitted to the Attorney-General, with the request that he reminds me of this application whenever, we shall make a judicial appointment in South Carolina or Georgia.   A. LINCOLN
Jan. 11. 1865.

[1] AES, DNA RG 60, Papers of Attorney General, Appointments, South Carolina, Box 866. Lincoln's endorsement is written on a recommendation signed by the presidential electors of New York in favor of the application of A. J. Dittenhoefer of New York City, a native of South Carolina, for judge of the U.S. District Court for South Carolina. No record of Dittenhoefer's appointment has been found.

To J. Bates Dickson[1]

Officer in command at   Executive Mansion,
Lexington,   Washington,
Kentucky   Jan'y 12th, 1865.

Suspend execution of sentence of death in case of Solomon Spiegel 9th Michigan cavalry until further orders, and forward record of trial for examination.   A. LINCOLN.

Maj. Eckert
Please send the above telegram.   JNO. G. NICOLAY

[1] D, DNA WR RG 107, Presidential Telegrams, I, 285. This telegram was written and signed by Nicolay. No reply or further reference has been found. Captain J. Bates Dickson was in command in the absence of Colonel Stephen G. Burbridge.

Endorsement[1]

These papers first seen or known of by me, Jan. 12, 1865   A. L.

[1] AES, DLC-RTL. Lincoln's endorsement is written on a letter from Amasa J. Parker, W. F. Allen, and William Kelly, New York state commissioners, November 3, 1864, concerning imprisoned citizens of New York. A letter from Stanton to Lincoln, November 2, 1864, requesting an audience for the New York commissioners is endorsed by John Hay: "At one o'clock, the President answered & they came." (*Ibid.*).

To Ulysses S. Grant[1]

Lieut. Gen. Grant   Executive Mansion,
City-Point, Va.   Washington, Jan. 12. 1865.

If Henry Stork of, 5th. Pa. Cavalry has been convicted of desertion, and is not yet executed, please stay till further order & send record.   A. LINCOLN

[212]

1 ALS, DNA WR RG 107, Presidential Telegrams, I, 287. On January 10, 1865, James K. Moorhead wrote Lincoln:

"I respectfully ask that the record in the case of Henry Stork private 5th Pa Cavalry tried at City Point for desertion some ten days since, be ordered here and execution of sentence deferred until approved.

"Please do this *promptly* and oblige. . . ." (DLC-RTL).

On January 13, Grant replied to Lincoln's telegram that he would stay execution of Henry Stork if he was still alive. (DLC-Grant Papers).

The roster of the Fifth Pennsylvania Cavalry lists Henry Stork of Company C as mustered out with the company on August 7, 1865.

To Joseph Holt[1]

January 12, 1865

Judge Advocate General please examine & report on this case.

Jan. 12. 1865   A. LINCOLN

So much of sentence as imposes confinement in the Penitentiary remitted.   A. LINCOLN

Jan. 23. 1865

1 AES, DNA WR RG 153, Judge Advocate General, NN 2627. Lincoln's endorsements are written on the court-martial record of Captain William McNally, Company G, Seventy-seventh New York Volunteers, convicted on charges of bribery and conduct prejudicial to good order and military discipline. Holt recommended remitting confinement.

To Montgomery C. Meigs[1]

January 12, 1865

Quarter-Master-General, please see Mr. Duncan, of Montreal, who wishes to exhibit a discovery for the protection of wooden structures against fire   A. LINCOLN

Jan. 12. 1865

1 ALS, owned by Charles W. Olsen, Chicago, Illinois. Duncan has not been further identified.

Order Concerning David Levy[1]

January 12, 1865

If David Levy shall enlist and serve faithfully for one year or until otherwise honorably discharged I will pardon him for the past.   A. LINCOLN.

Jan. 12, 1865.

1 Isaac Markens, *Abraham Lincoln and the Jews* (1909), p. 48. On January 10, 1865, James W. Bowen, provost marshal of the Tenth District, Pottstown, Pennsylvania, wrote Lincoln: "The bearer, Mrs. Maria Davis, of this District,

visits Washington, with the view of obtaining a pardon of her son, David Levy, a member of Co. L. 3d Regt. Penna. Cavalry, who is absent without leave. . . . From her statement . . . it will appear that he was induced to desert by an older comrade. . . . The family have already suffered, by the death of two of its members, a husband and son . . . while in the Service. . . ." (DLC-RTL).

According to Markens, in 1902 Levy's application for a pension was denied on the basis of his record of desertion; whereupon, "He immediately wrote to the Bureau that he was pardoned for that desertion by President Lincoln and as evidence of the fact he forwarded to the Pension Office a small card . . . whereon was written in his well-known handwriting: [text as above]

"Upon receipt of this Eugene F. Ware, the Commissioner of Pensions, ordered that the pardon be recognized. . . ."

To James Speed[1]

Attorney General please file & inform me at whose recommendation Duffield was appointed.   A. LINCOLN

    Jan. 12. 1865

[1] AES, RPB. Lincoln's endorsement is written on a letter from Charles D. Poston, delegate in congress from Arizona, January 10, 1865, recommending "Col. King S. Woolsey of Prescott Arizona as a Suitable person for United States Marshall of said Territory in place of Milton P. Duffield the present incumbent who is unworthy of the office. . . ." No reply has been found. Duffield is listed as "Milton H. Duffield" in the *U.S. Official Register* for 1865.

To Edwin M. Stanton[1]

Let the appointment within requested be made if it consistently can.   A. LINCOLN.

    Jan. 12, 1865

[1] Milton Kronovet Catalog 53, September 26, 1949. According to the catalog description, this endorsement appears on a letter to John P. Usher, December 30, 1864, recommending an officer for promotion.

To John P. Usher[1]

January 12, 1865

Will the Secretary of the Interior please have the Comr. of Pensions to make a particular report in this case, in order that it can be judged whether the man is or is not entitled to a pension?

    Jan. 12. 1865   A. LINCOLN

[1] AES, owned by Ray Henderson, Lakewood, Ohio. Lincoln's endorsement is written on a copy of a letter of Joseph H. Barrett to Dave Crone, Dover, Pennsylvania, November 25, 1864: "Your invalid pension claim No. 36,298 is rejected the disability for which you claim a pension is not found to have originated in the line of duty as a soldier in the Military Service of the United States."

To Gideon Welles[1]

Hon. Secretary of the Navy   Executive Mansion
Sir: Washington, Jan. 12. 1865
  If it is legally possible, let Frank C. Birney, son of the late Major
General Birney, be appointed to the Naval School. Yours truly
                                                    A. LINCOLN

[1] ALS, owned by John O. Needles, Baltimore, Maryland. Frank C. Birney,
son of Major General David B. Birney who died on October 18, 1864, entered the
Naval Academy in July, 1865, and graduated in June, 1869.

To Benjamin F. Butler[1]

Major General Butler   Executive Mansion,
Fort-Monroe, Va.   Washington, Jan. 13. 1865.
  Yours asking leave to come to Washington is received. You have
been summoned by the Committee on the Conduct of the War to
attend here, which of course you will do.   A. LINCOLN

[1] ALS, DNA WR RG 107, Presidential Telegrams, I, 288. The date of Butler's
telegram requesting "permission to visit Washington upon personal business to
adjust some accounts to get some vouchers and evidence in a suit commenced
against me. . . ." is given as received on January 3 and sent on January 1 (DLC-
RTL), but the date January 13 given in the *Official Records* (I, XLVI, II, 120)
seems more probable.

Memorandum[1]

  File as an application for District Attorney in Georgia, when
an appointment shall be made.   A. LINCOLN.
    Jan. 13, 1865

[1] Anderson Galleries Catalog 1423, April 16, 1919, No. 204. The application
is not identified in the source, and no appointment of U.S. attorney for Georgia
is listed in the *U.S. Official Register* for 1865.

To Leonard Myers[1]

                                              January 13, 1865
If Hon. Mr. Myers will request me in writing, on this sheet, to discharge this man on refunding any bounty received, I will do it,
because Mr. Myers requests it.   A. LINCOLN
    Jan. 13, 1865

Let this man be discharged on refunding any bounty received.
    Jan. 13, 1865   A. LINCOLN

[215]

¹ American Art Association Anderson Galleries Catalog 3823, February 25-26, 1930, No. 245. According to the catalog description, Lincoln's endorsements are written on the back of a letter from Leonard Myers, U.S. representative from Pennsylvania, asking for release of a soldier under arrest for receiving bounty money twice. Between the two endorsements Myers made the request in a second note.

To Ulysses S. Grant[1]

	Office U.S. Military Telegraph,
Lieut. Genl. Grant	War Department,
City-Point, Va.	Washington, D.C., January 14 1865.

You have perhaps seen in the papers that Ex. Senator Foote, with his family, attempted to escape from Richmond to Washington, and that he was pursued and taken back. His wife and child are now here. Please give me the earliest information you may receive concerning him—what is likely to be done with him &c.

A. LINCOLN

¹ ALS, DNA WR RG 107, Presidential Telegrams, I, 290. Concerning Henry S. Foote, formerly of Mississippi, but a member of the Confederate Congress from Tennessee, Grant replied on January 15: "I send you by telegraph message from Davis & other dispatches from Richmond Whig, concerning the arrest of Ex Senator Foote, which is all the information I have on the subject. Any further information that I obtain will be sent you what is likely to be done with him is difficult to conjecture. I suppose they will at furthest do nothing more than imprison him." (DLC-RTL).

Having resigned from the Confederate Congress, Foote was arrested at Occoquan, Virginia, on January 10, while attempting to pass through the lines (OR, II, VIII, 68-69). He arrived in New York City from Europe on April 6, 1865, only to be arrested by order of General Dix (ibid., p. 472). He was paroled on April 22 (ibid., p. 504).

To Andrew Johnson[1]

	Office U.S. Military Telegraph,
Gov. Johnson	War Department, Washington, D.C.,
Nashville, Tenn.	January 14th. 1865

Yours announcing ordinance of emancipation received. Thanks to the Convention and to you. When do you expect to be here? Would be glad to have your suggestions as to supplying your place of Military Governor.

A LINCOLN

¹ ALS, DNA WR RG 107, Presidential Telegrams, I, 289. The date is not in Lincoln's handwriting. On January 13, Governor Johnson had telegraphed Lincoln: "The Convention composed of more than five hundred delegates from all parts of the State have unanimously adopted an amendment to the constitution forever abolishing Slavery in this State and denying the power of the Legislature passing any law creating property in man. Thank God that the tyrants rod has been broken. This amendment is to be submitted to the people for ratification on the

birth day of the Father of his Country, when, without some reverse of arms, the state will be redeemed and the foul blot of Slavery erased from her escutcheon. . . ." (DLC-RTL).

On January 17, he replied to Lincoln's question:

"The ordinance abolishing slavery will be adopted by the people on the 22d of February. Legislature and the Governor will be elected on the 4th of March, and will meet on the first Monday in April, when the State will be organized & resume all the functions of a state in the Union. I would prefer remaining where I am until that time, and then hand it all over to the people. . . .

"I would rather have the pleasure and honor of turning over the state, organized . . . than be Vice President of the United States. At some convenient time after the first Monday in April, I could be qualified &c. There are precedents for qualifying Vice Presidents after the fourth of March. Give me your opinion on the subject. . . ." (Ibid.).

See further Lincoln to Johnson, January 24, infra.

To Grenville M. Dodge[1]

Major General Dodge.   Executive Mansion
St. Louis, Mo.   Washington, January 15, 1865

It is represented to me that there is so much irregular violence in Northern Missouri as to be driving away the people and almost depopulating it. Please gather information, and consider whether an appeal to the people there to go to their homes, and let one another alone, recognizing as a full right of protection for each, that he lets others alone, and banning only him who refuses to let others alone, may not enable you to withdraw the troops, their presence itself a cause of irritation and constant apprehension, and thus restore peace and quiet & returning prosperity. Please consider this and telegraph or write me.   A. LINCOLN

[1] ALS, DNA WR RG 107, Presidential Telegrams, I, 291. On January 16, General Dodge replied:

"I have the honor to acknowledge the receipt of your telegram of the 15th inst.

"Since I assumed command here the troubles in North Missouri have increased from the fact that the troops that were in those Counties, infested by guerilla bands, were nearly all withdrawn . . . to send to General Thomas; but there is no doubt that this country is now more quiet than it has been before for three years.

"Where these troubles exist the people are to a great extent disloyal and it is the protection, aid, and sympathy that they give to the enemy and to outlaws that causes these troubles. . . .

"Allow me to assure you that the course you propose would be protested against by the State authorities, the legislature, the convention and by nearly every undoubtedly loyal man in North Missouri, while it would receive the sanction of nearly every disloyal, semi-loyal, and non-committed person there, all such could, under that course live and should want to stay in that country, while every loyal man would have to leave these counties when the disloyal sentiment is in the ascendancy. . . ." (DLC-RTL).

Representative William A. Hall of Huntsville, Missouri, was apparently shown Dodge's letter, and wrote Lincoln on January 19:

"Gen Dodge is misinformed as to the state of things in North Missouri. The statements I made to you were within my own knowledge.

"Gov. King will lay before you many facts of the same character which I presented.

"Gen. Dodge probably derives his information through officers who are themselves in some degree to blame.

"I wish to be distinctly understood as not in any thing I have stated cast any censure on Gen. Dodge." (*Ibid.*).

Endorsement[1]

Let this boy be discharged on refunding any bounty received.

Jan. 16 1865.   A. LINCOLN

[1] John Heise Autographs, Catalog 2467, No. 58. According to the catalog description, Lincoln's endorsement appears on a letter from Samuel Latta, Friendship, New York, asking release of his son Emmett, who had enlisted when only fifteen years old.

Endorsement Concerning Ezekiel F. Clay[1]

Let this man be paroled according to the within.   A. LINCOLN

Jan. 16, 1865

[1] Parke-Bernet Catalog 611, December 4-5, 1944, No. 271. According to the catalog description, Lincoln's endorsement appears on a petition signed by senators and representatives from Kentucky requesting that Ezekiel F. Clay, a prisoner of war, be paroled.

Pass for Mrs. Harriet C. Bledsoe[1]

Allow the bearer, Mrs. Harriet C. Bledsoe, to pass our lines with ordinary baggage and go South.   A. LINCOLN

Jan. 16. 1865

[1] ADS-P, DLC-Bledsoe Papers. Harriet C. Bledsoe was the wife of Albert T. Bledsoe, who had served as acting assistant secretary of War of the Confederacy. According to a newspaper article concerning this pass, Mrs. Bledsoe "ran the blockade, hoping that in the North she could get clothing material for her children. . . . She had known Mr. and Mrs. Lincoln in her younger days in Springfield, Ill., and she wrote to Bishop Charles P. McIlvaine, of the Methodist Church . . . a relative of the Bledsoes by marriage, and he asked that President Lincoln should grant her an interview and hear her request for a pass. . . ." (Jersey City *Journal*, February 8, 1930).

Pass for John Eaton[1]

Allow Col. Eaton to pass to Gen. Grant's Head Quarters & return

Jan. 16. 1865.   A. LINCOLN

[1] AES-F, John Eaton, *Grant, Lincoln and the Freedmen*, p. 230.

[218]

To Joseph Holt[1]

January 17, 1865

Unexecuted part of sentence remitted, on condition that prisoner serves with his regiment to the end of it's term, if it has not already ended.   A. LINCOLN

Jan. 17. 1865.

[1] AES, DNA WR RG 153, Judge Advocate General, LL 2048. Lincoln's endorsement appears on the court-martial record of Isaac R. Simmons, Third Volunteer Cavalry, sentenced on charges of desertion, to dishonorable discharge, loss of pay, and imprisonment for three years on Dry Tortugas.

To Joseph Holt[1]

January 17, 1865

Pardon on condition of serving out his time faithfully in his regiment.   A. LINCOLN

Jan. 17. 1865

Pardon for unexecuted part of sentence.   A. LINCOLN

Jan. 23, 1865

[1] ES and AES, DNA WR RG 153, Judge Advocate General, NN 2361. Lincoln's endorsements appear on the court-martial record of Charles Brady, Twentieth Massachusetts Volunteers, sentenced for absence without leave, to three years' imprisonment at hard labor and to have branded on his left hip the letter "D" three inches high. Holt noted that the sentence was "excessively harsh." The first endorsement is in Hay's handwriting but signed by Lincoln.

Order Concerning Sisters of Charity of Nazareth[1]

January 17, 1865

Let no depredation be committed upon the property or possessions of the "Sisters of Charity" at Nazareth Academy, near Bardstown, Ky   A. LINCOLN

Jan. 17. 1865

[1] ADS, Sisters of Charity of Nazareth, Mother House, Nazareth, Kentucky. Accompanying Lincoln's small card in the Nazareth Archives is the following letter from Senator Lazarus W. Powell, January 17, 1865: "I received your letter of the 9th inst., two days ago. I called on the president this morning and presented your case for his consideration. He promptly gave me a safe-guard which I enclose herewith; it will protect you from further depredations. It affords me pleasure to serve you in this matter. If I can serve you further, command me."

To the Senate[1]

To the Senate of the United States: January 17, 1865

I herewith lay before the Senate, for its constitutional action thereon, a treaty concluded at the Isabella Indian Reservation, in

[219]

the State of Michigan, on the 18th day of October, 1864, between H. J. Alvord, special commissioner, and D. C. Leach, United States Indian agent, acting as commissioner on the part of the United States, and the chiefs and headmen of the Chippewas of Saginaw, Swan Creek, and Black River, in the State of Michigan, parties to the treaty of August 2, 1855, with amendments.

A letter of the Secretary of the Interior of the 12th instant and a copy of a communication of the Commissioner of Indian Affairs, of the 22d ultimo, with inclosure accompanying the treaty.

Executive Mansion,   ABRAHAM LINCOLN.
Washington, January 17, 1865.

[1] *Executive Journal*, XIV, 87. The treaty was ratified with amendments on May 22, 1866.

To Edwin M. Stanton[1]

Executive Mansion, Washington, D.C.,
Hon. Secretary of War   January 17, 1865.

My dear Sir: Some time last autumn (I think it was) Shelby made a raid into Missouri; and Gen. Brown had something to do in driving him out. If Gen. Brown's report of the matter is on file, please send me a copy of it. Yours truly,   A. LINCOLN.

[1] NH, X, 341. For General Egbert B. Brown's report of Confederate Colonel Joseph O. Shelby's raid, see OR, I, XLI, I, 344 ff.

To Edwin M. Stanton[1]

Please send me the papers in the case of Lieut. John T. Arnette.
Jan. 17. 1865   A. LINCOLN

[1] ALS, RPB. Lincoln's note is on a small card pasted on a letter from William Price, Baltimore, January 4, 1865:

"John T. Arnett is represented by his sisters as being a prisoner in Fort Delaware, having been a soldier in the army of the rebels, and captured with a rebel uniform on, at the time. These ladies say, that you promised to release their brother, if they would satisfy you of the truth of their statement, that they have two brothers in the land & naval service of the U. States and three first cousins in the same service.

"I am satisfied from the evidence adduced to me that their statement is correct, of which however you will be able to judge from the the [*sic*] depositions I have caused to be taken, & the other papers they will present to you."

To Francis P. Blair, Sr.[1]

F. P. Blair, Esq   Washington,
Sir: Jan. 18. 1865

Your having shown me Mr. Davis' letter to you of the 12th. Inst., you may say to him that I have constantly been, am now, and shall continue, ready to receive any agent whom he, or any other influential person now resisting the national authority, may informally send to me, with the view of securing peace to the people of our one common country. Yours &c   A. LINCOLN.

[1] ALS, IHi; ADfS, DLC-RTL; ALS copy, CSmH; ALS copy, NAuE. See Lincoln's communication to the House of Representatives, February 10, *infra*, for Jefferson Davis' letter and other related documents.

Cotton Permit for Mrs. R. I. Ward[1]

Executive Mansion   January 18 1865.

An authorized agent of the Treasury Department having with the approval of the Secretary of the Treasury, contracted for the cotton above mentioned and the party having agreed to sell and deliver the same to such agent.

It is ordered, that the cotton moving in compliance with and for fulfilment of said contract, and being transported to said agent, or under his direction, shall be free from seizure or detention by any officer of the Government, and commanders of military departments, districts posts and detachments naval stations, gunboats flotillas and fleets, will observe this order and give the said Mrs. R. I. Ward her agents and transports, free and unmolested passage, for the purpose of getting the said cotton, or any part thereof through the lines other than blockaded lines, and safe conduct within our lines while the same is moving in strict compliance with the regulations of the Secretary of the Treasury and for fulfilment of said contract with the agent of the Government.

ABRAHAM LINCOLN

[1] DS, RTL. Lincoln's permit is written on the certificate of the same date signed by Hanson A. Risley, supervising special agent of the Treasury, and issued to Mrs. R. I. Ward of Louisville, Kentucky, agreeing to purchase 1,000 bales of cotton. Both permit and certificate have "Cancelled" written across the face.

To ——— Goodwin[1]

Mr. ——— Goodwin   Executive Mansion,
Supreme Court Room   Washington, Jan. 18, 1865.

My dear Sir   Since talking with you I have concluded to appoint a successor to Mr. Larned at once. This is not because of any change of feeling for, or estimate of, Mr. Larned. Yours truly

A. LINCOLN

[1] ALS, owned by H. Gail Davis, South Bend, Indiana. See Lincoln to Speed, *infra*. Stephen A. Goodwin and Daniel Goodwin, Jr., were law partners of Edwin C. Larned in Chicago. Which of them Lincoln was addressing cannot be determined.

To Richard T. Jacob[1]

Hon. Richard T. Jacob   Executive Mansion,
Sir: Washington, Jan. 18, 1865.

You are at liberty to proceed to Kentucky, and to remain at large so far as relates to any cause now past. In what I now do, I decide nothing as to the right or wrong of your arrest, but act in the hope that there is less liability to misunderstanding among Union men now than there was at the time of the arrest. Respectfully

A. LINCOLN

[1] ADfS, DLC-RTL. See Lincoln to Grant, January 5, *supra.*

To George C. Miller[1]

Executive Mansion,
Washington, January 18, 1865

My Dear Sir—Please accept my cordial thanks for the cane you were so kind as to send me, and the letter by which it was accompanied. Yours truly,   A. LINCOLN

George C. Miller, Esq.

[1] *Cincinnati, Past and Present, Or, Its Industrial History* (M. Joblin and Company, Cincinnati, 1872), p. 33. George C. Miller, manufacturer of agricultural implements at Cincinnati, wrote Lincoln on December 30, 1864:

"My Father being a soldier of the Revolution and I haveing some knowledge of the War of Eighteen Hundred and Twelve, being Seventy Five years old on the above date. I have been Led to Fix a value upon the union, Liberty and Independence of the States above all other matters of an Earthly nature. Have twice voted for your Honor. . . . Beleaveing that you are the Man. that God has Raised up and appointed as Our Leader in the Putting Down of the Greatest and Wickedest Rebellion that has ever taken place in the World. . . .

"I have made and Desire to Present to you a Cane in some Measure Emblematical of What I hope Our Nation Will be, before your Second term Expires. Being Composed of as Maney Sections and Pieces as there Ware States, and of a verry Beautifull Curled White Oak Not of the kind that Could be Split into Railes with Mall and wedge Conveniently.

"The Sections are not Bound together by a Rope of Sand But With a Rod of Iron. . . ." (DLC-RTL).

To James Speed[1]

If Larned's resignation is on file, please send me nomination for Perkins Bass at once.   A. LINCOLN

Jan. 18. 1865

[1] AES, DNA RG 60, Papers of Attorney General, Appointments, Illinois, Box 373. Lincoln's endorsement appears on an envelope marked "Perkins Bass for U.S. Dist. Atty. for Northern Dist. of Illinois," which contains recommendations. Nominated on January 18, to succeed Edwin C. Larned, Bass was confirmed by the Senate on January 19, 1865. See Lincoln to Goodwin, *supra.*

To Grenville M. Dodge[1]

Major General Dodge   Executive Mansion
St. Louis, Mo.   Washington, Jan. 19. 1865

If Mrs. Beattie *alias* Mrs. Wolff, shall be sentenced to death, notify me, and postpone execution till further order.   A. Lincoln

[1] ALS, DNA WR RG 107, Presidential Telegrams, I, 292. General Dodge replied on the same day: "Mrs. Beattie has been sent to her friends in the rebel lines." (DLC-RTL). In a second telegram of the same date he queried: "Have you any orders for Maj Wolfe Had he not better be sent to Johnsons Island for exchange" (*ibid.*). The identity of Mrs. Beattie is not clarified but is indicated in an item appearing in the St. Louis *Missouri Republican*, November 22, 1864:
"Mrs. Kate Beattie.—A good deal of local interest has been excited within a few days past, in regard to a woman professing to be Mrs. Wolff—wife of the rebel Major condemned to be shot in retaliation for the murder of Maj. Wilson. All our readers know that she is now a prisoner, but the following advertisement from Memphis . . . will be of interest:
" 'Information Wanted: Fifty dollars reward will be given for information as to the whereabouts of Mrs. Kate Beattie, wife of Capt. Tuck. Beattie, of Lexington, Mo. . . . Mrs. Beattie is about five feet four inches tall, has light blue eyes, hair closely shingled, and a scar upon the right cheek. She is rather eccentric, intelligent, and prepossessing in manners.
" 'Address, W. W. Cason, Adams Street, Memphis, Tenn. . . .' "
Concerning Major Enoch O. Wolf, see Lincoln's communications to General Rosecrans, November 10 and 19, 1864, *supra*.

To Ulysses S. Grant[1]

         Executive Mansion, Washington,
Lieut. General Grant: Jan. 19, 1865.

Please read and answer this letter as though I was not President, but only a friend. My son, now in his twenty second year, having graduated at Harvard, wishes to see something of the war before it ends. I do not wish to put him in the ranks, nor yet to give him a commission, to which those who have already served long, are better entitled, and better qualified to hold. Could he, without embarrassment to you, or detriment to the service, go into your Military family with some nominal rank, I, and not the public, furnishing his necessary means? If no, say so without the least hesitation, because I am as anxious, and as deeply interested, that you shall not be encumbered as you can be yourself. Yours truly

                           A. Lincoln

[1] ALS, owned by Foreman M. Lebold, Chicago, Illinois; LS, DLC-Nicolay Papers. On January 21 Grant replied from Annapolis Junction, Maryland: "Your favor of this date in relation to your son serving in some Military capacity is received. I will be most happy to have him in my Military family in the manner you propose. The nominal rank given him is immaterial but I would suggest that of Capt. as I have three staff officers now, of conciderable service, in no

higher grade. Indeed I have one officer with only the rank of Lieut. who has been in the service from the begining of the war. This however will make no difference and I would still say give the rank of Capt. Please excuse my writing on a half sheet. I had no resource but to take the blank half of your letter."

Robert T. Lincoln was appointed captain and assistant adjutant general of Volunteers, February 11, 1865, and resigned June 10, 1865.

To Ethan A. Hitchcock[1]

Will Gen. Hitchcock please see and hear the bearer, Col. Coburn, on the subject within? A. LINCOLN
Jan. 19. 1865.

[1] AES, In. Lincoln's endorsement appears on the back of a four-page letter from Oliver P. Morton, January 12, 1865, presented by Colonel John Coburn, Thirty-third Indiana Volunteers, requesting immediate action in regard to exchanging Confederate prisoners in Indiana prisons for members of the Fifty-first and Seventy-third Indiana Regiments, suffering in Southern prisons.

To Joseph Holt[1]

January 19, 1865

Will the Judge Advocate General please give me his opinion whether it would be legally competent for the President to direct a new-trial in this case, and if yea, whether this is a proper case in which to so direct? A. LINCOLN
Jan. 19. 1865.

[1] AES, IHi. Lincoln's endorsement appears on the back of a long letter from A. G. Riddle and R. Stockett Mathews, counsel for Thomas W. Johnson and others, January 18, 1865, asking for a new trial of their clients, who had been convicted along with the notorious blockade runner Pardon Worsley. Chief ground for the request was new evidence and the fact that the defense had not been allowed to introduce witnesses to refute Worsley's testimony that Johnson supplied him with goods with full knowledge that he was trading with the rebels. See further Lincoln to Holt, February 17, *infra*.

To Edward O. C. Ord[1]

Executive Mansion, Washington,
Major General Ord. Jan. 19. 1865.

You have a man in arrest for desertion passing by the name of Stanley—William Stanley I think—but whose real name is different. He is the son of so close a friend of mine that I must not let him be executed. Please let me know what is his present and prospective condition. A. LINCOLN

[1] ALS, DNA WR RG 107, Presidential Telegrams, I, 293. See Lincoln's telegram to Butler, December 29, 1864, *supra*. No reply from General Ord has been found.

To Edwin M. Stanton[1]

Let this appointment be made.   A LINCOLN
Jan. 19. 1865

[1] AES, RPB. Lincoln's endorsement appears on a letter to Stanton signed by members of the Y.M.C.A. of Elmira, New York, November 4, 1864, recommending appointment of Reverend Thomas S. Dewing as hospital chaplain. Acting Surgeon General C. H. Crane, endorsed on January 17, 1865: "There is a General Hospital at Elmira, NY, to which no Chaplain has been appointed." Dewing was nominated as hospital chaplain at Elmira on January 23, and his appointment was confirmed on February 20.

To Edwin M. Stanton[1]

Hon. Sec. of War   Executive Mansion,
Dear Sir.   Washington, Jan. 19, 1865.

You remember that from time to time appeals have been made to us by persons claiming to have attempted to come through our lines with their effects to take the benefit of the Amnesty proclamation, and to have been despoiled of their effects under Gen. Butler's administration. Some of these claims have color of merit, and may be really meritorious. Please consider whether we can not set on foot an investigation, which may advance justice in the premises.
Yours truly   A LINCOLN
Jan. 19. 1865.

[1] ALS, IHi. No reply has been found.

To John P. Usher[1]

January 19, 1865
I personally know this man—Vital Jarrot—to be one of the best of men; & as I believe, having peculiar qualifications for the place— and I shall be glad to appoint him if no obstacle be known at the Department.   A. LINCOLN
Jan. 19. 1865

[1] AES, DNA NR RG 48, Appointments, Indian Agents, Box 72. Lincoln's endorsement appears on a letter of Vital Jarrot to Senator Lyman Trumbull, Philadelphia, January 16, 1865: "After reaching this place transacting some business here on my way to Washington City, I received a telegram, from my son in law, calling me back home immediately. You will therefore pardon me for calling upon you to represent me with the Executive. To be short—at the solicitations of the traders along the Platte I have consented to apply to Mr Lincoln for the Indian Agency of the Sious on the Platts. I am informed that said agency is now vacant and I am vain enough to concur, with the Indian traders I have seen, in believing that I could do much with the Indians in bringing them back to peaceful relations with us. To give what, I am informed, was the cause of their

present hostility would require more space than an ordinary letter. I shall therefor neither trouble you with the details of the origin, progress and present condition of the troubles with those Indians. Should you however please apply and procure me the apointment, it will be time for me then to lay all the information I have received on the subject, before the proper department. This is my only application I have ever made for executive favor of any kind and I do not think that I am expecting too much, to believe that the President on your recommendation will appoint me."

Vital Jarrot of St. Clair County, Illinois, who had followed his father Nicholas Jarrot in the Indian trade, had been known to Lincoln from the period of the Black Hawk War and had served with Lincoln in the Illinois House of Representatives in 1838-1839. He was nominated agent of the Upper Platte Agency on February 17 and confirmed by the Senate on March 3, 1865.

To John A. Dix[1]

Major General Dix   Executive Mansion
New-York.   Washington, Jan. 20. 1865
    Let W. N. Bilbo be discharged on his parole.   A. LINCOLN

[1] ALS, DNA WR RG 107, Presidential Telegrams, I, 294. William N. Bilbo, an old Whig of Tennessee, wrote Lincoln from New York on January 26, 1865: "Accept my unfeigned gratitude for my prompt release from the malicious or profoundly ignorant charge of being a southern spy. To those who know me the charge is simply ridiculous. I may be justly charged of being impulsive, defiant, and precipitant, but never as a hypocrite or spy—never never. Sir, I have written this for other purposes than a return of my grateful acknowledgement for your confidence and friendship. I have at last succeeded this evening through my friends in prevaling upon the 'World' the organ of the Democracy to declare on Saturday or friday that to vote *for* or *against* the 'Amend-ment' clause on Tuesday next was no test of Democracy a::d rather indirectly to advise the Democracy to vote for it. I was thus promised this evening by its Editor So you need not have any apprehension now upon its passage. Gov Seymour has declared that he had no interest upon the subject, and if it passed he would have no regrets. . . . Mr Seward first intrusted this matter to me, and I first won over Judge [Thomas A. R.] Nelson who introduced me to you and who has been indefatigable in his assiduous efforts to procure other Democrats to vote for it. The Bill will pass and thus I will have discharged my obligations to you & Mr Seward as an old line whig, and my paramount obligations to eternal justice and an universal humanity. Had you not better have the article of the 'World' copied in the Chronicle the next day, to ease the Democratic scruples of some members of congress."

To Ulysses S. Grant[1]

Lieut. Gen. Grant   Executive Mansion
City-Point, Va   Washington, Jan. 20. 1865
    If Thomas Lamplugh, of the first Delaware Regiment, has been sentenced to death, and is not yet executed, suspend & report the case to me.   A. LINCOLN

[1] ALS, DNA WR RG 107, Presidential Telegrams, I, 295. General John A. Rawlings replied on the same day: "The following dispatch has just been received from Genl Meade. . . . 'The proceedings in the case of private Lemplough first

(1st) Delaware Vols will be forwarded to the President and action in the case suspended till his orders are received.' " (DLC-RTL).

No further action has been found in the case of "Thomas Lamplaugh," alias Thomas Carey, sentenced to be shot for desertion. The court-martial record ends with Lincoln's suspension of sentence on January 20 (DNA WR RG 153, Judge Advocate General, NN 3380).

Order Concerning Export of Hay[1]

Executive Mansion,
Washington City, Jan. 20, 1865.

Ordered: That no clearances for the exportation of hay from the United States be granted until further orders, unless the same shall have been placed on shipboard before the publication hereof.
ABRAHAM LINCOLN.

[1] Stan. V. Henkels Catalog, October 16, 1930, No. 85; James D. Richardson, *Messages and Papers of the President*, VI, 275. According to the catalog description, this is a document signed.

Pass for H. P. Livingston[1]

Allow the bearer, H. P. Livingston, to pass from any Northern Port to Savannah Ga. & then report to the U.S. Military Commandant.
Jan. 20. 1865   A. LINCOLN

[1] ADS, owned by Richard Lufkin, Boston, Massachusetts.

Recommendation for L. J. Czapkay[1]

Executive Mansion,
Washington, January 20, 1865.

I am not personally acquainted with Dr. L. J. Czapkay, of whom the letter on the other half of this sheet is written; but the writer is one of our United States Senators, of high standing, whom I cheerfully indorse; and I add that I hope Dr. Czapkay may have a pleasant sojourn in Europe and may find all reasonable facilities for effecting the objects of his visit.   A. LINCOLN

[1] Copy, DLC-RTL. The copy of Lincoln's letter written on Executive Mansion stationery is in John Hay's handwriting. A copy of Senator John Conness' letter of January 19, also in Hay's handwriting, is as follows:

"The bearer of this letter is a citizen of the U.S. and of Cal and is one of our most ardent patriots and a gentleman of wealth and discretion He has a letter of Commissioner Newton to represent that Department at the coming 'International Exhibition' in Prussia. My object is to get an autograph letter from you with the condition precedent that no expense shall accrue from the proceeding," (*Ibid.*).

Reply to Baron de Wetterstedt[1]

January 20, 1865

BARON WETTERSTEDT: My memory does not recall an instance of disagreement between Sweden and the United States. Your predecessor was most agreeable in his intercourse with this Government, and I greet you with the same good feeling which was entertained for him while he resided with us. The consideration which your Government has manifested by raising the rank of its mission here, is acknowledged with sincere satisfaction. You may be assured that on my part every occasion will be improved to exhibit the sincere desire which this Government entertains for the prosperity and welfare of the Government and Kingdom of Sweden and Norway.

[1] Washington *Daily Morning Chronicle*, January 21, 1865. Lincoln replied to Baron de Wetterstedt, minister from Sweden and Norway, whose speech upon presenting his credentials called attention to the esteem which the King of Sweden and Norway expressed for the United States in "thus elevating his legation in America to the first rank of our diplomatic hierarchy."

To Joseph J. Reynolds[1]

Executive Mansion Washington,
Major General Reynolds.   Jan. 20. 1865

It would appear by the accompanying papers that Mrs. Mary E. Morton is the owner, independently of her husband, of a certain building, premises and furniture, which she, with her children, has been occupying and using peaceably during the war, until recently, when the Provost-Marshal, has, in the name of the U.S. government, seized the whole of said property, and ejected her from it. It also appears by her statement to me, that her husband went off in the rebellion at the beginning, wherein he still remains.

It would seem that this seizure has not been made for any Military object, as for a place of storage, a hospital, or the like, because this would not have required the seizure of the furniture, and especially not the return of furniture previously taken away.

The seizure must have been on some claim [of] *confiscation*, a matter of which the courts, and *not* the Provost-Marshals, or other military officers are to judge. In this very case, would probably be the questions "Is either the husband or wife a traitor?" "Does the property belong to the husband or to the wife?" "Is the property of the wife confiscable for the treason of the husband?" and other similar questions, all which it is ridiculous for a Provost-Marshal to assume to decide.

[228]

The true rule for the Military is to seize such property as is needed for Military uses and reasons, and let the rest alone. Cotton and other staple articles of commerce are seizable for military reasons. Dwelling-houses & furniture are seldom so. If Mrs. Morton is playing traitor, to the extent of practical injury, seize her, but leave her house to the courts. Please revise and adjust this case upon these principles. Yours &c   A. LINCOLN

1 ALS, DLC (on deposit); LS copy, DLC-RTL. This letter is incorrectly dated 1864 in Nicolay and Hay (IX, 287), as a result of the fact that the copy in the Lincoln Papers is misdated 1864. General Joseph J. Reynolds was in command of the Department of Arkansas. No further reference to this case has been found.

To Joseph Holt[1]

Let the order dishonorably dismissing Captn. Burrage be revoked.
Jan. 21, 1865   A. LINCOLN

1 Copy, DNA RG 130, U.S. Army Court Martial Cases, White House Office. Captain Henry S. Burrage, Company A, Thirty-sixth Massachusetts Volunteers, had been dismissed on charges of holding communication with the enemy. AGO *Special Orders No. 61*, February 7, 1865, ordered that he be restored to his command. He was mustered out of service on June 8, 1865.

To Joseph Holt[1]

January 21, 1865
Let the unexecuted portion of the sentence be remitted and the soldier be returned to duty with his regiment to serve his full enlistment including period of absence.   A. LINCOLN
Jan. 21. 1865

1 ES, DNA WR RG 153, Judge Advocate General, NN 2703. Lincoln's endorsement appears on the court-martial record of Private Vance Mason, Company C, Thirty-seventh Kentucky Volunteers, sentenced to be shot for desertion.

To Lewis Wallace[1]

Major General Wallace.   Executive Mansion
Baltimore, Md.   Washington, Jan. 21. 1865
Two weeks or ten days ago as I remember I gave direction for Levin L. Walters to be either tried at once or discharged. If he has not been tried, nor a trial of him progressing in good faith, discharge him at once.   A. LINCOLN

1 ALS, DNA WR RG 107, Presidential Telegrams, I, 296. See Lincoln to Stanton, January 4, *supra*. General Wallace replied on January 22: "I referred your telegram relative to Waters to Maj Genl [Edward M.] McCook President of the Military Commission and he replies as follows

[229]

" 'The trial of Levin L. Waters is progressing in good faith. The papers in his case were sent to the commission about ten (10) days ago. The accused asked to have thirty (30) witnesses summoned, then some more, which was ordered. These witnesses are now reporting and his trial commenced Monday night. I received no instructions from you to have him tried at once, or discharged but only received telegram from Mr Stanton to proceed without delay to have Waters tried The delay you will observe has been from a disposition to accomodate Waters. Remembering your former directions I have had the effort made to hasten the proceedings I assure you I would not thwart your wishes or trifle with a prisoners liberty Under these circumstances shall the trial proceed' " (DLC-RTL).

See further Lincoln to Wallace, January 22, *infra.*

Cotton Permit for John D. Champlin[1]

Executive Mansion, City of Washington.

January, [22?] 1865.

It having been made satisfactorily to appear to me that John D. Champlin of the City of New York, is the owner of a large amount of Cotton, now being in the vicinge of the Port of Galveston and City of Houston, State of Texas, amounting to Eleven Thousand Bales, which it is right and proper he should be permitted, and which it is the true policy of the United States that he be authorized together with any other Cotton of which he may obtain possession to take and carry away from said State of Texas.

Now therefore, it is hereby ordered that permission be and is hereby given to the said John D. Champlin by himself, his agents, servants and employees, by means of Steamers, Ships or other Vessels, to proceed to, and take such Cotton and transport the same from said Port of Galveston, to the Port of Havana, or any Port within the United States.

And said Steamers, Ships or other Vessels, with such Cotton, shall be and are hereby declared free and exempt from seizure or detention or any molestation by any Officer of the Government. And Commandants of Military Departments, Districts, Posts, Detachments, Naval Stations, Ships of War, Squadrons, Gun Boats, Flotillas, and Fleets will observe this order, and obey the same— and will give the said John D. Champlin, his agents, servants and employees, Steamers, Ships, Vessels and Transports free and unmolested way and right of way for the purpose of getting and taking away said Cotton or any part thereof from the place aforesaid.

The said John D. Champlin is not to carry into the Port of Galveston any article goods or merchandize contraband of war, but may take into said Port Bagging and Rope and such articles as are not contraband of war, for the purposes aforesaid.

[1] Df (copy?), DLC-RTL. The editors have not been able to determine whether Lincoln ever signed or issued this permit. The bracketed portion of the date is supplied on the basis of John D. Champlin's memorial of January 20, 1865:

"Your memorialist, John D. Champlin, of the city of New York respectfully represents as follows:

"I am a native of the State of Rhode Island and at present a resident of the City of New York For more than twenty years next preceding the . . . Rebellion, I was a resident of Louisiana and other Southern States. . . .

"I am now the owner of about Eleven Thousand Bales of Cotton, all at and in the vicinity of Galveston and Houston in the State of Texas.

"I desire to obtain from the United States authorities the requisite authority and permission to bring such cotton from Texas by the way of the Port of Galveston. . . ." (DLC-RTL).

Memorandum Concerning the Draft[1]

[c. January 22, 1865]

The draft matter complained of by Gov. Fenton is this, that in giving credits for part calls *one* three-years man is counted equal to *three* one-year men, while on the pending call each man is to count *one* and *only* one, whether he enlist for one, two, or three years. The practical difficulty may be illustrated by the following supposed case. The towns of A & B—before any enlisted, had each 100 men. On the late call A gave sixty six *one* year men, leaving only 34 at home, while B. gave 33 three-years men, leaving 67 at home. On the pending call each owes 100 men, subject to its credit. But while A gets credit for 66—it owes 34—taking the last man in it; while B gets credit for 99—owes one, and has sixty-six left quietly at home. This ugly conjuncture occurs in some sort accidentally, some towns putting in one years men and others three years men, while attaching no consequence to the difference, but which now burthens the one class absolutely beyond their immediate power to bear. While the above is only a supposed case, I am told there are realities that are even stranger—when there are not men enough in the town to answer it's quota. It gives no present relief that the one year men are to come home sooner than the three year men, as the former . . .[2]

[1] AD, RPB. This memorandum is written in pencil on a blotter. The date has been assigned on the assumption that Governor Reuben E. Fenton's conference with Lincoln, January 22-24, provided the data of which Lincoln takes notice. On January 26, upon returning to Albany, Governor Fenton wrote Lincoln: "Honorables James A. Bell, George H. Andrews, Thomas B. Van Buren, and E. C. Topliff, Members of the Legislature, visit you in regard to filling the quotas for our State. They will represent to you the public feeling, and what we deem just cause for complaint. I beg you consider favorably what they may say; and allow me again to earnestly renew my recommendations as to the mode of filling the present quota." (DLC-RTL).   See Lincoln to Stanton, *infra.*

[2] The last one and one-half lines are illegible.

To Edwin M. Stanton[1]

Executive Mansion.

Hon. Sec of War.   January 22, 1865.

The Governor has a pretty good case. I feel sure he is more than half right. We don't want him to feel cross and we in the wrong. Try and fix it with him.   A. LINCOLN

[1] Tracy, p. 251. See Lincoln's memorandum concerning the draft, *supra*.

To Lewis Wallace[1]

Major General Wallace   Executive Mansion
Baltimore, Md.   Washington Jan. 22. 1865

The case of Waters being as you state it, in your despatch of to-day, of course the trial will proceed.   A. LINCOLN

[1] ALS, DNA WR RG 107, Presidential Telegrams, I, 297. See Lincoln to Wallace, January 21, *supra*.

To Christopher C. Augur[1]

January 23, 1865

Returned to Gen. Augur for the exercise of his own discretion. And it is suggested that like cases be not refered to the President, unless it be such as he specially directs.   A. LINCOLN

Jan. 23. 1865.

[1] AES, DNA WR RG 153, Judge Advocate General, NN 2203. Lincoln's endorsement is written on the court-martial record of Private Frank Carpenter, alias Harry J. Carpenter, Third Vermont Volunteers, sentenced to be shot for desertion. General Augur had approved the sentence. Although Lincoln's later endorsement pardoning Carpenter is missing, the jacket covering the papers indicates that Carpenter was pardoned and returned to his regiment on March 7 (9?), and the Roster of Company K, Third Vermont Regiment, lists Franklin Carpenter as pardoned on March 9 and returned to his regiment on March 23, 1865.

To William O. Bartlett[1]

Office U.S. Military Telegraph,
W. O. Bartlett, Esq   War Department,
New-York.   Washington, D.C., Jan. 23. 1865

Please come and see me at once.   A. LINCOLN.

[1] ALS, DNA WR RG 107, Presidential Telegrams, I, 298. See Lincoln to Wakeman, January 26, *infra*.

Endorsement Concerning William F. Hinkle[1]

[c. January 23, 1865]

West-Point—An interesting testimonial.
William F. Hinkle.

1 AE, DNA WR RG 94, U.S. Military Academy, 1864, No. 75. Lincoln's endorsement appears on a letter from Charles Case, Washington, January 23, 1865, recommending William F. Hinkle for reappointment. An endorsement in another hand notes that Hinkle "failed to pass his entrance examination both in June & Sep. 1864." No record of Hinkle's reappointment has been found.

To Joseph Holt[1]

Pardon, on condition of re-inlisting and faithfully serving a term
Jan. 23, 1865. A. LINCOLN

1 AES, DNA WR RG 153, Judge Advocate General, NN 45. Lincoln's endorsement appears on the court-martial record of Private Llewellyn Sawyer, Fifth Maine Battery, sentenced to two years' imprisonment at hard labor, on charges of desertion. Lincoln's pardon of Sawyer was promulgated in AGO *Special Orders No. 63*, February 8, 1865.

To Joseph Holt[1]

Pardon, for unexecuted part of sentence on condition of serving out remainder of his term in his regiment. A. LINCOLN
Jan. 23. 1865

1 AES, DNA WR RG 153, Judge Advocate General, LL 316. Lincoln's endorsement appears on the court-martial record of Private Thomas McGrath, Company I, Twenty-sixth Massachusetts Volunteers, sentenced to fifteen years at hard labor on charges of drunkenness and striking an officer. McGrath was mustered out of service on August 26, 1865.

Order Concerning John Dugan and Christopher V. Hogan[1]

January 23, 1865

The within named Hogan, or Dugan was arrested and imprisoned by my authority. This writ of habeas corpus is suspended, and the officer having Hogan or Dugan in custody is directed not to produce his body, but to hold him in custody until further orders giving this order in his return to the court.

Jan. 23, 1865. A. LINCOLN

1 New York *Times*, January 25, 1865. The *Times* article in which this order appears relates the following:
"To-day was set apart for the return of writs of habeas corpus on the Superintendent of the Old Capitol Prison, commanding him to produce the bodies of Christopher V. Hogan and John Dugan, with the date and cause of their arrest. They were formerly employed as detectives on the Metropolitan Police force, and subsequently Hogan was a special detective of the Treasury Department. While so acting, a robbery was committed, in February last. The trunk of Major [Benjamin] Malone, a Paymaster in the Army, was robbed of nearly $2,000. Some time after, Hogan and Dugan were arrested by Superintendent Wood, on charge of being concerned in the robbery, and they have ever since been held in custody.

This morning, at the convening of the general term of the court, Mr. Wood appeared to answer the writ, and handed his return to the court. Superintendent Wood answered: 'The body of Hogan, or Dugan, is in my possession. He was arrested and imprisoned by authority of the President of the United States. I do not produce his body by reason of the order of the President of the United States indorsed upon said writ, to which reference is hereby respectfully made.' The indorsement of the President on each writ is as follows: [text as above]"

To Edwin M. Stanton[1]

January 23, 1865

Order of dismissal having been revoked and officer dismissed because Senate had not confirmed, now let him have his reappointment if vacancy has not been filled.   A. LINCOLN

Jan. 23, 1865

[1] Copy, DNA RG 130, U.S. Army Court Martial Cases, White House Office. The original of this order has not been found, but the transcript is preserved in the record of the case of First Lieutenant Isaac M. Beebe, Company A, Twelfth Regiment, Veteran Reserve Corps, dismissed for unofficer-like conduct and inattention to duty by reason of drunkenness. Beebe's reappointment was confirmed by the Senate on February 14, 1865.

To Grenville M. Dodge[1]

Major General Dodge   Executive Mansion
St. Louis, Mo   Washington, Jan. 24. 1865

It is said an old lady in Clay county, Mo, by name, Mrs. Winfred E. Price, is about being sent South. If she is not misbehaving let her remain   A. LINCOLN

[1] ALS, DNA WR RG 107, Presidential Telegrams, I, 300. General Dodge replied on January 26: "No order has been issued from these Head Quarters banishing Mrs Winfred E Price nor from any subordinate that I can learn of" (DLC-RTL).

Endorsement[1]

[January 24, 1865]

Charge to me   A. LINCOLN

[1] AES, ORB. Lincoln's endorsement appears on a telegram of Robert T. Lincoln to Fred P. Anderson, January 24, 1865.

Endorsement Concerning David Zimmerman[1]

A substitute will be accepted when mustered in for this man.

Jan. 24. 1865   A. LINCOLN

[1] AES, owned by R. E. Burdick, New York City. Lincoln's endorsement appears on a letter of J. H. Zimmerman, Stoystown, Pennsylvania, to Representative Alexander H. Coffroth, December 17, 1864, asking to be allowed to furnish a substitute for his brother David Zimmerman, Company G, Ninety-third Pennsylvania Volunteers. The roster of Company G lists David Zimmerman as not accounted for at muster out.

To Ulysses S. Grant[1]

Lieut. Gen. Grant   Executive Mansion
City-Point.   Washington Jan. 24. 1865

If Newell W. Root, of Conn. Heavy Artillery is under sentence of death please telegraph me briefly the circumstances.

A LINCOLN

[1] ALS, DNA WR RG 107, Presidential Telegrams, I, 299. On January 25, 1865, Captain and Judge Advocate P. T. Whitehead telegraphed: "I have the honor to report in regard to Private Newell W. Root alias Geo H Harris Co H 1st Conn Heavy Artillery, that he was tried by this Court on Dec 19th 1864 & convicted of 'deserting to the Enemy' & sentenced to be hung. His sentence is approved by General Meade & ordered to be carried into effect at City Point on Friday 27th inst. . . . Root deserted to the Enemy near Dutch Gap & gave himself up to the rebels as a union deserter; was released . . . and on making his way through . . . Ky represented himself as a rebel Deserter for the purpose of getting out of the service. he gave the name of Harris & came to City Point in arrest under that name. . . ." (DLC-RTL). See further, Lincoln's telegram to Grant, January 25, *infra*.

To Andrew Johnson[1]

Hon. Andrew Johnson   Executive Mansion
Nashville, Tenn.   Washington, Jan. 24. 1865

Several members of the Cabinet, with myself, considered the question to-day as to the time of your coming on here. While we fully appreciate your wish to remain in Tennessee until her State-Government shall be completely re-inaugerated, it is our unanamous conclusion that it is unsafe for you to not be here on the fourth of March. Be sure to reach here by that time.

A. LINCOLN

[1] ALS, DNA WR RG 107, Presidential Telegrams, I, 301. See Lincoln to Johnson, January 14, *supra*.

To William A. Menzies[1]

William Menzies, Esq.   Executive Mansion
Dear Sir   Washington, Jan. 24. 1865

Wilmington, N.C. is ours, of right and in fact   Yours truly
A. LINCOLN

1 ALS, The Rosenbach Company, Philadelphia and New York. No communication from Menzies related to this note has been found. William A. Menzies was a resident of Bourbon County, Kentucky, and the father of Representative John W. Menzies. An accompanying envelope carries Lincoln's endorsement: "William Menzies/New-York." Fort Fisher was captured on January 15, and the port of Wilmington which was to surrender on February 22, was blockaded.

Reply to Philadelphia Delegation[1]

January 24, 1865

REVEREND SIR, AND LADIES AND GENTLEMEN: I accept, with emotions of profoundest gratitude, the beautiful gift you have been pleased to present to me. You will, of course, expect that I acknowledge it. So much has been said about Gettysburg, and so well said, that for me to attempt to say more may, perhaps, only serve to weaken the force of that which has already been said. A most graceful and eloquent tribute was paid to the patriotism and self-denying labors of the American ladies, on the occasion of the consecration of the National Cemetery at Gettysburg, by our illustrious friend, Edward Everett, now, alas! departed from earth.[2] His life was a truly great one, and, I think, the greatest part of it was that which crowned its closing years. I wish you to read, if you have not already done so, the glowing, and eloquent, and truthful words which he then spoke of the women of America. Truly, the services they have rendered to the defenders of our country in this perilous time, and are yet rendering, can never be estimated as they ought to be. For your kind wishes to me, personally, I beg leave to render you, likewise, my sincerest thanks. I assure you they are reciprocated. And now, gentlemen and ladies, may God bless you all.

1 Washington *Daily Morning Chronicle*, January 25, 1865. This speech is incorrectly dated January 25, 1865, in Hertz, II, 960. Lincoln replied to a speech of Reverend William Suddards, delivered on presenting "a truly beautiful and superb vase of skeleton leaves, gathered from the battle-fields of Gettysburg."
2 Edward Everett died on January 15, 1865.

To Edwin M. Stanton[1]

January 24, 1865

I personally know Captn Winters & think he should have another chance. Let the order dismissing him be set aside upon his making right the matter of his accounts.

Jany 24. 1865

1 Copy, DNA RG 130, U.S. Army Court Martial Cases, White House Office. The transcript of Lincoln's endorsement is preserved on the White House regis-

ter of court-martial cases. Captain Gilbert E. Winters, commissary of subsistence of Volunteers, had been dismissed for inefficiency on September 16, 1863. He was reinstated on March 3, 1865.

To Ulysses S. Grant[1]

Office U.S. Military Telegraph,

Lieut. Genl. Grant   War Department,

City-Point, Va.   Washington, D.C., Jan. 25 1865

Having received the report in the case of Newell W. Root, I do not interfere further in the case.   A. LINCOLN

[1] ALS, DNA WR RG 107, Presidential Telegrams, I, 303. See Lincoln to Grant, January 24, *supra*. Newell W. Root was hanged on January 27, 1865.

Memoranda on Robert Burns[1]

[January 25, 1865]

I can not frame a toast to Burns. I can say nothing worthy of his generous heart, and transcendent genius   A. LINCOLN

I can not frame a toast to Burns. I can say nothing worthy of his generous heart and transcending genius. Thinking of what he has said, I can not say anything which seems worth saying

A. LINCOLN

[1] ADS-P, ISLA. Lincoln had been invited to attend the annual celebration of the Burns Club of Washington in 1864 (Robert Crawford to Lincoln, January 23, 1864, DLC-RTL). Alexander Williamson, a clerk in the Second Auditor's Office who had tutored "Willie" and "Tad" Lincoln, wrote again on January 24, 1865: "The 'Executive Committee of Management for the Celebration of the 106th Anniversary of the birth of Robert Burns' have instructed me as their Secretary to request the honor of your recognition of the genius of Scotland's bard, by either a toast, a sentiment, or in any other way you may deem proper. It takes place tomorrow." (*Ibid.*).

The Washington *Evening Star* of January 26, 1865, reported the meeting of the Burns Club on the previous evening: "Mr. Williamson, remarking that the President's pressing duties had prevented him writing a letter or a toast in response to the invitation to be present . . . read a hastily written memorandum which the President had sent him, in substance as follows

" 'I cannot now frame a toast to Burns or say to you aught worthy of his most generous heart and transcending genius.' "

To John F. Miller[1]

Officer in Command at   Executive Mansion

Nashville, Tenn.   Washington, Jan. 25. 1865

Do not allow ——— Elliott, under sentence of death to be executed without further order from me; and if an exchange of him

[237]

for Capt. S. T. Harris, now a prisoner, supposed to be at Columbia South-Carolina, can be effected, let it be done.   A. LINCOLN

¹ ALS, DNA WR RG 107, Presidential Telegrams, I, 302. See Lincoln to Miller, January 11, *supra*. General Miller replied on the same day: "Your orders suspending sentence of J W Elliott until further orders from yourself & authorizing Exchange of Capt J T Harris just recd" (DLC-RTL). Although Elliott appears in earlier correspondence also as "S. W. Elliott," "J. W." appear to be the correct initials.

To Edwin M. Stanton¹

Hon. Secretary of War.   Executive Mansion
My dear Sir.   Washington Jan. 25. 1865
    About Jews. I wish you would give Dr. Zacharie a pass to go to Savannah, remain a week and return, bringing with him, if he wishes, his father and sisters or any of them. This will spare me trouble and oblige me. I promised him long ago that he should be allowed this whenever Savannah should fall into our hands.
    Blumenberg, at Baltimore. I think he should have a hearing. He has suffered for us & served us well—had the rope around his neck for being our friend—raised troops—fought, and been wounded. He should not be dismissed in a way that disgraces and ruins him without a hearing. Yours truly   A. LINCOLN

¹ ALS, NHi. Stanton replied on the same day: "An order for leave to Zacharie as directed by you has been issued & sent to Mr Nicolay. In relation to [Leopold] Blumenburg—I had no knowledge of the proceedings in his case they having transpired during my absence, but the Provost Marshal reports that he was removed for cause of which a statement will be furnished you. Among other things one charge was cruelty in gaging men to make them confess they were deserters. This charge General Fry reports was fully established." (DLC-RTL).
    An undated letter from Dr. Isachar Zacharie (cataloged in the Lincoln Papers in December, 1864) seems certainly to have been written after January 25, 1865: "I leave on Saturday per steamship *Arago* for Savannah where I hope to find my Dear old Father and friends—if you have any matters that you would have properly attended to, I will consider it a favour for [you] to let me attend to it for you. . . ." (*Ibid.*).
    Major Leopold Blumenburg, Fifth Maryland Infantry, wounded at Antietam and later appointed provost marshal of the Third District in Maryland, had been dismissed from the service on January 17, 1865.

Endorsement¹

Pardon, on condition of returning to his regiment and faithfully serving to the end of the term of the regiment.   A. LINCOLN
    Jan. 26. 1865

¹ AES, IHi. This endorsement has been clipped from attendant papers.

To Ulysses S. Grant[1]

Executive Mansion, Washington,
Lieutenant General Grant   January 26, 1865.

Suspend execution of death sentence of William H. Jeffs Company B Fifty sixth Massachusetts volunteers until further orders, and forward record of trial for examination.   A. LINCOLN.

Maj. Eckert
Please send the above telegram   JNO. G. NICOLAY
Priv. Sec.

[1] D, DNA WR RG 107, Presidential Telegrams, I, 305. Across the top of this telegram appears a pencilled note: "Repeated Jany 28 '65 to Comdg Officer Norfolk Va." Grant replied on the same day, quoting a telegram from Major General John G. Parke: "No proceedings in the case of Wm. A Jeffs Co 'B' fifty sixth (56) Mass Vols have been recd at these HdQuarters   In case the sentence should be death the proceedings will be forwarded you" (DLC-RTL). See Lincoln's telegram to George F. Shepley, January 28, *infra*.

To Ulysses S. Grant[1]

Executive Mansion, Washington,
Lieutenant General Grant   Jan'y 26, 1865.

Suspend execution of Hamel Shaffer ordered to be shot at City-Point tomorrow, until further orders, and forward record of trial for examination   A. LINCOLN

[1] D, DNA WR RG 107, Presidential Telegrams, I, 306. On the received copy of this telegram appears Grant's endorsement to Major General John G. Parke: "The above just received. Please send proceedings to these Head Quarters." (DNA WR RG 108, Headquarters of the Army, Letters Received, P 25). A telegram from Nellie O. Shaffer, Concord (no state), January 26, 1865, asked: "My husband Hamel Shaffer is sentenced to be shot tomorrow at City Pt   Will you please delay the sentence until I reach him   answer immedy" (DLC-RTL). Efforts to identify Hamel Shaffer and locate the record of his case have failed, but see Lincoln's telegram to Grant, February 6, *infra*.

To Abram Wakeman[1]

"*Cypher*"   Office U.S. Military Telegraph,
Abram Wakeman.   War Department,
New-York.   Washington, D.C., January 26 1865

I have telegraphed W. O. Bartlett to come and see me. He neither comes, nor answers. Can you not send him?   A. LINCOLN

[1] ALS, DNA WR RG 107, Presidential Telegrams, I, 304. Wakeman replied on the same day: "Mr B only got your dispatch this morning   He will go over tonight" (DLC RTL). William O. Bartlett also replied: "Mr Wakeman was ab-

sent. Your telegram but just received. I will be there tomorrow." (*Ibid.*). Lincoln's business with James Gordon Bennett's close associate William O. Bartlett is suggested by Bartlett's letter to Bennett, November 4, 1864:

"My Dear Sir: I am from Washington, fresh from the bosom of Father Abraham. I had a full conversation with him, alone, on Tuesday evening, at the White House, in regard to yourself, among other subjects.

"I said to him: There are but few days now before the election. If Mr. Bennett is not *certainly* to have the offer of the French Mission, I want to know it *now*. It is important to me.

"We discussed the course which the *Herald* had pursued, at length, and I will tell you, verbally, at your convenience, what he said; but he concluded with the remark that in regard to the understanding between him and me, about Mr. Bennett, he had been a 'shut pan, to everybody'; and that he *expected to do that thing* (appoint you to France) *as much as he expected to live.* He repeated: '*I expect to do it as certainly as I do to be reelected myself.*'

"I wanted to see you; but I am obliged to do some work in Pennsylvania, about the election, and cannot till my return." (Oliver Carlson, *The Man Who Made the News, James Gordon Bennett*, p. 370).

See further, Lincoln to Bennett, February 20, *infra.*

To Gideon Welles[1]

Hon. Secretary of the Navy   Executive Mansion,
My dear Sir   Washington, Jan. 26. 1865.

I now understand that the record of the trial of Smith brothers at Boston is before you. Please do not let any execution of sentence take place, until the record shall have been before me. Yours truly

A. LINCOLN

[1] ALS, DNA WR NB RG 45, Executive Letters, No. 83. Concerning Benjamin G. and Franklin W. Smith, see Lincoln to Welles, August 28, 1864, *supra*, and the order annulling sentence in the case, March 18, 1865, *infra.*

To Ulysses S. Grant[1]

Executive Mansion, Washington,
Lt. General Grant   27 January, 1865.

Stay execution in case of Barney Roorke 15th New York Engineers until record can be examined here.   A. LINCOLN.

Send above dispatch and oblige   JOHN HAY A.A.G.

[1] D, DNA WR RG 107, Presidential Telegrams, I, 307. This telegram, including Lincoln's signature, is in John Hay's handwriting. Grant replied on the same day:

"Maj Gen Parke furnishes the following . . . in relation to Barney Rouke 15th N Y Engineers of whom you telegraphed this morning

"'Private Barney Rouke 15th N.Y. Engineers was not sentenced capitally. His sentence to be dishonorably discharged . . . and to be confined at hard labor for . . . ten (10) years . . . at Albany N.Y. . . . the record forwarded Jany 2nd 1865 to the Judge Advocate General for reference to the Secretary of War. . . .'" (DLC-RTL).

A petition in behalf of Barney Rourke, Company F, Fifteenth New York Engineers, sentenced for shooting a member of his company, was referred by Lincoln to Stanton on January 13, 1865, but is missing from the files (DNA WR RG 107, Secretary of War, Letters Received, P 69, Register).

To John F. Miller[1]

To the Commanding Officer
at Nashville Tenn

Executive Mansion,
Washington,
27 January, 1865.

Let execution in case of Cornelius E. Peacher be stayed until further orders.   A. LINCOLN

[1] LS, DNA WR RG 107, Presidential Telegrams, I, 308. See Lincoln to Miller, January 11, *supra*. Lincoln approved the sentence of Peacher on January 27 and ordered execution (DNA WR RG 153, Judge Advocate General, OO 1188), but sent this telegram afterwards. No record of further action by Lincoln has been found. General Miller telegraphed on January 31: "Your dispatch ordering that the execution of C. E. Peacher be stayed until further orders has been recd" (DLC-RTL).

Order Concerning Cornelius C. Van Arsdale[1]

Executive Mansion,
Washington, 27 January, 1865.

Let Cornelius C. Van Arsdale Prisoner of War be discharged on taking the oath of Dec. 8. 1863.   A. LINCOLN

[1] DS, RPB. This order, in John Hay's handwriting on Executive Mansion stationery, signed by Lincoln, is accompanied by an envelope addressed by Hay "For Mrs. C. W. Frazier." Van Arsdale and Mrs. Frazier have not been further identified.

Reply to Delegation of Christian Commission[1]

January 27, 1865

You owe me no thanks for what I have been able to do for you. If I may be permitted to say it, I owe you no thanks for what you have so excellently done for the country and for me; we are both alike working in the same cause, and it is because of the fact of its being a just one which gives us our mutual joy and reward in its service."

[1] New York *Tribune*, January 28, 1865. Lincoln replied to an address by George H. Stuart, who with "300 to 500 members of the Christian Commission called upon the President to-day, to thank him for his hearty co-operation with their labors in the field of war."

What appears to be another version of this reply is printed in Hertz (II, 879) as follows:

"We have been only doing our duty my friends, whatever we have been able to do together. You owe me no thanks for what I have done for the country, whatever that may be,—and I owe none, to you. We cannot repay the soldiers. (Jan. 1865)."

To the Senate[1]

To the Senate of the United States: January 27, 1865

In answer to a resolution of the Senate, dated January 23, 1865, returning to me certain nominations and requesting information whether the offices to which the persons named are respectively nominated are vacant, and, if so, how they became vacant, I herewith transmit a communication from the honorable the Attorney-General giving the information required.   ABRAHAM LINCOLN.

Executive Mansion,
January 27, 1865.

1 *Executive Journal*, XIV, 115. Attorney General James Speed's letter of January 26, submitted the following:

"1. Charles A. Peabody, nominated as attorney of the United States for the eastern district of Louisiana. Mr. Peabody was nominated in place of Rufus Waples, esq., the former incumbent, removed.

"2. Culver P. Chamberlin, nominated as attorney of the United States for the northern district of Florida.

"Mr. Chamberlin has been twice commissioned for this post in the recess of the Senate, once in April, 1863, and again in July, 1864, the post of the former incumbent, Chandler C. Yonge (appointed M'ch 14th, 1858), being, without inquiry as to the effect of the so-called secession of Florida, vacant by lapse of time.

"3. Delos Lake, nominated as attorney of the United States for the northern district of California. Mr. Lake was, on August 17th, 1864, commissioned to this post in the recess of the Senate, vice W. H. Sharp, removed.

"4. Charles P. Redmond, nominated as attorney of the United States for the eastern district of Arkansas. Mr. Redmond was commissioned in recess, on September 24, 1864, to fill a vacancy in this post caused by the removal of Charles E. Jordan, the former incumbent, who was commissioned July 29th, 1861.

"5. Bennett Pike, nominated as attorney of the United States for the western district of Mo. Mr. Pike was nominated in place of Robert J. Lackey, removed, and having been confirmed by the Senate on Dec. 13th, 1864, his commission has before this been issued.

"6. Cuthbert Bullitt, nominated as U.S. marshal for the eastern district of Louisiana. Mr. Bullitt was, on July 6th, 1864, in the recess of the Senate, commissioned in place of the former incumbent, James Graham, removed.

"7. William O. Stoddard, nominated as U.S. marshal for the eastern district of Arkansas. Mr. Stoddard was commissioned on Sept. 24th, 1864, the post then being, to say nothing as to the effect of the so-called secession of Arkansas, vacant by the expiration of the term of office of Samuel P. Haliburton, former incumbent, commissioned July 1st. 1859.

"8. John Gould, nominated as U.S. marshal for the district of Connecticut. Mr. Gould was appointed and commissioned on Dec. 1st, 1864, in recess, the post being then vacant by the resignation of Henry Hammond, the former incumbent.

"9. John A. Bingham, nominated as solicitor for the United States before the Court of Claims. Mr. Bingham was commissioned to this post July 27th, 1864, in recess, to fill a vacancy caused by the resignation of Mr. Gibson, the former incumbent.

"10. John J. Weed, nominated as assistant solicitor for the United States before the Court of Claims. Mr. Weed was commissioned to this post on July 27th, 1864, in recess, to fill a vacancy caused by the resignation of Mr. McPherson, the former incumbent.

"11. Sydney A. Hubbell, nominated as associate justice of the supreme court of the Territory of New Mexico. Mr. Hubbell was commissioned August 10th, 1864, in recess, in place of Judge Perry E. Brocchus, superseded."

Endorsement Concerning Francis P. Blair, Sr.[1]

January 28. 1865

To-day Mr. Blair tells me that on the 21st. Inst. he delivered to Mr. Davis the original of which the within is a copy, and left it with him; that at the time of delivering it, Mr. Davis read it over twice in Mr. Blair's presence, at the close of which he, Mr. B. remarked that the part about "our one common country" related to the part of Mr. D's letter about "the two countries" to which Mr. D. replied that he so understood it.   A. LINCOLN

[1] AES, DLC-RTL; AES copy, NAuE. Lincoln's endorsement is written on the copy of his letter to Blair of January 18, *supra.* See Lincoln's communication to the House of Representatives, February 10, *infra.*

To Edward O. C. Ord[1]

Executive Mansion,
Major General Ord   Washington,
Army of the James   28 January, 1865.

Give me a brief report in case of Charles Love, 7th New Hampshire, tried for desertion, & transmit record for my examination.
                    A. LINCOLN

[1] D, DNA WR RG 107, Presidential Telegrams, I, 309. This telegram, including Lincoln's signature, is in John Hay's handwriting. The roster of Company I, Seventh New Hampshire Volunteers, lists Charles Love as deserted April 28, 1864, returned to service April 4, 1865, and mustered out July 20, 1865. No reply from General Ord has been found, but see Lincoln to Grant, February 16, *infra.*

Order Concerning Fergus Peniston[1]

Executive Mansion
Washington January 28. 1865.

Mr Fergus Penniston of New Orleans claiming that he has bought products of the insurrectionary States under proper authorities of the Treasury Department issued prior to July 2, 1864, and proposing to get the Permits issued under said Authorities renewed or revived as provided in "Amended Regulation LV, series of July 29, 1864," dated January 4, 1865 signed by the Secretary of the Treasury, and approved by me, all officers of the Army and Navy and civil officers of the Government will respect all Permits to said Penniston renewed or revived in pursuance of said Amended Regulation, and cotton being transported under such renewed or revived Permits will be free from seizure detention or forfeiture, and be allowed free and unmolested passage as permitted by Agents of the Treasury Department in accordance with said amended Regulation.   ABRAHAM LINCOLN

[1] Copy preserved in the file of Cotton Case No. 562, U.S. Court, Southern District of Illinois, Springfield, Illinois. Fergus Peniston and William S. Pike were claimants for 956 bales of cotton taken by the U.S. Navy on the Ouachita expedition, about April, 1864. Lincoln's original order has not been found. See Lincoln's order of January 4, *supra*.

Pass for Mrs. J. B. Holliday[1]

Allow the bearer to visit her husband, Major J. B. Holliday, a prisoner of war, at Johnson's Island.   A. LINCOLN
    Jan. 28, 1865

[1] Anderson Galleries Catalog 2193, November 15, 1927, No. 285. A petition signed by citizens of Nicholas County, Kentucky, January 23, 1865, endorsed by Representative George H. Yeaman, asked that "Mrs. Lallie Holliday" be given a pass to visit her husband at Johnson's Island.

To William H. Seward[1]

Can the Sec. of State do any thing with this?
[January?] 28, 1865   A. LINCOLN

[1] AES, NAuE. Lincoln's endorsement appears on an envelope postmarked in 1864. The month date of Lincoln's endorsement is torn off. The undated letter in the envelope is from Madame de Give in Belgium: "It is now 13 months ago that my husband, Mr. Laurent de Give, belgian Consul left me in a great sorrow: he was obliged by heavy considerations to visit Atlanta, *Ga.* Since then, I have tried several times and by different ways to send him some news of the only beloved little child the Lord left us, but you know, Sir the blocade is such that it is absolutely impossible to force it. We are united by the laws, but how can I tell you the deep affection, the love, the mutual estimm which filled our hearts! Sir, be human and generous and take under your protection a poor lady, so sad and unhappy that no words could give you a just idea of her despair; she kneels before you and pry [*sic*] you by your mother, by all you love the most on this earth to send to his address the letter which follows."

To George F. Shepley[1]

U.S. Military Telegraph

To Commanding Officer   By Telegraph from Washington D.C
Norfolk   dated January 28th. 1865

Suspend execution of death sentence of Wm. H. Jeffs Co. "B" 56th. Mass Vols, until further orders, and forward record of the trial for examination.   A. LINCOLN

[1] Official copy, OFH. See the same telegram sent to General Grant, January 26, *supra.* General George F. Shepley replied on January 29: "Your order in reference to Wm. H. Jeffs . . . has been received. There is no such man at Norfolk and as far as I am informed no such man within this District I have communicated your order to the Major General Commanding the Department" (DLC-RTL).

On January 30, Shepley telegraphed again: "Wm B Jeffs . . . is not to be found in this District or Department The 56th Mass Vols is not in this Department & never has been." (*Ibid.*).

No further correspondence has been found. The roster of the Fifty-sixth Massachusetts Volunteers lists William H. Jeffs as mustered out of service on July 12, 1865.

To James Speed[1]

Will the Attorney General please give his opinion in writing on the legal points presented in this paper.   A. LINCOLN

Jan. 28. 1865

[1] AES, DNA GE RG 60, Papers of Attorney General, Segregated Lincoln Material. Lincoln's endorsement is written on a ten-page letter from Governor Andrew G. Curtin, January 25, 1865, protesting the violations of the Enrollment Act of March 3, 1863, by the Provost Marshal General's Office. Too long and involved to summarize or quote adequately, Curtin's letter and Attorney General Speed's opinion may be consulted in the *Official Records* (III, IV, 1076-80, 1158-61).

To George H. Stuart[1]

[January 29, 1865]

Near the close let us have "Your Mission" repeated by Mr. Philips. Dont say I called for it   LINCOLN

[1] AES, ORB. Lincoln's endorsement appears on the back of the printed program of the "Third Anniversary Meeting of the U.S. Christian Commission" held in the Hall of the House of Representatives at 7 P.M. on January 29, 1865. The order of exercises listed item 7, "SINGING—'YOUR MISSION'—By Mr. PHILIP PHILLIPS, of Cincinnati." An endorsement appears on the bottom of the program: "This is the *original* Programme used by *President Lincoln* in the Hall of the House of Representatives Washington on the occasion of the third anniversary of the U.S. Christian Commission January 29th. 1865 when *Mr. Philip Phillip* sang 'Your Mission' at the close of the Hymn the President

wrote on the other side with his own hand a request that it [be] repeated which was done between 11 & 12 O'clock P.M. GEO. H STUART."

George H. Stuart, chairman of the Commission, conducted the meeting. On January 30, Philip Phillips wrote Lincoln:

"I learn through Mr Geo H Stuart . . . that you made the request to him *in writing* for me to repeat my little song—'*Your Mission*' at our Aniversary last sunday night. The honor created in me a strong desire to have the request in writing as you gave it to him. But Mr S wanted it himself, and said I could apply to you for another and you to send it to me by mail.

"This little favor in *your own* hand writing I should appreciate nearly as highly as having *the honor* of singing *many* songs—togeather with *Two* (2) hearty votes for *you* during the last five years. . . .

"I will send to you my last little singing Book for your little Boy containing the Song '*Your Mission*' " (DLC-RTL).

No reply to Phillips' letter has been found. The text of "Your Mission" may be found in the *Annals of the Christian Commission*, pp. 256-57.

To Thomas T. Eckert[1]

Major T. T. Eckert   Executive Mansion
Sir   Washington, Jan. 30. 1865

You will proceed with the documents placed in your hands; and, on reaching Gen. Ord, will deliver him the letter addressed to him by the Secretary of War; then, by Gen. Ord's assistance, procure an interview with Messrs. Stephens, Hunter and Campbell, or any of them, deliver to him, or them, the paper on which your own letter is written,[2] note on the copy which you retain the time of delivery, and to whom delivered, receive their answer in writing, waiting a reasonable time for it, and which, if it contain their decision to come, through, without further condition, will be your warrant to ask Gen. Ord to pass them through as directed in the letter of the Secretary of War to him. If by their answer they decline to come, or propose other terms, do not have them passed through. And this being your whole duty return and report to me.
Yours truly   A. LINCOLN

[1] ALS, owned by Justin G. Turner, Los Angeles, California; ALS copy, DLC-RTL. See Lincoln's communication to the House of Representatives, February 10, *infra*, for other documents concerning the "Peace Mission."
[2] See to Stephens and others, *infra*.

To Joseph Holt[1]

Judge Advocate General, please procure record & report on this case
Jan. 30. 1865   A. LINCOLN

[1] AES, DNA WR RG 153, Judge Advocate General, NN 2032. Lincoln's endorsement appears on papers in the court-martial record of Captain Hooker A. DeLand, Company F, First Michigan Volunteers, cashiered and sentenced to Dry Tortugas until the end of his term of service, on charges of cowardice. Holt reported unfavorably.

To Edward O. C. Ord[1]

Major General Ord   Washington, D.C.,
Hd. Qrs. Army of James   Jan. 30, 1865.

By direction of the President you are instructed to inform the three gentlemen, Messrs. Stephens, Hunter, and Campbell, that a messenger will be despatched to them, at or near where they now are, without unnecessary delay.   Edwin M Stanton
                                         Sec of War

[1] AD, IHi. The body of this letter is in Lincoln's handwriting; the signature is Stanton's. See Lincoln's communication to the House of Representatives, February 10, *infra*, for related documents.

To Edward O. C. Ord[1]

Major General Ord.   [January 30, 1865]

Please procure for the bearer, Major Thomas T. Eckert an interview with Messrs. Stevens, Hunter and Campbell; and if on his return to you, he requests it, pass them through our lines to Fortress-Monroe, by such route, and under such other Military precautions as you may deem prudent, giving them protection and comfortable quarters while there. Let none of this have any effect upon your military movements or plans.

[1] ADf, NHi. This autograph draft of instructions to General Ord is written in pencil. On the bottom of the page appears an endorsement in another handwriting: "This paper was written by President Linclon [*sic*], January 30th. 1865, and was copied by Mr. Stanton and given to Gen. Eckert to deliver in person to Genl. Ord, and led to the interview which took place afterwards between the gentlemen herein named and the President." Stanton addressed the message to Grant instead of Ord. See Lincoln's communication to the House of Representatives, February 10, *infra*.

To William H. Seward[1]

                                      January 30, 1865

Will the Secretary of State please see and hear the bearer Mr. Ulrich & oblige him if he conveniently can? He is a young man raised in the place of my residence, and of a most respectable family, as he also is himself.   A. LINCOLN

Jan. 30. 1865.

[1] AES, DNA FS RG 59, Appointments, Box 395. Lincoln's endorsement appears on a petition signed by Richard J. Oglesby and others, dated incorrectly December 25, 1865, but written in December 1864, recommending appointment of Bartow A. Ulrich as consul or vice-consul. No record has been found of Ulrich's appointment.

To Alexander H. Stephens, John A. Campbell and Robert M. T. Hunter[1]

Messrs Alex H Stephens,   [January 30, 1865]
J. A. Campbell and R. M. T. Hunter.

Gentlemen I am instructed by the President of the United States to place this paper in your hands with the information that if you pass through the U.S. Military lines it will be understood that you do so for the purpose of an informal conference, on the basis of the letter, a copy of which is on the reverse side of this sheet; and that if you choose to pass on such understanding, and so notify me in writing, I will procure the Commanding General to pass you through the lines, and to Fortress-Monroe, under such military precautions as he may deem prudent; and, at which place you will be met in due time by some person or persons for the purpose of such informal conferrence. And further that you shall have protection, safe-conduct, and safe return, in all events.

THOS. T. ECKERT.
Maj & A.D.C.

[1] AD, CSmH. The body of the letter is in Lincoln's handwriting; the names of the persons addressed and the signature are in Eckert's autograph. On the verso is Lincoln's autograph copy of his letter to Blair, January 18, *supra*. Although supplied by Nicolay and Hay with the date February 1, 1865 (XI, 16), this letter was obviously given to Eckert on January 30 (see to Eckert, *supra*), and was delivered by him on February 1. On the verso of the copy retained by Eckert appears his endorsement dated at City Point, Virginia, February 1, 1865: "A copy of the above [Lincoln to Blair, January 18, 1865], also a copy of my letter to Messrs. Alex H. Stephens, J. A. Campbell & R. M. T. Hunter were delivered in person to Alex H. Stephens at 4.15 PM. by him read, then by Mr Campbell & then by Mr Hunter." (Original owned by Justin G. Turner, Los Angeles, California.) See Lincoln's communication to the House of Representatives, February 10, *infra*.

To James M. Ashley[1]

So far as I know, there are no peace commissioners in the city, or likely to be in it.   A. LINCOLN
Jan. 31. 1865.

[1] Copy, DLC-HW. The copy of Lincoln's endorsement is preserved with the copy of the letter of Representative James M. Ashley, January 31, 1865, on which it was written. Both copies were sent to Herndon by Ashley in a letter dated November 23, 1866. Ashley's letter of January 31, 1865, is as follows: "The report is in circulation in the House that Peace Commissioners are on their way or are in the city, and is being used against us. If it is true, I fear we shall loose the bill. Please authorize me to contradict it, if not true."

To George C. Cadwalader[1]

Officer in command
at Philadelphia, Pa.

Executive Mansion,
Washington,
January 31, 1865.

Suspend execution of death sentence of John Murphy, ordered for February 10th 1865 at Fort-Mifflin, until further orders, and forward record of trial for examination.   A. LINCOLN

Maj. Eckert
  Please send above telegram   JNO. G. NICOLAY   Priv. Sec.

[1] D, DNA WR RG 107, Presidential Telegrams, I, 313. This telegram is signed by Nicolay but not by Lincoln. General George Cadwalader replied on the same day: "Your telegram of this date suspending execution . . . of John Murphy ordered for February tenth next until further orders is received. The record of his trial was forwarded yesterday by mail to the Dept." (DLC-RTL).

Not the same John Murphy about whom Lincoln telegraphed General Meade on October 8 and 12, 1863, Private John Murphy, an unassigned substitute, had been sentenced to be shot for desertion. Appeals from his wife and others were endorsed by Lincoln: "Sentence commuted to hard labor during the war. Jan. 25. 1865. A. LINCOLN." (DNA WR RG 153, Judge Advocate General, NN 3237; AGO *Special Orders No. 68*, February 11, 1865). No record of further action by Lincoln has been found.

To Samuel S. Cox[1]

Executive Mansion, Washington,

Hon. Samuel S. Cox   Jan. 31, 1865.

Thank you for the speech. I sought it for the humor said to be in it; but while it meets expectations in that respect, it has a far higher merit, so far as I can judge by the hasty glance I have only found time to give it.   A. LINCOLN

[1] *The Collector*, April, 1950, p. 85; Parke-Bernet Catalog 1026, January 10-11, 1949, No. 53. The speech was probably Cox's speech of January 26, 1865, opposing House Resolution 214, which provided that heads of executive departments were entitled to seats on the floor of the House. See *Congressional Globe*, January 27, 1865, New Series No. 27, pp. 437-44. No correspondence from Cox in regard to a speech has been found.

To Ulysses S. Grant[1]

Lieut. General Grant
City-Point, Va.

Executive Mansion
Washington Jan. 31. 1865

A messenger is coming to you on the business contained in your despatch. Detain the gentleman in comfortable quarters until he arrives & then act upon the message he brings, as far as applicable, it having been made up to pass through Gen. Ord's hands, & when the gentlemen were supposed to be beyond our lines.

A. LINCOLN

[1] ALS, DNA WR RG 107, Presidential Telegrams, I, 312. For Grant's telegram of January 31 to which Lincoln is replying, see Lincoln's communication to the House of Representatives, February 10, *infra.*

To Hannibal Hamlin[1]

Hon. H. Hamlin,   Executive Mansion, Washington, D.C.,
President of the Senate,   January 31, 1865.

Sir, I transmit herewith a communication from the Secretary of war, covering papers bearing on the arrest and imprisonment of Colonel Richard T. Jacobs, Lieutenant Governor of the State of Kentucky, and Colonel Frank Wolford, one of the Presidential Electors of that State, requested by Resolution of the Senate, dated December 20, 1864. Very Respectfully, Yr. obdt. servant,

ABRAHAM LINCOLN

[1] LS, DNA RG 46, Senate 38A F2. The lengthy report from Stanton on the arrest and imprisonment of Richard T. Jacob and Frank Wolford may be found in Thirty-eighth Congress, Second Session, *Senate Executive Document No. 16.*

To William H. Seward[1]

Hon. William H. Seward   Executive Mansion
Secretary of State   Washington, Jan. 31. 1865

You will proceed to Fortress-Monroe, Virginia, there to meet, and informally confer with Messrs. Stephens, Hunter, and Campbell, on the basis of my letter to F. P. Blair, Esq., on Jan. 18. 1865, a copy of which you have.

You will make known to them that three things are indispensable, towit:

1. The restoration of the national authority throughout all the States.

2. No receding, by the Executive of the United States on the Slavery question, from the position assumed thereon, in the late Annual Message to Congress, and in preceding documents.

3. No cessation of hostilities short of an end of the war, and the disbanding of all forces hostile to the government.

You will inform them that all propositions of theirs not inconsistent with the above, will be considered and passed upon in a spirit of sincere liberality. You will hear all they may choose to say, and report it to me.

You will not assume to definitely consummate anything. Yours &c.   ABRAHAM LINCOLN.

[1] ALS, NAuE; ALS copy, DLC-RTL. See Lincoln's communication to the House of Representatives, February 10, *infra*.

To William H. Seward[1]

Hon. Sec. of State, please see this gentleman who is the gentleman from Canada spoken of yesterday.   A. LINCOLN
Jan. 31, 1865

[1] ALS, owned by Gordon A. Block, Philadelphia, Pennsylvania. The gentleman has not been identified.

To Lewis Wallace[1]

Office U.S. Military Telegraph,
Major General Wallace   War Department,
Baltimore, Md.   Washington, D.C., Jan. 31 1865

Suspend sending off of Charles E. Waters until further order & send record if it has not been already sent.   A. LINCOLN

[1] ALS, DNA WR RG 107, Presidential Telegrams, I, 310. This telegram is marked as sent at 10 A.M.   General Wallace replied: "Charles E. Waters left for Philadelphia on the Nine-twenty . . . train this A.M. He can be re arrested at Wilmington if you so direct

"If I hear from you at once, I will order the Commander at Wilmington to stop him" (DLC-RTL).

A second telegram from Wallace corrected the error: "I supposed your Telegram referred to Levin T. Waters, and was informed that he had gone North this A.M. as I telegraphed you—this is an error. he is at Annapolis Md   has taken his seat in the Senate. of Chas E. Waters we know nothing. Who is he?" (*Ibid.*).

Nicolay replied at 12:20 P.M.: "Your second dispatch in regard to Waters is received. The President's dispatch of this morning did not refer to Levin T. [L.] Waters, but to a man who it was represented had been convicted by a military commission of unlawful trade with the rebels or something of that kind, and was to be sent this morning to the Albany Penitentiary. His name was given as Chas. E. Waters. If such prisoner is on his way north let him be brought back and held as directed in the President's dispatch." (DNA WR RG 107, Presidential Telegrams, I, 311).

Wallace's reply was received at 1:45 P.M.: "The man Chas E Waters was tried & sentenced in Washington not Baltimore   I have telegraphed to General Dix at N York to send him back to Washington."

Archibald Stirling, Jr., counsel for Charles E. Waters, wrote Lincoln from Baltimore on February 11, 1865, asking a pardon for Waters, who had been convicted on testimony of the blockade runner Pardon Worsley.

To Thomas T. Eckert[1]

Major T. T. Eckert   Office U.S. Military Telegraph,
Care Gen. Grant   War Department,
City-Point, Va.   Washington, D.C., Feb. 1 1865

Call at Fortress-Monroe & put yourself under direction of Mr. S. whom you will find there.   A. LINCOLN

[1] ALS, DNA WR RG 107, Presidential Telegrams, I, 316. See Lincoln's instructions to Seward, January 31, *supra*, and his communication to the House of Representatives, February 10, *infra*.

To Ulysses S. Grant[1]

"Cypher"   Office U.S. Military Telegraph,
Lieut. Genl. Grant   War Department,
City-Point.   Washington, D.C., February 1. 1865

Let nothing which is transpiring, change, hinder, or delay your Military movements, or plans.   A LINCOLN

[1] ALS, DNA WR RG 107, Presidential Telegrams, I, 314. For Grant's reply, see Lincoln's communication to the House of Representatives, February 10, *infra*.

Order Concerning John S. Loveaire[1]

February 1, 1865

Let this man re-inlist for not less than two years, in any regiment, & upon faithfully serving out of which term, or until other wise honorably discharged, he is pardoned for all military offences now past.   A. LINCOLN

Feb. 1. 1865

[1] AES, IHi. Lincoln's endorsement appears on a letter from the Reverend E. D. Saunders, Philadelphia, January 24, 1865: "Mr. J. G. Loveaire, who desires to make a brief statement respecting his son, rendered me more service, in raising volunteers, than any other citizen of Philadelphia. He is the esteemed Lieutenant of Police in the 15th. Ward. . . ." The son was probably Private John S. Loveaire, Company B, Eighty-second Pennsylvania Volunteers, sentenced by court-martial on December 28, 1864, "to be confined at hard labor for the period of two years," on the charge of desertion (AGO *General Court Martial Orders No. 115*, February 25, 1865). No record of the promulgation of Lincoln's order has been found. On February 15, Reverend Saunders wrote Lincoln: "Your kind response to my application for the pardon of young Levaire (son of Mr. Levaire Lieutenant of Police 15th ward) has been very *thankfully* received. . . ." (DLC-RTL).

Order Concerning William Peacock[1]

February 1, 1865

Allow the bearer, William Peacock to enter any regiment having as much as two years to serve, and upon faithfully serving out his term in which he is pardoned for any desertions heretofore committed.   A. LINCOLN

Feb. 1, 1865

1 Parke-Bernet Catalog 1026, January 10-11, 1949, No. 54. According to the catalog description, this note appears on a card on the back of which General John A. Dix wrote on February 6, 1865, an order to General Lewis C. Hunt, commanding troops in the city and harbor of New York, to "execute the President's order."

Resolution Submitting the Thirteenth Amendment to the States[1]

February 1, 1865

Thirty-Eighth *Congress of the United States of America;*
At the second *Session,*
Begun and held at the City of Washington, on Monday, the fifth *day of December, one thousand eight hundred and sixty*-four.

A RESOLUTION

Submitting to the legislatures of the several States a proposition to amend the Constitution of the United States.

Resolved by the Senate and House of Representatives of the United States of America in Congress assembled, (two-thirds of both houses concurring), That the following article be proposed to the legislatures of the several States as an amendment to the constitution of the United States, which, when ratified by three-fourths of said Legislatures, shall be valid, to all intents and purposes, as a part of the said Constitution, namely: Article XIII. Section 1. Neither slavery nor involuntary servitude, except as a punishment for crime whereof the party shall have been duly convicted, shall exist within the United States, or any place subject to their jurisdiction. Section 2. Congress shall have power to enforce this article by appropriate legislation.

SCHUYLER COLFAX
Speaker of the House of Representatives.
H. HAMLIN
Vice President of the United States,
and President of the Senate.

Approved, February 1. 1865.   ABRAHAM LINCOLN

1 DS, DNA FS RG 11, Department of State. This printed form with blanks filled in by a clerk is the original resolution approved by Lincoln. Printed por-

tions are reproduced in italics. Engrossed copies bearing the signatures not only of Colfax, Hamlin, and Lincoln, but also of members of the Senate and House of Representatives, are in IHi and ORB. Presumably other signed copies may be in existence. Lincoln's approval of this resolution, although signed in accordance with his usual practice in approving resolutions and acts of congress, was unnecessary in the case of an amendment to the constitution. On February 7 the Senate passed a resolution declaring that "such approval was unnecessary," since the Supreme Court had decided in a case arising in 1798 that the president "has nothing to do with the proposition or adoption of amendments to the Constitution" (Remarks of Senator Trumbull, *Congressional Globe*, February 7, 1865, pp. 629-30). For an account of the adoption of the resolution, see Nicolay and Hay, *Abraham Lincoln: A History*, X, 72-90.

Response to a Serenade[1]

February 1, 1865

The President said he supposed the passage through Congress of the Constitutional amendment for the abolishment of Slavery throughout the United States, was the occasion to which he was indebted for the honor of this call. [Applause.] The occasion was one of congratulation to the country and to the whole world. But there is a task yet before us—to go forward and consummate by the votes of the States that which Congress so nobly began yesterday. [Applause and cries—"They will do it," &c.] He had the honor to inform those present that Illinois had already to-day done the work.[2] [Applause.] Maryland was about half through; but he felt proud that Illinois was a little ahead. He thought this measure was a very fitting if not an indispensable adjunct to the winding up of the great difficulty. He wished the reunion of all the States perfected and so effected as to remove all causes of disturbance in the future; and to attain this end it was necessary that the original disturbing cause should, if possible, be rooted out. He thought all would bear him witness that he had never shrunk from doing all that he could to eradicate Slavery by issuing an emancipation proclamation. [Applause.] But that proclamation falls far short of what the amendment will be when fully consummated. A question might be raised whether the proclamation was legally valid. It might be added that it only aided those who came into our lines and that it was inoperative as to those who did not give themselves up, or that it would have no effect upon the children of the slaves born hereafter. In fact it would be urged that it did not meet the evil. But this amendment is a King's cure for all the evils. [Applause.] It winds the whole thing up. He would repeat that it was the fitting if not indispensable adjunct to the consummation of the great game we are playing. He could not but congratulate all present, himself, the country and the whole world upon this great moral victory.

¹ New York *Tribune*, February 3, 1865, 5:3. The *Tribune* carried a less acceptable text of this speech on page one. Collation with the text appearing in the New York *Times* and *Herald* shows the page five text to be generally superior to either. Brackets are in the source. This response is misdated January 31 by Nicolay and Hay (X, 352).

² On February 1, Governor Richard J. Oglesby telegraphed Lincoln that the Illinois legislature had approved the amendment (DLC-RTL).

To George F. Shepley¹

Gen. Shepley   Executive Mansion
Norfolk, Va.   Washington, Feb. 1. 1865

It is said that Henry W. Young, private in 63rd. N.Y. Vols. Co. E. is in arrest for desertion. If he shall be tried and sentenced to any punishment, do not let sentence be executed until further order from me, meantime send me record of the trial.

                A LINCOLN

¹ ALS, DNA WR RG 107, Presidential Telegrams, I, 318. General Shepley replied on February 2: "Private Henry W Young Co E. sixty third 63 N York Vols is in arrest. has not been tried. His trial is delayed by the absence of the Judge Advocate under orders The record will be forwarded to you before sentence is executed if he shall be convicted." (DLC-RTL).

To Edwin M. Stanton¹

   Let Colonel Thomas be appointed.   A. LINCOLN
    Feb. 1. 1865.

¹ AES, RPB. Lincoln's endorsement appears on an envelope, labeled "Colonel Stephen Thomas, Vermont Vols, Brigadier General Vols, Recommended by Hon. J. S. Morrill, Hon. Collamer, Hon. Portus Baxter." Colonel Stephen Thomas, Eighth Vermont Infantry, was appointed brigadier general on February 1, 1865.

To Montgomery Blair¹

           Executive Mansion,
        Washington,   186 .

Mr. Blair will hereafter know that I ought not to stop now
  Feb'y 2d 1865.   A L.

¹ ADS, DLC-RTL. This note is written on Executive Mansion stationery. The date at bottom of the sheet is in Hay's handwriting, "2d" having been written over "1st." On the verso is Blair's unsigned and undated note: "Mr M Blair desires to see the President on several subjects of public importance, one of which

ought to have *immediate* attention He has been in attendance several days If the President can find an opportunity to see him, he would be much obliged." Presumably Hay added the date later, from memory of the fact that Blair sought his interview at the time of Lincoln's departure for the Hampton Roads conference, at or near 11 A.M., on February 2.

To Stephen G. Burbridge[1]

Officer in command   Executive Mansion,
at Frankfort, Kentucky   Washington, Feb'y 2, 1865.

Suspend execution of death sentence of W. E. Walker until further orders, and forward record of trial for examination.

A. LINCOLN.
Maj. Eckert

Please send the above telegram   JNO. G. NICOLAY Priv. Sec.

[1] D, DNA WR RG 107, Presidential Telegrams, I, 321. Nicolay's signature is autograph, but Lincoln's is not. Pierce B. Hawkins "late Colonel 11th Ky," telegraphed Lincoln on January 29: "In behalf of loyal parents & friends I ask the release of an inexperienced boy named W E Walker recently ordered to be shot without any chance of trial this boy will take the amnesty oath & adhere to every requirement of the same to the fulfillment of the promise I together with his friends pledge our lives" (DLC-RTL).

General Burbridge replied on February 4: "Execution of death sentence in case of W. E. Walker, guerrilla, has been suspended. He was ordered to be shot in retaliation for the murder of union citizens." (*Ibid.*).

See Lincoln to Hawkins, February 11, *infra.*

To Ulysses S. Grant[1]

"Cipher"   Office U.S. Military Telegraph,
Lieut. Genl. Grant   War Department,
City-Point, Va   Washington, D.C., Feb. 2, 1865.

Say to the gentlemen I will meet them personally at Fortress-Monroe, as soon as I can get there.   A. LINCOLN

[1] ALS, DNA WR RG 107, Presidential Telegrams, I, 320. For Grant's telegram and other related documents see Lincoln's communication to the House of Representatives, February 10, *infra.*

To William H. Seward[1]

"Cipher"   Office U.S. Military Telegraph,
Hon. W. H. Seward.   War Department,
Fortress-Monroe, Va   Washington, D.C., Feb. 2. 1865

Induced by a despatch of Gen. Grant, I join you at Fort-Monroe so soon as I can come.   A. LINCOLN

[1] ALS, DNA WR RG 107, Presidential Telegrams, I, 319. For Grant's telegram and related documents, see Lincoln's communication to the House of Representatives, February 10, *infra.*

To Edwin M. Stanton[1]

Let the within request be complied with, unless there be some insuperable objection not occurring to me.   A. LINCOLN

Feb. 2. 1865

[1] AES, owned by R. E. Burdick, New York City. See Lincoln's memorandum concerning the draft, January 22, *supra*. Lincoln's endorsement appears on the back of a statement dated February 1, 1865, signed by James A. Bell and George H. Andrews of the New York Senator

"In deference to the forcible objections urged by the Hon: Secy. of War to the proposition originally made by Governor Fenton, the undersigned have the honor to submit the following:

"That so much of the revised quota as was added to the State of New York by the orders of Jany. 24. 1865 say (16,000) be deferred for future investigation; this deferred portion of the quota to be deducted *pro rata* from the various districts of the State."

To John F. Driggs[1]

                              Executive Mansion, Washington,
My Dear Sir: 3d February, 1865.

I have received at your hands a very fine specimen of the Mackinaw Salmon Trout and I beg that you will convey to Mr. Williams my cordial thanks for his kind thoughtfulness; and accept my acknowledgments for your courtesy in the transmission of his present. I am, sir, very truly yours   A. LINCOLN.

Hon. J. F. Driggs   &c   &c

[1] LS, owned by Milton H. Shutes, Oakland, California. Written by John Hay, this letter was signed by Lincoln following his return from the Hampton Roads conference. Representative John F. Driggs of Saginaw, Michigan, wrote Lincoln on February 1: "I have the honor to present you with a fair specimen of our Mackinaw Salmon Trout. The Fish was sent me by Express, and came from Mr. Harvey Williams, one of my constituents who is eighty years of age, and who has followed fishing on Lake Huron for thirty or forty years. He has been a life long Democrat, but at the last Election made a trip of forty miles in one of his fishing boats to vote for you and the Union candidates. May I beg of you an autograph receipt to send to the old gentleman which I know he will highly prize." (DLC-RTL).

To Carl Schurz[1]

                              Executive Mansion,
General: Washington, Feb. 3d., 1865.

I have received your note of today. There will be no objection made to your leaving Washington for a few days, and returning upon the permission heretofore granted. Yours truly

Major General Carl Schurz   A. LINCOLN

[1] LS, DLC-Schurz Papers. The note from Schurz has not been found. He was engaged in organizing veterans' corps in various states (Schurz, *Reminiscences*, III, 108).

To James B. Fry[1]

This is too large a job for the officers to be encumbered with now in the midst of preparations for the approaching draft.

Feb. 4. 1865   A. LINCOLN

[1] AES, owned by Charles W. Olsen, Chicago, Illinois. Lincoln's endorsement appears on a letter to Fry from Orison Blunt and other members of the Committee of the Board of Supervisors of New York, February 4, 1865, asking for the figures and the manner of arriving at the quotas assigned on December 23, 1864. Stanton endorsed below "I concur with the President that the job is too large for the present but direct such force as can be, to be put on it. The draft will go on in the meantime."

This endorsement Stanton crossed out and continued: "The demand of the committee appears to me unreasonable & impracticable, but the Provost Marshal General will put on it such force as he can and in the meantime go on with the draft. Filling the army cannot be delayed by calls on the office of the Provost Marshal that will require months to fill and which can serve no other purpose than delay."

As printed in OR, III, IV, 1121, Lincoln's endorsement is preceded by an endorsement of the same date by Fry:

"Respectfully referred to the Secretary of War.

"The principles and figures upon which the quotas of the city of New York were assigned on the 24th ultimo, and which designate the number of men required, have been already examined by a committee on the part of the Board of Supervisors of New York, who approved of the same and reported that the revised quotas of January are correct, except that they allege an excessive enrollment. It is respectfully submitted that it is unnecessary now to inquire into the basis of previous assignments, which have now no practical bearing, when current business requires all the time of the office."

See Lincoln to Fry, February 6, *infra*.

To Ulysses S. Grant[1]

Lieut. Gen. Grant   Washington,
City-Point. Va.   Feb 4 1865

The President desires me to repeat that nothing transpired, or transpiring with the three gentlemen from Richmond, is to cause any change hindrance or delay, of your military plans or operations.

EDWIN M STANTON
Secretary of War

[1] AD, owned by Edwin C. Stone, Boston, Massachusetts. This telegram is in Lincoln's autograph, signed by Stanton. A copy in the Lincoln Papers is marked "Sent in Cipher at 12.20 P.M."

To Charles W. Hill[1]

Office U.S. Military Telegraph,
Officer in command at   War Department,
Johnson's Island, Ohio   Washington, D.C., Feb. 4, 1865

Parole Lieut. John A. Stephens, prisoner of War, to report to me here in person, and send him to me. It is in pursuance of an arrangement I made yesterday with his uncle, Hon. A. H. Stephens. Acknowledge receipt   A. LINCOLN

[1] ALS, DNA WR RG 107, Presidential Telegrams, I, 323. "Acknowledge receipt" is not in Lincoln's handwriting. Colonel Charles W. Hill replied on February 5: "Your telegram relating to Lieut Jno A Stevens is just received. He will leave Sandusky first train tomorrow to report to you" (DLC-RTL). See Lincoln to Alexander H. Stephens, February 10, *infra*.

To John F. Miller[1]

Officer in command   Executive Mansion,
at Nashville, Tennessee   Washington, February 4, 1865.

Suspend execution of death sentence of James R. Mallory until further orders.   A. LINCOLN

Maj. Eckert
Please send the above telegram   JNO. G. NICOLAY

[1] D, DNA WR RG 107, Presidential Telegrams, I, 322. Nicolay signed Lincoln's name as well as his own. See Lincoln to Miller, December 28, 1864, *supra*. On February 3, 1865, John S. Brien had telegraphed Lincoln from Nashville: "There are important papers prepared & will be forwarded to you signed by Brig Gen Jno F Miller. Gen Rousseau, Gov Johnson & others asking mitigation of the sentence of Jas R Mallery, for fear they may not reach you in time to have you answer by the tenth, the day for his execution, will you extend the time so as to make it certain you can act on the papers. . . ." (DLC-RTL).

General Miller acknowledged receipt of Lincoln's telegram on February 4 (*ibid.*). No further record of Lincoln's action in the case of James R. Mallory has been found, but on September 7, 1865, President Andrew Johnson directed that sentence be executed in the case of "James R. Mallory, alias Capt. James R. Mallory, of the so-called Confederate service, a murderer." (OR, II, VIII, 743).

To the Senate[1]

To, the Senate of the United States: February 4, 1865

In compliance with the Resolution of the Senate of the 13th. ultimo, requesting information upon the present condition of Mexico, and the case of the French war transport steamer "Rhine," I transmit a report from the Secretary of State, and the papers by which it was accompanied.   ABRAHAM LINCOLN

Washington, February. 4th. 1865.

1 DS, DNA RG 46, Senate 38A F2. Seward's report and accompanying papers are printed in Thirty-eighth Congress, Second Session, *Senate Executive Document No. 33.*

To Thomas E. Bramlette[1]

His Excellency   Office U.S. Military Telegraph,
Governor Bramlette   War Department,
Frankfort, Ky.   Washington, D.C., Feb. 5 1865

Your despatch received. Will send official copy of Constitutional amendment by mail to-morrow, this being Sunday. Precedents justify the Legislature to act on *ex-officio* notice, of congress having passed the proposed amendment; nevertheless I will send you the authenticated copy.   A. LINCOLN

1 ALS, DNA WR RG 107, Presidential Telegrams, I, 324. Governor Bramlette's telegram has not been found. Secretary Seward wrote Lincoln on February 5: "A certified copy of Constitutional Amendment was sent (as I had directed) to every Governor of every state on Wednesday last—Bramlette included. He will be so advised by telegraph to day." (DLC-RTL).

To the Senate and House of Representatives[1]

Fellow citizens of the Senate, and   [February 5, 1865]
House of Representatives.

I respectfully recommend that a Joint Resolution, substantially as follows, be adopted so soon as practicable, by your honorable bodies.

"Resolved by the Senate and House of Representatives, of the United States of America in congress assembled: That the President of the United States is hereby empowered, in his discretion, to pay four hundred millions of dollars to the States of Alabama, Arkansas, Delaware, Florida, Georgia, Kentucky, Louisiana, Maryland Mississippi, Missouri, North Carolina, South Carolina, Tennessee, Texas, Virginia, and West-Virginia, in the manner, and on the conditions following, towit: The payment to be made in six per cent government bonds, and to be distributed among said States *pro rata* on their respective slave populations, as shown by the census of 1860; and no part of said sum to be paid unless all resistance to the national authority shall be abandoned and cease, on or before the first day of April next; and upon such abandonment and ceasing of resistance, one half of said sum to be paid in manner aforesaid, and the remaining half to be paid only upon the amendment of the national constitution recently proposed by congress, becoming valid law, on or before the first day of July next, by the action thereon of the requisite number of States"

The adoption of such resolution is sought with a view to embody it, with other propositions, in a proclamation looking to peace and re-union.

Whereas a Joint Resolution has been adopted by congress in the words following, towit

Now therefore I, Abraham Lincoln, President of the United States, do proclaim, declare, and make known, that on the conditions therein stated, the power conferred on the Executive in and by said Joint Resolution, will be fully exercised; that war will cease, and armies be reduced to a basis of peace; that all political offences will be pardoned; that all property, except slaves, liable to confiscation or forfeiture, will be released therefrom, except in cases of intervening interests of third parties; and that liberality will be recommended to congress upon all points not lying within executive control.

[Endorsement]

Feb. 5. 1865

To-day these papers, which explain themselves, were drawn up and submitted to the Cabinet & unanamously disapproved by them.   A LINCOLN

[1] ADf, DLC-RTL. Lincoln's endorsement printed at the end of this communication appears on the verso of the autograph draft. Gideon Welles' *Diary* records under date of February 6: "There was a Cabinet-meeting last evening. The President had matured a scheme which he hoped would be successful in promoting peace. It was a proposition for paying the expenses of the war for two hundred days, or four hundred millions, to the Rebel States, to be for the extinguishment of slavery, or for such purpose as the States were disposed. . . . It did not meet with favor. . . . The earnest desire of the President to conciliate and effect peace was manifest, but there may be such a thing as so overdoing as to cause a distrust or adverse feeling. In the present temper of Congress the proposed measure, if a wise one, could not be carried through successfully. . . ."

To William Dennison[1]

February 6, 1865

Mr. Washburne has presented me all the papers in this case; and finding Mrs. Bushnell as well recommended as any other, & she being the widow of a soldier who fell in battle for the Union, let her be appointed.   A. LINCOLN

Feb. 6. 1865

[1] ALS, owned by Mrs. Karl Wentsel, Sterling, Illinois. Mrs. Emily J. C. Bushnell, widow of Major Douglas R. Bushnell, Thirteenth Illinois Volunteers, who

was killed on November 27, 1863, at the battle of Ringgold, Georgia, was appointed postmaster at Sterling, Illinois, to succeed L. K. Hawthorn (*U.S. Official Register*, 1865).

To James B. Fry[1]

Executive Mansion,
Provost-Marshal-General: Washington February 6, 1865.

These gentlemen distinctly say to me this morning that what they want is the means from your office of showing their people that the quota assigned to them is right. They think it will take but little time—two hours, they say. Please give them double the time and every facility you can. Yours, truly,   A. LINCOLN.

February 6, 1865.

The Provost-Marshal brings this letter back to me and says he cannot give the facility required without detriment to the service, and thereupon he is excused from doing it.   A. LINCOLN.

[1] OR, III, IV, 1142. Following receipt of Lincoln's endorsement of February 4, *supra,* James B. Fry wrote the Committee of the Board of Supervisors of New York on February 5 that having laid their request before the president and having "received their instructions to this effect, I beg you will excuse me from giving time to an investigation into the December assignment." (*Ibid.*, p. 1128).

To this letter the committee replied on the same date that they thought the figures necessary, "in order to show the occasion of the increase of the quotas assigned in January," but that they "desire now to be allowed to copy from the records the enrollment of the remaining Congressional districts of the loyal States. . . ." (*Ibid.*, pp. 1129-30).

Fry replied on the same day, quoting Lincoln's and Stanton's endorsement on the committee's letter of February 4, *supra* (ibid., 1132-33). On February 6, the committee interviewed the president and submitted their case in writing:

"*To His Excellency the President of the United States:*

"Under your call of Dec. 19, 1864, for 300,000 men, there was assigned to the County of New-York, on the 23d of December, a quota of 4,423 men.

"On the 24th of January, 1865, our quota was increased to 21,019 men.

"We ask:

"1. Inasmuch as the increase in our quota is due in great part to a reassignment of quotas after the correction of the enrollment in other districts, we think it but fair that our quota should be reassigned after the correction of our enrollment. We ask, therefore, that upon the completion of the correction of our enrollment, which will be in about twenty days, our quota be reassigned.

"2. In case our County shall keep her Provost-Marshals reasonably busy mustering in recruits, that the Provost Marshals be not withdrawn from that duty to enforce the draft.

"3. To satisfy our constituents as to the justice of this increase of our quota, we ask leave to copy the figures on which the quotas of December and January are based. As the quota of each district depends on the figures for every other district, we shall be obliged to copy the figures of all the districts of the loyal States. This we will do at any hour of day or night which may be least inconvenient to the War Department, and we will do it in less than two hours." (New York *Tribune*, February 9, 1865. The original document has not been found and does not appear in the *Official Records*).

The committee's account of Lincoln's response is as follows:

"Although your Committee received no positive assurance from the President to the two first points presented to him, they were led to believe that His Excellency saw their force and justice.

"In regard to the third point, however, in which our correspondence with the Provost-Marshal General had been so unsatisfactory, he remarked that it had been represented to him that we desired these figures for the purpose of showing that the Government was wrong. Your Committee assured him, however, that their only object was to be put in possession of the data on which they might satisfy themselves and their constituents that the quota assigned them was just." (*Ibid.*).

During the interview, Lincoln gave the committee the letter to Fry (as above). Upon receiving Lincoln's letter, Fry went to the president and obtained the endorsement excusing him at Lincoln's request. Fry addressed two further letters to the committee on February 6, refusing their request and dismissing the matter with the statement, "I have no further time at my disposal to devote to this subject." (OR, III, IV, 1144).

Much disgruntled, the committee returned to New York and published their report, including the correspondence exchanged with Provost Marshal Fry (New York *Tribune*, February 9, 1865).

To Ulysses S. Grant[1]

To Gen: Grant   February 6, 1865
Headquarters Armies of the U.S.

Suspend execution in case of Simon J. Schaffer 15th N.Y. Engineers until further orders and send me the record.

                      A LINCOLN

Send above
    JNO. G. NICOLAY   Priv. Sec.

[1] D, DNA WR RG 107, Presidential Telegrams, I, 326. The body of the telegram is in John Hay's handwriting. The date appears to have been added by a clerk. Lincoln's signature and the remainder is by Nicolay. Grant replied on the same day: "The execution in the case of Simon J Schaffer 155h N Y Engineers was suspended until further orders on the 27th January and the Record was forwarded to Washington on the following day" (DLC-RTL). The court-martial record in the case of Simon J. Shaffer, alias Samuel Jefferson, Fifteenth New York Engineers, sentenced February 4, 1865, to be shot for desertion, indicates that he was sent to Dry Tortugas (DNA WR RG 153, Judge Advocate General, NN 2455). Grant's reference to having sent the record on January 27 suggests that the "Hamel Shaffer" of Lincoln's telegram to Grant, January 26, *supra*, may have been confused with Simon J. Shaffer.

To Frederick Hassaurek[1]

             Office U.S. Military Telegraph,
Frederick Hassaurek.   War Department,
Cincinnati, O.   Washington, D.C., Feb. 6. 1865

A despatch from Gen. Grant says "Lieut. Markbeit has been released from prison, and is now on his way North."

                      A. LINCOLN

[1] ALS, DNA WR RG 107, Presidential Telegrams, I, 325. Concerning Lieutenant Leopold Markbreit, see Lincoln to Hitchcock, September 19, 1864, *supra*. Frederick Hassaurek replied to Lincoln's telegram on February 8: "It is with the deepest emotion that I acknowledge the receipt of your telegram of the 6th inst. communicating to me the release of my brother. Language cannot express my gratitude to you for this proof of your considerate kindness and sympathy. May God bless you for it as you are blessed by my mother, sisters, and by your most obed. servant." (DLC-RTL).

To Andrew Johnson[1]

Governor Andrew Johnson   Executive Mansion
Nashville Tennessee   Feb. 6. 1865

Let the matter of the McKendree Church remain as it is without further action until you see me.   A. LINCOLN

[1] D, DNA WR RG 107, Presidential Telegrams, I, 327. This telegram is entirely in John Hay's handwriting. On January 24, Governor Johnson wrote Lincoln, enclosing a copy of his decision dated January 23, 1865, in the case of the McKendree Methodist Church in Nashville, Tennessee:

"The Methodist Episcopal Church, denominated the 'McKindree Church,' in the City of Nashville, was taken possession of under an order of the Secretary of War, issued November 30th 1863, and is now held by Bishop Simpson in pursuance thereof

"Application has been made to the President of the United States, for the restoration of said Church, Parsonage, and other property pertaining to said Church therewith. The President thereupon referred the questions of restoration to me for consideration and decision   It appears from a statement of facts, which have been filed in this Office in reference to the Loyalty of the parties who make the application for the restoration, that Bishop [Joshua] Soule is and has been Loyal . . . and the Officiating Ministers and Trustees have long since taken the Amnesty Oath, and . . . there is . . . proof that . . . they have complied with the Constitution and Laws of the United States. . . .

"It is therefore my decision, that the Bishop and the Officiating Minister, and the Trustees . . . in whom the title and control is vested, are entitled to the possession of the 'McKindree Church,' and other property pertaining to the Same . . . and that they . . . be restored to the possession and occupation of the Same, until such time, as it shall be disposed of by regular proceedings in Court under the Confiscation Acts of Congress. . . ." (DLC-RTL).

Order to Make Corrections in the Draft[1]

Executive Mansion, Washington City.
February 6th. 1865.

Whereas complaints are made in some localities, respecting the assignments of quotas and credits allowed for the pending call of troops to fill up the armies—now, in order to determine all controversies in respect thereto, and to avoid any delay in filling up the armies—It is ordered—That the Attorney General, Brigadier General Richard Delafield, and Colonel C. W. Foster,[2] be, and they are hereby constituted, a Board to examine into the proper quotas and credits of the respective States and districts, under the call of December 19th. 1864, with directions that, if any errors be found therein, to make such corrections as the law and facts may require, and report their determination to the Provost Marshal General. The determination of said Board to be final and conclusive, and the draft to be made in conformity therewith.

2. The Provost Marshal General is ordered to make the draft in the respective districts, as speedily as the same can be done after the 15th. of this month.   ABRAHAM LINCOLN.

[1] DS, IHi.
[2] General Richard Delafield had succeeded General Joseph G. Totten as chief engineer of the U.S. Army Corps of Engineers; Colonel Charles W. Foster was assistant adjutant general of Volunteers.

To Thomas T. Eckert[1]

War Department
Major T. T. Eckert   Washington City,
Dear Sir.   Feb. 7 1865

Please furnish me copies of all despatches sent by the Secretary of War or myself, on or about the peace negotiation, from 29th. Ult. till I left on the 2nd. Inst. both inclusive.
So far as I can remember they will be
One by Sec. of War to Gen. Ord, sent after mid-night Sunday night & may be dated either 29th. or 30th.
One sent by him to Gen. Ord on 30th. written in my hand.
One sent by me to Gen. Grant on 31st.
One sent by me to Gen. Grant on 2nd. Inst.
One sent by me to Hon. W. H. Seward on 2nd. Inst.
You may add one sent by Sec. of War to Gen. Grant on my return on the 4th   Yours truly   A LINCOLN

[1] ALS, owned by Justin G. Turner, Los Angeles, California. See Lincoln's communication to the House of Representatives, February 10, *infra*.

To William Lloyd Garrison[1]

Executive Mansion, Washington,
My Dear Mr. Garrison   7 February, 1865.

I have your kind letter of the 21st of January, and can only beg that you will pardon the seeming neglect occasioned by my constant engagements. When I received the spirited and admirable painting "Waiting for the Hour" I directed my Secretary not to acknowledge its arrival at once, preferring to make my personal acknowledgment of the thoughtful kindness of the donors; and waiting for some leisure hour, I have committed the discourtesy of not replying at all.

I hope you will believe that my thanks though late, are most cordial, and I request that you will convey them to those associated with you in this flattering and generous gift.

I am very truly Your friend and Servant   A. LINCOLN.

Wm. Lloyd Garrison Esq

[1] LS, RPB; Df, DLC-RTL. This letter is misdated January 24, 1865, by Nicolay and Hay (X, 344). The body of the signed letter as well as the draft in the Lincoln Papers is entirely in John Hay's handwriting. On January 21, 1865, William Lloyd Garrison had written Lincoln:

"About the first of July, last year, what was deemed by critics . . . an admirable painting, was sent by Adams's Express to your address . . . accompanied by a letter from me in behalf of the donors, whose contributions to the object in view amounted to upwards of five hundred dollars. This meritorious picture . . . was entitled 'Watch Night—or, Waiting for the Hour.' It represented a group of negro men, women and children waiting . . . for the midnight hour of December 31, 1862, to pass, and the introduction of that new year which was to make them forever free. Many photographic copies were made of it, and it was by my advice that it was presented to you as the most fitting person in the world to receive it. . . .

"For some cause or other, no acknowledgment has been made . . . of the receipt of the picture, or of my letter, which contained the names of the donors. As . . . Mr. Sumner assured me . . . that he had seen the picture again and again at the White House, all anxiety has been relieved as to its safe arrival. . . . But as the money raised . . . was collected by ladies who desire that the donors may be officially apprised of its legitimate application, I write in their behalf to say that it would relieve them of much embarrassment if you would be so obliging . . . as to send me a line, stating that the painting . . . was duly received by you. . . ." (DLC-RTL).

To John Glenn[1]

"Cypher"

Lt. Col. Glenn.   Executive Mansion
Commanding Post at   Washington,
Henderson, Ky.   Feb. 7. 1865

Complaint is made to me that you are forcing negroes into the Military service, and even torturing them—riding them on rails and the like—to extort their consent. I hope this may be a mistake. The like must not be done by you, or any one under you. You must not force negroes any more than white men. Answer me on this.   A. LINCOLN

[1] ALS, DNA WR RG 107, Presidential Telegrams, I, 329. No reply from Lieutenant Colonel John Glenn, One Hundred Twentieth Colored Infantry, has been found. See Lincoln to Stanton, *infra.*

To Ulysses S. Grant[1]

Lieutenant General Grant: Executive Mansion,
City Point, Va.   Washington, February 7, 1865.

Gen. Singleton, who bears you this claims that, he already has arrangements made if you consent to bring a large amount of Southern produce through your lines. For its bearing on our finances I would be glad for this to be done if it can be without injuriously disturbing your military operations, or supplying the enemy. I wish you to be judge and master on these points. Please see and hear him fully, and decide whether anything, and if anything, what can be done in the premises. Yours truly,

                 A. LINCOLN

[1] DfS (copy?), DLC-RTL. The words "if you consent" in the first sentence and the signature are in Lincoln's autograph. See Lincoln's pass for James W. Singleton, January 5, *supra*, and communication to Grant, March 8, *infra*. Under dates of February 1, 7, 9, and 22, Orville H. Browning's *Diary* records the continuance of General Singleton's venture. The entry for February 9 is in part as follows: "At night I went to the Presidents. He had just prepared his answer to a resolution of Congress calling on him for information in relation to the recent peace conference . . . and read it all to me. He also gave me a letter to Genl. Grant, respecting the purch[a]ses of produce in the South by Singleton. The letter is dated the 7th. and is intended to be delivered by Singleton. . . ."

To Ulysses S. Grant[1]

                 Executive Mansion,
Lieut. Gen. Grant   Washington, Feb. [post 7], 1865.

Some time ago you telegraphed that you had stopped a Mr. Laws from passing our lines with a boat and cargo, and I directed you to be informed that you must be allowed to do as you please in such matters. To-night Mr. Laws calls on me, and I have told him, and now tell you that the matter, as to his passing the lines is under your control absolutely; and that he can have any relaxation you choose to give him & none other. Yours truly

                 A. LINCOLN

[1] ADfS, DLC-RTL. This letter is supplied with the date "February [1?], 1865, in Nicolay and Hay (X, 354), but must have been written after February 7, the date on which Grant telegraphed to Stanton: "A. M. Laws is here with a steamer partially loaded with sugar and coffee, and a permit from the Treasury Department to go through into Virginia and North Carolina, and to bring out 10,000 bales of cotton. I have positively refused to adopt this mode of feeding the Southern army unless it is the direct order of the President. It is a humiliating fact that speculators have represented the location of cotton at different points in the South, and obtained permits to bring it out, covering more than the entire amount of the staple in all the cotton-growing States. . . ." (OR, I, XLVI, II, 445).

Stanton replied on the same day: "The President directs that you will regard all trade permits, licenses, or privileges of every kind, by whomsoever signed . . . as subject to your authority and approval as commander of the U.S. forces in the field, and such permits as you deem prejudicial to the military service by feeding or supporting the rebel armies . . . you may disregard and annul, and if necessary to the public safety seize the property of the traders. In short, the President orders that you 'as being responsible for military results, must be allowed to be judge and master on the subject of trade with the enemy.' " (*Ibid.*).

No communication from Laws, or reply from Grant to Lincoln's letter, has been found, and it seems possible that Lincoln's undated draft was never sent.

Introduction for Mrs. Long[1]

Please see Mrs. Dr. Long   AL.

Feb. 7. 1865

[1] ADS, ORB. This note is written on a small card. Mrs. Long has not been identified.

To James Speed[1]

February 7, 1865

I have sufficient evidence that R. A. Gray, bearer of this, is a loyal man, and entitled to be treated as such, but I know nothing as to his rights concerning the property, or rents mentioned within.

Feb. 7. 1865   A. LINCOLN

[1] AES, DNA GE RG 60, Papers of Attorney General, Segregated Lincoln Material. Lincoln's endorsement appears on an unsigned document:

"It being represented to me that H. Jouette Gray, of Harrisonburg, Rockingham County, Virginia is the owner of a lot of land on the North side of Pearl street, between Western Row and Plum streets, now occupied by certain tenants under a lease originally made to one Alexander McKenzie; And it being further shown to my satisfaction that said Gray, although within the rebel lines, is nevertheless, loyal to the Federal Government, and has not in any [way] aided the rebellion, I do hereby authorize and permit the said Gray, personally or by attorney to collect the ground rents, due or to become due on said property, and to sell or otherwise dispose of said real estate in such manner as to him may seem right and proper, Washington January 1865"

To Edwin M. Stanton[1]

Hon. Sec. of War.   Executive Mansion,

Dear Sir   Washington, Feb. [7?], 1865.

Complaint is made to me that our recruiting officers at, and in vicinity of of [*sic*] Mayville, Ky. are *forcing* negroes into the service. Please enquire into this & stop it if true. Yours truly

A. LINCOLN

[1] ALS, owned by Joseph L. Block, Chicago, Illinois. The date is supplied on the basis of Lincoln's telegram to Glenn, *supra*. No reply from Stanton has been found.

To Alfred Sully[1]

Officer in command   Executive Mansion,
at Davenport Iowa: Washington, Feb'y 7, 1865.

Suspend execution of death sentence of John Davis alias John Lewis until further orders and forward record of trial for examination.   A. Lincoln

Maj. Eckert:

Please send the above telegram.   Jno. G. Nicolay

[1] D, DNA WR RG 107, Presidential Telegrams, I, 328. This telegram is in Nicolay's handwriting. Although General Alfred Sully is listed in the tables of organization as commanding officer of the District of Iowa, Captain J. F. Miller replied to Lincoln's telegram on February 8: "Your telegram relative to the suspension of Execution of Jno Davis Alias Jno Lewis recd no record of trial is here nor do I know where it can be found unless at Judge Advocate Generals office" (DLC-RTL). AGO *General Court Martial Orders No. 194*, April 14, 1865, promulgated the pardon of John Davis, alias John Lewis, substitute recruit, on condition that he serve out his term.

To William P. Fessenden[1]

February 8, 1865

As this letter is written by my old friend, who is one hundred and four years old, I sincerely desire that his friend, this young lady may obtain the employment he asks for her. Will the Sec. of the Treasury please see & hear her?   A. Lincoln

Feb. 8, 1865

[1] AES, CSmH. Lincoln's endorsement or note has been removed from attendant papers, and as a result neither the old friend nor the young lady can be identified. It is a guess, however, that Deacon John Phillips may have been the old friend. See Lincoln to Phillips, November 21, 1864, *supra*.

To Ulysses S. Grant[1]

Lieut. Gen. Grant   Executive Mansion
City Point, Va.   Washington, Feb. 8. 1865

I am called on by the House of Representatives to give an account of my interview with Messrs. Stephens, Hunter & Campbell; and it is very desireable to me to put in your despatch of Feb. 1st. to the Sec. of War, in which among other things you say "I fear now their going back without any expression from any one in authority will have a bad influence" I think the despatch does you credit while I do not see that it can embarrass you. May I use it?   A Lincoln

[1] ALS, DNA WR RG 107, Presidential Telegrams, I, 331. Grant replied on the same day:

"By all means use my dispatch, referred to in yours of this date, if you desire to do so.

"It was marked 'confidential' in contra distinction to official dispatches but not to prevent such use being made of it as you or the Secretary of War might think proper." (DLC-RTL).

Grant's telegram to Stanton of February 1 will be found in Lincoln's communication to the House of Representatives, February 10, *infra*.

To Joseph Holt[1]

February 8, 1865

Judge Advocate General please procure record & report on this case.   A. LINCOLN

Feb. 8, 1865

Pardon for unexecuted portion of sentence and discharge the Prisoner.   A. LINCOLN

Feb. 16, 1865

[1] AES and ES, DNA WR RG 153, Judge Advocate General, LL 2498. Lincoln's first endorsement appears on an envelope and the second on the record in the case of Franklin Wells, citizen of Maryland, sentenced to hard labor for eight years from May 17, 1864, or to be released upon payment of $1,000, on charges of violation of laws and customs of war. Holt recommended that the punishment already inflicted seemed sufficient.

To the Senate and House of Representatives[1]

To the Honorable, the Senate   February 8, 1865
and House of Representatives:

The Joint Resolution entitled, "Joint Resolution declaring certain States not entitled to representation in the Electoral College," has been signed by the Executive, in deference to the view of Congress implied in its passage and presentation to him. In his own view, however, the two Houses of Congress, convened under the Twelfth Article of the Constitution, have complete power to exclude from counting all electoral votes deemed by them to be illegal; and it is not competent for the Executive to defeat or obstruct that power by a veto, as would be the case if his action were at all essential in the matter. He disclaims all right of the Executive to interfere in any way in the matter of canvassing or counting electoral votes; and he also disclaims that by signing said Resolution he has expressed any opinion on the recitals of the preamble or any judgment of his own upon the subject of the Resolution.   ABRAHAM LINCOLN

Executive Mansion
February 8, 1865.

[1] DS, DNA RG 46, Senate 38A F2; DS, DNA RG 233, House Executive Document No. 56; ADf, DLC-RTL. The joint resolution (H.R. 126) approved on February 8, 1865, declared that Virginia, North Carolina, South Carolina, Georgia, Florida, Alabama, Mississippi, Louisiana, Texas, Arkansas, and Tennessee were in "such condition on the eighth day of November, eighteen hundred and sixty-four, that no valid election . . . was held" and that these states were not entitled to representation in the electoral college.

To the Senate and House of Representatives[1]

To the Senate   February 8, 1865
and House of Representatives:

I transmit to Congress a copy of a note of the 4th instant addressed by J. Hume Burnley, Esquire, Her Britannic Majestys Chargé d' Affaires to the Secretary of State, relative to a sword which it is proposed to present to Captain Henry S. Stellwagen, Commanding the United States frigate Constellation, as a mark of gratitude for his services to the British brigantine Mersey. The expediency of sanctioning the acceptance of the gift, is submitted to your consideration.   ABRAHAM LINCOLN

Washington, 8th. February, 1865.

[1] DS, DNA RG 46, Senate 38A F2; DS, DNA RG 233, House Executive Document No. 55. A joint resolution approved on March 3, 1865, authorized Captain Stellwagen to accept the sword. Burnley's letter of February 4 is in part as follows:

"Her Majesty's consul at St. Thomas has reported to his government the friendly and efficient assistance given by Captain Stellwagen . . . to the British brigantine Mersey, of Liverpool, which he fell in with in a disabled condition, and in a state of imminent peril from the effects of a severe hurricane. . . . Captain Stellwagen went on board the Mersey and most liberally supplied the wants of the ship and crew, thus enabling her master to bring her in safety to . . . St. Thomas.

"Her Majesty's government . . . have caused the accompanying sword of honor to be prepared . . . as a mark of their gratitude, and I am instructed . . . to deliver it to you, with a request that Captain Stellwagen may be permitted to accept it. . . ." (Ibid.).

To John G. Smith[1]

His Excellency   Executive Mansion,
Gov. Smith   Washington, Feb'y. 8th, 1865.

Complaint is made to me by Vermont that the assignment of her quota for the draft on the pending call is intrinsically unjust, and also in bad faith of the government's promise to fairly allow credits for men previously furnished. To illustrate a supposed case is stated as follows.

Vermont and New Hampshire must between them furnish 6000

men on the pending call,[2] and being equals each must furnish as many as the other in the long run. But the Government finds that on former calls, Vermont furnished a surplus of 500, and New Hampshire a surplus of 1500. These two surpluses making 2000 an[d] added to the 6000, making 8000 to be furnished by the two states or 4000 each less by fair credits. Then subtract Vermont's surplus of 500 from her 4000, leaves 3500 as her quota on the pending call; and likewise subtract New Hampshire's surplus of 1500 from her 4000 leaves 2500 as her quota on the pending call. These 3500 & 2500 make precisely the 6000 which the supposed case requires from the two states; and it is just—equal—for Vermont to furnish 1000 more *now* than New Hampshire, *because* New Hampshire has *heretofore* furnished a 1000 more than Vermont which equalizes the burthens of the two in the long run. And this result so far from being bad faith to Vermont is indispensable to keeping good faith with New Hampshire. By no other result can the 6000 men be obtained from the two states and at the same time deal justly and keep faith with both; and we do but confuse ourselves in questioning the process by which the right result is reached. The supposed case is perfect as an illustration.

The pending call is *not* for 300,000 men subject to fair credits, but is for 300,000 remaining after all fair credits have been deducted; and it is impossible to concede what Vermont asks, without coming out short of the 300,000 men, or making other localities pay for the partiality shown her.

This upon the case stated—if there be different reasons for making an allowance to Vermont let them be presented and considered. Yours truly

[1] Df (copy?), DLC-RTL. Although cataloged as a draft in the Lincoln Papers, this document may possibly be a copy made from Lincoln's original letter and corrected by him. A single phrase, as noted, appears in Lincoln's autograph. Governor Smith, who had been in Washington several days conferring with Provost Marshal General James B. Fry about the draft quotas, wrote Lincoln on February 10 before his departure: "Will you allow me to publish your letter of yesterday in reference to the call for three hundred thousand volunteers, in the papers in Vermont." (DLC-RTL). No reply from Lincoln has been found.

[2] "On the pending call," inserted in Lincoln's handwriting.

To Edwin M. Stanton[1]

February 8, 1865.

Hon. E. M. Stanton, Secretary of War.

Do not fail to have an interview with this most extraordinary and intelligent black man.   A. LINCOLN.

[1] Frank A. Rollin, *Life and Public Services of Martin R. Delany* (1883), p. 171. According to the source, Martin R. Delany, Negro doctor and editor of Pittsburgh, Pennsylvania, proposed to Lincoln that Negro officers of colored troops be appointed as a means of enlisting Southern Negroes in the army. AGO *Special Orders No. 98*, February 27, 1865, directed: "Major Martin R. Delany, U.S. Colored Troops, now in this city, will report in person, without delay, to Brevet Major-General Saxton, U.S. Volunteers, Superintendent of Recruitment and Organization of Colored Troops, Department of the South, at Beaufort, South Carolina, or wherever he may be."

To George C. Cadwalader[1]

Major General Cadwallader　　　　　　Executive Mansion,
Philadelphia　　　　　　Washington, 9 February, 1865.

Please suspend execution in case of Thomas Adams, 186th Pa Vols & send record to me.　　　　　　A. LINCOLN

Maj: Eckert
Please send above telegram　　JNO. G. NICOLAY

[1] D, DNA WR RG 107, Presidential Telegrams, I, 332. This telegram is in John Hay's handwriting, with Lincoln's signature and instructions to Eckert added in Nicolay's handwriting. General George Cadwalader replied on the same day: "Your telegram directing the suspension of execution in the case of Thomas Adams, One hundred & Eighty Sixth 186 Penna Vols is received and shall be complied with. The record of the case was forwarded to the Judge Advocate General of the Army February Second. . . ." (DLC-RTL). The roster of Company D, One Hundred Eighty-sixth Pennsylvania Volunteers, lists Thomas Adams as dishonorably discharged on August 23, 1865.

To George W. Getty[1]

Commanding General　　　　　　Executive Mansion,
Sixth Army Corps,　　　　　　Washington, February 9th., 1865.

Suspend the execution of the sentence of Private James L. Hycks 67 Pa Vols, until further orders.　　　　　　A. LINCOLN

Major Eckert
The President requests that you will send the above. The man was to have been executed on 10th inst. EDW D NEILL
　　　　　　Sec: to Pres: US. etc

[1] LS, DNA WR RG 107, Presidential Telegrams, I, 333. Brigadier General Getty replied the same day: "I have the honor to acknowledge receipt of your telegram of this date suspending the execution of Private Hicks 67th Pa Vols" (DLC-RTL).

On the court-martial record in the case of Private James L. Hicks, sentenced on charges of desertion, appears Lincoln's endorsement, "Pardon, March 22. 1865 A. LINCOLN." (DNA WR RG 153, Judge Advocate General, LL 3119). The roster of the Sixty-sixth Pennsylvania Volunteers shows Hicks as mustered out with his regiment on July 14, 1865.

To Ulysses S. Grant[1]

Executive Mansion, Washington,
Lieutenant General Grant: February 9, 1865.
Suspend execution of death sentence of Hugh F. Riley, eleventh
Mass Vols. now in front of Petersburg, until further orders, and
forward record for examination.   A. LINCOLN.

Maj: Eckert
Please send above telegram   JNO. G. NICOLAY

[1] D, DNA WR RG 107, Presidential Telegrams, I, 334. This telegram is in
Nicolay's handwriting, including Lincoln's signature. Governor John A. Andrew
telegraphed Lincoln on February 9: "I earnestly pray you to order by telegraph
delay of execution of Hugh F Riley of Eleventh Battalion Mass Volunteers before Petersburg under sentence to be shot. . . . He is an old soldier though only
a boy   Please telegraph reply." (DLC-RTL). Nicolay replied: "The President
has today sent a dispatch ordering that the execution of Hugh F. Riley . . . be
suspended until further orders. . . ." (D, DNA WR RG 107, Presidential Telegrams, I, 335). The roster of the Eleventh Massachusetts Volunteers lists Riley
as dishonorably discharged on October 31, 1865.

To John Eaton[1]

Col Eaton: February 10, 1865
You will continue your supervision of Freedmen over the same
territory & on the same principles as in the past, making such improvements as experiences may suggest, until legislation shall require some farther change   A. LINCOLN
Feb. 10. 1865

[1] LS-F, Eaton, *Grant, Lincoln and the Freedmen*, p. 230. According to Eaton's
account, the dispute in congress over shifting the Freedmen's Bureau from the
War Department to the Treasury prompted him to consult the president: "I
asked Mr. Lincoln if he would give me a word over his own signature to
strengthen me against the difficulties I felt might still be encountered. To this he
agreed . . . and asked me to write out an order which I deemed would be most
useful for my purposes. I wrote the following informal order, summarizing the
verbal instructions he had already given me. . . ." (*Ibid.*, p. 231).

To the House of Representatives[1]

February 10, 1865
To the Honorable, the House of Representatives.
In response to your resolution of the 8th. Inst. requesting infor-
mation in relation to a conference recently held in Hampton Roads

[1] AD, DLC-RTL; DS, DNA RG 233, House Executive Document No. 59. On
February 8, Schuyler Colfax wrote Lincoln: "The Senate have been hesitating
for two days about Mr. Sumner's resolution, asking for information as to the

[274]

I have the honor to state that on the day of the date I gave Francis
P. Blair *sent* a card written on as follows, towit:[2]

Allow the bearer, F. P. Blair, Senr. to pass our lines, go South and return
Dec. 28. 1864   A. LINCOLN

That at the time I was informed that Mr. Blair sought the card as
a means of getting to Richmond, Va. but he was given no authority to speak or act for the government; nor was I informed of any
thing he would say or do on his own account, or otherwise. Afterwards Mr. Blair told me that he had been to Richmond, and had
seen Mr. Jefferson Davis; and he Mr. B. at the same time left with
me a manuscript letter, as follows, towit:[3]

F. P. Blair Esqr.   Richmond Va
Sir: 12 Jany 65
    I have deemed it proper and probably desirable to you to give you in
this form the substance of remarks made by me to be repeated by you
to Presdt. Lincoln &c &c
    I have no disposition to find obstacles in forms, and am willing now as
heretofore to enter into negociations for the restoration of Peace; am
ready to send a commission whenever I have reason to suppose it will
be received, or to receive a commission if the U.S. Govt. shall choose to
send one. That notwithstanding the rejection of our former offers, I
would if you could promise, that a Commissioner, Minister or other
Agent would be received, appoint one immediately and renew the effort
to enter into conference with a view to secure peace to the two countries.
Yrs &c   JEFFN DAVIS

Afterwards, and with the view that it should be shown to Mr.
Davis I wrote and delivered to Mr. Blair a letter as follows, to-wit:[4]

F. P. Blair, Esq   Washington,
Sir: Jan. 18. 1865
    Your having shown me Mr. Davis' letter to you of the 12th. Inst. you
may say to him that I have constantly been, am now, and shall con-

---

recent Conference at Hampton Roads. . . . I stated . . . to Mr. [Thaddeus]
Stevens this morning that I understood from you that you had no objection to
communicating the information, & a resolution has been passed unanimously,
asking for it. . . . Under the circumstances, even if the Senate pass the resolution today, I hope you will reply to the House Resolution, in duplicate, if you
feel required to answer the delayed Senate Resolution to that Body. I know the
answer cannot fail to increase the confidence of the American people in you."
(DLC-RTL).
    The autograph manuscript of Lincoln's communication is composed of Lin-
coln's autograph letters, telegrams received, etc., which he collected for the purpose. In succeeding footnotes each document is described as it appears in Lincoln's
manuscript. Peculiarities of punctuation and spelling follow Lincoln's original
manuscript rather than the signed document sent to the House of Representatives.
    [2] ADS.   [3] ALS.   [4] ALS copy.

tinue, ready to receive any agent whom he, or any other influential person now resisting the national authority, may informally send to me with the view of securing peace to the people of our one common country. Yours &c   A. LINCOLN.

Afterwards Mr. Blair dictated for and authorized me to make an entry on the back of my retained copy of the letter last above recited, which entry is as follows.[5]

January 28. 1865

To-day Mr. Blair tells me that on the 21st. Inst. he delivered to Mr. Davis the original of which the within is a copy, and left it with him; that at the time of delivering it, Mr. Davis read it over twice in Mr. Blair's presence, at the close of which he, Mr. B. remarked that the part about "our one common country" related to the part of Mr. D's letter about "the two countries" to which Mr. D. replied that he so understood it.   A. LINCOLN

Afterwards the Secretary of War placed in my hands the following telegram, indorsed by him, as appears.[6]

Office U.S. Military Telegraph,
Cipher   War Department.
The following Telegram received at Washington, M. Jan 29. 1865.
From Hd Qrs Army of James 6.30 pm 1865.
Hon. Edwin M. Stanton. Secretary of War.   Jan. 29.
The following dispatch just rec'd from Maj. Gen. Parke, who refers it to me for my action. I refer it to you in Lieut Gen. Grant's absence.
E. O. C. ORD   Maj. Gen. Comd'g

"Hd Qrs A of Potomac   4 P.M. Jan. 29. 1865.
Maj. Gen. E. O. C. Ord   Hd Qrs A of J.
The following dispatch is forwarded to you, for your action. Since I have no knowledge of Gen. Grant's having had any understanding of this kind I refer the matter to you as the ranking officer present in the two Armies.   Signed JNO. G. PARKE   "Maj. Gen. Comd'g."

"From Hd Qrs 9th A. Corps 29.
Maj. Gen. Jno. G. Parke, Hd Qrs A. of P.
Alex H. Stevens, R. M. T. Hunter & W. J. A. Campbell desire to cross my lines in accordance with an understanding claimed to exist with Lt. Gen Grant, on their way to Washington as peace Commissioners. Shall they be admitted? They desire an early answer to come through immediately   Would like to reach City Point tonight if they can. If they cannot do this they would like to come through at 10 A.M. to-morrow morning.
Signed O. B. WILCOX   Maj Gen. Cmdg   "9th Corps"

Respectfully referred to the President for his instructions as he may be pleased to give   EDWIN M STANTON   Sec of War
8.30 PM Jan. 29. 1865

5 AES.   6 Received telegram endorsed in Stanton's autograph.

It appears that about the time of placing the foregoing telegram in my hands, the Secretary of War despached Gen. Ord as follows, to-wit: [7]

Copy   War Department Washington City
Maj Gen Ord.   Jany 29th 1865 10. P.M
This Department has no knowledge of any understanding by Genl Grant to allow any person to come within his lines as commissioners of any sort. You will therefore allow no one to come into your lines under such character or profession, until you receive the President's instructions, to whom your telegram will be submitted for his directions
              (signed) EDWIN M. STANTON   Sec'y of War
    Sent in Cipher at 2. A.M. 30th

Afterwards, by my direction, the Secretary of War telegraphed Gen. Ord as follows, towit: [8]

Copy.
Maj. Gen. E. O. C. Ord,   War Department   Washington D.C.
Hd. Qrs. Army James.   10.30 A.M. January 30. 1865.
By direction of the President you are instructed to inform the three gentlemen, Messrs Stephens, Hunter and Campbell, that a messenger will be dispatched to them at, or near where they now are, without unnecessary delay.   Signed EDWIN M. STANTON   Secretary of War.

Afterwards I prepared and put into the hands of Major Thomas T. Eckert, the following instructions and message. [9]

Major T. T. Eckert   Executive Mansion
Sir.   Washington, Jan. 30. 1865
You will proceed with the documents placed in your hands; and, on reaching Gen. Ord, will deliver him the letter addressed to him by the Secretary of War; then, by Gen. Ord's assistance, procure an interview with Messrs. Stephens Hunter and Campbell, or any of them, deliver to him or them the paper on which your own letter is written, note on the copy which you retain, the time of delivery and to whom delivered, receive their answer in writing waiting a reasonable time for it, and which, if it contain their decision to come through, without further condition, will be your warrant to ask Gen Ord to pass them through as directed in the letter of the Secretary of War to him. If by their answer they decline to come, or propose other terms, do not not [*sic*] have the[m] passed through. And this being your whole duty, return and report to me. Yours truly   A. LINCOLN

Messrs Alex H. Stephens, J. A. Campbell & R. M. T. Hunter
Gentlemen: I am instructed by the President of the United States to place this paper in your hands with the information that if you pass through the U.S. Military lines it will be understood that you do so for the purpose of an informal conference, on the basis of the letter, a

---

[7] Copy.   [8] Copy.
[9] ALS copy and copy. The original autographs of these two documents, carried by Eckert, are described under their respective dates, *supra*.

copy of which is on the reverse side of this sheet, and that if you choose to pass on such understanding, and so notify me in writing, I will procure the Commanding General to pass you through the lines, and to Fortress-Monroe, under such military precautions as he may deem prudent; and, at which place you will be met in due time by some person or persons for the purpose of such informal conference. And further that you shall have protection, safe-conduct, and safe return, in all events. THOS. T. ECKERT.

City Point Va. Maj & A.D.C.

February 1st. 1865.

Afterwards, but before Major Eckert had departed, the following despatch was received from Gen. Grant[10]

Office U.S. Military Telegraph,
Cipher War Department.

The following Telegram received at Washington, M. Jan. 31. 1865.

His Excellency Abraham Lincoln. From City Point Va.

President of the U.S. 10.30 AM Jan. 31. 1865.

The following communication was received here last evening.

"Lieut. Gen. U. S. Grant Petersburg Va.

Comd'g Armies U.S. Jan. 30. 1865.

Sir: We desire to pass your lines under safe conduct and to proceed to Washington to hold a conference with President Lincoln upon the subject of the existing war, and with a view of ascertaining upon what terms it may be terminated, in pursuance of the course indicated by him in his letter to Mr Blair of January 18th. 1865, of which we presume you have a copy, and if not, we wish to see you in person if convenient, and to confer with you upon the subject. Signed, Very Respy Yours ALEXANDER STEVENS

J. A. CAMPBELL

R. M. T. HUNTER"

I have sent directions to receive these gentlemen and expect to have them at my Quarters this evening awaiting your instructions.

U. S. GRANT Lieut Genl Comdg Armies US

This, it will be perceived, transferred Gen. Ord's agency in the matter to Gen. Grant. I resolved, however to send Major Eckert forward with his Message, and accordingly telegraphed Gen. Grant as follows, towit:[11]

Telegram Copy.

Lieut Genl Grant Executive Mansion

City Point Va. Washington Jany 31st. 1865

A messenger is coming to you on the business contained in your despatch. Detain the gentlemen in comfortable quarters until he arrives and then act upon the message he brings, as far as applicable, it having been made up to pass through Genl Ord's hands, and when the gentlemen were supposed to be beyond our lines (signed) A. LINCOLN

Sent in Cipher at 1.30. P.M.

[10] Telegram received. An autograph copy in Lincoln's handwriting is in the Seward Papers, NAuE. [11] Copy.

When Major Eckert departed he bore with him a letter of the Secretary of War to Gen. Grant as follows, towit:[12]

Letter   *Copy*   War Department   Washington D.C.
Lt Genl Grant   Comd'g &c.   Jany 30th 1865
General: The President desires that you will please procure for the bearer, Major Thomas T. Eckert, an interview with Messrs Stephens, Hunter, & Campbell,—and if on his return to you he requests it—pass them through our lines to Fortress Monroe by such. route and under such Military precautions as you may deem prudent, giving them protection & comfortable quarters while there; and that you let none of this, have any effect upon your movements or plans.
  By order of the President
              (signed)   EDWIN M. STANTON   Secretary of War

Supposing the proper point to be then reached I despatched the Secretary of State with the following instructions, Major Eckert, however, going ahead of him.[13]

Hon. William H. Seward.   Executive Mansion
Secretary of State.   Washington, Jan. 31. 1865
  You will proceed to Fortress-Monroe, Virginia, there to meet, and informally confer with Messrs. Stephens, Hunter, and Campbell, on the basis of my letter to F. P. Blair, Esq. of Jan. 18. 1865, a copy of which you have.
  You will make known to them that three things are indispensable, towit:
1 The restoration of the National authority throughout all the States.
2 No receding by the Executive of the United States, on the Slavery question, from the position assumed thereon, in the late Annual Message to Congress, and on preceding documents.
3. No cessation of hostilities short of an end of the war, and the disbanding of all forces hostile to the government.

[12] Copy.
[13] ALS copy.
Not included in Lincoln's report but important to the narrative is the following:
          "Head Quarters Armies of the United States,
              "January 31st 1865.
"Hon. Alexander H. Stephens, J. A Campbell, and R. M. T Hunter
  "Gentlemen! Your communication of yesterday requesting an interview with myself and a safe conduct to Washington and return, is received. I will instruct the Commanding Officer of the forces near Petersburg to receive you, notifying you at what point of the line and the time when and where conveyance will be ready for you.
  "Your letter to me has been telegraphed to Washington for instructions. I have no doubt but that before you arrive at my Headquarters an answer will be received directing me to comply with your request. Should a different reply be received I promise you a safe and immediate return within your own lines. I am, very respectfully   (sgd) U. S. GRANT
  "Official   Lieutenant General.
       "T. S. Bowers.
       "Asst. Adjt. Gen'l." (Copy, owned by Justin G. Turner, Los Angeles, California).

You will inform them that all propositions of theirs, not inconsistent with the above, will be considered and passed upon, in a spirit of sincere liberality.

You will hear all they may choose to say, and report it to me.

You will not assume to definitely consummate any thing. Yours &c
ABRAHAM LINCOLN.

On the day of it's date the following telegram was sent to Gen. Grant.[14]

Telegram   Copy.
Lieut Genl Grant   War Department   Washington D.C.
City Point Va.   Feby 1st. 1865
Let nothing which is transpiring, change, hinder, or delay your Military movements, or plans   (signed) A. LINCOLN
Sent in cipher at 9.30 a.m

Afterwards the following despatch was received from Gen. Grant.[15]

In Cipher   Office U.S. Military Telegraph,
                                              War Department.
The following Telegram received at Washington,
    2.30 P.M. Feby 1st. 1865
His Excellency A. Lincoln   From City Point Va
Prest U.S.   Feb'y 1st. 12.30 P.M 1865
Your despatch received; there will be no armistice in consequence of the presence of Mr Stephens and others within our lines. The troops are kept in readiness to move at the shortest notice if occasion should justify it   U. S. GRANT   Lieut Genl

To notify Major Eckert that the Secretary of State would be at Fortress-Monroe, and to put them in communication the following despatch was sent.[16]

Telegram   Copy
Maj T. T. Eckert   War Department   Washington D.C.
Care Genl Grant   City Point Va.   Feby 1st. 1865
Call at Fortress Monroe & put yourself under direction of Mr S. whom you will find there   (signed) A. LINCOLN
Sent in cipher at 5.30 P.M.

On the morning of the 2nd. Inst. the following telegrams were received by me respectively from the Secretary of State and Major Eckert.[17]

Recd 4 30 AM   Feb 2nd   United States Military Telegraph,
    In cipher   War Department.
The President U.S.   Fort Monroe Va 11 30 PM Feb 1. 1865
Arrived at ten (10) this evening. Richmond party not here. I remain here.   WM H. SEWARD

[14] Copy.   [15] Telegram received.   [16] Copy.
[17] Telegrams received.

Recd   United States Military Telegraph,
In cipher Feb 2nd.   War Department.
His Excellency A Lincoln   City Point Va
President U.S.   10 PM Feb 1. 1865

I have the honor to report the delivery of your communication and my letter at four fifteen 4.15 this afternoon, to which I received a reply at six (6) P.M, but not satisfactory.

At eight (8) PM the following note addressed to Genl Grant was received.[18]

To "Lt Gen Grant,   City Point Va
Sir,   Feb 1. 1865"

"We desire to go to Washington City to confer informally with the President personally in reference to the matters mentioned in his letter to Mr Blair of the eighteenth 18th January ultimo, without any personal compromise on any question in the letter.

"We have the permission to do so from the authorities in Richmond."
Very Respectfully Yours"   (signed)   "ALEX H. STEPHENS
                                        "R. M T. HUNTER
                                        "J. A CAMPBELL."

At nine thirty (9.30) P.M I notified them that they could not proceed further unless they complied with the terms expressed in my letter. The point of meeting designated, in above note, would not in my opinion, be insisted upon   Think Fort Monroe would be acceptable. Having complied with my instructions, I will return to Washington to-morrow unless otherwise ordered.   THos T. ECKERT   Maj &c

On reading this despatch of Major Eckert I was about to recall him and the Secretary of State when the following telegram of Gen. Grant to the Secretary of War was shown me.[19]

---

[18] The original note signed by Stephens, Hunter, and Campbell, as well as the autograph draft of Eckert's telegram, is now owned by Justin G. Turner, Los Angeles, California.

[19] Telegram received. Not included by Lincoln in his report but important to the narrative is the following telegram:

                         "City Point Va Feby 1st. 1865
"Hon Edwin M Stanton.   "10.30 PM

"In reply to the letters delivered by me to Messrs Stephens, Campbell & Hunter, they give a copy of their instructions from Jefferson Davis, which I think is a verbatim copy of that now in the Presidents possession, am posative about the last two words, which differs from the ending of copy delivered by me & to which the President called my particular attention.

"After giving object of conference they add, 'Our instructions contemplate a personal interview with President L at Washington, but with this explanation we are ready to meet any person or persons that President L. may appoint at such place as he may designate. Our earnest desire is that a just & honorable peace may be agreed upon & we are prepared to receive or to submit propositions which may possibly lead to the attainment of that end. Signed Alex H Stephens, R M T Hunter & J A Campbell.' They say the ending of letter I delivered to them is the only objectionable point & one that, in their opinion,

Office U.S. Military Telegraph,
In cipher   War Department.

The following Telegram received at Washington,
    4.35 A.M. Feby 2nd. 1865
        From City Point Va. Feby 1st. 10.30 P.M 1865

Hon Edwin M Stanton   Secy of War.

Now that the interview between Maj. Eckert, under his written instructions, and Mr Stevens & party, has ended I will state confidentially, but not officially to become a matter of record, that I am convinced, upon conversation with Messrs Stevens & Hunter that their intentions are good and their desire sincere to restore peace and union. I have not felt myself at liberty to express even views of my own or to account for my reticency. This has placed me in an awkward position which I could have avoided by not seeing them in the first instance. I fear now their going back without any expression from any one in authority will have a bad influence. At the same time I recognize the difficulties in the way of receiving these informal commissioners at this time and do not know what to recommend. I am sorry however that Mr Lincoln cannot have an interview with the two named in this despatch if not all three now within our lines. Their letter to me was all that the Presidents instructions contemplated, to secure their safe conduct if they had used the same language to Maj Eckert   (signed)   U.S. GRANT Lt Genl

This despatch of Gen. Grant changed my purpose; and, accordingly, I telegraphed him and the Secretary of State respectively as follow.[20]

Copy.   War Department
Lieut Genl Grant   Washington D.C.
City Point Va.   Feby 2nd. 1865

    Say to the gentlemen I will meet them personally at Fortress Monroe as soon as I can get there   (signed)   A. LINCOLN
    sent in cipher at 9. A.M.

Copy.   War Department
Hon Wm. H. Seward   Washington D.C.
Fortress Monroe Va.   Feby 2nd. 1865

    Induced by a despatch from Genl Grant, I join you at Fort Monroe as soon as I can come   (signed)   A. LINCOLN
    Sent in cipher at 9. A.M.

Before starting the following despatch was shown me; I proceeded nevertheless.[21]

---

should be left out of both, the letter they bring as well as the one they receive, adding if they accept the latter & terms are not agreed upon, it would be an acknowledgement that might prejudice future interests of people they represent. THOS. T. ECKERT." (ALS, owned by Justin G. Turner, Los Angeles, California).

[20] Copies.   [21] Telegram received.

Office U.S. Military Telegraph,

Cipher   War Department.

The following Telegram received at Washington, M. Feby. 2d. 1865

From City Point Va 9 A.M. Feby. 2d. 1865

Hon Wm. H. Seward   Secretary of State   Ft. Monroe

Copy to Hon. Edwin M. Stanton   Secretary of War   Wash.

The gentlemen here have accepted the proposed terms and will leave for Ft. Monroe at 9.30 A.M.   U. S. GRANT   Lt. Genl.

On the night of the 2nd, I reached Hampton Roads found the Secretary of State and Major Eckert on a Steamer anchored off shore, and learned of them that the Richmond gentlemen were on another Steamer also anchored off shore in the Roads, and that the Secretary of State had not yet seen, or communicated with them. Here I ascertained that Major Eckert had litterally complied with his instructructions [sic] and I saw, for the first, the answer of the Richmond gentlemen to him, which in his despatch to me of the 1st. he characterizes as "not satisfactory.["] That answer is as follows, towit: [22]

Copy

Thomas J. [T.] Eckert   City Point Va.

Major & A.D.C.   Feby 1st. 1865

Major.   Your note delivered by yourself this day has been considered. In reply we have to say that we were furnished with a copy of the letter of President Lincoln to Francis P. Blair Esq of the 18th of Jany ult. another copy of which is appended to your note.

Our instructions are contained in a letter of which the following is a copy.

"Richmond Jany 28th 1865

"In conformity with the letter of Mr Lincoln of which the foregoing is a copy, you are to proceed to Washington City for informal conference with him upon the issues involved in the existing war and for the purpose of securing peace to the two countries. With great respect Your ob't Servt   (signed)   JEFFERSON DAVIS"

The substantial object to be obtained by the informal conference is, to ascertain upon what terms the existing war can be terminated honorably.

Our instructions contemplate a personal interview between President Lincoln and ourselves at Washington City, but with this explanation we are ready to meet any person or persons that President Lincoln may appoint, at such place as he may designate.

Our earnest desire is that a just and honorable peace may be agreed upon, and we are prepared to receive or to submit propositions which may, possibly, lead to the attainment of that end. Very Respectfully Yours   (signed)   ALEXANDER H. STEPHENS

R. M. T. HUNTER

JOHN A. CAMPBELL

[22] Copy. The original manuscript of this letter is owned by Justin G. Turner, Los Angeles, California.

A note of these gentlemen, subsequently addressed to Gen. Grant, has already been given in Major Eckert's despatch of the 1st. Inst. I also here saw, for the first [time], the following note addressed by the Richmond gentlemen to Major Eckert:[23]

Copy.

Thomas C. [T.] Eckert   City Point Va.
Major & A.D.C.   Feby 2nd. 1865
    Major. In reply to your verbal statement that your instructions did not allow you to alter the conditions upon which a passport could be given to us, we say that we are willing to proceed to Fortress Monroe and there to have an informal conference with any person or persons that President Lincoln may appoint on the basis of his letter to Francis P. Blair of the 18th of Jan'y ult. or upon any other terms, or conditions that he may hereafter propose not inconsistent with the essential principles of self government and popular rights upon which our institutions are founded.
    It is our earnest wish to ascertain after a free interchange of ideas and information, upon what principles and terms, if any, a just and honorable peace can be established without the further effusion of blood, and to contribute our utmost efforts to accomplish such a result.
    We think it better to add that in accepting your passport we are not to be understood as committing ourselves to anything, but to carry to this informal conference the views and feelings above expressed. Very Respectfully Yours &c   (signed)   ALEXANDER H. STEPHENS
                                                                   J. A. CAMPBELL
                                                                   R. M. T. HUNTER

Note
The above communication was delivered to me at Fort Monroe at 4.30 P.M. Feby 2nd. by Lieut Col Babcock of Gen'l Grants Staff
                    (signed)   THOS T. ECKERT   Maj & A.D.C

On the morning of the 3rd., the three gentlemen, Messrs Stephens, Hunter and Campbell, came aboard of our Steamer and had an interview with the Secretary of State and myself of several hours duration. No question of preliminaries to the meeting was then and there made or mentioned. No other person was present; no papers were exchanged, or produced; and it was, in advance, agreed that the conversation was to be informal, and verbal merely.[24] On our part, the whole substance of the instructions to the Secretary of State, herein before recited, was stated and insisted upon, and nothing was said inconsistently therewith; while, by the other party it was not said that, in any event, or on any condition, they *ever* would consent to re-union, and yet they

[23] Copy. The original manuscript of this letter is owned by Justin G. Turner, Los Angeles, California.
[24] Lincoln deleted four lines at this point: "and that no one was to be committed by it. Perhaps a pledge of secrecy, as to particulars, was implied, though not expressed. I believe, however, there can be no impropriety in stating that."

equally omitted to declare that they *never* would so consent. They seemed to desire a postponement of that question, and the adoption of some other course first, which, as some of them, seemed to argue, might, or might not, lead to re-union, but which course, we thought, would amount to an indefinite postponement. The conferrence ended without result. The foregoing, containing, as is believed, all the information sought, is respectfully submitted.[25]

Executive Mansion,   ABRAHAM LINCOLN
February 10th, 1865.

[25] The autograph manuscript ends without the date and signature which appear on the signed copy sent to the House of Representatives.

To Edward O. C. Ord[1]

Will Gen. Ord please see & hear these ladies on the within?
Feb. 10, 1865   A. LINCOLN

[1] Anderson Auction Company-Metropolitan Art Association Catalog 1110, October 22, 1914, No. 434. According to the catalog description, Lincoln's endorsement is written on a petition of two ladies (unnamed) to have their property, taken from them by General Butler, restored.

Order Concerning E. R. Scott[1]

Executive Mansion, Feb. 10, 1865
Let Captain Scott be paroled and bailed to Lieutenant General Scott.   A. LINCOLN

[1] Clipping, ICHi-MacChesney Scrapbook, XXXIII, 8028. According to the source, Lincoln's endorsement appears on the back of a letter from Winfield Scott, February 8, 1865, concerning his great-nephew Captain E. R. Scott.

To David D. Porter[1]

Executive Mansion, February 10, 1865.
Sir: It is made my agreeable duty to enclose herewith the joint resolution approved 24th January, 1865, tendering the thanks of Congress to yourself, the officers and men under your command, for their gallantry and good conduct in the capture of Fort Fisher, and through you to all who participated in that brilliant and decisive victory under your command. Very respectfully,

Rear-Admiral David D. Porter,   ABRAHAM LINCOLN.
Commanding North Atlantic Squadron,
Hampton Roads, Virginia.

[1] OR, I, XI, 459. The resolution of thanks was approved by Lincoln on January 24, 1865.

To the Senate[1]

To the Senate of the United States.   February 10, 1865

In answer to the Resolution of the Senate of the 8th instant, requesting information concerning recent conversations or communications with insurgents, under executive sanction, I transmit a Report from the Secretary of State, to whom the Resolution was referred.   ABRAHAM LINCOLN

Washington,
10th February, 1865.

[1] DS, DNA RG 46, Senate 38A F2. See Lincoln's communication to the House of Representatives, *supra*. The resolution introduced in the House by Thaddeus Stevens and the resolution introduced in the Senate by Charles Sumner were both adopted on February 8. Lincoln's reply was directed to the House as a result of the request of Schuyler Colfax. The report of Secretary Seward, dated February 10, 1865, pointed out that "the Senate may properly be referred to a special message of the President bearing upon the subject of the resolution and transmitted to the House this day. Appended to this report is a copy of an instruction which has been addressed to Charles Francis Adams, Esq., envoy extraordinary and minister plenipotentiary of the United States at London, and which is the only correspondence found in this department touching the subject referred to in the resolution. . . ."

The extract from Seward's letter to Adams, February 7, follows:

"On the morning of the 3d, the President, attended by the Secretary, received Messrs. Stephens, Hunter, and Campbell on board the United States steam transport *River Queen* in Hampton Roads. The conference was altogether informal. There was no attendance of secretaries, clerks, or other witnesses. Nothing was written or read. The conversation, although earnest and free, was calm, and courteous, and kind on both sides. The Richmond party approached the discussion rather indirectly, and at no time did they either make categorical demands, or tender formal stipulations or absolute refusals. Nevertheless, during the conference, which lasted four hours, the several points at issue between the government and the insurgents were distinctly raised, and discussed fully, intelligently, and in an amicable spirit. What the insurgent party seemed chiefly to favor was a postponement of the question of separation, upon which the war is waged, and a mutual direction of efforts of the government, as well as those of the insurgents, to some extrinsic policy or scheme for a season during which passions might be expected to subside, and the armies be reduced, and trade and intercourse between the people of both sections resumed. It was suggested by them that through such postponement we might now have immediate peace, with some not very certain prospect of an ultimate satisfactory adjustment of political relations between this government and the States, section, or people now engaged in conflict with it.

"This suggestion, though deliberately considered, was nevertheless regarded by the President as one of armistice or truce, and he announced that we can agree to no cessation or suspension of hostilities, except on the basis of the disbandment of the insurgent forces, and the restoration of the national authority throughout all the States in the Union. Collaterally, and in subordination to the proposition which was thus announced, the antislavery policy of the United States was reviewed in all its bearings, and the President announced that he must not be expected to depart from the positions he had heretofore assumed in his proclamation of emancipation and other documents, as these positions were reiterated in his last annual message. It was further declared by the President

[286]

that the complete restoration of the national authority was an indispensable condition of any assent on our part to whatever form of peace might be proposed. The President assured the other party that, while he must adhere to these positions, he would be prepared, so far as power is lodged with the executive, to exercise liberality. His power, however, is limited by the Constitution; and when peace should be made, Congress must necessarily act in regard to appropriations of money and to the admission of representatives from the insurrectionary States. The Richmond party were then informed that Congress had, on the 31st ultimo, adopted by a constitutional majority a joint resolution submitting to the several States the proposition to abolish slavery throughout the Union, and that there is every reason to expect that it will be soon accepted by three-fourths of the States, so as to become a party of the national organic law.

"The conference came to an end by mutual acquiescence, without producing an agreement of views upon the several matters discussed, or any of them. Nevertheless, it is perhaps of some importance that we have been able to submit our opinions and views directly to prominent insurgents, and to hear them in answer in a courteous and not unfriendly manner." (Thirty-eighth Congress, Second Session, *Senate Executive Document No. 18*).

To James Speed[1]

Please file. I have sent to the Senate a nomination of Richard W. Thompson of Indiana to fill the vacancy.   A. LINCOLN

Feb. 10. 1865.

[1] AES, DNA RG 60, Papers of Attorney General, 1865, Box 125. Lincoln's endorsement appears on a letter of resignation signed by James Hughes, Judge of the U.S. Court of Claims, February 3, 1865. On February 13, Richard W. Thompson wrote from Terre Haute, Indiana: "I learned, on Saturday, by telegram from Messrs [Henry S.] Lane & [John D.] Defrees, that you had appointed me Judge of the Court of Claims. Since then I have given the subject much reflection, and am constrained, by a sense of duty to my family, to decline it. The office would require me to be away from home a greater part of the time, which is so contrary to all the calculations I have made for the future, that I could not discharge its duties without violating others which I have no right to disregard. . . ." (DLC-RTL).

On February 21, Lincoln nominated Charles C. Nott in place of Thompson, and the Senate confirmed Nott's appointment on February 22, 1865.

To Alexander H. Stephens[1]

Executive Mansion
Hon. A. H. Stephens   Washington, Feb. 10, 1865

According to our agreement, your nephew, Lieut. Stephens, goes to you, bearing this note. Please, in return, to select and send to me, that officer of the same rank, imprisoned at Richmond, whose physical condition most urgently requires his release   Respectfully
          A. LINCOLN

[1] ADfS (copy?), NNP; ALS, owned by Robert G. Stephens, Washington, Georgia. The autograph draft, or autograph copy, was given to J. Pierpont Morgan by Robert Todd Lincoln in 1908, accompanied by Alexander H.

Stephens' autograph notation of his nephew's name and address, which Stephens gave Lincoln during the Hampton Roads Conference. See Lincoln to Charles W. Hill, February 4, *supra*.

To Henry B. Anthony and William Sprague[1]

February 11, 1865

I would like to give Mr. Hammond some tolerably good appointment; but understanding that giving him the place of Internal Revenue Collector in his District, would be embarrassing or disagreeable to Senators Anthony and Sprague, I will thank them to make an effort to find something respectable for him which, would not be disagreeable to them.   A. LINCOLN

Feb. 11. 1865.

[1] AES, MH-Slattery Collection. This endorsement appears to have been cut from a letter. George T. Hammond, editor of the Newport, Rhode Island, *Daily News*, had written Lincoln on September 14, 1864:

"Can I have a private or unembarrassed interview with you for a *few* moments if I go to Washington on purpose?

"If so when shall I come?

"My paper has supported the Republican party from its formation and your administration from its beginning without reward, and if this is a sufficient reason to grant me the favor which I ask, more for your benefit than my own, you will favor me with an early reply. . . ." (DLC-RTL).

No record of his appointment to a federal job has been found, but see Lincoln's notes to Heads of Departments, and to Welles, *infra*.

To Ulysses S. Grant[1]

Executive Mansion,

Lieut Genl. Grant   Washington Feby [c.11] 1865.

City Point.   Dr. Ray whom you know will talk to you about a certain matter about which I would like your opinion informally expressed. Yours Very Respectfully   A LINCOLN.

[1] Copy, DLC-RTL (4070-22). The bracketed portion of the date has been supplied on the basis of the date of Grant's reply, which is described in the transcript preserved in the Lincoln Papers as appearing on the same sheet as Lincoln's note:

"Trade will be subject to the approval of the Dept. Commanders so far as left for the military to control. I see less objection to whiskey being introduced into the South than to any other one article. Dr. Ray has asked my opinion particularly as to the propriety of taking this article up White river, the Yazoo and the St. Francis. Gen Dana will have to be referred to in matters of trade on the Yazoo, and Gen Reynolds when permits are desired on the other two streams.

"Washington D.C.   U. S. GRANT

"Feby 11th 1865.   Lt. Genl."

On January 17, Governor Richard J. Oglesby had written Lincoln: "Dr C H

Ray formerly of the Tribune is here and I believe is being approached with an offer to engage in an enterprise at Chicago Ills which may lead to a chism in our cause in this State, he desires to turn his attention towards other matters in the border or Rebel States, I really hope you may be able to give the Doctor such privilidges as may induce him to abide by his wishes in this respect and relieve him from the pursuasions of his friends to return just now to the editorial chair. I would like to see him do well and shall be verry much pleased if you can find it agreeable to respond to his wishes. The excitement growing out of the Senatorial contest is still unabated. I think it would be wise to favor any policy to abate it." (DLC-RTL).

See further Lincoln's authorization for Ray, February 15, *infra.*

To Pierce B. Hawkins[1]

P. B. Hawkins   Executive Mansion
Frankfort, Ky   Washington Feb. 11. 1865
  Gen. Burbridge may discharge W. E. Waller, if he thinks fit.
                            A. LINCOLN

[1] ALS, DNA WR RG 107, Presidential Telegrams, I, 337. In Lincoln's telegram to Burbridge, February 2, *supra,* the name was "Walker," but Hawkins telegraphed Lincoln on February 11: "Genl Burbridge says he would release W E Waller if he had the power   Aching hearts ask it of you. he ought to be" (DLC-RTL). No further record of the case has been found.

To Heads of Departments[1]

                        Washington, Feb. 11, 1865.
  Will the Head of any Department to whom this card may be presented, give the bearer, Mr. Hammond, an interview?
                            A. LINCOLN.

[1] NH, XI, 32. See Lincoln's communication to Anthony and Sprague, *supra,* and to Welles, *infra.*

To Edward O. C. Ord[1]

Major Genl. Ord   Executive Mansion,
Army of James.   Washington, Feb. 11, 1865
  Suspend execution of sentence in case of Major T. C. Jameson & send me the record.   A. LINCOLN

[1] ALS, DNA WR RG 107, Presidential Telegrams, I, 336. General Ord replied the same day: "Your dispatch is received. The matter will be attended to" (DLC-RTL).

On February 13, William Lloyd Garrison wrote Lincoln enclosing a clipping of his speech celebrating the passage of the Thirteenth Amendment (delivered on February 4) and acknowledging receipt of Lincoln's letter of February 7, *supra*. Garrison added a request for clemency in the case of Major Thorndike C. Jameson, Fifth Rhode Island Artillery, dishonorably discharged, fined $8,000, and sentenced to three years' imprisonment on charges of fraud (DLC-Nicolay Papers). AGO *General Court Martial Orders No. 149*, March 17, 1865, promulgated Jameson's pardon and release from imprisonment.

Pass for Abraham U. Colby[1]

Let this gentleman & wife pass from New York to Savannah.
Feb. 11, 1865.   A. LINCOLN

[1] Newark Galleries Catalog 128, December 5, 1930, No. 161. According to the catalog description, Lincoln's note accompanies an affidavit of Dr. Robert Watts endorsed by Dr. Willard Parker and Representative William H. Randall of Kentucky, that Abraham U. Colby was suffering from a disease of the lungs.

Pass for John T. Heard[1]

Surgeon J. Theodore Heard is allowed to visit Washington, D.C, provided he does not overstay his Leave of Absence.
Feb. 11. 1865   A. LINCOLN

[1] ADS, IHi. The leave of absence of Surgeon John T. Heard, medical director of the Fourth Army Corps, was extended ten days by AGO *Special Orders No. 91*, February 24, 1865.

To James Speed[1]

Atty. Genl. make out pardon for unexpired part of sentence.
Feb. 11, 1865.   A. LINCOLN

[1] AES, DNA RG 204, U.S. Pardon Attorney, A 583. Lincoln's endorsement appears on a letter of M. J. Payne, Jefferson City, Missouri, to Austin A. King, February 1, 1865, asking pardon for George Walkey convicted of counterfeiting.

To Edwin M. Stanton[1]

Will the Sec. of War please see & hear the bearer & do as well for those he represents as we have heretofore done for "Friends"?
Feb. 11. 1865.   A. LINCOLN

[1] AES, NHi. Lincoln's endorsement appears on a letter from Oliver L. Davis, Danville, Illinois, January 30, 1865, introducing Jonah M. Davis of Ridge Farm, who is "on his way to Washington to obtain, if possible, some relief for the Society of Friends of Ellwood Township. The township is unable to raise sufficient funds, without the aid of the 'Friends' to obtain volunteers to fill their quota, and the 'Friends' are not only conscientiously opposed to bearing arms, but they are opposed to voluntarily furnishing money to pay others. . . ."

To Edwin M. Stanton[1]

Hon. Sec. of War   Executive Mansion,
Sir   Washington, Feb. 11, 1865.

On a petition presented to me I have concluded to not allow the death penalty to be enforced on Norman L. King; but I wish to see Mr. Holt's review of the evidence, before finally disposing of the case. Please have it made and sent to me. Yours truly

A. LINCOLN

[1] ALS, IHi. Norman L. King, citizen of Washington, D.C., had been sentenced to death on January 19, 1865, for violating laws and customs of war. Joseph Holt's report was adverse to the petition for clemency, but a note on the jacket of the court-martial record dated April 28, 1865, indicates a pardon "by the late President." (DNA WR RG 153, Judge Advocate General, NN 3306). On February 17, Reverend Phineas D. Gurley wrote Lincoln: "My esteemed friend and neighbor Mr. King, the life of whose son you have recently saved, will call to-morrow with Senator Pomeroy to see you further about the case. . . . I deeply and fully sympathize with them in their desire that he should be released from his imprisonment as well as saved from death. . . ." (DLC-RTL).

To Gideon Welles[1]

[c. February 11, 1865?]

Hon. Sec. of Navy, please give the bearer, Mr. Hammond, a short interview   A. LINCOLN

[1] ALS, owned by Joseph L. Block, Chicago, Illinois. See Lincoln's notes to Anthony and Sprague and to Heads of Departments, *supra*.

Endorsement Concerning Daniel M. Taylor[1]

West Point. Daniel Morgan Taylor. This is a good letter, written by the boy himself.   A. LINCOLN.

Feb. 12, 1865.

[1] Copy, DNA WR RG 94, U.S. Military Academy, 1865, No. 325. The copy of Lincoln's endorsement appears on a copy of a letter from Daniel Morgan Taylor, Washington City, January 6, 1865. Taylor entered West Point in July 1865 and graduated in June 1869.

To Joseph Hooker[1]

Major General Hooker   Executive Mansion
Cincinnati, O.   Washington, Feb. 12. 1865

Is it Lieut. Samuel B. Davis whose death sentence is commuted? If not, done, let it be done. Is there not an associate of his also in trouble? Please answer.   A. LINCOLN

[291]

[1] ALS, DNA WR RG 107, Presidential Telegrams, I, 339. Hooker replied on the same day: "It is Lieut Saml B. Davis whose death sentence has been commuted to confinement at hard labor at Ft Delaware. No associate of his is in any immediate danger that I know of" (DLC-RTL).

Lieutenant Samuel Boyer Davis, CSA, was ordered released from confinement at Fort Warren (AGO *General Court Martial Orders No. 660*, December 20, 1865). On February 7, 1865, Senator George R. Riddle and Senator Willard Saulsbury of Delaware had written Lincoln asking clemency for Davis (DLC-RTL). A letter from Hooker to Lincoln dated February 7 indicates that Davis had been arrested in Cincinnati on charges of being a spy, and sentenced to death by a military commission "now in session in this city. The sentence was approved by me, with the view of commuting it to confinement . . . during the war, which was done day before yesterday." (OR, II, VIII, 191-92).

Pass for Mrs. Edward Byrne[1]

Allow Mrs. Edward Byrne to pass our lines Northward, and go to Louisville, Ky.   A. LINCOLN

Feb. 12. 1865

[1] ADS, ICHi. Mrs. Edward Byrne has not been identified.

Pass for Mrs. Willis F. Jones[1]

Allow Mrs. Willis F. Jones to pass our lines with ordinary baggage, go South & return.   A. LINCOLN

Feb. 12. 1865

[1] ADS, owned by William H. Townsend, Lexington, Kentucky. This pass written on a small card accompanies a letter to Lincoln from Martha M. Jones, Versailles, Kentucky, February 1, 1865:

"My husband, Maj. Willis F. Jones, Adgnt Gen of [Charles W.] Field's Division of the Confederate Army was killed in battle before Richmond on the 13th of October last. I have been separated from him for two long years, during which time I have experienced almost every conceivable trial—the most severe of which resulted from the unsuccessful applications made in my behalf to the War Department by many of the most eminent military and professional men of this state for permission for me to visit him there during a dangerous and protracted illness.

"I now address your Excellency and entreat you to grant me the privilege of going to Richmond that I may visit his tomb, and the friends who attended his last moments and received his personal effects which are of sacred and inestimable value to me; and also permission to bring from the South his man servant, whom I desire to manumit in consideration of his fidelity to his master. . . ."

To John Pope[1]

Major Genl. Pope   Executive Mansion,
St. Louis, Mo.   Washington, Feb. 12, 1865.

I understand that Provost-Marshals in different parts of Missouri are assuming to decide that the conditions of bonds are forfeited, and thereupon are seizing and selling property to pay damages. This, if true, is both outrageous and ridiculous. Do not allow it. The courts and not Provost-Marshals, are to decide such questions, only when military necessity makes an exception. Also excuse John Ecton of Clay Co. & Wesley Martin of Platte from being sent South & let them go East, if anywhere.

A LINCOLN

[1] ALS, DNA WR RG 107, Presidential Telegrams, I, 998. General John Pope had been placed in command of the Department of the Missouri to succeed General Samuel R. Curtis who was transferred to the Department of the Northwest (AGO *General Orders No. 11*, January 30, 1865). He replied on February 13: "Dispatch recd & attended to Provost Marshal system in Mo is oppressive and absurd I am examining into & will correct the whole matter" (DLC-RTL).

On February 11, Austin A. King had written Lincoln:

"I ask the President for a despatch to Gen. Pope changing the order for the banishment of John Ecton of Clay County, and Wesley Martin of Platte County, from being sent South—and at their options, to be banished to the state of Illinois, or some other loyal state, East of the Mississippi—and that Ecton's personal property only—be sold by the U.S. Marshal—when required to do so, by the proper order made under the confiscation act—and not under a military order, and by a Military Provost Marshal.

"I respectfully ask for this order by a despatch as early as you conveniently can."

See further, Lincoln to Pope, February 14, *infra.*

To Edwin M. Stanton[1]

February 12, 1865

In a long verbal conversation with me Judge Fisher assured, as within, of his confident belief that Dr. Worrell is partially insane. I suppose that on this ground, he should be discharged.

Feb. 12. 1865   A. LINCOLN

[1] AES, owned by Dale Carnegie, New York City. Lincoln's endorsement appears to have been clipped from a document. The register of letters received by the adjutant general lists an application of George P. Fisher for relatives of Dr. E. Worrell, which is missing from the file (DNA WR RG 94, Adjutant General Letters Received, P 226). The court-martial record in the case of Edward Worrell, citizen of Delaware, sentenced to imprisonment for one year for violating laws of war and aiding a prisoner to escape from Fort Delaware, shows that this application was denied on January 25, 1865, but a later endorsement, probably the one of February 12, appears to have been cut from the record (DNA WR RG 153, Judge Advocate General, NN 2475).

Endorsement Concerning Garrett Davis[1]

February 13, 1865

I personally know Senator Davis to be of the highest moral character, and I still wish these prisoners discharged, because he asks it, notwithstanding others, or another may have attempted wrong in the matter.   A. LINCOLN

Feb. 13. 1865

[1] AES-P, ISLA. Lincoln's endorsement appears on a letter from Garrett Davis, February 10, 1865:

"I herewith inclose to you the bundle of papers you handed me this morning just as they were, except I have attatched my name to the list of prisoners whose release I asked for, and which I inadvertently omitted to do when I handed the list to you.

"I acknowledge my increased respect for you because of the frank manner in which you brought the matter to my attention this morning. I am free to say, as I did say to you, that the letter of Mr. Simmons was inadvertently put into the bundle, and if I had observed it at the time I should have withheld it. I am however gratified that it turned out otherwise, and I ask that you will have this note placed in the same file.

"I have recd. several letters makeing to me a similar overture to that of Mr. Simmons; but to him, & the other writers, I replied, I never had, and never would receive a cent for any such services   As I said this morning, I now report to you, that in the course of 40 years, as lawyer, member of the Legislature, representative & senator in Congress I have in a great many cases rendered services to soldiers, their widows, children, pensioners & prisoners; and I have made it the rule of my life, never to charge or receive a dollar for any such services, and I have faithfuly lived up to that rule. If ever there was a man invulnerable to all imputations of peculation, extortion, or the raising of money without equivalent, or for services which the most scrupulous would say money ought not to be received, I claim to be that man.

"You will remember, Mr President, that until within the last month I had not asked for the release of a single confederate prisoner. I had heard that many persons were interveneing to obtain the release of such prisoners, & extorting from their friends large sums of money. It was to prevent, to some extent, such extortions that I sought interviews with & asked you to make orders that certain prisoners applying, should have the benefit of the amnesty proclamation. I never applied for any one that I did not believe would faithfully keep his pledges. I determined then, & I inflexibly [?] adhere to the purpose, on my return home, unspareingly to denounce those extortioners; and I would prefer to enter upon this task, with all my correspondence, received & sent, in relation to these topics, to be on file in the war office."

To Military Officers Commanding in West Tennessee[1]

To the Military Officers   Washington,
Commanding in West-Tennessee.   Feb. 13. 1865

While I can not order as within requested, allow me to say that it is my wish for you to relieve the people from all burthens, harrassments, and oppressions, so far as is possible, consistently with your Military necessities; that the object of the war being to restore and maintain the blessings of peace and good government, I desire you to help, and not hinder, every advance in that direc-

[294]

tion. Of your Military necessities you must judge and execute; but please do so in the spirit and with the purpose above indicated.

A. LINCOLN.

1 AES, DLC-RTL. Lincoln's endorsement appears on the back of the following printed document:

"MR. PRESIDENT: In accordance with your direction, we now state in writing the relief which the people of the District of West Tennessee ask at your hands, viz:

"1st.   To be relieved from all interference of the military authorities with the administration of justice by the civil courts.

"And to this end, 1st, that the judges of the courts and all officers thereof be left entirely free, in the discharge of their several functions of office, from the control or interference of the military authorities; and that they be declared exempt from all military duty, whether of the regular or militia service; and, 2d, that all jurors, witnesses, and parties and their counsel, attending said courts, lawfully summoned thereto, or prosecuting or defending their rights therein, shall be exempt from such military duty while so in attendance.

"2d.   That said military authorities be prohibited from imposing upon the people assessments, taxes, duties, or charges, of any kind whatever, and collecting the same, unless authorized so to do specifically by the President or Secretary of War.

"3d.   That all officers and soldiers who have served in the armies of the United States and have been honorably discharged from said service, on account of physical disability, and also all such officers and soldiers as shall have served out the term of their enlistment, the same being for three years, shall be held exempt from all military duty, whether militia or otherwise.

"4th.   That all persons who have come within the lines of the United States army and taken the oath of amnesty, in good faith, under, and trusting to the assurances of, General Grant's general order No. 10, shall be exempt from such military duty, and so long as they continue to be quiet citizens and obedient to the laws shall be permitted to remain.

"5th.   That the people be relieved from the imposition of any other draft than such as is in accordance with law; they do not ask to be exempt from draft, but insist that it be levied upon them in accordance with the laws of the United States and administered by the same rules and regulations as elsewhere in the United States.

"6th.   That the President give assurances that so soon as Tennessee shall have ratified the amendments to her Constitution made by the Convention of Nashville, and now being submitted to the people, he will, by proclamation, so far as he lawfully may, declare the State of Tennessee no longer in insurrection against the authority of the United States.

"7th.   That all persons who have furnished acceptable Substitutes be exempt from all military Service. [This seventh request is inserted, not in Lincoln's autograph, on the right-hand margin of the document.]

"Mr. President, the granting of the relief above asked for, it is believed, will so powerfully impress public sentiment as to enable us, by a splendid vote and overwhelming majority, to carry the above-mentioned amendments of the State Constitution—to regenerate the State, and to restore her to her place in the Union. Respectfully, your obedient servants,   "WM. WALLACE,
"JOHN CALDWELL,
"P. E. BLAND."

Accompanying the document is a letter from Bland and Wallace, Executive Mansion, Washington, Feb. 11, 1865:

"Having learned this morning that Brig. Genl. [Benjamin H.] Grierson will probably call on you during the day; and knowing him to be more thoroughly

[295]

acquainted with the condition and wants of our people than perhaps any other man in the public service, as also the character and probable worth or worth-lessness of the Memphis Millitia as at present organized and the oppressive exactions imposed in its name upon the people—and also how odious to the people is the proposed draft made as they believe without the sanction of law—We beseech you, if any doubts remain in your mind, to question him concerning the matters of relief asked for by us in the printed paper which we had the honor to submit to you several days since. . . ."

If Lincoln's endorsement was sent as a letter or order, the original has not been found. It may have been handed to Grierson during the interview.

Order Concerning Waller R. Bulloch[1]

Allow Lieut. Waller R. Bulloch to be paroled and go to his parents in Baltimore, and remain there until well enough to be exchanged.

Feb. 13, 1865   A. LINCOLN.

[1] John M. Bulloch, "President Lincoln's Visiting Card," *The Century Magazine*, LV (February, 1898), 568. According to the source, Lincoln's order was written on a card and given to John M. Bulloch, whose brother Waller R. Bulloch, was a prisoner on Johnson's Island.

To the Senate and House of Representatives[1]

February 13, 1865

To the Senate and House of Representatives.

I transmit to Congress a copy of a despatch of the 12th. ultimo addressed to the Secretary of State by the Minister Resident of the United States at Stockholm, relating to an International Exhibition to be held at Bergen, in Norway, during the coming summer. The expediency of any legislation upon the subject is submitted for your consideration.   ABRAHAM LINCOLN

Washington,
February 13th. 1865.

[1] DS, DNA RG 46, Senate 38A F2. Lincoln's enclosures are printed in Thirty-eighth Congress, Second Session, *Senate Executive Document No. 20*. A joint resolution charging the president to make known and invite participation in the expositions to be held at Bergen, Norway, and Oporto, Portugal, but with no governmental expense to be incurred, was approved on March 3, 1865.

To the Senate and House of Representatives[1]

February 13, 1865

To the Senate and House of Representatives,

I transmit to Congress a copy of a note of the 2nd. instant addressed to the Secretary of State by the Commander J. C. de

Figaniere e Morai, Envoy Extraordinary and Minister Plenipotentiary of His Most Faithful Majesty the King of Portugal, calling
attention to a proposed International Exhibition at the City of
Oporto, to be opened in August next, and inviting contributions
thereto of the products of American manufactures and industry.
The expediency of any legislation upon the subject is submitted
for your consideration.   ABRAHAM LINCOLN
   Washington,
   February 13th. 1865.

   [1] DS, DNA RG 46, Senate 38A F2. Lincoln's enclosures are printed in Thirty-
eighth Congress, Second Session, *Senate Executive Document No. 21.*

To Philip H. Sheridan[1]

Major General Sheridan   Executive Mansion,
Winchester Va.   Washington, 13 February, 1865.
   Suspend execution of sentence in case of James Lynch alias
Hennessy, until further orders and send record to me. Please ac-
knowledge receipt of this.   A. LINCOLN.

Maj. Eckert
   Please send above Telegram   JNO. G. NICOLAY

   [1] D, DNA WR RG 107, Presidential Telegrams, I, 340. John Hay wrote the
telegram, and Nicolay signed Lincoln's name and added the note to Eckert. A
clerk inserted "Winchester Va." General Sheridan's reply was received on the
same day at 2 P.M.: "Telegram in the case of Jas Linch recd   order issued suspending execution of sentence until further orders" (DLC-RTL).
   A second telegram from Sheridan was received at 4:30 P.M.: "James Lynch
was tried by a General Court Martial convened by Genl Crook and the proceedings in his case must now be on file in the War Dept" (*ibid.*).
   The court-martial record in the case of Private James Lynch, Second New
York Cavalry, sentenced to be shot for desertion, shows no action by Lincoln
(DNA WR RG 153, Judge Advocate General, OO 158).

To John Pope[1]

Major Genl. Pope.   Executive Mansion
St. Louis, Mo.   Washington, Feb. 14. 1865
   Yours of yesterday about Provost-Marshal system, received. As
part of the same subject let me say I am now pressed in regard to
a pending assessment in St. Louis County. Please examine & satisfy yourself whether this assessment should proceed or be abandoned, and if you decide that it is to proceed, please examine as
to the propriety of its application to a gentleman by the name of
Charles McLaran.   A. LINCOLN

[1] ALS, DNA WR RG 107, Presidential Telegrams, I, 342. See Lincoln to Pope, February 12, *supra*. On February 24, General Grenville M. Dodge, in command of the Division of the Missouri, reported to Pope's adjutant, Captain Joseph M. Bell: "I have the honor to report in relation to the assessment in Saint Louis that when I assumed command here I found a large number of refugees being supported here by the Government. Houses over the city for their occupation had been seized and rents accumulating that the Government would have to pay. . . . General Halleck . . . instructed that where the local authorities would not protect and support . . . refugees the disloyal should be assessed to do it. . . . The Sanitary Commission proposed to take charge . . . provided I would fix up the old Lawson Hospital. . . . This was done at a cost of about $10,000. . . . This assessment of $10,000 was made to reimburse the quartermaster's department . . . and if stopped will bring the whole matter back on Government. . . . The assessment on Colonel McLaran I considered too much, and have ordered it reduced $1,500. He was colonel of the Minute Men when the war commenced. . . ." (OR, I, XLVIII, I, 966).

Pope telegraphed his reply to Lincoln on February 25: "Have examined into the assessment as directed in your telegram of 14th instant. It was ordered by General Dodge before I took command. Full report of the facts sent by mail." (*Ibid.*, p. 978).

See further Lincoln to Pope, March 7, *infra*.

To Philip H. Sheridan[1]

Major General Sheridan: Executive Mansion, Washington, Feb'y 14, 1865.

Suspend execution of death sentence of James Brown, fixed for the 17th inst., at Harpers Ferry, until further orders and forward record for examination.   A. LINCOLN

Maj. Eckert
Please send above telegram   JNO. G. NICOLAY

[1] D, DNA WR RG 107, Presidential Telegrams, I, 343. Nicolay wrote this telegram and signed Lincoln's name. No reply or further reference has been found.

To James Speed[1]

Please make a commutation of this case as suggested within.
Feb. 14. 1865   A. LINCOLN
Atty. Genl.

[1] AES, DNA RG 204, U.S. Pardon Attorney, A 573. Lincoln's endorsement appears on a letter from Nathan Clifford, Washington, February 13, 1865, asking commutation of sentence of death to life imprisonment for Jose Bente Dias, alias Joseph Bent, convicted of murder on the high seas.

To Alfred Sully[1]

To the Commanding Officer,   Executive Mansion, Davenport, Iowa,   Washington, February 14, 1865.

Suspend execution of death sentence of John C. Brown alias Wm

A. Craven, and of John Ble alias Cohoe until further orders and send records for examination   A. LINCOLN

Major Eckert
    Please send the above dispatch   JNO. G. NICOLAY   Priv: Sec:

[1] D, DNA WR RG 107, Presidential Telegrams, I, 341. The body of this telegram is in the handwriting of Edward Neill. Lincoln's signature and Nicolay's signature are in Nicolay's autograph. On February 12, 1865, John C. Brown, under sentence for desertion, wrote Lincoln from Camp McClellan, Davenport, Iowa, stating his case and asking for a reprieve. An endorsement by N. B. Baker, adjutant general for Iowa, appears on the letter, recommending a reprieve until Brown's friends "have an opportunity to show the whole case." (DLC-RTL). On February 13, Baker telegraphed Lincoln: "I ask that Jno C Brown whose real name is Wm A Craven formerly acting Adjutant for three months of second Mo Cavalry & now under sentence of death at this point for desertion be reprieved until papers showing his prior services & a full statement of the case be furnished to you   he wishes to refer to Lt Col Jas H Crane second Missouri Cavalry & to Col Moore of twenty first Mo infy" (*ibid.*).
See further, Lincoln to Sully, February 17 and 20, *infra*.

Authorization for Charles H. Ray[1]

February 15, 1865
    With the approval in writing of the Department commanders whose lines are to be crossed, and not without, Charles H Ray, of Illinois, is authorized to take beyond said lines such articles, not contraband, nor capable of aiding or sustaining the army or forces of the enemy, as he may choose; and to bring products in return, subject to Treasury regulations and not otherwise; and to move both ways, while acting only in strict accordance with this permission, without seizure or molestation.   A LINCOLN
    Feby 15th 1865.

[1] Copy, DLC-RTL. See Lincoln to Grant, February 11, *supra*. On April 1, 1865, Dr. Charles H. Ray wrote Lincoln from Memphis, Tennessee: "On my arrival here with the Special Order, given to me by request of Gov. [Richard J.] Oglesby, authorizing me to carry on certain trade, I found that the purpose for which it was given had already been served by the many traders on the river, and that whisky & all its compounds were at a discount. Unwilling to give up the enterprise, more on account of those who are associated with me than for any hope of personal profit, I was uncertain what to do; but visiting Gen [Napoleon T. J.] Dana, at Vicksburg, I found that he was willing to allow me [to] take up the Yazoo certain articles like bale-rope & bagging, queensware, calico, womens' shoes, stationery & the like, all strictly within the limit of non-contraband articles, and, on your authorization, to bring out products in return. This I am about to avail myself of; the boat with part of her cargo aboard is now lying at the levee here; but as this is outside of the original purpose for which the permit was granted . . . I have thought proper to advise you . . . so as to give you the opportunity, if you choose, of stopping operations at once. . . ." (*Ibid.*).

Order Concerning Prisoners[1]

Executive Mansion, Washington City, D.C.
February 15. 1865.

The Penitentiary at Albany, N.Y.; the State Prison at Clinton, N.Y.; the Penitentiary at Columbus, Ohio; the Penitentiary at Jefferson City, Missouri; and such other prisons as the Secretary of War may designate for the confinement of prisoners under sentence of Courts Martial shall be deemed and taken to be military prisons.   ABRAHAM LINCOLN

[1] DS, IHi.

To John Pope[1]

Major General Pope.   Executive Mansion,
St. Louis, Mo.   Washington, Feb. 15, 1865.
    Please ascertain whether Gen. Fisk's administration is as good as it might be, and answer me.   A. LINCOLN

[1] ALS, DNA WR RG 107, Presidential Telegrams, I, 345. Pope replied from Milwaukee on February 20: "Your dispatch asking about General Fisk met me here, where I had come to meet General Curtis. I return to Saint Louis to-morrow, and will endeavor to answer your inquiry. I have not been long enough in command to find out fully about men and their proceedings, but shall find out soon." (OR, I, XLVIII, I, 921).
No report from Pope on General Clinton B. Fisk has been found.

To Hanson A. Risley[1]

February 15, 1865
    Will Mr. Risley please see and hear Mrs. Baldwin, the bearer, who is of the McCook family, so many of whom have gallantly fallen in this war?   A. LINCOLN.
    Feb. 15, 1865

[1] Dayton, Ohio, *Daily News*, July 25, 1951. According to the newspaper article, Lincoln's autograph note appears on a small card. Concerning Mary McCook Baldwin, see Lincoln's telegram of August 24, 1864, *supra*.

To Philip H. Sheridan[1]

Major Genl. Sheridan   Executive Mansion,
    &c   &c   Washington, 15 February, 1865.
    Suspend execution in case of Luther T. Palmer 5th N.Y. Artillery for fourteen (14) days and send record to me for examination.
    John Hay   A.A.G.   A LINCOLN

[1] D, DNA WR RG 107, Presidential Telegrams, I, 344. This telegram is entirely in Hay's handwriting. On February 13, A. P. Case, Vernon, New York, had written Representative Francis Kernan: "The bearer is the wife of Luther T. Palmer a Private in 5th N.Y. Artillery, who now lies at Harper's Ferry under sentence of death, for desertion. He is to be shot on the 17th Feb. She wishes an immediate interview with the President, that she make a personal appeal for a pardon. . . ." (DLC-RTL).

General Sheridan replied to Lincoln's telegram on the same day: "Dispatch in the case of Luther T Palmer received and order issued suspending the sentence" (*ibid.*).

See further, Lincoln to Stevenson, February 28, *infra*.

To Philip H. Sheridan[1]

Executive Mansion,
Major General Sheridan   Washington, Feb'y 15, 1865.

Suspend execution of death sentence of William Randall, at Harper's Ferry, of 5th N.Y. Heavy Artillery, until further orders, and forward record of trial for examination.   A. LINCOLN.

Maj: Eckert
Please send the above telegram   JNO. G. NICOLAY

[1] D, DNA WR RG 107, Presidential Telegrams, I, 346. This telegram is entirely in Nicolay's handwriting. General William H. Emory replied on the same day: "Telegram received suspending Sentence in the case of Wm. Randall and order issued" (DLC-RTL).

See further, Lincoln to Stevenson, February 17, *infra*.

Endorsement[1]

If the services are needed let this appointment be made.
Feb. 16. 1865   A. LINCOLN

[1] AES-P, ISLA. Lincoln's endorsement has been clipped from attendant papers.

To Ulysses S. Grant[1]

Executive Mansion,
Lieutenant General Grant   Washington, Feb'y 16, 1865.

Suspend execution of death sentence of George W. Brown, Company A fifteenth New-York Engineers, now at City-Point, until further orders, and forward record for examination

A. LINCOLN.
Maj. Eckert
Please send the above telegram   JNO. G. NICOLAY

[1] D, DNA WR RG 107, Presidential Telegrams, I, 347. No reply or further reference has been found.

To Ulysses S. Grant[1]

Executive Mansion,
Lieutenant General Grant: Washington, Feb'y 16, 1865.
Suspend execution of death sentence of Charles Love, Seventh
New-Hampshire Vols. at City-Point until further orders, and for-
ward record for examination   A. LINCOLN

Major Eckert
Please send the above telegram   JNO. G. NICOLAY

[1] D, DNA WR RG 107, Presidential Telegrams, I, 348. See Lincoln to Ord,
January 28, *supra*. No reply from Grant has been found.

To Edward D. Neill[1]

Mr. Neill may have this.   A. LINCOLN.
February 16, 1865.

[1] Copy, ISLA. This endorsement was written on the back of a petition dated
March 4, 1862, and signed by prominent citizens of New York, recommending
consideration of James L. Pettigru of South Carolina as successor to Associate
Justice John A. Campbell of the Supreme Court.

Order Concerning R. H. Baptist[1]

Executive Mansion,
Washington, February 16, 1865.
Let Captain R. H. Baptiste, a Prisoner of War at Johnson's Island,
be paroled for special Exchanges and suffered to go South. This
order is given at the special request of Mr. George D. Prentice.
                                   A. LINCOLN

[1] DS, owned by W. Easton Louttit, Jr., Providence, Rhode Island. A letter of
Captain R. H. Baptist, October 22, 1864, to George D. Prentice, offering to give
evidence in the forthcoming trial of Colonel Clarence J. Prentice, CSA, was
enclosed by George D. Prentice to Secretary Seward on October 25, 1864: "Capt
Babtist, who formerly served under my son . . . and is now a prisoner . . . at
Johnson's Island, writes to me some facts which would be of vast importance to
my erring child in his approaching trial . . . and which Capt. B. says he would
state on oath . . . if he could be paroled to the Southern Confederacy or exchanged. . . . I think that the exchange of Capt Babtist would subserve the
cause of truth, humanity and justice. . . ." (DLC-RTL).
Clarence J. Prentice was tried for murder of a man named White at Abingdon, Virginia, and was acquitted.

Pass for Mrs. John F. Slaughter[1]

Allow Mrs. Slaughter, children & servant, with ordinary baggage,
to pass our lines and go South.   A. LINCOLN
Feb. 16, 1865.

[1] ADS, ViU. Mrs. John F. Slaughter of Lynchburg, Virginia, had taken her son to Philadelphia for medical treatment. See Rosalie S. Morton, *A Woman Surgeon* (New York, 1937), p. 6.

To Charles A. Dana[1]

Let Capt. Burgoyne be paroled in the way that Senator Collamer may ask.   A. LINCOLN.

   Feb. 17. 1865

[1] American Art Association Catalog, February 20-21, 1928, No. 265. According to the catalog description, Lincoln's endorsement appears on a letter of A. O. Aldis to Senator Jacob Collamer, February 9, 1865, asking parole of Captain W. H. S. Burgoyne. Dana endorsed on February 17, "Referred with directions to send Captain Burgoyne forward in the first body of officers who are exchanged."

To Joseph Holt[1]

                             Executive Mansion

Judge Advocate General   Washington, Feb. 17. 1865

In regard to the Baltimore and Washington Merchants—clothes dealers—convicted mostly on the testimony of one Worsley (I believe) I have not been quite satisfied. I can not say that the presumption in favor of their innocence has not been shaken; and yet it is very unsatisfactory to me that so many men of fair character should be convicted principally on the testimony of one single man & he of not quite fair character. It occurs to me that they have suffered enough, even if guilty, and enough for example I propose giving them a jubilee, in which course the Sec. of War inclines to concur; but he tells me you are opposed. I write this to ask your cheerful concurrence. Yours truly

                             A. LINCOLN

[1] ALS, owned by Joseph H. Rose, Pasadena, California. See Lincoln to Holt, January 19, *supra*. On February 11, Lincoln seems to have written a further memorandum on the case of Thomas W. Johnson and others, but the text is not available (offered for sale, Chicago Book & Art Auctions Catalog 45, November 27, 1934, No. 134—memorandum attached to petition of Baltimore merchants and letter of J. W. Garrett, concerning release of Johnson and R. M. Sutton).

Holt replied to Lincoln's letter of February 17 on the same day: "I certainly have no disposition to oppose the impulses of your kind heart, in the matter referred to in your note just received. In a conversation with the Secty of War this morning, I said, in allusion to your anticipated action, that I thought the sentence resting in large part on a finding of guilt of attempt to bribe an officer of the government, might, in the exercise of your clemency, be well distinguished from the other cases in which no such criminality was averred. . . ." (DLC-RTL).

On February 18, Stanton wrote and Assistant Adjutant General Edward D. Townsend signed, the following order pardoning Thomas W. Johnson, Robert M. Sutton, and eight other merchants of Baltimore who had been sentenced to from one to five years' imprisonment and fines of $1,000 to $15,000: "The President directs that in consideration of the punishment already undergone by the persons specified in the foregoing list (except Moses Weisenfeldt) they be released from further imprisonment during their good behaviour under these respective sentences, and that the fines stand as security for their good behavior and that they engage in no illicit trade nor furnish any aid or comfort to the enemies of the United States and hold no intercourse with them during the war." (DNA WR RG 94, Adjutant General, Letters Received, P 269).

Order Concerning Joseph D. Hart[1]

If Joseph D Hart shall pass through Baltimore as a prisoner, allow him to be paroled and remain there with his sister two days.
Feb. 17. 1865   A. LINCOLN

[1] ADS, ORB. Miss Margaret Hart of Baltimore persuaded Lincoln to give the order to her brother, a Confederate prisoner in Old Capitol Prison, who was being transferred to Governor's Island in New York harbor (Chicago *Tribune*, February 7, 1909).

Proclamation Convening the Senate in Extra Session[1]

February 17, 1865
By the President of the United States of America:

A Proclamation.

Whereas objects of interest to the United States require that the Senate should be convened at twelve o'clock on the Fourth of March next, to receive and act upon such communications as may be made to it on the part of the Executive:

Now, therefore, I, Abraham Lincoln, President of the United States, have considered it to be my duty to issue this my Proclamation, declaring that an extraordinary occasion requires the Senate of the United States to convene for the transaction of business at the Capitol, in the city of Washington, on the Fourth day of March next, at twelve o'clock at noon on that day, of which all who shall at that time be entitled to act as members of that body, are hereby required to take notice.

Given under my hand and the seal of the United States at Washington, the seventeenth day of February, in the [L.S.]   year of our Lord one thousand eight hundred and sixty-five, and of the Independence of the United States of America, the eighty-ninth.   ABRAHAM LINCOLN
By the President:
WILLIAM H. SEWARD Secretary of State.

[1] DS, DNA FS RG 11, Proclamations.

To John D. Stevenson[1]

Officer in command   Executive Mansion,
at Harper's Ferry   Washington, February 17, 1865.

Chaplain Fitzgibbon yesterday sent me a dispatch invoking clemency for Jackson Stewart and Randall who are to be shot to-day   The dispatch is so vague that there is no means here of ascertaining, whether or not the execution of sentence of one or more of them may not already have been ordered. If not suspend execution of sentence in their cases until further orders and forward records of trials for examination.   A. LINCOLN

Maj. Eckert
     Please send above telegram   JNO. G. NICOLAY

[1] D, DNA WR RG 107, Presidential Telegrams, I, 350. This telegram is entirely in Nicolay's handwriting. The communication from Chaplain James Fitzgibbon has not been found. Brigadier General John D. Stevenson replied to Lincoln's telegram on the same day: "I have the honor to report in accordance with telegram of this date the order suspending the execution of Jackson Stewart & Randall has been duly obeyed." (DLC-RTL).

Concerning William Randall, see Lincoln to Sheridan, February 15, *supra*. No further reference has been found and the other men have not been identified.

To Alfred Sully[1]

Officer in command at   Executive Mansion,
Davenport Iowa.   Washington, February 17, 1865.

Suspend execution of death sentence of Wm A. Craven for four weeks, and forward record for examination.   A. LINCOLN

Maj. Eckert
     Please send above telegram   JNO. G. NICOLAY

[1] D, DNA WR RG 107, Presidential Telegrams, I, 349. Nicolay wrote this telegram and signed Lincoln's name. See Lincoln's telegram to Sully, February 14, *supra*. No reply has been found. AGO *General Court Martial Orders No. 140,* March 14, 1865, directed: "Private William A. Craven, *alias* John C. Brown, substitute, sentenced by a General Court Martial 'To be shot . . .' as promulgated in General Orders, No. 4, Headquarters, Department of the Northwest, Milwaukee, Wisconsin, January 31, 1865, is pardoned on condition of his faithfully serving out his term."

To Napoleon J. T. Dana[1]

Major General Dana;   Washington, Feb 18. 1865

Allow the bearers of this paper to prove to you if they can, that the foregoing statement of facts made on their representation, by the Secretary of the Treasury is substantially true; and on their doing so to your satisfaction, in a reasonable degree, allow them to bring out the products in the manner, and on the terms indicated by the Secretary of the Treasury in the foregoing letter.

The change of lines, if true as stated, justifies the dealing with the case, and similar cases, as special ones. Yours &c

A. LINCOLN

[1] Copy, DLC-RTL. The copy of Lincoln's letter in Edward D. Neill's handwriting accompanies Neill's copy of William P. Fessenden's letter to D. A. Nunn and W. P. Bond of Nashville, Tennessee, February 17, 1865:

"I have received your communications, making application for permission to ship to a loyal State certain cotton alleged to have been raised by you, upon your own plantations, situated within the State of Tennessee.

"If I understand the statements made in your letters the facts are these; that you are the owners of plantations lying in the State of Tennessee, to the north of the City of Memphis; that while such plantations were within the military lines of the United States forces, you planted your crop, but before its maturity the lines of military occupation were contracted, and you were thus thrown beyond them; that the crop was raised in part by your slave labor, notwithstanding which such slave labor was compensated by you in money, in addition to the support and clothing which previous to the rebellion it was customary to allow such laborers, and that the rest of the crop was cultivated by labor, compensated by you.

"You therefore claim under the Act of July 2, 1864, the right under the Regulations, to ship that cotton to a loyal State, upon the payment of the prescribed fees and taxes; but represent that objections are made to such shipment, on the part of the military. The Regulations under the law direct the officers of this Department to grant permits for the shipment to loyal States of the products of insurrectionary States, when such products at the date of the law, or subsequently were within the lines of military occupation provided that such officers are satisfied that such products were raised by the applicants own labor, or the labor of freedmen or others paid by them; and so far as the officers of this Department are concerned, such permits on application by you, would doubtless be granted, on their being satisfied that the provisions of law were fully complied with.

"If however, objections to moving the cotton are presented by the military, it is not in the province of this Department, to control their decision."

Endorsement Concerning Edwin Sprague[1]

February 18, 1865

Upon this boy's faithfully serving out his enlistment in the Naval service he is pardoned for any desertion from the army heretofore committed.   A. LINCOLN

Feb. 18. 1865

[1] AES, owned by Alexander W. Armour, Princeton, New Jersey. Lincoln's endorsement appears on a letter from Senator Nathan A. Farwell, February 17, 1865, asking pardon for Edwin Sprague, Thirtieth Maine Volunteers, who had deserted and enlisted in the Navy. Lincoln's pardon of Sprague was promulgated in AGO *Special Orders No. 94*, February 25, 1865.

Pass[1]

Allow Mrs.   daughter of Judge Young to pass our lines and come to Washington.   A. LINCOLN
   Feb. 18, 1865

[1] Anderson Galleries Catalog 2166, May 4, 1927, No. 123. According to the catalog description, this pass is written on a small card. Judge Young was probably the late Richard M. Young of Washington, D.C., associate justice of the Illinois Supreme Court (1843-1847) and U.S. senator from Illinois (1837-1843). His daughter Matilda was the wife of Major Robert A. Matthews, CSA.

To Edwin M. Stanton[1]

February 19, 1865

I know nothing of Col. Briscoe; nor have I taken any supervision in the organization of Hancock's new Corps.[2] Hence I submit these papers to the Sec. of War, simply remarking that they seem to be good and ample.   A. LINCOLN
   Feb. 19. 1865.

[1] AES, owned by Verne Miners, Chicago, Illinois. Lincoln's endorsement has been removed from attendant papers. Colonel James C. Briscoe of the One Hundred Ninety-ninth Pennsylvania Volunteers was brevetted brigadier general from March 13, 1865.
[2] The First Army Corps was reorganized under the command of Major General Winfield S. Hancock, November 28, 1864.

To Edwin M. Stanton[1]

Will the Sec. of War please do one or the other, for Gen. Orme as requested?   A. LINCOLN
   Feb. 19. 1865.

[1] AES, DLC-Stanton Papers. Lincoln's endorsement appears on a letter of General William W. Orme to Ward H. Lamon, January 24, 1865, asking that William McCullough, unfit for duty, be relieved. Private William A. McCullough, Fifth Illinois Cavalry, was the brother of Fanny McCullough to whom Lincoln wrote on December 23, 1862, *supra*. No record of action in his relief has been found. AGO *Special Orders No. 396*, July 25, 1865, directed his discharge at Memphis, Tennessee, "upon receipt of this order."

To James G. Bennett[1]

James G. Bennett, Esq.   Executive Mansion
Dear Sir: Washington, Feb. 20, 1865

I propose, at some convenient, and not distant day, to nominate you to the United States' Senate, as Minister to France. Your Obt. Servt.   A. LINCOLN.

1 ADfS, DLC-RTL. See Lincoln to Wakeman, January 26, *supra*. On February 28, William O. Bartlett wrote Lincoln:

"Mr. J.G.B. informed me this morning that he would give me his answer Monday next. . . .

"I propose to leave for Washington with it, the same evening, and to call on you Tuesday morning. . . ." (DLC-RTL).

On March 6, James Gordon Bennett replied:

"I have received your kind note in which you propose to appoint me Minister Plenipotentiary to . . . France. I trust that I estimate, at its full value, the high consideration which the President . . . entertains and expresses for me by proposing so distinguished an honor. Accept my sincere thanks for that honor. I am sorry however to say that at my age I am afraid of assuming the labors and responsibilities of such an important position. Besides, in the present relations of France and the United States, I am of the decided opinion that I can be of more service to the country in the present position I occupy.

"Which, therefore, entertaining the highest consideration for the offer you have made, permit me most respectfully to decline the service for the reasons assigned. . . ." (*Ibid.*).

See further, Lincoln to Bartlett, March 9, *infra*.

To Thomas C. Fletcher[1]

His Excellency   Executive Mansion
Gov. Fletcher,   Washington Feb 20 1865

It seems that there is now no organized military force of the enemy in Missouri and yet that destruction of property and life is rampant every where. Is not the cure for this within easy reach of the people themselves? It cannot but be that every man, not naturally a robber or cut-throat would gladly put an end to this state of things. A large majority in every locality must feel alike upon this subject; and if so they only need to reach an understanding one with another. Each leaving all others alone solves the problem. And surely each would do this but for his apprehension that others will not leave him alone. Can not this mischievous distrust be removed? Let neighborhood meetings be every where called and held, of all entertaining a sincere purpose for mutual security in the future, whatever they may heretofore have thought, said or done about the war or about anything else. Let all such meet and waiving all else pledge each to cease harassing others and to make common cause against whomever persists in making, aiding or encouraging further disturbance. The practical means they will best know how to adopt and apply. At such meetings old friendships will cross the memory; and honor and Christian Charity will come in to help.

Please consider whether it may not be well to suggest this to the now afflicted people of Missouri. Yours truly [A. LINCOLN.]

1 Copy, DLC-RTL. For Governor Fletcher's reply, see Lincoln to Fletcher, February 27, *infra*.

[308]

To Joseph Holt[1]

Pardon on condition of faithfully serving out his term.

Feb. 20. 1865   A. LINCOLN

[1] AES, DNA WR RG 153, Judge Advocate General, NN 1266. Lincoln's endorsement appears on the court-martial record of Thomas Woods and Beverley Johnson, Company E, Eighteenth Missouri Volunteers, convicted of assault and battery with intent to kill.

To Ella Steele[1]

                                Executive Mansion

Miss Ella Steele   Washington, Feb. 20. 1865

  With pleasure I send the autograph. Yours truly

                                A. LINCOLN.

[1] ALS-F, ISLA. An accompanying facsimile of an autograph letter from Stanton is addressed to "Miss Ella Steele, New York," dated March 4, 1865. She has not been further identified.

To Alfred Sully[1]

Officer in Command at   Executive Mansion

Davenport, Iowa.   Washington, Feb. 20. 1865

  Suspend execution of Henry Cole *alias* Henry Cohe, until further order, and send record.   A. LINCOLN

[1] ALS, DNA WR RG 107, Presidential Telegrams, I, 351. See Lincoln to Sully, February 14 and 17, *supra.* No reply or further reference has been found.

To James Speed[1]

The Attorney General will please cause a pardon in this case to be prepared.   A. LINCOLN

  Feb. 21, 1865

[1] ES, DNA RG 204, U.S. Pardon Attorney, A 585. Lincoln's endorsement appears on the record of the conviction by the U.S. District Court of Southern New York of William Rogerson and Asa Marvin for counterfeiting.

To Stephen G. Burbridge[1]

Officer in command at   Executive Mansion,

Lexington, Ky.   Washington, Feb. 22. 1865.

  Send forthwith record of the trial of C. K. Johnson.

                                A. LINCOLN

[1] ALS, DNA WR RG 107, Presidential Telegrams, I, 352. No reply has been found from Burbridge or any other officer. Burbridge was relieved of his command on February 22 (OR, I, XLIX, I, 756). Burbridge had telegraphed General John C. Breckinridge, Department of West Virginia, on February 14, that C. K. Johnson, claiming to be a Lieutenant Colonel in the Confederate Army, had been tried on charges of being a spy (OR, II, VIII, 223). AGO *General Court Martial Orders No. 314*, June 19, 1865, confirmed the death sentence in Johnson's case and ordered his execution.

Endorsement[1]

Let this appointment be made, if the service is needed.

Feb. 22, 1865   A. LINCOLN

[1] AES, owned by Dale Carnegie, New York City. Lincoln's endorsement appears on a fragment of a letter from William Lilley, asking promotion of an assistant quartermaster (unnamed) to a captaincy. Senator James Dixon's endorsement asking the appointment appears above Lincoln's.

To William P. Fessenden[1]

Executive Mansion,

My Dear Sir: Washington, 22 February, 1865.

Allow me to introduce the Honorable William Pickering, Governor of Washington Territory, who desires to see you upon official business. Your Obt. Servt.,   A. LINCOLN.

The Secretary of the Treasury.

[1] Walter Colyer, "Times When Lincoln Remembered Albion," *Journal of the Illinois State Historical Society*, IX (January, 1917), 495. On January 14, 1865, Governor Pickering had telegraphed Lincoln: "Official duty calls me to Washington. Please send leave immediately" (DLC-RTL).

To Ethan A. Hitchcock[1]

February 22, 1865

This case is respectfully submitted to Gen Hitchcock, with the remark that I would be pleased for Dr. English to be obliged if it can be done without detriment   A. LINCOLN

Feb. 22. 1865

[1] AES, DLC-Hitchcock Papers. Lincoln's endorsement appears on a letter from Charles D. Pennebaker, agent for the State of Kentucky, February 18, 1865, forwarding a copy of a letter from Major W. D. Ray, Fourth Kentucky Cavalry, CSA, a prisoner of war on Johnson's Island, addressed to Dr. John B. English, January 22, 1865. Ray proposed that if his parole could be arranged he would return to Richmond and find out what had happened to the son of Dr. English, Major Duval English, Eleventh Kentucky Cavalry, USA. Pennebacker wrote as follows:

"The reason why this parole is asked, is briefly this. In Sept. 64, an order was issued by the Secty of War for the special exchange of Maj. Duval English 11th. Ky. Cav. On the 11th. day of December, Col. Jno. E. Mulford wrote to Dr. J. B. English New Liberty, Ky. saying, 'I have this day effected the release of Maj. Duval English 4th. Ky. Cav. who will be at once forwarded to Anapolis: Md. when he will get leave of absence & return home.'

"Col. [T. H.] Butler 5th Ind Cav. reports about the middle of December, when on his way to east Tenn, after his escape from Prison, that he received a Message from Maj. English, while crossing the mountains. Nothing has been heard from Maj. English since. It is sincerely apprehended by his friends, that he was recaptured or that some unexplained mistake has occured in his special exchange. Maj. Ray is a man of honor, & will, if liberated under these circumstances execute the conditions of his parole faithfully."

To Ethan A. Hitchcock[1]

I shall be glad for Gen. Paul to be obliged in this matter, if it can be without detriment.   A. LINCOLN

Feb. 22. 1865

[1] AES, IHi. Lincoln's endorsement appears on a letter of General Gabriel R. Paul, Newport, Kentucky, to Green C. Smith, January 5, 1865, asking assistance in obtaining the exchange of his son, Captain Augustus C. Paul, captured at the Battle of Spotsylvania. General Paul's letter concludes: "I can write but a little being completely blind from the effects of the wound I received in battle [at Gettysburg]—but I trust I have said enough to interest you in the case." Augustus C. Paul remained a prisoner until the end of the war.

To ——— King[1]

Let Mr. King bring the papers of Lewis B. Dougherty

Feb. 22. 1865   A. LINCOLN

[1] ALS, owned by C. M. Rogers, Chicago, Illinois. Perhaps this note was meant for Austin A. King. Lewis B. Dougherty has not been identified.

To Edwin M. Stanton[1]

I know not what to do with this persistent appeal. Can any thing be done?   A. LINCOLN

Feb. 22. 1865

[1] AES, DLC-RTL. Lincoln's endorsement appears on the following letter, dated February 22, 1865:

"The Provost Marshal General proposes to enforce the Draft tomorrow in Philadelphia.

"If this were an order for the whole U.S. we could ask no exception that other places were not allowed.

"In New York and many other cities the draft is not yet to be enforced.

"*The moment the Draft commences our City Bounty of $400 for one year &c. ceases.*

"Philadelphia has always done her duty and furnished her full complement

[311]

of men. The Citizens are bending every exertion to raise our quota and we have no doubt that hereafter 100 men per day or more can be raised. We now ask a weeks delay in the enforcement of the draft *and promise 100 men per day in that week*—asking a like further delay if the promise be kept. We are sir   Very Respectfully yours.   "WM D KELLEY   M RUSSELL THAYER
"LEONARD MYERS.   SAM. J. RANDALL
"CHAS. ONEILL   E. D. SAUNDERS,
"On behalf of the citizens of Philadelphia."

Pasted on the bottom of the letter is the following clipping:

THE DRAFT.
The following correspondence explains itself:
OFFICE OF THE MAYOR OF THE CITY OF
PHILADELPHIA, February 18, 1865.
Professor E. D. Saunders, D.D.:
MY DEAR SIR: The efficient services that you have heretofore rendered to the community in aiding to fill its quota of recruits, induce the hope that you will again afford the benefit of your time and valued efforts, that this city may still be spared from military draft. I am, very respectfully,
ALEXANDER HENRY,
Mayor of Philadelphia.

We concur in the foregoing remarks.   JOHN ASHHURST, Chairman,
J. G. ROSENGARTEN, Secretary,
City Bounty Fund Commission.

PHILADELPHIA, February 20, 1865.
*To His Honor Alexander Henry, Mayor of Philadelphia,
and City Bounty Commission:*
GENTLEMEN: In view of the certainty and nearness of the military draft about to take place unless extraordinary efforts shall be made to obtain recruits, I accede to your request. Yours, truly,   E. D. SAUNDERS.

Beside the clipping John W. Forney endorsed: "This is a case I would beg of you to favor if I were not too ill to do so in person. I ask it now in writing. J. W. FORNEY"
Stanton endorsed below Lincoln's endorsement:
"Mr President
"1st   I think the draft will not be enforced in any State City County or district if this application is yielded to. It presents no ground that may not be urged with equal or greater force in every district   The fate of the war therefore may depend upon enforcing the law
"2.   You will observe that the application is not made by any City or district authority but only by members of Congress a fraction of a State delegation who have no authority to make a pledge and no promise to keep but who may get a little weak popularity by standing between their constituents and the execution of the law. The connection of [E. D.] Saunders with the matter gives it no strength but excites suspicion of a job in which his fingers are used by men who are unwilling to face the music, or stand bound for his pledges and those of five Congressmen who have no right to pledge any body.
"It is worth your while to notice the printed letter of the Mayor to Saunders pasted on the letter. It asks him to aid *in getting recruits*—not to paddle off to Washington to postpone the draft. I repeat no local authority nor any respectable citizen save the very respectable delegation in Congress and Mr Forney ask to have the draft suspended or pledge a man to be furnished   Saunders is the whole concern.

[312]

"I am respectfully constrained to advise most earnestly against your interference with the draft in Philadelphia unless you are prepared to give it up altogether. I write on my back in bed but hope you may be able to read what is written."

Endorsement
Concerning William B. Williamson[1]

Let him be discharged.   A. Lincoln
Feb. 23. 1865

[1] AES, owned by Charles E. Barber, Alhambra, California. Lincoln's endorsement appears on a letter from Alexander Williamson, February 23, 1865, asking discharge of his son William B. Williamson, a private acting as messenger in the Military Telegraph Bureau.

To Ulysses S. Grant[1]

Executive Mansion, Washington,
Lieutenant General Grant   Feb'y 23, 1865.
Suspend execution of death sentence of George A. Maynard, Co. A 46th New-York Veteran Volunteers until further orders and forward record for examination.   A. Lincoln

Maj. Eckert
Please send the above telegram.   Jno. G. Nicolay   Priv. Sec.

[1] D, DNA WR RG 107, Presidential Telegrams, I, 353. No reply has been found. See Lincoln to Holt, April 12, *infra*.

To Joseph Holt[1]

Pardon, for unexecuted part of sentence & disability removed.
Feb. 23. 1865   A. Lincoln

[1] AES, DNA WR RG 153, Judge Advocate General, LL 1666. Lincoln's endorsement appears on the court-martial record of Major Alexander S. Hill, Eighteenth Corps d'Afrique, dishonorably dismissed for conduct unbecoming an officer and gentleman, etc.

Endorsement Concerning Elias Davis[1]

Let Elias Davis, mentioned herein, be excepted from the operation of the order of Feb. 1. 1865 within made.   A. Lincoln
Feb. 24. 1865.

[1] ES, Herbert Wells Fay Collection. The endorsement, in John Hay's handwriting and signed by Lincoln, has been cut from attendant papers. Elias Davis has not been identified.

Endorsement Concerning James S. Martin[1]

I would like for the Brevet to be given.   A. LINCOLN

Feb. 24, 1865

[1] American Art Association Anderson Galleries Catalog 3955, March 4, 1932, No. 136. According to the catalog description, Lincoln's endorsement appears on a letter from Isham N. Haynie asking the brevet rank of brigadier general for Colonel James S. Martin, One Hundred Eleventh Illinois Volunteers. Martin became brevet brigadier general as of February 28, 1865.

To Ulysses S. Grant[1]

Cipher[2]   Office U.S. Military Telegraph,
Lieut. Genl. Grant   War Department,
City-Point, Va.   Washington, D.C., Feb. 24 1865

I am in a little perplexity. I was induced to authorize a gentleman to bring R. A. Pryor here with a view of effecting an exchange of him. But since then I have seen a despatch of yours showing that you specially object to his exchange. Meantime he has reached here & reported to me. It is an ungracious thing for me to send him back to prison, and yet inadmissable for him to remain here long. Can not you help me out with it? I can conceive that there may be difference to you in days; and I can keep him a few days to accommodate on that point. I have not heard of my son's reaching you.   A LINCOLN

[1] ALS, DNA WR RG 107, Presidential Telegrams, I, 354. Grant replied on February 25: "Send Pryor on here and we will exchange him; He can do us no harm now. Capt Lincoln reported on the 22nd and was assigned to duty at my Head Quarters" (DLC-RTL).

On February 6, Horace Greeley had written Lincoln: "Roger A. Pryor, now a prisoner of war in Fort Lafayette, was captured under circumstances which seem to give him special claims to exchange. My friend Mr. W[ashington] Mc-Lean of Cincinnati is authorized to offer any reasonable exchange for Mr. Pryor, and I hope it may be effected." (*Ibid.*).

On February 7, Grant had notified William Hoffman, commissary general of prisoners:

"The prisoners you have at Fort Delaware may be forwarded direct to City Point. The proportion of officers is not material. . . .

"I think Pryor . . . now at Point Lookout, should not be exchanged so long as we hold a prisoner." (Copy, DLC-RTL).

On February 15, Joshua F. Speed had written Lincoln:

"Mr McClean of Cincinati is very anxious to get Roger Pryor . . . now at Fort Lafayette exchanged. He says that he would stake his fortune on Pryors complying with any promise he would make or for the fulfilment of the terms upon which he accepts a parole. . . ." (*Ibid.*).

On February 18, John W. Forney also had appealed to Lincoln: "I do not think that the release of Roger A. Prior, according to your generous card given to Washington McClain yesterday, would be followed by any but the very best consequences. He has Mr. Greeley's letter to you asking for his deliverance. A fair and honorable exchange is offered by his friends. I am full of sorrow that Mr. Stanton should object to the fulfillment of your promise in his behalf, and I now write this note in the hope that you will permit your own wishes to be carried out. . . ." (*Ibid.*).

Washington McLean, publisher of the Cincinnati *Inquirer*, obtained the pass on February 25 (*infra*).

2 Inserted by telegrapher.

Order Concerning Hiram Hibbard[1]

Executive Mansion
Washington Feb. 24 1865

To-day Hiram Hibbard calls voluntarily under apprehension of being punished as a deserter Now on condition that he faithfully serves out his term Co. A. in 50th N Y. Engineers, he is fully pardoned for any supposed desertion A. LINCOLN

1 ADS, ORB. AGO *Special Orders No. 114*, March 8, 1865, promulgated the pardon of Hiram Hibbard.

To John M. Palmer[1]

Office U.S. Military Telegraph,
War Department,
Washington, D.C., Feb. 24 1865

Major Genl. Palmer
Louisville, Ky.

Please telegraph me an exact copy of the order of John C. Breckinridge borne by Col. Robert J. Breckinridge. A. LINCOLN

1 ALS, DNA WR RG 107, Presidential Telegrams, I, 355. On February 24, General John M. Palmer telegraphed Stanton: "Robert J. Breckinridge, colonel in the rebel army, was captured near Versailles, Ky., on the 22d instant, with orders from John C. Breckinridge ordering all Confederate officers and men out of the State, under the penalty of being reported to the Federal authorities as guerrillas. Breckinridge came into the State secretly. When he surrendered was in uniform—probably put on for the occasion. What shall be done with him?" (OR, I, XLIX, I, 764).

On February 25, Palmer replied to Lincoln's telegram:

"In obedience to your orders I have the honor to forward you the following copy of the order found on Col. R. J. Breckinridge. . . .

'General Orders,   Hdqrs. West Virginia and East Tennessee
No. 2.   Wytheville, Va., January 6, 1865.

'All officers and men now in Kentucky upon military service under authority other than that of the Secretary of War, are required to report to Robert J. Breckinridge, whose orders they are commanded to obey. All who have authority from the Secretary of War prior to April 4, 1864, or from these headquarters, whose time has expired, will report to their respective commands or these headquarters. All who fail to obey this order promptly will be at once reported to the existing authorities in Kentucky as not recognized by the Confederate Government as prisoners of war, if captured.

'By command of Major-General Breckinridge.' " (*Ibid.*, p. 770).

To John Pope[1]

Major General Pope.   Executive Mansion,
St. Louis, Mo.   Washington, Feb. 24. 1865.

Please inquire and report to me whether there is any propriety of longer keeping in Gratiott Street prison, a man said to be there by the name of Riley Whiting.   A. LINCOLN

[1] ALS, DNA WR RG 107, Presidential Telegrams, I, 356. No reply has been found. On February 20, John Hogan wrote Lincoln asking that Riley Whiting either be brought to trial or released (DNA WR RG 107, Secretary of War, Letters Received, P 525).

To Edwin M. Stanton[1]

February 24, 1865

This letter is written by Gen. Palmer; & I personally know Dr. Stephenson & believe him to be a good man. I know nothing else about the case & refer it to the Secretary of War.   A. LINCOLN.
Feb. 24, 1865.

[1] American Art Association Anderson Galleries Catalog 4020, February 21, 1933, No. 158. According to the catalog description, Lincoln's endorsement appears on the back of a letter from John M. Palmer, recommending Dr. Stephenson for a sutlership at Camp Butler, Illinois. Dr. Benjamin F. Stephenson had served as surgeon of the Fourteenth Illinois Volunteers from April, 1862 to June, 1864.

To Ulysses S. Grant[1]

"Cypher"   Office U.S. Military Telegraph,
Lieut. Genl. Grant   War Department,
City-Point, Va.   Washington, D.C., Feb. 25 1865

Gen. Sheridan's despatch to you of to-day, in which he says he "will be off on Monday" and that he "will leave behind about two thousand men" causes the Secretary of War and myself considerable anxiety. Have you well considered whether you do not again leave open the Shenandoah-valley entrance to Maryland and Pennsylvania?—or, at least, to the B & O. Railroad?

A. LINCOLN.

[1] ALS, DNA WR RG 107, Presidential Telegrams, I, 357. Sheridan telegraphed Grant on February 25: "I could not get off to-day . . . but will be off on Monday. . . . The cavalry officers say the cavalry never was in such good condition. I will leave behind about 2,000 men, which will increase to 3,000 in a short time." (OR, I, XLVI, II, 701).

Grant replied to Lincoln's telegram on February 26:

"Two thousand cavalry and that to be increased to three thousand, besides all his Infantry is what Genl. Sheridan means.

"His movement is in the direction of the enemy & the tendency will be to protect the B. & O. road and to prevent an attempt to invade Maryland and Penna." (DLC-RTL).

Sheridan reported to Stanton on February 26: "There is on the Baltimore and Ohio . . . not including Harper's Ferry, between 12,000 and 14,000 men. . . . There will be in the Shenandoah Valley, after I leave . . . not less than 2,000 men . . . increased by men at Remount Camp; then there will be the division . . . at Winchester. . . . This seems to me to be ample for the defense of this frontier. . . ." (OR, I, XLVI, II, 711-12).

See further, Lincoln to Grant, February 27, *infra*.

Pass for Roger A. Pryor[1]

Allow the bearer, Roger A. Pryor, to pass to Gen. Grant, and report to him for exchange.   A. LINCOLN

Feb. 25. 1865

[1] ADS, owned by George W. Wild, Farmingdale, New York. See Lincoln to Grant, February 24, *supra*.

To the Senate[1]

To the Senate of the United States: February 25, 1865

In compliance with the Resolution of the Senate of the 23d. instant, I transmit herewith a report from the Secretary of War, with the accompanying General Orders No. 23, issued by Major General Banks, at New Orleans, February 3d, 1864.

Washington,   ABRAHAM LINCOLN

February 25, 1864 [1865].

[1] DS, DNA RG 46, Senate 38A F2. Nathaniel P. Banks' order of February 3, 1865, promulgating regulations concerning compensated plantation labor are printed with Lincoln's communication in Thirty-eighth Congress, Second Session, *Senate Executive Document No. 29*.

To James Speed[1]

Atty. Genl. please make out pardons in one or two cases which Col. Netherland will name.   A. LINCOLN

Feb. 25. 1865

[1] AES, CSmH. Lincoln's endorsement appears on a petition of D. B. Childress, of New Market, Tennessee, asking to take the oath of allegiance and be pardoned. Following Lincoln's endorsement is a note in unidentified handwriting: "Requisition in the case of Childress made out Feby 25. In the other named case, (Judge McKinney) requisition withheld till further orders—by command of the President."

John Netherland was a citizen of Rogersville, Tennessee.

To Henry W. Beecher[1]

Rev. H. W. Beecher   Executive Mansion
My dear Sir   Washington, Feb. 27. 1865

Yours of the 4th. and the 21st. reached me together only two days ago. I now thank you for both. Since you wrote the former the whole matter of the negotiations, if it can be so called, has been published, and you, doubtless, have seen it. When you were with me on the evening of the 1st. I had no thought of going in person to meet the Richmond gentlemen. Yours truly   A. Lincoln

[1] ADfS, DLC-RTL. Following his interview with Lincoln on February 1, Reverend Henry Ward Beecher wrote on February 4:

"The interview and information which you gave me, not only relieved me *then*, but has, ever since, given me great faith. Even your unexpected visit to Ft Munroe did not stagger me. *It has been much criticized.* The *pride of the* nation, is liable to be hurt. Anything that looks like the humiliation of our Government, would be bitterly felt.

"*But, I do not criticize it.* Knowing the ground on which you stand, and the *bases* of any negotiation, I am more than willing that, as you will sacrifice *no substantial* element you should wave any mere formality So that the inside of the hand is solid *bone*, I am willing to have the outside *flesh* soft as velvet.

"And I clearly perceive that, whether you gain any point with the *south* or not, the very extraordinary step, of the Head of a nation, leaving the Capital, and going *to* the rebels, is an act of condescension which *will stop the mouths* of *Northern enemies.*

"No man on earth, was ever before so *impregnably* placed, as you are. Look at the facts.

"1. The south is exhausted and defeated. The military *result is sure.*

"2. Every step which you have, one by one taken, toward emancipation & national liberty is now confirmed beyond all change.

"3. You have brought the most dangerous and extraordinary rebellion in history, not only to a successful end, but, have done it without sacrificing *republican government* even in its forms. It is wonderful, and a sign of Divine help, that democratic institutions & feelings, are stronger *today*—after four years of War, and military administration as enlarged as when all Europe was one camp,— than when you began.

"The north is renovated. Heresy is purged out. Treason is wounded to the death. Our Constitution has felt the hand of God laid upon it, as He said, 'Be thou clean' & the leprosy is departed You have now done all that your enemies, even, could ask to shew your desire for peace, & *more* than many of your friends would wish. Your position is eminent & impregnable. I am only anxious that you should not lose that place. *I do not believe that you will.* But it is more dangerous *to make peace than to make war.*

"Why then do I write to you?

"1. Because, it seemed to me, that a man in public office, seeing chiefly political & official people, might be cheered to hear from a private citizen. . . .

"2. Because, I wish to suggest, that, these *rumors of peace,* and this feverish suspense about commissioners & negotiations, is injurious, in so far as replenishing the army is concerned. . . .

"Would it not be well if the country could be told, deffinitely how the case stands? An address to the army, or to the nation, declaring that *peace can come only by arms,* if in your judgement the fact is so, would end these feverish uncertainties & give the spring campaign renewed vigor.

"My dear Mr Lincoln, I have written to you, as a friend to a friend. I am

grateful to God, for raising you up. I believe that you are in His hand. That he may guide you is my daily & almost hourly prayer.

"I hope that it will not seem intrusive in me to write to you. If I add nothing to your wisdom, I might I hope, sometimes cheer you under your great cares." (DLC-RTL).

On February 21, Beecher wrote:

"You have enough political reading, & I thought it might serve as a variety to present you another sort. I extract a passage from a letter just received from . . . *Persia* . . . from Wm. J. Perkins, formerly my tutor in College, now a Missionary.

" 'We are just now cheered amazingly by the intelligence of President Lincoln's reelection It reached us when our Mission were assembled in a business meeting; and for the first ti ne in thirty years, our sober body was so electrified as to greet the news with a long and loud demonstration of clapping the hands We hail this result as an earnest of the salvation of our beloved country, in the permanent restoration of the Union, and the effectual overthrow of slavery. . . .' " (*Ibid.*).

To ——— Dickson[1]

Will Mr. Dickson, Chief Engineer of Hibernia please pump the water out of a certain well, which Tad will show?

Feb. 27, 1865   A LINCOLN

[1] ALS-F, Wayne Whipple, *The Story-Life of Lincoln*, p. 616. According to Whipple, the *Hibernia* was a fire engine sent from Philadelphia to Washington with "some of its company . . . during the War and remained at the Capital for some time to be in readiness for any emergency" (p. 615).

To Thomas C. Fletcher[1]

Gov. Fletcher   Executive Mansion,
Jefferson City, Mo.   Washington, Feb. 27, 1865.

Have you received my letter of the 20th.? I think some such thing as therein suggested, is needed. If you put it before the people, I will direct the Military to co-operate. Please answer.

                                                  A. LINCOLN

[1] ALS, DNA WR RG 107, Presidential Telegrams, I, 359. Governor Fletcher replied on the same day: "Your letter of 20th instant has been received. I will diligently, faithfully, and honestly try the policy you suggest, letting none know my utter want of confidence in its success, and preparing for the only other policy as best I can. I will write you to-night. Please withhold any public directions to the military until you receive my letter." (OR, I, XLVIII, I, 997).

Fletcher's letter of the same date is as follows:

"I have the honor to acknowledge the receipt of your letter of the 20th Inst. . . .

"I have to say: That the destruction of life and property in every part of Missouri which has been going on for nearly four years and which is yet going on, is not the result of the immediate action of men who can be reached by any amicable propositions. The State being infested with thousands of outlaws who are naturally and practically 'robbers' and 'cut-throats,' no good man desires to reach any understanding with them. . . . I have every confidence in our ability, when properly organized, to assert by force the supremacy of the law . . . and thus give security to . . . every man who is willing to aid in enforcing the law, or to recognize its authority. . . . In almost every neighborhood . . . the loyal men have worked in parties for the last three summers, some standing guard while others ploughed, and all at night sleeping in the woods. No theatre of war has presented scenes of murder and outrage such as we have witnessed in Missouri. . . . Every man in Missouri knows his neighbor. Four years standing guard with or against him leaves no room to doubt the position of each. An agreement to leave 'all others alone' would be kept by the good, and only result in advantages to the men who can neither be bound by oaths nor agreements. It would but madden the true men of this State to talk to them of reliance on the 'honor' and 'christian charity' of these fiends in human shape. When we have sworn them, they have violated their oaths; when we have armed them by agreement to assist in our mutual defence, they have turned their arms against us; when we sought to enrol them for militia duty, they took their guns and either joined Price or went into the bushes to become banditti. . . .

"I am satisfied, Mr. President, that if you could see and fully understand what we have done and suffered in Missouri . . . you would agree . . . that we want no peace with rebels but the peace which comes of unconditional submission to the authority of the law. . . .

"My request by telegraph to-day to withhold any public instructions to the military on the subject of your letter, was prompted by the belief that our soldiers—a majority of whom are soldiers because they cannot live at home in safety—would be exasperated beyond control at the announcement that the men who have driven them from their homes were to be let alone. . . .

"I will go to St Louis tomorrow, and confer with Generals Pope and Dodge as to the best method of fully testing the policy suggested by you, and in the earnest hope that I may be mistaken as to the result. . . ." (DLC-RTL).

On March 7, Fletcher issued a proclamation:

"Whereas there no longer exists within the State of Missouri any organized force of the enemies of the Government of the United States, recognized as entitled to the usages of war among civilized nations; and

"Whereas the supremacy of the civil law is the desire of all good citizens and its protection to those who obey, and its infliction of known and just punishments on those who violate it, are the ends for which governments are established, and the restoration of its power is the sole purpose of the armed forces of the United States and the State of Missouri.

"Now, therefore, I, Thomas C. Fletcher, governor . . . desiring to give to every citizen an opportunity of uniting with the civil authorities for the restoration of peace and order on the basis of the administration of justice, as embodied in the civil law, before the commencement of active operations by the military force now being organized to effect the common object, do invite all men who have not made themselves infamous by crime to unite together for the support of the authority of the officers and laws and to make common cause against whomsoever shall persist in making, aiding, or encouraging any description of lawlessness. . . ." (OR, I, XLVIII, I, 1115).

To Ulysses S. Grant[1]

Office U.S. Military Telegraph,
War Department.,

Lieut. Gen. Grant
City-Point, Va.

Washington, D.C., Feb. 27 1865

Subsequent reflection, conference with Gen. Halleck, your despatch, and one from Gen. Sheridan, have relieved my anxiety; and so I beg that you will dismiss any concern you may have on my account, in the matter of my last despatch.   A LINCOLN

[1] ALS, DNA WR RG 107, Presidential Telegrams, I, 358. See Lincoln to Grant, February 24, *supra*.

To Joseph Holt[1]

Executive Mansion,
Judge Advocate General   Washington, Feb. 27, 1865.
Please procure the record, and report to me on the case of Edward Donahoe, Jr. about election frauds. Yours truly
A. LINCOLN

[1] Anderson Galleries Catalog, October 16, 1928, No. 98. According to the catalog description, this item is an autograph letter signed. Edward J. Donahue, Jr., was appointed by Governor Horatio Seymour to act as an inspector for the Democratic party in obtaining votes of New York soldiers in the field. Arrested on October 26, 1864, he was tried on charges of fraudulently signing names of soldiers on voting blanks and sentenced to imprisonment for life. Sentence was remitted three years later. No record of Lincoln's further action has been found. See Josiah H. Benton, *Voting in the Field* (Boston, 1915) and Stewart Mitchell, *Horatio Seymour of New York* (Cambridge, Massachusetts, 1938).

Recommendation for Charles C. Leigh[1]

I heartily commend Mr. Leigh's object, and bid him God speed in it.   A. LINCOLN
Feb. 27. 1865.

[1] ADS, NBLiHi. Lincoln's endorsement appears on a War Department pass issued to C. C. Leigh of the National Freedmen's Relief Association, to Norfolk, Charleston, Savannah, and return. Above Lincoln's recommendation appears: "Transportation free   E M STANTON Sec of War." Below appears: "Pass Mr. C. C. Leigh through all the Armies of the United States.   U. S. GRANT Lt. Gen. City Point, Va. March 2d 1865."

Recommendation for Frederick Tompkins[1]

I heartily commend Dr. Tomkin's object, and bid him God-speed in it.   A. LINCOLN
Feb. 27. 1865.

[1] AES-F, ISLA. Lincoln's recommendation appears on the back of a War Department pass issued to Frederick Tompkins, secretary of the National Freedmen's Aid Society of London, to Norfolk, Charleston, Savannah, and return. Both Stanton and Grant endorsed as on the pass to Leigh, *supra*. On February 23, Henry Ward Beecher wrote Lincoln:
"The bearer Mr Fred. Tompkins is a fast friend of the north, tho an Englishman. He has been restlessly active in England for us. He comes now to collect facts about the freedmen that he may aid us still more on his return.
"He is worthy of entire confidence" (DLC-RTL).

To the Senate[1]

To the Senate of the United States: February 27, 1865

I herewith lay before the Senate, for its constitutional action thereon, a treaty made and concluded with the Klamath and Modoc tribes of Indians of Oregon, at Fort Klamath, on the 5th [15th] day of October, 1864.

A letter of the Secretary of the Interior, of this date, a copy of the report of the Commissioner of Indian Affairs of the 24th instant, and a communication of the superintendent of Indian affairs in Oregon accompany the treaty.   ABRAHAM LINCOLN.

Executive Mansion,
Washington, February 27, 1865.

[1] *Executive Journal*, XIV, 214. The treaty was ratified with amendments on July 2, 1866.

To Edwin M. Stanton[1]

Hon. Sec. of War   Executive Mansion,
Dear Sir   Washington, Feb. 27, 1865.

More than a year ago, as I remember, one Hall at Indianapolis was convicted of something in connection with a horse-contract, but Mr. Holt held the conviction to be illegal, and yet you thought the service would suffer by at once announcing the conviction null, and so it has been held along. Senator Hendricks,[2] knowing of Mr. Holt's decision, has frequently been pressing me, until about three months ago I promised, *almost*, to discharge the case, about this time. Can we not now do it, without detriment to the service? Yours truly   A. LINCOLN

[1] ALS, IHi. On March 6, Stanton replied: "In Halls case I am not aware of any objection to his receiving any clemency you may think proper to extend to him." (DLC-RTL). AGO *General Court Martial Orders No. 119*, March 6, 1865, remitted the sentence and discharged Charles W. Hall, citizen, ordered "To pay . . . a fine of ten thousand dollars, and to be imprisoned . . . 'as promulgated in General Orders, No. 186, Headquarters, Department of the Ohio, November 24, 1863.'"
[2] Thomas A. Hendricks of Indiana.

To Charles A. Dana[1]

Does Mr. Dana know about this case?   A. LINCOLN
Feb. 28. 1865.

[1] AES, ORB. Lincoln's endorsement appears on a letter from Salmon P. Chase, February 26, 1865: "William H Stabler, of Maryland, a member of the Society of friends intercedes for the release of the son of Walter W. Bowie a planter of

Prince George's County. Young Bowie has been in the rebel service; and is now a prisoner in the old Capitol; but willing to take the oath. His father was one of my scholars when I taught school here. If possible I hope his son may be released." No reply or further reference has been found.

To William Dennison[1]

February 28, 1865

I know what our friend Corwine wants. He wants me to decide a matter in favor of his client, which I might possibly do if we were nearer the end of the war, but which, if driven to decide now, I should have to decide against him.   A. LINCOLN

Feb. 28. 1865.

[1] AES, ORB. Lincoln's endorsement appears on the back of a letter from William Dennison asking Lincoln to grant Richard M. Corwine an interview. Concerning E. A. Smith, see Lincoln to Eastman, November 24, 1863, and to Corwine, March 30, 1864, *supra.*

On March 6, Corwine wrote:

"After your declination to see me this last week, I would not make another effort in that direction, if I did not feel that you have misunderstood the import of my business. I wish not to ask you at present to decide Smith's case any further than you have, but I did then and do now wish to make a suggestion, with respect to it . . . which cannot fail to meet your approbation. . . .

"I shall make no further effort to see you unless you intimate . . . that my presence will be agreeable. . . ." (DLC-RTL).

On March 8, Corwine wrote again: "There is a ballance coming to E. A. Smith for horses furnished . . . at Cincinnati and Louisville amounting to . . . Forty thousand Dollars. The accounting officers refuse to pay him as long as the court martial fine, for $20,000 remains in force. Aware of your policy in this class of cases, I have no disposition now and have not had since I learned what your policy was, to press any further consideration of his case, but I respectfully submit that an order might be made by you, directing the payment of any *just* claim he has without respect to this fine. . . . I take the liberty to enclose the copy of such an order as I have referred to. Had you found it convenient to grant me an interview, this is all I had designed to propose." (*Ibid.*).

AGO *General Court Martial Orders No. 640*, December 9, 1865, directed remission of one-half the fine of $20,000, and Smith to be discharged upon payment of the $10,000 to a quartermaster of the U.S. Army.

To Thomas D. Eliot[1]

February 28, 1865

If a majority of the Massachusetts delegation in Congress will, in writing on this sheet, request the pardon of this man, it shall be granted.   A. LINCOLN

Feb. 28. 1865

Attorney General please make out a pardon in this case.

March. 2. 1865   A. LINCOLN

[323]

1 AES, DNA RG 204, U.S. Pardon Attorney, A 562. Lincoln's endorsements appear on a letter from Thomas D. Eliot, February 28, 1865, enclosing a petition for pardon for Zeno Kelley of New Bedford, Massachusetts, convicted on charges of fitting out a vessel to be engaged in the slave trade. Eliot and nine other members of congress signed the request which Lincoln required.

To Hannibal Hamlin[1]

Executive Mansion,
Washington, D.C., February 28, 1865.

Sir: In reply to the resolution of the Senate, dated February 14, 1865, I transmit herewith a communication from the Secretary of War, forwarding a copy of the report of the court of inquiry in respect to the explosion of the mine in front of Petersburg. I am, sir, very respectfully, your obedient servant,

Hon. H. Hamlin ABRAHAM LINCOLN.
President United States Senate.

1 *Senate Journal*, March 1, 1865, pp. 267-68. See the *Report of the Joint Committee on the Conduct of the War* (1865) for the reports of the court of inquiry and of the investigation by congress.

To Ethan A. Hitchcock[1]

Will Gen. Hitchcock please see & hear the bearer, Hon. A. A. C. Rogers, of Arkansas? A. LINCOLN
Feb. 28. 1865.

1 AES, IHi. Lincoln's endorsement appears on a letter from J. N. H. Patrick, Anthony A. C. Rogers, and J. C. Mills, Washington, February 28, 1865, asking exchange of "Maj McCauly of the 1 Indiana Cavalry . . . held as prisoner of war at Camden in Arkansas." No record of the exchange of Major Mark McCauley has been found.

To James Speed[1]

Attorney General, please see Mr. King & make out the pardon he asks. A. LINCOLN
Feb. 28. 1865.

1 AES-P, ISLA. Lincoln's endorsement appears on a letter of Prince L. Hudgins to Austin A. King, St. Louis, January 27, 1865, asking assistance in procuring a pardon. Hudgins had been indicted for conspiracy but not tried. King endorsed recommending the pardon.

To James Speed[1]

February 28, 1865

Of course it is not proper for me to indulge my personal feelings exclusively in this matter, but I am very partial to Mr. Root.

[1] Anderson Galleries Catalog 1214, March 29, 1916, No. 703. According to the catalog description, this is part of the text of an autograph letter concerning "J. M. Root" for district attorney in Ohio. Thomas M. Root is listed as U.S. attorney for the Northern District of Ohio in the *U.S. Official Register,* 1865.

To John D. Stevenson[1]

Commanding Officer   Executive Mansion,
Harpers Ferry Va   Washington, 28 February, 1865.

Let the sentence in case of Luther T. Palmer be suspended till further order.   A. LINCOLN

John Hay   A.A.G.

[1] D, DNA WR RG 107, Presidential Telegrams, I, 360. This telegram was written and signed by John Hay. See Lincoln to Sheridan, February 15, *supra.* On April 10, Lincoln pardoned Private Luther T. Palmer, Company C, Fifth New York Heavy Artillery, sentenced to be shot for desertion, but the record is missing from the file (DNA WR RG 153, Judge Advocate General, OO 158).

To John P. Usher[1]

[c. March, 1865]

This application is made on the idea that the incumbent is to go out at the end of four years.   A.L.

[1] AES, DNA NR RG 48, Department of Interior, Superintendent of Indian Affairs, Miscellaneous, Box 87. Lincoln's endorsement appears on an envelope labeled "Hon. G. A. Colton, Paola, Kansas. Application for the office of Superintendent of Southern Indian Affairs." The *U.S. Official Register,* 1865, lists Elijah Sells of Iowa as superintendent of the Southern Agency.

To Thomas W. Conway[1]

Mr. Thomas W. Conway,   Executive Mansion,
General Superintendent   Washington, D.C.,
Freedmen, Department of the Gulf: March 1st, 1865.

Sir: Your statement to Major-General Hurlbut of the condition of the freedmen of your department, and of your success in the work of their moral and physical elevation, has reached me and given me much pleasure.

That we shall be entirely successful in our efforts I firmly believe.

The blessing of God and the efforts of good and faithful men will bring us an earlier and happier consummation than the most sanguine friends of the freedmen could reasonably expect. Yours,

                     A. LINCOLN.

[1] New York *Evening Post,* December 13, 1865. As printed in the *Post,* the communication is introduced merely as an unpublished letter, with no explanation or comment. Conway's statement to Stephen A. Hurlbut has not been found.

Endorsement[1]

[March 1, 1865]

Please send   A. LINCOLN

[1] AES, IHi. Lincoln's endorsement appears on a telegram of Robert T. Lincoln to Woodward Emery, Cambridge, Massachusetts: "Letter just received. I will be here until next Tuesday & will be glad to see you."

To Joseph Holt[1]

Judge Advocate General please examine & report.

Mar. 1, 1865   A. LINCOLN

[1] AES, DNA WR RG 153, Judge Advocate General, NN 1884. Lincoln's endorsement appears on an envelope in the record of Christian Emerick of Baltimore, sentenced to imprisonment for the duration of the war on charges of recruiting for the rebel service. Holt recommended that an army surgeon should examine and report if confinement would result in death, and if so, that Emerick should be pardoned upon taking the oath and giving bond. AGO *General Court Martial Orders, No. 277*, June 10, 1865, directed discharge of Christian Emerick from Albany Penitentiary upon his taking the oath of allegiance.

Reply to Notification Committee[1]

[March 1, 1865]

Having served four years in the depths of a great, and yet unended national peril, I can view this call to a second term, in nowise more flatteringly to myself, than as an expression of the public judgment, that I may better finish a difficult work, in which I have labored from the first, than could any one less severely schooled to the task.

In this view, and with assured reliance on that Almighty Ruler who has so graceously sustained us thus far; and with increased gratitude to the generous people for their continued confidence, I accept the renewed trust, with it's yet onerous and perplexing duties and responsibilities.

Please communicate this to the two Houses of Congress.

[1] AD, IaHA. This speech has been the subject of much confusion. Nicolay and Hay, instead of printing the above text, printed a copy of Lincoln's reply on a similar occasion in 1861 (*vide supra*, February 26, 1861), incorrectly dating it February 9, 1865 (*Complete Works*, XI, 10). The same error appears in Nicolay and Hay, *Abraham Lincoln: A History* (X, 142), with an appended footnote explaining that the text which appeared in the *Congressional Globe* and the newspapers on March 2, 1865, was incorrect, "having apparently been written out from memory." The text appearing in the *Congressional Globe*, New York *Times*, and other papers on March 2, was inaccurate to a minor extent, but did follow Lincoln's spoken words better than Nicolay and Hay realized in their

belief that their 1861 speech was the 1865 speech. The errors in the newspapers of March 2, 1865, arose from the fact that an inaccurate and hastily prepared copy was transmitted to congress in lieu of Lincoln's autograph manuscript, which was retained by Representative James F. Wilson of Iowa, who together with Senator Lyman Trumbull and Representative John L. Dawson of Pennsylvania, comprised the notification committee. For a discussion of the inaccurate copy received by congress, see *The Collector*, XLVIII (January, 1934), 25-27. Further error arose when Hertz printed the newspaper text under date of "March 4, 1865," (I, 143-44).

The autograph manuscript bears on the bottom of the page James F. Wilson's endorsement. "The above is the original manuscript of Abraham Lincoln's acceptance of his second presidential term, in his own hand writing delivered to the joint committee of Congress appointed to inform him officially of his election.

"The committee consisted of
"Senator Lyman Trumbull of Ill.
"Representative J. F. Wilson of Iowa, and Rep. John L. Dawson of Penna."

To Winfield Scott and Others[1]

Gentlemen: March 1, 1865

I have received your address on the part of the Bureau for the employment of disabled and discharged soldiers which has recently been established in connection with the Protective War Claim Association of the Sanitary Commission.

It gives me pleasure to assure you of my hearty concurrence with the purposes you announce, and I shall at all times be ready to recognize the paramount claims of the soldiers of the nation, in the disposition of public trusts. I shall be glad also to make these suggestions to the several Heads of Departments. I am very truly Your Obt. Servt A LINCOLN

Lt. Gen Winfield Scott Presdt
Howard Potter
W E Dodge Jr
Theodore Roosevelt

[1] Df, DLC-RTL. The draft is in John Hay's handwriting. On January 24, 1865, Theodore Roosevelt, Sr., wrote John G. Nicolay, enclosing a letter signed by General Winfield Scott and others, dated January 17:

"We address you on the part of the Bureau for the employment of disabled and discharged Soldiers which has recently been established in connection with this association

"The promise of employment which a large City is supposed to hold out, & other influences, have operated to congregate in this City many of that class, whose condition is such as to challenge immediate attention to their claims to employment & support, & it is our desire to find ways of satisfying those claims which shall not compromise the self-respect & independence of men who, having done and suffered so much for the country, should be considered by all her citizens as having a preferred claim to such employments as they are still fit for.

"This preference . . . cannot of course be secured to them by legislation, but we think much may be done towards educating public sentiment to that end if the Government would set the example of conferring upon these . . . veterans such offices within its gift, as they might be found qualified to fill, &, if your Excellency approve the plan, we would ask of you such instructions to the Heads of the Several Departments . . . as may serve that purpose. . . ." (DLC-RTL).

To Schuyler Colfax[1]

Executive Mansion.
Sir: Washington D.C. March 2d. 1865.
   I transmit herewith the report of the Secretary of War, which with my permission has been delayed until the present time to enable the Lieutenant General to furnish his report.
   Hon. Schuyler Colfax,   ABRAHAM LINCOLN
   Speaker   House of Representatives.

[1] LS, DNA RG 233, House Executive Document No. 83. The annual report of the Secretary of War which should have accompanied Lincoln's Annual Message of December 6, 1864, *supra*, had been delayed for the reason indicated.

To Samuel S. Cox[1]

Will see Hon. S. S. Cox at 9½ A.M. tomorrow, if he pleases to call.
   March 2. 1865   A. LINCOLN

[1] ALS, RPB.

To James B. Fry[1]

These two of my men—Crook & Alexander are drafted & I can not spare them. P.M.G. please fix.   A. LINCOLN
   March 2. 1865

[1] ALS-F, ICHi-MacChesney Scrapbook, XXXII, 7484. William H. Crook and Alexander Smith were members of Lincoln's bodyguard. The circumstances surrounding Lincoln's request were related by Crook:
   "I was drafted, and the other guards with me. Frankly, I didn't want to go. I had served in the army already; I had a young wife and a young son at home to hold me. I couldn't afford to pay a substitute. So I joined the ranks of the people with grievances whom for some time I had been watching and went to the President. I found him in his own room, in dressing-gown and slippers. I told him that I had been drafted, and asked him if he could do anything in my case and in that of Alexander Smith, who was my special friend on the force. He listened to my story as patiently as if he had not heard hundreds like it. I like to remember how kindly he looked at me. When I had finished, he said:
   " 'Well, I can't spare you. Come into my office.'
   "I followed him. . . . He seated himself at the desk and wrote on a small card a note to Provost-Marshal Frye and told me to take it to him and get the answer. Years after this the Hon. Robert T. Lincoln gave me the card when he was Secretary of War, and I have it still. It reads: [as above]" (*Through Five Administrations, Reminiscences of Colonel William H. Crook*, pp. 25-26).

[328]

To Ulysses S. Grant[1]

"Cypher"   Office U.S. Military Telegraph,
Lieut. Genl. Grant   War Department,
City Point, Va.   Washington, D.C., March 2 1865
    You have not sent contents of Richmond papers for Tuesday
or Wednesday.
    Did you not receive them? If not, does it indicate anything?
                                                    A. LINCOLN

    [1] ALS, DNA WR RG 107, Presidential Telegrams, I, 361. Grant replied at
12:30 P.M.: "Richmond papers received daily. No bulletins were sent Tuesday
or Wednesday because there was not an item of either good or bad news in them.
There is every indication that Genl Sherman is perfectly safe. I am looking every
day for direct news from him." (DLC-RTL).

To Hannibal Hamlin[1]

                                          Executive Mansion,
Sir: Washington D.C. March 2d. 1865
    I transmit herewith the report of the Secretary of War, which,
with my permission, has been delayed until the present time to
enable the Lieutenant General to furnish his report.
    Hon. Hannibal Hamlin   ABRAHAM LINCOLN
    President of the Senate.

    [1] LS, DNA RG 46, Senate 38A F4. See Lincoln to Colfax, *supra.*

To Joseph Holt[1]

I do not see sufficient reasons in this case to interfere with the action of the Department.   A. LINCOLN
    Mar. 2, 1865.

    [1] Copy, DNA RG 130, U.S. Army Court Martial Cases, White House Office,
Register. The copy of Lincoln's endorsement is recorded in the register as a notation on the case of Henry F. Liebenau, Twenty-fifth New York Cavalry, excluded
from mustering in a regiment on charges of having received considerations for
appointments granted to applicants for commissions.

To Edwin M. Stanton[1]

James M. Scovel, being a member of the New-Jersey Senate, now
in session, if drafted, let him be discharged from the draft.
    March 2. 1865.   A. LINCOLN

    [1] ADS, owned by Gordon A. Block, Philadelphia, Pennsylvania.

Cotton Permit for Charles E. Fuller[1]

Executive Mansion   March 3. 1865.

An authorized agent of the Treasury Department, having with the approval of the Secretary of the Treasury contracted for the Cotton above mentioned and the party having agreed to sell and deliver the same to such agent:

It is ordered that the cotton moving in compliance with and for fulfilment of said contract, and being transported to said agent, or under his direction, shall be free from seizure or detention by any officer of the Government, and commandants of military departments, districts ports and detachments, naval stations, gunboats flotillas and fleets will observe this order, and give the said Charles E. Fuller his agents and transports, free and unmolested passage for the purpose of getting the said Cotton, or any part thereof through the lines, other than blockaded lines, and safe conduct within our lines while the same is moving in strict compliance with the Regulations of the Secretary of the Treasury and for fulfilment of said contract with the agent of the Government.

ABRAHAM LINCOLN

[1] DS, IHi. Lincoln's permit accompanies an agreement of Hanson A. Risley, March 3, 1865, to purchase ten thousand bales of cotton from Charles E. Fuller.

To William Dennison[1]

Post-Master-General please see Mrs. Ellis, & file her papers which are within.   A. LINCOLN

March 3. 1865

[1] AES, IHi. Lincoln's endorsement appears to have been clipped from an envelope. The widow of Lieutenant Colonel Edward F. W. Ellis, Fifteenth Illinois Volunteers, killed at Shiloh, sought to be appointed postmaster at Rockford, Illinois. Annie M. Smith (see Lincoln to Montgomery Blair, July 24, 1863, *supra*) served as postmaster at Rockford until May 10, 1865, and Anson S. Miller succeeded her.

To Ulysses S. Grant[1]

Lieutenant General Grant   March 3. 1865

The President directs me to say to you that he wishes you to have no conference with General Lee unless it be for the capitulation of Gen. Lee's army, or on some minor, and purely, military matter. He instructs me to say that you are not to decide, discuss, or confer upon any political question. Such questions the Presi-

dent holds in his own hands; and will submit them to no military conferences or conventions. Meantime you are to press to the utmost, your military advantages.　　　EDWIN M STANTON
Secretary of War

[1] AD-F, ISLA. The body of this telegram is in Lincoln's autograph, the date, salutation, and signature having been written by Stanton. On March 2, Grant had telegraphed Stanton:
"The following communication has just been received from Genl Lee

"'Lt Gen U S Grant　　　　　　　　　　　　　　H'd Qrs C S Armies
"'Comd'g US Armies　　　　　　　　　　　　　　　Mch 2d 1865
"'General: Lieut Genl Longstreet has informed me that in a recent conversation between himself and Maj Genl Ord as to the possibility of arriving at a satisfactory adjustment of the present unhappy difficulties, by means of a military convention. Genl Ord stated that if I desired to have an interview with you on the subject you would not decline, provided I had authority to act. Sincerely desiring to leave nothing untried which may put an end to the calamities of war, I propose to meet you at such convenient time and place as you may designate with the hope that upon an interchange of views it may be found practicable to submit the subjects of controversy between belligerents to a convention of the kind mentioned.
"'In such event I am authorized to do whatever the result of the proposed interview may render necessary or advisable　Should you accede to this proposition, I would suggest if agreeable to you, we meet at the place selected by Genls Ord and Longstreet for their interview at 11 A M on Monday next　Very Respy　Your Obdt Servt　　　　　　　　　　　(signed) R E LEE'
"Genl Ord met Genl Longstreet a few days since at the request of the latter to arrange for the exchange of citizen prisoners. . . .
"He had my authority to do so and to arrange definitely for such as were confined in his Dept. arrangements for all others to be submitted for approval.
"A general conversation ensued on the subject of the war and it has induced the above letter. I have not returned any reply but promised to do so at noon tomorrow. I respectfully request instructions" (DLC-RTL).

Response to Serenade[1]

March 3, 1865

Sherman went in at Atlanta and came out right. He has gone in again at Savannah, and I propose three cheers for his coming out gloriously.

[1] New York *Tribune*, March 4, 1865. Lincoln's remarks were made in response to a serenade by "a large delegation of New-Yorkers and Poughkeepsians, accompanied by Eastman's Business College band of Poughkeepsie." No more complete text of Lincoln's response has been found.

To the Senate and House of Representatives[1]

March 3, 1865

To The Senate and House of Representatives:

I herewith transmit to Congress a Report dated 1st. instant, with the accompanying papers, received from the Secretary of

State, in compliance with the requirements of the 18th. Section of the Act entitled "An Act to regulate the Diplomatic and Consular Systems of the United States," Approved August 18th. 1856.

Washi[ngton, March 3, 1865]   [ABRAHAM LINCOLN]

---

[1] DS, DNA RG 46, Senate 38A F3. Part of the date and signature have been torn from the document. The accompanying report may be found in Thirty-eighth Congress, Second Session, *Senate Executive Document No. 32.*

Second Inaugural Address[1]

[Fellow Countrymen:]   March 4, 1865

At this second appearing to take the oath of the presidential office, there is less occasion for an extended address than there was at the first. Then a statement, somewhat in detail, of a course to be pursued, seemed fitting and proper. Now, at the expiration of four years, during which public declarations have been constantly called forth on every point and phase of the great contest which still absorbs the attention, and engrosses the enerergies [*sic*] of the nation, little that is new could be presented. The progress of our arms, upon which all else chiefly depends, is as well known to the public as to myself; and it is, I trust, reasonably satisfactory and encouraging to all. With high hope for the future, no prediction in regard to it is ventured.

On the occasion corresponding to this four years ago, all thoughts were anxiously directed to an impending civil-war. All dreaded it—all sought to avert it. While the inaugeral address was being delivered from this place, devoted altogether to *saving* the Union without war, insurgent agents were in the city seeking to *destroy* it without war—seeking to dissol[v]e the Union, and divide effects, by negotiation. Both parties deprecated war; but one of them would *make* war rather than let the nation survive; and the other would *accept* war rather than let it perish. And the war came.

One eighth of the whole population were colored slaves, not distributed generally over the Union, but localized in the Southern part[2] of it. These slaves constituted a peculiar and powerful interest. All knew that this interest was, somehow, the cause of the war. To strengthen, perpetuate, and extend this interest was the object for which the insurgents would rend the Union, even by war; while the government claimed no right to do more than to restrict the territorial enlargement of it. Neither party expected for the war, the magnitude, or the duration, which it has already

[332]

attained. Neither anticipated that the *cause* of the conflict might cease with, or even before, the conflict itself should cease. Each looked for an easier triumph, and a result less fundamental and astounding. Both read the same Bible, and pray to the same God; and each invokes His aid against the other. It may seem strange that any men should dare to ask a just God's assistance in wringing their bread from the sweat of other men's faces; but let us judge not that we be not judged. The prayers of both could not be answered; that of neither has been answered fully. The Almighty has His own purposes. "Woe unto the world because of offences! for it must needs be that offences come; but woe to that man by whom the offence cometh!" If we shall suppose that American Slavery is one of those offences which, in the providence of God, must needs come, but which, having continued through His appointed time, He now wills to remove, and that He gives to both North and South, this terrible war, as the woe due to those by whom the offence came, shall we discern therein any departure from those divine attributes which the believers in a Living God always ascribe to Him? Fondly do we hope—fervently do we pray—that this mighty scourge of war may speedily pass away. Yet, if God wills that it continue, until all the wealth piled by the bond-man's two hundred and fifty years of unrequited toil shall be sunk, and until every drop of blood drawn with the lash, shall be paid by another drawn with the sword, as was said three[3] thousand years ago, so still it must be said "the judgments of the Lord, are true and righteous altogether"

With malice toward none; with charity for all; with firmness in the right, as God gives us to see the right, let us strive on to finish the work we are in; to bind up the nation's wounds; to care for him who shall have borne the battle, and for his widow, and his orphan—to do all which may achieve and cherish a just, and a lasting peace, among ourselves, and with all nations.[4]

[Endorsement]

Original manuscript of second Inaugeral presented to Major John Hay.   A. LINCOLN
    April 10. 1865

---

[1] AD, DLC. The salutation is not in Lincoln's handwriting. An autograph copy of the final paragraph, written by Lincoln at the request of Mrs. John P. Usher, is now owned by Arthur Wendell, Rahway, New Jersey.
    [2] Lincoln deleted "half" and inserted "part."
    [3] Lincoln first wrote "four," erased it and substituted "three."
    [4] Lincoln deleted "the world" and inserted "all nations."

To Schuyler Colfax[1]

Mr. Speaker Colfax   Executive Mansion
My dear Sir.   Washington, March 5. 1865
    I should be pleased for you to accompany us to-morrow evening at ten o'clock, on a visit of half an hour to the Inaugeral-ball. I inclose a ticket. Yours truly   A. LINCOLN

[1] ALS, In. The ball was held on the evening of March 6 in the Patent Office. "At half-past ten the Presidential party was announced, and as they entered the bands struck up 'Hail to the Chief,' and the company formed in lines, leading to the Presidential platform. The President and Speaker Colfax led the party. Mrs. Lincoln was escorted by Senator Sumner, Secretary Seward and Mrs. Fred Seward, Secretary Usher and Mrs. Usher, Senator Wilson and Mrs. Wilson, and other notables followed. . . ." (New York *Herald*, March 8, 1865).

To Edwin M. Stanton[1]

Please file as a West-Point application.   A. LINCOLN
    Mar. 5, 1865.

[1] AES, DNA WR RG 94, U.S. Military Academy, 1865, No. 36. Lincoln's endorsement appears on a letter of B. H. Bressler to Simon Cameron, February 28, 1865, recommending Ferdinand Bressler for a cadetship. No record of an appointment has been found.

To Charles Sumner[1]

Hon. C. Sumner.   Executive Mansion
My dear Sir   Washington, March 5/65
    I should be pleased for you to accompany us to-morrow evening at ten o'clock, on a visit of half an hour to the Inaugeral-ball. I inclose a ticket. Our carriage will call for you at half past nine. Yours truly   A. LINCOLN

[1] ALS, MH. See Lincoln to Colfax, *supra*.

Order Concerning Amos C. and William Babcock[1]

                 Executive Mansion   March 6. 1865.
    Whereas, Amos C. Babcock and William Babcock of Fulton County, Illinois, claim to own or control Products of the insurrectionary States in Florida, Louisiana, Mississippi, Alabama and Arkansas, and have arrangements with parties in the insurrec-

tionary States by which they will be able to bring such Products within the national military lines and sell and deliver the same to agents authorised to purchase for the United States under the Act of Congress of July 2. 1865 and the Regulations of the Secretary of the Treasury

It is ordered, that all such Products which an authorised agent of the Government has agreed to purchase and the said Amos C and William Babcock have stipulated to deliver as shown by the certificate of said agent issued under Regulation VIII. (Form No. 1 of Regulations) attached hereto by such agent, and being transported or in store awaiting transportation for fulfillment of said stipulation and in pursuance of the Regulations of the Secretary of the Treasury, shall be free from detention seizure or forfeiture to the United States; and officers of the Army and Navy and civil officers of the Government will observe this order, and will give the said Amos C. and William Babcock their agents and means of transportation and said Products, free and unmolested passage through the lines other than blockaded lines, and safe conduct within the lines, while going for or returning with said Products, or while said Products are in store awaiting transportation for the purposes aforesaid.   ABRAHAM LINCOLN

[1] DS, The Rosenbach Company, Philadelphia and New York.

Order Concerning Lion and Frank Silverman[1]

Executive Mansion March 6. 1865

Whereas, Lion Silverman and Frank Silverman claim to own or control Products of the insurrectionary states on and near White River in Arkansas and the Yazoo River in Mississippi, which they propose to sell and deliver to Agents authorised to purchase the same for the United States under the Act of Congress of July 2, 1864 and the Regulations of the Secretary of the Treasury;

It is ordered, that all such Products which a Purchasing Agent of the Government has agreed to purchase and the said Lion and Frank Silverman have stipulated to deliver as shown by the certificate of the Purchasing Agent authorised by Regulation VIII. (Form No. 1. appended to Regulations) attached hereto by such agent, and being transported or in store awaiting transportation for fulfillment of said stipulations and in pursuance of the Regulations of the Secretary of the Treasury shall be free from seizure detention or forfeiture to the United States; and officers of the

Army and Navy and Civil officers of the Government, will observe this order, and will give the said Lion and Frank Silverman their agents and means of transportation and said Products free and unmolested passage through the lines, other than blockaded lines, and safe conduct within the lines, while going for or returning with said Products, or while said Products are in store awaiting transportation for the purposes aforesaid.

ABRAHAM LINCOLN

[1] DS, IHi. At the bottom of the second page appears an endorsement: "By the President of the United States and to be respected accordingly by all under my Command   S. P. LEE
"Black Hawk, Cairo Ills.   A. R. Admiral
"April 8th. 1865.   Com'g Miss. Squadron"

Order Concerning Samuel P. Walker[1]

Executive Mansion March 6. 1865

Whereas, Samuel P. Walker of Memphis, Tenn. claims to own Products of the insurrectionary states near Grenada and Canton Miss; and Montgomery and Selma Alabama, and has arrangements with parties in the same vicinities for other Product[s] of the insurrectionary states all which he proposes to sell and deliver to Agents authorised to purchase for the United States the Products of the insurrectionary states under the Act of Congress of July 2, 1864 and the Regulations of the Secretary of the Treasury;

It is ordered, that all such Products which a Purchasing Agent of the Government has agreed to purchase and the said Walker has stipulated to deliver, as shown by the certificate of the Purchasing Agent authorised by Regulation VIII. (Form No. 1. appended to Regulations) attached hereto by such Agent, and being transported or in store awaiting transportation for fulfillment of said stipulations and in pursuance of the Regulations of the secretary of the Treasury, shall be free from seizure detention or forfeiture to the United States; and officers of the Army and Navy and civil officers of the Government will observe this Order, and will give the said Walker his agents and means of transportation and said Products, free and unmolested passage through the lines, other than blockaded lines, and safe conduct within the lines, while going for or returning with said Products, or while said Products are in store awaiting transportation for the purposes aforesaid.   ABRAHAM LINCOLN

[1] DS, DNA RG 56, Cotton and Captured Property Records, No. 3869.

To Hanson A. Risley[1]

Will Mr. Risley please see & hear the bearer, Hon. John T. Stuart.
March 6. 1865   A. LINCOLN

[1] ALS-F, ISLA. Lincoln's first law partner, John Todd Stuart, who had just completed a term in congress, was probably interested in consulting Risley about a cotton contract, but no references to his business have been found.

To William H. Seward[1]

Hon. Sec. of State   Executive Mansion,
My dear Sir.   Washington, March 6. 1865.
I have some wish that Thomas D. Jones, of Cincinnati, and John J. Piatt, now in this city, should have some of those moderate sized consulates which facilitate artists a little [in] their profession. Please watch for chances. Yours truly   A. LINCOLN

[1] ALS, NAuE. Thomas D. Jones was a sculptor, and John J. Piatt a poet who had been secretary to George D. Prentice of the Louisville *Journal*, and later a clerk in the Treasury Department (1861-1867). No consular appointment is of record for either man until Piatt became consul at Cork, Ireland, 1882-1892.

To Charles Sumner[1]

Dear Mr. Sumner:—   March 6, 1865
Unless you send me word to the contrary, I shall this evening call with my carriage at your house, to take you with me to the Inauguration Ball. Sincerely Yours,   ABRAHAM LINCOLN.

[1] Hertz, II, 963. See Lincoln to Colfax and to Sumner, March 5, *supra*.

To David Tod[1]

"Cypher"   Office U.S. Military Telegraph,
Hon. David Tod   War Department,
Cleveland, O.   Washington, D.C., March 6. 1865
I have yours about Grannis, and am compelled to say there is a complication in the way.   A. LINCOLN

[1] ALS, DNA WR RG 107, Presidential Telegrams, I, 362. Tod's telegram has not been found, but has been listed for sale as bearing Lincoln's endorsement "File. A.L. March 11, 1865" (Anderson Auction Company Catalog 941, February 27, 1912, No. 609). See Lincoln to Speed, February 28, *supra*, and endorsement concerning John C. Grannis, March 9, *infra*.

Endorsement
Concerning Charles C. Coffenberry[1]

[c. March 7, 1865]
At end of term.

[1] AE, DNA NR RG 48, Department of Interior, Appointments, Indian Agencies, Box 67. Lincoln's endorsement appears on a letter from Senator James H. Lane, Representative Sidney Clarke, and Governor Samuel J. Crawford, March 7, 1865, recommending Charles C. Coffenberry of Lincoln, Kansas, for agent of the Otoe Indians. No record of Coffenberry's appointment has been found.

Endorsement Concerning M. R. Dutton[1]

[c. March 7, 1865]
This application assumes that the incumbent is wholly incompetent. 				A.L.

[1] AES, DNA NR RG 48, Department of Interior, Appointments, Indian Agencies, Box 62. Lincoln's endorsement appears on a letter of James H. Lane, Sidney Clarke, and Samuel J. Crawford, March 7, 1865, recommending M. R. Dutton of Oskaloosa, Kansas, for agent of the Kickapoo Indians. No record of Dutton's appointment has been found.

Endorsement Concerning Alexander Low[1]

[c. March 7, 1865]
This on idea that incumbent is to go out at end of four years.

[1] AE, DNA NR RG 48, Department of Interior, Appointments, Indian Agencies, Box 61. Lincoln's endorsement appears on a letter from James H. Lane, Samuel J. Crawford, and Sidney Clarke, March 7, 1865, recommending Alexander Low of Doniphan, Kansas, for agent of the Nimeha (Nemaha) Indians. No record of Low's appointment has been found.

Endorsement Concerning F. W. Potter[1]

[c. March 7, 1865]
This application made on the idea that the present incumbent is to go out at the end of four years from his appointment. 		AL.

[1] AES, DNA NR RG 48, Department of Interior, Appointments, Indian Agencies, Box 62. Lincoln's endorsement appears on a letter from James H. Lane, Sidney Clarke, and Samuel J. Crawford, March 7, 1865, recommending F. W. Potter of Burlington, Kansas, for agent of the Kansas Indians. No record of Potter's appointment has been found.

Endorsement Concerning Phillip C. Schuyler[1]

[c. March 7, 1865]

Kansas folks for removal—but Mr. Dole opposed.   A.L.

Incumbent is brother-in-law to Gov. Morton & this morning Sec. of Interior brings a reappointment commission.

[1] AES, DNA NR RG 48, Department of Interior, Appointments, Indian Agencies, Box 70. Lincoln's endorsement appears on a letter from James H. Lane, Sidney Clarke, and Samuel J. Crawford, March 7, 1865, recommending Phillip C. Schuyler of Burlingame, Kansas, for agent of the Sac and Fox Indians. Henry W. Martin was reappointed to the agency.

To Ulysses S. Grant[1]

Executive Mansion, Washington,

Lieutenant General Grant: March 7, 1865.

In accordance with a Joint Resolution of Congress, approved December 17, 1863, I now have the honor of transmitting, and presenting to you, in the name of the People of the United States of America, a copy of said resolution, engrossed on parchment, together with the gold medal therein ordered and directed.

Please accept, for yourself and all under your command, the renewed expression of my gratitude for your and their arduous and well-performed public service. Your Obt. Servt.

A LINCOLN

[1] LS copy, DLC-RTL. The joint resolution approved December 17, 1863, extended the thanks of congress to Grant and "through him to the officers and soldiers who have fought under his command," and instructed the president to cause a gold medal to be struck and presented to Grant along with a copy of the joint resolution, engrossed on parchment.

Order Concerning James Andrews[1]

Executive Mansion, March 7th 1865.

Whereas, James Andrews, of Pittsburgh Pennsylvania, claims to own or control products of the insurrectionary States, and to have arrangements whereby he will be able to bring such products within the national military lines, and sell and deliver them to Agents authorized to purchase for the United States, under the Act of Congress of July 2nd 1864 and the Regulations of the Secretary of the Treasury.

It is ordered, that all such products which an authorized Agent of the Government shall have agreed to purchase and the said Andrews shall have stipulated to deliver as shown by certificate of the Agent prescribed by Regulation VIII (Form No 1. Regulations) attached hereto by such Agent and being transported or in store awaiting transportation in fulfillment of said stipulations and in pursuance of Regulations of the Secretary of the Treasury shall be free from seizure detention or forfeiture to the United States and Officers of the Army and Navy and civil Officers of the Government will observe this order and will give the said Andrews and his Agents and means of transportation and said products free and unmolested passage through the lines, other than blockaded lines, and safe-conduct within the lines, while going for or returning with said products or while the said products are in store awaiting transportation for the purposes aforesaid.

ABRAHAM LINCOLN

1 DS-P, ISLA.

Order Concerning Mrs. Charlotte Hough[1]

Executive Mansion, March 7th. 1865.

Whereas, Mrs. Charlotte Hough of New York claims to own or control products of the insurrectionary States and to have arrangements whereby she will be able to bring such products within the National military lines and sell and deliver them to Agents authorized to purchase for the United States under the Act of Congress of July 2nd 1864, and the Regulations of the Secretary of the Treasury

It is ordered, that all such products which an authorized Agent of the Government shall have agreed to purchase and the said Charlotte Hough shall have stipulated to deliver as shown by Certificate of the Agent prescribed by Regulation VIII (Form No 1. Regulations) attached hereto by such Agent and being transported or in store awaiting transportation in fulfillment of said stipulations and in pursuance of said Regulations of the Secretary of the Treasury, shall be free from seizure detention or forfeiture to the United States; and Officers of the Army and Navy and civil Officers of the Government will observe this order and will give the said Charlotte Hough and her Agents means of transportation and said products free and unmolested passage through the lines, other than blockaded lines, and safe conduct within the lines, while going for or returning with said products or while the said products are in store awaiting transportation for the purposes aforesaid.

ABRAHAM LINCOLN

1 DS, RPB.

Order Concerning Samuel H. Jones and John Talbot[1]

Executive Mansion, March 7th 1865.

Whereas, Samuel H. Jones and John Talbot of Missouri, claim to own or control products of the insurrectionary States and to have arrangements whereby they will be able to bring such products within the National Military lines and sell and deliver them to Agents authorized to purchase for the United States under the Act of Congress of July 2nd. 1864, and the Regulations of the *Secretary of the Treasury,*

It is ordered, that all such products which an authorized Agent of the Government shall have agreed to purchase and the said *Jones and Talbot* shall have stipulated to deliver as shown by the certificate of the Agent prescribed by Regulation VIII, (Form No 1. Regulations) attached hereto by such Agent or being transported or in store awaiting transportation in fulfillment of said stipulations and in pursuance of Regulations of the *Secretary of the Treasury,* shall be free from seizure detention or forfeiture to the *United States* and *Officers of the Army* and *Navy and civil Officers of the Government will observe this order,* and will give the said *Jones and Talbot* and their Agents and means of transportation and said products free and unmolested passage through the lines, other than blockaded lines, and safe-conduct within the lines while going for or returning with said products or while the said products are in store awaiting transportation for the purposes aforesaid.   ABRAHAM LINCOLN

[1] DS, owned by Mrs. Logan Hay, Springfield, Illinois.

Order Concerning Lucius H. Terry[1]

Executive Mansion   March 7. 1865

Whereas, Lucius H. Terry of St. Louis claims to own or control products of the insurrectionary states and to have arrangements whereby he will be able to bring such products within the national military lines and sell and deliver them to agents authorised to purchase for the United States under the Act of Congress of July 2, 1864 and the Regulations of the Secretary of the Treasury,

It is Ordered, that all such products which an authorised agent of the Government shall have agreed to purchase and the said Terry shall have stipulated to deliver as shown by certificate of the agent prescribed by Regulation VIII. (Form No. 1. Regulations) attached hereto by such agent, and being transported or in store awaiting transportation for fulfillment of said stipulations and in pursuance of Regulations of the Secretary of the Treasury shall be free from seizure detention or forfeiture to the United States; and officers of the Army and Navy and civil officers of the Government will observe this order, and will give the said Terry and his agents and means of transportation and said products free and unmolested passage through the lines other than blockaded lines and safe conduct within the lines, while going for or returning with said products, or while said products are in store awaiting transportation for the purposes aforesaid.

ABRAHAM LINCOLN

1 DS, CSmH.

Pass for Judge Dixon[1]

March 7, 1865

Allow the bearer, Judge Dixon to pass to the Officer in Command at Nashville, Tenn. to whom the Judge is commended, as worthy of reasonable facilities for passing about Kentucky & Tennessee.

March 7, 1865   A. LINCOLN

1 ADS, InFtwL. Judge Dixon has not been identified, but Lincoln may have misspelled the name inadvertently in writing the pass for Judge William M. Dickson of Cincinnati.

To John Pope[1]

Major Genl. Pope   Executive Mansion,
St. Louis, Mo.   Washington, March 7, 1865.

Please state briefly by telegraph what you concluded about the assessments in St. Louis county. Early in the war one Samuel B. Churchill was sent from St. Louis to Louisville, where I have quite satisfactory evidence that he has not misbehaved. Still, I am told his property at St. Louis is subjected to this assessment, which I think it ought not to be. Still, I wish to know what you think.

A. LINCOLN

1 ALS, DNA WR RG 107, Presidential Telegrams, I, 363. See Lincoln to Pope, February 14, *supra.* Pope replied on March 8: "I wrote fully concerning assessment to the Secy of War on the twenty sixth 26 Feby. I submitted the question to War Dept, as the authority for assessment originated in Washington

& the order was made before I came here   there are strong reasons given for making it given me by Genl Dodge which are communicated in my letter. . . . that letter must be in War Dept and I respectfully invite your attention to it." (DLC-RTL). Pope's letter of February 26 has not been found.

To Gideon Welles[1]

Private   Executive Mansion,
To the Honorable   Washington,
The Secretary of the Navy   7 March, 1865.

M. de Mareil who bears this, is the Editor of the Messager-Franco-Americain, a French Newspaper published in the City of New York, which has sustained the Union cause during this war with great ability and energy.

I hope that any advertising which can be legally and appropriately given to a journal of this class, may be given to M. Mareil.
Yours truly   A. LINCOLN

[1] LS, RPB. This letter is in John Hay's handwriting, marked *"Private"* and signed by Lincoln. No record of Navy advertising in Monsieur H. De Mareil's paper has been found.

Endorsement Concerning Daniel J. Pinckney[1]

A good case.   A. LINCOLN
March. 8. 1865

[1] AES, DNA FS RG 59, Appointments, Box 363. Lincoln's endorsement appears on a letter from David Davis, February 21, 1865, recommending Professor Daniel J. Pinckney of Rock River Seminary, Mount Morris, Illinois, for a suitable appointment "in the South of Europe." No record of his appointment has been found.

To Ulysses S. Grant[1]

"Cypher"   Office U.S. Military Telegraph,
Lieut. Genl. Grant   War Department,
City-Point, Va.   Washington, D.C., March 8. 1865

Your two despatches to the Secretary of War—one relating to supplies for the enemy going by the Blackwater, and the other to Gen. Singleton and Judge Hughes—have been laid before me by him. As to Singleton and Hughes, I think they are not in Richmond by any authority, unless it be from you. I remember nothing from me which could aid them in getting there except a letter to you as follows, towit:

"Lieut. Genl. Grant   Executive Mansion
City-Point, Va.   Washington City Feb. 7. 1865

Gen. Singleton who bears you this, claims that, he already has arrangements made, if you consent, to bring a large amount of Southern produce through your lines. For it's bearing on our finances, I would be glad for this to be done, if it can be, without injuriously disturbing your military operations, or supplying the enemy. I wish you to be judge and master on these points. Please see and hear him fully; and decide whether anything & if anything, what can be done in the premises. Yours truly

A. LINCOLN.["]

I believe I gave Hughes a card putting him with Singleton, on the same letter.

However this may be I now authorize you to get Singleton and Hughes away from Richmond, if you choose, and can. I also authorize you, by an order, or in what form you choose, to suspend all operations on the Treasury-trade-permits, in all places South Eastward of the Alleghenies. If you make such order, notify me of it, giving a copy, so that I can give corresponding direction to the Navy.   A LINCOLN

1 ALS, DNA WR RG 107, Presidential Telegrams, I, 364-66. On March 8, Grant telegraphed Stanton at 11:30 A.M.:

"We have got supplies going out by Norfolk to the rebel army stopped, but information received shows that large amounts still go by way of the Blackwater. They no doubt go on the Treasury permits heretofore given under Act of Congress regulating trade with states in insurrection

"I would respectfully recommend that orders be sent to the Army and Navy everywhere, to stop supplies going to the interior and annulling all permits for such trade heretofore given" (DLC-RTL).

A second telegram from Grant to Stanton is as follows:

"I believe Genl [James W.] Singleton should be ordered to return from Richmond and all permits he may have should be revoked. Our friends in Richmond . . . send word that Tobacco is being exchanged on the Potomac for Bacon, and they believe Singleton to be at the bottom of it.

"I am also of the opinion that all permits issued to Judge [James] Hughes should be cancelled. I think the same of all other permits heretofore granted, but in the case of Singleton and Judge Hughes, I believe there is a deep laid plan for making millions and they will sacrifice every interest of the country to succeed. I do not know Hughes personally never having seen him but once, but the conviction here expressed is forced upon me" (ibid.).

On March 10, Grant issued his Special Orders No. 48:

"The operations on all Treasury Trade Permits, and all other trade permits and licenses to trade, by whomsoever granted, within the State of Virginia, except that portion known as the Eastern Shore, and the States of North Carolina and South Carolina, and that portion of the State of Georgia immediately bordering on the Atlantic, including the city of Savannah, are hereby suspended until further orders. All contracts and agreements made under or by virtue of any trade permit or license within any of said States or parts of States, during the existence of this order, will be deemed void, and the subject of such contracts or agreements will be seized by the military authorities for the benefit of the

Government, whether the same is at the time of such contracts or agreements within their reach or at any time thereafter comes within their reach, either by the operations of war or the acts of the contracting parties or their agents. The delivery of all goods contracted for and not delivered before the publication of this order is prohibited.

"Supplies of all kinds are prohibited from passing into any of said States or parts of States, except such as are absolutely necessary for the wants of those living within the lines of actual military occupation, and under no circumstances will military commanders allow them to pass beyond the lines they actually hold."

See further, Lincoln's telegram to Grant, March 13, *infra.*

To George Harrington[1]

Executive Mansion,
Dear Sir: Washington, March 8, 1865.

Please detail a good clerk from your Department, to report to my Private Secretary for temporary duty in the Executive Office. Yours truly   A. LINCOLN

George Harrington Esq
Secretary of the Treasury *ad interim.*

[1] LS, OClWHi. No reply has been found.

To the Senate[1]

To the Senate of the United States: March 8, 1865

The 4th section of the law of 16 January, 1857, provides that reserved officers may be promoted on the reserved list, by and with the advice and consent of the Senate, and under this authority various officers of the Navy have been promoted one grade from time to time.

I therefore nominate Commander John J. Young, now on the reserved list, to be a captain in the Navy on the reserved list, from the 12th August, 1854, the date when he was entitled to his regular promotion had he not been overslaughed. It is due to this officer to state that he was passed over in consequence of physical disability, this disability having occurred in the discharge of his duties; and prior to his misfortune he bore the reputation of an efficient and correct officer, and subsequently has evinced a willingness to perform whatever duties were assigned him.

Washington, D.C., 8 March, 1865.   ABRAHAM LINCOLN.

[1] *Executive Journal*, XIV, 256. The Senate confirmed Young's promotion on March 10, 1865.

To the Senate[1]

To the Senate of the United States   March 8, 1865

In answer to the Senate's Resolution of the 6th. instant requesting the return of a certain Joint Resolution, I transmit a Report from the Secretary of State   ABRAHAM LINCOLN

Washington 8th. March, 1865.

[1] DS, DNA RG 46, Senate 38A F3. A resolution passed on March 6, requested the president "to return to the Senate the joint resolution (H.R. 161) in relation to certain railroads, which was presented to him through mistake." H.R. 161 did not pass the Senate, but by mistake was signed by Vice-president Johnson and transmitted to Lincoln for approval.

To William O. Bartlett[1]

W. O. Bartlett,   Office U.S. Military Telegraph,
Philadelphia   War Department, Washington, D.C.,
(Probably at Continental)   March 9 1865

It will soon be too late, if you are not here.   A. LINCOLN

[1] ALS, DNA WR RG 107, Presidential Telegrams, I, 369. Bartlett had telegraphed on March 7, "Been lying this side the Susquehanna all night. Blocked by ice. Shall reach Washington as soon as possible." (DLC-RTL). Bartlett was carrying James Gordon Bennett's letter of March 6 in reply to Lincoln's letter of February 20, *supra*. The Senate was to adjourn on March 11, and hence Lincoln could not have his nomination of Bennett confirmed if further delayed.

Endorsement Concerning Hayden De Lany[1]

Let this case be filed & considered when this subject shall be acted upon.   A. LINCOLN

March 9. 1865.

[1] AES, DNA WR RG 94, U.S. Military Academy, 1865, No. 93. Lincoln's endorsement appears on an envelope from John A. Bingham with recommendations of Corporal Hayden De Lany, Thirtieth Ohio Volunteers, for West Point. Lincoln also endorsed an envelope containing additional recommendations: "West-Point—a good case." (*Ibid.*). De Lany entered West Point in July, 1865, and was commissioned second lieutenant in the Ninth U.S. Infantry on September 11, 1867.

Endorsement Concerning John C. Grannis[1]

March 9, 1865

This came to me March 9. 1865 at ½ past 3. PM. & after, nomination for Dist. Atty had been made   A L

¹ AES, CSmH. Lincoln's endorsement appears on a letter from Representative Rufus P. Spalding, asking appointment of John C. Grannis as district attorney. See Lincoln to Tod, March 6, *supra*. On March 11, Senator John Sherman wrote Lincoln:

"I have learnt how you can settle the disappointment of our Cleveland friends about Root & the Dist Atty of N. Dist of Ohio.

"The present collector of customs at Cleveland will by common consent have to go out and John C Grannis will accept.

"I have talked with Spalding about it & it will be very satisfactory to him to Gov. Tod—Col. [George B.] Senter & all our friends" (DLC-RTL).

Grannis received the appointment as collector of customs.

Endorsement Concerning John P. Usher¹

Accepted to take effect, May 15th. 1865   A. LINCOLN
    March 9. 1865

¹ AES, DLC-RTL. Lincoln's endorsement appears on a letter from John P. Usher, March 8, 1865, tendering his resignation as secretary of Interior. Usher's covering letter of the same date is as follows: "I thought it possible that the letter of resignation might be published; and I feared it would appear a little inconsistent to tender it, to take effect at so distant a day. I send it up by Mr. Dole, and, at his suggestion will name the 15th day of May as the date when the resignation shall take effect. If that pleases you the letter could be so endorsed and the nomination of my successor could be made to the Senate with a view to his appt. at that time. . . ." (*Ibid.*).

To Ulysses S. Grant¹

Office U.S. Military Telegraph,
Lieut. Genl. Grant   War Department,
City-Point, Va.   Washington, D.C., March 9. 1865

I see your despatch to the Sec. of War, objecting to rebel prisoners being allowed to take the oath and go free. Supposing that I am responsible for what is done in this way, I think fit to say that there is no general rule, or action, allowing prisoners to be discharged merely on taking the oath. What has been done is that Members of Congress come to me from time to time with lists of names alleging that from personal knowledge, and evidence of reliable persons they are satisfied that it is safe to discharge the particular persons named on the lists, and I have ordered their discharge. These Members are chiefly from the border states; and those they get discharged are their neighbors and neighbors sons. They tell me that they do not bring to me one tenth of the names which are brought to them, bringing only such as their knowledge or the proof satisfies them about. I have, on the same principle, discharged some on the representations of others than Members of Congress, as, for instance, Gov. Johnson of Tennessee. The number I have discharged has been rather larger than I liked

—reaching I should think an average of fifty a day, since the recent general exchange commenced. On the same grounds, last year, I discharged quite a number at different times, aggregating perhaps a thousand, Missourians and Kentuckians; and their Members returning here since the prisoner's return to their homes, report to me only two cases of proving false. Doubtless some more have proved false; but, on the whole I believe what I have done in this way has done good rather than harm.   A. LINCOLN

¹ ALS, DNA WR RG 107, Presidential Telegrams, I, 367-68. On March 8, Grant had telegraphed Stanton: "I understand that rebel prisoners in the North are allowed to take the oath of allegiance and go free. I think this is wrong. No one should be liberated on taking the oath . . . who has been captured while bearing arms against us, except where persons of known loyalty vouch for them. Men who desire to take the oath are the best men to exchange. They can afterward come into our lines if they do not wish to fight." (OR, I, XLVI, II, 887).

At 5 P.M. on March 9, he replied to Lincoln's telegram: "Your dispatch of this morning shows that prisoners of war are being discharged only in accordance with the rule I proposed. I questioned the officers from Camp Morton & Rock Island who arrived here yesterday in charge of prisoners for exchange and they told me that great numbers were being discharged on taking the oath of allegiance. They thought all who desired to do so are permitted to obtain their liberty in this way. I supposed this was in pursuance of a general policy which you knew nothing about and I wanted it changed so that none would be allowed to take the oath . . . except by special permission" (DLC-RTL).

Memorandum
Concerning Maryland Appointments¹

March 9, 1865

To-day Gov. Swann, Mayor Chapman, & Hon Mr. Webster personally complain of me about my action in regard to the offices in Maryland.

1. Blumenberg.
2. Sands— Collector of 5 Dist.
3. Ridgeley—this, not objected to.
4. Stuart. this objected.—removal of Thompson.

Changes made in Custom-House with a view of economy —15 dropped—12 my friends—on whose designation dropped.

¹ AD, DLC-RTL. Lincoln's callers were: Governor Thomas Swann, Mayor John L. Chapman of Baltimore, and former congressman Edwin H. Webster, who is listed in the *U.S. Official Register,* 1865, as collector of customs at Baltimore. Leopold Blumenberg is listed as superintendent of warehouses in the customhouse at Baltimore, James L. Ridgely as collector of internal revenue at Baltimore, and Joseph J. Stewart (Stuart?) as assessor of internal revenue at Baltimore. William Thomson (Thompson?) is listed in the 1863 *Register* as a clerk in the Baltimore customhouse. Sands has not been found in the *Register,* but was probably George W. Sands of Ellicott Mills, (now Ellicott City), Maryland.

To James Speed[1]

Send me a nomination for Caspar E. Yost, of Nebraska—to fill the vacancy caused by this resignation.   A. LINCOLN

    March 9. 1865

[1] AES, DNA RG 60, Papers of Attorney General, 1864, Box 122. Lincoln's endorsement appears on a letter of resignation from Phineas W. Hitchcock, U.S. marshal for Nebraska. Yost's appointment was confirmed by the Senate on March 11, 1865.

To Edwin M. Stanton[1]

Hon. Secretary of War   Executive Mansion,
Dear Sir.   Washington, March 9, 1865.

I have long thought that Col. Lewis B. Parsons of the Quarter-Master's Department, ought to be promoted; and this impression has been deepened by his great success in the recent matter of transporting troops from the West to the East. Is there any legal obstacle in the way? If not, let the promotion be made at once.
Yours truly   A. LINCOLN

[1] ALS, IHi. A note pencilled on the bottom of this letter by Lewis B. Parsons indicates that it was given to him by John Hay. The letter was apparently not sent to Stanton, but its text was incorporated in Lincoln's letter to Stanton, March 17, *infra*. In January, 1865, Colonel Parsons had superintended the transportation of the Twenty-third Army Corps (twenty thousand men, with animals and full equipment) from Mississippi to Washington.

Proclamation Offering Pardon to Deserters[1]

March 11, 1865
By the President of the United States of America:

A Proclamation.

Whereas, the twenty-first section of the act of Congress approved on the third instant, entitled "An act to amend the several acts heretofore passed to provide for the enrolling and calling out the national forces and for other purposes," requires, "that in addition to the other lawful penalties of the crime of desertion from the military or naval service, all persons who have deserted the military or naval service of the United States who shall not return to said service, or report themselves to a Provost Marshal within sixty days after the proclamation hereinafter mentioned shall be deemed and taken to have voluntarily relinquished and forfeited their rights of citizenship, and their rights to become citizens, and such deserters shall be forever incapable of holding any office of trust or profit under the United States, or of exercising any rights of citizens thereof, and all persons who shall hereafter desert the military or naval service, and all persons who, being duly enrolled, shall depart the jurisdiction of the district in which he is enrolled, or go beyond the limits of the United States with intent to avoid any draft into the military or naval service, duly ordered, shall be liable to the penalties of this Section. And the President is hereby authorized and required, forthwith on the passage of this Act, to issue his proclamation setting forth the provisions of this Section, in which proclamation the President is requested to notify all deserters returning within sixty days, as aforesaid that they shall be pardoned on condition of returning to their regiments and companies or to such other organizations as they may be assigned to, until they shall have served for a period of time equal to their original term of enlistment:"

Now, therefore, be it known that I, Abraham Lincoln, President of the United States, do issue this my Proclamation, as required by said act, ordering and requiring all deserters to return to their proper posts, and I do hereby notify them that all deserters, who shall, within sixty days from the date of this proclamation, viz: on or before the tenth day of May 1865, return to service or report themselves to a Provost Marshal, shall be pardoned, on condition that they return to their regiments and companies, or to such other organizations as they may be assigned to, and serve the remainder of their original terms of enlistment, and, in addition thereto, a period equal to the time lost by desertion.

In testimony whereof, I have hereunto set my hand, and caused the seal of the United States to be affixed.

Done at the City of Washington, this eleventh day of March, in the year of our Lord one thousand eight hundred and [L.S.]   sixty-five, and of the Independence of the United States the eighty-ninth.   ABRAHAM LINCOLN

By the President:

WILLIAM H SEWARD Secretary of State.

[1] DS, DNA FS RG 11, Proclamations.

To the Senate[1]

March 11, 1865

I withdraw the nomination of [Hugh M.] Herrick, as Assessor of Internal Revenue for the 9th. Collection District of New-York, in place of Homer Franklin; and substitute therefor a nomination of said Herrick for said office, to take effect March 20th. 1865.

[1] AD (ADf?), DLC. Bracketed portion is not in Lincoln's autograph. The circumstances which prompted Lincoln to renominate Herrick are not clear. A regular nomination for Herrick to replace Homer Franklin, dated March 10, 1865, appears in the *Executive Journal* (XIV, 274). The withdrawal and re-nomination as above, but bearing Lincoln's signature, appears in the *Executive Journal* on March 11 (XIV, 293). The Senate did not confirm the appointment.

To Edwin M. Stanton[1]

I shall be glad if the Secretary of War will allow this gentleman, —Wm. Van Dalsan—a pass to go to Wilmington N.C.

March 11. 1865   A. LINCOLN

[1] ALS, CSmH. William Van Dalsan has not been identified.

To Henry T. Blow[1]

Hon. Henry T. Blow   Washington,
St. Louis Mo.   March 13. 1865

A Miss. E. Snodgrass, who was banished from St. Louis in May 1863, wishes to take the oath and return home. What say you?

A. LINCOLN

[1] ALS, DNA WR RG 107, Presidential Telegrams, I, 370. Above the date "13" as written by Lincoln someone has written "12," but there is no other evidence that this is the correct date. Henry T. Blow replied on March 15: "Have been sick. What I learn of Miss Snodgrass is favorable and I recommend her return" (DLC-RTL). Miss E. Snodgrass was banished as a secret rebel mail agent (St. Louis *Republican*, May 14, 1863). A pass for Miss Snodgrass "to report to Gen. Pope," dated March 18, 1865, has been listed for sale in American Art Association Anderson Catalog 4306, March 4, 1937, No. 144.

Endorsement Concerning General Ames[1]

If there be no legal obstacle, let the recommendation of Gen. Ames be carried into effect.   A. LINCOLN

Mar. 13, 1865

[1] Carnegie Book Shop Catalog 119, No. 84. According to the catalog description, Lincoln's autograph endorsement appears on the verso of the concluding portion of a letter of General Ames. Whether Brigadier General Adelbert Ames of Maine, or Brigadier General John W. Ames of Massachusetts, was the writer, is not stated.

To John Z. Goodrich[1]

Hon. John Z. Goodrich   Executive Mansion,
My dear Sir: Washington, March 13. 1865.

Your official term expires about this time. I know not whether you desire a re-appointment; and I am not aware of any objection to you personal, political, or official. Yet if it be true, as I have been informed, that the office is of no pecuniary consequence to you, it would be quite a relief to me to have it at my disposal. Yours truly

A LINCOLN

¹ ADfS, DLC-RTL. John Z. Goodrich, collector of customs at Boston, replied on March 13:

"Your letter of the 13th was handed to me yesterday by your messenger. You say you know of no personal, political or official objection to my re-appointment. From other parts of your letter I am lead to infer that you think I may not care about being re-appointed because the office is of no pecuniary consequence to me. If this be so you would be glad to have the disposal of it, & to ascertain whether it be so is the purpose of your letter. As you are one of the frankest of men, I assume that you desire the utmost frankness from me. You desire me to state as between friends, & confidentially, precisely what the fact is on these points. . . . So understanding your letter I say frankly & truly—that I do desire a re-appointment, & one of the strong reasons for this desire . . . is that the office is a matter of 'pecuniary' importance to me, and have entertained the hope that it will be. Hitherto, as I will explain, it has not been.

"I entered the office comparatively poor. I had some factory property . . . but no supplies or working capital. . . . In about a year the factory began to make money & continued to do a successful business till about six months ago. . . .

"During the time of my greatest prosperity I made a donation to Williams College. . . . I have said to my wife once or twice that if part of it had not been made, I should not make it now. . . . Part was a large Gymnasium Building which I agreed to erect, at a cost not to exceed $15,000. . . . It is now perhaps ¾ down & the cost . . . will reach $25,000. I have several times comforted myself with the hope . . . that if I should be allowed to keep my office another term, I might in that way make up this extra $10,000. . . . I say . . . that I have made nothing hitherto by my office, nor do I think there is a man in Boston who believes I have. Still I feel . . . that should the war close soon . . . I shall be fairly entitled to the pecuniary advantages of it for the remainder of another term. But of this you will judge. There is no man living I would sooner relieve from embarrassment than yourself. . . ." (DLC-RTL).

Lincoln probably wished to find a place for retiring Vice-president Hannibal Hamlin. Charles Sumner's letter to Hamlin, August 22, 1865, explained how Hamlin got the appointment later from President Johnson:

"It seemed to [Henry] Wilson and myself that before deciding on your course you ought to know the history of the recent change at our custom-house, and we hoped for an opportunity of speaking of it freely in a personal interview. As you may not be here very soon, I will give the narrative.

"Some time ago Mr. Hooper [Representative Samuel Hooper of Boston] received a letter from the Secretary of the Treasury, stating that the administration desired to change the three officers at the custom-house whose salaries were large, and he asked him to confer with the two senators and Mr. [Alexander H.] Rice, and send him the names which we should agree upon for the places. We concluded to confine the conference to those indicated, and I invited the whole delegation to meet at my house. . . .

"At the meeting . . . I stated that, on general grounds, I was against a change —that I doubted its policy, but that I should cooperate cheerfully . . . in making the desired recommendations. I then proceeded to propose Mr. Hamlin for collector. It was evident at once that there was a strong disposition in all the delegation towards Mr. Hamlin; but it was remarked that the naval office was easier in its duties . . . the delegation overruled my proposition and recommended Mr. Hamlin for naval officer. . . . Some days later Mr. Hooper received a letter from the secretary stating that the President wished to offer Mr. Hamlin the alternative of these two offices. This is all we know. . . ." (Charles Eugene Hamlin, *The Life and Times of Hannibal Hamlin*, pp. 501-502).

To Ulysses S. Grant[1]

Executive Mansion

Lieut. Gen'l Grant.   March 13, 1865.

I think it will tend to remove some injurious misunderstanding for you to have another interview with Judge Hughes. I do not wish to modify anything I have heretofore said, as to you having entire control whether anything in the way of trade shall pass either way through your lines. I do say, however, that having known Judge Hughes intimately during the whole of the rebellion, I do not believe he would knowingly betray any interest of the country and attempt to deceive you in the slightest degree. Please see him again. Yours truly,   A. LINCOLN.

[1] Angle, p. 372. See Lincoln to Grant, March 8, *supra*. Orville H. Browning's *Diary* records under date of March 11:

"Saw in the papers this morning the statement that 200,000 pounds of tobacco purchased by Genl Singleton in Richmond and sent to Fredericksburgh had been destroyed by our troops. . . . Knowing . . . that Singleton had written authority from the President to go to Richmond & purchase and bring out produce . . . I was greatly surprised. . . . Just at night I took Judge Hughes with me, and went to the Presidents. . . . The President at once showed us despatches from Genl Grant . . . saying substantially that Genl Singleton and Judge Hughes were at Richmond engaged in a stupendous scheme to make millions . . . that they were willing to sacrifice the interests of the Country to the accomplishment of their purpose. . . . This astonished me greatly. Hughes had not been in Richmond. All that Singleton had done had been open and above board. . . . The President had not seen the paper Grant had given to Singleton authorising him to send products to Fredericksburg, and guarantying protection. I had a copy . . . which I showed to the President, and I think he was not less amazed at Grants subsequent conduct than I was. He seemed troubled and perplexed . . . and manifested a desire to keep faith, and save Singleton from ruin if he could, but at the same time gave me the impression that he was afraid to take the responsibility.

"I thought he was afraid of Secy Stanton, although he said Stanton had always been in favor of getting out products. I suggested that I would see, and converse, with Mr Stanton upon the subject, and he urged me to do so. He also thought that Judge Hughes ought to go down and see Grant, saying he would give him a pass to go, and also write a letter to Grant. . . ."

Under date of March 21, Browning records a conversation with Stanton, in which it was developed that the tobacco destroyed did not belong to James W. Singleton and James Hughes.

To Joseph Holt[1]

[c. March 13, 1865]

Although this is an old case I do not perceive that the Judge Advocate General has reported on it. Will he please report on the evidence, fully, as to the 3rd. Charge and Specification, which seems to me to be the controlling one? A. LINCOLN

[1] AES, DNA WR RG 153, Judge Advocate General, NN 1785. Lincoln's endorsement appears on a letter of Lafayette S. Foster, March 13, 1865, in behalf of John H. Lester, convicted on charges of manufacturing arms for the enemy, endeavoring to give aid and comfort to the enemy, and treasonable and disloyal conduct. He was sentenced to imprisonment at hard labor for ten years and to forfeit all property. Lincoln had referred the papers in this case to Holt on January 12 (DNA WR RG 153, Judge Advocate General, NN 1785). See Lincoln to Lorenzo Thomas, March 16, *infra*.

Endorsement Concerning Thomas B. Lincoln[1]

Sent me by the Sec. of State to procure a pass South, which I gave.
March. 15. 1865. A. LINCOLN

[1] AES, DLC-RTL. Lincoln's endorsement has been torn from the letter on which it was originally written but is accompanied by an envelope endorsed "Thomas B. Lincoln." See the pass for Thomas B. Lincoln, *infra*.

To Hugh McCulloch

I shall be glad if S. James Johnson, the bearer, could get a little promotion. A. LINCOLN
March. 15. 1865

[1] ALS, CSmH. See Lincoln to Chase, January 28, 1864, *supra*. Solomon James Johnson, a laborer in the Treasury Department, was made a clerk in 1867.

To Ulysses S. Grant[1]

Lieutenant Gen: Grant
Please allow the bearer, Robert E. Coxe, to pass through our lines to go South and return A. LINCOLN
March 15. 1865

[1] Copy, ORB. The original document has not been located. See Lincoln's order concerning Robert E. Coxe, January 5, 1865, *supra*. According to Hanson A. Risley's statement, this pass was not given him until March 16, though dated March 15. Orville H. Browning's *Diary*, under date of March 16, relates that Browning procured the pass for Coxe on March 15 and that "the signature alone was in the President's hand writing—the rest in Mr Nicolay's."

Pass for Thomas B. Lincoln[1]

Allow the bearer, Thomas B. Lincoln, with ordinary baggage, to pass our lines and go South. A. LINCOLN
March 15. 1865

[1] ADS, owned by Ray W. Davis, Circleville, Ohio. See the endorsement concerning Thomas B. Lincoln, *supra*.

Reply to Count Wydenbruck[1]

March 15, 1865

COUNT WYDENBRUCK: I sincerely hope that you may find your residence in our country an agreeable one. During a period in which our relations with several of the foreign powers have been a subject of especial care, if not of anxiety, the friendly intercourse between your great country and ours has been free not only from disturbance, but even from every form of irritation or annoyance. Your sovereign has been discreet, frank, and friendly, and has thus won the confidence and good will of the American people.

[1] Washington *Daily Morning Chronicle*, March 16, 1865. Lincoln replied to a brief speech made by Count Wydenbruck, minister from Austria, upon presenting his credentials.

To James Speed[1]

Executive Mansion,
Hon. Attorney General   Washington, March 15, 1865.
    Appoint Judge Caleb Baldwin of Iowa to be District Attorney for the District of Iowa. Yours truly   A. LINCOLN

[1] ALS, DNA GE RG 60, Papers of Attorney General, Segregated Lincoln Material. Caleb Baldwin of Council Bluffs, was appointed to succeed William H. F. Gurley of Davenport.

To John P. Usher[1]

[c. March 15, 1865]
Let these appointments be made as agreed on by Senators Pomeroy & Lane.   A. LINCOLN

[1] AES, DNA NR RG 48, Appointments, Indian Agencies, Miscellaneous, 1857-1869, Box 1269. Lincoln's endorsement appears on a letter from Samuel C. Pomeroy and Sidney Clarke, endorsed by James H. Lane and Samuel J. Crawford, March 15, 1865, recommending George A. Reynolds for agent of the Seminole Indians. Reynolds is listed as agent of the Seminoles in the *U.S. Official Register*, 1865.

To John P. Usher[1]

Let this appointment, being to fill a vacancy, be made.
March. 15. 1865.   A. LINCOLN

1 AES, DNA NR RG 48, Department of Interior, Appointments, Land Offices, Osage District, Kansas—Independence, California, Box 25. Lincoln's endorsement appears on an envelope labeled "Watson Stewart, Humbolt, Kansas. Application for the appointment of Register Land Office Humbolt, Kansas." Stewart is listed as register at the Humboldt Land Office in the *U.S. Official Register*, 1865.

To Thurlow Weed[1]

Thurlow Weed, Esq   Executive Mansion,
My dear Sir.   Washington, March 15, 1865.

Every one likes a compliment. Thank you for yours on my little notification speech, and on the recent Inaugeral Address. I expect the latter to wear as well as—perhaps better than—any thing I have produced; but I believe it is not immediately popular. Men are not flattered by being shown that there has been a difference of purpose between the Almighty and them. To deny it, however, in this case, is to deny that there is a God governing the world. It is a truth which I thought needed to be told; and as whatever of humiliation there is in it, falls most directly on myself, I thought others might afford for me to tell it. Yours truly

A. LINCOLN

1 ALS, NRU. Thurlow Weed had written Lincoln on March 4:
"The sour Weather has spoiled the Celebration, so I send you my Badge. It is prettily got up, though with by no means a flattered reflext of our President. . . .
"The reply to the Committee of Congress, informing of your re-election, is not only the *neatest* but the most pregnant and effective use to which the English Language was ever put." (DLC-RTL).
No letter of Weed mentioning the Second Inaugural Address has been found, and it seems probable that Lincoln misread or misrecollected Weed's reference to the "prettily got up" badge.

To John Evans[1]

                            Executive Mansion,
Gov. Evans.   Washington, March 16. 1865.

As you are Governor of the Territory of Colorado, and Hon. J. M. Ashley, of Ohio is, and probably will again be, Chairman of the Committee on Territories, of the H.R. there is no objection to your corresponding with him about territorial matters. Yours truly

A. LINCOLN

1 ALS, CoHi; ADfS, DLC-RTL. On March 6, Governor John Evans wrote Lincoln seven letters concerning appointments in Colorado, and on March 14 wrote six letters to James M. Ashley, bringing charges against territorial officers in Colorado and recommending appointments (DLC-RTL).

To Joseph Holt[1]

Judge Advocate General please report upon this case.

Mar. 16, 1865   A. LINCOLN

[1] AES, DNA WR RG 153, Judge Advocate General, NN 3355. Lincoln's endorsement appears in the court-martial record of William M. Patterson, chaplain, CSA, sentenced to imprisonment for the duration of the war on charges of violating laws of war and being a spy. Holt recommended pardon upon taking the oath, and Lincoln approved on March 22, 1865.

To Edward O. C. Ord[1]

Executive Mansion

Major General Ord.   Washington, March 16, 1865

Suspend execution of Lieut. Henry A. Meck, of 1st. U.S. Colored Cavalry until further order from here. Answer

A. LINCOLN

[1] ALS, DNA WR RG 107, Presidential Telegrams, I, 371. Lincoln endorsed the court-martial record of Henry A. Meck "Sentence approved Jan. 25. 1865 A. LINCOLN." (DNA WR RG 153, Judge Advocate General, NN 2357). Meck's sentence of death was for conviction on charges of murder and breach of arrest. An undated letter from I. N. Baylor, Norfolk, Virginia, is as follows:

"May I be allowed the liberty of addressing your Honor a few lines, in favor of Henry A Meck from Pennsylvania . . . at this time under Sentence of death in this city by hanging, about the middle of next week or 14th of *March next*.

"H. A. Meck was formerly a lieutenant in a Regiment of negro Soldiers— Stationed here. About June 1864 . . . Meck was under the influence of Spirituous liquors—and while in that Situation with some of his black soldiers unfortunately attacked a Sutlers Store here. The Sutler defended his property, drew a pistol and Shot Meck, wounding him severely: Meck ordered one of his black Soldiers to return the fire, which was done, Shooting the Sutler, who soon deceased. Meck has been in prison ever Since—I think—and Shows a very contrite heart. . . ." (DLC-RTL).

General Ord replied to Lincoln's telegram on the same day: "Orders have been issued suspending execution of Lieut Henry A. Mecker 1st U.S. Colored Cavalry until further orders. . . ." (*Ibid.*).

To Lorenzo Thomas[1]

March 16, 1865

Let this man Lester take the oath and give bond as suggested by the Judge Advocate General upon doing which he is fully pardoned and the money taken from him or from his wife to be refunded.

Mar. 16. 1865   A. LINCOLN

[1] Copy, DNA RG 130, U.S. Army Court Martial Cases, White House Office, Register. This endorsement or order concerning John H. Lester is missing from the files of the Adjutant General (DNA WR RG 94, Letters Received, P 457 with 552 L, 1864). See Lincoln to Holt, March 13, *supra*.

To John P. Usher[1]

Appoint according to within.   A. LINCOLN

March 16. 1865

[1] AES, DNA NR RG 48, Applications, Indian Agencies, Box 1274. Lincoln's endorsement appears on a letter from James Harlan, James W. Grimes, James F. Wilson and others, February 23, 1865, recommending Patrick H. Conger of Iowa for agent of Sioux Indians at Yankton, Dakota Territory.

To John P. Usher[1]

Hold on till Senators return.   A L.

March 16. 1865

[1] AES, DNA NR RG 48, Applications, Indian Agencies, Miscellaneous, 1857-1869, Box 1269. Lincoln's endorsement appears on a letter from Representative Ignatius Donnelly of Minnesota, March 16, 1865, asking that no Minnesota appointments be made until the senators from his state should return from Charleston, South Carolina.

To John P. Usher[1]

Appoint according to within.   A. LINCOLN

March 16. 1865

[1] AES, DNA NR RG 48, Department of Interior, Appointments, Indian Agencies, Box 73. Lincoln's endorsement appears on a petition from the Union members of the Dakota legislative assembly, endorsed by Walter A. Burleigh, delegate in congress, and others, asking appointment of Joseph R. Hanson as agent of the Upper Missouri Indian Agency. Hanson seems not to have been appointed; Samuel N. Latta is listed as agent in the *U.S. Official Register* for both 1863 and 1865.

To John P. Usher[1]

Let this appointment be made.   A. LINCOLN

March 16. 1865.

[1] AES, DNA NR RG 48, Department of Interior, Appointments, Land Offices, Boonville, Missouri, etc., Box 13. Lincoln's endorsement appears on a letter from James W. Nye, William M. Stewart, and U. G. Worthington, March 13, 1865, recommending David L. Gregg for receiver at the land office, Carson City, Nevada. Gregg received the appointment.

To John P. Usher[1]

Appoint according to within.   A. LINCOLN

March 16. 1865

¹ AES, DNA NR RG 48, Applications, Indian Agencies, Ponca, Box 1271. Lincoln's endorsement appears on a petition from the Union members of the Dakota legislative assembly, asking appointment of Dr. Joel A. Potter of Dakota as agent of the Ponca Indians. Potter received the appointment.

To John P. Usher¹

Appoint Owen Wade, of Oregon, to fill this vacancy.

March. 16. 1865   A. LINCOLN

¹ AES, DNA NR RG 48, Department of Interior, Appointments, Land Office, New Ulm, Minnesota, etc., Box 36. Lincoln's endorsement appears on a letter from William A. Starkweather, February 1, 1865, resigning as register of the land office at Oregon City, Oregon. Owen Wade received the appointment.

To Rosell M. Hough and Others¹

                              Office U.S. Military Telegraph,
Col. R. M. Hough & others   War Department,
Chicago, Illinois   Washington, D.C., March 17 1865

Yours received. The best I can do with it is to refer it to the War Department. The Rock-Island case referred to, was my individual enterprize; and it caused so much difficulty in so many ways that I promised to never undertake another.   A. LINCOLN

¹ ALS, DNA WR RG 107, Presidential Telegrams, I, 372. The letter from Rosell M. Hough, president of the Chicago Board of Trade, has not been found. It probably referred to Lincoln's order to Huidekoper, September 1, 1864, supra.

Proclamation Concerning Trade with Indians¹

March 17, 1865

By the President of the United States of America:

A Proclamation.

Whereas, reliable information has been received that hostile Indians within the limits of the United States have been furnished with arms and munitions of war by persons dwelling in conterminous foreign territory, and are thereby enabled to prosecute their savage warfare upon the exposed and sparse settlements of the frontier.

Now, therefore, be it known that I, Abraham Lincoln, President of the United States of America, do hereby proclaim and direct that all persons detected in that nefarious traffic, shall be arrested and tried by Court Martial at the nearest military post, and, if convicted, shall receive the punishment due to their deserts.

In witness whereof, I have hereunto set my hand and caused the seal of the United States to be affixed.

Done at the City of Washington this seventeenth day of March, in the year of our Lord one thousand eight hundred and [L.S.]   sixty-five, and of the Independence of the United States the eighty-ninth.   ABRAHAM LINCOLN

By the President:

WILLIAM H SEWARD Secretary of State.

¹ DS, DNA FS RG 11, Proclamations.

To William H. Seward¹

Submitted to Sec. of State to be considered, if & when vacancy occurs.   A. LINCOLN

March 17. 1865

¹ AES, DNA FS RG 59, Appointments, Box 343. Lincoln's endorsement appears on a letter of Calvin S. Mattoon, Department of Interior, to Robert C. Schenck, March 15, 1865, forwarding recommendations for "my appointment as Consul at Honolulu. . . ." Schenck endorsed in recommendation of the appointment. No record of Mattoon's appointment has been found.

Speech to One Hundred Fortieth Indiana Regiment¹

March 17, 1865

[Autograph Draft]

FELLOW CITIZENS. A few words only. I was born in Kentucky, raised in Indiana, reside in Illinois, and now here, it is my duty to care equally for the good people of all the States. I am to-day glad of seeing it in the power of an Indianana regiment to present this captured flag to the good governor of their State. And yet I would not wish to compliment Indiana above other states, remembering that all have done so well. There are but few aspects of this great war on which I have not already expressed my views by speaking or writing. There is one—the recent effort of our erring bretheren, sometimes so-called, to employ the slaves in their armies. The great question with them has been; "will the negro fight for them?" They ought to know better than we; and, doubtless, do know better than we. I may incidentally remark, however, that having, in my life, heard many arguments,—or strings of words meant to pass for arguments,—intended to show that the negro ought to be a slave, that if he shall now really fight to keep himself a slave, it will be a far better argument why [he] should remain a slave than I have ever before heard. He, perhaps, ought to be a slave, if he desires it ardently enough to fight for it. Or, if one out of four will, for his own freedom, fight to keep the other three in slavery, he ought to be a slave for his selfish meanness. I have always thought that all men should be free; but if any should be slaves it should be first those who desire it for *themselves*, and secondly those who *desire* it for *others*. Whenever [I] hear any one,[2] arguing for slavery I feel a strong impulse to see it tried on him personally.

There is one thing about the negroes fighting for the rebels which we can know as well [as] they can; and that is that they can not, at [the] same time fight in their armies, and stay at home and make bread for them. And this being known and remembered we can have but little concern whether they become soldiers or not. I am rather in favor of the measure; and would at any time if I could, have loaned them a vote to carry it. We have to reach the bottom of the insurgent resources; and that they employ, or seriously think of employing, the slaves as soldiers, gives us glimpses of the bottom. Therefore I am glad of what we learn on this subject.

[Newspaper Version]

FELLOW CITIZENS—It will be but a very few words that I shall undertake to say. I was born in Kentucky, raised in Indiana and lived in Illinois. (Laughter.) And now I am here, where it is my business to care equally for the good people of all the States. I am glad to see an Indiana regiment on this day able to present the captured flag to the Governor of Indiana. (Applause.) I am not disposed, in saying this, to make a distinction between the States, for all have done equally well. (Applause.) There are but few views or aspects of this great war upon which I have not said or written something whereby my own opinions might be known. But there is one—the recent attempt of our erring brethren, as they are sometimes called—(laughter)—to employ the negro to fight for them. I have neither written nor made a speech on that subject, because that was their business, not mine; and if I had a wish upon the subject I had not the power to introduce it, or make it effective. The great question with them was, whether the negro, being put into the army, would fight for them. I do not know, and therefore cannot decide. (Laughter.) They ought to know better than we. I have in my lifetime heard many arguments why the negroes ought to be slaves; but if they fight for those who would keep them in slavery it will be a better argument than any I have yet heard.

(Laughter and applause.) He who will fight for that ought to be a slave. (Applause.) They have concluded at last to take one out of four of the slaves, and put them in the army; and that one out of the four who will fight to keep the others in slavery ought to be a slave himself unless he is killed in a fight. (Applause.) While I have often said that all men ought to be free, yet I would allow those colored persons to be slaves who want to be; and next to them those white persons who argue in favor of making other people slaves. (Applause.) I am in favor of giving an opportunity to such white men to try it on for themselves. (Applause.) I will say one thing in regard to the negro being employed to fight for them. I do know he cannot fight and stay at home and make bread too— (laughter and applause)—and as one is about as important as the other to them, I don't care which they do. (Renewed applause.) I am rather in favor of[3] having them try them as soldiers. (Applause.) They lack one vote of doing that, and I wish I could send my vote over the river so that I might cast it in favor of allowing the negro to fight. (Applause.) But they cannot fight and work both. We must now see the bottom of the enemy's resources. They will stand out as long as they can, and if the negro will fight for them, they must allow him to fight. They have drawn upon their last branch of resources. (Applause.) And we can now see the bottom. (Applause.) I am glad to see the end so near at hand. (Applause.) I have said now more than I intended, and will therefore bid you goodby.

[1] AD, DLC-Nicolay Papers. Since the newspaper report of this speech differs widely from the manuscript, both versions are reproduced. The newspaper version is primarily from the New York *Herald*, March 18, 1865, with a variant as noted from the New York *Tribune* of the same date.

[2] Lincoln had written "even a preacher," but deleted it.

[3] *Tribune* reads "of allowing them to try."

To Edwin M. Stanton[1]

Hon. Secretary of War.   Executive Mansion,
Dear Sir: Washington D C Mch 17th. 1865

I have long thought Col. Lewis B. Parsons ought to be promoted, and intended it should have been sooner done. His long service and the uniform testimony to the ability with which he has discharged his very responsible and extended duties render it but just and proper his services should be acknowledged, and more especially so since his great success in executing your orders for the recent movement of Troops from the West.

You will therefore at once promote Col. Parsons to the rank of a Brigadier General, if there is a vacancy which can be given to the Quarter-Master's Department,[2] and if not, you will so promote him when the first vacancy occurs. Yours Truly   A. LINCOLN

[1] LS, IHi. See Lincoln to Stanton, March 9, *supra.* Preserved with Lincoln's letter is a copy of Lewis B. Parsons' letter to Lincoln, also dated March 17: "I regret to annoy you. I would not do so but for your long and decidedly expressed opinion that I am well entitled to all that is asked an opinion for nearly two years fully endorsed by Gen [Robert] Allen and Gen Meigs, no less than by all conversant with the facts. There are 12 Brigadiers from my Dept—all but one from the Regular army. Is this just? I can not comprehend it. My only hope is in your order. It will be positive and *I trust your influence with this administration may be equal to the occasion.*"
[2] "Which can be given to the Quarter-Master's Department," inserted by Lincoln.

To John P. Usher[1]

Let the appointment be made.   A. LINCOLN
March 17. 1865.

[1] AES, owned by Emily Brown, Burbank, California. Lincoln's endorsement appears on a letter from Representative William Windom, March 15, 1865, enclosing the resignation of Abner Tibbetts as register of the land office at St. Peter, Minnesota, and requesting that Charles T. Brown be appointed to the office. James Harlan endorsed in concurrence, but Henry A. Swift received the appointment as listed in the U.S. *Official Register,* 1865.

To Edward R. S. Canby[1]

March 18, 1865
Gen. Canby is authorized, but not ordered, to give Rev. Mr. Teasdale such facilities in the within matters, as he, in his discretion, may see fit.   A. LINCOLN.
March 18, 1865.

[1] Thomas C. Teasdale, *Reminiscences and Incidents of a Long Life* (St. Louis, 1891), pp. 202-203. Reverend Teasdale was a Baptist minister formerly in Springfield, Illinois, who was seeking to raise funds for the Orphans' Home of the State of Mississippi. See the pass for Teasdale, *infra.*

Endorsement Concerning Charles T. Dorsett[1]

March 18, 1865
Mr. Dorset, the father, says he already has two substitutes in the army, that he yet has three unmarried sons subject to draft, who

will not shrink, and that he has still another son a prisoner among the rebels. He asks that this married son, now drafted, may be discharged. Let it be done.   A. LINCOLN

March 18, 1865

¹ Thomas F. Madigan, *A Catalogue of Lincolniana* (1929), p. 34. According to the source, this autograph endorsement appears on the back of a two-page letter. AGO *Special Orders No. 133*, March 18, 1865, directed the discharge of "Private Charles T. Dorsett, a drafted man from the District of Columbia, now supposed to be at the Headquarters of that District . . . upon the receipt of this Order. . . ."

Order Annulling Sentence of Benjamin G. and Franklin W. Smith[1]

March 18, 1865

I am unwilling for the sentence to stand and be executed, to any extent in this case. In the absence of a more adequate motive than the evidence discloses, I am wholly unable to believe in the existence of criminal or fraudulent intent on the part of one of such well established good character as is the accused. If the evidence went as far toward establishing a guilty profit of one or two hundred thousand dollars, as it does of one or two hundred dollars, the case would, on the question of guilt, bear a far different aspect. That on this contract, involving from one million to twelve hundred thousand dollars, the contractors should attempt a fraud which at the most could profit them only one or two hundred, or even one thousand dollars, is to my mind beyond the power of rational belief. That they did not, in such a case, strike for greater gains proves that they did not, with guilty, or fraudulent intent, strike at all. The judgment and sentence are disapproved, and declared null, and the accused ordered to be discharged.

March 18. 1865   A. LINCOLN

¹ ADS-F, Franklin W. Smith, *The Conspiracy in the U.S. Navy Department.* . . . (1890), p. 56; ADf, DLC-RTL. The order as printed here was considerably revised from the wording in the autograph draft. See Lincoln to Welles, January 26, *supra.* Franklin W. Smith's account of the injustice of his trial and Senator Charles Sumner's account (Edward L. Pierce, *Memoir and Letters of Charles Sumner*, IV, 232-33) give one side of this case. Gideon Welles' *Diary*, March 18, 1865, and *passim*, gives the other.

Order Concerning George Burr[1]

At the request of Hon. Mr. Hotchkiss & upon his representation the order of dismissal in this case is revoked   A. LINCOLN

March 18. 1865.

[1] AES, owned by Milton H. Shutes, Oakland, California. Lincoln's endorsement appears on a letter from Dr. George Burr, January 29, 1865, who had been dismissed from the army as surgeon on November 18, 1862. Giles W. Hotchkiss was U.S. representative from Binghamton, New York.

Pass for Thomas C. Teasdale[1]

Pass the Rev. Thomas Teasdale through our lines going South, with convenient baggage.   A. LINCOLN
    March 18, 1865

[1] Thomas C. Teasdale, *Reminiscences and Incidents of a Long Life*, pp. 201-202. See Lincoln to Canby, *supra*.

To John Pope[1]

Major General Pope   Executive Mansion,
St. Louis, Mo.   Washington, March 19, 1865
    Understanding that the plan of action for Missouri, contained in your letter to the Governor of that State, and your other letter to me, is concurred in by the Governor, it is approved by me, and you will be sustained in proceeding upon it.   A. LINCOLN

[1] ALS, DNA WR RG 107, Presidential Telegrams, I, 373. On March 2, Governor Thomas C. Fletcher had written Pope for his views as to "the best uses of the military forces in this Department, and their relation to the present and prospective condition of this State." (DLC-RTL). Pope's lengthy reply of March 3 may be found in OR, I, XLVIII, I, 1070-77. In substance it sets forth that the civil authority should recognize its responsibilities and perform its duties.

On March 8, Pope had written Lincoln:
"I . . . transmit . . . a printed copy [clipping from the *Missouri Republican*, March 8, 1865] of a letter addressed by me to the Governor of Missouri. . . .

"In addition to what is set forth in the letter . . . I . . . submit for your consideration a few . . . suggestions, which it was perhaps well not to make public in my letter to Gov. Fletcher. I ask your consideration of these suggestions and of those contained in the printed letter, and if they meet your approval I . . . request that I may be so notified. . . .

"It is . . . desirable that . . . the General Government be relieved from all concern in the civil affairs of the State, and be required only to defend it against armed invasion. So long as United States troops remain in Missouri . . . they will be a constant source of embarassment and a difficult obstacle to the renewal of civil administration. . . . So long as the troops remain and . . . Martial Law obtains the people will feel a constant desire to appeal from the State Executive and the Civil laws, to the Military Authorities and to the General Government; and no step will be taken toward a resumption of local civil administration. . . . Remove that source of difficulty, and they will soon learn, that they must depend upon themselves and their state government, as their final resort for justice.

"I do not propose to change the present condition of the military suddenly, but . . . cautiously and gradually, as follows.

"The term of the Missouri State Militia . . . paid by the General Government and . . . under officers of the United States is about to expire. . . . Under no circumstances should these troops be reorganized or employed in the same manner. . . . No authority should be given to raise troops for service in Missouri. If these recommendations be adopted, we shall be left . . . within a few months, with nothing but a few regiments of Volunteers from other States. These . . . I will push down to the Southern border of the State. . . .

"In many counties . . . the civil courts are in full operation. In those . . . I propose to suspend Martial law, not by any public order, but simply by private instructions to commanding officers to withdraw their Provost Marshals and to refrain . . . from any interference with citizens. . . . Slowly, county by county, the military forces of the United States can thus be withdrawn from all connection with the . . . civil affairs of the State. If troops or Martial Law are afterwards required . . . let the Governor take the responsibility of declaring Martial Law and enforcing it by his State Militia. . . .

"There is a loyal State executive and civil officers and a large loyal majority in the State and I cannot see why it is not abundantly able to settle all controversies between its own citizens, without referring them to the Administration at Washington. . . ." (DLC-RTL).

To Edwin M. Stanton[1]

Hon. Sec. of War, please, see & hear Hon. H. P. H. Bromwell, one of our new Union M.Cs from Illinois.   A. LINCOLN
March 19, 1865

[1] ALS, DLC-Bromwell Papers. Henry P. H. Bromwell was U.S. representative from Charleston, Illinois.

Endorsement Concerning Nathaniel P. Banks[1]

Gen. Banks remained in Washington from some time last autumn, until this date by my consent and direction.   A. LINCOLN
March 20, 1865

[1] AES, IHi. Lincoln's endorsement appears on the back of original manuscript copy of AGO *Special Orders No. 132*, March 18, 1865, directing that "Major General N. P. Banks, US Volunteers, will repair to New Orleans, and resume command of the Department of the Gulf."

Endorsement Concerning William D. Briggs[1]

March 20, 1865

This boy is pardoned for any desertion from the land service heretofore committed upon condition of faithfully serving out his term in the Naval service   A. LINCOLN
March 20, 1865

[1] AES, IHi. Lincoln's endorsement appears on a letter of John R. Briggs, Jr., assistant clerk of the House of Representatives, to Senator James Harlan, March 14, 1865, asking his influence to obtain a pardon for his son William D.

Briggs, who had deserted from Company M, Second Illinois Light Artillery, and enlisted in the Navy in March, 1864. Lincoln's pardon was promulgated in AGO *Special Orders No. 156*, April 1, 1865.

To Ulysses S. Grant[1]

"*Cypher*" Office U.S. Military Telegraph,
Lieut. Genl. Grant War Department,
City-Point, Va. Washington, D.C., March 20 1865

Your kind invitation received. Had already thought of going immediately after the next rain. Will go sooner if any reason for it. Mrs. L. and a few others will probably accompany me. Will notify you of exact time, once it shall be fixed upon.

A. LINCOLN

[1] ALS, DNA WR RG 107, Presidential Telegrams, I, 375. Grant telegraphed Lincoln at 10 A.M. on March 20: "Can you not visit City Point for a day or two? I would like very much to see you and I think the rest would do you good" (DLC-RTL).

To Mrs. Amanda H. Hall[1]

Mrs. Amanda H. Hall Executive Mansion,
Madam Washington, March 20. 1865.

Induced by a letter of yours to your brother, and shown me by him, I send you what follows below. Respectfully

A. LINCOLN

"Fondly do we hope—fervently do we pray—that this mighty scourge of war may speedily pass away. Yet, if God wills that it continue until all the wealth piled by the bondman's two hundred and fifty years of unrequited toil shall be sunk, and until every drop of blood drawn with the lash shall be paid by another drawn with the sword, as was said three thousand years ago, so still it must be said:

"The judgments of the Lord are true, and righteous altogether."

ABRAHAM LINCOLN

[1] ALS-F, ISLA. Numerous facsimiles of this letter have been supposed by their owners to be the original autograph manuscript written by Lincoln because they were printed many years ago and have the appearance of genuine manuscripts. The editors have not been able to certify the present location or ownership of the original letter, but there seems to be no doubt that the facsimiles were made from a genuine letter. Mrs. Amanda H. Hall was the daughter of Reverend William M. Ferry, an early settler of Ottawa County, Michigan. Her husband was Henry C. Hall of Ashfield, Massachusetts. Her brother was Representative Thomas W. Ferry of Michigan. See William M. Ferry, "Ottawa's Old Settlers," *Michigan Pioneer and Historical Collections*, XXX (1905), 572-73.

To Joseph Holt[1]

Will the Judge Advocate General please procure proper record and papers & report on the case as soon as practicable?

March 20. 1865   A. LINCOLN

[1] AES, DNA WR RG 153, Judge Advocate General, LL 3189. Lincoln's endorsement appears in the court-martial file of Sergeant Omar L. Rosenkrans, Twenty-eighth Independent Battery, New York Volunteers, sentenced for desertion to imprisonment at hard labor for two years. No further action by Lincoln has been found.

To Edward O. C. Ord[1]

Major General Ord   Executive Mansion,
Army of the James.   Washington, May [March] 20. 1865.

Is it true that George W. Lane is detained at Norfolk without any charge against him? And if so, why is it done?

A. LINCOLN

[1] ALS, DNA WR RG 107, Presidential Telegrams, I, 376. Lincoln plainly misdated this telegram "May 20." General Ord replied on March 21: "It is not true that Geo W Lane is detained at Norfolk without any charges against him Charges of a very serious nature are before the Secy of War against Lane of which [one] is that he made use of your name to cover flagrant violations of law thereby betraying the confidence bestowed in him &c &c" (DLC-RTL).

George W. Lane of Baltimore had procured a permit to bring out cotton from the Chowan River in North Carolina. His cargo and ship were seized at Norfolk, Virginia, where he was imprisoned by order of a military commission (*Private and Official Correspondence of Benjamin F. Butler*, V, 550, 577). See further, Lincoln to Gordon, April 11, *infra*.

Order Concerning Peter Lake[1]

Executive Mansion
Washington, Mar. 20, 1865

Hon. Thomas T. Davis, now present, asks that Peter Lake, now a prisoner of War at Elmira, N.Y, may be discharged on taking the oath of Dec. 8, 1863. Let it be done.   A. LINCOLN

[1] Copy, ISLA.

To James Speed[1]

Executive Mansion,
Hon. Attorney General   Washington, March 20. 1865.

Let Hewett, Wyche & Oliphant, be reappointed as Judges in Washington Territory. Yours truly   A. LINCOLN

[1] ALS, DNA RG 60, Papers of Attorney General, 1865, Box 124. C. C. Hewitt, James E. Wyche, and Ethelbert P. Oliphant were duly reappointed, but Oliphant resigned before the Senate confirmed his appointment.

To James Speed[1]

Attorney General please report on this case, with reference to a pardon, with as little delay as possible   A. LINCOLN

   March 20. 1865

[1] AES, DNA RG 204, U.S. Pardon Attorney, A 467. Lincoln's endorsement appears on the jacket of a copy of the record in "The United States vs. James S. Williams, Minutes of Examination January, 1860." Williams had been convicted of taking a letter from the post office. No report has been found.

To Thomas Swann[1]

Gov. Swann.   Executive Mansion
Baltimore, Md.   Washington, March 20. 1865

   I wish you would find Cresswell and bring him with you and see me to-morrow.   A. LINCOLN

[1] ALS, DNA WR RG 107, Presidential Telegrams, I, 374. Governor Swann replied on the same day: "Have sent for Mr Cresswell Will telegraph again as soon as I hear from him & will see you as requested" (DLC-RTL). John A. J. Cresswell had been elected to the Senate to fill the vacancy left by death of Senator Thomas H. Hicks on February 14, 1865. See the memorandum concerning Maryland appointments, March 9, *supra*.

To Robert T. Lincoln[1]

Cipher   Office U.S. Military Telegraph,
Capt. R. T. Lincoln   War Department,
City-Point, Va   Washington, D.C., March 21 1865

   We now think of starting to you about One P.M. Thursday. Dont make public.   A. LINCOLN

[1] ALS, DNA WR RG 107, Presidential Telegrams, I, 378. See Lincoln to Grant, March 20, *supra*, and March 23, *infra*.

Memorandum[1]

I met my friend Benton at the door. I can do no better than I have already said. It is useless for him to importune me.

   March 21 1865   A. LINCOLN

[1] Copy, ISLA. Benton has not been identified.

To Walter B. Scates[1]

Hon. Walter B. Scates   Executive Mansion
Centralia, Ills.   Washington, March 21. 1865

   If you choose to go to New-Mexico, and reside, I will appoint you Chief Justice there. What say you? Please answer.

                      A. LINCOLN

¹ ALS, DNA WR RG 107, Presidential Telegrams, I, 377. Walter B. Scates telegraphed from Cincinnati, Ohio, on March 25: "Most respectfully declined reason by letter" (DLC-RTL). Scates' letter of March 25, 1865, was referred to James Speed by John Hay on April 11 (DNA RG 60, Papers of Attorney General, Appointments, New Mexico, Box 660). Scates had been chief justice of the Illinois Supreme Court (1853-1857).

To James Speed¹

Pardon, for unexecuted part of sentence.   A. LINCOLN
    March 21. 1865

¹ AES, DNA RG 204, U.S. Pardon Attorney, B 5. Lincoln's endorsement appears on a letter of "R. Barrette," Syracuse, New York, to Representative Thomas T. Davis, February 20, 1865, reminding him of a petition for pardon. Davis endorsed: "Robert Barnett [*sic*] was convicted . . . for two years for discouraging enlistments. . . . I respectfully ask for his release. . . ."

To John P. Usher¹

File. Appt. made   A. L
    March 21, 1865

¹ AES, DNA NR RG 48, Department of Interior, Appointments, Indian Agencies, Box 74. Lincoln's endorsement appears on a letter from Usher, March 18, 1865, enclosing a commission for reappointment of Saint A. D. Balcombe of Minnesota as agent of the Winnebago Indians in Minnesota. The *U.S. Official Register*, 1865, lists Charles Mathewson of Connecticut as agent of the Winnebago Indians.

Endorsement Concerning James M. Campbell¹

On the representation of Vice-President Johnson, it is ordered that special pardon be made out in this case.   A. LINCOLN
    March 22. 1865

¹ AES, CSmH. Lincoln's endorsement appears on a letter to Andrew Johnson from James Britton, Knoxville, Tennessee, March 2, 1865, enclosing an application for special pardon of James M. Campbell of Green County, Tennessee.

To Winfield S. Hancock¹

                                        Office U.S. Military Telegraph,
Major Gen. Hancock,   War Department,
Winchester, Va.   Washington, D.C., March 22. 1865.
    Seeing your despatch about Gen. Crook, and fearing that, through misapprehension, something unpleasant may occur, I send you below two despatches of Gen. Grant, which I suppose will fully explain Gen. Crook's movements.   A. LINCOLN

[370]

1 ALS, DNA WR RG 107, Presidential Telegrams, I, 379. Major General George Crook had been in command of the Department of West Virginia when he was captured at Cumberland on February 21, 1865. On March 20, Edward D. Townsend notified Crook: "Your exchange has been effected. The general-in-chief directs that you immediately return to command of your department. . . ." (OR, I, XLVI, III, 59). On March 21, Major General Winfield S. Hancock telegraphed Halleck: "I learn to-night . . . that Major-General Crook has assumed command of the Department of West Virginia, with headquarters at Cumberland. The headquarters of the department are at this place, and I am in command by the assignment of the President. I have no other official knowledge of General Crook's being in this division. I have ordered him, if he has assumed command, to replace matters as he found them, and report at Frederick, Md., in arrest, and will prefer charges against him as soon as practicable." (Ibid., p. 69).

Townsend replied to Hancock on the same day: "The Secretary of War directs that Maj. Gen. George Crook be immediately relieved from command of the Department of the Cumberland and ordered to report in person without delay to Lieutenant-General Grant for assignment to a command. . . ." (Ibid.).

Crook relinquished command on March 22, and Hancock ordered him in obedience to orders from the Secretary of War to report to Grant (ibid., p. 85).

The two telegrams from Grant which Lincoln forwarded to Hancock as indicated above were: (1) to Townsend, March 18: "Please notify General Crook that his exchange has been effected, and order him back to his department. As soon as he goes on duty I will have him relieved and ordered at once to command the cavalry of the Army of the Potomac" (ibid., p. 28); and (2) to Stanton, March 21: "I would recommend relieving Crook from command of his department and ordering him to command the cavalry of the Army of the Potomac. . . ." (Ibid., p. 61).

Hancock's reply to Lincoln's telegrams was received at 11:20 A.M. on March 22: "There can be no trouble in Genl Crooks' case if he has observed my order to restore matters as he found them and to proceed to Frederick in arrest. Where my order suspending his arrest, and ordering him to report to Lt Genl Grant will reach him. According to just military principle I could pursue no other course, & there will be no delay on my part in the execution of the order of the Department to send General Crook to City Point" (DLC-RTL).

Memorandum
Concerning the Duchess of Argyll[1]

Executive Mansion,
Washington, March 22, 1865.

Senator Sumner shows me a letter from the Dutchess of Argyle, of date, March 2. 1865, from which I extract the following.

"I do not know what your opinion is as to giving the Franchise to the negroes of the Slave States. One wd. be inclined to think that that [sic] there ought to be some realization first of their new condition.

We feel great confidence in the President. It is sad to hear of the Abolition party so much divided since his nomination

Has Goldwin Smith made you understand more than you did, the mist before the eyes of Englishmen? I like his Article in McMil-

lan on the Prest. and think the speech at the Gettysburg Cemetery
must live." A. LINCOLN

[1] ADS, DLC-RTL. Concerning the letter of Elizabeth Georgiana Granville, Duchess of Argyll, see Pierce, *Memoir and Letters of Charles Sumner*, IV, 241.

To Grenville M. Dodge[1]

Executive Mansion,
Washington, Mch 23. 1865.

Allow Mrs. R S Ewell the benefit of my amnesty proclamation on
her taking the oath A. LINCOLN

Genl Dodge
Comg &c St Louis Mo

[1] LS, DNA WR RG 107, Presidential Telegrams, I, 380. The sequel to this telegram is interesting. On April 21, Stanton telegraphed General George H. Thomas at Nashville: "You are directed to arrest Mrs. General [Richard S.] Ewell, who is reported to be in Nashville and cause her to be removed immediately to Saint Louis, and enjoined to remain there until further orders." (OR, II, VIII, 507).

General Thomas replied on April 23: "Mrs. R. S. Ewell has just reported to me . . . that being permitted by the President to take the amnesty oath, on the 23d of March she appeared before Lieut. George H. Richardson, assistant provost-marshal-general . . . at Saint Louis, and subscribed to the oath; and believing she had under that amnesty the right to come to this place quietly and attend to . . . her private affairs, she left Saint Louis on the 31st of March, and came for that purpose. . . . Since taking the oath . . . she claims to have conducted herself as . . . a loyal citizen . . . and also as a woman under personal obligations to Mr. Lincoln, and therefore that she had the right to return to Saint Louis without military surveillance. . . . I respectfully recommend that she be permitted to remain in Nashville until next Saturday . . . and then be permitted to return . . . free from military surveillance en route." (*Ibid.*).

To this Stanton gave an immediate reply: "You will please execute the order heretofore given in reference to Mrs. General Ewell, without regard to her representations and without unnecessary delay. . . ." (*Ibid.*).

To Ulysses S. Grant[1]

Cipher Executive Mansion,
Lieut. Gen. Grant Washington,
City-Point, Va. March 23, 1865

We start to you at One P.M. to-day. May lie over during the dark
hours of the night. Very small party of us. A. LINCOLN

[1] ALS, DNA WR RG 107, Presidential Telegrams, I, 381. *"Cipher"* is in the handwriting of the telegrapher. See Lincoln's telegrams to Grant, March 20, and to Robert T. Lincoln, March 21, *supra*. Lincoln was accompanied by Mrs. Lincoln and her maid, his son "Tad," the bodyguard William H. Crook, and Captain Charles B. Penrose who had been detailed by Stanton to accompany the president. The party were on the *River Queen*, accompanied by the *Bat*, the lat-

ter having been intended as Lincoln's conveyance until it was learned that Mrs. Lincoln intended to accompany him.

Stanton telegraphed Lincoln on March 23: "I reached the Arsenal with Mrs. Stanton to see you depart a few minutes after you had got under way. I hope you have reached Point Lookout safely not-withstanding the furious gale that came on soon after you started. . . . No news from any Quarter has come in today. . . . Please let me hear from you at Point Lookout and how you and Mrs. Lincoln stand the voyage" (DLC-RTL).

Upon arrival at City Point, Captain Penrose telegraphed Stanton (received 12:30 P.M. on March 24): "The President desires me to say he has just arrived at this point safely, and is now feeling well, having had a pretty fair passage. Your telegram he received" (OR, I, XLVI, III, 96).

To William L. James[1]

March 24, 1865

I am not at all impatient, and hope Major James will not reproach himself or deal harshly with the officer having the matter in charge. Doubtless he, too, has met some unexpected difficulty.

March 24, 1865.   A. LINCOLN.

[1] *Store Chat*, February, 1931. According to the source, Lincoln's endorsement appears on the back of a letter from Major William L. James, acting quartermaster at Fort Monroe, March 24, 1865: "I am exceedingly mortified at the delay which you have experienced in obtaining the water you desire. I have sent several messengers already to the officer to make all possible haste, and that he should have delayed so is exceedingly annoying to me. I shall certainly call him to account for his bad management."

Lincoln had an upset stomach, which he attributed to the drinking water on the *River Queen*.

To Edwin M. Stanton[1]

Hon. Sec. of War.   City Point, Va.
Washington, D.C.   March 25, 1865. 8/30 A.M.

Arrived here, all safe about 9 P.M. yesterday. No war news. Gen. Grant does not seem to know very much about Yeatman, but thinks very well of him so far as he does know.

I like Mr. Whiting very much, and hence would wish him to remain or resign as best suits himself. Hearing this much from me, do as you think best in the matter. Gen. Lee has sent the Russell letter back, concluding, as I understand from Grant, that their dignity does not admit of their receiving the document from us. Robert just now tells me there was a little rumpus up the line this morning, ending about where it began.   A. LINCOLN

[1] ALS, DLC-Stanton Papers. Stanton had telegraphed Lincoln on March 24: "I was glad to hear your safe arrival at Fortress Monroe and hope that by this time you and Mrs Lincoln have reached General Grants Head Quarters in

health and comfort. Nothing new has transpired here. Your tormentors have taken wings and departed. Mr [William] Whiting Solicitor of this Department has tendered his resignation which with your permission I will accept. From absence and ill health he has been of no service for many months. What does General Grant say about Mr [James E.] Yeatman?

"The weather here is cold windy and very disagreeable so that I think you went to the sunny south in good time. I would be glad to receive a telegram from you dated at Richmond before you return. Compliments to Mrs Lincoln." (DLC-RTL).

The office of solicitor for the War Department remained vacant for some time after William Whiting's resignation. James E. Yeatman was under consideration for appointment as head of the Freedmen's Bureau, which had been reorganized under an act approved on March 3, 1865. Yeatman declined the appointment according to the *Dictionary of American Biography*.

Concerning Earl John Russell's communication to the Confederate States, General Robert E. Lee wrote Confederate Secretary of War John C. Breckinridge on March 16, 1865:

"I have received the papers recently forwarded by me, with the instructions to return them to General Grant. . . . At the time General Grant sent the papers to me I only acknowledged the receipt of them without saying what disposition I would make of them. I hoped that this would render it unnecessary to take any further notice of the matter, but as it is deemed proper to reply, and the fact that the communication of Earl Russell was forwarded at his request may render a reply necessary, I beg leave . . . to suggest that the refusal of the Government to hold intercourse with neutral nations through the medium selected by Lord Russell, would seem to be sufficient for all purposes.

"The addition of a doubt as to the authenticity of the document would seem to be unnecessary after such a general refusal to receive any communication through the channel selected, and may weaken the force of that refusal, by leading to the inference that a duly authenticated paper would be received, if forwarded in the objectionable manner, through the hands and under the inspection of the enemy. . . ." (OR, I, XLVI, III, 1315-16).

To Edwin M. Stanton[1]

Hon. Sec. of War.   Meade's Hd. Qrs.
Washington D C.   March 25. 1/25. 1865

I am here within five miles of the scene of this morning's action. I have nothing to add to what Gen. Meade reports, except that I have seen the prisoners myself and they look like there might be the number he states—1600.   A LINCOLN

[1] ALS, CtY-Webb Papers. Stanton replied to Lincoln's telegram at 8:30 P.M.

"Your telegram and Genl. Parkes report of the 'Scrimmage' this morning are received. The rebel rooster looks a little the worse as he could not hold the fence.

"We have nothing new here; now you are away everything is quiet and the tormentors vanished. I hope you will remember Gen. Harrison's advice to his men at Tippecanoe, that they 'can see as well a little further off.' " (DLC-RTL).

General John G. Parke's telegram is as follows: "The enemy attacked my front this morning at about 4.30 with three divisions under command of General [John B.] Gordon. By a sudden rush they seized the line . . . to the right of Fort Stedman, wheeled, and . . . took possession of the fort. . . . Our troops on either flank stood firm . . . the enemy were driven out of the fort, with the loss of a number of prisoners, estimated at about 1,600. . . ." (OR, I, XLVI, III, 109).

To Edwin M. Stanton[1]

Hon. Sec. of War.   City Point, Va
Washington D.C   March 26. 1865. 9. A.M

I approve your Fort-Sumpter programme. Grant dont seem to know Yeatman very well, but thinks very well of him so far as he knows—thinks it probable that Y. is best man for the place. I told you this yesterday, as well as that you should do as you think best about Mr. Whiting's resignation, but I suppose you did not receive the despatch. I am on the boat, and have no later war news than went to you last-night.   A. LINCOLN

[1] ALS, CSmH. Stanton had telegraphed Lincoln on March 25: "I have invited Henry Ward Beecher to deliver an address on raising the flag upon Fort Sumter and will give directions to Genl Gilmore to make all suitable military arrangements for the occasion and fire a salute of five hundred Guns. The flag will be raised by Genl Anderson. Please let me know if these arrangements have your approval. What does Genl Grant say about Yeatman? I congratulate you and Genl Grant on the operations of today" (DLC-RTL).

His reply to Lincoln's telegram was received at 1:45 P.M.: "Your telegram of this day received we have no news but what comes from you & Gen Grant. Yeatman is not hurt no application has been made by him on his behalf he was suggested by General Halleck and had two (2) or three times occurred to me . . . . the weather here is very cold windy & disagreeable Your military news warms the blood or we would be in danger of a march chill." (*Ibid.*).

To Edwin M. Stanton[1]

Hon. Sec. of War.   City Point, Va.
Washington, D.C.   March 27. 1865. 3/35. PM.

Yours inclosing Fort-Sumpter order received. I think of but one suggestion. I feel quite confident that Sumpter fell on the thirteenth (13th.) and not on the fourteenth (14th.) of April as you have it. It fell on Saturday the 13th.—the first call for troops on our part was got up on Sunday the 14th. and given date, and issued on Monday the 15th. Look up the old Almanac & other data and see if I am not right.   A. LINCOLN

[1] ALS-P, ISLA. Stanton telegraphed Lincoln on March 27:
"Every thing goes on smoothly here. We have no news from any quarter except what comes from Gen Grant. I send you a copy of the official order [*General Orders No. 50*] in relation to fort Sumter

" 'Ordered first. That at the hour of noon on the 14th day of April 1865 Brevet Maj Gen [Robert] Anderson will raise & plant upon the ruins of Fort Sumter in Charleston harbor the same United States flag which floated over the Battlements of that fort during the rebel assault & which was lowered & saluted by him and the small force of his command, when the works were evacuated on the 14th day of April 1861. Second. That the flag when raised be saluted by one hundred guns from fort Sumter & by a National salute from every fort & rebel battery that fired upon fort Sumter. Third. That suitable ceremonies be had upon the occasion under the direction of Maj. Gen Wm. T. Sherman whose military operations compelled the Rebels to evacuate Charleston, or in his absence under the charge of Maj Gen Q. A. Gillmore Comdg the Dept. Among the ceremonies will be the delivery of a public address by the Rev H. W. Beecher. Fourth. That the naval forces at Charleston & their commander on that station be invited to participate in the ceremonies of the occasion

" 'By order of The Pres't. of the U.S.

" 'EDWIN M STANTON

" 'Sec of War' " (DLC-RTL).

Stanton's reply to Lincoln's telegram was received at 6:30 P.M.: "My own impression agreed with yours that the surrender of Fort Sumter was on the 13th of April. But the official report of Maj Anderson to the Sec of War states that he 'marched out of the fort on sunday afternoon the 14th inst with colors flying and Drums beating bringing away private property and saluting my flag with fifty guns' The attack was made on the 12th at 4.30 continued the next day & during the afternoon of the 13th The surrender was agreed upon but the evacuation actually took place on the afternoon of sunday the fourteenth 14 It may be a question of what time should be selected to raise the old flag. I should be glad to have your views. I had contemplated the time of actual evacuation on the 14th. Please let me know which you deem most proper the 13th or 14th" (*ibid.*).

To Edwin M. Stanton[1]

Hon. Sec. of War.   City-Point, Va
Washington D.C.   March 28. 1865. 12. M.

After your explanation, I think it is little or no difference whether the Fort-Sumpter ceremony takes place on the 13th. or 14th.

Gen. Sherman tells me he is well acquainted with James Yeatman, & that he thinks him almost the best man in the country for anything he will undertake.   A. LINCOLN

[1] ALS-P, ISLA. General William T. Sherman arrived at City Point on March 27, 1865, to confer with Grant.

To Ulysses S. Grant[1]

U.S. Military Telegraph.
Gen. Grant.   City Point, March 29, 1865

Your three despatches received. From what direction did the enemy come that attacked Griffin? How do things look now?

A LINCOLN

[1] ALS, ORB. Grant's first telegram is as follows: "Just arrived here 11 15 A.M. Nothing heard of from the front yet. No firing. I start in a few minutes. Sheridan got off at 3 this morning" (DLC-RTL).

The second telegram was sent from "Gravelly Run": "The 2d Corps are in the position designated for them for today No oposition has yet been met but a few pickets & scouts have been picked up Nothing heard from Sheridan yet

[Gouverneur K.] Warren must now be in the place laid down for him in orders I will remain here until morning if nothing transpires" (*ibid.*).

The third from "Gravelley Creek," was received at 5:10 P.M.: "The enemy attacked [Charles] Griffin Div 5 AC near where the Quaker road intersects the Boydtown road about 4 P.M. The enemy were repulsed leaving about 60 prisoners in our hands There was some loss of life on both sides" (*ibid.*).

Grant's reply to Lincoln's telegram was received at 9 P.M.: "Griffin was attacked near where the Quaker road intersects the Boydtown Plank—at 5.50 P.M. Warren reports the fighting pretty severe but the enemy repulsed leaving one hundred prisoners in our hands. Warren advanced to attack at the hour named but found the enemy gone He thinks inside of his main works. Warren's Pickets on his left along Boydtown Plank road reported the enemys cavalry moving rapidly Northward & they thought, Sheridan after them. Sheridan was in Dinwiddie this P.M." (*Ibid.*).

To Godfrey Weitzel[1]

U.S. Military Telegraph.

Gen. Weitzel   City Point, March 29 1865

What, if any thing, have you observed, on your front to-day?

A LINCOLN

[1] ALS-F, ISLA. General Weitzel's reply was received at 8:20 P.M.: "I have only heard that Fitz Hugh Lees cavalry passed through Richmond yesterday & at 11.25 this morning it was seen passing Port Walthal Junction towards Petersburg at a fast gait No movements have been observed other than the above. I expect deserters every moment & as soon as I hear anything new I will telegraph you" (DLC-RTL).

A second telegram from Weitzel was received at 12:20 A.M. on March 30: "A Lieutenant & 2 men have just come in from the Enemy they report no change on this front up to the time they left" (*ibid.*).

To Edwin M. Stanton[1]

City Point, Va., March 30, 1865–7.30 p.m.

Hon. Secretary of War: I begin to feel that I ought to be at home, and yet I dislike to leave without seeing nearer to the end of General Grant's present movement. He has now been out since yesterday morning, and although he has not been diverted from his programme, no considerable effect has yet been produced, so far as we know here. Last night at 10.15, when it was dark as a rainy night without a moon could be, a furious cannonade, soon joined in by a heavy musketry-fire, opened near Petersburg and lasted about two hours. The sound was very distinct here, as also were the flashes of the guns upon the clouds. It seemed to me a great battle, but the older hands here scarcely noticed it, and, sure enough, this morning it was found that very little had been done.   A. LINCOLN.

¹ OR, I, XLVI, III, 280. General John G. Parke telegraphed Colonel Theodore S. Bowers on March 30: "The enemy drove in our pickets on line in vicinity of steadman & made demonstration on other portions of the line. Signal Rockets were thrown up by enemy & general cannonading ensued accompanied with heavy musketry on both sides The main line was not touched, & the picket line re established. The casualties not yet reported. . . ." (DLC-RTL).

Stanton replied on March 31: "I hope you will stay to see it out, or for a few days at least. I have strong faith that your presence will have great influence in inducing exertions that will bring Richmond; compared to that no other duty can weigh a feather. There is . . . nothing to be done here but petty private ends that you should not be annoyed with. A pause by the army now would do harm; if you are on the ground there will be no pause. All well here." (OR, I, XLVI, III, 332).

To Edwin M. Stanton¹

Hon. Edwin M. Stanton, City Point, Va.,
Secretary of War: March 31, 1865—8.30 p.m.

At 12.30 p.m. to-day General Grant telegraphed me as follows:

There has been much hard fighting this morning. The enemy drove our left from near Dabney's house back well toward the Boydton plank road. We are now about to take the offensive at that point, and I hope will more than recover the lost ground.

Later he telegraphed again as follows:

Our troops, after being driven back on the Boydton plank road, turned and drove the enemy in turn and took the White Oak road, which we now have. This gives us the ground occupied by the enemy this morning. I will send you a rebel flag captured by our troops in driving the enemy back. There have been four flags captured to-day.

Judging by the two points from which General Grant telegraphs, I infer that he moved his headquarters about one mile since he sent the first of the two dispatches. A. LINCOLN.

¹ OR, I, XLVI, III, 332. The time of this telegram is given as 3 P.M. in NH (XI, 64). Grant's telegrams quoted by Lincoln vary slightly from Lincoln's text. The first is marked as sent at Gravelly Run, 12:50 P.M., rather than 12:30 P.M., and as received at 4 P.M.: "There has been much hard fighting this morning the Enemy drove our left from near W Dabney house back well towards the Boydton plank Road We are now about to take the offensive at that point & I hope will more than recover the lost ground the heavy Rain & horrid roads have prevented the Execution of my designs or attempting them up to this time Gen Ords reports the capture of some prisoners this morning but does not say how many" (DLC-RTL).

The second is marked as sent from Boydton Road and received at 7 P.M.: "Our troops after being driven back on to Boydton plank road turned & drove the Enemy in turn & took the White Oak Road which we now have. This gives us the ground occupied by the Enemy this morning I will send you a rebel flag captured by our troops in driving the Enemy back. There has been four (4) flags captured today. The one I send you was taken from a Va Regiment of Hunters Brigade" (*ibid.*).

To Ulysses S. Grant[1]

U.S. Military Telegraph.

Lt Gen Grant   City Point   Apl 1 1865

Yours to Col Bowers about the secretary of War is shown to me. He is not here nor have I any notice that he is coming. I presume the mistake comes of the fact that the secy of state was here. He started back to Washington this morning. I have your two despatches of this morning and am anxious to hear from Sheridan

A LINCOLN

[1] D, DNA WR RG 108, HQA, Letters Received, P 214. Grant telegraphed Colonel Theodore S. Bowers from Dabney's Mill at 11:10 A.M.: "I understand the Secretary of War is at City Point. Present my respects to him, and say we would have had Petersburg before this but for the rain which unfortunately set in the first night we were out." (OR, I, XLVI, III, 393).

To Ulysses S. Grant[1]

Head Quarters Armies of the United States,

City-Point,

Lieut. General Grant.   April 1. 5/45. P.M. 1865

Yours showing Sheridan's success of to-day is just received, & highly appreciated. Having no great deal to do here, I am still sending the substance of your despatches to the Secretary of War.

A. LINCOLN

[1] ALS, owned by Joseph Block, Chicago, Illinois. Three telegrams were received from Grant on April 1, the first at 9:15 A.M.: "Yesterday as reported the left of the 5th Corps attempted to push north so as to cross the White Oak Road about W Dabneys House but were driven back Sheridan at the same time was pushing up the right branch of the 2 Roads from J. Boisseaus North to the same Road he was at the same time holding Dinwiddie C H & the line of Chamberlain Creek he was met by all the Enemys Cavalry & four or five brigades of Infantry & gradually forced back until at 8 P.M. last Evening he was holding a line from Chamberlain Creek to the Boydton Road probably not more than one mile from the C.H. after [the] falling back of two Divisions of the 5th Corps they again pushed forward and gained the position on the White Oak road first sought finding however the situation Sheridan was in, orders were sent to [Gouverneur K.] Warren after dark to leave the position he held & to push two (2) Divisions down by J Boisseaus & one down the Boydton Road to his relief I had much hopes of destroying the force detached by the Enemy so far to our rear I have not yet heard the result but I know that Sheridan took the offensive this A.M. Ord yesterday pushed the Enemys pickets from the left

of his (Ords) line next to Hatchers Run Capturing 189 men & 2 officers with but very little loss to us this puts Ord so close to the Enemy that he cannot put out pickets in front this Morning before day the Enemy attempted to drive him from this position but was repulsed without loss on our side and leaving over 60 prisoners in our hands" (DLC-RTL).

The second telegram was received at 11:24 A.M.: "In my dispatch this morning I made a mistake in saying Ord lost nothing in the attack made on him this AM his casualties were about 30 killed & wounded he reported no casualties in [John W.] Turners Division which led me into the Errer. The quicksand of this section exceeds anything I have ever seen roads have to be corduroyed in front of teams and Artillery as they advance We were 56 hours moving 600 teams 5 miles with 1200 men to help them through the woods when it is perfectly dry for infantry horses will go through so deep as to scarcely be able to extricate themselves I have nothing special to report at this hour." (*Ibid.*).

The third was received at 5:05 P.M.: "The following dispatch is just recd from Col [Horace] Porter of my staff who was sent to communicate with Gen Sheridan You remember I told you the 5th Corps was sent to him last evening. . . . 'Gen Sheridan's HQrs J. Boisseaus Cross Roads April 1st 1865 2 P.M. . . . Divens [Thomas C. Devin's] Div of Cavalry has just carried the barricade at the five forks held by [George E.] Pickett's Div capturing about two hundred prisoners. The enemy now seem to hold a line across the ford & White Oak roads The whole 5th Corps is now moving from here up to five forks & Gen S. will attack the enemy with every thing the Head of Warrens column is now about a mile & a half from five forks moving up rapidly Our men have never fought better. All are in excellent spirits and anxious to go in The enemy is said by all the officers to be fighting badly giving away constantly before our dismounted Cavy The enemys loss yesterday was very heavy many of their dead are lying in the woods I [saw?] several old men with heads perfectly bald. The enemy threw away many arms in their retreat & seem to have been pretty much demoralized H. PORTER Lt Col A.D.C.' " (*Ibid.*).

To William H. Seward[1]

Head Quarters Armies of the United States,

Hon. W. H. Seward   City-Point,
Fort-Monroe, Va.   April 1. 5/30 [P.M.] 1865

Despatch just received, showing that Sheridan, aided by Warren, had at 2. P.M. pushed the enemy back so as to retake the five forks, and bring his own Head Quarters up to J. Boissau's. The five forks were barricaded by the enemy, and carried by Devin's[2] Division of Cavalry. This part of the enemy seem to now be trying to work along the White Oak Road, to join the main force in front of Grant, while Sheridan & Warren are pressing them as closely as possible.

A LINCOLN

[1] ALS, The Rosenbach Company, Philadelphia and New York. See footnote, Lincoln to Grant, *supra*. As printed in OR, I, XLVI, III, 392, this telegram is followed by a parenthesis: "(Same to Hon. Edwin M. Stanton, Secretary of War.)." Seward probably forwarded the copy to Stanton, for Lincoln's telegram to Stanton of this date refers to receiving "two dispatches from Gen. Grant since my last to you," which would probably refer to Lincoln's telegram of 8:30 P.M.

March 31, *supra,* and the telegrams from Grant received on April 1 at 9:15 and 11:24 A.M. See Lincoln to Grant, 5:45 P.M., *supra.*

2 Brigadier General Thomas C. Devin.

To Edwin M. Stanton[1]

Head Quarters Armies of the United States,

Hon. Sec. of War   City Point,

Washington, D.C.   April 1. 12/50 PM 1865.

    I have had two despatches from Gen. Grant since my last to you, but they contain little additional except that Sheridan also had pretty hot work yesterday, that infantry was sent to his support during the night, and that he, Grant, has not since heard from Sheridan.

    Mrs. L. has started home; and I will thank you to see that our coachman is at the Arsenal wharf at Eight (8) o'clock to-morrow morning, there wait until she arrives.[2]   A. LINCOLN

    1 ALS (copy?), DLC-RTL. See Lincoln to Grant, 5:45 P.M., *supra.*

    2 Stanton telegraphed on April 2 that Mrs. Lincoln "arrived safely this morning" (DLC-RTL). A telegram from Lincoln to the coachman Alfonso Donn, April 1, 1865, has not been found, but according to its description in a sale catalog, Lincoln told Donn "to have the enclosed carriage sent to the arsenal wharf at 8 o'clock Sunday Morning & remain until Mrs. Lincoln's arrival" (Stan. V. Henkels Catalog 1345, February 19, 1924, No. 153).

To Mary Todd Lincoln[1]

Head Quarters Armies of the United States,

Mrs. A. Lincoln,   City-Point,

Washington, D.C.   April 2. 7/45 [A.M.] 1865 [2]

    Last night Gen. Grant telegraphed that Sheridan with his Cavalry and the 5th. Corps had captured three brigades of Infantry, a train of wagons, and several batteries, prisoners amounting to several thousands. This morning Gen. Grant, having ordered an attack along the whole line telegraphs as follows

    "Both Wright and Parke[3] got through the enemies lines. The battle now rages furiously. Sheridan with his Cavalry, the 5th. Corps, & Miles[4] Division of the 2nd. Corps, which was sent to him since 1. this A.M. is now sweeping down from the West. All now looks highly favorable. Ord is engaged, but I have not yet heard the result in his front"

    Robert yesterday wrote a little cheerful note to Capt. Penrose, which is all I have heard of him since you left.[5] Copy to Secretary of War[6]   A LINCOLN

¹ ALS-F, ISLA. Grant telegraphed Colonel Theodore S. Bowers at 9:30 P.M. on April 1: "I have just heard from Sheridan. He has carried everything before him. Captain [Peter T.] Hudson has just returned from him and reports that he has captured three brigades of infantry and a train of wagons and is now pushing up his success. I have ordered everything else to advance and prevent a concentration of the enemy against Sheridan. Several batteries were captured. The prisoners captured will amount to several thousand." (OR, I, XLVI, III, 394).

Grant's telegram to Bowers, as quoted by Lincoln is dated April 2, 6:40 A.M. (*ibid.*, p. 448).

² Telegrams of this date are given in order of time rather than alphabetical according to person addressed.

³ Horatio G. Wright and John G. Parke.

⁴ Major General Nelson A. Miles.

⁵ Robert T. Lincoln's note to Charles B. Penrose has not been found.

⁶ As printed by Nicolay and Hay (XI, 68), this telegram is also addressed to Stanton, and the time given is 8:30 A.M., but the autograph telegram was addressed to Mrs. Lincoln.

To Edwin M. Stanton¹

Hon. Edwin M. Stanton, City Point, Va.,
Secretary of War: April 2, 1865—11 a.m.

Dispatches frequently coming in. All going finely. Parke, Wright, and Ord, extending from the Appomattox to Hatcher's Run, have all broken through the enemy's intrenched lines, taking some forts, guns, and prisoners. Sheridan, with his own cavalry, Fifth Corps, and part of the Second, is coming in from the west on the enemy's flank, and Wright is already tearing up the South Side Railroad. A. LINCOLN.

¹ OR, I, XLVI, III, 446. Grant telegraphed Theodore S. Bowers at 8:25 A.M.: "Wright has gone through the enemy's line, and now has a regiment tearing up the track on the South Side road west of Petersburg. [Andrew A.] Humphreys, with two divisions, is south of Hatcher's Run crossing the Boydton road. Sheridan with his cavalry, the Fifth Corps, and one division of the Second Corps, is moving from the west toward Petersburg   Ord has gone in with Wright. I do not see how the portion of the rebel army south of where Wright broke through . . . are to escape. . . ." (*Ibid.*, p. 448).

To Edwin M. Stanton¹

Hon. Edwin M. Stanton, City Point, Va.,
Secretary of War: April 2, 1865—2 p.m.

At 10.45 a.m. General Grant telegraphed as follows:

Everything has been carried from the left of the Ninth Corps. The Sixth Corps alone captured more than 3,000 prisoners. The Second and Twenty-fourth Corps both captured forts, guns, and prisoners from the enemy, but I cannot tell the number. We are now closing around the works of the line immediately enveloping Petersburg. All looks remarkably well. I have not yet heard from Sheridan.

His headquarters have been moved up to T. Banks' house, near the Boydton road, about three miles southwest of Petersburg.

A. LINCOLN.

1 OR, I, XLVI, III, 447. A forgery of this telegram is in NN, but the original telegram has not been found. Grant's telegram to Theodore S. Bowers, quoted by Lincoln, was sent at 10:45 A.M. (*ibid.*).

To Ulysses S. Grant[1]

Head Quarters Armies of the United States,

City-Point,

Lieut. General Grant.   April. 2. 8/15 P.M. 1865.

Allow me to tender to you, and all with you, the nations grateful thanks for this additional, and magnificent success. At your kind suggestion, I think I will visit you to-morrow.   A. LINCOLN

1 ALS, ORB. Grant's telegram to Theodore S. Bowers, which carried the information for which Lincoln was thanking Grant, is quoted by Lincoln in the telegram to Stanton, 8:30 P.M., *infra*. As printed in OR, I, XLVI, III, 449, Grant's telegram to Bowers has an additional sentence not quoted by Lincoln: "I think the President might come out and pay us a visit to-morrow."

Robert T. Lincoln telegraphed his father on April 3, "I am awaiting you at Hancock Station." (DLC-RTL).

To Edwin M. Stanton[1]

Hon. Edwin M. Stanton,   City Point, Va.,
Secretary of War: April 2, 1865—8.30 p.m.

At 4.30 p.m. to-day General Grant telegraphed as follows:

We are now up, and have a continuous line of troops, and in a few hours will be intrenched from the Appomattox, below Petersburg, to the river above. [Henry] Heth's[2] and [Cadmus M.] Wilcox's divisions—such part of them as were not captured—were cut off from town, either designedly on their part or because they could not help it. Sheridan, with the cavalry and Fifth Corps, is above them. Miles' division, Second Corps, was sent from the White Oak road to Sullivan [Sutherland's][3] Station, on the South Side Railroad, where he met them, and at last accounts was engaged with them. Not knowing whether Sheridan would get up in time Humphreys was sent with another division from here.

The whole captures since the army started out will not amount to

[383]

less than 12,000 men, and probably 50 pieces of artillery. I do not know the number of men and guns accurately, however. A portion of [Robert S.] Foster's division, Twenty-fourth Corps, made a most gallant charge this afternoon, and captured a very important fort from the enemy, with its entire garrison. All seems well with us, and everything quiet just now. A. LINCOLN.

1 OR, I, XLVI, III, 447.

2 As printed in Nicolay and Hay (XI, 69-70) the remainder of this paragraph is omitted, probably because their text was derived from the newspapers which omitted the passage (see New York *Tribune*, April 3, 1865).

3 "Sutherland's" is bracketed in the source.

To Mary Todd Lincoln[1]

City Point, Va., April 2, 1865.

Mrs. Lincoln: At 4:30 p.m. to-day General Grant telegraphs that he has Petersburg completely enveloped from river below to river above, and has captured, since he started last Wednesday, about 12,000 prisoners and 50 guns. He suggests that I shall go out and see him in the morning, which I think I will do. Tad and I are both well, and will be glad to see you and your party here at the time you name. A. LINCOLN.

1 OR, I, XLVI, III, 447-48. Apparently Mrs. Lincoln had telegraphed that she was returning to City Point, but her telegram has not been found.

To Edwin M. Stanton[1]

Head Quarters Armies of the United States.

Hon. Sec. of War   City-Point,
Washington D.C   April 3. 8/00 A.M. 1865

This morning Gen. Grant reports Petersburg evacuated; and he is confident Richmond also is. He is pushing forward to cut off if possible, the retreating army. I start to him in a few minutes.

A. LINCOLN

1 ALS-F, ISLA. Grant had telegraphed Theodore S. Bowers: "Petersburg was evacuated last night. Pursuit will be immediately made." (OR, I, XLVI, III, 509). A second telegram from Grant to Bowers followed: "Say to the President that an officer and escort will attend him, but as to myself I start toward the Danville road with the army. I want to cut off as much of Lee's army as possible." (*Ibid.*).

Stanton replied to Lincoln's telegram: "I congratulate you and the nation on the glorious news in your telegram just recd. Allow me respectfully to ask you to consider whether you ought to expose the nation to the consequence of any disaster to yourself in the pursuit of a treacherous and dangerous enemy like the rebel army. If it was a question concerning yourself only I should not presume to say a word. Commanding Generals are in the line of their duty in running such risks. But is the political head of a nation in the same condition" (DLC-RTL).

To Edwin M. Stanton[1]

Head Quarters Armies of the United States,

Hon. Sec. of War   City-Point,
Washington, D.C.   April 3. 5. P.M. 1865

Yours received. Thanks for your caution; but I have already been to Petersburg, staid with Gen. Grant an hour & a half and returned here. It is certain now that Richmond is in our hands, and I think I will go there to-morrow. I will take care of myself.

A LINCOLN

[1] ALS-F, ISLA.

To Edwin M. Stanton[1]

Head Quarters Armies of the United States,

Hon. Sec. of War.   City-Point,
Washington, D.C.   April 4. 7/30 A.M. 1865

Weitzel telegraphs from Richmond that of Railroad stock, he found there twenty-eight (28) Locomotives, forty-four passenger & baggage cars, and two hundred and six freight cars.[2] At 3/20 this morning Grant, from Southerland station, ten miles from Petersburg towards Burkesville, telegraphs as follows, towit:[3]

A. LINCOLN

"General Sheridan picked up 1,200 prisoners to-day and from 300 to 500 more have been gathered by other troops. The majority of the arms that were left in the hands of the remnant of Lee's army are now scattered between Richmond and where his troops are. The country is also full of stragglers, the line of retreat marked with artillery, ammunition, burned or charred wagons, caissons, ambulances, &c."

[1] ALS, IHi; OR, I, XLVI, III, 544. The portion of this telegram quoted from Grant is missing from the original manuscript.

[2] Godfrey Weitzel to Grant, April 3 (OR, I, XLVI, III, 534).

[3] Grant's telegram has not been found. As printed in the *Official Records*, Lincoln's telegram reads "at 3:30 this evening" instead of "at 3/20 this morning," and an explanatory note opines that it was "probably written before midnight of April 3." In view of Lincoln's autograph telegram, the *Official Records* must

be in error as to the time. Supporting the correctness of Lincoln's autograph telegram is the fact that Sheridan's telegram to Grant, to which Grant referred, was sent at 4:10 P.M. on April 3 (OR, I, XLVI, III, 529).

To Nathaniel P. Banks[1]

Cipher   Office U. S. Military Telegraph,
Maj Gen N P Banks   War Department.
New York   City Point 7 30 pm Apl 5th 1865

Yours of today just rec'd   I have been so much occupied with other thoughts that I really have no directions to give you.

You may go at once and you and I will correspond, when desired by either   A LINCOLN
                                                                                    Prest

[1] D, DNA WR RG 107, Presidential Telegrams, I, 382. Banks telegraphed on April 5: "You directed me to telegraph at Washington when I was ready to leave for New Orleans. I have been detained by the serious illness of my daughter and have waited a few days your return to the Capital   I am ready and desire any directions you may have. The fall of Richmond & the destruction of the Rebel Army fill all hearts with inexpressible joy." (DLC-RTL).

To John A. Campbell[1]

[April 5, 1865]

As to peace, I have said before, and now repeat, that three things are indispensable.

1. The restoration of the national authority throughout all the States.
2. No receding by the Executive of the United States on the slavery question, from the position assumed thereon, in the late Annual Message to Congress, and in preceding documents.
3. No cessation of hostilities short of an end of the war, and the disbanding of all force hostile to the government.

That all propositions coming from those now in hostility to the government; and not inconsistent with the foregoing, will be respectfully considered, and passed upon in a spirit of sincere liberality.

I now add that it seems useless for me to be more specific with those who will not say they are ready for the indispensable terms, even on conditions to be named by themselves. If there be any who are ready for those indispensable terms, on any conditions whatever, let them say so, and state their conditions, so that such conditions can be distinctly known, and considered.

It is further added that, the remission of confiscations being within the executive power, if the war be now further persisted in, by those opposing the government, the making of confiscated property at the least to bear the additional cost, will be insisted on; but that confiscations (except in cases of third party intervening interests) will be remitted to the people of any State which shall now promptly, and in good faith, withdraw it's troops and other support, from further resistance to the government.

What is now said as to remission of confiscations has no reference to supposed property in slaves.

[1] AD, DLC. This document is misdated April 13 in Hertz, II, 967. Charles A. Dana telegraphed Stanton at 4 P.M.: "Judge Campbell . . . had an interview with the President here this morning to consider how Virginia can be brought back to the Union. All they ask is an amnesty and a military convention, to cover appearances. Slavery they admit to be defunct. General Weitzel, who was present, tells me that the President did not promise the amnesty, but told them he had the pardoning power, and would save any repentant sinner from hanging. They . . . are sure if amnesty could be offered the rebel army would dissolve and all the States return. The President went to City Point this morning, and I have not been able to see him." (OR, I, XLVI, III, 575).

On April 7, Dana telegraphed Stanton further: "Meeting of five members of the Virginia legislature held here to-day upon the President's propositions to Judge Campbell. The President showed me the papers confidentially to-day. They are two in number, one without address [supra], the other . . . to General Weitzel [April 6, infra]. The one states sine qua non of reunion, and does not differ essentially from previous statements. The second authorizes Weitzel to allow members of the body claiming to be legislature of Virginia to meet here for purpose of recalling Virginia soldiers from rebel armies, with safe conduct to them, so long as they do and say nothing hostile to the United States. Judge Campbell laid these papers before the five men. . . . The President told me this morning that Sheridan seemed to be getting Virginia soldiers out of the war faster than this legislature could think. . . ." (Ibid., p. 619).

See Lincoln to Grant, April 6, infra.

To William H. Seward[1]

Hon. Secretary of State: City Point, Va., April 5, 1865.

Yours of to-day received. I think there is no probability of my remaining here more than two days longer. If that is too long come down. I passed last night at Richmond and have just returned.

A. LINCOLN.

[1] OR, I, XLVI, III, 572. This telegram appears in NH, XI, 73, erroneously addressed "Hon. Secretary of War." Stanton may have received a copy, but Seward's telegram to Lincoln on April 5 indicates the correctness of the address in the Official Records: "We need your personal sanction to several matters here which are important and urgent in conducting the Government but not at all critical or serious. Are you coming up or shall I go down to you with the papers. The public interest will not suffer by you remaining where you are" (DLC-RTL).

To Ulysses S. Grant[1]

Head Quarters Armies of the United States,

Lieut. Genl. Grant   City-Point,
In the Field.   April. 6. 12. M. 1865

Secretary Seward was thrown from his carriage yesterday and seriously injured. This, with other matters, will take me to Washington soon. I was at Richmond yesterday and the day before, when and where Judge Campbell (who was with Messrs. Hunter and Stephens in February) called on me and made such representations as induced me to put in his hands an informal paper, repeating the propositions in my letter of instructions to Mr. Seward (which you remember) and adding that if the war be now further persisted in by the rebels, confiscated property shall, at the least, bear the additional cost; and that confiscations shall be remitted to the people of any State which will now promptly, and in good faith, withdraw its troops and other support, from resistance to the government. Judge Campbell thought it not impossible that the rebel Legislature of Virginia would do the latter, if permitted; and accordingly, I addressed a private letter to Gen. Weitzel (with permission for Judge Campbell to see it) telling him, Gen. W. that if they attempt this, to permit and protect them, unless they attempt something hostile to the United States, in which case to give them notice and time to leave, and to arrest any remaining after such time.

I do not think it very probable that anything will come of this; but I have thought best to notify you, so that if you should see signs, you may understand them. From your recent despatches it seems that you are pretty effectually withdrawing the Virginia troops from opposition to the government. Nothing I have done, or probably shall do, is to delay, hinder, or interfere with you in your work. Yours truly   A. LINCOLN

[1] ALS, The Rosenbach Company, Philadelphia and New York. Stanton telegraphed Lincoln on April 5 at 6 P.M.: "About two hours ago Mr Seward was thrown from his carriage his shoulder bone at the head of the joint broken off. his head and face much bruised and he is in my opinion dangerously injured. I think your presence here is needed. Mrs Lincoln with a party of friends left here this morning . . . for City Point. Please let me know when you may be expected" (DLC-RTL).

On April 6, Stanton sent Lincoln further reports, and to Mrs. Lincoln en route to City Point, the following: "Mr Seward although severely injured is not in danger. I telegraphed the Prest. last night that you were on the road and also that the Surgeon Genl saw no reason for alarm. There can be no objection to the President remaining at City Point until your arrival there and I have so telegraphed him" (*ibid.*).

Mrs. Lincoln endorsed the telegram in pencil, presumably to forward it to Lincoln: "We will be ready to leave tomorrow eve 6 o'clock do wait & return with us. M.L."

To Godfrey Weitzel[1]

Head Quarters Armies of the United States,

Major General Weitzel   City-Point,
Richmond, Va.   April 6. 1865

It has been intimated to me that the gentlemen who have acted as the Legislature of Virginia, in support of the rebellion, may now now [sic] desire to assemble at Richmond, and take measures to withdraw the Virginia troops, and other support from resistance to the General government. If they attempt it, give them permission and protection, until, if at all, they attempt some action hostile to the United States, in which case you will notify them and give them reasonable time to leave; & at the end of which time, arrest any who may remain. Allow Judge Campbell to see this, but do not make it public. Yours &c.   A. LINCOLN.

[1] ALS, DLC. See Lincoln's memorandum to Campbell, April 5, *supra*.

To Edwin M. Stanton[1]

City Point, April 7, 1865—8.35 a.m.

Hon. Secretary of War: At 11.15 p.m. yesterday, at Burkeville Station, General Grant sends me the following from General Sheridan.   A. LINCOLN.

April 6.

Lieutenant-General Grant: I have the honor to report that the enemy made a stand at the intersection of the Burke's Station road with the road upon which they were retreating. I attacked them with two divisions of the Sixth Army Corps and routed them handsomely, making a connection with the cavalry. I am still pressing on with both cavalry and infantry. Up to the present time we have captured Generals Ewell, Kershaw, Barton, Corse, DuBose, and Custis Lee,[2] several thousand prisoners, 14 pieces of artillery with caissons and a large number of wagons. If the thing is pressed I think Lee will surrender.   P. H. SHERIDAN,
Major-General, Commanding.

[1] OR, I, XLVI, III, 640 and 610; New York *Tribune*, April 8, 1865. As printed in the *Official Records*, Lincoln's telegram appears (p. 640) without Sheridan's telegram, but with a note referring to it as appearing earlier (p. 610). The New York *Tribune* prints the two as incorporated in a telegram from Stanton to John A. Dix of the same date.

Stanton replied to Lincoln's telegram at 1 P.M. "Accept my congratulations on the glorious news of this morning Mr. Seward continues to be doing as well as could be expected from the nature of his injuries. His spirits are good. Your news stimulates him better than anything the apothecary could give and his surgeons say he will soon be able to sit up" (DLC-RTL).

2 The names of the Confederate generals are garbled in the sources and have been corrected by the editors from available information: Richard S. Ewell, Joseph B. Kershaw, Seth M. Barton, Montgomery D. Corse, Dudley M. DuBose, and G. W. Custis Lee, were the generals captured.

To Edwin M. Stanton[1]

Hon. Secretary of War:

City Point,

April 7, 1865—9 a.m.

The following further just received.　　　　　A. LINCOLN.

A. Lincoln　　　　　　　　　　　　　　　　Burkeville

The following Telegrams respectfully forwarded for your Information　　　U. S. GRANT　Lt Gen

2d ac 7.30 PM 6th

Bt Maj Gen A. S. Webb

Our last fight just before dark at Sailors Creek gave us two (2) guns 3 flags considerable number of prisoners 200 wagons 70 ambulances with mules & horses to about one half the wagons & ambulances. There are between 30 & 50 wagons in addition abandoned & destroyed along the road some batty wagons forges[?] & limbers　I have already reported to you the capture 1 gun 2 flags & some prisoners & the fact that the Road for over 2 miles is strewed with tents baggage cooking utensils some ammunition some material of all kinds　the wagons [are] across the approach to the bridge & it will take some time to clear it　The Enemy is in position on the heigth beyond, with 6 artillery the bridge partially destroyed & the approaches on other side are of soft bottom land　We cannot advance tomorrow in the same manner we have today. as soon as I get my troops up a little　we are considerably mixed　I might push a column down the road & deploy it but [it] is Evident that I cannot follow rapidly during the night

A A HUMPHREYS

Maj Gen

Meades Hd Qrs 10 P.M Apl 6

Lt Gen Grant

At daylight this morning I moved the 2d 5 & 6th Corps along the R R in the direction of Amelia C.H　soon after moving reliable Intelligence was received that the Enemy was moving toward Farmville [and] the direction [of] the 2d & 5th Corps was immedidiately changed from a northerly to a north westerly direction the directing Corps the 2d moving on Deatonville & the 5th hertofore in the centre moved on the right of the 2d & the 6th facing about and moving by the left flank taking position on left of the 2d it was understood the Cavalry would operate on the extreme left the changes were promptly made the 2d corps soon becoming engaged with the Enemy near Deatonville driving him by night across sailor Creek to the appomatox the 5th corps made a long march but its position prevented its striking the Enemys column before it had passed. The 6th Corps came up with the Enemy about 4 PM & in conjunction with the 2d on its right & cavalry on its left attacked & routed the Enemy Capturing many prisoners among the[m] Lt Gen Ewell & Gen Custis Lee. I transmit dispatch[es] both from Gen Humphreys & Wright which in justice to these distinguished officers & the gallant Corps they command I beg may be sent to the War Dept for immediate publication. it is impossible at this moment to give any estimate in [of] the casualties in either side or of the number of prisoners taken but it is evident todays[2] works is going to be one of the most important of the recent brilliant operations The pursuit will be continued so soon as the men have a little rest [Charles] Griffin with 5th Corps will be moved by the left & Wright & Humphreys continue the direct pursuit as long as it promises success

GEO. G. MEADE
Maj Gen

Hd Qrs 6th 10 PM Apl 6
Maj Gen Webb

In pursuance with instruction of this morning from Maj Gen Meade I moved via Jetersville by the shortest practicable road to the left of Deatonville with the object of there taking position on left of the 2d Corps striking the road running from Deatonsville to Burkes Station at a point a little to the south ward of the former place. I found that the 2d Corps was engaged to the front & right & the Cavalry heavily to my left moving down the road towards Burks Station perhaps a mile & turning sharp to right I proceeded across toward a nearly paralel road on which the Enemy was moving & along which he had thrown up a line of entrenchments as soon as the leading Division Gen [Truman] Seymours could be formed it was moved upon the road held by the Enemy which was carried then turning to the left it was advanced down the road against a pretty strong resistance by this time [Frank] Wheatons Division was put in position as rapidly as possible on Seymours left the lines were again advanced & we swept down the road for a distance of about 2 miles arriving at a Deep & difficult creek we found the Enemy had reformed his line on the opposite side where we attacked & drove him to a point a distance of a half mile further In the 1st attack a portion of the Cavalry operated on our right flank in its subsequent attacks the mass of cavalry operated on our left & right flank of the Enemy. The result has been a complete success. The combined forces captured 5 General officers among them Gen Ewell & Custis Lee & large numbers of other prisoners I shall go in camp about 2 miles beyond this point & await instructions the 1st & 3d Divisions Wheatons & Seymours & the artillery Engaged today behaved splendidly a return of casualties will be forwarded as soon as possible The Corps has nobly sustained the reputation it earned on the 2d inst as well as upon its many previous hard fought battle fields

H G. WRIGHT
M.G.

[1] OR, I, XLVI, III, 640. As printed in the *Official Records*, the enclosures are omitted, but a footnote cites the pages where they may be found. Nicolay and Hay (XI, 76-77) printed only the first of the enclosures. The text for the enclosures as given above is taken from the telegram which Lincoln received from Grant (DLC-RTL).

[2] The remainder of this sentence appears in OR (I, XLVI, III, 596) as follows: "to-day's work is not going to be one of the least important in the recent brilliant operations."

To Ulysses S. Grant[1]

Head Quarters Armies of the United States,

City-Point,

Lieut Gen. Grant.   April 7. 11 AM. 1865

Gen. Sheridan says "If the thing is pressed I think that Lee will surrender." Let the *thing* be pressed.   A LINCOLN

[1] ALS, ICHi. The text of Sheridan's telegram is quoted in Lincoln's telegrams to Stanton of 8:35 A.M., *supra*.

To Francis H. Peirpoint[1]

Gov. Pierpoint   Executive Mansion
Alexandria, Va.   Washington, April 10. 1865

Please come up and see me at once.   A. LINCOLN

[1] ALS, DNA WR RG 107, Presidential Telegrams, I, 383. For an account of Lincoln's conference with Governor Peirpoint, see Charles H. Ambler, *Francis H. Pierpont* (1937), p. 255 ff.

Response to Serenade[1]

April 10, 1865

"FELLOW CITIZENS: I am very greatly rejoiced to find that an occasion has occurred so pleasurable that the people cannot restrain themselves. [Cheers.] I suppose that arrangements are being made for some sort of a formal demonstration, this, or perhaps, to-morrow night. [Cries of 'We can't wait,' 'We want it now,' &c.] If there should be such a demonstration, I, of course, will be called upon to respond, and I shall have nothing to say if you dribble it all out of me before. [Laughter and applause.] I see you have a band of music with you. [Voices, 'We have two or three.'] I propose closing up this interview by the band performing a particular tune which I will name. Before this is done, however, I wish to mention one or two little circumstances connected with it. I have always thought 'Dixie' one of the best tunes I have ever heard. Our adversaries over the way attempted to appropriate it, but I insisted yesterday that we fairly captured it. [Applause.] I presented the question to the Attorney General, and he gave it as his legal opinion that it is our lawful prize. [Laughter and applause.] I now request the band to favor me with its performance."

[1] Washington *Daily National Intelligencer*, April 11, 1865. Brackets are in the source. Lincoln's remarks were reported substantially the same in other papers (Washington *Daily Morning Chronicle*, New York *Herald*, etc.), but with considerable minor verbal variation. The *Intelligencer's* account of the occasion is as follows:

"The procession proceeded along Pennsylvania avenue gaining accessions at every step, despite the mud and rain, and when it turned up Fifteenth street it is estimated that there were over three thousand persons in the crowd. The procession proper—that is, those who had come from the Navy Yard—and a portion of the crowd proceeded to the residence of Secretary Welles, while the other portion kept along Pennsylvania avenue to the White House and the War Department. At the latter place the band of the Quartermaster's regiment, Capt. Tompkins, under the leadership of Prof. Blish, and the band of the Fourteenth regiment V.R.C., were stationed, and their excellent music attracted an immense concourse of people, who called again loudly for Secretary Stanton, but failing to get him out, the crowd, preceded by the Quartermaster's band, moved toward the White House, and in a few moments an immense number of people were assembled, and completely filled the portico, the carriageway, and pavements on either side, while many were forced to content themselves with a stand-up place in the mud. The bands played, the howitzers belched forth their thunder, and the people cheered. Call after call was made for the President, and his failure to appear only made the people cry out the louder. Master Tad Lincoln, who was at the window, appeared to hugely enjoy the shouting, cheering, and swaying to and fro of the crowd, who evinced a determination not to depart until the Chief Magistrate acknowledged their greeting by his presence. At length, after persistent effort, the presence of Mr. Lincoln was secured. Three loud and hearty cheers were given, after which the President said: [as above]

"In accordance with the request, the band struck up 'Dixie,' and at its conclusion played 'Yankee Doodle,' the President remaining at the window meanwhile.

"The President then said: 'Now give three good hearty cheers for General Grant and all under his command.' These were given with a will, after which Mr. Lincoln requested 'three more cheers for our gallant Navy,' which request was also readily granted.

"The President then disappeared from the window, amid the cheers of those below. The crowd then moved back to the War Department, and loud calls were again made for Secretary Stanton."

Response to Serenade[1]

April 10, 1865

My Friends: I am informed that you have assembled here this afternoon under the impression that I had made an appointment to speak at this time. This is a mistake. I have made no such appointment. More or less persons have been gathering here at different times during the day, and in the exuberance of their feeling, and for all of which they are greatly justified, calling upon me to say something; and I have, from time to time, been sending out what I supposed was proper to disperse them for the present. [Laughter and applause.]

I said to a larger audience this morning what I desire now to repeat. It is this: That I supposed in consequence of the glorious news we have been receiving lately, there is to be some general demonstration, either on this or to-morrow evening, when I will be expected, I presume, to say something. Just here I will remark that I would much prefer having this demonstration take place to-morrow evening, as I would then be much better prepared to say what I have to say than I am now or can be this evening. [A voice—"And we will then have heard from Johnston."]

I therefore say to you that I shall be quite willing, and I hope ready, to say something then; whereas just now I am not ready to say anything that one in my position ought to say. Everything I say, you know, goes into print. [Laughter and applause.] If I make a mistake it doesn't merely affect me nor you but the country. I, therefore, ought at least try not to make mistakes. [Voices—"You have made no mistakes yet."]

If, then, a general demonstration be made to-morrow evening, and it is agreeable, I will endeavor to say something, and not make a mistake, without at least trying carefully to avoid it. [Laughter and applause.] Thanking you for the compliment of this call, I bid you good evening.

[1] Washington *Daily National Republican*, April 11, 1865. Brackets are in the source. According to the *Republican*, Lincoln delivered this speech between five

and six o'clock in the afternoon. Other Washington newspapers reported it with only minor verbal variations. The text in the New York *Herald, Times,* etc., is less extensive.

To Edwin M. Stanton[1]

Hon. Sec. of War.

Tad wants some flags. Can he be accommodated.

April 10. 1865   A. LINCOLN

[1] ALS, ORB. No reply has been found.

To Gideon Welles[1]

[April 10, 1865?]

Let Master Tad have a Navy sword.   A. LINCOLN

[1] ALS, ORB. Written on a small card, without date, this note seems to have been written at the same time as the note to Stanton, *supra.*

To George H. Gordon[1]

Brig. Gen. G. H. Gordon   Executive Mansion,
Norfolk, Va.   Washington, April 11. 1865

Send to me at once a full statement as to the cause or causes for which, and by authority of what tribunal, George W. Lane,[2] Charles Whitlock, Ezra Baker, J. M. Renshaw, & others, are restrained of their liberty. Do this promptly & fully.

A. LINCOLN

[1] ALS, DNA WR RG 107, Presidential Telegrams, I, 384. On March 31, Charles Whitlock and Ezra Baker and associates petitioned Lincoln for return of goods seized by military authorities, release from arrest, and trial before a civil tribunal (*Private and Official Correspondence of Benjamin F. Butler,* V, 589 ff.). No reply from Gordon has been found.
[2] See Lincoln to Ord, March 20, *supra.*

Pass for Ward H. Lamon[1]

Allow the bearer, W. H. Lamon & friend, with ordinary baggage to pass from Washington to Richmond and return.

April 11. 1865   A. LINCOLN

[1] ADS, CSmH. Lamon's friend has not been identified.

[395]

Proclamation Concerning Blockade[1]

April 11, 1865

By the President of the United States of America:

A Proclamation.

Whereas, by my Proclamations of the nineteenth and twenty seventh days of April, one thousand eight hundred and sixty-one, the ports of the United States in the States of Virginia, North Carolina, South Carolina, Georgia, Florida, Alabama, Mississippi, Louisiana and Texas, were declared to be subject to blockade; but whereas the said blockade has, in consequence of actual military occupation by this Government, since been conditionally set aside or relaxed in respect to the ports of Norfolk and Alexandria, in the State of Virginia, Beaufort in the State of North Carolina, Port Royal in the State of South Carolina, Pensacola and Fernandina in the State of Florida, and New Orleans in the State of Louisiana:

And, whereas, by the fourth section of the Act of Congress approved on the thirteenth of July eighteen hundred and sixty one, entitled "An act further to provide for the collection of duties on imports and for other purposes," the President, for the reasons therein set forth, is authorized to close certain ports of entry;

Now, therefore, be it known, that I, Abraham Lincoln, President of the United States, do hereby proclaim that the ports of Richmond, Tappahannock, Cherrystone, Yorktown and Petersburg in Virginia; of Camden, (Elizabeth City,) Edenton, Plymouth, Washington, Newbern, Ocracoke and Wilmington, in North Carolina; of Charleston, Georgetown and Beaufort in South Carolina; of Savannah, St. Mary's and Brunswick, (Darien) in Georgia; of Mobile in Alabama; of Pearl River, (Shieldsborough,) Natchez and Vicksburg in Mississippi; of St. Augustine, Key West, St. Marks, (Port Leon,) St. John's, (Jacksonville,) and Apalachicola, in Florida; of Teché, (Franklin) in Louisiana; of Galveston, La Salle, Brazos de Santiago, (Point Isabel,) and Brownsville, in Texas, are hereby closed, and all right of importation, warehousing, and other privileges shall, in respect to the ports aforesaid, cease until they shall have again been opened by order of the President; and if, while said ports are so closed, any ship or vessel from beyond the United States or having on board any articles subject to duties, shall attempt to enter any such port, the same, together with its tackle, apparel, furniture and cargo, shall be forfeited to the United States.

In witness whereof, I have hereunto set my hand, and caused the seal of the United States to be affixed.

Done at the City of Washington, this eleventh day of April, in the year of our Lord one thousand eight hundred and [L.S.]   sixty-five, and of the Independence of the United States of America the eighty-ninth.   ABRAHAM LINCOLN

By the President:

WILLIAM H SEWARD   Secretary of State.

[1] DS, DNA FS RG 11, Proclamations. See the modifying proclamations, *infra*.

Proclamation Modifying Blockade of Key West, Florida[1]

April 11, 1865

By the President of the United States of America:

A Proclamation.

Whereas, by my Proclamation of this date, the port of Key West, in the State of Florida, was inadvertently included among those which are not open to commerce:

Now, therefore, be it known that I, Abraham Lincoln, President of the United States, do hereby declare and make known that the said port of Key West is and shall remain open to foreign and domestic commerce upon the same conditions by which that commerce has there hitherto been governed.

In testimony whereof, I have hereunto set my hand and caused the seal of the United States to be affixed.

Done at the City of Washington this eleventh day of April, in the year of our Lord one thousand eight hundred and [L.S.]   sixty-five, and of the Independence of the United States of America the eighty ninth.

By the President: ABRAHAM LINCOLN

WILLIAM H SEWARD   Secretary of State.

[1] DS, DNA FS RG 11, Proclamations.

Proclamation Concerning Foreign Port Privileges[1]

April 11, 1865

By the President of the United States of America:

A Proclamation.

Whereas, for some time past, vessels of war of the United States have been refused in certain foreign ports, privileges and immunities to which they were entitled by treaty, public law or the comity of nations, at the same time that vessels of war of the country wherein the said privileges and immunities have been withheld have enjoyed them fully and uninterruptedly in ports of the United States; which condition of things has not always been forcibly resisted by the United States, although, on the other hand, they have not at any time failed to protest against and declare their dissatisfaction with the same. In the view of the United States no condition any longer exists which can be claimed to justify the denial to them by any one of such nations of customary naval rights, as has heretofore been so unnecessarily persisted in:

Now, therefore, I, Abraham Lincoln, President of the United States, do hereby make known that, if after a reasonable time shall have elapsed for intelligence of this Proclamation to have reached any foreign country in whose ports the said privileges and immunities shall have been refused as aforesaid, they shall continue to be so refused, then and thenceforth the same privileges and immunities shall be refused to the vessels of war of that country in the ports of the United States, and this refusal shall continue until war vessels of the United States shall have been placed upon an entire equality in the foreign ports aforesaid with similar vessels of other countries—the United States, whatever claim or pretence may have existed heretofore, are now, at least, entitled to claim and concede an entire and friendly equality of rights and hospitalities with all maritime nations.

In witness whereof, I have hereunto set my hand and caused the seal of the United States to be affixed.

Done at the City of Washington this eleventh day of April, in the year of our Lord one thousand eight hundred and
[L.S.]   sixty-five, and of the Independence of the United States of America the eighty-ninth.   ABRAHAM LINCOLN

By the President:

WILLIAM H. SEWARD, Secretary of State.

[1] DS, DNA FS RG 11, Proclamations.

To James Speed[1]

Pardon & send to tribe.   A. LINCOLN
April 11. 1865

[1] AES, DNA RG 204, U.S. Pardon Attorney, B 9. Lincoln's endorsement appears on a letter from G. C. Snow, agent for the Seminole Indians, but working among the refugee Indians, Washington, March 24, 1865: "I beg leave to submit the following statement in relation to Robert P Lombard who is now a prisoner

at Ft Smith as I am informed under sentence of a Court Martial upon a charge of stealing cattle from the Indian Territory. This man Lombard is a half breed Quawpaw Indian and is my interpreter for said tribe and has a family with said tribe. He is exceedingly useful to the Agent as interpreter, and I do not see how the affairs of the tribe are to be managed without his assistance. . . ."

Last Public Address[1]

April 11, 1865

We meet this evening, not in sorrow, but in gladness of heart. The evacuation of Petersburg and Richmond, and the surrender of the principal insurgent army, give hope of a righteous and speedy peace whose joyous expression can not be restrained. In the midst of this, however, He, from Whom all blessings flow, must not be forgotten. A call for a national thanksgiving is being

[1] AD-P, ISLA. On April 11, Salmon P. Chase had written Lincoln at length about reconstruction:

"I am very anxious about the future: and most about the principles which are to govern reconstruction for as these principles are sound or unsound so will be the work & its results. . . .

"And first as to Virginia.

"By the action of every branch of the Government we are committed to the recognition & maintenance of the State organization of which Governor Pierpont is the head. You know all the facts. . . . There will be a pressure for the recognition of the rebel organization on condition of profession of loyalty. It will be far easier and wiser, in my judgment, to stand by the loyal organization already recognized.

"And next as to the other rebel States:

"The easiest & safest way seems to me to be the enrollment of the loyal citizens without regard to complexion and encouragement & support to them in the reorganization of State Governments under constitutions securing suffrage to all citizens. . . . This you know has long been my opinion. . . .

"This way is recommended by its simplicity, facility & above all, justice. It will be, hereafter, counted equally a crime & a folly if the colored loyalists of the rebel states shall be left to the control of restored rebels, not likely, in that case, to be either wise or just, until taught both wisdom and justice by new calamities.

"The application of this principle to Louisiana is made somewhat difficult by the organization which has already taken place: but happily the Constitution enables the Legislature to extend the right of suffrage. . . .

"The same result can be assured in Arkansas by an amendment of the state constitution; or what would be better, I think, by a new Convention . . . without distinction of color. To all the other states the general principle may be easily applied. . . ." (DLC-RTL).

On the morning after Lincoln's speech, Chase wrote again:

"The American of this morning contains your speech of last evening. Seeing that you say something on the subject of my letter to you yesterday—reconstruction—, & refer, though without naming me, to the suggestions I made in relation to the Amnesty Proclamation, when you brought it before the Heads of Departments, I will ask your permission to add some observations to what I have already written.

"I recollect the suggestions you mention; my impression is that they were in writing. There was another which you do not mention and which, I think, was not in writing. It is distinct in my memory; though doubtless forgotten by you.

prepared, and will be duly promulgated. Nor must those whose harder part gives us the cause of rejoicing, be overlooked. Their honors must not be parcelled out with others. I myself, was near the front, and had the high pleasure of transmitting much of the good news to you; but no part of the honor, for plan or execution, is mine. To Gen. Grant, his skilful officers, and brave men, all belongs. The gallant Navy stood ready, but was not in reach to take active part.

By these recent successes the re-inauguration of the national authority—reconstruction—which has had a large share of thought from the first, is pressed much more closely upon our attention. It is fraught with great difficulty. Unlike the case of a war between independent nations, there is no authorized organ for us to treat with. No one man has authority to give up the rebellion for any other man. We simply must begin with, and

It was an objection to the restriction of participation in reorganization to persons having the qualifications of voters under the laws of their several states just before rebellion.

"Ever since questions of reconstruction have been talked about, it has been my opinion that the colored loyalists ought to be allowed to participate in it and it was because of this opinion that I was anxious to have this question left open. I did not however say much about the restriction. I was the only one who expressed a wish for its omission; & I did not desire to seem pertinacious.

"You will remember, doubtless, that the first order ever issued for enrollment with a view to reconstruction went to General Shepley & directed the enrollment of all loyal citizens; and I suppose that, since the opinion of Attorney General Bates, no one, connected with your administration, has questioned the citizenship of free colored men more than that of free white men. The restriction in the amnesty proclamation operated as a revocation of the order to General Shepley:—but, as I understood you not to be wedded to any particular plan of reconstruction, I hoped & believed that reflection & observation would probably satisfy you that the restriction should not be adhered to.

"I fully sympathized with your desire for the restoration of the Union by the change of rebel slave States into Union free States; and was willing, if I could not get exactly the plan I thought best, to take the plan you thought best, & to trust the future for modifications. I welcomed, therefore, with joy the prospects of good results from the cooperation of General Banks with the free state men of Louisiana. I think General Banks' error, & I have said so to him, was in not acting through instead of over the Free State Committee. This Committee had already shown itself disposed to a degree of liberality towards the colored people quite remarkable at that time. They had admitted delegates from the creole colored population into their free State Convention, & had evinced a readiness to admit intelligent colored citizens of that class to the rights of suffrage. I have *no* doubt that great & satisfactory progress would have been made in the same direction had not the work been taken out of their hands. This created the impression that the advocates of general suffrage were to be treated with disfavor by the representatives of the Government. Discouragement & disinterest were the natural consequences.

"For one I was glad of all the good that was done; and, naturally, wanted more. So when I came to Washington last winter I saw Gen Banks: and, being now more deeply than ever persuaded of the necessity of universal suffrage, I begged him to write himself & to induce the Senators & Representatives elect

mould from, disorganized and discordant elements. Nor is it a small additional embarrassment that we, the loyal people, differ among ourselves as to the mode, manner, and means of reconstruction.

As a general rule, I abstain from reading the reports of attacks upon myself, wishing not to be provoked by that to which I can not properly offer an answer. In spite of this precaution, however, it comes to my knowledge that I am much censured for some supposed agency in setting up, and seeking to sustain, the new State Government of Louisiana. In this I have done just so much as, and no more than, the public knows. In the Annual Message of Dec. 1863 and accompanying Proclamation, I presented *a* plan of re-construction (as the phrase goes) which, I promised, if adopted by any State, should be acceptable to, and sustained by, the Executive government of the nation. I distinctly stated that this was

from Louisiana to write to members of the Legislature and urge them to exercise their power under the constitution by passing an act extending suffrage to colored citizens. I knew that many of our best men in and out of Congress had become thoroughly convinced of the impolicy and injustice of allowing representation in Congress to States which had been in rebellion and were not yet prepared to concede equal political rights to all loyal citizens. They felt that if such representation should be allowed & such states reinstated in all their former rights as loyal members of the Union, the colored population would be practically abandoned to the disposition of the white population, with every probability against them; and this, they believed would be equally unjust & dangerous.

"I shared their sentiment & was therefore extremely desirous that General Banks should take the action I urged upon him. I thought indeed that he concurred, mainly, in my views, & would to some extent at least act upon them. I must have been mistaken, for I never heard that he did anything in that direction.

"I know you attach much importance to the admission of Louisiana, or rather to the recognition of her right to representation in Congress as a loyal State in the Union. If I am not misinformed there is nothing in the way except the indisposition of her Legislature to give satisfactory proof of loyalty by a sufficient guaranty of safety & justice to colored citizens through the extension to loyal colored men of the right of suffrage. Why not, then, as almost every loyal man concurs with you as to the desirableness of that recognition, take the shortest road to it by causing every proper representation to be made to the Louisiana Legislature of the importance of such extension.

"I most earnestly wish you could have read the New Orleans papers for the last few months. Your duties have not allowed it. I have read them a good deal —quite enough to be satisfied that, if you had read what I have, your feelings of humanity & justice would not let you rest till *all* loyalists are made equal in the right of self protection by suffrage.

"Once I should have been, if not satisfied, reasonably contented by suffrage for the more intelligent & for those who have been soldiers; now I am convinced that universal suffrage is demanded by sound policy and impartial justice alike.

"I have written too much already & will not trouble you with my reasons for this conclusion. I shall return to Washington in a day or two & perhaps it will not be disagreeable to you to have the whole subject talked over. . . ." (DLC-RTL).

not the only plan which might possibly be acceptable; and I also distinctly protested that the Executive claimed no right to say when, or whether members should be admitted to seats in Congress from such States. This plan was, in advance, submitted to the then Cabinet, and distinctly approved by every member of it. One of them suggested that I should then, and in that connection, apply the Emancipation Proclamation to the theretofore excepted parts of Virginia and Louisiana; that I should drop the suggestion about apprenticeship for freed-people, and that I should omit the protest against my own power, in regard to the admission of members to Congress; but even he approved every part and parcel of the plan which has since been employed or touched by the action of Louisiana. The new constitution of Louisiana, declaring emancipation for the whole State, practically applies the Proclamation to the part previously excepted. It does not adopt apprenticeship for freed-people; and it is silent, as it could not well be otherwise, about the admission of members to Congress. So that, as it applies to Louisiana, every member of the Cabinet fully approved the plan. The Message went to Congress, and I received many commendations of the plan, written and verbal; and not a single objection to it, from any professed emancipationist, came to my knowledge, until after the news reached Washington that the people of Louisiana had begun to move in accordance with it. From about July 1862, I had corresponded with different persons, supposed to be interested, seeking a reconstruction of a State government for Louisiana. When the Message of 1863, with the plan before mentioned, reached New-Orleans, Gen. Banks wrote me that he was confident the people, with his military co-operation, would reconstruct, substantially on that plan. I wrote him, and some of them to try it; they tried it, and the result is known. Such only has been my agency in getting up the Louisiana government. As to sustaining it, my promise is out, as before stated. But, as bad promises are better broken than kept, I shall treat this as a bad promise, and break it, whenever I shall be convinced that keeping it is adverse to the public interest. But I have not yet been so convinced.

I have been shown a letter on this subject, supposed to be an able one, in which the writer expresses regret that my mind has not seemed to be definitely fixed on the question whether the seceded States, so called, are in the Union or out of it. It would perhaps, add astonishment to his regret, were he to learn that since I have found professed Union men endeavoring to make that question, I have *purposely* forborne any public expression upon it. As appears to me that question has not been, nor yet is, a practically material one, and that any discussion of it, while it thus remains practically immaterial, could have no effect other than the mischievous one of dividing our friends. As yet, whatever it may hereafter become, that question is bad, as the basis of a controversy, and good for nothing at all—a merely pernicious abstraction.

We all agree that the seceded States, so called, are out of their proper practical relation with the Union; and that the sole object of the government, civil and military, in regard to those States is to again get them into that proper practical relation. I believe it is not only possible, but in fact, easier, to do this, without deciding, or even considering, whether these states have even been out of the Union, than with it. Finding themselves safely at home, it would be utterly immaterial whether they had ever been abroad. Let us all join in doing the acts necessary to restoring the proper practical relations between these states and the Union; and each forever after, innocently indulge his own opinion whether, in doing the acts, he brought the States from without, into the Union, or only gave them proper assistance, they never having been out of it.

The amount of constituency, so to to [sic] speak, on which the new Louisiana government rests, would be more satisfactory to all, if it contained fifty, thirty, or even twenty thousand, instead of only about twelve thousand, as it does. It is also unsatisfactory to some that the elective franchise is not given to the colored man. I would myself prefer that it were now conferred on the very intelligent, and on those who serve our cause as soldiers. Still the question is not whether the Louisiana government, as it stands, is quite all that is desirable. The question is "Will it be wiser to take it as it is, and help to improve it; or to reject, and disperse it?" "Can Louisiana be brought into proper practical relation with the Union *sooner* by *sustaining*, or by *discarding* her new State Government?"

Some twelve thousand voters in the heretofore slave-state of Louisiana have sworn allegiance to the Union, assumed to be the rightful political power of the State, held elections, organized a State government, adopted a free-state constitution, giving the benefit of public schools equally to black and white, and empowering the Legislature to confer the elective franchise upon the colored man. Their Legislature has already voted to ratify the constitutional amendment recently passed by Congress, abolishing slavery throughout the nation. These twelve thousand persons are thus fully committed to the Union, and to perpetual freedom in the state—committed to the very things, and nearly all the things the nation wants—and they ask the nations recognition, and it's assistance to make good their committal. Now, if we reject, and spurn them, we do our utmost to disorganize and disperse them. We in effect say to the white men "You are worthless, or worse— we will neither help you, nor be helped by you." To the blacks we say "This cup of liberty which these, your old masters, hold to your lips, we will dash from you, and leave you to the chances of gathering the spilled and scattered contents in some vague and undefined when, where, and how." If this course, discouraging and paralyzing both white and black, has any tendency to bring Louisiana into proper practical relations with the Union, I have, so far, been unable to perceive it. If, on the contrary, we recognize, and sustain the new government of Louisiana the converse of all this is made true. We encourage the hearts, and nerve the arms of the twelve thousand to adhere to their work, and argue for it, and proselyte for it, and fight for it, and feed it, and grow it, and ripen it to a complete success. The colored man too, in seeing all united for him, is inspired with vigilance, and energy, and daring, to the same end. Grant that he desires the elective franchise, will he not attain it sooner by saving the already advanced steps toward it, than by running backward over them? Concede that the new government of Louisiana is only to what it should be as the egg is to the fowl, we shall sooner have the fowl by hatching the egg than by smashing it? Again, if we reject Louisiana, we also reject one vote in favor of the proposed amendment to the national constitution. To meet this proposition, it has been argued that no more than three fourths of those States which have not attempted secession are necessary to validly ratify the amendment. I do not commit myself against this, further than to say that such a ratification would be questionable, and sure to be persistently questioned; while a ratification by three fourths of all the States would be unquestioned and unquestionable.

I repeat the question. "Can Louisiana be brought into proper practical relation with the Union *sooner* by *sustaining* or by *discarding* her new State Government?

What has been said of Louisiana will apply generally to other States. And yet so great peculiarities pertain to each state; and such important and sudden changes occur in the same state; and, withal, so new and unprecedented is the whole case, that no exclusive, and inflexible plan can safely be prescribed as to details and colatterals. Such exclusive, and inflexible plan, would surely

[404]

become a new entanglement. Important principles may, and must, be inflexible.

In the present *"situation"* as the phrase goes, it may be my duty to make some new announcement to the people of the South. I am considering, and shall not fail to act, when satisfied that action will be proper.

To Joseph Holt[1]

Let the Prisoner be pardoned and returned to his Regiment.
April 12. 1865   A. Lincoln

[1] ES, DNA WR RG 153, Judge Advocate General, NN 3617. Lincoln's endorsement is written on the court-martial record of Private George Maynard, Forty-sixth New York Volunteers, sentenced to death for desertion. See Lincoln to Grant, February 23, *supra.*

To Edwin M. Stanton[1]

I would be glad, if convenient, for Isaac G. Wilson of Ills. to be an Examiner at West-Point.   A. Lincoln
April 12. 1865.

[1] ALS, ORB. No record of Isaac G. Wilson's appointment has been found.

To Godfrey Weitzel[1]

"Cypher"   Office U.S. Military Telegraph,
Major General Weitzel   War Department,
Richmond, Va.   Washington, D.C., April 12. 1865

I have seen your despatch to Col. Hardie about the matter of prayers. I do not remember hearing prayers spoken of while I was in Richmond; but I have no doubt you have acted in what appeared to you to be the spirit and temper manifested by me while there.

Is there any sign of the rebel Legislature coming together on the understanding of my letter to you? If there is any such sign, inform me what it is; if there is no such sign you may as [well] withdraw the offer.   A. Lincoln

[1] ALS, DNA WR RG 107, Presidential Telegrams, I, 385. The time of this telegram is marked by the clerk as 9 A.M. On April 9, Charles A. Dana had telegraphed Stanton from Richmond: "On Friday evening I asked Weitzel . . . what he was going to do about opening the churches on Sunday. He answered that all were to be allowed to be opened on condition that no disloyalty should be uttered and that the Episcopal ministers would be required to read the prayer

for the President. . . . I told him this was all right. Last evening he sent [George F.] Shepley to me to ask that this order might be relaxed, so that the clergy would only be required not to pray for Jeff. Davis. Shepley said this was what had been determined on by . . . Weitzel before I gave orders to the contrary. I answered I had given no orders at all . . . and that Weitzel must act in the matter entirely on his own judgment. It appears that Judge Campbell thought it very desirable that a loyal prayer should not be exacted, and that Weitzel had consented to it; but when I asked him the question . . . he gave me an answer opposite to the reality. I report the fact, confessing that it shakes a good deal my confidence in Weitzel. . . ." (OR, I, XLVI, III, 677).

Whereupon Stanton telegraphed Weitzel: "It has just been reported to this Department that you have, at the instance of Mr. Campbell, consented that service should be performed in the Episcopal churches of Richmond to-day without the usual prayer said in loyal churches of that denomination for the President . . . and that you have even agreed to waive that condition. If such has been your action it is strongly condemned by this Department . . . you are directed immediately to report by telegraph your action in relation to religious services in Richmond . . . and also to state what took place between you and Mr. Campbell on the subject. . . ." (Ibid., p. 678).

Weitzel replied the next day: "The orders in relation to religious services in Richmond were verbal, and were applicable alike to all religious denominations. . . . They were, in substance, that no expression would be allowed in any part of the church service . . . which in any way implied a recognition of any other authority than that of the United States. . . . No orders were given as to what would be preached or prayed for, but only as to what would not be permitted. . . . I have had personally but three interviews with Judge Campbell—two of them in the presence of, and the other by the written command of, the President. In neither of these interviews was any question discussed in relation to church or prayers. . . ." (Ibid., pp. 696-97).

On April 11, James A. Hardie telegraphed Weitzel: "The Secretary of War directs me to say that your explanation . . . is not satisfactory. . . . The Secretary also directs me to instruct you that officers commanding in Richmond are expected to require from all religious denominations in that city, in regard to their rituals and prayers, no less respect for the President . . . than they practiced toward the rebel chief . . . before he was driven from the capital." (Ibid., p. 711).

Weitzel's reply to Lincoln's telegram of April 12 was received at 3 P.M.: "You spoke of not pressing little points. You said you would not order me, but if you were in my place you would not press them. The passports have gone out for the legislature, and it is common talk that they will come together." (Ibid., p. 724).

To Godfrey Weitzel[1]

"*Cypher*"   Office U.S. Military Telegraph,
Major General Weitzel   War Department,
Richmond, Va   Washington, D.C., April 12. 1865

I have just seen Judge Campbell's letter to you of the 7th. He assumes as appears to me that I have called the insurgent Legislature of Virginia together, as the rightful Legislature of the State, to settle all differences with the United States. I have done no such thing. I spoke of them not as a Legislature, but as "the gentlemen who have *acted* as the Legislature of Virginia in support of the rebellion." I did this on purpose to exclude the assumption that I was recognizing them as a *rightful* body. I dealt with them as men having power *de facto* to do a specific thing, towit, "to withdraw the Virginia troops, and other support from resistance to the General Government," for which in the paper handed Judge Campbell I promised a specific equivalent, to wit, a remission to the people of the State, except in certain cases, the confiscation of their property. I meant this and no more. In as much however as Judge Campbell misconstrues this, and is still pressing for an armistice, contrary to the explicit statement of the paper I gave him; and particularly as Gen. Grant has since captured the Virginia troops, so that giving a consideration for their withdrawal is no longer applicable, let my letter to you, and the paper to Judge Campbell both be withdrawn or, countermanded, and he be notified of it. Do not now allow them to assemble; but if any have come, allow them safe-return to their homes.   A. LINCOLN

[1] ALS, DNA WR RG 107, Presidential Telegrams, I, 386-87. The time of this telegram is marked by the clerk as 6 P.M. See Lincoln's memorandum to Campbell, April 5, and communications to Grant and to Weitzel, April 6, *supra*. On April 7, Judge Campbell wrote Weitzel:

"The events of the war have placed under the military control of the United States the natural and artificial channels of communication of the Confederate States, their emporiums of commerce and intercourse, and all the places that have any special importance in a military point of view. The armies of the Confederacy are diminished in point of numbers, and debilitated from the want of adequate equipments, transportation, and supplies. The spirit of the people is not broken and the resources of the country allow of a prolonged and embarrassing resistance. Humanity as well as patriotism requires that such a contest, which must be in the end fruitless, should be averted. To do this is the province of enlarged and [wise] statesmanship. The obstacles to an immediate accommodation arise [from the] condition of the Confederate Government and nature of the questions involved [in] the war. The Confederate Government has made no provision [for] the possibility of its failure. Its functionaries don't understand how [they] can negotiate for the subversion or overthrow of their [Government]. All the powers of negotiation are in the hands of the [President], and he is not willing to employ them for such [a] result. The affections and hopes of the people are concentrated [in] the Army, and it will be difficult to bring them [to] take action without the co-operation and counsel of their [brethren] of the army. Thus while reflecting persons are convinced that the [cause] of the Confederate States can't be achieved, and they are predisposed [to] an adjustment, there is a great difficulty in obtaining an [acknowledgment] of this conviction from a legally constituted authority. I [think] that an armistice would obviate much of this difficulty, nor [do] I believe that there would be any danger of a [delay] in securing peace by this temporary cessation of hostilities. The [disbanding] of the armies would be the probable, I may say the [certain], result of such a measure.

"The legislature of Virginia [will or should] be immediately convened. The legislature of South Carolina will meet according [to] adjournment in May.

"The President of the United States in his memorandum left with [me] states three indispensable conditions to peace, which when examined are [all] included in the single one of the restoration of the Union by [the] consent of the seceding States. If his proclamations upon the subject of slavery have the force of law I suppose that it became operative when it was issued, and that rights were vested under it. I do not presume that his revocation of that proclamation could destroy the rights thus acquired.

"The acceptance of the Union involves acceptance of his proclamation, if it be valid as a law. In Virginia the question of limits is one of great concern and interest, and in both States the averages of taxes, the confiscation acts, the bills of pains and penalties, the oaths of allegiance, the right to representation in Congress, and the condition of the slave population, are subjects of importance. I do not very well see how these matters can be adjusted without a very grave, important, and patient inquiry between the parties; that is, the United States and the authorities of the States. I have stated that the regular session of the legislature of South Carolina will be held in May. I would recommend that all the facilities offered in Virginia to the assembling of their legislature be extended to that State, and that it be invited to send commissioners to adjust the questions that are supposed to require adjustment.

"I have made a statement of the practical difficulties that exist in order to encourage you to persevere in the course of patience, moderation, forbearance, and conciliation that has marked your conduct since you entered Richmond. Many of the difficulties will be removed or lessened by such a course, and I do not know of any that will not be aggravated by the adoption of the opposite." (OR, I, XLVI, III, 657. Brackets are in the source.)

To Hugh McCulloch[1]

Hon. Sec. of the Treasury,   Executive Mansion,
Dear Sir.   Washington, April 13, 1865.

The office of Collector of Internal Revenue for the 5th. Collection District of California is vacant by the resignation of Charles Maltby. I would like to oblige Gen. Schenck by the appointment of his nephew, William C. S. Smith, long a resident of the District, to fill the vacancy. I am satisfied that he is competent, and of good character; and that his appointment will be satisfactory in the district & State. Unless you know some valid objection, send me an appointment for him. Yours truly   A. LINCOLN

[1] ALS, owned by Ross McCulloch, Fort Wayne, Indiana. On March 7, Hugh McCulloch's nomination as secretary of the Treasury in place of William P. Fessenden was confirmed by the Senate. William C. S. Smith of Napa City, California, is listed as collector for the Fifth District in the *U.S. Official Register*, 1865.

Memorandum Respecting Reduction of the Regular Army[1]

[c. April 13, 1865?]

At the close of the last British war,—in 1815—the Regular army was reduced and fixed at 14,000, which was about one soldier to 602 souls. In 1821 the army was again reduced to 10,000, which was about one soldier to 963 souls. It is proposed that at the end

[408]

of this struggle, the Regular Army shall be reduced to, and fixed at, one soldier to 1000 souls—the reduction to be in the regiments now created, all privates, thus discharged, to receive half pay from their discharge to the end of their several terms of enlistment; all officers thus discharged, who were taken from civil life, to receive one years full pay after discharge; and all who were taken from the old regular Army, to receive   pay for life, according to their several ranks, at the time of their discharge, and without promotion, Congress to provide a mode of designating what officers, and what privates, are to be discharged at the time of the reduction.

[1] AD, DLC-RTL. This memorandum is cataloged in the Lincoln Papers with a supplied date "[1864]." It seems more likely, however, to have been written in April, 1865, following Lee's surrender. On April 13, Stanton issued his order to stop drafting and recruiting, to curtail purchases, to reduce the number of general and staff officers, and to remove all military restrictions. By summer, demobilization was well under way, but the organization of the postwar Regular Army, with a maximum force of 76,000 men, was not established until the Act of July 28, 1866.

Pass for A. B. Darling[1]

Allow the bearer, A. B. Darling, to pass to, and visit Mobile, if, and when the city shall be in our possession.   A. LINCOLN
April 13, 1865.

[1] Newspaper clipping, ISLA. The pass is described in a United Press release, East Burke, Vermont, October 23, 1943, as being in "a collection . . . of the late A. B. Darling, owner and once proprietor of New York's old Fifth Avenue hotel."

Pass for G. T. Jenkins and J. M. Hiatt[1]

Allow the bearers, G. T. Jenkins & J. M. Hiatt, with ordinary baggage, to pass our lines into Virginia & return.
April 13. 1865.   A. LINCOLN

[1] ADS-P, ISLA. On January 12, 1865, James Harlan, Edwin H. Webster, and Thomas H. Hicks wrote Lincoln recommending that G. Taylor Jenkins be permitted to visit Richmond. Jenkins and Hiatt have not been identified further, but were probably citizens of Maryland.

Pass for Robert C. Schenck[1]

And to Richmond if he chooses.   A. LINCOLN
April 13. 1865.

[1] AES-P, ISLA. Lincoln's endorsement appears on a War Department pass "to City Point & back in Government transport free," signed by Edwin M. Stanton, April 11, 1865.

Pass for James W. Singleton[1]

Allow Gen. Singleton to pass to Richmond & return

April 13, 1865   A. LINCOLN

[1] ADS-F, ISLA. See Lincoln's telegrams to Grant, March 8 and 13, *supra*.

To James Speed[1]

Attorney General   Executive Mansion,
Dear Sir.   Washington, April 13. 1865

Send me a Commission for William Kellogg, to be Judge in Nebraska in place of W. P. Kellogg resigned. Yours truly

A LINCOLN

[1] ALS, DNA GE RG 60. Papers of Attorney General, Segregated Lincoln Material. William Pitt Kellogg was commissioned collector of the Port of New Orleans on April 13, 1865. Former congressman William Kellogg, fifth cousin of William Pitt Kellogg, was nominated chief justice of Nebraska Territory by President Johnson on December 20, 1865, and was confirmed by the Senate on January 15, 1866.

Concerning Passes to Richmond[1]

[April 14, 1865?]

No pass is necessary now to authorize any one to go to & return from Petersburg & Richmond. People go & return just as they did before the war.   A LINCOLN

[1] ADS, DLM. This undated manuscript would seem to have been written on April 14, 1865.

To William P. Dole[1]

Commissioner of Indian Affairs.   Executive Mansion,
My dear Sir   Washington, April 14. 1865

Please do not send off the commission of W. T. Howell, as Indian agent in Michigan, until the return of Mr. Harlan, and hearing from me again. Yours truly   A. LINCOLN

[1] ALS, owned by William H. Townsend, Lexington, Kentucky. On March 10, Lincoln nominated William T. Howell of Michigan to be agent for the Indians in Michigan, succeeding DeWitt C. Leach, and the Senate confirmed the nomination on March 11. James Harlan had been nominated and confirmed secretary of the Interior on March 9, but had not yet taken office. Lincoln wished to delay the commission, perhaps, until Harlan could approve Howell's appointment. Richard M. Smith, rather than Howell, received the appointment.

To Ulysses S. Grant[1]

Executive Mansion, Washington,
Lieut. Genl. Grant   April 14. 1865
Please call at 11. A.M. to-day instead of 9. as agreed last evening.
Yours truly   A. LINCOLN

[1] ALS, owned by John S. M. Glidden, Natick, Massachusetts. See Lincoln to Seward, *infra.*

Memorandum
Concerning Maryland Appointments[1]

Gov. Swann & Senator Cresswell present the above to-day, which they do on a plan suggested by me.   A.L.
April 14. 1865.

[1] AES, DNA FI RG 56, General Records of the Treasury Department, Series AB, 1865, Letters Received from Executive Officers, I, 6. Lincoln's endorsement appears on the following list of appointees:

"For Collector	Edwin H. Webster
	Bel-Air, Harford Coy, Md
" Post Master	Genl Andrew W Denison
	Baltimore, Md
" Surveyor	Edington Fulton
	Baltimore, Md
" Naval Officer	Samuel M. Evans
	Baltimore Md
" Marshal	James W. Clayton
	Baltimore, Md
" District Attorney	Wm J. Jones
	Elkton, Cecil County, Md
" Navy Agent	Doctr Thomas King Carroll
	Cambridge, Md
" Appraiser	Robert G. Proud
	Baltimore, Md
" "	Thomas A. Smith
	Urbana, Frederick Coy
" "	Ephraim F. Anderson
	Hagerstown, Washington County, Md"

Of these only Edwin H. Webster, Edington Fulton, William J. Jones, and Ephraim F. Anderson are listed in the *U.S. Official Register*, 1865.

Order Concerning Thomas Geary[1]

Let Thomas Geary be discharged from the service on refunding any bounty received.   A. LINCOLN.
April 14, 1865.

[1] Thomas F. Madigan, *A Catalogue of Lincolniana* (1929), No. 72. According to the catalog description, this order was written by John Hay and signed by Lincoln on an appeal of Geary's mother, a widow from Richmond, Maine, that Thomas was only seventeen years of age.

[411]

Order Concerning Benjamin F. Twilley[1]

Let it be done.   A. LINCOLN
April 14. 1865

[1] AES-F, ISLA. Lincoln's endorsement appears on the back of a letter of Benjamin F. Twilley, a prisoner at Point Lookout, Maryland, March 26, 1865, asking his cousin to persuade Senator John A. J. Creswell to secure his release. Creswell endorsed, "I respectfully ask that the within named Benjn F. Twilley be discharged on the usual terms."

To William H. Seward[1]

Hon. Sec. of State   Executive Mansion,
Sir: Washington, April 14, 1865.
    Please assemble the Cabinet at 11. A.M. to-day.
    Gen. Grant will meet with us. Yours truly   A. LINCOLN

[1] ALS, NAuE. Secretary William H. Seward was confined by his injuries, and his secretary son, Frederick W. Seward, was conducting routine duties. For an account of the cabinet meeting on problems of reconstruction, see Welles' *Diary* under this date.

To James Speed[1]

Appoint.   A. LINCOLN
April 14. 1865

[1] AES, DNA GE RG 60, Papers of Attorney General, Segregated Lincoln Material. Lincoln's endorsement appears on a letter from William H. Wallace, Washington, April 12, 1865: "I would respectfully recomend James H Alvord for the office of Marshall of the Territory of Idaho made vacant by the removal of Dolphus S Payne."
Alvord was nominated by President Johnson on December 20, 1865, and was confirmed by the Senate on January 18, 1866.

To James Speed[1]

If it is definitely concluded to accept Judge Parks' resignation, as I understand it is, let the within appointment be made
April 14. 1865.   A. LINCOLN

[1] AES, DLC. Lincoln's endorsement appears on a letter from William H. Wallace, Washington, April 12, 1865: "I would respectfully recomend Milton Kelley of Idaho for the position of Associate Justice of the Supreme Court of the Territory of Idaho, made vacant by the resignation of Samuel C Parks." Kelley was nominated by President Johnson on December 20, 1865, and was confirmed by the Senate on January 15, 1866.

To Edwin M. Stanton[1]

Hon. Secretary of War, please see and hear Hon. Mr. Rollins, & oblige him if you consistently can. A. LINCOLN
April 14. 1865.

[1] ALS-P, ISLA. Lincoln's endorsement appears on a petition addressed to the Secretary of War, presented by Congressman Edward H. Rollins of New Hampshire: "About five o'clock in the afternoon of April 14, 1865, Rollins called upon the President to secure his endorsement on a petition from New Hampshire addressed to the Secretary of War. Lincoln had finished his day's business and left his office in the White House, going up-stairs. On receiving Rollins' card, he returned to meet him. Lincoln took the petition on his knee and wrote his endorsement, dated it, and signed his name. . . . Rollins did not present the petition, but kept it as a memento . . . forwarding the request of his New Hampshire constituents in another way. . . ." (James O. Lyford, *Life of Edward H. Rollins*, pp. 187-88).

To James H. Van Alen[1]

Washington, April 14th, 1865.
My dear Sir: I intend to adopt the advice of my friends and use due precaution. . . . I thank you for the assurance you give me that I shall be supported by conservative men like yourself, in the efforts I may make to restore the Union, so as to make it, to use your language, a Union of hearts and hands as well as of States.
Yours truly, A. LINCOLN.

[1] NH, XI, 94. No trace of the original letter has been found, and the text in the source is open to question. A footnote in the source is as follows: "General Van Alen wrote Lincoln, requesting him, for the sake of his friends and the nation, to guard his life and not expose it to assassination as he had by going to Richmond. The above reply was written on the very day Lincoln was assassinated. Its discovery is due to the enthusiastic research of Mr. Gilbert A. Tracy, of Putnam, Conn." The purported letter from Van Alen is not in the Lincoln Papers.

Card of Admission for George Ashmun[1]

Allow Mr. Ashmun & friend to come in at 9. A.M. to-morrow.
April 14. 1865. A. LINCOLN

[1] ADS, DLC. Framed with a portrait of Lincoln, this card is accompanied by another card on which Ashmun wrote: "The above is the last autograph of President Lincoln. It was written & given to me at half past 8 P.M. April 14, 1865, just as he & Mrs Lincoln were starting for the Theatre where he was assasinated."

APPENDIX I

THE items of this appendix are those received too late for inclusion in their proper chronological order and those to which the editors have been unable to assign a date with accuracy.

Petition of Anson G. Henry[1]

December 15, 1847

To the Honorable, the Senate and House of Representatives of the United States of America in Congress assembled:

Your Petitioner, Anson G. Henry, of Pekin, Illinois, respectfully represents that in June 1846 he furnished supplies, transportation &c. to Capt. Edward Jones' company of volunteers, before they were mustered into the service of the United States, to the value of   that his claim has been submitted to, and finally disallowed, by the accounting officers of the Government, except as to the sum of   which has been allowed & paid

Your Petitioner herewith presents what he hopes will be deemed ample evidence of the justice of his claim; and respectfully prays that the unpaid ballance of the same be allowed him; and as in duty bound &c.   Decr. 15. 1847   A. G. HENRY.

[1] ADS, DNA RG 233, HR 30 AF 3 (7). This petition, entirely in Lincoln's autograph, is endorsed by a clerk: "Decr 20 1847. Referred to the Committee of Claims/Feby 29 1848   Bill 246." On the latter date, H.R. 246, "for the relief of Dr. A. G. Henry of Illinois," was "read the first and second time" and passed (*House Journal*). In the Senate, H.R. 246 was reported from the committee on military affairs without amendment on June 20, but no further action was taken (*Senate Journal*).

To William H. Seward[1]

Hon: W. H. Seward   Springfield, Ills.
Dear Sir: June 4. 1849

Would you as soon I should have the General Land Office as any other Illinoian? If you would, please write me to that effect at Washington, where I expect to be soon. A private despach says the appointment has been postponed three weeks from the first of June for my benefit. No time to lose. Your Obt. Servt.

A. LINCOLN

[1] ALS, NAuE. No reply from Seward has been found. See Lincoln's similar letters of June 3 and 4, 1849, *supra* (II, 52-53).

Receipt to Department of Interior[1]

Department of the Interior
June 22 1849.

Received from the files of this Department a Letter written by myself, in favor of Mr Thomas for Marshal of Ill. dated May 12 1849.   A. LINCOLN

[1] DS, DNA RG 59, Appointments, Charles G. Thomas. See Lincoln's letter to Clayton, March 10, 1849, *supra* (II, 36-37). Lincoln's letter to Clayton in favor of Charles G. Thomas has not been found.

To Thomas J. Turner[1]

Hon: Thos. J. Turner: Springfield,
Dear Sir: April 26. 1850.

I came home from the circuit four days ago, and found your letter in waiting. To-day I made some corrections of mistakes in the descriptions of the land and filed the Bill. Process is issued. In this court we can not bring in non-resident defendants by publication as we do in the State courts; but I [think] service can be had on Kemper, as he was here a few days since, and has gone to the Rock River country looking after this very land. If not, I suppose both he and Bradshaw will enter their appearance. In haste, yours as ever   A. LINCOLN

[1] ALS, IFre. See Lincoln's letter to Thomas J. Turner, February 8, 1850, *supra* (II, 72).

To Daniel A. Cheever[1]

D. A. Cheever, Esq.,   Springfield,
Dear Sir: Aug. 11, 1858.

I have had my last Springfield speech printed in pamphlet form, and now send you 250 of them. If you find them useful, more of them can be had by writing here. Address J. O. Johnson,[2] of this place, as I shall be absent after today. Yours as ever,

      A. LINCOLN.

[1] Concord, New Hampshire, *Daily Monitor and N. H. Patriot*, February 12, 1925. According to the source, this original autograph letter was presented to Governor John G. Winant by John C. Thorne. See Lincoln to Cheever, July 25, 1858, *supra* (II, 522).

[2] Concerning John O. Johnson, see Lincoln to Yates, September 30, 1857, *supra* (II, 424).

To Joseph Gillespie[1]

Illinois Central Railroad Company,

Hon: J. Gillespie   Superintendent's Office,

My dear Sir   Centralia, Sept. 16. 1858.

Since parting with you I see by the papers that the Americans and Republicans of New-York failed to form a union, and have nominated seperate tickets. This fact may be seized upon to help prevent a union in Madison Co., and I am more than ever anxious that you should be at home Saturday to do what you can. Please do not fail to go.

The meeting at Jonesborough yesterday was not large; but, in other matters, altogether respectable. I will venture to say that our friends were a little better satisfied with the result than our adversaries. You will see particulars in the papers.

Be sure to go home to the meeting on Saturday. Yours as ever

A. LINCOLN.

[1] ALS, owned by Mrs. J. L. Chapman, Jr., Van Nuys, California. No reply from Gillespie has been found. Lincoln saw Gillespie when he spoke at Edwardsville, Illinois, on September 11.

To Simon Cameron[1]

[March 8, 1861]

If the appointment herein sought, meets the approbation of Gen. Scott, and violates no rule of the army, let it be made, in which case let a blank appointment be sent me.   A. LINCOLN

[1] AES, RPB. Lincoln's endorsement appears on a true copy (March 5, 1861) of a letter from Winfield Scott to Joseph Holt, February 18, 1861:

"If the new vacancy in the Adjutant General's Department is to be filled, I know of no Lieutenant in the army who combines such strong claims—of good service long service and familiarity with the special duties of the office— as Lieutenant Fry, now commanding a battery here. It is very important that officers for this branch of the staff should be selected with a view to peculiar qualification."

An accompanying letter of James B. Fry indicated by the clerk's endorsement of March 8 is no longer with the true copy bearing Lincoln's endorsement. Fry was appointed brevet captain and assistant adjutant general as of March 16, 1861.

To William H. Seward[1]

Hon. W. H. Seward.   Executive Mansion

My dear Sir   April 17. 1861

The bearer of this, Mr. Geo. T. Whittington, of Alexandria Va. would go to Richmond, and make observations for us, if we would

bear his expenses. I think it would be well for him to go, and if you concur with me, please fit him out. Yours truly   A. LINCOLN

[1] ALS-P, ISLA. No reply from Seward or further reference to George T. Whittington has been found.

To Simon Cameron[1]

Hon. Sec. of War   Executive Mansion
My dear Sir   August 6. 1861
    Mr. Senator Latham wishes Judson Haycock to be a 2nd. Lieut. of 1st. Dragoons, in place Charles Stewart Brooks rejected by the Senate. If this place is open, as Mr. Latham thinks, oblige him in this matter. Yours truly   A. LINCOLN

[1] ALS, owned by Paul B. Freeland, Crowley, Louisiana. On the letter appears an unsigned endorsement, "To be done." According to Senator Milton S. Latham's request, Judson Haycock was appointed second lieutenant to date from August 16, 1861, and was confirmed by the Senate on February 3, 1862. The appointment of Charles Stewart Brooks was rejected by the Senate on August 5, 1861.

To Edwin M. Stanton[1]

The enclosed request from Dr. Perkins is respectfully referred to the most favorable consideration of the Secretary of War.
    March 13. 1862.   A. LINCOLN

[1] ES, RPB. The body of the endorsement is in John Hay's handwriting; the date and signature are in Lincoln's autograph. The letter of Tarrant A. Perkins, Charleston, Virginia, March 6, 1862, on which the endorsement appears, requests transfer to Missouri. Dr. Perkins was brigade surgeon on the staff of Brigadier General Jacob D. Cox, commanding the District of Kanawha. A further endorsement of the Adjutant General's Office reads: "This officer's resignation has been accepted, to take effect March 24/62." See Lincoln's letter to Stanton, May 22, 1862, *supra* (V, 229-30).

Order Concerning Mr. Garton[1]

Executive Mansion,
Washington, September 23. 1862
Mr. Garton is represented to me by good authority to have done valuable service for the Government, and to have made many sacrifices. I think his account is a very reasonable one and ought to be paid. Let no merely technical objection stand in the way of the payment.   A. LINCOLN

[1] DS, IHi. This document is in Hay's handwriting except for the last sentence and signature in Lincoln's autograph. Mr. Garton has not been identified.

To Edwin M. Stanton[1]

Executive Mansion
September 22. 1863

Respectfully referred to the Hon: Secretary of War.

The statements made by Maj. Tracy which are fully sustained by the strong testimonials he presents from the leading citizens of East Tennessee, seem to me to entitle his application to very favorable consideration. A. LINCOLN

[1] ES, RPB. The heading and body of this endorsement are in John Hay's handwriting. The endorsement appears on a letter from William R. Tracy of Hamilton County, Tennessee, September 17, 1863:

"I respectfully submit the enclosed recommendation from the principal officers in the service from East Tennessee, for the position of Paymaster in the Army. I present the paper myself, as we have at present neither Senator, or Representative in Congress, from our section of the country. I would state to you that there are *Fourteen (14)* Regiments now in the field, in the service of the United States, and that there is no Paymaster appointed for Tennessee, the above *14* Regts. being all from East Tennessee. I have served my country in the field faithfully, for nearly two years. And should your Excellency see fit to comply with the wishes of my friends, I will still do my utmost duty. I am an exile from my home in East Tennessee which I left at the commencement of the War, and I have lost all the property I left behind me.

"From a private soldier in the ranks, with no influence but my exertions I rose to the rank of Major in the 1st. East Tennessee Cavalry. . . ."

Tracy was appointed captain and commissary of subsistence of Volunteers, June 30, 1864, but no record has been found of his appointment as paymaster.

To Lorenzo Thomas[1]

On the within report, the petition of M. Van Buren Boker is refused. A. LINCOLN

August 26, 1864.

[1] ES, RPB. Lincoln's endorsement appears on a report of Robert B. Carnahan, U.S. District Attorney, Pittsburgh, Pennsylvania, August 16, 1864, recommending refusal of the petition of citizens of Washington County, Pennsylvania, on behalf of M. Van Buren Boker, convicted of resisting the draft.

To Edwin M. Stanton[1]

If it would be no detriment to the service I would be glad for General Grierson to remain here two days longer. A. LINCOLN.

February 13th, 1865.

[1] *Record of Services Rendered the Government by B. H. Grierson in 1865* (privately printed), p. 185. According to the source, this note was on a small card on the back of which Stanton wrote: "General [Benjamin H.] Grierson has permission to remain at Washington two days." See Lincoln to military officers commanding in West Tennessee, *supra* (VIII, 294-96).

To ———[1]

It is a matter of great personal consequence to me that our Illinois Rail Road bill should be acted on this session. May I hope you will help me suspend the rule to take it up? A LINCOLN

[1] ALS, owned by Robert G. Hopkins, Cincinnati, Ohio. This note was probably written while Lincoln was in congress. On January 17, 1848, Representative Robert Smith of Illinois, introduced H.R. 87, a bill to grant to the State of Illinois a right of way through the public lands, to aid in the construction of the Northern Cross Railroad. The bill was referred to the committee on public lands, but was never reported. On February 8, 1849, S. 13, another bill to grant the State of Illinois a right of way through public lands was laid before the House and referred to the committee on public lands. Representative Jacob Collamer reported the bill and moved that it should pass. There was no second. On February 28, Representative Samuel F. Vinton moved that the bill be reconsidered. Consideration was postponed. On March 3, Representative John Wentworth moved to consider Vinton's motion of February 28, but following debate the motion was tabled and the bill died.

To ———[1]

A. LINCOLN

Want to see you, but will, call again if you are busy.

[1] ALS, CSmH. This note appears on Lincoln's printed visiting card.

To ———[1]

My dear Sir

Herewith is the resolution we talked of yesterday. I think my answer should include one from the Sec. of War, as well as from you. If you send me back a copy of the resolution I will lay it before him. Yours truly A LINCOLN.

[1] Copy, ISLA. The date and the name of the recipient have been cut from the top of the letter.

To Mr. Atkinson[1]

Mr. Atkinson: I can not think of any cotton question to ask & I am really very tired. Will Mr. Atkinson please excuse me?

A. LINCOLN.

[1] Charles F. Heartman Catalog, April 2, 1927, No. 214. According to the catalog description, Lincoln's note is written on both sides of a visiting card. Atkinson may have been Robert J. Atkinson, who resigned as Third Auditor of the Treasury in June, 1864. See Lincoln to Chase, June 15, 1864, *supra* (VII, 392).

To Nathaniel P. Banks[1]

Will Gov. Banks please call and see me at once?   A. LINCOLN

[1] ALS-P, ISLA. This note was probably written prior to May 16, 1861, when Banks was commissioned a major general.

Bass-Ackwards[1]

He said he was riding *bass-ackwards* on a *jass-ack*, through a *patton-cotch*, on a pair of *baddle-sags*, stuffed full of *binger-gred*, when the animal *steered* at a *scump*, and the *lirrup-steather* broke, and throwed him in the *forner* of the *kence* and broke his *pishing-fole*. He said he would not have minded it much, but he fell right in a great *tow-curd*; in fact, he said it give him a right smart *sick* of *fitness*—he had the *molera-corbus* pretty bad. He said, about *bray dake* he come to himself, ran home, seized up a *stick* of *wood* and split the *axe* to make a light, rushed into the house, and found the *door* sick abed, and his *wife* standing open. But thank goodness she is getting right *hat* and *farty* again.

[1] AD-P, ISLA. In transcribing a copy of this piece of foolery, Jesse W. Weik identified it merely as "a 'piece' which Lincoln wrote and gave to the bailiff of one of the Springfield courts" (Hertz, *The Hidden Lincoln*, p. 400). Whether or not it was original with Lincoln has not been established.

F. S. Bougan[1]

F. S. Bougan—wants to [be] Q.M. Com. or something of the sort
I think after all, but am not sure, that he is a drunken loafer.

[1] AE, DLC-Nicolay Papers. Lincoln's undated endorsement, written between 1861 and 1865, has been cut from an envelope. F. S. Bougan has not been identified.

Cabinet Meeting[1]

Please come to Cabinet ½ past ten to-day.   A LINCOLN

[1] ALS, DLC-Nicolay Papers. Lincoln's note is written on a small card.

California Appointments[1]

Would like to have your brief for California appointments.
                                        LINCOLN.

[1] Stan. V. Henkels Catalog 1364, November 18, 1924, No. 291. According to the catalog description, this item is an autograph note signed, damaged by fire.

To Simon Cameron[1]

The Secretary of the Treasury and the President will call on the Secretary of War at 12:15, noon, today. A. LINCOLN

[1] Julia Taft Bayne, *Tad Lincoln's Father* (1931), p. 90. According to the source, Lincoln's note was written on a card, delivered to Secretary Cameron by Horatio N. Taft, Jr., and retrieved by him when Cameron threw it on the floor after reading it.

To Simon Cameron[1]

Sec. of War, please see Rev. Mr. Griffith of Alabama.
A. LINCOLN

[1] ALS, DLC-Cameron Papers. The Reverend Mr. Griffith has not been identified.

John Constant[1]

I have been at a good deal of pains to get the information you want. As I now understand it, Shandy assigned to Fogg, three notes on Constant, two of them for $150 each, one due one year after date, & the other due in two years, both dated May 9th. 1839,— the other for $45—due one year after date, dated May 10th. 1839 —on the last, there is a credit of $18.00, as of June 16th. 1841. Constant had a mortgage against White to secure four notes, three of them, for $250 each, and the fourth for $450—he sold three of the notes & retained one of the $250 ones. The mortgaged property was sold on the 27th. day of August 1844. for $550—and it has not been redeemed. It was sold for the ratable benefit of these four notes; and consequently the ratio of the 250 note retained by Constant goes to Fogg. It's ratio, as I count it, is $114.58⅓ cents, to be credited on the Shandy notes as of date 27th August 1844. The ballance of those notes remain unpaid. This

[1] AD, owned by Mrs. Edna Orendorff Macpherson, Springfield, Illinois. The top and bottom of this letter have been cut off. From the contents, the letter appears to have been written after August 27, 1844. In the case of John Constant *v.* John White, Logan and Lincoln obtained judgment for the plaintiff in the amount of $1,200, on November 16, 1843.

Draft of Telegram[1]

If any vessel has been cleared from New-York for Mobile within this year, send by mail immediately copies of every paper and entry you have, about it. If no such clearance has been given, simply say "No" by telegraph.

1 AD, OClWHi. The following endorsement written in pencil, appears on the bottom of the sheet:

"The above was written by Mr Lincoln in my presence as the substance of a letter sent to Collr. of N.Y. GEO HARRINGTON

"no com next day by Tel"

This document was probably written sometime after the fall of Fort Morgan on August 5, 1864.

Jesse K. Dubois[1]

My acquaintance first began with him in 1836. He was a member from Lawrence and Coles. Our friendship has continued and strengthened. When I first saw him he was a slim handsome young man, with auburn hair and sky-blue eyes, with the elegant manners of a Frenchman, from which nation he had his descent.

You may safely confide in him and in all he would advise you to confide in.

1 Helen L. Allen, "A Sketch of the Dubois Family, Pioneers of Indiana and Illinois," *Journal of the Illinois State Historical Society*, V (April, 1912), 62-63. Neither fragment is dated, but the second is described as being in a letter of recommendation written while Lincoln was a candidate for the presidency. No further reference to the documents has been found.

To ——— Edwards[1]

Will Mr. Edwards please attend to this case, and notify me?

A LINCOLN

1 ALS, THaroL. Lincoln's note has been removed from the attendant papers. Mr. Edwards may have been Ninian W. Edwards.

Endorsement[1]

. . . He was one of Col. Ellsworth's nearest friends, & is a good officer.

1 Parke-Bernet Catalog 134, October 25, 1939, No. 244. According to the catalog description, Lincoln's endorsement appears on a letter of Isaac N. Arnold concerning an army appointment for E. M. Ellsworth. E. M. Ellsworth has not been identified. The initials may be in error for Edward A. Ellsworth; see Lincoln to Cameron, August 8, 1861, *supra* (IV, 479).

Endorsement[1]

Let no merely technical objection stand in the way of payment.

A. LINCOLN

1 *The Flying Quill*, January-March, 1952, No. 19. According to the catalog description, this undated endorsement appears following a memorandum by John G. Nicolay concerning a citizen (unnamed) seeking pay for his services, written on Executive Mansion stationery, 1862.

Endorsement[1]

poem—I like this

[1] Herndon, II, 321. According to Herndon, Lincoln's endorsement was written on an envelope containing a copy of Charles Mackay's poem "The Enquiry," and addressed to Lincoln "in an unmistakable female hand." No trace has been found of the original.

To Gustavus V. Fox[1]

Will Mr. Fox please call and see me at once.   A. LINCOLN

[1] ALS, RPB.

To Friends of Missing Persons[1]

To the friends of missing persons; Miss Clara Barton has kindly offered to search for the missing prisoners of War. Please address her at Annapolis, Maryland giving name, regiment, and company of any missing prisoner.   A. LINCOLN

[1] Corra Bacon-Foster, "Clara Barton, Humanitarian," *Records of Columbia Historical Society*, XXI (1918), 296. No trace of the original manuscript of this item has been found.

To Charles S. Hempstead and Elihu B. Washburne[1]

Gentlemen:

Enclosed is a draft for the pension of Victoria Crowder. On your urgent request, *and merely to oblige you*, I have retained $2.00 out of it. Yours as ever   A. LINCOLN

[1] Copy, ISLA. This letter, probably written to the law firm of Hempstead & Washburne, was formerly among the papers of Elihu B. Washburne, but its present location is unknown. Victoria Crowder has not been identified.

To Thomas H. Hicks[1]

The lady who is making application is not known to me but I would be pleased if she could find a suitable position.

A. LINCOLN

[1] Copy, ISLA.

To Joseph Holt[1]

Come at 7, this evening.

[1] AE, DLC. Lincoln's endorsement appears on the back of Joseph Holt's card on which Holt had written: "I find it necessary to leave for St. Louis tomorrow. Could the Prest indicate an hour this evening or night at which he would see me." It was probably written prior to Holt's appointment as judge advocate general, September 3, 1862.

Henry C. Kerr[1]

This is filed as an application by Capt H. C. Kerr, to be Provost-Marshall of the in [sic] Judge Kelly's Dist. Penn.

[1] AE, RPB. Lincoln's endorsement has been removed from the attendant papers. Henry C. Kerr's appointment as captain of the Veteran Reserve Corps, as of May 29, 1863, was confirmed by the Senate on June 30, 1864, but no reference has been found to his appointment as provost marshal.

To James H. Lane[1]

Will Senator Lane please excuse me tonight?   A. LINCOLN.

[1] ALS, owned by Mrs. A. D. Johnson, Lawrence, Kansas. Lincoln's note appears on James H. Lane's calling card.

List of Names[1]

Bishop McIlvaine
Judge Otto
Barney Williams
Lady at Baltimore
Gen. Haupt.

[1] AD, THaroL. There is no clue to the significance of this list.

To Montgomery C. Meigs[1]

Tad wishes to see Gen. Meigs about getting cloth caps for the . . . .

[1] Parke-Bernet Catalog 1352, May 27, 1952, No. 188. According to the catalog description, this incomplete text is from an autograph note signed, including the signature of Thomas "Tad" Lincoln certified by James W. Somers.

Memorandum[1]

When you can't find *it* any where else look into this

[1] AD, PHi. Herndon relates the following: "Lincoln had always on the top of our desk a bundle of papers into which he slipped anything he wished to keep

and afterwards refer to. It was a receptacle of general information. Some years ago, on removing the furniture from the office, I took down the bundle and blew from the top the liberal coat of dust that had accumulated thereon. Immediately underneath the string was a slip bearing this endorsement, in his hand: "When you can't find it anywhere else, look in [sic] this." (Herndon, II, 315n.).

Order[1]

Let these boots go through to Richmond immediately, as directed.

A. LINCOLN

[1] New York *Sun,* February 12, 1934. According to the newspaper article, Lincoln wrote this order on a small card at the request of Green Clay Smith for Mrs. Lindsey Hamilton, whose brother, a Confederate soldier wounded in the ankle, needed the specially made boots to prevent his becoming a permanent cripple.

Order Concerning Edward W. Kinsley[1]

To All Officers of the Army of the Potomac:

You will allow the bearer, Mr. Edward W. Kinsley, to pass inside our lines at whatever time he may choose and at any point he may desire, and officers will see that he has proper escort.

ABRAHAM LINCOLN.

[1] Bowdoin S. Parker, *History of Edward W. Kinsley Post No. 113, Department of Massachusetts, Grand Army of the Republic* . . . (Norwood, Massachusetts, 1913), p. 144. This order is without date in the source, but the time is indicated as the latter part of the war, when Kinsley, a Boston merchant, was the confidential agent of Governor John A. Andrew.

Pardon of Doll Jack[1]

The Doll Jack is pardoned by order of the President.

A. LINCOLN

[1] Julia Taft Bayne, *Tad Lincoln's Father* (1931), p. 137. For circumstances, see the source.

O. H. Platt[1]

O. H. Platt, trying to resign an office which he does not hold.

[1] AE, DLC-Nicolay Papers. Lincoln's endorsement has been cut from an envelope. Orville H. Platt, a lawyer and legislator of West Meriden, Connecticut, may have been the man referred to (see Welles' *Diary,* August 15, 1862), but Obadiah H. Platt of Missouri, appointed additional paymaster, June 1, 1861, and dismissed June 21, 1862, is another possibility.

To the Secretary of War[1]

Hon. Sec. of War. Please make the Hospital Chaplaincy appointment for Senator Foot which he asks for. Yours truly,

A. LINCOLN.

[1] Carnegie Book Shop Catalog 142, May, 1949, No. 250. According to the catalog description, this is an autograph letter signed.

To the Secretary of War[1]

Sec. of War. Please see Mr. Edwards a moment.　　A.L.

[1] American Art Association Catalog, April 11-12, 1922, No. 491. Mr. Edwards may have been Ninian W. Edwards.

To William H. Seward[1]

Sec. of State, please see Mrs. Handy & send her out of the country if you can.　　A. LINCOLN.

[1] ALS, NAuE. Lincoln's undated note appears on a card with an envelope endorsed by Seward, "Note to Mrs. Handy/For self/84 North Charles Street/& 3 children/Baltimore, Md."

To William H. Seward[1]

I know nothing of the gentleman recommend[ed] within; but the lady (Mrs. Walworth) in whose hands I find the paper is an old friend and acquaintance, and I would like for her to to [sic] be obliged, in the way named, or some similar one.

A. LINCOLN

[1] AES, NAuE. Lincoln's undated endorsement has been removed from attendant papers. A bracketed date in pencil, "March, 1861," has been added by someone. Mrs. Walworth was probably Sarah Ellen (Smith) Hardin, the widow of John J. Hardin, who in 1851 had married Reuben H. Walworth, member of congress (1821-1823) and chancellor of New York (1828-1848).

To Edwin M. Stanton[1]

Has anything been heard from Buell lately? Is anything being done for East Tennessee?　　A. LINCOLN

[1] Anderson Galleries Catalog 1270, January 25, 1917, No. 196. According to the catalog description, this undated autograph note is written in pencil on a card. It was probably written during September, 1862, when General Don C. Buell was attempting to check General Braxton Bragg's invasion of Tennessee.

To Edwin M. Stanton[1]

If approved by the Secretary of War I request the court to turn the arms within mentioned over to United States Ordnance Department.

[1] Copy, ISLA. No further description available.

To Edwin M. Stanton[1]

Please see Mr. Goggin.   A. L.

[1] AES, owned by Van Dyk MacBride, Newark, New Jersey. Lincoln's endorsement appears on a printed envelope to "The Secretary of War," which is also endorsed by Stanton: "Mr Goggin/Application to bring person from Richmond." William L. Goggin had served in congress with Lincoln in 1847-1849.

To Lyman Trumbull[1]

Impossible

[1] AE, NHi. Lincoln's endorsement appears on an empty envelope addressed to President Lincoln by Senator Lyman Trumbull.

Elias T. Turney[1]

We take pleasure in certifying that Hon. Elias T. Turney is a gentleman of good moral character.   A. LINCOLN,

WARD H. LAMON

[1] Howard F. Dyson, "Lincoln in Rushville," *Transactions of the Illinois State Historical Society* (1903), p. 225. Turney was an applicant for a license to practice law. No record has been found of his admission to practice.

To Gideon Welles[1]

Secretary Welles,—

The United States don't need the services of boys who disobey their parents. Let both Snyder and Ratcliffe be discharged.

A. LINCOLN.

[1] Tracy, p. 237. Snyder and Ratcliffe have not been identified.

To Gideon Welles (?)[1]

No remark, except I was informed the vessel *had* proceeded to sea yesterday. Now she *is* to go to-day.   A.L.

[1] ADS, NHi. Lincoln's note is written on a small card.

To Gideon Welles[1]

. . . desires to have a portion of the Marine force. Let him have it at once, unless you think there is some insuperable objection, in which case call and see me at once. Yours truly   A. LINCOLN

[1] Stan. V. Henkels Catalog 1342, January 4, 1924, No. 37. According to the catalog description the upper portion of this autograph letter has been destroyed by fire.

To Whom It May Concern[1]

To Whom It May Concern:
On application of the Sisters of Mercy in charge of the Military Hospital in Washington furnish such provisions as they desire to purchase, and charge same to the War Department.
ABRAHAM LINCOLN.

[1] Ellen Ryan Jolly, *Nuns of the Battlefield* (1927), p. 245. The original manuscript has not been found.

To Whom It May Concern[1]

To Whom It May Concern:
On application of the Sisters of Mercy of Chicago, furnish such provisions as they desire to purchase and charge the same to the War Department.   ABRAHAM LINCOLN.

[1] Ellen Ryan Jolly, *Nuns of the Battlefield* (1927), p. 236. The original manuscript has not been found.

To Mrs. W. C. Williams[1]

I only know by the despatch from Camp Chase, which Mrs. W. has.   A.L.

[1] Anderson Galleries Catalog 2193, November 15, 1927, No. 290; Swann Auction Galleries Catalog, March 3, 1949, No. 235. The second source gives the text of the note to which Lincoln replied: "Will President Lincoln please give me the name of the Commandant at Camp Chase. MRS. W. C. WILLIAMS."

———— Woodruff[1]

Mr. Woodruff personally tells me he has tried the business and knows he can succeed . . . thinks someone should be appointed at once.

[1] *The Flying Quill*, January-February, 1951, No. 18. According to the catalog description, Lincoln's endorsement appears on an envelope addressed to "His Excellency, A. Lincoln, President of United States." Mr. Woodruff has not been identified.

To the People of Sangamon County[1]

TO THE PEOPLE OF SANGAMON COUNTY

Fellow Citizens:

I have this moment been shown a handbill signed "Truth Teller," in which my name is done up in large capitals. No one can doubt the object of this attack at this late hour. An effort is now made to show that John T. Stuart and myself opposed the passage of the bill by which the Wiggins loan was paid. The handbill says—"The only vote taken on the bill when the yeas and nays were taken, was upon engrossing the bill for a third reading." That's a lie. Let the reader refer to pages, 124, 125 & 126 of the Journal,[2] and he will see that the yeas and nays were taken *twice* upon the bill *after* the vote referred to by this lying Truth Teller. And he will also see that my course toward the bill was anything but unfriendly. It is impossible to make a lengthy answer at this late hour. All I have to say is that the author is a *liar* and a *scoundrel,* and that if he will avow the authorship to me, I promise to give his proboscis a good wringing. A. LINCOLN.

[1] Copy, IHi. This copy is in the handwriting of Joseph Wallace who states in a postscript that it is a "copy of an Election Handbill issud by Mr Lincoln . . . found among the old papers of the late Archer G. Herndon of Springfield [Illinois]. It is without date, but was probably issued on the eve of the [congressional] election in 1836." Another copy in Wallace's handwriting is owned by Mrs. Edna Orendorff Macpherson, Springfield, Illinois.

[2] *House Journal,* Dec. 22, 1835.

APPENDIX II

IN this, index the editors have listed chronologically writings for which no text has been found, forgeries and spurious or dubious items attributed to Lincoln, certain routine communications issued on Lincoln's authority, and routine endorsements. Although the editors have tried to list all those items which in their opinion would be of service to the student, the list is necessarily selective. Except in particular cases, the following categories of documents have *not* been listed: nominations, land grants, discharge papers, ships' papers, routine pardon and clemency endorsements, draft orders, approvals, appointments, authorizations, and commissions.

Abbreviations are the same as those used throughout the *Complete Works* except for an additional symbol NE adopted specifically for this list. The symbol NE indicates that, in so far as the editors have been able to determine, the item is not extant.

1818

c. Oct. 5. To David Elkin, NE, purported, Chittenden, *Personal Reminiscences*, 346.

1824–1826

——. Poem: "Adam and Eve's Wedding Song," purported, Herndon, I, 43
——. Essay on American Government, NE, purported, *ibid.*, 61

1828

——. Poem: "Let auld acquaintance be forgot," purported, *ibid.*, 57
——. Essay on Temperance, NE, purported, *ibid.*, 61

1829

——. Chronicles of Reuben, purported, *ibid.*, 52
——. Poem: "I will tell you a joke about Joel and Mary," purported, *ibid.*, 55

1830

Summer. Speech at Decatur, Ill., NE, purported, Howells, *Lincoln*, 28

1831

Sept. 2. Witness, William Batterton to Denton Offutt, DS, Sangamon Co. Deed Book E, 297

Oct. 20. Attests, James Richardson to John Ferguson, DS, IHi
Dec. 9. Witness, John M. Camron to John McNamar, DS, Sangamon
Co. Deed Book F, 48, 49 (two deeds)
Dec. 19. Witness, John M. Camron to David Whary, DS, *ibid.*, Book
E, 309

1832

———. To Charles P. Cabanis, NE, *see* George E. Cabanis to Lincoln,
Aug 12, 1860, DLC-RTL
Jan. 16. Witness, John Jones, Sr., to John Watkins, Sr., DS, Sangamon
Co. Deed Book E, 433
Apr. 21. Remarks accepting captaincy, Black Hawk War, NE, pur-
ported, Herndon, I, 104
c. July. Speech at Pappsville, Ill., purported, *see* A. Y. Ellis to Hern-
don, June 5, 1866, DLC-HW
Aug. 4. Speech at Springfield, Ill., NE, *see* Bulletin 12, ISLA
Aug. 30. Certification of David Rutledge's service in Black Hawk War,
DS, Fern Nance Pond, Petersburg, Ill.
Sept. 3. Witness, Ranson Lane to James Goldsby, DS, Sangamon Co.
Deed Book F, 240
Sept. 21. Certification of Lewis W. Farmer's service in Black Hawk
War, DS-F, ISLA
Sept. 26. Certification of David M. Pantier's service in Black Hawk
War, DS, CSmH
Sept. 29. Certification of Travice Elmore's service in Black Hawk War,
DS-F, ISLA

1833

Jan. 10. Witness, George Warburton to Hezekiah King, DS, Sanga-
mon Co. Deed Book F, 433-34 (two deeds)
Mar. 6. William F. Berry signs Lincoln's name to bond for license to
sell liquor at Berry-Lincoln store at New Salem, D, IHi
June 4. Witness, Hiram L. Allen to Hawkins Taylor, DS, Sangamon
Co. Deed Book I, 478
July 13. Witness, Joseph Watkins to Thomas Dowell, DS, *ibid.*, Book
T, 185
July 13. Witness, Thomas Dowell to Joseph Watkins, DS, *ibid.*, Book
G, 143
Nov. 29. Witness, Silas Watkins to Charles Bell, DS, *ibid.*, Book G, 230

1834

———. To Elmore Johnson [Johnson Elmore], NE, purported, Lamon,
Lincoln, 149
———. Essay on Religion, NE, purported, Herndon, III, 439
———. "Lincoln's Field Notes and Plat," forgery, AD, ICHi
Feb. 14. Plat of survey of Section 16, copy, Sangamon Co. Supt. of
Schools, Record Book A, 63
Apr. 3. Promissory note to Waltam E. Grassel, forgery, ADS-P, ISLA
Apr. 30. Promissory note to Waltam E. Grassel, forgery, ADS-P, ISLA

Aug. 25. Witness, John F. and Parthena Harrison to Robert McNabb, DS, Sangamon Co. Deed Book H, 101

Sept. 30. Survey of New Boston, Ill., copy, Warren Co. Deed Records, I, 308

Dec. 10. Pseudonymous "Our Correspondent" letter, attributed on insufficient evidence, *Sangamo Journal*, Dec. 13, 1834

Dec. 24. Remarks in Ill. legislature concerning bill to limit jurisdiction of justices of peace, mentioned, *Illinois Advocate*, Dec. 27, 1834

1835

Jan. 23. Anonymous letter to "Mr. Editor," attributed on insufficient evidence, *Sangamo Journal*, Jan. 31, 1835

Jan. 28. Pseudonymous "Our Correspondent" letter, attributed on insufficient evidence, *ibid.*, Feb. 7, 1835

Mar. 16. Copy of an act relative to a state road (*see* Jan. 29, 1835) made for Sangamon Co. Commissioners Court, AD, IHi

Apr. 25. Witness, John Jones, Sr. and Lydia Jones to John Jones, Jr., DS, Sangamon Co. Deed Book H, 365

May 16. Witness, bans of matrimony, William Taylor and Emaline Johnson, forgery, DS, ICHi

May 27. Copy of an act to change state road from Springfield to Alton, Ill., introduced by John T. Stuart, Jan. 17, 1835, AD, IHi

June 19. Witness, Alexander Latine to Henry Anno, DS, Sangamon Co. Deed Book H, 393

Sept. 22. Letter franked "Free. A. Lincoln P.M." to George M. Marsh, Portsmouth, N. H., from Matthew S. Marsh, New Salem, Ill., DS, ORB

Sept. 24. Survey of timber land, William Green to Matthew S. Marsh, ADS, ORB

Dec. 7. Pseudonymous "Our Correspondent" letter, attributed on insufficient evidence, *Sangamo Journal*, Dec. 12, 1835

Dec. 7. Anonymous letter "From a Member of the Legislature," attributed on insufficient evidence, *ibid.*, Dec. 19, 1835

Dec. 13. Anonymous letter on "The Canal Bill," attributed on insufficient evidence, *ibid.*

Dec. 14. Pseudonymous "Our Correspondent" letter, attributed on insufficient evidence, *ibid.*

Dec. 18. Motion "to fill the blank with 8500" (Apportionment Bill), Ill. *House Journal*, 107

Dec. 26. Pseudonymous "Our Correspondent" letter, attributed on insufficient evidence, *Sangamo Journal*, Jan. 2, 1836

Dec. 28. Anonymous letter, "Sequel of the Van Buren State Convention," attributed on insufficient evidence, *ibid.*, Feb. 6, 13, 20, 1836

Dec. 29. Anonymous letter, "This evening we made Noel's tobacco fly again," attributed on insufficient evidence, *ibid.*, Jan. 9, 1836

1836

——. To Postmaster General Amos Kendall, letter returning twenty-five cents owed the government, NE, purported, Boston *Globe*, Feb. 5, 1926

——. Inscription on flyleaf of *The Works of William Paley:* "A. Lincoln—Presented by his friend, N. W. Edwards." ADS-F, ISLA

Jan. 4. Anonymous letter, "I have been rather remiss," attributed on insufficient evidence, *Sangamo Journal,* Jan. 9, 1836

Jan. 6. Anonymous letter, "In my last I mentioned," attributed on insufficient evidence, *ibid.,* Jan. 16, 1836

Jan. 7. Anonymous letter, "I am gratified," attributed on insufficient evidence, *ibid.*

Feb. 13. Speech at Petersburg, Ill., mentioned, *ibid.,* Feb. 20, 1836

Feb. 17. Certificate of survey of Petersburg, Ill., copy, Sangamon Co. Deed Book I, 293

Feb. 17. Pseudonymous letter, "Johnny Blubberhead," attributed on insufficient evidence, *Sangamo Journal,* Feb. 20, 1836

Apr. 9. List of 64 unclaimed letters at New Salem Post Office, *ibid.,* Apr. 9 and 16, 1836

July 9. List of 48 unclaimed letters at New Salem Post Office, *ibid.,* July 9 and 16, 1836

July 14. Speech at Salisbury, Ill., mentioned, *ibid.,* July 16, 1836

July 16. Speech at Athens, Ill., announced, *ibid.*

July 18. Speech at Varsell's farm on Sugar Creek, Ill., announced, *ibid.*

July 19. Speech at Mechanicsburg, Ill., announced, *ibid.*

July 20. Speech at Cotton Hill, Ill., announced, *ibid.*

July 21. Speech at New Salem, Ill., announced, *ibid.*

July 23. Speech at Allenton, Ill., announced, *ibid.,* July 23, 1836

July 25. Speech at Berlin, Ill., announced, *ibid.*

July 26. Speech at Thomas Campbell farm on Lick Creek, Ill., announced, *ibid.*

July 27. Speech at Petersburg, Ill., announced, *ibid.*

July 29. Speech at Isaac Spear farm (six miles from Springfield, Ill.), announced, *ibid.*

July 30. Speech at Springfield, Ill., announced, *ibid.,* July 16, 1836; in reply to George Forquer tells lightning rod story (Herndon, I, 172)

c. Sept. 7. Survey of school section in northeast Cass Co., mentioned, Morgan Co. Commissioners Record

Nov. 1. Survey of Bath, Ill., copy, Mason County plat records, Book I, 42

Dec. 5. Pseudonymous letter, "Illinois Patriot," attributed on insufficient evidence, *Sangamo Journal,* Dec. 24, 1836

Dec. 11. Anonymous letter, "As yet little business," attributed on insufficient evidence, *ibid.,* Dec. 17, 1836

Dec. 17. Anonymous letter, "This is the close," attributed on insufficient evidence, *ibid.,* Dec. 24, 1836

Dec. 22. Pseudonymous letter, "A Citizen of Sangamon," attributed on insufficient evidence, *ibid.,* Jan. 7, 1837

Dec. 22. Remarks in Ill. legislature on formation of new county of Van Buren, mentioned, *Ill. State Register,* Jan. 12, 1837

Dec. 25. Pseudonymous "Our Correspondent" letter attributed on insufficient evidence, *Sangamo Journal,* Dec. 31, 1836

Dec. 25. Anonymous letter, "All communication," attributed on insufficient evidence, *ibid.*

Dec. 30. Anonymous letter, "I have a most unpleasant task," attributed on insufficient evidence, *ibid.*, Jan. 6, 1837

1837

Jan. 18. Motion to amend Usher F. Linder's bank resolution, Ill. *House Journal*, 290

Jan. 20. Motion to amend resolution concerning slavery in the District of Columbia, *ibid.*, 309

Feb. 24. Motion to amend bill locating state capital, *ibid.*, 702

Apr. 20. Deed to Josephus Hewett and Edward D. Baker, copy, Sangamon Co. Deed Book K, 616

May 9. Deed to Gershom Jayne, copy, *ibid.*, Book K, 686

June 6. Certification of map of John Bennett's addition to Petersburg, Ill., copy, *ibid.*, Book L, 198

June 14. Pseudonymous letter, "Sampson's Ghost," attributed on insufficient evidence, *Sangamo Journal*, June 17, 1837

June 21. Pseudonymous letter, "Sampson's Ghost," attributed on insufficient evidence, *ibid.*, June 24, 1837

July 1. Anonymous letter, "To the Voters Sangamon County," attributed on insufficient evidence, *ibid.*, July 1, 1837

July 4. Pseudonymous letter, "Sampson's Ghost," attributed on insufficient evidence, *ibid.*, July 8, 1837

July 8. Receipt on back of note of Pollard Simmons for $213.62: "Received on the within $80." AES, DLC-HW

July 12. Pseudonymous letter, "Sampson's Ghost," attributed on insufficient evidence, *Sangamo Journal*, July 15, 1837

July 15. Anonymous skit, "A Ghost!" attributed on insufficient evidence, *ibid.*

July 15. Attest, note of Samuel Hurst to William Butler, DS, IHi

July 16. Anonymous letter, "The various subjects," attributed on insufficient evidence, *Sangamo Journal*, July 22, 1837

July 20. Pseudonymous letter, "Sampson's Ghost," attributed on insufficient evidence, *ibid.*

July 26. Pseudonymous letter, "Sampson's Ghost," attributed on insufficient evidence, *ibid.*, July 29, 1837

Aug. 5. Anonymous anecdote, General James Adams and the calf, attributed on insufficient evidence, *ibid.*, Aug. 5, 1837

Aug. 7. Benjamin Talbott's testimony on deed, Joseph Anderson to General Adams, purported, *ibid.*, Aug. 19, 1837

Aug. 15. Signs bond of Charles R. Matheny as clerk of county commissioners court, DS, Sangamon Co. Record D, 355

Sept. 27. Witness, Samuel Neale, Sr. to Archer G. Herndon, DS, Sangamon Co. Deed Book M, 247

Sept. 30. Pseudonymous letter, "An Old Settler," attributed on insufficient evidence, *Sangamo Journal*, Sept. 30, 1837

Oct. 7. Pseudonymous letter, "An Old Settler," attributed on insufficient evidence, *ibid.*, Oct. 7, 1837

Oct. 14. Anonymous letter, "An Old Settler," attributed on insufficient evidence, *ibid.*, Oct. 14, 1837

Dec. 29. Receipt on note of H. Garret & Co. to Anderson, Bell & Co. for $1,049.72: "Received on the within $305.50 cents," AE, DLC-HW

1838

——. Poem: "Whatever spiteful fools may say," purported, Herndon, I, 244

Jan. 12. Pseudonymous letter, "The Conservative," attributed on insufficient evidence, *Sangamo Journal*, Jan. 12, 1838

Jan. 19. Temperance pledge, attributed on insufficient evidence, *The Interior*, Feb. 11, 1909

Jan. 20. Anonymous letter, "Lost Townships," attributed on insufficient evidence, *Sangamo Journal*, Feb. 10, 1838

Jan. 27. Pseudonymous letter, "The Conservative—No. 2" attributed on insufficient evidence, *ibid.*, Jan 27, 1838

Feb. 3. Pseudonymous, "Addendum—to Conservative, No. 2," attributed on insufficient evidence, *ibid.*, Feb. 3, 1838

Feb. 10. Pseudonymous letter, "The Conservative—No. 3," attributed on insufficient evidence, *ibid.*, Feb. 10, 1838

Mar. 15. To B. C. Marshall, forgery, ALS, NN

Apr. 25. Anonymous letter, "Lost Townships," attributed on insufficient evidence, *Sangamo Journal*, May 5, 1838

May 7. Anonymous letter, "Lost Townships," attributed on insufficient evidence, *ibid.*, May 26, 1838

c. May 10. Speech at Bloomington, Ill., mentioned by Henry Stevens in Bloomington *Pantagraph*, Mar. 12, 1898

June 16. Speech at Bartell's on Sugar Creek, Ill., mentioned, *Sangamo Journal*, June 23, 1838

June 18. Signs bond of Charles R. Matheny as clerk of county commissioners court, Sangamo Co. Record D, 434

June 22. Speech at William Colburn's Mill on Lick Creek (Loami), Ill., mentioned, *Sangamo Journal*, June 23, 1838

June 23. Speech at Berlin, Ill., mentioned, *ibid.*

June 30. Speech at Waters' Camp Ground on Spring Creek, Ill., announced, *ibid.*

July 22. To Jesse W. Fell, NE (*see* Lincoln to Fell, July 23, 1838)

Aug. 11. Editorial, "At the result of this election," attributed on insufficient evidence, *Sangamo Journal*, Aug. 11, 1838

Aug. 22. Certification of payment of mortgage by William L. May for Henry B. Truett, AES, Sangamo Co. Deed Book M, 413

Aug. 27. Anonymous letter, "Lost Townships," attributed on insufficient evidence, *Sangamo Journal*, Sept. 7, 1838

Sept. 6. Anonymous letter, "Lost Townships," attributed on insufficient evidence, *ibid.*, Sept. 15, 1838

Sept. 29. Speech at Springfield, Ill., mentioned, *ibid.*, Oct. 6, 1838

Nov. 3. Editorial excusing Whigs for passing up Clay and Webster as nominees, attributed on insufficient evidence, *ibid.*, Nov. 3, 1838

Dec. 15. Remarks in legislature opposing settler's right to collect for improvements on public lands, mentioned, Vandalia *Free Press*, Dec. 27, 1838

Dec. 18. Committee report by Archibald Williams opposing Van Buren's sub-treasury plan, attributed on insufficient evidence, Ill. *House Journal*, 98-103

1839

——. Inscription in Gibbon's *Decline and Fall of the Roman Empire:* "A. Lincoln—Presented by his friend, N. W. Edwards." ADS, CSmH

Jan. 16. Remarks in legislature on bill to regulate elections: "Mr. Lincoln would ask a question. Would not the suspected persons be entitled to a trial by jury? And would not a jury inquire into the *intention* of persons thus tried? If so, the amendment was unnecessary." Vandalia *Free Press,* Jan. 24, 1839

Jan. 18. Motions to amend bill establishing counties of Menard, Logan and Dane (Christian), Ill. *House Journal,* 234-35

Jan. 18. Remarks in legislature on bill authorizing land patents to be admitted to record: "Mr. Lincoln said that the difficulty to be remedied is already provided for; and therefore the last clause of the bill is irrelevant." Vandalia *Free Press,* Jan. 24, 1839

Jan. 21. Remarks in legislature on bill to change judicial circuits, mentioned, *ibid.*

Jan. 22. Speech in legislature on sub-treasury, mentioned, Quincy *Whig,* Feb. 2, 1839; Vandalia *Free Press,* Jan. 24, 1839

Feb. 13. Remarks in legislature opposing bill to distribute school fund, mentioned, Vandalia *Free Press,* Feb. 21, 1839

Feb. 19. Bill in legislature to incorporate Santa Fe Railroad, attributed on insufficient evidence, D, I-Ar

Feb. 20. Bill in legislature to incorporate Franklin Institute introduced by Lincoln, but attributed on insufficient evidence, D, I-Ar

Feb. 22. Remarks in legislature on bill changing judicial circuits: "Mr. Lincoln would go for the bill, although he would have preferred that amendment which was lost yesterday evening; and he thought that others of the Sangamon delegation would do the same." Vandalia *Free Press,* Feb. 28, 1839

Feb. 23. Motion to amend title of act for relief of clerk of circuit court of Sangamon Co., Ill. *House Journal,* 492

Feb. 26. Motion to amend title of act for limitation of actions and for avoiding law suits, *ibid.,* 530

Apr. ——Indenture (printed form) partially filled out by Lincoln for Martin G. and Lucy Pulliam, AD, owned by Harry E. Pratt, Springfield, Ill.

Spring. Debate at Lewistown, Ill., mentioned in Harvey L. Ross, *Lincoln's First Years in Illinois,* 33-34

Oct. 7. Preamble and resolutions adopted at Whig State convention at Springfield, Ill., attributed on insufficient evidence, Wilson, *Uncollected Works,* I, 631-33

Oct. 28. Pseudonymous article, "A Looker-on," attributed on insufficient evidence, *Sangamo Journal,* Nov. 8, 1839; *Ill. State Register,* Nov. 16, 1839

Nov. 19. Speech at Springfield, Ill., mentioned, *ibid.,* Nov. 23, 1839

Nov. 20. Speech at Springfield, Ill., mentioned, *ibid.*

Nov. 29. Anonymous article, "The Contested Election" (Stuart *vs.* Douglas for congress), attributed on insufficient evidence, *Sangamo Journal,* Nov. 29, 1839

Dec. 9. Remarks in legislature on propriety of seating Oscar Love, mentioned, *ibid.*, Dec. 10, 1839

Dec. 13. Motion to amend resolution concerning Oscar Love and Richard Kerr: "Mr. Lincoln moved to amend the amendment by adding, 'and that until this contest be determined, neither of the contesting parties be entitled to a seat in this House:' which was agreed to." Ill. *House Journal*, 39.

Dec. 16. Motion to amend resolution concerning Oscar Love and Richard Kerr: "Mr. Lincoln moved to amend, by striking out the following words in the resolution just adopted, 'until further testimony is heard on the subject,' which was agreed to." *Ibid.*, 43

Dec. 21. Motion to amend resolution reserving Hall of H.R.: "Mr. Lincoln moved to strike out 'every night' and insert Mondays, Wednesdays and Fridays; which was agreed to." *Ibid.*, 74

Dec. 26. Remarks in legislature concerning bill licensing taverns and groceries: "Mr. Lincoln said it was but just, either that towns should have nothing to do with the matter, or if burthened with it, that they should have the proceeds of the Licenses they granted." *Sangamo Journal*, Dec. 31, 1839

Dec. 26. Motion to amend liquor bill: "Mr. Lincoln moved to amend the report by striking out the third section, and the words 'and trustees of incorporated towns' whenever they occur in the report; which was agreed to." Ill. *House Journal*, 86

1840

——. Speech on history of the drama and against a high license fee for theatricals before town council of Springfield, Ill., purported in Joseph Jefferson, *Autobiography*, 29-30

Jan. 11. Endorsement, "A Lincoln (true, as I believe)" on Edward D. Baker's remonstrance against acquittal of John Pearson, AES, I-Ar

Jan. 11. Remarks in legislature concerning John Pearson, mentioned, *Sangamo Journal*, Jan. 17, 1840

Jan. 16. Corrections on petition written by Thomas Moffett for divorce of Sarah Martin from Nathaniel Martin, D, I-Ar

Jan. 17. Remarks in legislature on bill to abolish Board of Public Works: "Mr. Lincoln said he had a word to say to the original friends of the system, and that is, if they will come forward and go for the above proposition, he will also go for it. In other words, he is willing to classify, if those gentlemen will agree upon that road. Ill. *State Register*, Jan. 22, 1840

Jan. 20. An act to amend acts in relation to constables, incorrectly attributed to Lincoln, but introduced by him, D, I-Ar

Feb. 1. Act to amend laws in relation to Illinois and Michigan Canal, incorrectly attributed, Wilson, I, 489-92

Feb. 1. Amendment limiting tenure of the secretary of state, mentioned, *Sangamo Journal*, Feb. 7, 1840

Feb. 10. Speech at Peoria, Ill., mentioned, Peoria *Reg. and N. W. Gazetteer*, Feb. 15, 1840

Mar. 17. Speech at Jacksonville, Ill., mentioned, *Ill. State Reg.*, Mar. 27, 1840

Apr. 6. Speech at Carlinville, Ill., mentioned, Alton *Telegraph*, Apr. 11, 1840; *Sangamo Journal*, Apr. 24, 1840

Apr. 9. Speech at Alton, Ill., mentioned, Alton *Telegraph*, Apr. 11, 1840

Apr. 11. Speech at Belleville, Ill., mentioned, *Missouri Republican*, Apr. 13, 1840; Belleville *Advocate*, Apr. 18, 1840

June 3. Speech at state Whig convention, Springfield, Ill., mentioned, Burlington, Iowa, *Hawk Eye*, June 11, 1840

June 3-4. Report of Whig convention in *The Old Soldier*, June 15, 1840, incorrectly attributed, Wilson, I, 543-46

June 27. Speech at Shelbyville, Ill., mentioned, *Ill. State Reg.*, July 10, 1840

July 20. Debate at Springfield, Ill. with Jesse B. Thomas over authorship of "The Conservative" letters, mentioned, *ibid.*, July 24, 1840

Aug. 22?. Speech at Belleville, Ill., mentioned, Belleville *Advocate*, Aug. 29, 1840

Aug. 25. Speech at Waterloo, Ill., mentioned, *Ill. State Reg.*, Sept. 4, 1840

Aug. 28?. Debate with John A. McClernand at Mt. Vernon, Ill., mentioned, *Recollections of Rev. John Johnson* (1869), 259

Sept. 1. Speech at Carmi, Ill., mentioned, Pratt, *Lincoln 1840-1846*, 36

Sept. 3. Speech at Mt. Carmel, Ill., mentioned, *ibid.*

Sept. 5. Debate with John A. McClernand at Shawneetown, Ill., mentioned, *Ill. State Reg.*, Sept. 25, 1840

Sept. 7?. Debate with Josiah Lamborn at Equality, Ill., mentioned, *ibid.*

Sept. 7?. Debate with Josiah Lamborn at Shawneetown, Ill., mentioned, *ibid.*

Sept. 8?. Speech at Morganfield, Ky., purported, Pratt, *Lincoln 1840-1846*, 38

Sept. 17. Speech in reply to Josiah Lamborn at Equality, Ill., mentioned, *Ill. State Reg.*, Oct. 2, 1840

Sept. 19. Speech at Marshall, Ill., purported by George W. Smith, Pratt, *Lincoln 1840-1846*, 38

Sept. 19. Speech at Casey, Ill., purported, *ibid.*

Sept. 26. To Isaac Underhill & Frisby & Metcalf, forgery, ALS-P, ISLA

Oct. 20?. Speech at Albion, Ill., purported, Gibson W. Harris, "My Recollections. . . ." *Farm & Fireside*, Dec. 1, 1904

Dec. 1. Speech in legislature on law repealing Board of Public Works: "Mr. Lincoln was of opinion that the bill, having come from the committee on finance, ought now be referred to a different committee; it was, he thought, a question of great moment, and a select committee might have new views." *Ill. State Reg.*, Dec. 4, 1840

Dec. 2. Remarks on resolution that no reports or communication other than Auditor's, Treasurer's, or select or standing committees, be printed in *House Journal:* "Mr. Lincoln understood that if this resolution did not pass, the clerk was bound to put every report on the Journal." *Ibid.*, Dec. 11, 1840

Dec. 3. Remarks on resolution to investigate conduct of canal commissioners at Lockport, Ill., "Mr. Lincoln . . . wishes to know from some other gentleman what time the investigation would take. . . ." *Ibid.*

Dec. 5. Remarks on bill for manufacture of salt in Gallatin and Saline counties: "Mr. Lincoln was willing to go for the bill if he could be satisfied that we were not making a bad bargain." *Ibid.*

Dec. 10. Remarks on motion to print bill to provide for payment of January interest: "Mr. Lincoln was opposed to the printing; he questioned if the bill was of sufficient importance." *Ibid.*, Dec. 18, 1840

Dec. 17. Resolution in legislature to give control of jails to county commissioners, incorrectly attributed, *ibid.*, Dec. 23, 1840; *see* Ill. *House Journal*, 129

Dec. 18. Remarks in legislature concerning Norman H. Purple, mentioned, *Sangamo Journal*, Dec. 22, 1840; *Ill. State Reg.*, Dec. 23, 1840

1841

——. To Dr. Daniel Drake, purported, Joshua F. Speed to William H. Herndon, Nov. 30, 1866, DLC-HW

——. Poem on suicide, purported, Herndon, II, 216

Jan. 29. Last line of an act to amend an act incorporating agricultural societies, "whether he be a member of a county society or not," D, I-Ar

Feb. 1. Remarks in legislature on Peoria ferry bill, mentioned, *Sangamo Journal*, Feb. 5, 1841

Feb. 9. Remarks in legislature on distributing moneys from Vermilion saline lands, mentioned, *ibid.*, Feb. 12, 1841

Feb. 16. Remarks in legislature on apportionment bill, mentioned, *Ill. State Reg.*, Feb. 26, 1841

Feb. 18. Remarks in legislature on extending boundaries of Menard County, mentioned, *Sangamo Journal*, Feb. 26, 1841

Feb. 25. Remarks in legislature on incorporation of the Springfield and Alton Turnpike Co., mentioned, *ibid.*, Mar. 5, 1841

Apr. 14. Notice of dissolution of partnership of Lincoln & Stuart, forgery, D, ICHi

July 8. Certified Josiah McRoberts and John H. Murphy qualified to be licensed as lawyers, DS, Clerk's Record, Ill. Supreme Court

July 29. Address to Springfield Mechanics Union, announced, Minutes, July 8, 1841

1842

Jan. 10. Announces death of William J. Gatewood at meeting of bar of the Ill. Supreme Court, *Sangamo Journal*, Jan. 14, 1842

c. Feb. 13. To Mrs. Joshua F. Speed, NE, mentioned, Lincoln to Speed, Feb. 13, 1842

Feb. 15. Remarks at funeral of Bowling Green, mentioned, Herndon, I, 140

Feb. 18. Tribute to Bowling Green, attributed on insufficient evidence, *Sangamo Journal*, Feb. 18, 1842

Feb. 22. Extracts from letter to George E. Pickett, forgery, Tarbell (Appendix), 287-88

Feb. 28. Indenture between Francis Webster and William Butler, AD, Parke-Bernet Catalog 1352, May 27, 1952, No. 155

Apr. 25. Witness, note of Peter Rickard to William Butler and Philip C. Latham, DS, IHi

May 6. Speech at Cincinnati, Ohio, incorrectly attributed, Hertz, II, 531. Speech was made by Salmon P. Chase, May 6, 1845

July 13. Speech at Clay Club organization meeting, mentioned, *Ill. State Reg.*, July 15, 1842

July 20. Speech at Clay Club meeting, Springfield, Ill., mentioned, *Sangamo Journal*, July 22, 1842

Aug. 10. Pseudonymous letter, "Rebecca," incorrectly attributed, *ibid.*, Aug. 19, 1842

Aug. 28, 29. Pseudonymous letter, "Rebecca," incorrectly attributed, *ibid.*, Sept. 9, 1842

Sept. 3. Address at Masonic obsequies of Bowling Green at Petersburg, Ill., announced, *ibid.*, Aug. 26, 1842

Sept. 8. Pseudonymous letter, "Rebecca," incorrectly attributed, *ibid.*, Sept. 9, 1842

Sept. 16. Pseudonymous verse, "Cathleen," incorrectly attributed, *ibid.*, Sept. 16, 1842

c. Oct. 28. To John Hanks on Lincoln's approaching marriage, purported, Sandburg, *Prairie Years*, I, 291

Dec. 31. Preamble and resolutions presented to the legislature by Orville H. Browning in the case of Thomas C. Browne, attributed on insufficient evidence, Ill. *House Journal*, 132-33

1843

———. Excerpt "from Baxter," forgery, ADS, ICHi

Mar. 1. Speech at Whig meeting, Springfield, Ill., concerning the party convention system, Lacon *Ill. Gazette*, Mar. 18, 1843

Mar. 1. To M. D. Browning, forgery, ALS-P, ISLA

Mar. 20. Speech to Whigs at Springfield, Ill., mentioned, Alton *Telegraph*, Apr. 1, 1843

Mar. 23. To Joshua F. Speed, NE, mentioned, Speed to Lincoln, Apr. 3, 1843, ALS-P, ISLA

Apr. 11. "I dreamed last night that I was dead . . . ," forgery, AD-F, ISLA

Apr. 15. To Martin S. Morris, forged copy of authentic letter of Apr. 14, dated Apr. 15, 1843, ICHi

May 1. Remarks at Whig convention, Pekin, Ill., withdrawing Edward D. Baker's name, mentioned, *Sangamo Journal*, May 11, 1843

Aug. 19. Speech at Whig convention, Springfield, Ill., mentioned, Quincy *Whig*, Aug. 30, 1843

Dec. 12. Speech at Whig state convention, Springfield, Ill., mentioned, *Ill. State Reg.*, Dec. 15, 1843

1844

Feb. 14. To Henry E. Dummer, Stephen T. Logan for Logan & Lincoln, incorrectly attributed, Wilson, II, 548

Mar. 2. Speech at flag raising over Whig Cabin, Springfield, Ill., mentioned, *Sangamo Journal*, Mar. 7, 1844

Mar. 9. Speech at Rochester, Ill., announced, *ibid.*

Apr. 6. Speech to Clay Club, Peoria, Ill., mentioned, Peoria *Register*, Apr. 19, 1844

Apr. 8?. Speeches in Tazewell County, mentioned, *Ill. State Reg.*, Apr. 19, 1844

Apr. 13. Speech at Peoria, Ill. in reply to John Calhoun, mentioned, Peoria *Reg.*, Apr. 19, 1844

Apr. 23. Signs with his wife deed to Adams St. lot in part payment of home purchased from Charles Dresser, NE, Sangamon Co. Deed Record

June 3. Speech on tariff to Clay Club, Petersburg, Ill., mentioned, *Sangamo Journal*, June 13, 1844

June 14?. Speech at Springfield, Ill., in reply to Ebenezer Peck, mentioned, *ibid.*, July 4, 1844

June 19. Speech at Whig meeting in Peoria, Ill., mentioned, *ibid.*, June 27, 1844

July 17. Speech at Whig convention, Vandalia, Ill., mentioned, *ibid.*, July 25 and Aug. 8, 1844

July 19. Speech at Whig convention, Vandalia, Ill., mentioned, *ibid.*, July 25, 1844

July 20. Speech at Hillsboro, Ill., mentioned, *ibid.*

July 21. Speech at Whig Cabin, Springfield, Ill., mentioned, *ibid.*

Oct. —. Speech at Gentryville, Ind., purported by Nathaniel Grigsby, Hertz, *Hidden Lincoln*, 356, 368

Oct. 3. Speech at Whig barbecue, Jacksonville, Ill., mentioned, *Sangamo Journal*, Oct. 10, 1844

Oct. 9. Speech at Whig meeting, Decatur, Ill., announced, *ibid.*, Sept. 26, 1844

Oct. 15-17. Debate with William L. May at Peoria, Ill., purported, Thomas J. Pickett in Rock Island *Weekly Register*, May 30, 1860

Oct. 24. Speech at Bruceville, Ind., purported, *Lincoln Lore*, No. 271

Oct. 25. Speech at Washington, Ind., purported, *ibid.*

Nov. 1. Speech at Evansville, Ind., purported, *ibid.*

Nov. 2. Speech at Carter Township, Ind., purported, *ibid.*

1845

Apr. 12. Resolutions on death of William H. Wilmot, mentioned, Tazewell Circuit Court Record D, 423-24

July 4. Speech at State House at Springfield, Ill., announced, *Sangamo Journal*, July 3, 1845

Aug. 28. Editorial, "Beautiful consistency. . . ." attributed on insufficient evidence, *ibid.*, Aug. 28, 1845

1846

c. Jan. 16. To Benjamin F. Dickinson, NE, mentioned, Lincoln to Benjamin F. James, Jan. 16, 1846

c. Jan. 16. To Anson G. Henry, NE, mentioned, Lincoln to James, Jan. 16, 1846

c. Jan. 27. To Anson G. Henry, NE, mentioned, Lincoln to James, Jan. 27, 1846

c. Apr. 20. To James Berdan, NE, mentioned, Lincoln to Berdan, Apr. 26, 1846
c. May 1. Speech to Juvenile Society, Springfield, Ill., mentioned in minutes of Sangamon Co. Temperance Union, IHi
May 25. Speech at Jacksonville, Ill., mentioned, Lincoln to Berdan, May 7, 1846
May 30. Speech at Mexican War rally, Springfield, Ill., mentioned, *Sangamo Journal,* June 4, 1846
July 20. Speech at Bonham farm near Henry, Ill., purported, Bonham, *Fifty Years Recollections,* 161
July 22?. Speech at Hennepin, Ill., purported by John F. Nash, in C. C. Tisler, *Lincoln's Ottawa*
July 24. Speech at Mackinaw, Ill., announced, *Tazewell Whig* (Tremont), July 18, 1846
July 25. Speech at Delavan, Ill., announced, *ibid.*

1847

1847. Ordinances adopted by City of Springfield granting right of way to Alton and Sangamon railroad, attributed to Lincoln
Apr. 6. Signature, "Abram Lincoln," in unidentified hand, on petition for pardon of John Huffman, D, I-Ar
c. Apr. 30. Temperance address at South Fork Schoolhouse, Ill., mentioned in minutes of Sangamon Co. Temperance Union, IHi
c. May 16. Temperance address at Middle Lick Creek, Ill., mentioned, *ibid.*
June 20. Temperance address at Langston's Settlement, Ill., mentioned, *ibid.*
July 6. Speech at River and Harbor Convention, Chicago, Ill., mentioned, N.Y. *Tribune,* July 17, 1847
Sept. 2. Map and endorsement "By act of the General Assembly— June 1847. . . ." forgery, ADS, Speed Museum, Louisville, Ky.
Nov. 11. To John Mortimore, forgery, ALS-P, ISLA
c. Dec. 1847–1848. To Andrew W. Leggatz, NE, envelope addressed and franked "A. Lincoln, M.C.," ADS, RPB
c. Dec. 1847–1848. Page of 33 signatures of U.S. congressmen headed by: "We concur in the above. A LINCOLN, Ills." DS, RPB
Dec. 2. Signs register, Brown's Hotel, Washington, D.C., "A. Lincoln & Lady Illinois/ 2 Children Do." Anderson Auction Catalog 421, Dec. 8, 1905, No. 392
Dec. 12. To Thomas J. Henderson, NE, fragment quoted, *Journal of Ill. State Hist. Soc.,* IV, 74
Dec. 20. Notice of bill to amend the act to raise an additional military force approved Feb. 11, 1847, U.S. *House Journal,* 47-48 (bill not located)
c. Dec. 22. Endorsement on petition: "Memorial of citizens of Illinois asking a pre-emption right to certain lands and in the construction of the Central Rail Road in the State of Illinois." AE, DNA RG 233 HR 30A F 18 (1) Comm. on Public Lands
c. Dec. 29. To Anson Henry, NE, mentioned, Henry to Lincoln, Dec. 29, 1847, DLC-RTL

Dec. 29. Signs petition to James K. Polk, asking appointment of Francis B. Thompson as assistant army surgeon, Thomas Madigan, *Catalogue of Lincolniana* (1935), No. 233

1848

c. Jan. 1. Endorsement: "Memorial of Uriah Brown praying for a further testing of his discovery of 'liquid fire.' " AE, DNA RG 233 HR 30A F13 (1) Comm. on Naval Affairs

c. Jan. 25. Endorsement: "*Illinois*. The Petition of sundry citizens of Scott county, Illinois, asking for the establishment of a Post-Road therein named," AE, DNA RG 233 HR 30A F15 (3) Comm. on Post Offices

c. Jan. 25. Endorsement: "Petition of Danl. Wadsworth, P.M. at Auburn, Illinois—praying legislation in relation to the compensation of Post Masters." AE, *ibid.*, (7) Comm. on Post-Roads

c. Feb. 7. Endorsement: "The Petition of sundry citizens of [Tazewell County] the State of *Illinois*, praying a reduction of postages on small news-papers." AE, *ibid.*, (5) Comm. on Post Offices

c. Feb. 14. Endorsement: "Petition of Citizens of Illinois, asking bounty lands for soldiers of the War of 1812." AE, *ibid.*, F18 (2) Comm. on Public Lands

c. Feb. 14. Endorsement on petition of citizens of Illinois for grant of lands to aid in construction of a railroad to connect the upper and lower Mississippi with the Great Lakes: "Refer to committee on Public Lands." AE, *ibid.*

c. Feb. 18. Endorsement: "The Petition of sundry citizens of [Edgar County] Illinois praying a distinction be made in the postage of large & small news-papers," AE, *ibid.*, 30A F15 (5) Comm. on Post Offices

c. Feb. 28. Endorsement: "Petition of J. M. Sturtevant & others, citizens of Morgan County, Illinois, praying for the abolition of the slave trade in the District of Columbia." AE, *ibid.*, F5 (3) Feb. 17, 1849

c. Mar. Signature on order for copies of Elisha Embree's speech concerning bounty lands for soldiers, "A. Lincoln 200." DS, IHi

c. Mar. Endorsement: "Petition of certain citizens of Illinois for a post road from Virginia in Cass county to Petersburg in Menard county." AE, DNA RG 233 HR 30A F15 (9) Comm. on Post Offices

Mar. 6. Petition of Hickox & Brothers to congress for compensation for transporting Illinois Volunteers, AD, missing from DNA RG 233

Mar. 9. Report to accompany H.R. Bill No. 301, submitted by Lincoln (*Cong. Globe*, Mar. 16, 1848, p. 449) but not written by him, and included in previous compilations (NH, II, 4-10) in error. The original document (Report No. 325, DNA RG 233 HR 30A D15) is not in Lincoln's autograph.

Apr. 9. To Mary Todd Lincoln, NE, mentioned, Lincoln to Mary Todd Lincoln, Apr. 16, 1848

May 12. Remarks in H.R. on claim of Richard W. Meade, mentioned, *Cong. Globe*, 762

May 21. To Mary Todd Lincoln, NE, mentioned, Lincoln to Mary Todd Lincoln, May 24, 1848

c. June 20. To James Berdan, NE, envelope, AD, IaDaM

c. June 22. Signed subscription list for copies of John I. Slingerland's speech on internal improvements, "A. Lincoln, 100," DS, Parke-Bernet Catalog 1352, May 27, 1952, No. 157

Aug. 2. Remarks in H.R. concerning bill to grant public lands for railroad connecting the Mississippi and Great Lakes in Illinois, mentioned, *Cong. Globe*, 1027

Aug. 8. Remarks in H.R. on reorganization of Post Office, mentioned, *ibid.*, 1049

Aug. 24. Speech at Seneca, Md., mentioned, Frederick, Md., *Republican Citizen*, Sept. 1, 1848

Aug. 26. Speech at Rockville, Md., mentioned, *Natl. Intelligencer*, Aug. 29, 1848

Aug. 31. Speech at Washington, D.C., mentioned, Baltimore *Clipper*, Sept. 2, 1848

Sept. 5. Speech at Washington, D.C., announced, *Natl. Intelligencer*, Sept. 5, 1848

Sept. 14. Speech at New Bedford, Mass., mentioned, New Bedford *Daily Mercury*, Sept. 15, 1848

Sept. 18. Speech at Dorchester, Mass., announced, Boston *Atlas*, Sept. 16, 1848

Sept. 19. Speech at Chelsea, Mass., mentioned, *ibid.*, Sept. 20, 1848

Sept. 20. Speech (afternoon) at Dedham, Mass., mentioned, *ibid.*, Sept. 22, 1848

Sept. 20. Speech (evening) at Cambridge, Mass., mentioned, *ibid.*

Sept. 22. Speech at Boston, Mass., mentioned, *ibid.*, Sept. 23, 1848

Oct. 9. Speech at Peoria, Ill., mentioned, Peoria *Democratic Press*, Oct. 11, 1848

Oct. 19. Speech at Beardstown, Ill., mentioned, Beardstown *Gazette*, Oct. 25, 1848

Oct. 23. Speech at Petersburg, Ill., mentioned, *Ill. St. Register*, Nov. 3, 1848

Oct. 28. Speech at Bloomington, Ill., announced, Lacon *Ill. Gazette*, Sept. 23, 1848

Oct. 30. Speech at Metamora, Ill., mentioned, *Ill. Journal*, Nov. 1, 1848

Oct. 31. Speech (afternoon) at Magnolia, Ill., announced, *ibid.*

Oct. 31. Speech (evening) at Hennepin, Ill., announced, *ibid.*

Nov. 2. Speech at Washington, Ill., announced, *ibid.*

Nov. 3. Speech at Tremont, Ill., announced, *ibid.*

Nov. 4. Speech (afternoon) at Pekin, Ill., announced, *ibid.*

Nov. 4. Speech (evening) at Peoria, Ill., mentioned, Peoria *Dem. Press*, Nov. 8, 1848

c. Dec. Endorsement: "Petition of Allen Withers & others, citizens of McLean county, Illinois, asking a grant of land to aid in constructing a Rail road from the Upper & Lower Mississippi to Chicago in said state/ Refer to committee on Public Lands. A LINCOLN," AES, DNA RG 233 HR 30A F18 (4) Comm. on Public Lands

1849

——. Endorsement: "Petition of John Epler & others citizens of Illinois asking the passage of laws to facilitate emigration to California. Refer to committee on Teritories. A. LINCOLN," AES, DLC-RTL

Jan. 8. Notice of intention to introduce a bill in relation to school lands, U.S. *House Journal*, 215

Jan. 13. Notice of intention to introduce a bill to abolish slavery in the District of Columbia, U.S. *House Journal*, 242

c. Jan. 20. Endorsement: "Petition of Wm. C. Greenleaf, and others, citizens of Sangamon county, Illinois, asking a grant of lands to aid in the construction of a Rail Road from the Upper & Lower Miss[iss]ippi to Chicago, in said state/ Refer to Committee on Public Lands. A LINCOLN," AES, DNA RG 233 HR 30A F18 (5) Comm. on Public Lands

Jan. 24. To E. P. Oliphant, NE, mentioned, Oliphant to Lincoln, May 8, 1849, DLC-RTL

c. Jan. 29. Endorsement: "A petition of certain citizens of the State of Illinois, praying a grant of Lands to aid in the construction of a Rail Road." AE, DNA RG 233 HR 30A F18 (5) Comm. on Public Lands

c. Feb. Endorsement: "The Petition of certain citizens of Cass county Illinois, praying to be allowed to select other lands in lieu of certain valueless school lands &c. &c. Refer to Comm. on Public Lands. A. LINCOLN," AES, *ibid.*, (6)

c. Feb. Endorsement: "Petition of Ezekiel Bowman & others, citizens of Logan county, Illinois asking a grant of Lands to aid in the construction of a Rail Road from the upper & Lower Mississippi to Chicago in said state. Refer to Committee on Public Lands. A LINCOLN." AES, *ibid.*

c. Feb. 1. Endorsement: "Petition of A. H. H. Perkins & others, asking a grant of lands to aid in the construction of a Rail Road from the Upper & Lower Mississippi to Chicago in said State. Refer to Committee on Public Lands. A LINCOLN," AES, DNA RG 233 HR 30A F18 (6) Comm. on Public Lands

Feb. 12. To David Davis, NE, mentioned, Davis to Lincoln, Feb. 21, 1849, DLC-RTL

Feb. 12. Endorsement on check of Corcoran & Riggs, drawn in favor of Lincoln for $105, "Pay to the order of Joseph H. Berry, of Winchester, Ills. A LINCOLN," AES, CSmH

Feb. 15. To Cyrus Edwards, NE, mentioned, Edwards to Justin Butterfield, *Jnl. Ill. St. Hist. Soc.*, XXV, 143

c. Feb. 19. Endorsement: "The petition of citizens of Tazewell county, Illinois praying protection for the emigrants to California." AE, DNA RG 233 HR 30A F23 Comm. on Territories

c. Feb. 20. Endorsement on Robert S. Todd to Lincoln, Feb. 20, 1849, concerning appointment of Thomas M. Campbell, "Recommendation sent to Home Dept.," AE, DLC-RTL

c. Feb. 21. To Richard Yates, NE, mentioned, William K. Lindsay to Lincoln, Feb. 21, 1849, *ibid.*

c. Feb. 21. Endorsement on envelope, William F. Elkin to Lincoln, Feb. 21, 1849, "Within are recommendations that Turner R. King be appointed Register of Land Office at Springfield, Illinois." AE, DNA NR RG 48, Appointments, Land Offices in Springfield, Box 44

Mar. 6. To J. L. Edwards, NE, mentioned, Edwards to Lincoln, Mar. 28, 1849, DLC-RTL

c. Mar. 11. Filled out Baltimore & Ohio Railroad blank for shipment of two boxes of books from clerk of the H.R. "directed to the Hon A Lincoln Springfield Illinois, care of L Levering St Louis Missouri. . . ." Am. Art Assn. Catalog, Mar. 13, 1918, No. 184

Mar. 27. To Cyrus Edwards, NE, mentioned in Edwards to Butterfield, June 11, 1849, *Jnl. Ill. St. Hist. Soc.*, XXV, 143

c. Apr. To Henry Eddy, NE, mentioned, John W. Norton to Lincoln, May 1, 1849, DLC-RTL

Apr. 4. To Harrison Dills, NE, mentioned, Dills to Lincoln, Apr. 10, 1849, *ibid.*

c. Apr. 5. To Daniel Clapp, NE, Clapp to Lincoln, Apr. 5, 1849, endorsed "Ansd.," AE, *ibid.*

Apr. 5. To George W. Dole, NE, mentioned, Dole to Lincoln, Apr. 11, 1849, *ibid.*

c. Apr. 9. To James M. Davis, NE, Davis to Lincoln, Apr. 9, 1849, endorsed "Ansd before written." AE, *ibid.*

c. Apr. 12. To William W. Bennett, NE, Bennett to Lincoln, Apr. 12, 1849, endorsed "Ansd," AE, *ibid.*

Apr. 13. To John A. Jones, NE, mentioned, Jones to Lincoln, Apr. 17, 1849, *ibid*

Apr. 13. To Timothy P. Andrews, NE, mentioned, Andrews to Lincoln, Apr. 25, 1849, *ibid.*

Apr. 15?. To Joseph T. Eccles, NE, mentioned, Eccles to Lincoln, Apr. 20, 1849, *ibid.*

Apr. 22. To Josiah M. Lucas, NE, mentioned, Lincoln to Lucas, Apr. 25, 1849

c. Apr. 23. To P. H. Thompson, NE, mentioned, Thompson to Lincoln, Apr. 23, 1849, DLC-RTL

c. Apr. 29. To Benjamin F. James, NE, mentioned, (envelope) James to Lincoln, Apr. 29, 1849, *ibid.*

Apr. 30. To Cyrus Edwards, NE, mentioned in Edwards to Butterfield, June 11, 1849, *Jnl. Ill. St. Hist. Soc.*, XXV, 144

May —. To ——— Kannady (?), NE, mentioned, Frederick Remann to Lincoln, May 29, 1849, DLC-RTL

May —. To William K. Lindsay, NE, mentioned, Lindsay to Lincoln, May 15, 1849, *ibid.*

May 1?. To Thomas Ewing, missing from recommendations of William S. Wallace for pension agent at Springfield, Ill., DNA NR RG 48, Appointments, Pension Agents, Box 89

c. May 9. To William A. Grimshaw, NE, Grimshaw to Lincoln, May 9, 1849, endorsed "Grimshaw authorized to endorse," AE, DLC-RTL

May 12. To John M. Clayton, NE, mentioned, receipt to Dept. of Interior, June 22, 1849

May 13. To James W. Chickering, NE, mentioned, Chickering to Lincoln, May 14, 1849, DLC-RTL

May 26. To William Chumasero, NE, mentioned, Chumasero to Lincoln, May 29, 1849, *ibid.*

June —. To E. O. (A?) Smith, NE, mentioned, Smith to Lincoln, June 16, 1849, *ibid.*

June 3. To Robert Boal, NE, mentioned, Boal to Lincoln, June 7, 1849, *ibid.*

June 3?. To Charles H. Constable and Dr. Reuben Baker, NE, mentioned, Constable to Lincoln, June 10, 1849, *ibid.*

June 3. To Benjamin F. James, NE, mentioned, James to Lincoln, June 5, 1849, *ibid.*

June 4. To Chester Butler, NE, mentioned, Butler to Lincoln, June 18, 1849, *ibid*

c. June 4. To Alexander Evans, NE, mentioned, Evans to Lincoln, June 18, 1849, *ibid*

June 4. To Abraham R. McIlvaine, NE, mentioned, McIlvaine to Lincoln, June 18, 1849, *ibid.*

c. June 4. To James Pollock, NE, mentioned, Pollock to Lincoln, June 18, 1849, *ibid.*

c. June 4. To John A. Rockwell, mentioned, Rockwell to Lincoln, June 18, 1849, *ibid.*

June 5. To William Alt, NE, mentioned, Alt to Lincoln, June 15, 1849, *ibid.*

June 5. To W. Barrow, NE, mentioned, I. Shelby to Lincoln, June 13, 1849, *ibid.*

June 5. To Nathan K. Hall, NE, mentioned, Hall to Lincoln, June 13, 1849, *ibid.*

c. June 5. To ———— Knapp, NE, mentioned in A. L. and C. H. Knapp to Lincoln, June 5, 1849, *ibid.*

June 5. To William Nelson, *see* same form letter to Duff Green, June 5, 1849

c. June 19. To the Cabinet, NE, mentioned, Nathaniel G. Wilcox to Lincoln, June 6, 1864, DLC-RTL

Sept. 23?. To Thomas Ewing, NE, mentioned, index to Ewing Papers, DLC

Dec. 24. To Peter Hitchcock, forgery, Tracy, 40; *see* Bulletin 21, ISLA

1850

Jan. 25. To Zachary Taylor, NE, recommending Stephen T. Logan for U.S. district judge, mentioned, Lincoln to Taylor, Jan. 25, 1850

c. Feb. 25. To Zachary Taylor, NE, mentioned, Lincoln to Murray, Feb. 25, 1850

May 24. Signature, forgery, on genuine letter, J. I. Case to Samuel Dodds, DS-P, ISLA

c. Nov. 6. To Postmaster General Nathan K. Hall, NE, mentioned, Lincoln to Isaac Onstott, Nov. 6, 1850

1851

June 1. To E. H. Peck, forgery, ALS, NN

1852

Jan. 8. Speech at Kossuth meeting, mentioned, *Ill. Journal*, Jan. 12, 1852

c. June. To B. C. Collins, forgery, ALS-P, ISLA

June 1. To J. Edwards, forgery, ALS-P, ISLA

June 1. To N. W. Edwards, forgery, ALS-P, ISLA

Sept. 2. Inscription concerning the death of Henry Clay, inscribed on verso of first page of *Report of the Committee of Arrangements of the Common Council of New York, of the Obsequies in Memory of the Hon. Henry Clay* (New York, 1852), spurious, AD, copy in Parke-Bernet Catalog 488, Oct. 30, 1940, No. 425

Sept. 20. Speech at Pekin, Ill., mentioned, *Ill. St. Reg.*, Sept. 25, 1852

Oct. 28. Speech at Springfield, Ill., mentioned, *Ill. Journal*, Oct. 30, 1852

Oct. 30. Speech to Scott Club at Springfield, Ill., announced, *ibid.*

1853

1853. To Macedonio Melloni, forgery, Hertz, II, 623

June 13. Petition to City Council of Springfield, Ill., to have sidewalk on east side of Eighth St. between Cook and Adams, graded and paved or planked, City Council minutes

c. June 21. To William Weir and Jesse K. Dubois, NE, mentioned, Lincoln to Nathaniel Coffin, June 21, 1853

c. Aug. 20. To Ward H. Lamon, NE, envelope, AD, CSmH

Aug. 30. Speech on Negro colonization, Springfield, Ill., announced, *Ill. St. Reg.*, Aug. 30, 1853

1854

——. Speech at dedication of Ill. State University, Springfield, Ill., purported, *Week by Week in Springfield*, Jan. 2, 1932

June 14. Remarks introducing Millard Fillmore, Springfield, Ill., mentioned, *Ill. St. Reg.*, June 15, 1854

Sept. 2. Speech at Jacksonville, Ill., mentioned, *Ill. St. Reg.*, Sept. 6, 1854

Sept. 27. To George Gage, NE, mentioned, Gage to Lincoln, Oct. 4, 1854, DLC-RTL

Oct. 24. Speech at Urbana, Ill., mentioned, Urbana *Union*, Oct. 26, 1854. Text in Whitney, *Life on the Circuit* and Hertz, II, 627ff., spurious.

Nov. 4?. Speech at Carlinville, Ill., mentioned, Lincoln to Richard Yates, Oct. 31, 1854

Nov. 10. To A. G. Jones, NE, mentioned, Jones to Lincoln, Nov. 22, 1854, DLC-RTL

Nov. 10. To James Knox, NE, mentioned, Knox to Lincoln, Nov. 17, 1854, *ibid.*

Nov. 10. To Ward H. Lamon, NE, mentioned, Lamon to Lincoln, Nov. 21, 1854, *ibid.*

Nov. 10. To E. N. Powell, NE, mentioned, Powell to Lincoln, Nov. 16, 1854, *ibid.*

Nov. 11. To J. M. Ruggles, NE, mentioned, Ruggles to Lincoln, Nov. 20, 1854, *ibid.*

Nov. 12. To Robert Boal, NE, mentioned, Boal to Lincoln, Nov. 15, 1854, *ibid.*

Nov. 13. To Henry Grove, NE, mentioned, Grove to Lincoln, Nov. 18, 1854, *ibid.*

c. Nov. 15. To H. C. Johns, NE, mentioned, Johns to Lincoln, Nov. 15, 1854, *ibid.*

c. Nov. 20. To William Fithian, NE, mentioned, Fithian to Lincoln, Nov. 20, 1854, *ibid.*

Nov. 27. To W. B. Archer, NE, mentioned, Archer to Lincoln, Dec. 3, 1854, *ibid.*

Nov. 27. To Abraham Jonas, NE, mentioned, Jonas to Lincoln, Dec. 2, 1854, *ibid.*

Nov. 27. To Andrew McCallen, NE, mentioned, McCallen to Lincoln, Dec. 19, 1854, *ibid.*

Nov. 27. To Richard B. Servant, NE, mentioned, Servant to Lincoln, Dec. 2, 1854, *ibid.*

Nov. 29. To Robert Boal, NE, mentioned, Boal to Lincoln, Dec. 7, 1854, *ibid.*

Nov. 29. To William H. Randolph, NE, mentioned, Randolph to Lincoln, Dec. 4, 1854, *ibid.*

Dec. —. To William B. Archer, NE, mentioned, Charles L. Duncan to Lincoln, Dec. 8, 1854, *ibid.*

Dec. —. To Burton C. Cook, NE, mentioned, Cook to Lincoln, Dec. 25, 1854, *ibid.*

Dec. —. To David Davis, NE, mentioned, Davis to Lincoln, Dec. 19, 1854, *ibid.*

Dec. —. To James E. McClure, NE, mentioned, McClure to Lincoln, Dec. 10, 1854, *ibid.*

Dec. —. To Jesse O. Norton, NE, mentioned, Norton to Lincoln, Dec. 12, 1854, *ibid.*

Dec. —. To Samuel C. Parks, NE, mentioned, Parks to Lincoln, Dec. 13, 1854, *ibid.*

Dec. —. To Silas Ramsey, NE, mentioned, Ramsey to Lincoln, Dec. 23, 1854, *ibid.*

Dec. —. To Henry Riblett, NE, mentioned, Riblett to Lincoln, Dec. 13, 1854, *ibid.*

Dec. —. To J. Young Scammon, NE, mentioned, Scammon to Lincoln, Dec. 16, 1854, *ibid.*

Dec. 4. To William D. Henderson, NE, mentioned, Henderson to Lincoln, Dec. 11, 1854, *ibid.*

Dec. 4. To Thomas A. Marshall, NE, mentioned, Marshall to Lincoln, Dec. 8, 1854, *ibid.*

Dec. 5. To Augustus Adams, NE, mentioned, Adams to Lincoln, Dec. 17, 1854, *ibid.*

Dec. 5. To Daniel H. Whitney, NE, mentioned, Whitney to Lincoln, Dec. 19, 1854, *ibid.*

Dec. 6. To ——— Gooden, NE, mentioned, J. F. McDougall to Lincoln, Dec. 11, 1854, *ibid.*

Dec. 6. To Thomas B. Talcott, NE, mentioned, Talcott to Lincoln, Dec. 14, 1854, *ibid.*

Dec. 8. To William H. Randolph, NE, mentioned, Randolph to Lincoln, Dec. 13, 1854, *ibid.*

Dec. 21. To Eleazer A. Paine, NE, mentioned, Paine to Lincoln, Dec. 28, 1854, *ibid.*

Dec. 26. To William H. Randolph, NE, mentioned, Randolph to Lincoln, Dec. 28, 1854, *ibid.*

1855

Jan. 4. Speech at Springfield, Ill., to the African Colonization Society, mentioned, Chicago *Dem. Press*, Jan. 8, 1855

c. Feb. 24. To Lyman Trumbull, NE, mentioned, Trumbull to Lincoln, Feb. 24, 1855, DLC-RTL

May 4. Signs recommendation of Stephen A. Corneau for clerk of Ill. Supreme Court, *DeWitt Courier*, May 25, 1855

June 7. To John O. Johnson, forgery, ALS-P, ISLA

c. July. To John M. Walker, NE, mentioned, Lincoln to Orville H. Browning, Dec. 15, 1856, DLC-RTL

Sept. 18. List of notes left with Adams Bank, forgery, ADS, ICHi

Oct. 31. Speech at Danville, Ill., mentioned, *Ill. State Reg.*, Nov. 6, 1855

Nov. 24. Check to "Self" for $37, DS, IHi

Dec. 13. To T. L. Harris, forgery, Tarbell (Appendix), 306

Dec. 19. Check to "W. W. Watson & Son," confectioners, for $41.72, DS, owned by H. K. Hoblit, Springfield, Mo.

1856

Jan. 18. Check to "Self" for $53.64, DS, Parke-Bernet Catalog, Apr. 4, 1939, No. 294

Jan. 30. To James M. Loughborough, ALS, Metropolitan Art Assn. Catalog, Jan. 14, 1914, No. 447

Feb. 11?. Speech at Springfield, Ill., purported, Lamon, *Lincoln*, 372-73; Herndon, II, 379-80

May 10. To William H. Herndon, NE, mentioned, Herndon, II, 382-83

June —. To Elihu B. Washburne, purported, Seitz, *Lincoln*, 97-98

June 4. Speech at Decatur, Ill., mentioned, *Ill. St. Chronicle*, June 5, 1856

June 23. Speech at Urbana, Ill., mentioned, Urbana *Union*, June 26, 1856

July 17. Speech at Dixon, Ill., mentioned, Chicago *Dem. Press*, July 19, 1856

July 18. Speech at Sterling, Ill., mentioned, *ibid.*

July 26. To Harry P. Merriman, NE, mentioned, Merriman to Lincoln, July 29, 1856, U.S. Circuit Court Files, E-F

Aug. 2. Speech at Springfield, Ill., mentioned, *Ill. St. Journal*, Aug. 4, 1856

Aug. 7. Speech at Grand View, Ill., mentioned, Paris *Prairie Beacon*, Aug. 8, 1856

Aug. 8. Speech at Charleston, Ill., mentioned, Alton *Weekly Courier*, Aug. 11, 1856

Aug. 16. Speech at Oregon, Ill., mentioned, Chicago *Dem. Press*, Aug. 22, 1856

Aug. 22. Speech at Danville, Ill., announced, Chicago *Tribune*, Aug. 7, 1856

Sept. — . Speech at Monticello, Ill., mentioned, Chicago *Press and Tribune*, Sept. 9, 1858

Sept. 2. Speech at Lincoln, Ill., mentioned, *Ill. St. Journal*, Sept. 4, 1856

Sept. 2. Annotated map of Illinois Judicial Districts, forgery, ADS, NN

Sept. 4. Speech at Atlanta, Ill., mentioned, *Ill. State Journal*, Sept. 5. 1856

Sept. 6. Speech (evening) at "The Kansas Meeting," Springfield, Ill., mentioned, *ibid.*, Sept. 8, 1856

Sept. 7. To L. U. Reavis, concerning speech at Beardstown, Ill., ALS, Anderson Galleries Catalog 3941, Jan. 12, 1932

Sept. 8. Speech at "The Kansas Meeting," Springfield, Ill., mentioned, *Ill. State Journal*, Sept. 9, 1856 (Lincoln was member of committee which drew up adopted resolution favoring admission of Kansas as a free state)

Sept. 9. To John Hawes (form letter to Fillmore men), mentioned, Hawes to Lincoln, Sept. 15, 1856, DLC-HW

Sept. 9. To William Ryan (form letter to Fillmore men), IBloHi

Sept. 15. To ——— (form letter to Fillmore men), *Ill. State Reg.*, Oct. 13, 1856

Sept. 16. Speech at Bloomington, Ill., mentioned, Bloomington *Pantagraph*, Sept. 24, 1856

Sept. 17. To T. A. Brittenham (form letter to Fillmore men), owned by Sarah J. Brittenham, Chicago, Ill.

Sept. 17. Speech at Urbana, Ill., mentioned, *Ill. State Journal*, Sept. 22, 1856

Sept. 24. Speech at Decatur, Ill., mentioned, Chicago *Dem. Press*, Sept. 27, 1856

Sept. 25. Speech at Springfield, Ill., mentioned, *Ill. State Journal*, Sept. 26, 1856

Sept. 29. To Col. James Patton (form letter to Fillmore men), F-ISLA

Sept. 30. Speech at Lacon, Ill., mentioned, Chicago *Journal*, Oct. 6, 1856

Oct. 2. Speech at Alton, Ill., mentioned, *Ill. State Journal*, Oct. 4, 1856

Oct. 7. Speech at Ottawa, Ill., mentioned, Chicago *Journal*, Oct. 8, 1856

Oct. 8. Speech at Joliet, Ill., mentioned, *ibid.*, Oct. 9, 1856

Oct. 13. Speech at Clinton, Ill., mentioned, Bloomington *Pantagraph*, Oct. 22, 1856

Oct. 16. Speech at Freeport, Ill., announced, Dixon *Telegraph*, Oct. 4, 1856

Oct. 17. Speech at Mendota, Ill., announced, Bloomington *Pantagraph*, Oct. 15, 1856

Oct. 20. Speech at Urbana, Ill., mentioned, Urbana *Union*, Oct. 23, 1856

Oct. 21. Speech at West Urbana, Ill., mentioned, Urbana *Union,* Oct. 23, 1856

Oct. 23. Speeches at Atlanta, Ill., mentioned, Bloomington *Pantagraph,* Nov. 5, 1856

Oct. 27. Speech at Pittsfield, Ill., mentioned, *Pike Co. Free Press,* Oct. 30, 1856

Oct. 29. Speech at Springfield, Ill., mentioned, *Ill. State Journal,* Oct. 30, 1856

Oct. 31. Speech at Springfield, Ill., mentioned, *ibid.,* Nov. 1, 1856

Nov. 1. Speech at Jacksonville, Ill., mentioned, *ibid.,* Nov. 3, 1856

c. Nov. 4. Tabulation of election returns for Illinois, AD, DLC-RTL

c. Dec. 16. Check to Mrs. Maria L. Bullock for $970 (money collected on her loans), copy, ISLA

Dec. 22. Speech to New England Society at Springfield, Ill., mentioned, *Ill. State Journal,* Dec. 24, 1856

Dec. 31. Speech at meeting for establishing a female seminary at Springfield, Ill., mentioned, *ibid.,* Jan. 1, 1857

1857

c. 1857. To Gustave Koerner, concerning Illinois Central fee, NE, mentioned in *Memoirs of Gustave Koerner,* II, 111-12

Jan. 12. Speech at Gov. Bissell's inauguration, Springfield, Ill., mentioned, *Ill. State Journal,* Jan. 13, 1857

Mar. 2. To James Lemen, forgery, Tracy, 71

Mar. 14. To Zimri A. Enos, "I concur in the foregoing opinion of Judge Logan. A. LINCOLN," endorsement on Stephen T. Logan to Enos, Mar. 14, 1857, AES-P, ISLA

Mar. 21. Receipt on mortgage of Nathaniel Hay to Maria L. Bullock, Sangamon Co. Deed Book 55, p. 500

Mar. 21. Receipt on mortgage of Patrick Keily to Maria L. Bullock, *ibid.,* Book 1, p. 78

May 27. To Benjamin F. Jonas, NE, mentioned, Jonas to Lincoln, June 4, 1857, DLC-RTL

June 15. Guaranty bond for Ill. Normal University, Bloomington, Ill., signed by Jesse Fell and 84 others, AD, copy in *Hist. of McLean County* (1879), 430

July 21. Receipt on mortgage of John Connelley to Maria L. Bullock, Sangamon Co. Deed Book 55, p. 497

Aug. 28. Check to Joel A. Matteson for $200, DS-P, ISLA

Aug. 31. Check to "Self" for $4,800 (Ill. Central Railroad fee), copy, ISLA

Sept. To Hannah Armstrong, forgery, Tracy, 79

Sept. 27. Check to William H. Herndon for $23, DS, owned by Mrs. Mary Edwards Brown, Springfield, Ill.

Sept. 28. Check to Bailhache & Baker for $10 for subscription to *Ill. State Journal,* DS-P, ISLA

Sept. 28. Check to J. Bunn for $16.68, DS, owned by Springfield Marine Bank, Springfield, Ill.

Sept. 28. Check to John Hutchinson for $11 for furniture, DS, ORB

Sept. 29. Check to Jacob Ruckel for $200, DS-F, ISLA

c. Oct. 25. To William Brown, NE, mentioned, Lincoln to Gustave Koerner, Oct. 25, 1857

c. Oct. 25. To Richard Yates, NE, mentioned, *ibid.*

Dec. — . To David Davis, NE, mentioned, Davis to Lincoln, Jan. 1, 1858, DLC-RTL

1858

Feb. 25. To Mark Carley, forgery, NH, XI, 104

Mar. 2. To J. C. Eccles, forgery, ALS-P, ISLA

Mar. 27. To Jackson Grimshaw, NE, mentioned, Grimshaw to Lincoln, Apr. 3, 1858, U.S. Circuit Court files

Apr. 19. To Blatchford, Seward, & Griswold, NE, mentioned in their letter to Lincoln, Apr. 23, 1858, DLC-RTL

c. Apr. 19. To John Wentworth, NE, mentioned, Wentworth to Lincoln, Apr. 19, 1858, *ibid.*

Apr. 23?. To George W. Rives, NE, mentioned, Rives to Lincoln, May 15, 1858, *ibid.*

Spring. To Franklin Blades, NE, mentioned, Isaac N. Phillips, *Recollections*, p. 109

May 2. To Blatchford, Seward, & Griswold, NE, mentioned in their letter to Lincoln, Dec. 9, 1858, DLC-RTL

c. May 3. To C. B. Hitt, NE, Hitt to Lincoln, May 3, 1858, endorsed "About Charles Hardin Answered," AE, *ibid.*

c. May 7. To Friend S. Rutherford, NE, Rutherford to Lincoln, May 7, 1858, endorsed "Answered," AE, *ibid.*

c. May 15. To George W. Rives, NE, Rives to Lincoln, May 15, 1858, endorsed "Ansd.," AE, *ibid.;* mentioned, Rives to Lincoln, May 22, 1858, *ibid.*

c. May 17. Endorsement, William M. Fishback to Lincoln, May 17, 1858, "W. Fishback Needs no answer," AE, *ibid.*

May 17. To Elihu B. Washburne, NE, mentioned, Washburne to Lincoln, May 22, 1858, *ibid.*

c. May 18. To E. T. Bridges, NE, Bridges to Lincoln, May 18, 1858, endorsed "Ansd," AE, *ibid.*

c. May 18. To Martin S. Morris, NE, Morris to Lincoln, May 18, 1858, endorsed "Answered," AE, *ibid.*

May 20. To Oliver L. Davis, NE, mentioned, Davis to Lincoln, June 3, 1858, *ibid.*

c. May 22. To George W. Rives, NE, Rives to Lincoln, May 22, 1858, endorsed "Ansd." AE, *ibid.;* mentioned, Rives to Lincoln, June 4, 1858, *ibid.*

c. May 24. To C. D. Hay, NE, Hay to Lincoln, May 24, 1858, endorsed "Ansd," AE, *ibid.*

May 31. Map of quarter section of land drawn on back of Samuel A. Harvey's letter to Lincoln, May 15, 1858, ADS-P, ISLA

c. May 31. To Anthony Thornton, NE, Thornton to Lincoln, May 31, 1858, endorsed "Ansd." AE, DLC-RTL

c. June 1. To Norman B. Judd, NE, mentioned, Judd to Lincoln, June 1, 1858, *ibid.*

c. June 2. To Patrick J. Nagle, NE, Nagle to Lincoln, June 2, 1858, endorsed "Ansd." AE, *ibid.*

June 4. To Abraham Smith, NE, mentioned, Smith to Lincoln, May 31, 1858, *ibid.*

June 11. To Henry Wert, NE, mentioned, Wert to Lincoln, June 16, 1858, *ibid.*

June 14. To D. P. Roberts, NE, mentioned, Roberts to Lincoln, June 29, 1858, *ibid.*

June 26. To William D. Henderson, NE, mentioned, Henderson to Lincoln, July 12, 1858, *ibid.*

July — . To Henry E. Dummer, NE, mentioned, Dummer to Lincoln, July 10, 1858, *ibid.*

July ? Newspaper article in Paris, Ill., *Prairie Beacon* (?), purported, Lincoln to Robert Moseley, July 2, 1858, and Leander Munsell to Lincoln, Aug. 16, 1858, DLC-RTL

July 2. To T. L. McEvers, NE, mentioned, McEvers to Lincoln, July 11, 1858, *ibid.*

c. July 9. To J. H. Reed, NE, mentioned, Reed to Lincoln, July 9, 1858, *ibid.*

July 19. To Thomas A. Marshall, NE, mentioned, Marshall to Lincoln, July 22, 1858, *ibid.*

July 20. To Thomas J. Turner, NE, mentioned, Turner to Lincoln, July 27, 1858, *ibid.*

c. July 23. To Anderson, Lamoreux & Co., NE, their letter to Lincoln, July 23, 1858, endorsed "Ansd," AE, *ibid.*

July 23. To T. A. Howland, NE, mentioned, Howland to Lincoln, July 27, 1858, *ibid.*

c. July 24. Copy in Lincoln's autograph, of a letter from Horace Greeley to Joseph Medill, July 24, 1858, *ibid.*

c. July 27. To Thomas J. Turner, NE, Turner to Lincoln, July 27, 1858, endorsed "Ansd," AE, *ibid.*

c. July 30. To David Davis, NE, Davis to Lincoln, July 30, 1858, endorsed "Ansd." AE, *ibid.*

July 30. To Nathan C. Geer, NE, mentioned, Geer to Lincoln, Aug. 2, 1858, *ibid.*

July 30. To William C. Hobbs, NE, mentioned, Hobbs to Lincoln, Aug. 2, 1858, *ibid.*

July 30. To Frank W. Tracy, NE, mentioned, Tracy to Lincoln, Aug. 3, 1858, *ibid.*

July 30. To William Walker, NE, mentioned, Walker to Lincoln, Aug. 2, 1858, *ibid.*

Aug. — . To B. M. Davenport, NE, mentioned, Davenport to Lincoln, June 17, 1860, *ibid.*

c. Aug. 1. To William Kellogg, NE, mentioned, Kellogg to Lincoln, Aug. 4, 1858, *ibid.*

c. Aug. 1. To F. S. Potter and others, NE, mentioned, Potter and others to Lincoln, Aug. 9, 1858, *ibid.*

c. Aug. 1. To H. P. Sloan, NE, mentioned, Sloan to Lincoln, Aug. 10, 1858, *ibid.*

Aug. 2. To John M. Bush, NE, mentioned, Bush to Lincoln, Aug. 5, 1858, *ibid.*

Aug. 2. To John A. Jones, NE, mentioned, Jones to Lincoln, Aug. 7, 1858, *ibid.*

Aug. 2. To Owen Lovejoy, NE, mentioned, Lovejoy to Lincoln, Aug. 4, 1858, *ibid.*

Aug. 2. To Thomas J. Pickett, NE, mentioned, Pickett to Lincoln, Aug. 5 (?), 1858, *ibid.*

Aug. 9. To J. B. McKinley, NE, mentioned, McKinley to Lincoln, Aug. 11, 1858, *ibid.*

Aug. 9. To Clifton H. Moore, NE, mentioned, Moore to Lincoln, Aug. 10, 1858, *ibid.*

Aug. 9. To Samuel C. Parks, NE, mentioned, Parks to Lincoln, Aug. 9, 1858, *ibid.*

Aug. 12. To Lyman Trumbull, NE, mentioned, Ozias M. Hatch to Lincoln, Aug. 17, 1858, *ibid.*

c. Aug. 16. To Mattoon, Ill. Republican Club, NE, Mattoon Rep. Club to Lincoln, Aug. 16, 1858, endorsed "Ansd," AE, *ibid.*

Aug. 19. Speech at Peoria, Ill., mentioned, *Ill. State Journal,* Aug. 21, 1858

Aug. 23. Speech at Henry, Ill., mentioned, Ottawa *Republican,* Aug. 28, 1858

Aug. 24. Speech at Galesburg, Ill., mentioned, Chicago *Press & Tribune,* Aug. 26, 1858

Aug. 26. Speech at Amboy, Ill., purported, Angle, *Lincoln 1854-1861,* p. 243

Aug. 28. Speech at El Paso, Ill., mentioned, Chicago *Press & Tribune,* Sept. 3, 1858

c. Sept. To John F. Farnsworth, NE, mentioned, Farnsworth to Lincoln, Sept. 20, 1858, DLC-RTL

c. Sept. To Sydney Spring, NE, Spring to Lincoln, Sept. ?, 1858, endorsed "Ansd," AE, *ibid.*

Sept. 2. To Ninian W. Edwards, forgery, Swann Auction Galleries Catalog 303, Dec. 6, 1951

Sept. 6. Speech at Monticello, Ill., mentioned, Chicago *Press & Tribune,* Sept. 9, 1858

Sept. 7. Speech at Tolono, Ill., mentioned, *ibid.,* Sept. 11, 1858

Sept. 7. Speech at Mattoon, Ill., mentioned, *ibid.*

Sept. 9. Speech at Hillsboro, Ill., mentioned, *ibid.,* Sept. 14, 1858

Sept. 11. Speech at Highland, Ill., mentioned, *ibid.,* Sept. 15, 1858

Sept. 20. Speech at Sullivan, Ill., mentioned, *Ill. State Journal,* Oct. 4, 1858

Sept. 21. Speech at Danville, Ill., mentioned, Chicago *Press & Tribune,* Sept. 24, 1858

Sept. 22. Speech at Danville, Ill., mentioned, *ibid.,* Sept. 27, 1858

Sept. 24. Speech at Urbana, Ill., mentioned, *ibid.,* Sept. 28, 1858

Sept. 27. Speech at Jacksonville, Ill., mentioned, Jacksonville *Sentinel,* Oct. 1, 1858

Sept. 28. Speech at Winchester, Ill., mentioned, *Ill. State Journal,* Oct. 2, 1858

Sept. 29. Speech at Winchester, Ill., mentioned, *Chicago Press & Tribune,* Oct. 5, 1858

Oct. 1. Speech at Pittsfield, Ill., mentioned, Quincy *Whig,* Oct. 5, 1858

c. Oct. 3. To Hawkins Taylor, NE, Taylor to Lincoln, Oct. 3, 1858, endorsed "Answered," AE, DLC-RTL

Oct. 4. Speech at Metamora, Ill., announced, *Ill. State Journal*, Sept. 2, 1858

Oct. 8. Speech at Toulon, Ill., purported, Angle, *Lincoln 1854-1861*, p. 249

Oct. 9. Speech at Burlington, Iowa, mentioned, Burlington *Hawk Eye*, Oct. 11, 1858

Oct. 9. Speech at Oquawka, Ill., mentioned, Oquawka *Spectator*, Oct. 14, 1858

Oct. 16. Speech at Lincoln, Ill., mentioned, *Ill. State Journal*, Oct. 18, 1858

Oct. 18. Speech at Naples, Ill., mentioned, Jacksonville *Sentinel*, Oct. 22, 1858

Oct. 19. Speech at Mt. Sterling, Ill., announced, *Ill. State Journal*, Oct. 5, 1858

Oct. 23. Speech at Dallas City, Ill., mentioned, Carthage *Republican*, Oct. 28, 1858

Oct. 23. Speech at La Harpe, Ill., purported, Angle, *Lincoln 1854-1861*, p. 251

Oct. 27. Speech at Vermont, Ill., announced, *Ill. State Journal*, Sept. 2, 1858

c. Oct. 30. To Chester P. Dewey, NE, Dewey to Lincoln, Oct. 30, 1858, endorsed "Ansd." AE, DLC-RTL

Nov. 1. Speech at Decatur, Ill., announced, Chicago *Democrat*, Oct. 29, 1858

c. Nov. 5. To William H. Hanna and John H. Wickizer, NE, Hanna and Wickizer to Lincoln, Nov. 5, 1858, endorsed "Ansd.," AE, DLC-RTL

c. Nov. 5. To George W. Searle, NE, Searle to Lincoln, Nov. 5, 1858, endorsed "Ansd," AE, *ibid.*

c. Nov. 7. To David Davis, NE, Davis to Lincoln, Nov. 7, 1858, endorsed "Ansd.," AE, *ibid.*

Nov. 11. To J. W. Crisfield, forgery, ALS, NN

c. Nov. 11. To William A. Grimshaw, NE, Grimshaw to Lincoln, Nov. 11, 1858, endorsed "Ansd.," AE, DLC-RTL

c. Nov. 12. To Henry C. Whitney, NE, Whitney to Lincoln, Nov. 12, 1858, endorsed "Ansd," AE, *ibid.*

c. Nov. 15. To George W. Rives, NE, Rives to Lincoln, Nov. 15, 1858, endorsed "Ansd." AE, DLC-RTL

c. Nov. 22. To Charles H. Gordon, NE, Gordon to Lincoln, Nov. 22, 1858, endorsed "Ansd." AE, *ibid.*

c. Nov. 23. To Eleazer A. Paine, NE, Paine to Lincoln, Nov. 23, 1858, endorsed "Ansd," AE, *ibid.*

Dec. 2. To N. W. Edwards, forgery, ALS, NN

Dec. 2. To W. E. Stuart, forgery, ALS-P, ISLA

c. Dec. 4. To A. and J. Haines, NE, their letter to Lincoln, Dec. 4, 1858, endorsed "A. & J. Haines Ansd," AE, DLC-RTL

Dec. 10. To Hopkins, Hays, Palmer & Co., NE, mentioned in their letter to Lincoln, Dec. 16, 1858, *ibid.*

Dec. 10. To ———— Matheny, forgery, ALS, NN

Dec. 11. To William Kellogg, NE, mentioned, Kellogg to Lincoln, Dec. 15, 1858, DLC-RTL

c. Dec. 14. To Thomas C. W. Sale, NE, Sale to Lincoln, Dec. 14, 1858, endorsed "Ans'd," AE, *ibid.*

c. Dec. 23. To William H. Marshall, NE, mentioned, Marshall to Lincoln, Dec. 23, 1858, *ibid.*

Dec. 24. To Sidney Breese, NE, mentioned, Breese to Lincoln, Dec. 29, 1858, *ibid.*

Dec. 24. To William H. Carlin, NE, mentioned, Carlin to Lincoln, Dec. 29, 1858, *ibid.*

Dec. 24. To John Dougherty, NE, mentioned, Dougherty to Lincoln, Dec. 28, 1858, *ibid.*

Dec. 24?. To Henry S. Fitch, NE, mentioned, Fitch to Lincoln, Jan. 7, 1859, *ibid.*

Dec. 24. To O. C. Skinner, NE, mentioned, Skinner to Lincoln, Dec. 28, 1858, *ibid.*

c. Dec. 28. To John Reynolds, NE, mentioned, Reynolds to Lincoln, Dec. 28, 1858, *ibid.*

c. Dec. 30. To Thomas S. Halbach, mentioned, Halbach to Lincoln, Dec. 30, 1859, *ibid.*

1859

c. 1859. Inscription on flyleaf of Lanman's *Dict. of U. S. Cong.*, "Hon. David Fisher From his friend A. LINCOLN," spurious, ADS, CSmH

c. Jan. 10. Endorsement on envelope of letter from J. B. Jones to Lincoln, Jan. 10, 1859, "J. B. Jones—Boy in jail." AE, DLC-RTL

Feb. 5. To William Randolph, NE, mentioned, Randolph to Lincoln, Feb. 15, 1859, *ibid.*

Feb. 14. To Peter Ambos, NE, mentioned, Ambos to Lincoln, Feb. 17, 1859, *ibid.*

Feb. 16. Check to Bressmer, McQuinton, & Matheny (dry goods) for $7.21, copy, ISLA

c. Feb. 16. Check to John Williams & Co. (dry goods and groceries) for $26.03, *ibid.*

c. Feb. 19. To C. P. Danforth and N. H. Nashua, NE, mentioned, Danforth to Lincoln, Feb. 19, 1859, DLC-RTL

Feb. 21. Check for draft on H. A. Tucker & Co. for $25 to pay S. Little for guarantee to Henry Chew, copy, ISLA

Feb. 21. Check to Van Ness & Co. (chinaware and lamps) for $35.75, *ibid.*

Feb. 21. Lecture on Discoveries and Inventions, delivered at Springfield, Ill. (same as lecture at Jacksonville, Feb. 11, 1859)

Mar. 4. To Martin F. Conway and K. T. Lawrence, NE, mentioned, Conway to Lincoln, Mar. 16, 1859, DLC-RTL

Mar. 5. To Thomas J. Pickett, spurious, Tracy, p. 104; Pickett to William H. Herndon, Nov. 29, 1866, DLC-HW

Mar. 12. Subscribes $10 to Young Men's Republican Assn. of Springfield, Ill., DS-P, ISLA

c. Mar. 15. Check to C. M. & S. Smith (dry goods and groceries) for $407.72, copy, ISLA

Mar. 19. Endorsement on bill for subscription to Lacon *Gazette*, "$3.00 Sent, this 19. March 1859" AE, DLC-RTL

c. Apr. 29. To J. H. Reid, NE, letter from Reid, April 29, 1859, endorsed, "J. H. Reid—Ansd," AE, DLC-RTL

May 2. Check to Robert T. Lincoln for $6, DS-P, ISLA

c. May 11. To Benjamin F. James, NE, James to Lincoln, May 11, 1859, endorsed "B. F. James Ansd." AE, DLC-RTL

c. May 11. To Clifton H. Moore, NE, Moore to Lincoln, May 11, 1859, endorsed "C. H. Moore Ansd," AE, *ibid.*

c. May 13. To Norman B. Judd, NE, mentioned, Judd to Lincoln, May 13, 1859, *ibid.*

May 14. To Martin F. Conway, NE (*see* Lincoln to Mark W. Delahay this date)

May 14. To Jefferson L. Dugger, NE (*see* Lincoln to Mark W. Delahay this date)

c. May 21. Endorsement on envelope from John Livingston containing prospectus of *Livingston's United States Law Register,* "Too deep for me," AE, DLC-RTL

c. June 1. To Nathaniel P. Banks, NE, mentioned, Henry C. Whitney to Banks, June 1, 1859, Banks MSS., IHi

June 10. Check to W. B. Farnham for $30.45, DS-P, ISLA

c. June 15. To Norman B. Judd, NE, mentioned, Judd to Lincoln, June 15, 1859, DLC-RTL

June 15. Check for draft on H. A. Tucker & Co. for $7 to pay subscription for Chicago *Press & Tribune,* copy, ISLA

c. June 29. Check to Clifton H. Moore for $1.60 for taxes on land in Tama Co., Iowa, *ibid.*

July 4. Speech at Atlanta, Ill., mentioned, *Ill. State Journal,* July 9, 1859

July 4. Speech (evening) at Atlanta, Ill., mentioned, Lincoln, Ill., *Herald,* July 6, 1859, "Lincoln . . . talked about eating"

July 13. To T. A. Howland, NE, mentioned, Howland to Lincoln, July 16, 1859, DLC-RTL

c. July 25. To Joseph and David Gillespie, NE, mentioned in their letter to Lincoln, July 25, 1859, *ibid.*

c. Aug. 1. To A. B. Pikard, NE, mentioned, Pikard to Lincoln, Aug. 6, 1859, *ibid.*

c. Aug. 7. To Mark W. Delahay, NE, mentioned, Delahay to Lincoln, Aug. 7, 1859, *ibid.*

Aug. 10. To S. S. Cowan, NE, mentioned, Cowan to Lincoln, Sept. 13, 1859, *ibid.*

Aug. 19. To John Taffe, NE, mentioned, Taffe to Lincoln, June 15, 1860, *ibid.*

c. Aug. 22. To Norman B. Judd, NE, mentioned, Judd to Lincoln, Aug. 22, 1859, *ibid.*

Aug. 23. To William H. Brown, NE, mentioned, Brown to Lincoln, Sept. 10, 1859, *ibid.*

c. Aug. 26. To Theophilus L. Dickey, NE, mentioned, Dickey to Lincoln, Aug. 26, 1859, *ibid.*

c. Sept. 6. To William T. Bascom, letter and telegram, NE, mentioned, Bascom to Lincoln, Sept. 9, 1859, *ibid.*

Sept. 9. To Richard H. Lloyd, NE, mentioned, Lloyd to Lincoln, Sept. 16, 1859, *ibid.*

Sept. 16. Speech (evening) at Columbus, Ohio, to Young Men's Republican Club, mentioned in Ryan, *Lincoln and Ohio*, 35

Sept. 17. Speech at Hamilton, Ohio, mentioned, *ibid.*, 67-68

Sept. 21. To Richard H. Lloyd, NE, mentioned, Lloyd to Lincoln, Sept. 26, 1859, DLC-RTL.

Sept. 22. To Theophilus L. Dickey, NE, mentioned, Dickey to Lincoln, Oct. 3, 1859, *ibid.*

c. Sept. 25. To Thomas Corwin, NE, mentioned, Corwin to Lincoln, Sept. 25, 1859, *ibid.*

Sept. 25. To M. A. Northrup, NE, mentioned, Northrup to Lincoln, Sept. 29, 1859, *ibid.*

Sept. 30. To William T. Bascom, NE, mentioned, Bascom to Lincoln, Oct. 3, 1859, *ibid.*

Sept. 30. Remarks at Newhall House, Milwaukee, Wis., mentioned, Milwaukee *Sentinel*, Oct. 1, 1859

Oct. 11. To P. Wyckoff, NE, mentioned, Wyckoff to Lincoln, Oct. 18, 1859, DLC-RTL

c. Oct. 17. To Thomas Corwin, NE, mentioned, Corwin to Lincoln, Oct. 17, 1859, *ibid.*

c. Oct. 18. To Francis P. Blair, Jr., NE, mentioned, Blair to Lincoln, Oct. 18, 1859, *ibid.*

c. Oct. 23. To Horatio M. Vandeveer, NE, mentioned, Vandeveer to Lincoln, Oct. 23, 1859, *ibid.*

c. Oct. 26. Endorsement on envelope of invitation of Oct. 26, 1859 to speak at ratification meeting at Cooper Institute on Nov. 3, 1859, "New York Centl. Com." AE, DLC-Nicolay Papers

Oct. 27. Speech at Springfield, Ill., mentioned, *Ill. State Journal*, Oct. 27, 1859

c. Nov. 1. To Samuel Galloway, NE, mentioned, Galloway to Lincoln, Nov. 1, 1859, DLC-RTL

Nov. 8. To William T. Page, NE, mentioned, Page to Lincoln, Nov. 11, 1859, *ibid.*

c. Nov. 14. To Mark W. Delahay, NE, mentioned, Delahay to Lincoln, Nov. 14, 1859, *ibid.*

Nov. 16. Endorsement on letter of Burton C. Cook to Lincoln, Nov. 12, 1859: "Suit commenced by me this day—Nov. 16. 1859," AE, *ibid.*

Nov. 16. Check for draft on Metropolitan Bank for $50.75 for Robert T. Lincoln, copy, ISLA

Nov. 22. Check for draft on Ketchum, Howe & Co. for $25 for Robert T. Lincoln, *ibid.*

Dec. 2. Speech at Troy, Kansas, purported, Sandburg, *Prairie Years*, II, 193

Dec. 2. Speech at Doniphan, Kansas, mentioned, *Ill. State Journal*, Dec. 10, 1859

Dec. 2. Speech at Atchison, Kansas, mentioned, *ibid.*

Dec. 12. Inscriptions in a copy of Helper's *Impending Crisis, passim*, purportedly a gift to Alexander Williamson, forgery, AD-P, ISLA

Dec. 14. To Blatchford, Seward, & Griswold, NE, mentioned in their letter to Lincoln, Feb. 11, 1860, DLC-RTL

Dec. 14?. Copy in Lincoln's autograph of a letter from George W. Dole, Gurdon S. Hubbard, and William H. Brown, Dec. 12, 1859, AD, *ibid.*

Dec. 16. To C. W. Green & Co., NE, mentioned, Green to Lincoln, Dec. 19, 1859, *ibid.*

Dec. 16. Check for draft on Ketchum, Howe & Co. for $25.25 for Robert T. Lincoln, copy, ISLA

c. Dec. 18. To Van H. Higgins, NE, mentioned, Higgins to Lincoln, Dec. 18, 1859, DLC-RTL

Dec. 22. To John J. Crittenden, forgery, Tracy, p. 120

c. Dec. 30. Endorsement on envelope of letter from Thomas S. Halbach to Lincoln, Dec. 30, 1859, "Dutch Justice, at Rock-run," AE, DLC-RTL

1860

——. To Alexander K. McClure, NE, letter introducing Leonard Swett and David Davis, mentioned, McClure, *Abraham Lincoln and Men of War-times*, 39

——. To George A. Wenck, NE, letter written prior to November, 1860, mentioned, Wenck to Lincoln, Sept. 21, 1861, DLC-RTL

c. Jan. 6. To Charles H. Heard, NE, mentioned, Heard to Lincoln & Herndon, Jan. 6, 1860, *ibid.*

Jan. 18. To Peter Ambos, NE, mentioned, Ambos to Lincoln, Jan. 21, 1860, *ibid.*

Jan. 19. To Alexander H. Stephens, forgery, Tracy, 123

Jan. 23. To Glover, Cook & Campbell, NE, mentioned, in their letter to Lincoln, Jan. 28, 1860, DLC-RTL

Jan. 24. To George M. Parsons, NE, mentioned, Parsons to Lincoln, Jan. 30, 1860, *ibid.*

c. Jan. 27. To Norman B. Judd, NE, mentioned, Judd to Lincoln, Jan. 27, 1860, *ibid.*

Jan. 27. Lecture on Discoveries and Inventions, at Pontiac, Ill. (same as lecture at Jacksonville, Feb. 11, 1859), Pratt, ed., *Concerning Mr. Lincoln*, 21

Feb. 1. Check to Bressmer, McQuinton & Matheny (dry goods) for $6.46, copy, ISLA

Feb. 1. Check for draft to Officer & Pusey for $5 to have deed recorded, *ibid.*

Feb. 1. Check to "First Church" [First Presbyterian Church, Springfield, Ill.] for $10, DS-P, ISLA

c. Feb. 1. To Carl Schurz, NE, mentioned, Schurz to Lincoln, Feb. 23, 1860, DLC-RTL

Feb. 1. Speech at Springfield, mentioned, *Ill. State Journal*, Feb. 2, 1860

Feb. 2. To Officer & Pusey, NE, mentioned, Officer & Pusey to Lincoln, May 2, 1860, copy, ISLA

Feb. 2. Check for draft on Metropolitan Bank for $15.25 for self, *ibid.*

c. Feb. 2. Check to John Williams & Co. (dry goods and groceries) for $17.28, *ibid.*

Feb. 5. To Peter Ambos, NE, mentioned, Ambos to Lincoln, Feb. 8, 1860, DLC-RTL

c. Feb. 7. To John Wentworth, NE, mentioned, Wentworth to Lincoln, Feb. 7, 1860, *ibid.*

c. Feb. 8. To Van H. Higgins, NE, mentioned, Higgins to Lincoln, Feb. 8, 1860, *ibid.*

c. Feb. 11. To John Wentworth, NE, mentioned, Wentworth to Lincoln, Feb. 11, 1860, *ibid.*

c. Feb. 13. To Charles Billinghurst, NE, mentioned, Lincoln to Horace White, Feb. 13, 1860

Feb. 22. Check for draft on Ketchum, Son & Co. for $50 for self, copy, ISLA

c. Feb. 26. To David Wilmot, NE, mentioned, Lincoln to Simon Cameron, Feb. 26, 1860

Mar. 1. Speech at Concord, N.H., mentioned, Manchester *Daily Republican*, Mar. 2, 1860

Mar. 3. Speech at Exeter, N.H., mentioned, *Ill. State Journal*, Mar. 16, 1860, citing Concord, N.H., *Independent Democrat*

Mar. 6. To John Gorden, NE, mentioned, Gorden to Lincoln, June 15, 1860, DLC-RTL

Mar. 7. Speech at Meriden, Conn., mentioned in New Haven *Palladium*, cited by Chicago *Press & Tribune*, Mar. 14, 1860

Mar. 8. Speech at Woonsocket, R.I., mentioned, Providence *Journal*, Mar. 9, 1860

Mar. 9. Speech at Norwich, Conn., mentioned, Norwich *Daily Aurora*, Mar. 10, 1860 (same as New Haven speech of Mar. 6, 1860)

Mar. 10. Speech at Bridgeport, Conn., mentioned, *Ill. State Journal*, Mar. 16, 1860

Mar. 11. Speech at Five Points House of Industry, Brooklyn, N.Y., mentioned, New York *Tribune*, May 30, 1860

c. Mar. 15. Inscription in *Debates*, "To Hon. Abraham Jonas, with respects of A. Lincoln," ADS, IHi

c. Mar. 15. Inscription in *Debates*, "Samuel N. Shoup Esq From A. Lincoln," ADS, MiU-C

Mar. 15. To —— Wilkinson, NE, mentioned, Joseph H. Jackson to Lincoln, March 19, 1860, DLC-RTL

Mar. 19. Check for draft on Ketchum, Son & Co. for $25 for Robert T. Lincoln, copy, ISLA

c. Apr. 1. Speech at Evanston, Ill., mentioned in Currey, *Lincoln's Visit to Evanston*

Apr. 2. Speech at Waukegan, Ill., mentioned, James S. Frazear to Elihu B. Washburne, Apr. 3, 1860, Washburne Papers, IHi

c. Apr. 20. To Samuel C. Parks, NE, mentioned, Parks to Lincoln, Apr. 20, 1860, DLC-RTL

Apr. 26. Lecture on Discoveries and Inventions, at Springfield, Ill., mentioned, *Ill. State Journal*, Apr. 28, 1860 (same as lecture at Jacksonville, Feb. 11, 1859)

c. May 2. Copy in Lincoln's autograph of Richard M. Corwine's letter to Lincoln of Apr. 30, 1860, AD, DLC-RTL

May 17. Purported telegram to member of the Illinois delegation to the Republican National Convention: "I authorize no bargains and will be bound by none." Lapsley, VII, 397

May 17. To Mark W. Delahay, purported telegram agreeing to accept vice-presidential nomination, mentioned in Barton, *Life of Lincoln*, I, 431

May 22. To John M. Douglass, NE, mentioned, Douglass to Lincoln, May 23, 1860, DLC-RTL

c. May 26. To Clark E. Carr, NE, Carr's letter to Lincoln of May 26, 1860, endorsed "Ack," AE, *ibid.*

May 26. To Richard W. Thompson, NE, mentioned, Thompson to Lincoln, June 12, 1860, *ibid.*

May 27. To William H. Pratt, forgery, ALS, ICHi

May 28. To a New England collector, form letter sending autograph, copy, ISLA

May 28. To William C. Baker, form letter sending autograph, ALS, RPB

c. May 28. Endorsement on letter from G. W. Miller to Lincoln, May 28, 1860, "Lincoln family (uncles?)," AE, DLC-RTL

May 31. To James E. Harvey, NE, mentioned, Harvey to Lincoln, June 5, 1860, *ibid.*

June. To Cassius M. Clay, letter offering cabinet post, mentioned in *The Life, Memoirs, Writings and Speeches of Cassius M. Clay*, I, 250, 303n.

c. June 1. Endorsement on letter from Elihu B. Washburne to Lincoln, May 22, 1860, "Gave letter to Butler—June 1," AE, DLC-RTL

June 2. To Edward Herrick, Jr., form letter sending autograph, ALS, MH-Nolen Collection

June 4. To Edwin A. Palmer, Jr., form letter sending autograph, ALS, InFtwL

June 7. To Charles E. Alling, form letter sending autograph, LS, NBuHi

June 7. To Albert Daggett, form letter sending autograph, LS, Am. Art Assn. Catalog, Mar. 12, 1920, No. 536

c. June 8. Check to Obed Lewis, carriagemaker, for $75, copy, ISLA

June 9. To George M. Harrison, Nicolay for Lincoln, DLC-RTL

June 9. To Russell F. Hicks, NE, mentioned, Hicks to Lincoln, June 22, 1860, *ibid.*

June 18. To John M. Burt, form letter sending autograph, copy, ISLA

c. June 19. To Richard M. Corwine, NE, mentioned, Corwine to Lincoln, June 19, 1860, DLC-RTL

June 19. To Thomas R. Proctor, form letter sending autograph, LS-P, Munson-Williams-Proctor Institute, Utica, N.Y.

June 22. Signature on letter of Ozias M. Hatch to Charles F. Ulbrich, RPB

June 28. To Henry T. Coates, form letter sending autograph, LS-P, ISLA

June 28. To Alexander K. McClure, NE, mentioned, McClure to Lincoln, July 2, 1860, DLC-RTL

June 30. Check for $153 for draft on Metropolitan Bank for Robert T. Lincoln to enroll at Harvard College, copy, ISLA

June 30. To George W. Lewis, form letter sending autograph, LS, RPB

July. Marginal corrections in Samuel C. Parks' copy of *Lives and Speeches of Abraham Lincoln and Hannibal Hamlin* by William D. Howells, IHi

c. July. To David Wilder, Jr., NE, mentioned, Wilder to Lincoln, Oct. 22, 1862, DLC-RTL

July 2. To E. E. Bradbury, form letter sending autograph, Goodspeed's Catalog, n.d.

July 4. To David Wilmot, NE, mentioned, Wilmot to Lincoln, July 11, 1860, DLC-RTL

July 9. To ———— Ralph, forgery, ALS, DLC

July 10. To ————, form letter sending autograph, LS, RPB

July 10. To II. L. Haines, form letter sending autograph, King V. Hostick Catalog 10

July 16. To Richard M. Corwine, ALS, Parke-Bernet Catalog 398, Oct. 25-26, 1939, No. 232, ". . . The whole field looks well now. . . ."

July 24. Inscription in *Debates* to Carl Schurz, Angle, *Lincoln 1854–1861*, p. 343

July 28. To M. S. Mackenzie, form letter sending autograph, LS-P, ISLA

July 28. Autograph check to Mrs. Barbara Dinkel for $5, ADS, Reredel Corp., New York City

c. July 29. To David Davis, NE, mentioned, Davis to Lincoln, July 29, 1860, DLC-RTL

July 30. To John C. Richardson, NE, mentioned, Richardson to Lincoln, July 31, 1860, *ibid.*

c. Aug. 1. To Norman B. Judd, NE, mentioned, Judd to Lincoln, Aug. 1, 1860, *ibid.*

Aug. 9. Speech to Rosamond Wide Awakes at Springfield, Ill., mentioned, *Ill. State Journal*, Aug. 10, 1860

Aug. 14. To G. W. Wilson, form letter sending autograph, LS, owned by H. E. Luhrs, Shippensburg, Pa.

Aug. 24. To F. W. Ely, form letter sending autograph, LS, Parke-Bernet Catalog 505, Nov. 30-Dec. 1, 1943, No. 194

Aug. 25. To W. S. Howard, form letter sending autograph, LS, *ibid.*, Catalog 1352, May 27, 1952, No. 164

Aug. 30. To C. H. Bowen, form letter sending autograph, LS, IHi

Aug. 30. To Alexander K. McClure, NE, mentioned, McClure to Lincoln, Sept. 27, 1860, DLC-RTL

Aug. 31. To P. D. Richards, form letter sending autograph, LS, ORB

Sept. 3. Children's Village, memorandum, purported (incorrect as to date and questionable as to text), Hertz, II, 784

Sept. 4. To Elihu B. Washburne, NE, mentioned, Washburne to Lincoln, Sept. 11, 1860, DLC-RTL

c. Sept. 9. To Elbridge G. Spaulding, NE, mentioned, Spaulding to Lincoln, Sept. 9, 1860, *ibid.*

Sept. 11. To Samuel T. Glover, NE, mentioned, Glover to Lincoln, Sept. 17, 1860, *ibid.*

Sept. 15. To Aaron H. Greenwood, form letter sending autograph, LS, Vassar College Library, Poughkeepsie, N.Y.

Sept. 21. To Isaac Newton, NE, mentioned, Newton to Lincoln, Oct. 29, 1860, DLC-RTL

Sept. 22. To Jason Yurann, form letter sending autograph, copy, ISLA

Sept. 24. To R. L. Miller, Nicolay for Lincoln, concerning Robert Rutledge, DLC-RTL

Sept. 25. To E. S. Bradford, form letter sending autograph, LS, MSHi

Sept. 26. To Thomas L. Thornell, NE, mentioned, Thornell to Lincoln, Oct. 4, 1860, DLC-RTL

Sept. 28. To Elliott F. Shepard, NE, mentioned, Shepard to Lincoln, Oct. 15, 1860, *ibid.*

Sept. 30 (misdated Oct. 30 by Lincoln). To Clark R. Wheeler, NE, mentioned, Wheeler to Lincoln, Oct. 19, 1860, *ibid.*

c. Oct. 1. To Eli C. Blankenship, NE, mentioned, Blankenship to Lincoln, Oct. 1, 1860, *ibid.*

c. Oct. 1. To Charles W. House, NE, mentioned, House to Lincoln, Oct. 1, 1860, *ibid.*

Oct. 2. Check to Henry C. Latham, DS, Anderson Auction Co. Catalog 1025, April 16, 1914, No. 408

Oct. 6. To Prentis Dow, form letter sending autograph, LS, owned by John W. Dow, Reading, Vt.

Oct. 13. To R. B. Church, form letter sending autograph, LS, OClWHi

Oct. 16. To Luke Boone, form letter sending autograph, ALS-F, ISLA

Oct. 29. To Charles G. Dill, form letter sending autograph, LS, Stan. V. Henkels Catalog 1262, July 1, 1920, No. 269

Oct. 29. To C. H. Fisher, NE, mentioned, Fisher to Lincoln, Nov. 1, 1860, DLC-RTL

Oct. 30. *See* to Clark R. Wheeler, Sept. 30, 1860, *supra*

Nov. 2. To George F. Smith, form letter sending autograph and signed photograph, owned by Harold C. Brooks, Marshall, Mich.

Nov. 2. To "Young Lady No. 2," letter sending autograph owned by Mrs. L. B. Dabney, Vicksburg, Miss.

Nov. 8. To K. Clark, form letter sending autograph, LS, Swann Auction Gallery Catalog 141, Jan. 31, 1946, No. 95

Nov. 8. To James T. Matteson, form letter sending autograph, owned by C. L. Mulfinger, Los Angeles, Calif.

c. Nov. 9. To Charles Gibson, NE, letter from Gibson to Orville H. Browning (enclosed in Browning to Lincoln, Nov. 9, 1860) endorsed "C. Gibson Nov. 9. 1860 Ansd.," AE, DLC-RTL

Nov. 10. To Lizzie S. Weeden, form letter sending autograph, LS, owned by Mark R. Bittner, Allentown, Pa.

c. Nov. 12. Endorsement on Rauch to Conkling: "E. H. Rauch *to* James C. Conkling Nov 12, 1860 Recommends Gnl. Cameron for Secy. of Treasury." AE, DLC-RTL

Nov. 16. To L. S. Benedict, note for $35, forgery, ADS-F, ISLA

Nov. 16. To the Secretaries of the St. Marie Brass Band & St. Cecilia Society, forgery, ALS-F, St. Louis *Globe-Democrat*, Jan. 27, 1929

Nov. 17. To E. D. Loud, form letter sending autograph, LS, copy, ISLA

Nov. 17. To Charles Roberts, form letter sending autograph, LS, PHC

Nov. 19. To H. P. Main, form letter sending autograph, LS, MH

Nov. 19. To W. F. Stone, form letter sending autograph, ALS-P, ISLA

Nov. 21. To Fred W. French, form letter sending autograph, LS, RPB

c. Nov. 22. Check to Elkin & Davis (dry goods) for $150, copy, ISLA

Nov. 24. To G. D. Rumsey, form letter sending autograph, ALS-P, ISLA

Nov. 25. Speech to Mission Sabbath School, Chicago, Ill., mentioned, Chicago *Daily Journal*, Nov. 26, 1860

Nov. 26. To R. B. Rogers, form letter sending autograph, LS, InFtwL

Nov. 30. To R. R. Donnelley, form letter sending autograph, LS, Am. Art Assn. Catalog, Nov. 16, 1922, No. 288

c. Dec. 5. To Peter S. Mather, NE, letter from Mather to Lincoln, Dec. 5, 1860, endorsed "Answered," AE, DLC-RTL

Dec. 6. Endorsement on contract with Theodore Canisius, conveying "type, paper and good will" to Canisius, mentioned in Barton, *Life of Lincoln*, I, 423

Dec. 10. To ———, form letter sending autograph, LS, Madigan Catalog, June, 1928

Dec. 11. To Thomas Ewing, spurious, newspaper clipping, DLC-Nicolay Papers

c. Dec. 12. Check to E. B. Hawley & Co. (dry goods) for $13.20, copy, ISLA

c. Dec. 15. To Thomas Corwin, NE, mentioned, Lincoln to Lyman Trumbull, Dec. 17, 1860, and Lincoln to Gilmer, Dec. 15, 1860

Dec. 17. To B. F. Jacobs, form letter sending autograph, LS, owned by Benjamin F. Stein, Waukegan, Ill.

Dec. 17. To Worthington G. Snethen, NE, mentioned, Snethen to Lincoln, Dec. 21, 1860, DLC-RTL

Dec. 19. To Horace Greeley, NE, mentioned, Greeley to Lincoln, Dec. 22, 1860, *ibid.*

Dec. 21. To Henry Faxon, form letter sending autograph, LS, owned by Theodore Sheldon, Chicago, Ill.

Dec. 21. To John A. Gilmer, telegram and letter, NE, mentioned, Gilmer to Lincoln, Dec. 29, 1860, DLC-RTL

Dec. 22. To Kinsley S. Bingham, NE, mentioned, Bingham to Lincoln, Dec. 26, 1860, DLC-Nicolay Papers

Dec. 31. To Isabella B. Eustis, form letter sending autograph, ALS, MSHi

1861

———. Endorsement on letter of Martin Welker, 1861, *The Collector*, Oct. 1919, No. 77

———. To William H. Seward, Hay for Lincoln, 1861, NAuE

Jan. 1. To Mrs. Atwater, form letter sending autograph, LS, ICHi

c. Jan. 1. To Alexander K. McClure, NE, mentioned in McClure, *Abraham Lincoln and Men of War-times*, 41

Jan. 2. To J. A. Spencer, spurious, Charleston, S. C. *Mercury*, Jan. 30, 1861, copied in *Ill. State Journal*, Feb. 8, 1861

Jan. 4. To Alexander K. McClure, NE, mentioned, McClure to Lincoln, Jan. 11, 1861, DLC-Nicolay Papers

c. Jan. 5. To Charles D. Cleveland, NE, mentioned, Cleveland to Lincoln, Jan. 5, 1861, DLC-RTL

Jan. 7. Check to Bressmer, McQuinton & Matheny (dry goods) for $10.97, copy, ISLA

Jan. 12. To ———, form letter sending autograph, LS, Merwin Sales Co. Catalog, Mar. 9, 1915, No. 285

Jan. 15. To ———, form letter sending autograph, LS, C. F. Libbie Catalog, Oct. 17, 1905

Jan. 18. To William H. Seward, "James Churchman has rendered the cause very efficient service during the past campaign. . . ." LS, Anderson Auction Co. and Metropolitan Art Assn. Catalog 1110, Oct. 22, 1914, No. 431

Jan. 21. To E. Spring, form letter sending autograph, LS, *The Collector*, Feb. 1949, No. 322

Jan. 22. Check to Charles W. Matheny & Co. for $10.97 (duplicate payment, *see* Jan. 7, 1861), DS, DLC-RTL

Jan. 23. To Edwin C. Wilson, Nicolay for Lincoln, DLC-Nicolay Papers

Jan. 26. To Mrs. C. W. Pratt, form letter sending autograph, LS, RPB

Jan. 28. To Edward Bates, Nicolay for Lincoln, copy, DLC-RTL

Jan. 28. To James Fonda, form letter sending autograph, *The Collector*, Jan. 1928, No. 9890

Jan. 28. To J. W. Tillman, Nicolay for Lincoln, NH, VI, 100-101

c. Jan. 29. To Winfield Scott, NE, mentioned in Elliott, *Winfield Scott*, 688

c. Feb. To Abraham Kohn, NE, mentioned in Korn, *Am. Jewry and the Civil War*, 204-205

Feb. 1. Preamble and resolutions adopted by Illinois legislature, attributed on insufficient evidence, Phillips, *Abraham Lincoln by Some Men Who Knew Him* (1950), 93-95

Feb. 1. To Edwin D. Morgan, Nicolay for Lincoln, copy, DLC-RTL

Feb. 5. To ———, check for [$149.] 94, partial DS, InFtwL

Feb. 5. To Edward Bates, Nicolay for Lincoln, NH, VI, 106

c. Feb. 6. Check for fifty cents for taxes on lot in Lincoln, Ill., copy, ISLA

Feb. 7. To ———, form letter sending autograph, LS, C. F. Libbie Catalog, May 9, 1911, No. 803

c. Feb. 7. Endorsement on letter of John M. Wilson, Feb. 7, 1861, asking appointment of Joseph Knox as U.S. district attorney for Ill., "The only thing Mr [John F.] Farnsworth asks." AE, DNA RG 60, Papers of Atty. Gen., Appointments, Box 372

c. Feb. 8. Check for $26 for insurance on house and outbuildings, copy, ISLA

Feb. 8. To ———, form letter sending autograph, *The Collector*, Jan. 1931

Feb. 8. Editorial in *Ill. State Journal*, Feb. 8, 1861, denouncing forgery of letter to J. A. Spencer, Jan. 2, 1861, attributed in Barton, *Lincoln*, p. 144, but apparently only authorized, not written, by Lincoln

Feb. 10. To Isaac R. Diller, spurious, Hertz, II, 804

c. Feb. 11. Three checks for $100 each for drafts on Metropolitan Bank for self, copy, ISLA

c. Feb. 11. Check for self for $100, *ibid.*

Feb. 11. Speech at Decatur, Ill., as recollected by John Quinlan, Decatur, Ill., *Review*, Aug. 26, 1900; stop at Decatur, mentioned, New York *Tribune* and *Herald*, Feb. 12, 1861

Feb. 11. Remarks at Lebanon Station, Ind., mentioned, New York *Herald*, Feb. 12, 1861: "At Lebanon station, while being led out to bow to a congregation of ladies, he remarked that he was always glad to demonstrate how well he understood the poetry of motion."

Feb. 12. Speech at Indianapolis, Ind., from balcony of Bates House before leaving for Cincinnati, mentioned, New York *Herald* and Cincinnati *Commercial*, Feb. 13, 1861

Feb. 12. Speech at Shelbyville, Ind., mentioned, New York *Herald*, Feb. 13, 1861

Feb. 12. Speech at Greensburg, Ind., mentioned, *ibid.*

Feb. 12. Speech at Morris, Ind., mentioned, *ibid.*

Feb. 13. Speech at Milford, Ohio, mentioned, *ibid.*, Feb. 14, 1861

Feb. 13. Speech at Miamiville, Ohio, mentioned, New York *Tribune*, Feb. 14, 1861

Feb. 13. Speech at Loveland, Ohio, mentioned, New York *Herald*, Feb. 14, 1861

Feb. 13. Speech at Morrow, Ohio, mentioned, *ibid.*

Feb. 13. Speech at Corwin, Ohio, mentioned, New York *Tribune*, Feb. 14, 1861

Feb. 13. Speech at Xenia, Ohio, mentioned, *ibid.*

Feb. 13. To John Kent, Sr., purported note written on cardboard and given to Kent, who was engineer of the presidential train from Cincinnati to Columbus, "I am your friend. A. LINCOLN," copy, ISLA

Feb. 14. Speech at Port Washington, Ohio, recollection of Jacob Baringer, Coshocton, Ohio, *Age*, Feb. 4, 1909

Feb. 16. Speech at Willoughby, Ohio, mentioned, Cleveland *Plain Dealer*, Feb. 16, 1861

Feb. 16. Speech at Madison, Ohio, mentioned, *ibid.*

Feb. 16. Speech at Geneva, Ohio, mentioned, *ibid.*

Feb. 22. Speech at Downingtown, Pa., mentioned, New York *Tribune*, Feb. 23, 1861

Mar. 1. To J. Grey Jewell, Nicolay for Lincoln, DNA FS RG 59, Appointments, Box 318

Mar. 2. Purported remarks to callers at Willard's Hotel: "Gentlemen, it is evident that some one must take the responsibility of these appointments, and I will do it. My Cabinet is completed. The positions are not definitely assigned, and will not be until I announce them privately to the gentlemen whom I have selected as my Constitutional advisers," New York *Times*, Mar. 4, 1861 (misdated March 3 in Lapsley, V, 252)

Mar. 4. To James Buchanan, forgery, ALS, InFtwL

Mar. 5. Reply to Michigan delegation, mentioned, Washington *Evening Star*, Mar. 6, 1861

Mar. 6. Reply to Indiana delegation, mentioned, New York *Herald*, Mar. 7, 1861

Mar. 6. Reply to Maine delegation, mentioned, *ibid.*

Mar. 6. Reply to Ohio delegation, mentioned, New York *Tribune*, Mar. 7, 1861

Mar. 6. Reply to California delegation, mentioned, *ibid.*

Mar. 6. Reply to Vermont delegation, mentioned, *ibid.*

Mar. 7. To Gideon Welles, Nicolay for Lincoln, DNA WR NB RG 45, Exec. Letter No. 38

Mar. 8. To (Stephen A.) Douglas, forgery, copy, ISLA

Mar. 11. To Simon Cameron, directing appointment of James B. Fry as assistant adjutant general, missing from DNA WR RG 94, Adj. Gen. Letters Received, P 46

c. Mar. 12. Endorsement on letter from Charles Sumner to Lincoln, Mar. 12, 1861, "Senator Sumner's request that Mr. [Theodore S.] Fay be retained as Minister at Switzerland." AE, DNA FS RG 59, Appointments, Box 283

Mar. 14. To President of Costa Rica, same as to President of Nicaragua, Mar. 18, 1861

Mar. 16. To Governors of all states, form letter transmitting joint resolution to amend the constitution, approved on Mar. 2, 1861, by James Buchanan, LS. To: Governor of Mississippi (NN); of New Hampshire (Am. Art Assn. Catalog, Apr. 28-29, 1925, No. 526); of North Carolina (State Archives, Raleigh, N.C.); of Pennsylvania (PHi); of Rhode Island (State Archives, Providence, R.I.); of Vermont (Sec. of State's Office, Montpelier, Vt.); of other states, not located

Mar. 18. To the President of Nicaragua, withdrawal of Alexander Dimitry as minister, copy, DNA FS RG .59, Communications to Foreign Sovereigns and States, III, 124

c. Mar. 18. Endorsement on letter from William H. Seward, March 18, 1861, concerning appointment of territorial governors: "Seward wants to review as to Territory," AE, DLC-RTL

Mar. 19. To Leopold, King of the Belgians, withdrawal of Elisha Y. Fair as minister, copy, DNA FS RG 59, Communications to Foreign Sovereigns and States, III, 163

Mar. 19. To Leopold, King of the Belgians, appointing Henry S. Sanford as minister, copy, *ibid.*, Credences, IV, 378

Mar. 20. To William I, King of Prussia, appointing Norman B. Judd as minister, copy, *ibid.*, 379

Mar. 21. To Napoleon III, Emperor of France, withdrawal of Charles J. Faulkner as minister, copy, *ibid.*, Communications to Foreign Sovereigns and States, III, 120-21

Mar. 23. To the President of Guatemala, appointing Elisha O. Crosby as minister, National Archives of Guatemala, Autógrafas de Soberanos y Presidentes, T.I. 1850-1870 (B99-7-3-2; 4678)

Mar. 23. To Napoleon III, Emperor of France, appointing William L. Dayton as minister, copy, DNA FS RG 59, Credences, IV, 319

Mar. 25. To Charles XV, King of Sweden and Norway, withdrawal of Benjamin F. Angel as minister, copy, *ibid.*, Communications to Foreign Sovereigns and States, III, 168

Mar. 25. To Charles XV, King of Sweden and Norway, appointing Jacob S. Haldeman as minister, copy, *ibid.*, Credences, IV, 380

c. Mar. 25. Endorsement on letter from Fletcher P. Cuppy, March 25, 1861, "Cuppy, of Dayton—for Consulship. Mr. [Robert C.] Schenck recommends." AE, *ibid.*, Appointments, Box 265

c. Mar. 25. Endorsement on letter from William C. Jewett to Lincoln, Mar. 25, 1861, "Foolishness," DLC-RTL

Mar. 25. To Isabel II, Queen of Spain, withdrawal of William Preston as minister, copy, DNA FS RG 59, Communications to Foreign Sovereigns and States, III, 166

Mar. 25. To William I, King of Prussia, withdrawal of Joseph A. Wright as minister, copy, *ibid.*, 167

Mar. 27. To Victoria, Queen of the United Kingdom, withdrawal of George M. Dallas as minister, copy, *ibid.*, 121-22

Mar. 27. To Victoria, Queen of the United Kingdom, appointing Charles F. Adams as minister, copy, *ibid.*, Credences, IV, 317

c. Mar. 27. Endorsement on letter of John S. Watts, Mar. 27, 1861, "Judge Watts' recommendations as to vacancies in Indian agencies in New-Mexico." AE, DNA NR RG 48, Applications, Indian Agencies, Misc., Box 1268

Mar. 28. To the Senate, authorization for John G. Nicolay to make corrections in list of New Hampshire postmasters, DS, DLC-RTL

Mar. 29. To the Minister of Foreign Affairs of Hawaii, withdrawal of James W. Borden as commissioner, Seward for Lincoln, copy, DNA FS RG 59, Communications to Foreign Sovereigns and States, III, 126

Mar. 29. To Isabel II, Queen of Spain, appointing Carl Schurz as minister, Hertz, II, 824

Mar. 29. To Pedro V, King of Portugal, withdrawal of George W. Morgan as minister, copy, DNA FS RG 59, Communications to Foreign Sovereigns and States, III, 169

Mar. 30. To Pedro V, King of Portugal, appointment of James E. Harvey as minister, copy, *ibid.*, Credences, IV, 382

Apr. To William Bebb, NE, mentioned, Bebb to Lincoln, June 12, 1861, DLC-RTL

c. Apr. 1. Endorsement on list of senators and representatives, "Judge Abram D. Smith, of Wisconsin, Backers' for Minister to Rome. A.L.," AES, DNA FS RG 59, Appointments, Box 382

c. Apr. 1. To Pope Pius IX, withdrawal of John P. Stockton as minister, copy, *ibid.*, Communications to Foreign Sovereigns and States, III, 174-75

Apr. 1. To William III, King of the Netherlands, withdrawal of Henry C. Murphy as minister, copy, *ibid.*, 122-23

Apr. 1. To William III, King of the Netherlands, appointment of James S. Pike as minister, copy, *ibid.*, Credences, IV, 318

Apr. 2. To C. D. Chase, form letter sending autograph, LS, owned by N. Doss, Chicago, Ill.

c. Apr. 4. Endorsement on letter of G. W. Kinzer to Edward D. Baker, Apr. 4, 1861, "Kinzer vindicates [Willard B.] Farwell," AE, DLC-RTL

c. Apr. 5. Endorsement on letter from Patrick Crowley to Lincoln, Apr. 5, 1861, "Patrick Crowley, asking to be Warden of Penitentiary in the district." AE, *ibid.*

Apr. 6. To the President of the Argentine Confederation, appointment of Robert M. Palmer as minister, copy, DNA FS RG 59, Credences, IV, 325

Apr. 6. To the President of Bolivia, appointing David K. Cartter as minister, copy, *ibid.*, 325

Apr. 6. To the President of Ecuador, appointment of Frederick Hassaurek as minister, copy, *ibid.*

Apr. 6. To the President of Ecuador, withdrawal of Charles R. Buckalew as minister, copy, *ibid.*, Communications to Foreign Sovereigns and States, III, 127

Apr. 6. To the President of Mexico, appointment of Thomas Corwin as minister, copy, *ibid.*, Credences, IV, 324

Apr. 6. To the President of Mexico, withdrawal of John B. Weller as minister, copy, *ibid.*, Communications to Foreign Sovereigns and States, III, 128

Apr. 6. To the President of Nicaragua, appointment of Andrew B. Dickinson as minister, copy, *ibid.*, Credences, IV, 325

Apr. 8. To Alexander II, Emperor of the Russias, withdrawal of John Appleton as minister, copy, *ibid.*, Communications to Foreign Sovereigns and States, III, 123

Apr. 8. To Alexander II, Emperor of the Russias, appointment of Cassius M. Clay as minister, copy, *ibid.*, Credences, IV, 320

Apr. 8. To Salmon P. Chase, Nicolay for Lincoln, requesting applications for appointments in Washington Territory, DNA FI RG 56, Letters from Exec. Officers, Series AB, II, 1

Apr. 8. To Caleb B. Smith, Nicolay for Lincoln, requesting applications for appointments in Washington Territory, DNA NR RG 48, Appointments, Surveyors General, Box 9

Apr. 10. To Edward Bates, concerning appointment of John B. D. Coggswell as U.S. district attorney and D. C. Jackson as U.S. marshal of Wisconsin, ALS, Am. Art Assn. Anderson Galleries Catalog 4201, Nov. 13-14, 1935, No. 250

Apr. 10. To the Pacha of Egypt, appointment of William S. Thayer as consul general, copy, DNA FS RG 59, Credences, IV, 384

Apr. 10. To Francis Joseph I, Emperor of Austria, withdrawal of J. Glancy Jones as minister, copy, *ibid.*, Communications to Foreign Sovereigns and States, III, 170

Apr. 10. To Frederick VII, King of Denmark, withdrawal of James M. Buchanan as minister, copy, *ibid.*, 171

Apr. 10. To Frederick VII, King of Denmark, appointment of Bradford R. Wood as minister, copy, *ibid.*, Credences, IV, 383

c. Apr. 10. To Pope Pius IX, appointment of Rufus King as minister, NE, but authorization to affix seal on this letter is dated Apr. 10, 1861, DS, OClWHi

Apr. 11. To Gideon Welles, concerning a Navy appointment, partial ALS, Parke-Bernet Catalog 611, Dec. 4-5, 1944, No. 255

Apr. 12. To Charles XV, King of Sweden and Norway, acknowledgment of withdrawal of Baron N. G. de Wetterstedt, copy, DNA FS RG 59, Communications to Foreign Sovereigns and States, III, 172

c. Apr. 12?. Endorsement on letter of John B. S. Todd to Lincoln, Apr. 2, 1861, recommending John B. Hoffman for agent of Ponca Indians, "Personally requested by Capt. Todd," AE, DNA NR RG 48, Applications, Indian Agencies, Box 1272

c. Apr. 15. To Fernando Wood, NE, mentioned, Wood to Lincoln, Aug. 20, 1862, DLC-RTL

Apr. 16. To Victor Emmanuel II, King of Italy, appointment of George P. Marsh as minister, DNA FS RG 59, Credences, IV, 384-85

Apr. 19. To Edward Bates, Nicolay for Lincoln, designating *National Republican* to receive federal advertising, DNA RG 60, Papers of Atty. Gen., Box 99

Apr. 19. To Simon Cameron, Nicolay for Lincoln, same as to Bates, copy, DNA WR RG 156, Office of Chief of Ordnance, WD 321 (see Z)

Apr. 19. To Salmon P. Chase, Nicolay for Lincoln, same as to Bates, DNA FI RG 56, Letters from Exec. Officers, Series AB, II, 3

Apr. 19. To Parke Godwin, NE, mentioned, Godwin to Lincoln concerning George W. Denison, Apr. 20, 1861, DLC-Nicolay Papers

Apr. 20. To Edward Bates, Nicolay for Lincoln, requesting commissions for William Millward as marshal and George A. Coffey as attorney for Eastern Dist. of Pa., DNA RG 60, Papers of Atty. Gen., Box 99

Apr. 22. To Thomas H. Hicks, Seward for Lincoln, NH, VI, 252-54

Apr. 22. To Gideon Welles, Nicolay for Lincoln, calling cabinet meeting, DLC Welles Papers

c. Apr. 25. Endorsement on articles clipped from New York *Times*, Apr. 25, 1861, "Villainous articles," AE, DLC-RTL

c. Apr. 29. Endorsement, W. H. Lingenfelter to Lincoln and his cabinet, Apr. 29, 1861, concerning military and political problems, "To be submitted to the Cabinet," AE, *ibid.*

Apr. 29. Remarks to Committee from New York, mentioned, New York *Tribune*, May 1, 1861

May 1. To George W. Caldwell, Nicolay for Lincoln, NH, V, 260-61

May 6. To George Gibson, referring letter of William R. Nevins, missing from DNA WR RG 192, Comm. Gen. of Subsistence, L 9

May 6. To John M. Johnson, Hay for Lincoln, NH, VI, 266

May 7. To Salmon P. Chase, concerning letter of J. C. Smith of N.Y. on customs house officials doing military duty, missing from DNA RG 56, Misc. Letters, Register 32, P 8

May 9. To Hiram Barney concerning William Ward, NE, mentioned, Barney to Lincoln, May 11, 1861, DLC-RTL

May 9. To George Gibson, referring letter of John F. Omberton of May 3, 1861, missing from DNA WR RG 192, Comm. Gen. of Subsistence, L 11

May 17. Check to William for $8, DS, ORB

c. May 17. To Charles Russell, NE, mentioned, Lincoln to Edwin D. Morgan, May 20, 1861

May 21. Endorsement on letter of W. H. Botts, Carnegie Book Shop Catalog 119, No. 85

May 25. To Washington A. Bartlett, NE, mentioned, Bartlett to Lincoln, May 27, 1861, DLC-RTL

May 25. Endorsement on letter from Mrs. Edwin D. Morgan, concerning promotion of Chauncey McKeever, "I concur," William D. Morley Catalog, Oct. 22, 1943, No. 296

May 25. To Edwin M. Stanton, concerning death of Ephraim Elmer Ellsworth, forgery, ALS-P, ISLA

May 29. To the President of Granadian Confederacy, appointment of Allen A. Burton as minister, copy, DNA FS RG 59, Credences, IV, 348

May 30. To Edward Bates, Nicolay for Lincoln, forwarding resignation of John A. Campbell, DNA RG 60, Appts., Supreme Court

June 4. AGO *General Orders No. 29*, attributed, Milton, *Eve of Conflict*, 569

c. June 5. Draft of an order concerning Gen. McClellan, NE, mentioned, Lincoln to Cameron, June 5, 1861

June 5. To Pedro II, Emperor of Brazil, appointment of James W. Webb as minister, copy, DNA FS RG 59, Credences, IV, 349

June 7. To George Gibson, referring letter of William M. Dickson recommending Peter A. White, May 25, 1861, missing from DNA WR RG 192, Comm. Gen. of Subsistence, L 10

June 12. To the President of Costa Rica, appointment of Charles N. Riotte as minister, copy, DNA FS RG 59, Credences, IV, 350

June 17. Endorsement on bill rendered by William H. Carryl & Bro., "Approved, and referred to the Secretary of the Treasury for settlement. A. LINCOLN," AES, DNA RG 217, Gen. Accounting Office, No. 140775

June 20. To Simon Cameron, concerning an additional N.Y. regiment, G. A. Baker Catalog 101, May 4, 1943, No. 48

June 29. To Joseph G. Totten, Nicolay for Lincoln, concerning William H. Redwood, Jr., and James B. Breese, DNA WR RG 94, U.S. Mil. Acad., 1861, No. 67

June 29. To the Bey of Tripoli, appointment of William Porter as consul, copy, DNA FS RG 59, Credences, IV, 387

July 1. To Edward Bates, Hay for Lincoln, asking return of papers of M. Russell Thayer for U.S. district attorney at Philadelphia, DNA RG 60, Papers of Atty. Gen., Box 97

c. July 2. To Archibald Williams, NE, mentioned, Williams to Lincoln, July 2, 1861, DLC-RTL

c. July 3. To Simon Cameron, recommending Bronson Murray for sutlership, missing from DNA WR RG 107, Sec. of War, Personnel Appts., Box 4

July 3. To Joseph G. Totten, Nicolay for Lincoln, appointment of Charles Morris of Mass., DNA WR RG 94, U.S. Mil. Acad., 1861, No. 597

c. July 6. To Salmon P. Chase, NE, mentioned, Chase to Lincoln concerning recommendations made by Preston King, July 6, 1861, DLC-RTL

c. July 6. Endorsement on letter of Jefferson Davis to Lincoln, July 6, 1861, "Jeff. Davis about crew of Savannah," AE, *ibid.*

July 8. To Edward Bates concerning pardon of three seamen, NE, mentioned, Bates to Lincoln, July 9, 1861, *ibid.*

July 8. To Lorenzo Thomas, requesting list of nominations made in the War Dept. during Senate recess, missing from DNA WR RG 94, Adj. Gen. Letters Received, P 273

July 8. Endorsement on letter from H. W. Blodgett concerning appointment of Joseph Willard, Nicolay for Lincoln, "desires . . . this case called to his special attention . . . ," DNA WR RG 94, U.S. Mil. Acad., 1861, No. 932

c. July 13. To Simon Cameron, referring letters on want of protection for Union men in Missouri, missing from DNA WR RG 107, Sec. of War Letters Received, P 140

July 13. Endorsements on list of candidates for New Mexico and Utah appointments, passim, AE, DLC-RTL

July 18. To Hiram Barney, NE, mentioned, Barney to Lincoln, July 20, 1861, *ibid.*

July 18. To Edward Bates, Nicolay for Lincoln, referring petition for pardon of Stephen Brooks, DNA RG 204, U.S. Pardon Atty., A 329

July 18. To Simon Cameron, referring letter of Timothy Howe to Lincoln, July 10, 1861, recommending military appointments in letter of James R. Doolittle of same date, "Respectfully submitted to War Dept. A.L." AES, copy, ISLA

July 18. To Simon Cameron, referring letter recommending George J. Stealy for captain in U.S. Army, "Respectfully submitted to War Dept. A.L." AES, IHi

c. July 20. To Simon Cameron, NE, mentioned, Robert Smith to Lincoln, July 20, 1861, DLC-RTL

c. July 20. To Simon Cameron, referring letter of William R. Hanson, July 20, 1861, "Respectfully referred to the War Department A.L." AES, RPB

July 20. To Timothy O. Howe, NE, mentioned, Howe to Lincoln, July 22, 1861, DLC-RTL

July 21. To Edward Bates, on petition of citizens of Tuscola County, Mich., for pardon of Thomas Lean, "Attorney General please examine this. A. LINCOLN," AES, DNA RG 204, U.S. Pardon Atty., A 353

c. July 21. Endorsement on letter of Edwin D. Morgan to Hiram Berdan, mentioned, Berdan to Lincoln, July 21, 1861, DLC-RTL

July 21. To Edwin D. Morgan, NE, mentioned, Morgan to Lincoln, July 23, 1861, ibid.

July 22. Endorsement concerning a N.Y. rifle regiment, "Let it be accepted. A. LINCOLN," AES, RPB

July 22. To the President of Chile, appointment of Thomas H. Nelson as minister, copy, DNA FS RG 59, Credences, IV, 354

July 23. To Salmon P. Chase, approval of bill for $1500 rendered by A. P. Zimandy for White House glassware, "Approved and referred to the proper accounting officers for settlement. A. LINCOLN," AES, DNA RG 217, Gen. Accounting Office, No. 141158

July 24. To Hiram Barney, NE, mentioned, Barney to Lincoln, July 25, 1861, DLC-RTL

July 26. To Salmon P. Chase, purported in a dubious reminiscence, Whitney, Life of Lincoln, II, 24

July 26. Speech to Brigade of General William T. Sherman, mentioned in Sherman's Memoirs, I, 218

July 27. To Simon Cameron, on letter from Thomas Carbery to Lincoln, recommending C. S. Jones, July 15, 1861, "Respectfully submitted to the Secretary of War. A. L.," AES, DNA WR RG 107, Sec. of War Personnel Appts., Box 3

July 29. To Salmon P. Chase, Nicolay for Lincoln, concerning Senate refusal of nomination of James Jeffrey as appraiser at Baltimore, DNA FI RG 56, Letters from Exec. Officers, Series AB, II, 4

July 30. To the Emperor of China, appointment of Anson Burlingame as minister, copy, DNA FS RG 59, Credences, IV, 366

July 30. To A. G. Shaver, Hay for Lincoln, note of thanks, ALS, THaroL

July 31. To Alexander D. Bache, Nicolay for Lincoln, appointment at 9 P.M., DLC-Bache Papers

c. July 31. Endorsement on letter of John S. Carlile to Lincoln, July, 31, 1861, recommending James E. Wharton for consul, "To be respectfully considered in due time." AE, DLC-RTL

c. Aug. To John A. Dix, NE, mentioned, Dix to Lincoln, Aug. 28, 1861, ibid.

Aug. 2. To Charles C. Hoskins, sending autograph, LS, RPB

Aug. 2. To Caleb B. Smith, Nicolay for Lincoln, concerning nominations of Jonathan H. Charles and Clinton C. Hutchinson, DNA NR RG 48, Applications, Indian Agencies, Misc., Box 1268

c. Aug. 5. To Simon Cameron, recommending Henry V. Sullivan, missing from DNA WR RG 107, Sec. of War Personnel Appts., Box 5

Aug. 5. To Simon Cameron, endorsement on letter from Orville H. Browning to Lincoln, Aug. 5, 1861, recommending Charles C. Briggs for a lieutenancy, "I indorse the above. A. LINCOLN," AES, owned by Irving Dilliard, Collinsville, Ill.

c. Aug. 5. To Simon Cameron, endorsement by Nicolay for Lincoln on letter from David G. Farragut to Lincoln, Aug. 5, 1861, asking cadetship for his son Loyall, "The President desires this case to be remembered . . . ," DNA WR RG 94, U.S. Mil. Acad. 1861, No. 887

Aug. 5. To John C. Frémont, Nicolay for Lincoln, concerning situation in Cairo, Ill., New York *Tribune*, Mar. 4, 1862

Aug. 6. To Winfield Scott, Nicolay for Lincoln, enclosing Frémont's answer to Lincoln's telegram of Aug. 5, 1861, DNA WR RG 108, H.Q.A., P 255, Box 54

Aug. 7. To Simon Cameron, referring letter of Seymour Voullaire to Lincoln, July 29, 1861, recommending Capt. George A. Schaeffer for appointment in the regular Army, "Respectfully submitted to War Department. AL.," AES, owned by L. E. Dicke, Evanston, Ill.

c. Aug. 7. To Simon Cameron, on letter of J. D. Rynard to Cameron, Aug. 7, 1861, asking appointment as paymaster, "Respectfully submitted to War Department. A. LINCOLN," AES, IHi

Aug. 8. To Benjamin F. Watson, NE, mentioned in *Abraham Lincoln Tributes*, 139

c. Aug. 9. To Salmon P. Chase, on statement of G. S. Humphrey & Co. for $116.50, May 21, 1861, "Approved and referred to the proper accounting officers for settlement. A. LINCOLN," AES, DNA RG 217, Gen. Accounting Office, No. 141263

c. Aug. 9. To Salmon P. Chase, on bills totaling $1006, rendered by Alexander T. Stewart & Co., "Approved and referred to the proper accounting officers for settlement. A. LINCOLN," AES, *ibid.*, No. 141262

c. Aug. 11. Endorsement concerning George Barrell, NE, mentioned, Barrell to Lincoln, Aug. 11, 1861, DLC-RTL

c. Aug. 12. To Simon Cameron, referral of letter from Gen. John C. Frémont concerning a general order, Aug. 6, 1861, missing from DNA WR RG 107, Sec. of War Letters Received, P 227

Aug. 12. To Simon Cameron, on letter from Francis H. Peirpoint to Lincoln, Aug. 10, 1861, concerning appointment of Audley W. Gaggam, "Respectfully submitted to the War Department, A.L.," AES, IHi

Aug. 15. To Simon Cameron, on letter from R. S. Canley to Lincoln, June 27, 1861, recommending Andrew Gardner, "Respectfully submitted to the War Department. A. LINCOLN," AES, DNA WR RG 107, Sec. of War Personnel Appts., Box 2

Aug. 15. To Francis Joseph I, Emperor of Austria, appointment of John L. Motley as minister, DNA FS RG 59, Credences, IV, 389

c. Aug. 16. Endorsement on visiting card of William H. Seward, "Clarence Darling, 16, past—Son of an elector of 1860." AE, DNA WR RG 94, U. S. Mil. Acad., 1862, No. 75

c. Aug. 17. To Ormsby M. Mitchel, concerning appointment, NE, mentioned, Mitchel to Lincoln, Aug. 17, 1861, DLC-RTL

Aug. 17. To Lorenzo Thomas, referring request and directing appointment of William H. Powell as second lieutenant on recommendation of Rev. John C. Smith, missing from DNA WR RG 94, Adj. Gen. Letters Received, P 894 (for entry 1865)

Aug. 19. To Edward Bates, on letter from Benjamin F. Hall to Lincoln, July 21, 1861, asking leave of absence, "Respectfully submitted to the Atty. Genl. A.L.," AES, DNA GE RG 60, Papers of Atty. Gen., Segregated Lincoln Material

Aug. 19. To Montgomery C. Meigs, Hay for Lincoln, forwarding telegram from quartermaster of Fire Zouaves, ALS, owned by W. Easton Louttit, Jr., Providence, R.I.

Aug. 20. To Lorenzo Thomas, directing appointment of Lt. Redfield Proctor and Lt. A. V. Plumb, missing from DNA WR RG 94, Adj. Gen. Letters Received, P 899 (for entry 1865)

c. Aug. 22. To Nathaniel P. Banks, concerning "disappearance of Captain Smith," NE, mentioned, Banks to Lincoln, Aug. 22, 1861, DLC-RTL

c. Aug. 22. To Hamilton R. Gamble, NE, mentioned, Edward Bates to Lincoln, Aug. 24, 1861, *ibid.*

Aug. 22. To the Padischah, Sultan of the Empire of the Ottoman Family, appointment of Edward J. Morris as minister, DNA FS RG 59, Credences, IV, 390

Aug. 26. To Lorenzo Thomas (or Simon Cameron), concerning additional paymasters, missing from DNA WR RG 94, Adj. Gen. Letters Received, P 697

c. Aug. 28. Endorsement to Simon Cameron, "Respectfully submitted to the Sec. of War." AES, Stan. V. Henkels Catalog, Jan. 23, 1915, No. 65

Aug. 28. To Simon Cameron, on letter from Alfred H. Jones to Lincoln, Aug. 19, 1861, applying for office, "Respectfully submitted to the War Department. A. LINCOLN.," AES, DNA WR RG 107, Sec. of War Personnel Appts., Box 13

Aug. 28. Check to "Mr. Johns (a sick man)" for $3, DS-P, ISLA

Aug. 28. To Lorenzo Thomas (or Simon Cameron), approving proposal of Postmaster General Montgomery Blair and Sec. of War Cameron that officers of grade of captain and below be furnished to Volunteers, those now acting with Volunteers to number of 100 to remain, their places to be supplied by appointment of cadets as lieutenants; missing from DNA WR RG 94, Adj. Gen. Letters Received, P 343

Aug. 29. To Simon Cameron, on letter of William Sprague *et al*, recommending Ellery Eddy, "Respectfully submitted to the Sec. of War. A. LINCOLN," AES, owned by Frederick M. Dearborn, New York City

Aug. 29. To George Gibson, referring letter of recommendation for Henry Taimer for local commissary, missing from DNA WR RG 192, Comm. Gen. of Subsistence, L 13

Aug. 30. To John C. Frémont, NE, mentioned, Frémont to A. J. Dezeyk, Sept. 4, 1861, DLC-RTL

Sept. 1. To Benjamin F. Butler, Nicolay for Lincoln, concerning victory at Fort Hatteras, DLC-Butler Papers

Sept. 4. To George Gibson, referring letter of Israel Champion, Aug. 27, 1861, applying for commissary, missing from DNA WR RG 192, Comm. Gen. of Subsistence, L 14

Sept. 5. To Simon Cameron, on letter from James O'Grady to Lincoln offering services, Sept. 2, 1861, "Respectfully submitted to the War Dept. A. LINCOLN," AES, DNA WR RG 107, Sec. of War Personnel Appts., Box 4

c. Sept. 5. To Simon Cameron, referring letter of Hiram Barney to Lincoln, Aug. 28, 1861, enclosing letter of Mrs. Julia M. Sands to Barney, Aug. 26, 1861, with charges against Paymaster Samuel S. Williams, missing from *ibid.*, Letters Received, P 330 referred to Gen. McClellan

Sept. 5. To George Gibson, referring letter of B. S. (?) Fullerton, Aug. 27, 1861, complaining of scarcity of provisions in camp of 18th N.Y. Volunteers, missing from DNA WR RG 192, Comm. Gen. of Subsistence, L 15

Sept. 6. To Simon Cameron, on letter of David Webb to Major Watts, "Respectfully submitted to the War Department. A. LINCOLN," John Heise Catalog 2474

Sept. 6. To George Gibson, referring letter of Worthington G. Snethen to Lincoln, Aug. 13, 1861, asking that quartermasters be required to purchase supplies from loyal merchants, missing from DNA WR RG 192, Comm. Gen. of Subsistence, L 16

Sept. 6. To George Gibson, referring letter of Robert Kirkham, Aug. 27, 1861, applying for brigade commissary, missing from *ibid.*, L 17

Sept. 6. Check to "Master Tad" for "one gold" dollar, DS-P, ISLA

c. Sept. 7. To Simon Cameron, on letter of John A. Andrew to Lincoln, Sept. 7, 1861, "Respectfully submitted to the War Department. A. LINCOLN.," OR, III, I, 815

c. Sept. 7. Endorsement on letter of Edward Wallace to Lincoln, Sept. 7, 1861, City Book Auction Catalog, May, 1942, No. 47

c. Sept. 9. To Simon Cameron, missing from DNA WR RG 107, Sec. of War Letters Received, P 336, see B 308

Sept. 10. To George Gibson, referring letter of Ninian W. Edwards to Lincoln, Aug. 24, 1861, suggesting that he and commissary at St. Louis act together in purchasing supplies, missing from DNA WR RG 192, Comm. Gen. of Subsistence, L 19

Sept. 11. To Joseph Holt, Nicolay for Lincoln, acknowledging receipt of Holt's letter of Sept. 3, 1861, DLC-Holt Papers

Sept. 12. To George Gibson, referring letter of William H. Perrince, applying for commissary or paymaster, missing from DNA WR RG 192, Comm. Gen. of Subsistence, L 20

Sept. 14. To "Editor Lewistown Democrat," spurious letter published in Fulton, Ill., *Democrat,* July 12, 1922

Sept. 16. To Hiram Barney, NE, mentioned, Barney to Lincoln, Sept. 20, 1861, concerning Samuel A. Hopkins, DLC-RTL

c. Sept. 16. To Simon Cameron, referring documents concerning Samuel S. Williams, missing from DNA WR RG 107, Sec. of War Letters Received, P 360

Sept. 16. Endorsement on letter of Gen. Benjamin F. Kelley concerning Lieut. George H. Crosman, Stan. V. Henkels Catalog, Oct. 21, 1936, No. 111

c. Sept. 16. To Montgomery C. Meigs, NE, mentioned, Meigs to Lincoln, Sept. 16, 1861, DLC-RTL

c. Sept. 17. To S. J. Anderson, NE, mentioned, Anderson to Lincoln, Sept. 17, 1861, *ibid.*

Sept. 17. To Simon Cameron, on letter of William G. Tackaberry to Lincoln, Aug. 20, 1861, concerning a commission, "Respectfully submitted to the War Department. A. Lincoln," AES, owned by R. E. Burdick, New York City

Sept. 17. To Simon Cameron, on letter from Seward to Lincoln, Aug. 22, 1861, concerning "Mr. Wall and Col. McConnell," "Respectfully submitted to the War Department A. Lincoln," AES, IIIi

Sept. 18. To Chief Clerk of Judiciary Dept., Nicolay for Lincoln, forwarding papers of John O. Mott, DNA RG 60, Papers of Atty. Gen., Appointments, N.Y., North, Box 694

Sept. 18. To George Gibson, referring letter of S. B. (or "B. S.") Fullerton, Aug. 27 (second reference), missing from DNA WR RG 192, Comm. Gen. of Subsistence, L 18

Sept. 19. To Hiram Barney, concerning B. F. Sherman as appraiser, NE, mentioned, Barney to Lincoln, Sept. 20, 1861, DLC-RTL

Sept. 19. Endorsement on envelope, "West-Point. Joseph Dennie Meredith. Nephew of Hon. W. M. Meredith.," AE, DNA WR RG 94, U.S. Mil. Acad., 1861, No. 580

c. Sept. 20. To Robert Anderson, concerning Gen. William Nelson, NE, mentioned, Anderson to Lincoln, Sept. 20, 1861, DLC-RTL

c. Sept. 20. To Simon Cameron, concerning John B. S. Todd, NE, mentioned, Lincoln to Cameron, Sept. 20, 1861

Sept. 23. Endorsement on letter from Gen. John E. Wool, AES, William D. Morley Catalog, Apr. 28, 1944, No. 196

Sept. 25. To Rev. John G. Butler, NE, *see* form letter, Dec. 3, 1861

Sept. 25. To Rev. G. G. Goss, NE, *ibid.*

Sept. 25. To Rev. Henry Hopkins, NE, *ibid.*

Sept. 25. Endorsement on letter of Gen. Ormsby M. Mitchel, approving an appointment to his staff, Parke-Bernet Catalog 223, Oct. 30–Nov. 1, 1940, No. 412

c. Sept. 25. Endorsement on envelope, "Samuel A. Pancoast for P. Marshall, Hampshire Co., West Va." *The Flying Quill,* Feb.–Mar. 1950, No. 58

Sept. 27. Endorsement on letter of John P. Hall and others, Carnegie Book Shop Catalog No. (?), Item 198

Sept. 27. To Charles E. Mix, NE, mentioned, Mix to Lincoln concerning John B. Hoffman, Sept. 27, 1861, DLC-RTL

Sept. 30. Endorsement on letter of Mary Lambert to Mrs. Lincoln concerning her brother, Sergt. Meagher, "his sister kindly tells his story within" (incomplete), Carnegie Book Shop Catalog 93, No. 360

c. Oct. 1. Endorsement on envelope of recommendations for Horace B. Thompson, "West Point. Young man now Post-Master in Sickles' Brigade, & his father Commissary.," AE, DNA WR RG 94, U.S. Mil. Acad., 1861, No. 865

Oct. 1. Order, "The six New England States. . . ." AGO *General Orders No. 86,* attributed on insufficient evidence, *Private and Official Correspondence of Benjamin F. Butler,* I, 245-46

Oct. 2. Endorsement, Nicolay for Lincoln, concerning Francis F. Jones for cadetship at West Point, DNA WR RG 94, U.S. Mil. Acad., 1861, No. 443

Oct. 2. To Philip Kearney, forgery, CtY-Jackson Collection

Oct. 2. To George D. Ramsay, on letter from Daniel Moran to Lincoln, Oct. 2, 1861, "Respectfully to Maj. Ramsey. A. LINCOLN," AES, DLC-RTL

Oct. 4. To Simon Cameron, on letter from Daniel E. Sickles to Lincoln, Oct. 2, 1861, concerning appointment of William L. Wiley and Lovell Purdy, "Respectfully submitted to the War Department. A. LINCOLN," AES, RPB

Oct. 4. To Simon Cameron, on letter from John A. Gurley to Lincoln, Oct. 1, 1861, reporting on Frémont's actions, "Respectfully submitted to the War Department. A. LINCOLN," AES, DNA WR RG 107, Sec. of War Letters Received, P 434

Oct. 4. To Emperor of Morocco, appointment of James DeLong as consul, copy, DNA FS RG 59, Credences, IV, 391

Oct. 7. To Simon Cameron, on letter from Leonard Swett and William W. Orme to Lincoln, Sept. 11, 1861, recommending Alexander Briscoe, "Respectfully submitted to War Department, A. L." AES, DNA WR RG 107, Sec. of War Personnel Appts., Box 1

Oct. 9. To Captain (Quincy A. ?) Gillmore, concerning General (Thomas W. ?) Sherman, Bangs & Co. Catalog, Nov. 22, 1900, No. 284

c. Oct. 10. To Simon Cameron, Hay for Lincoln, on letter of Emmanuel J. Pleyel, Oct. 10, 1861, referred, DNA WR RG 107, Sec. of War Letters Received, P 464

Oct. 10. To the President of Venezuela, appointment of Henry T. Blow as minister, copy, DNA FS RG 59, Credences, IV, 360

Oct. 10. To the President of Venezuela, withdrawal of Edward A. Turpin, *ibid.*, Communications to Foreign Sovereigns and States, III, 133

c. Oct. 12. To John C. Frémont, NE, mentioned, Cameron to Lincoln, Oct. 12, 1861, DLC-RTL

Oct. 14. To Benjamin B. French, concerning Thomas Stackpole, NE, mentioned, French to Lincoln, Oct. 15, 1861, *ibid.*

Oct. 15. To Simon Cameron, referring reports of Nathaniel P. Banks and John W. Geary on Mrs. Louisa Hartshorne, missing from DNA WR RG 107, Sec. of War Letters Received, P 404

c. Oct. 17. To Robert Anderson, engraved invitation from "The President & Mrs. Lincoln" to dinner on Oct. 17, 1861, D, DLC-Anderson Papers

c. Oct. 17. To Caleb B. Smith, engraved invitation from "The President & Mrs. Lincoln" to dinner on Oct. 17, 1861, D, InFtwL

Oct. 18. To William H. Seward, on petition of James Pollock and others to Lincoln, Oct. 5, 1861, for appointment of George Gerard, "Respectfully submitted to the Secretary of State. A. LINCOLN," DNA FS RG 59, Appointments, Box 292

c. Oct. 19. To Simon Cameron, on letter from Orville H. Browning, Oct. 11, 1861, concerning appointment of H. M. Woodyard as Col. 2d. Mo. Vols., missing from DNA WR RG 107, Sec. of War Letters Received, P 456

c. Oct. 21. To Simon Cameron, referring letter of John J. Crittenden, Oct. 21, 1861, asking commission for Charles D. Morris, *ibid.*, P 492

Oct. 21. To Gideon Welles, endorsement removed from attendant papers, "Respectfully submitted to the Sec. of Navy. A. LINCOLN," AES, CtHi

c. Oct. 22. To Simon Cameron, referring letter from Higgins & Friehaus of Liege offering percussion muskets, missing from DNA WR RG 107, Sec. of War Letters Received, P 463

c. Oct. 24. To Nelson B. Sweitzer, concerning Gen. McClellan, NE, mentioned, Sweitzer to Lincoln, Oct. 24, 1861, DLC-RTL

Oct. 26. To Ninian W. Edwards, NE, mentioned, Edwards to Lincoln, Oct. 27, 1861, *ibid.;* mentioned Thomas A. Scott to Lincoln, Oct. 26, 1861, *ibid.*

c. Oct. 28. To Simon Cameron, referring letter of Daniel McCook concerning appointments to his staff, missing from DNA WR RG 107, Sec. of War Letters Received, P 477

Oct. 29. To Simon Cameron, referring letter from Hendrick B. Wright to Lincoln, Oct. 21, 1861, asking suspension of sentence of John Lanigan, missing from *ibid.*, P 482, 487

Oct. 30. To Rev. F. E. Boyle, NE, *see* form letter, Dec. 3, 1861

Nov. 2. To Montgomery C. Meigs, on telegram of Brig. Gen. William K. Strong to Lincoln, Nov. 1, 1861, concerning funds for quartermaster, "Respectfully submitted Quarter-Master General. A. LINCOLN," AES, IHi

Nov. 4. To Simon Cameron, Hay for Lincoln, forwarding letter of Z. T. Galt to Lincoln, Nov. 2, 1861, concerning Missouri campaign, DNA WR RG 108, H.Q.A., P 265, Box 54

Nov. 4. To Benjamin F. Isherwood, concerning "Perkins Steam Gun," NE, mentioned, Isherwood to Lincoln, Dec. 4, 1861, DLC-RTL

Nov. 4. To William H. Seward, referring letter from Washington Bonifant to Lincoln, Oct. 30, 1861, recommending D. A. Rich, "Respectfully submitted to the Sec. of State. A. LINCOLN," AES, DNA FS RG 59, Appointments, Box 370

Nov. 7. To Rev. William Y. Brown, NE, *see* form letter, Dec. 3, 1861

Nov. 7. To Simon Cameron, on letter of Col. Chester Harding, Jr. to Edward Bates, Nov. 2, 1861, concerning his staff, "Respectfully submitted to War Department. A. LINCOLN," AES, RPB

c. Nov. 7. To Simon Cameron, referring letter from C. Gibson to Lincoln, Nov. 7, 1861, recommending Horace A. Conant for major of cavalry, Ben Bloomfield Catalog DI-4, No. 116

Nov. 7. To Rev. John C. Smith, NE, *see* form letter, Dec. 3, 1861

c. Nov. 7. To Lorenzo Thomas, referring papers of Gurden Chapin, missing from DNA WR RG 94, Adj. Gen. Letters Received, P 591

Nov. 8. To James W. Ripley, introducing Judge Wilson who wants arms for Ill. Regt., missing from DNA WR RG 156, Office of Chief of Ordnance, WD 1802 (*see* Z)

c. Nov. 9. Autograph copy by Lincoln of letter from Salmon P. Chase to Lincoln, Nov. 9, 1861, DLC-Nicolay Papers

Nov. 9. To S. N. Holmes, Hay for Lincoln, acknowledging gift of fruit, ALS, owned by William Steiger, St. Petersburg, Fla.

Nov. 11. To the President of Peru, appointment of Christopher Robinson as minister, DNA FS RG 59, Credences, IV, 361

Nov. 11. To L. B. Wyman, chairman, Hay for Lincoln, declining invitation for Dec. 22, ALS, RPB

c. Nov. 12. To Lorenzo Thomas, directing appointment of Col. Thomas J. Wood and Capt. Richard W. Johnson as brigadier generals, missing from DNA WR RG 94, Adj. Gen. Letters Received, P 611

Nov. 13. To Simon Cameron, referring letter of Judge Dean Caton, AES, Am. Art Assn. Anderson Galleries Catalog 4298, Feb. 3-4, 1937, No. 287

Nov. 13. To William H. Seward, on letter from C. H. Blood to Lincoln, Nov. 8, 1861, applying for office, "Respectfully submitted to the State Department. A. LINCOLN," AES, DNA FS RG 59, Appointments, Box 233

Nov. 14. To the Tycoon of Japan, appointment of Robert H. Pruyn as minister, *ibid.*, Credences, IV, 391-92

Nov. 14. To the Tycoon of Japan, withdrawal of Townsend Harris, *ibid.*, Communications to Foreign Sovereigns and States, III, 182

Nov. 15. To James W. Ripley, directing purchases, missing from DNA WR RG 156, Office of Chief of Ordnance, WD 1842 (*see* Z)

c. Nov. 15. To Lorenzo Thomas, directing appointments to Gen. Wood's brigade, missing from DNA WR RG 94, Adj. Gen. Letters Received, P 613

Nov. 16. To Simon Cameron, on petition of Mrs. Agnes J. Fair for commutation of sentence of her husband, John Fair, 2d U.S. Infantry, "Respectfully submitted to the War Department. A. LINCOLN," AES, IHi

Nov. 19. To Simon Cameron, Hay for Lincoln, referring letter from George C. Thomas to Lincoln, Nov. 11, 1861, asking authority to organize a home guard to defend the capital, DNA WR RG 107, Sec. of War Letters Received, P 520

Nov. 19. To James W. Ripley, "Please see Mr. Morton of N. York & letter of W. A. Newell. A. LINCOLN," copy, DNA WR RG 156, WD 1889 (*see* Z) Register notation

Nov. 20. To Edward Bates, Hay for Lincoln, referring letter from H. Davies to Lincoln, Nov. 15, 1861, recommending Jonathan E. Field, DNA RG 60, Appts., South Carolina, Box 866

Nov. 21. To ———, concerning a military pass, ALS, Anderson Galleries Catalog 1248, Nov. 13, 1916, No. 173

Nov. 21. To Edward Bates, on letter from Montgomery Blair to Lincoln, Nov. 14, 1861, recommending Thomas S. Nelson, "Respectfully submitted to the Attorney General. A. LINCOLN," AES, DNA RG 60, Appts., New Mexico, Box 659

Nov. 21. To Simon Cameron, submitting proposal of Metropolitan Railroad Co. to build from Georgetown to Hagerstown, missing from DNA WR RG 107, Sec. of War Letters Received, P 528

Nov. 21. To William H. Seward, on letter of Thomas H. Hicks to Lincoln, Nov. 16, 1861, concerning appointment of John B. Kerr to Peru, "Respectfully submitted to the Sec. of State A. LINCOLN," AES, DNA FS RG 59, Appointments, Box 322

Nov. 21. To Robert J. Walker, purported (inaccurate or spurious) in James R. Gilmore, *Personal Recollections*, p. 54

c. Nov. 23. To William H. Seward, Nicolay for Lincoln, referring letter from Comte de Jondreville de Villarceau to Lincoln, Nov. 23, 1861, offering services, DLC-McClellan Papers

Nov. 27. To Edward Bates, Nicolay for Lincoln, referring letter from Alexander Ramsey to Lincoln, Nov. 19, 1861, asking pardon for Luther Preston, DNA RG 204, U.S. Pardon Atty., A 385

Nov. 27. To Presbyterian Synod (Old School) of N.Y. and N.J., Seward for Lincoln, McPherson, *The Political History of the United States* . . . , 468

Nov. 28. To Lorenzo Thomas, Hay for Lincoln, referring letter from Henry Beard to Lincoln, Nov. 26, 1861, DNA WR RG 94, Adj. Gen. Letters Received, P 712

Nov. 30. To William H. Seward, Nicolay for Lincoln, referring application of Thomas Hickling to Lincoln, Oct. 21, 1861, for consulate, DNA FS RG 59, Appointments, Box 308

c. Dec. To Carl Schurz, NE, mentioned, Schurz to Lincoln, Dec. 23, 1861, DLC-RTL

Dec. 4. To Simon Cameron, "Respectfully submitted to the War Department. A. LINCOLN," on letter from John J. Speed to Joshua F. Speed, Nov. 19, 1861, copy, ISLA

Dec. 4. To George B. McClellan, Seward for Lincoln, concerning arrest of slaves from Confederate states, ". . . their arrests as fugitives from labor or service should be immediately followed by military arrests of the parties making the seizure. Copies of this communication . . . sent to the Mayor of the City of Washington and to the Marshal. . . ." New York *Herald*, Dec. 6, 1861

Dec. 7. To Edward Bates, Hay for Lincoln, referring letter from J. Blodget Britton to Lincoln, Dec. 4, 1861, applying for office, DNA RG 60, Papers of Atty. Gen., Appointments, Louisiana, Box 504

Dec. 7. To Simon Cameron, asking appointment of John M. Palmer as brigadier general, offered for sale by F. G. Sweet in 1949

Dec. 9. To Simon Cameron, on letter of Uri Manly to Lincoln, Dec. 5, 1861, asking an appointment, "Respectfully submitted to the War Department. A. LINCOLN," AES, IHi

Dec. 9. To George B. McClellan, ALS, offered for sale by F. G. Sweet in 1949

c. Dec. 9. To John E. Wool, concerning Col. [Julian ?] Allen, NE, mentioned, Wool to Lincoln, Dec. 9, 1861, DLC-RTL

Dec. 12. To Dr. P. Kohler, forgery, ALS-F, ISLA

Dec. 12. To William H. Seward, on letter from Henry J. Adams, Thomas W. Sweney and others to Lincoln, Dec. 1861, recommending Remington Fairland, "Respectfully submitted to the Secretary of State. A. LINCOLN," AES, DNA FS RG 59, Appointments, Box 282

Dec. 13. Signature on purported tracing of Lincoln's feet by Dr. P. Kohler, spurious, DS-F, ISLA

Dec. 13. To John F. Lee, referring letter of A. B. Ely, counsel for Gen. Henry W. Benham, missing from DNA WR RG 153, Judge Adv. Gen. Letters Received, No. 97

Dec. 14. To Salmon P. Chase: "How goes the plan for sending a Court to Port-Royal?" partial text, ALS, Chicago Book and Art Auctions Catalog 45, Nov. 27, 1934, No. 131

Dec. 14. Endorsement on letter of Phineas D. Gurley recommending Dr. Frederick B. Culver for paymaster, F. H. Sweet List 58, No. 106

Dec. 14. To House of Representatives, draft of letter of transmittal in reply to resolution of Dec. 9, 1861, not in Lincoln's hand and never signed or sent, DLC-RTL

Dec. 14. To William H. Seward, Hay for Lincoln, referring letter from Preston King to Lincoln, Dec. 12, 1861, recommending Asa Mahan, DNA FS RG 59, Appointments, Box 340

Dec. 16. To Simon Cameron on letter from Mary Cassidy asking discharge of her son Patrick, a minor, in Co. C, 4th Cavalry, "Respectfully submitted to War Department. A. LINCOLN," AES, IHi

c. Dec. 17. To Simon Cameron, NE, mentioned, John N. King to Lincoln, Dec. 17, 1861, DLC-RTL

Dec. 18. To Francis E. Spinner, sending autograph "for your friend," ALS, PHC

Dec. 20. To Joseph G. Totten, inquiring about fortification of Lime Point, missing from DNA WR RG 77, Office of Chief of Engineers, P 1056

Dec. 23. Endorsement on letter from Don C. Buell, Parke-Bernet Catalog 223, Oct. 30–Nov. 1, 1940, No. 413

Dec. 24. To S. H. Kauffman, sending autograph "for your friend," ALS, DLC

Dec. 24. To F. W. Thayer, sending autograph "for your lady-friend," ALS, Am. Art Assn. Catalog, Feb. 20-21, 1928, No. 259

Dec. 27. To Simon Cameron, on letter of Will P. Thomasson to Robert Mallory, Dec. 18, 1861, asking about appointment of his son Charles, "Respectfully submitted to the War Department. A. LINCOLN," AES, DNA WR RG 107, Sec. of War Personnel Appts., Box 5

c. Dec. 28. To Ambrose E. Burnside, NE, mentioned in telegram from Burnside, Dec. 28, 1861, DLC-RTL

Dec. 31. To Lorenzo Thomas, directing appointment of Major Frederick Steele and Napoleon J. T. Dana as brigadier generals, missing from DNA WR RG 94, Adj. Gen. Letters Received, P 749

1862

——. To Ira Rankin, concerning C. H. Gaubert, NE, mentioned Rankin to Lincoln, Apr. 21, 1862, DLC-RTL

c. Jan. 1. To Don C. Buell, NE, mentioned in Lincoln's telegram to Buell, Jan. 1, 1862

c. Jan. 1. To George D. Prentice, NE, mentioned, Prentice to Lincoln, Jan. 1, 1862, DLC-RTL

Jan. 2. To George B. McClellan, Hay for Lincoln, referring report of Farrelly Alden that rebels plan to capture port of Guaymas, DNA WR RG 108, H.Q.A., Doc. File 1862, P 1

Jan. 2. To James Speed, concerning resolutions on slavery in Kentucky legislature, NE, mentioned, Speed to Lincoln, Jan. 6, 1862, DLC-RTL

c. Jan. 2. To Lorenzo Thomas, referring petition of citizens of Southwest Michigan for assignment of troops to that section, missing from DNA WR RG 94, Adj. Gen. Letters Received, P 752

c. Jan. 3. To Edward Bates, on letter from Leonard Swett to Lincoln, Jan. 3, 1862, "David Brier—for Judge somewhere." AE, DNA RG 60, Papers of Atty. Gen., Box 107

Jan. 6. To Luiz I, King of Portugal, appointment of James E. Harvey as minister, DNA FS RG 59, Credences, IV, 392-93

Jan. 6. Endorsement approving a printed circular of the New York Ladies' Educational Union with preceding endorsements by Cameron, Chase, and John C. Smith, "And also mine/A. LINCOLN," AES, CSmII

c. Jan. 7. To Winfield Scott, concerning Lt. Col. Robert C. Buchanan, NE, mentioned, Scott to Lincoln, Jan. 21, 1862, DLC-RTL

Jan. 8. To Lorenzo Thomas, requesting that if Capt. James Totten has refused appointment of assistant inspector, to give the place to Capt. Edward R. Platt, missing from DNA WR RG 94, Adj. Gen. Letters Received, P 34

Jan. 10. To Simon Cameron, on letter from Squire Moon to Lincoln, Jan. 2, 1862, tendering his services, "Respectfully submitted to the War Department. A. LINCOLN," AES, IHi

Jan. 16. To Simon Cameron, referring letter from William P. Fessenden concerning promotion of Maj. James L. Donaldson, missing from DNA WR RG 107, Sec. of War Letters Received, P 3

Jan. 16. To Salmon P. Chase, introducing Col. Dick Taylor, of doubtful authenticity, NH, XI, 122

Jan. 16. To George B. McClellan, on letter from Gen. Charles F. Smith, "Sent for Gen. McClellan's perusal. A.L. Jan. 16, 1862," Am. Art Assn. Anderson Catalog, Jan. 14-15, 1936, No. 353

Jan. 16. To Mrs. Ellen M. Otis, sending autograph, LS, F. H. Sweet List, Nov. 1937, No. 45

c. Jan. 16. Endorsement on letter of Simon Cameron to Lincoln, Jan. 16, 1862, "Thomas Williams, for a Port-Royal Judge Rec. by Gen. Cameron." AE, DNA RG 60, Papers of Atty. Gen., Box 107

c. Jan. 17. To Simon Cameron, letter announcing his nomination as minister to Russia, purported in Lamon, *Lincoln*, 461n

Jan. 18. To William W. H. Davis, on Provost Marshal's receipt for a prisoner, spurious, Argosy Book Shop Catalog, April, 1942, No. 20

Jan. 18. To Edwin M. Stanton, referring letter concerning Capt. Asher R. Eddy, missing from DNA WR RG 107, Sec. of War Letters Received, P 69 in Irregular Book 5

Jan. 18. To Edwin M. Stanton, "Good testimonials respectfully submitted to the Sec. of War. A. LINCOLN," Parke-Bernet Catalog 905, Dec. 1-2, 1947, No. 276

Jan. 20. To Andrew Johnson, Hay for Lincoln, directing him to forward a despatch received from Baltimore, DLC-Johnson Papers

Jan. 20. To George B. McClellan, as printed in NH (VII, 87) and OR (II, II, 193) this letter is incorrectly dated and addressed to McClellan. *See* under date of June 20, 1861, correctly addressed to Winfield Scott

c. Jan. 20. To Edwin M. Stanton, asking appointment of Cassius M. Clay as major general of Volunteers, offered for sale by F. G. Sweet, 1948

Jan. 20. To Edwin M. Stanton, on letter from T. B. McFalls and John C. Smith to Lincoln, Jan. 20, 1862, recommending Benjamin

F. McFalls, "Respectfully submitted to the War Department. A. LINCOLN," AES, DNA WR RG 107, Sec. of War Personnel Appts., Box 15

Jan. 21. Endorsement on letter from N.Y. members of the House of Representatives, Morley Catalog, Apr. 28, 1944, No. 201

c. Jan. 21. To Edwin M. Stanton, ―――― for Lincoln, endorsement referring letter of Nathan Ranney to Lincoln, Jan. 21, 1862, DNA WR RG 107, Sec. of War Letters Received, P 9

Jan. 23. To Frederick W. Seward, Nicolay for Lincoln, asking return of recommendations for Dr. A. H. Myers, DNA FS RG 59, Appointments, Box 351

Jan. 24. To Edwin M. Stanton, on application from Lt. Col. John Burke, 37th N.Y. Vols., for captaincy in Regular Army, "Respectfully submitted to the War Department, as good and ample recommendations," AES, owned by R. E. Burdick, New York City

Jan. 25. To Edward Bates, Nicolay for Lincoln, sending Senate resolution returning the nomination of Albert W. Archibald as marshal for New Mexico, DNA RG 60, Papers of Atty. Gen., Box 104

Jan. 25. To Edwin M. Stanton, concerning vacancies of second lieutenancies in 5th and 2nd Cavalry, missing from DNA WR RG 107, Sec. of War Letters Received, P 6

c. Jan. 25. To Lorenzo Thomas, directing appointment of Charles M. Cornell if Lieut. Alexander Carolin, 4th Inf., resigns, missing from DNA WR RG 94, Adj. Gen. Letters Received, P 43

c. Jan. 27. Endorsement on recommendations from senators and representatives from Missouri for Edward E. Sharp, "West-Point Everett Sharp A very strong case." AE, DNA WR RG 94, U.S. Mil. Acad., 1861, No. 750

Jan. 28. To Edward Bates, on petition of George Dower to Lincoln, Jan. 1862, for remission of sentence, "Respectfully submitted to the Attorney General requesting early attention to it. A. LINCOLN," AES, DNA RG 204, U.S. Pardon Atty., A 396

Jan. 28. To Ambrose E. Burnside, misdated by Lincoln, see Jan. 28, 1863

Feb. 1. To Edward Bates, Hay for Lincoln, referring letter concerning Charles N. Pine from Thomas Hoyne to Lincoln, Jan. 24, 1862, DNA RG 60, Papers of Atty. Gen., Box 104

Feb. 1. To William H. Seward, on letter from Alexander R. McKee to Lincoln, Jan. 4, 1862, recommending Charles Mackie, "Respectfully submitted to the State Department. A. LINCOLN," AES, DNA FS RG 59, Appointments, Box 339

Feb. 1. To Edwin M. Stanton, asking appointment of Mr. Hannah and that a commission be sent to John Law, missing from DNA WR RG 107, Sec. of War Letters Received, P 5

Feb. 1. To Edwin M. Stanton, ordering appointment of Thomas L. Price as brigadier general to date from Sept. 21, 1861, ALS, Am. Art Assn. Anderson Galleries Catalog 3955, Mar. 4, 1932, No. 122

Feb. 4. To Edward Bates, NE, mentioned, Bates to Lincoln, Feb. 4, 1862, DLC-RTL

Feb. 4. To George B. McClellan, Hay for Lincoln, referring petition by George A. Cutler of Creeks and Seminoles that James H. Lane be placed in command of expedition to their country, DNA WR RG 108, H.Q.A., P 13, Box 58

Feb. 5. To Joseph G. Totten, Nicolay for Lincoln, concerning applications for West Point, DNA WR RG 77, Office of Chief of Engineers, P 1082

Feb. 6. To Mrs. M. E. Dowman, forgery, ALS, ICHi

Feb. 6. To Edwin M. Stanton, on application from James D. Johnston to Lincoln, Jan. 28, 1862, DNA WR RG 107, Sec. of War Personnel Appts., Box 13

Feb. 7. To Edwin M. Stanton, returning letters of L. H. Walker and Dr. S. Hagadorn concerning exchange of prisoners, missing from DNA WR RG 107, Sec. of War Letters Received, P 2

Feb. 9. To Don C. Buell, Stanton for Lincoln, approving Buell's plan of operations, OR, I, VII, 937-38

c. Feb. 10. To William H. Seward, Hay for Lincoln, referring letter from A. Holbrook to Lincoln, Feb. 10, 1862, opposed to Thomas J. Dryer's commissionership of Sandwich Islands, DNA FS RG 59, Appointments, Box 276

Feb. 11. To Lorenzo Thomas, Hay for Lincoln, referring letter from Ninian W. Edwards concerning discharge of John H. Southwick, a minor, DNA WR RG 94, Adj. Gen. Letters Received, P 108

Feb. 13. Endorsement on letter from John E. Wool approving appointment of an aide-de-camp, Am. Art Assn. Anderson Galleries Catalog 4298, Feb. 3-4, 1937, No. 288

Feb. 14. Order of amnesty, Stanton for Lincoln, clipping, DNA WR RG 94, Adj. Gen. Letters Received, P 1337

Feb. 15. To Edwin M. Stanton, enclosing telegram from Capt. Montgomery concerning shipment of mortarbeds to Cairo, Ill., missing from DNA WR RG 107, Sec. of War Letters Received, P 8; ALS, Am. Art Assn. Anderson Galleries Catalog 3995, Nov. 10, 1932, No. 63

Feb. 15. To Mrs. Taylor, sending autograph, LS, owned by C. Norton Owen, Chicago, Ill.

Feb. 15. To Benjamin F. Wade, Nicolay for Lincoln, appointment for conference, ALS, DLC-Wade Papers

Feb. 17. To Frederick W. Lander, Stanton for Lincoln, commending his command, copy, DLC-Lander Papers

c. Feb. 17. Endorsement on request of Charles F. Thayer to Col. W. W. H. Davis, Feb. 17, 1862, to visit Washington, "Permit Capt and Mrs Thayer to come to me. A. LINCOLN," forgery, AES, NN

Feb. 18. To Edwin M. Stanton, endorsed by Hay for Lincoln, forwarding letter from Garrett Davis, Feb. 17, 1862, enclosing letter of Theophilus T. Garrard, DNA WR RG 107, Sec. of War Letters Received, P 16

c. Feb. 21. To Mrs. Cornelia Fonda, NE, mentioned, Mrs. Fonda to Lincoln, Jan. 28, 1864, DLC-RTL

Feb. 21. To the President of Honduras, appointment of James R. Partridge as minister, copy, DNA FS RG 59, Credences, IV, 363

Feb. 26. To William H. Seward, on letter from David Tod to Lincoln, Jan. 20, 1862, recommending Robert C. Kirk, "Respectfully submitted to the State Department. A. LINCOLN," AES, ibid., Appointments, Box 324

Feb. 26. To Lorenzo Thomas, withdrawal of nomination of Charles Case for assistant quartermaster in favor of George F. Clark, missing from DNA WR RG 94, Adj. Gen. Letters Received, P 128

Feb. 27. Executive Order No. 2, Stanton for Lincoln, copy, *ibid.*, P 1250

Feb. 27. To Edwin M. Stanton, directing appointment of Charles H. Gaubert as brigade quartermaster, ALS, Am. Art Assn. Anderson Galleries Catalog 3955, Mar. 4, 1932, No. 123

Feb. 27. To Edwin M. Stanton, referral of letter of Welles & Co. concerning saltpetre in Tennessee, missing from DNA WR RG 107, Sec. of War Letters Received, P 110, Irregular Book 5

Mar. —. To Anson G. Henry, NE, mentioned, Henry to Lincoln, Oct. 17, 1862, DLC-RTL

c. Mar. To Edwin M. Stanton, on recommendation of George A. Rowley, "Respectfully submitted to the War Department. A. LINCOLN," AES, DNA WR RG 107, Sec. of War Personnel Appts., Box 17

Mar. 4. To Edward Bates, Hay for Lincoln, referring petition of citizens of Steuben Co., N.Y., Jan. 2, 1862, for pardon of Reuben Decker, alias George Stephens, DNA RG 204, U.S. Pardon Atty., A 407

Mar. 4. To Montgomery C. Meigs, concerning payment for services of Juan N. Zerman, missing from DNA WR RG 92, Q.M. Gen., P 72

Mar. 4. To William H. Seward, Nicolay for Lincoln, enclosing H.R. Resolution of Inquiry, ALS, DNA FS RG 59, Misc. Letters

Mar. 5. To Koedze Samatano and Ando Isvesimano Kami (foreign ministers of Japan), Seward for Lincoln, concerning Townsend Harris, DNA FS RG 59, Communications to Foreign Sovereigns and States, III, 188-89

Mar. 5. To Edwin M. Stanton, Nicolay for Lincoln, requesting commission for William Phelps, DNA WR RG 107, ALS, Sec. of War Letters Received, P 18½

Mar. 5. To Edwin M. Stanton, Nicolay for Lincoln, requesting commissions for Cyrus K. Sanborn, E. P. Liscombe, and Moses T. Willard, ALS, *ibid.*, P 18

Mar. 7. To ———, sending autograph at request of "Mr. Wynne," Madigan, *Catalogue of Lincolniana*, 17

Mar. 7. To Anson G. Henry, Hay for Lincoln, acknowledging Henry's letter of Dec. 30, 1861, ALS, ORB

Mar. 7. To Edwin M. Stanton, on letter from Garrett Davis to Lincoln, Mar. 7, 1862, "Railroad matters—Mr. Stone—Respectfully submitted to the War Department. A. LINCOLN," AES, IHi

Mar. 7. To Edwin M. Stanton, on letter from Andrew G. Curtin to Lincoln, Feb. 28, 1862, recommending Isaac I. Hayes, "Respectfully submitted to the War Department A. LINCOLN," AES, DNA WR RG 107, Sec. of War Personnel Appts., Box 12

Mar. 7. Endorsement on letter of Francis Thomas to Montgomery Blair, Carnegie Book Shop Catalog 138, No. 171

Mar. 8. To Don C. Buell, Stanton for Lincoln, concerning commercial intercourse with states in rebellion, OR, I, X, II, 19

Mar. 8. To Henry W. Halleck, same as to Buell, *supra*

Mar. 8. To Edwin M. Stanton, Hay for Lincoln, referring recommendations of Ferdinand F. Remple, Feb. 7, 1862, DNA WR RG 107, Sec. of War Personnel Appts., Box 17

Mar. 10. To Andrew G. Curtin, forgery, ALS, NN

Mar. 10. To Gustavus V. Fox, Welles for Lincoln, concerning exposure of *Monitor, Naval Records,* I, VII, 83

Mar. 10. To Edwin M. Stanton, on letter of Pinckney H. Walker recommending William H. McCalister, Feb. 19, 1862, "Respectfully submitted to War Department. A. LINCOLN," AES, IHi.

Mar. 11. To the President of the Argentine Confederation, withdrawal of Robert M. Palmer, DNA FS RG 59, Communications to Foreign Sovereigns and States, III, 135-36

Mar. 11. Check to "William Johnson (colored)" for $5, DS-F, ISLA

Mar. 11. To Edwin M. Stanton, on recommendation for James L. Quait, Jan. 13, 1862, "Respectfully submitted to the War Department. A. LINCOLN," AES, DNA WR RG 107, Sec. of War Personnel Appts., Box 17

Mar. 11. To Edwin M. Stanton, referring letter of Charles H. Gaubert concerning appointment, missing from *ibid.,* Letters Received, P 19

Mar. 11. To Elisha Whittlesey, concerning White House accounts, NE, mentioned, Whittlesey to Lincoln, March 12, 1862, DLC-RTL

Mar. 12. To William H. Seward, on envelope, "Respectfully submitted to the State Department. A. LINCOLN," Anderson Galleries Catalog 90, Feb. 17, 1902, No. 4058

Mar. 14. To William H. Seward, on letter from Edward Bates to Lincoln, Mar. 13, 1862, recommending Charles Bunker, March 13, "Respectfully submitted to the Sec. of State. A. LINCOLN," AES, DNA FS RG 59, Appointments, Box 243

Mar. 14. To Watton J. Smith, appointment as acting secretary of Interior, Metropolitan Art Assn. Catalog, Apr. 1, 1914, No. 566

Mar. 14. To Edwin M. Stanton, secretary for Lincoln, referring letter from J. P. Durbin to Lincoln, Mar. 13, 1862, asking permission to send a missionary to Negroes at Port Royal, S.C., DNA WR RG 107, Sec. of War Letters Received, P 22

Mar. 15. To John A. Dix, NE, mentioned, Dix to Lincoln, Mar. 15, 1862, DLC-RTL

Mar. 15. To Edwin M. Stanton, referring application for transfer of Lt. Joseph F. Baker, missing from DNA WR RG 107, Sec. of War Letters Received, P 27

Mar. 16. To Edwin M. Stanton, NE, mentioned, Peter H. Watson to Lincoln, Mar. 16, 1862, DLC-RTL

Mar. 17. To Benjamin N. Reed, NE, mentioned, Reed to Lincoln, May 16, 1862, IHi

c. Mar. 18. To Edwin M. Stanton, recommending Maj. C. H. Larrabee, missing from DNA WR RG 107, Sec. of War Personnel Appts., Box 14

c. Mar. 20. To William H. Seward, Nicolay for Lincoln, referring application of David P. Brown to Lincoln, Mar. 20, 1862, DNA FS RG 75, Appointments, Box 240

Mar. 23. To Edwin M. Stanton, secretary for Lincoln, referring letter of Preston King to Lincoln, Mar. 22, 1862, enclosing letter from

John S. Richards in opposition to appointment of George M. Lanman, DNA WR RG 107, Sec. of War Letters Received, P 26

Mar. 25. To Edwin M. Stanton, on envelope addressed to Lincoln, "Respectfully submitted to the War Department. A. LINCOLN," AES, RPB

Mar. 25. To Edwin M. Stanton, on letter from Schuyler Colfax to Lincoln, Mar. 25, 1862, "Respectfully submitted to the Secretary of War. A. LINCOLN," OR, II, III, 403

Mar. 26. To Edwin D. Morgan, concerning Lt. Col. La Fayette Bingham, NE, mentioned, Morgan to Lincoln, Mar. 31, 1862, DLC-RTL

Mar. 26. To Edwin M. Stanton, Meigs for Lincoln, directing appointment of a commission to investigate debts of Q.M. Capt. Reuben B. Hatch, LS, DNA WR RG 107, Sec. of War Letters Received, P 80

Mar. 27. To the President of the Argentine Confederation, appointment of Robert C. Kirk as minister, DNA FS RG 59, Credences, IV, 364

Mar. 27. To Edward Bates, on letter from E. R. Glascock to Lincoln, Mar. 8, 1862, asking if he is still U.S. Marshal at Nashville, Tenn., "Respectfully submitted to the Attorney General. A. LINCOLN," AES, DNA RG 60, Papers of Atty. Gen., Appts., Box 886

Mar. 27. To Edwin M. Stanton, on letter from F. T. Fox, Jr., asking for discharge, "Respectfully submitted to the War Department. A. LINCOLN," copy, ISLA

Mar. 27. To Edwin M. Stanton, referring letter from William Barr concerning services performed in Savannah, missing from DNA WR RG 107, Sec. of War Letters Received, P 5, Irregular Book 5

Mar. 27. To Edwin M. Stanton, Nicolay for Lincoln, referring letter from Shelby M. Cullom to Lincoln, Mar. 14, 1862, concerning transport of gunpowder to mines in Colorado, ibid., P 24

Mar. 27. To Edwin M. Stanton, on letter from James F. Wilson, directing appointment of William A. Warren as quartermaster, Ben Bloomfield List DI-4, No. 114

Mar. 27. To Lorenzo Thomas, directing appointments of brigadier generals, missing from DNA WR RG 94, Adj. Gen. Letters Received, P 210

Mar. 28. To Edward Bates, on letter from James H. Lane to Lincoln, Mar. 27, 1862, recommending Abraham Cutler, "Respectfully submitted to the Attorney General. A. LINCOLN," AES, DNA GE RG 60, Papers of Atty. Gen., Segregated Lincoln Papers

Mar. 29. Endorsement on letter from William W. Tompkins recommending Maj. Henry C. Lockwood of Westchester, N.Y., Carnegie Book Shop Catalog 157, Feb., 1951, No. 265

Mar. 31. To Edward Bates, on letter of Douglas Stirling to James N. Muller applying for office, Mar. 29, 1862, "Respectfully submitted to the Attorney General." A. LINCOLN, AES, DNA RG 60, Papers of Atty. Gen., Appts., Maryland, Box 527

Mar. 31. To Joseph G. Totten, Hay for Lincoln, on letter from James W. Nesmith to Lincoln, Mar. 25, 1862, enclosing letter of Simeon Francis, Nov. 1, 1861, concerning West Point Cadet James Stephens, Jr., DNA WR RG 77, Office of Chief of Engineers, P 1096

c. Apr. To Lorenzo Thomas, referral of letter from officers of James

H. Lane's staff concerning pay, missing from DNA WR RG 94, Adj. Gen. Letters Received, P 347 (referred to Gen. W. E. Prince, May 9, 1862)

Apr. 1. To James C. Conkling, about Mackinac Island fortifications, NE, mentioned, Conkling to his son Clinton, Apr. 2, 1862, IHi

Apr. 1. To George B. McClellan, forgery of a genuine letter to Grant dated Jan. 25, 1864 (*q.v.*), ALS, NN

Apr. 1?. To Peter Sweat, spurious, Peoria, Ill., *Daily Record*, Apr. 1, 1940

Apr. 2. To Silas Casey, purported inscription on front cover of *Instructions for Officers on Outpost* . . . , of dubious authenticity, Argosy Book Store Catalog of William W. H. Davis Collection, April, 1942

Apr. 2. Order for release of John Morris, Jr., and John H. Pleasants, NE, mentioned in Bates' *Diary*, 245

Apr. 4. Check to John Hay for $1002.19, DS, Chase National Bank, New York

Apr. 4. To George B. McClellan, Stanton for Lincoln, concerning removal of McDowell's Corps from McClellan's command, Gorham, *Stanton*, p. 380

Apr. 4. To Edwin M. Stanton, contents unknown, ALS, offered for sale by F. G. Sweet, 1949

Apr. 7. To Pope Pius IX, appointment of Alexander W. Randall as minister, DNA FS RG 59, Credences, IV, 394

Apr. 8. To Alexander II, Emperor of the Russias, appointment of Simon Cameron as minister, *ibid.*, 368

Apr. 8. To Alexander II, Emperor of the Russias, withdrawal of Cassius M. Clay, *ibid.*, Communications to Foreign Sovereigns and States, III, 139

Apr. 8. To Lizzie A. Whipple, sending autograph (also Mrs. Lincoln's), ALS, CCamStJ

Apr. 9. To Gertrude F. McNamee, sending autograph at request of Owen Lovejoy, ALS-P, ISLA

Apr. 12. Check to "Self for Robert," for $25 (?), owned by J. Kenneth Foulke, Aurora, Ill.

Apr. 16. To Edwin M. Stanton, secretary for Lincoln, referring letter of William G. Brown to Lincoln, Mar. 29, 1862, asking parole for Richard E. Bird, DNA WR RG 107, Sec. of War Letters Received, P 28

Apr. 16. To Edwin M. Stanton, referring request of Seth G. Wood to Lincoln, Apr. 4, 1862, for a pass to Norfolk, Va., missing from *ibid.*, P 29

Apr. 19. To Edwin M. Stanton, Hay for Lincoln, requesting return of resolution confirming appointment of Lieut. Louis C. Bailey, ALS, *ibid.*, P 37

Apr. 20. To Mrs. Margarethe M. Schurz, Hay for Lincoln, granting an interview on Apr. 21, DLC-Schurz Papers

Apr. 21. To Edward Bates, on letter from George C. Bates to Lincoln, Apr. 15, 1862, applying for judgeship, "Respectfully submitted to the Attorney General. A. LINCOLN," AES, DNA RG 60, Papers of Atty. Gen., Appts., Colorado Territory

Apr. 21. To Carl Schurz, NE, mentioned, Schurz to Lincoln, Apr. 23, 1862, DLC-RTL

Apr. 21. To Edwin M. Stanton, referring letter from Garrett Davis with letters of R. B. Bowler and M. C. Johnson, missing from DNA WR RG 107, Sec. of War Letters Received, P 34

Apr. 23. To Henry W. Halleck, Stanton for Lincoln, OR, I, X, I, 98-99

Apr. 23. To Irvin McDowell, Stanton for Lincoln, "you should not throw your forces across the Rappahannock at present," Senate *Reports*, No. 108, 37th Cong. 3d Session, I, 271

Apr. 23. To the Emperor of Morocco, appointment of Jesse H. McMath as consul, DNA FS RG 59, Credences, IV, 397

Apr. 24. To Edwin M. Stanton, on letter of Alexander Ramsey to Lincoln, Mar. 3, 1862, recommending Alexander R. Nininger, "Respectfully submitted to the War Department. A. LINCOLN," AES, DNA WR RG 107, Sec. of War Personnel Appts., Box 16

Apr. 26. To Edward Bates, Hay for Lincoln, referring petition for pardon of Albert M. Batchelder, DNA RG 204, U.S. Pardon Atty., A 416

Apr. 27. To Edwin M. Stanton, endorsement removed from attendant papers, "Respectfully submitted to the War Department. A. LINCOLN," AES, ORB

Apr. 28. To Caleb B. Smith, on letter from James H. Lane and Samuel C. Pomeroy, Apr. 24, 1862, recommending W. Davis and Francis P. Baker for land office at Denver, "Respectfully submitted to the Secretary of the Interior. A. LINCOLN," AES, DNA NR RG 48, Applications, Registers and Receivers, Gen. Land Office, Colorado Territory, Box 1276

Apr. 28. To Edwin M. Stanton, on letter from Francis P. Blair, Jr., to Lincoln, Apr. 27, 1862, recommending Charles Hutawa, "Respectfully submitted to the Sec. of War. A. LINCOLN," AES, DNA WR RG 107, Sec. of War Personnel Appts., Box 12

Apr. 29. To Edwin M. Stanton, Hay for Lincoln, asking for return of a Senate resolution and appointments called for, DNA WR RG 107, Sec. of War Letters Received, P 40

May 1. To Peter H. Watson, Nicolay for Lincoln, requesting copy of Senate resolution of inquiry on arrest of Gen. Charles P. Stone, ALS, DNA WR RG 107, Sec. of War Letters Received, P 41

c. May 2. To John C. Frémont, NE, mentioned, in dispatch from Frémont to Lincoln, May 2, 1862, DLC-RTL

c. May 4. To Edward Bates, requesting a visit at 7:30 P.M. on May 4, 1862, ALS, Walpole Galleries Catalog, June 26, 1916, No. 243

May 4. To John E. Wool, Stanton for Lincoln, OR, I, XI, III, 138

c. May 5. To Gideon Welles, concerning "Mr. Pierces Sub Marine Propellor," NE, mentioned, Joseph Smith and Samuel Pook to Welles, May 5, 1862, DLC-RTL

May 5. To Gideon Welles, forgery, ALS-P, ISLA

May 8. To Montgomery C. Meigs, recommending John H. Dike, missing from DNA WR RG 92, Q.M. Gen., P 280, D 287

May 11. To John E. Wool, Stanton for Lincoln, order of thanks for capture of Norfolk, Va., OR, I, XI, I, 635

May 12. To Maj. Goodman, sending autograph, ALS, Anderson Galleries Catalog 2026, Jan. 19-20, 1926, No. 879

May 12. To Mushir Mohammed El Sadar, Possessor of the Kingdom of Tunis, appointment of Amos Perry as consul, DNA FS RG 59, Credences, IV, 397-98

May 12. To Edwin M. Stanton, ordering appointment of Major Robert W. Allen as brigadier general, ALS, Am. Art Assn. Anderson Galleries Catalog 3955, Mar. 4, 1932, No. 125

May 12. To Edwin M. Stanton, secretary for Lincoln, referring letter from George P. Blakey to Lincoln, May 8, 1862, asking release of two prisoners of war, DNA WR RG 107, Sec. of War Letters Received, P 44

May 13. To Montgomery C. Meigs, introducing Charles D. Chase, missing from DNA WR RG 92, Q.M. Gen., P 301, C 602

May 13. To Edwin M. Stanton, referring telegram from Francis H. Peirpoint that Gen. Beckley, prisoner at Camp Chase, should be released, missing from DNA WR RG 107, Sec. of War Letters Received, P 54

May 14. Speech to Twentieth Indiana Regiment, mentioned, Chicago *Tribune*, May 15, 1862, but in error for speech to 12th Indiana on May 13

May 15. To William H. Seward, on letter from William G. Brownlow to Lincoln, May 6, 1862, recommending Balie Peyton, "Respectfully submitted to the Secretary of State. A. LINCOLN," AES, DNA FS RG 59, Appointments, Box 362

May 15. To Edwin M. Stanton, on letter of Archbishop John Hughes to Mrs. A. C. Rodriguez, Aug. 21, 1861, concerning promotion of her son, "Respectfully submitted to the Secretary of War. A. LINCOLN," DNA WR RG 107, Sec. of War Personnel Appts., Box 17

May 15. To Lorenzo Thomas, requesting data on arrests in Kentucky, missing from DNA WR RG 94, Adj. Gen. Letters Received, *see* 376R

May 16. To John C. Frémont, Stanton for Lincoln, OR, I, XII, I, 10

May 16. To Edwin M. Stanton, on letter from W. Kerner to Lincoln, Apr. 30, 1862, applying for reappointment as an officer, "Respectfully submitted to the War Department, A. LINCOLN," AES, THaroL

May 18. To George B. McClellan, Stanton for Lincoln, OR, I, XI, I, 27; recd. copy, DLC-McClellan Papers

May 19. To Hiram Ketchum, Hay for Lincoln, acknowledging receipt of letter of Ketchum to Lincoln, May 18, 1862, copy, DLC-Crittenden Papers

May 20. To Edward Bates, on letter from Leland Stanford to Lincoln, Apr. 10, 1862, recommending Edwin B. Crocker, "Respectfully submitted to the Attorney General. A. LINCOLN," AES, DNA RG 60, Papers of Atty. Gen., Appts., Calif.

May 20. To Edwin M. Stanton, ordering appointment of Alfred B. Farnsworth as second lieutenant, Am. Art Assn. Anderson Galleries Catalog 3955, Mar. 4, 1932, No. 128

May 24. To Nathaniel P. Banks, telegram not in Lincoln's autograph, "What new about the Enemy being between you & Winchester. Answer," Parke-Bernet Catalog 635, Feb. 19, 1945, No. 358

May 24. To Nathaniel P. Banks, Stanton for Lincoln, OR, I, XII, I, 527

May 25. Order taking possession of railroads, Meigs for Lincoln, OR, III, II, 69-70

May 26. To James B. Ricketts, Stanton for Lincoln, OR, I, XII, III, 244

May 27. To John A. Andrew, Stanton for Lincoln, OR, III, II, 85

May 27. To Edwin M. Stanton, referring telegram of Hamilton R. Gamble to Edward Bates asking for authorization of more troops for Missouri, missing from DNA WR RG 107, Sec. of War Letters Received, P 78

May 28. To John C. Frémont, Stanton for Lincoln, *ibid.*, 645

May 28. To John C. Frémont, Stanton for Lincoln, *ibid.*, 645-46

May 28. To John C. Frémont, Stanton for Lincoln, *ibid.*, 646

c. May 29. Copy in Lincoln's autograph of letter from John C. Frémont to Lincoln, May 29, 1862, DLC-RTL

May 30. To Lorenzo Thomas, directing detail of Maj. Ernest F. Hoffmann and Capt. Sproul to Gen. Schurz' staff, missing from DNA WR RG 94, Adj. Gen. Letters Received, P 461

May 31. To George A. McCall, Stanton for Lincoln, OR, I, XII, III, 306

June. Draft of letter to unknown person, Stanton for Lincoln, concerning conversion of the White House (New Kent, Va.) to hospital purposes, DLC-Stanton Papers, VIII, 51712

June 1. To Nathaniel P. Banks, Stanton for Lincoln, OR, I, XII, I, 538

June 3. To John F. Lee, Nicolay for Lincoln, concerning pardon of William Griffin, ALS, DNA WR RG 153, Judge Adv. Gen. Letters Received, No. 158

June 4. To Edward Bates, on letter of Amos Pettijohn to Chase concerning U.S. marshal in Arizona, May 19, 1862, "Respectfully submitted to the Attorney General," copy, ISLA

June 4. To Montgomery Blair, concerning Dennis F. Hanks, NE, mentioned, Blair to Lincoln, June 12, 1862, DLC-RTL

June 4. To John F. Lee, Nicolay for Lincoln, copy, IHi-Nicolay and Hay Papers

June 5. To John F. Lee, Nicolay for Lincoln, referring cases of Privates C. A. Hamilton and McMahon, ALS, DNA WR RG 153, Judge Adv. Gen. Letters Received, No. 153

June 6. To Irvin McDowell, Stanton for Lincoln, OR, I, XI, III, 216

June 6. To Edwin M. Stanton, on letter from Allen C. Fuller to Lincoln, May 24, 1862, concerning sick and wounded soldiers, "Respectfully submitted to the Surgeon-General, through the Sec. of War. A. LINCOLN," AES, NHi

June 7. To Edward Bates, on recommendation of Sherrard Clemens, "Respectfully submitted to the Attorney General. A. LINCOLN," AES, DNA RG 60, Papers of Atty. Gen., Appts., Louisiana, Box 504

June 7. To Andrew Johnson, Stanton for Lincoln, OR, II, III, 659

June 8. Endorsement on communication of Gen. Casey, forgery, AES, NN

June 8. To Thaddeus V. Taber, forgery, AES, NN

June 9. To Ambrose E. Burnside, Stanton for Lincoln, OR, I, IX, 399

June 9. To John A. Dahlgren, concerning examination of a new gun, ALS, Am. Art Assn. Anderson Galleries Catalog 3955, Mar. 4, 1932, No. 124

June 9. To New School Presbyterian Assembly, Seward for Lincoln, N.Y. *Tribune*, June 21, 1862

June 9. To Edwin D. Morgan, on application of Maj. W. Newby for reinstatement after court-martial, June 6, 1862, AES, Metropolitan Art Assn. Catalog, Mar. 9, 1914, No. 635

June 9. To William H. Seward, on recommendations of Francis D. Parish, "Respectfully submitted to the State Department. A. LIN-COLN," AES, DNA FS RG 59, Appointments, Box 358

June 10. To Edwin M. Stanton, directing appointment of Richard B. Owen as quartermaster, ALS, Am Art Assn. Anderson Galleries Catalog 3955, Mar. 4, 1932, No. 129

June 11. To Edwin M. Stanton, secretary for Lincoln, referring letter of Susie P. and David O. Allen to Lincoln, June 3, 1862, asking pardon of Charles H. Smith, DNA WR RG 107, Sec. of War Letters Received, P 71

June 12. To John C. Frémont, Stanton for Lincoln, OR, I, XII, I, 657

June 12. To the Senate and House of Representatives, same communication as that dated June 13, ADfS, IHi

June 12. To Franz Sigel, Stanton for Lincoln, OR, I, XII, III, 378

June 13. Endorsement on 4th Corps, General Orders, June 13, 1862, "Approved. A. LINCOLN," forgery, AES, NN

c. June 15. To Edwin M. Stanton, referring letter of Charles Rogers, missing from DNA WR RG 107, Sec. of War Personnel Appts., Box 17

June 17. To Franz Sigel, Stanton for Lincoln, OR, I, XII, III, 401

June 17. To Edwin M. Stanton, on letter from J. W. Bryant to Lincoln, June 16, 1862, forwarding petition of John S. Fyler, "Respectfully submitted to the Secretary of War. A. LINCOLN," AES, DNA WR RG 107, Sec. of War Letters Received, P 79

June 18. Endorsement on *Special Orders No. 184*, Army of Potomac, "Approved, with good wishes to Capt. [L.D.] Ellsworth. A. LIN-COLN," forgery, AES, NN

June 18. To John F. Lee, Nicolay for Lincoln, referring petition of William Somers for pardon, DNA WR RG 153, Judge Adv. Gen. Letters Received, No. 154

June 19. To Edwin M. Stanton, referring letter from R. E. Constable to Lincoln, June 10, 1862, asking exchange of his sick son, missing from DNA WR RG 107, Sec. of War Letters Received, P 76

June 21. Endorsement on *General Orders No. 187*, Army of Potomac, "Approved. A. LINCOLN," AES, forgery, NN

June 22. To William H. Seward, on letter from John Sherman to Lincoln, June 21, 1862, recommending Francis D. Parish, "Respectfully submitted to the Secretary of State. A. LINCOLN," AES, DNA FS RG 59, Appointments, Box 358

June 26. To William H. Seward, on letter from Warner L. Underwood to Lincoln, June 23, 1862, "Warner L. Underwood, recommended for Min[is]ter to Bolivia. Respectfully submitted to the

State Department. A. LINCOLN," AES, DNA FS RG 59, Appointments, Box 395

c. June 27. To Edward Bates, on petition of June 27, 1862, for pardon of Joseph Dobson imprisoned for mutiny, "Let a pardon be made out in this case. Yours Truly. A. LINCOLN," AES, DNA RG 204, U.S. Pardon Atty., A 410

June 28. To Ambrose E. Burnside, Stanton for Lincoln, OR, I, XI, III, 271

June 28. To Henry W. Halleck, Stanton for Lincoln, OR, I, XVI, II, 69

June 28. To James W. Ripley, referring Senate resolution of June 27, 1862, report of Holt and Owen on ordnance and gun contracts, missing from DNA WR RG 156, Office of Chief of Ordnance, WD 1238 (see Z)

June 30. To Edward Bates, Nicolay for Lincoln, correcting name of Benjamin C. Whiting to Billington C. Whiting for U.S. district attorney for California, ALS, DNA GE RG 60, Papers of Atty. Gen., Segregated Lincoln Material

June 30. To Henry W. Halleck, Stanton for Lincoln, OR, I, XVI, II, 75

c. July. To Benjamin H. Brewster, NE, mentioned, Brewster to Lincoln, Sept. 1, 1862, DLC-RTL

c. July. To Lorenzo Thomas, Nicolay for Lincoln, requesting a corrected list of hospitals, ALS, DNA WR RG 94, Adj. Gen. Letters Received, P 568

July 1. To Carl Schurz, NE, mentioned, Schurz to Lincoln, July 2, 1862, DLC-Nicolay Papers.

July 1. To Edwin M. Stanton, referring complaint by citizens of Delaware that commander at Fort Delaware was rebel sympathizer, AES, Parke-Bernet Catalog 251, Jan. 22-24, 1941, No. 432

July 2. To the President of San Salvador, appointment of James R. Partridge as minister, copy, DNA FS RG 59, Credences, IV, 374

July 3. To Benjamin F. Butler, Stanton for Lincoln, OR, III, II, 200

July 4. To Edwin M. Stanton, referring letter from George D. Conyers offering services of himself and son Vernon, missing from DNA WR RG 107, Sec. of War Letters Received, P 82

July 6. To Gen. Naglee, forgery, AES, NN

c. July 8. To William H. Seward, Hay for Lincoln, referring letter from John C. Ten Eyck to Lincoln, July 8, 1862, recommending Elisha O. Crosby, DNA FS RG 59, Appointments, Box 264

July 9. To Salmon P. Chase, Hay for Lincoln, returning appointment papers under internal revenue law, DNA FI RG 56, Treas. Dept., Letters from Exec. Officers, Series AB, I, 2C

July 11. To Congregationalist Convention of Vermont, Seward for Lincoln, McPherson, *Political History of the U.S.*, 481

July 12. To Edwin M. Stanton, referring letter from L. P. Sanger concerning raising a regiment, missing from DNA WR RG 107, Sec. of War Letters Received, P 97

July 12. To Edwin M. Stanton, on letter of John E. Wool recommending Lieut. Stephen E. Jones, "Respectfully submitted to the Sec. of War. A. LINCOLN," AES, IHi

July 12. To Lorenzo Thomas, referring letters from Paul Coleman and Abner Doubleday, June 19, 1862, asking reinstatement of Doubleday and Maj. LaRhett L. Livingston, missing from DNA WR RG 94, Adj. Gen. Letters Received, P 1340

July 12. To Lorenzo Thomas, requesting compliance with Gen. John E. Wool's request on promise of a staff, missing from *ibid.*, P 675 with 877 W

July 13. To William A. Hammond, concerning Protestant and Catholic nurses, NE, mentioned, Hammond to Lincoln, July 16, 1862, DLC-RTL.

July 13. To William H. Seward, on letter of Samuel N. Castle to Charles Sumner, July 3, 1862, recommending James F. B. Marshall, "Respectfully submitted to the Sec. of State. A. LINCOLN," DNA FS RG 59, Appointments, Box 341

July 15. To Edwin M. Stanton, Nicolay for Lincoln, referring request of Senate for reasons for arrest of Col. D. R. Anthony, DNA WR RG 107, Sec. of War Letters Received, P 164

July 16. To Edwin M. Stanton, referring letter from Ninian W. Edwards on raising troops, missing from *ibid.*, P 93

July 19. To Watton J. Smith, appointment as acting secretary of Interior, Stan. V. Henkels Catalog, Apr. 10, 1908, No. 47

July 21. To Edwin M. Stanton, on envelope of application of Edward Everett, "Respectfully submitted to the War Department. A. LINCOLN," AES, DNA WR RG 107, Sec. of War Personnel Appts., Box 10

July 22. Order authorizing employment of contrabands, Stanton for Lincoln, ADf, DLC-Stanton Papers; DS, DNA WR RG 94, Adj. Gen. Letters Received, P 1329

July 22. To Edwin M. Stanton, referring telegram from Henry T. Blow that Leitch is not a union man, missing from DNA WR RG 107, Sec. of War Letters Received, P 91

July 23. To G. Julian Harney, Channel Islands, Great Britain, NE, mentioned, Harney to Lincoln, October 11, 1862, DLC-Nicolay Papers

July 23. To William H. Seward, Nicolay for Lincoln, "I showed your note to the President, and he replied 'Tell him I can't say that just now. Ask him to talk to Mr. Chase.'" ALS, NAuE

July 23. To Edwin M. Stanton, referring letter from R. N. Shurtliff asking reinstatement, missing from DNA WR RG 107, Sec. of War Letters Received, P 10, Irregular Book 5

July 25. To Edwin M. Stanton, Hay for Lincoln, referring letter of Samuel Shellabarger to Lincoln, July 21, 1862, *ibid.*, in favor of draft, P 99

July 25. To Edwin M. Stanton, on telegram from J. B. Temple and others to Lincoln, July 25, 1862, concerning raising a Kentucky regiment, "Respectfully submitted to the Secretary of War. A. LINCOLN," AES, NHi

July 27. To Edwin M. Stanton, referring application of G. W. Blount for discharge of W. E. Van Wyck, missing from DNA WR RG 107, Sec. of War Letters Received, P 112

July 28. To William P. Dole, on letter from James H. Lane to Lincoln, July 25, 1862, concerning retention of Fielding W. Johnson as Delaware Indian Agent, "Respectfully submitted to the Comr. of Indian Affairs. A. LINCOLN," AES, DNA NR RG 48, Indian Agencies, Delawares of Kansas, Box 1271

July 28. To Edwin M. Stanton, secretary for Lincoln, referring letter from Chauncey Shaffer to Lincoln, July 26, 1862, requesting authority to raise a brigade, DNA WR RG 107, Sec. of War Letters Received, P 121

July 28. To Edwin M. Stanton, secretary for Lincoln, referring letter from Henry T. Blow opposing appointment of "Mr. Leitch" as medical storekeeper, *ibid.*, P 150

c. July 29. To Mark W. Delahay, NE, but letter from Delahay, n.d., is endorsed by Hay "Answered July 29, declining to suggest any course of action—preferring to rely upon intelligence & patriotism of friends." DLC-RTL

July 29. To Edwin M. Stanton, referring letter of Samuel Kirkwood to Lincoln, July 28, 1862, "Respectfully submitted to the War Department. A. LINCOLN," OR, II, IV, 295

July 29. To Edwin M. Stanton, referring letter of Benjamin Johnson to Lincoln, July 13, 1862, protesting cutting of canal at Vicksburg, Miss., missing from DNA WR RG 107, Sec. of War Letters Received, P 101

July 30. To Edwin M. Stanton, referring letter of Orison Blunt to Col. J. S. Loomis concerning arms captured on board the *Nassau*, missing from *ibid.*, P 149

July 30. To Edwin M. Stanton, referring letter from George Opdyke concerning appointment of Theo. O. Ebaugh as paymaster, "Respectfully submitted to the Sec. of War. A. LINCOLN," AES, Anderson Galleries Catalog 2193, Nov. 15, 1927, No. 261

July 30. To Edwin M. Stanton, concerning Gov. Richard Yates' request for attention to application of Lieut. Col. John S. Loomis for rifles and muskets for Illinois regiments, missing from DNA WR RG 107, Sec. of War Letters Received, P 153

July 30. To Joseph P. Taylor, referring letter from James Harlan concerning lack of vegetables and soft bread in Army of Potomac, missing from DNA WR RG 192, Comm. Gen. of Subsistence, L 2

July 31. To Edward Bates, on letter from Phillip Fraser recommending Joseph Remington for marshal of Northern Florida, "Respectfully submitted to the Attorney General. A. LINCOLN," AES, DNA RG 60, Papers of Atty. Gen., Appts., Florida

July 31. To Montgomery C. Meigs, concerning Major Cross, missing from DNA WR RG 92, Q.M. Gen., P 211, S 758

July 31. To Edwin M. Stanton, referring letter from Surgeon H. M. McAleer concerning burial of dead and proper marking of graves, missing from DNA WR RG 107, Sec. of War Letters Received, P 118

July 31. To Edwin M. Stanton, referring letter from Mrs. H. A. Thurber to Lincoln, July 25, 1862, asking whether she can go to Gordonsville, Va., missing from *ibid.*, P 119

July 31. To Edwin M. Stanton, referring letter from B. E. Harrison asking exemption from Gen. Pope's *Order No. 11*, missing from *ibid.*, P 120

Aug. To H. F. Colby, Hay for Lincoln, sending Lincoln's autograph, ALS, RPB

Aug. 2. To Isaac Newton, NE, mentioned, Daniel E. Groux to Lincoln, Mar. 17, 1863, DLC-RTL

Aug. 2. To William H. Seward, Hay for Lincoln, referring letter from Charles Sumner to Lincoln, July 30, 1862, concerning appointment of James H. Holmes, DNA FS RG 59, Appointments, Box 310

c. Aug. 2. To Edwin M. Stanton, on letter from J. H. Van Winkle to Lincoln, Aug. 2, 1862, offering his services, "Respectfully submitted to the Secretary of War. A. LINCOLN," AES, DNA WR RG 107, Sec. of War Personnel Appts., Box 19

Aug. 4. Order for 300,000 militia, drafted by Seward and signed by Stanton for Lincoln, DS, ORB

Aug. 4. To James W. Ripley, referring letter from T. G. Boettig on iron field casements, missing from DNA WR RG 156, Office of Chief of Ordnance, Inventions, Misc., No. 332, Box 51

Aug. 4. To Edwin M. Stanton, on letter from David Labbez & Co., Rheims, France, offering an invention to protect soldiers, "Submitted to the War Department. A. LINCOLN," AES, DNA WR RG 156, Office of Chief of Ordnance, Inventions, Misc., No. 329

Aug. 4. To Edwin M. Stanton, on recommendation for Charles M. Brower, "Respectfully submitted to War Department. A. LINCOLN," AES, DNA WR RG 107, Sec. of War Personnel Appts., Box 7

c. Aug. 4. To Lorenzo Thomas, referring letter from Francis A. Miller asking a commission, missing from DNA WR RG 94, Adj. Gen. Letters Received, P 1339

c. Aug. 6. To James C. Conkling, printed invitation from "The President & Mrs. Lincoln," to dinner, Aug. 6, 1862, D-P, ISLA

Aug. 6. To Edwin M. Stanton, referring letter from W. C. Beardsley about raising troops, missing from DNA WR RG 107, Sec. of War Letters Received, P 91, Irregular Book 5

Aug. 6 To Edwin M. Stanton, referring letter from Laurel F. Brockway reporting officers at St. Louis unfit for duty, missing from *ibid.*, P 127

Aug. 6. To President of Venezuela, appointment of Erastus D. Culver as minister, copy, DNA FS RG 59, Credences, IV, 375

Aug. 9. To Edwin M. Stanton, referring report on case of Surgeon H. K. Neff, missing from DNA WR RG 107, Sec. of War Letters Received, 134

Aug. 11. To Salmon P. Chase, on bill for $113 from T. J. Crowen for books, "Correct for this amount A. LINCOLN," AES, DNA RG 217, Gen. Accounting Office, No. 145073

Aug. 11. To Edwin M. Stanton, approving appointment of John Finkelheimer to Gen. Louis Blenker's staff, AES, Carnegie Book Shop Catalog 129, No. 162

c. Aug. 11. To Edwin M. Stanton, referring letter from H. P. Cochran about enrolling a regiment, missing from DNA WR RG 107, Sec. of War Letters Received, P 137

Aug. 11. To Edwin M. Stanton, referring request of William A. Wheeler for appointment of A. Sutin as paymaster, missing from *ibid.*, P 136 (*see* AB)

Aug. 11. To Edwin M. Stanton, Hay for Lincoln, referring letter from Elihu B. Washburne to Lincoln, Aug. 7, 1862, requesting that J. Russell Jones be given same powers in northern district as marshal of southern district of Ill., *ibid.*, P 155

c. Aug. 12. To Salmon P. Chase, on bill from William F. Richstein for $16.25 for books, "Correct A. LINCOLN," AES, DNA RG 217, Gen. Accounting Office, No. 145073

Aug. 12. To Isabel II, Queen of Spain, appointment of Gustave P. Koerner as minister, copy (misdated 1861), DNA FS RG 59, Credences, IV, 398

Aug. 12. To Joseph P. Taylor, referring letter from E. E. Larned and others about scurvy among soldiers in Tenn., missing from DNA WR RG 192, Comm. Gen. of Subsistence, L 3

Aug. 14. To Salmon P. Chase, enclosing papers, Am. Art Assn. Anderson Galleries Catalog 4330, May 18-19, 1937, No. 225

Aug. 15. To Montgomery C. Meigs, referring request of I. F. Payson for reappointment as assistant quartermaster, missing from DNA WR RG 92, Q.M. Gen., P 262-63

Aug. 15. To Edwin M. Stanton, referring offer of Prince Felix Salm-Salm and Otto Corvin to raise German recruits in Europe, DNA WR RG 107, Sec. of War Letters Received, P 146

Aug. 15. To Edwin M. Stanton, referring request of H. Addison and others that Col. J. A. Peck be appointed to recruit troops, missing from *ibid.*, P 147

Aug. 15. To Edwin M. Stanton, on letter from Richard Yates and others to Lincoln, Aug. 9, 1862, recommending Levin W. Shepherd for quartermaster, "Respectfully submitted to the Sec. of War. A. LINCOLN," AES, IHi

Aug. 18. To Henry W. Halleck, Hay for Lincoln, referring request of John A. McClernand to Lincoln, Aug. 12, 1862, for leave of absence, DNA WR RG 107, H.Q.A. Letters Received, M 612, Box 58

Aug. 19. To Edwin M. Stanton, referring letter from Mark W. Delahay and Thomas Ewing, Jr., Aug. 6, 1862, opposing removal of Gen. James G. Blunt, missing from DNA WR RG 107, Sec. of War Letters Received, P 148

Aug. 19. To Edwin M. Stanton, referring letter from H. B. Armstrong offering services, missing from *ibid.*, P 11, Irregular Book 5

Aug. 20. To Fernando Wood, NE, mentioned in list of letters, IHi-Nicolay and Hay Papers

Aug. 21. To Montgomery C. Meigs, concerning Reuben B. Hatch, missing from DNA WR RG 92, Q.M. Gen., P 262, S 1014

Aug. 21. To Edward Stanly, NE, mentioned, Stanly to Lincoln, Sept. 2, 1862, DLC-RTL

Aug. 21. To Edwin M. Stanton, on letter from James L. Cramer to Lincoln, Aug. 20, 1862, applying for appointment as paymaster, "Submitted to the Sec. of War. A. LINCOLN," AES, IHi

Aug. 21. To Edwin M. Stanton, on letter from John C. Crowley to Lincoln, Aug. 18, 1862, offering services, "Submitted to Sec. of War A. LINCOLN," AES, DNA WR RG 107, Sec. of War Personnel Appts., Box 8

Aug. 22. To Edwin M. Stanton, referring letter from F. N. Haller to

Lincoln, Aug. 20, 1862, recommending G. O. Haller, missing from *ibid.*, Letters Received, P 154

Aug. 23. To Edward Bates, Nicolay for Lincoln, referring letter for Burt Van Horn to Lincoln, Aug. 18, 1862, asking pardon for John Quinlan convicted of counterfeiting, AE, DNA RG 204, U.S. Pardon Atty., A 431

Aug. 24. To Edwin M. Stanton, referring letter from Edmund J. Davis and John P. [L.] Haynes in regard to arming Unionists on the Rio Grande, missing from DNA WR RG 107, Sec. of War Letters Received, P 113, Irregular Book 5

Aug. 25. To Edwin M. Stanton, asking appointment of a quartermaster on request of John S. Phelps, Am. Art Assn. Anderson Galleries Catalog 3955, Mar. 4, 1932, No. 130

Aug. 27. To David Davis, NE, mentioned, Davis to Lincoln, Sept. 1, 1862, DLC-RTL

Aug. 27. To Edwin M. Stanton, referring letter from Robert B. Allen offering to give evidence against secession sympathizers in Burlington, N.J., missing from DNA WR RG 107, Sec. of War Letters Received, P 156

Aug. 27. To Edwin M. Stanton, referring petition of John P. Vincent and others to report on frontier defenses, etc., missing from *ibid.*, P 157

Aug. 28. To Edwin M. Stanton, referring letter from George P. Fisher concerning military appointments, missing from *ibid.*, P 160

Aug. 28. To Edwin M. Stanton, referring letter from Richard D. Goodwin concerning recruiting practices in N.Y., missing from *ibid.*, P 159

Aug. 28. To Edwin M. Stanton, referring letter from Mrs. J. S. Delano to Lincoln, Aug. 22, 1862, asking to accompany her husband if he is drafted or to serve as his substitute, missing from *ibid.*, P 161

Aug. 28. To Edwin M. Stanton, referring letter from E. A. Parmenter to Lincoln, Aug. 21, 1862, for permission to demonstrate an incendiary weapon, missing from *ibid.*, P 158

Aug. 29. To Edwin M. Stanton, ALS, for sale by dealer, 1949

Aug. 30. To Edwin M. Stanton, secretary for Lincoln, referring telegram from S. Newton Pettis to Lincoln, about raising troops for Northwest frontier, DNA WR RG 107, Sec. of War Letters Received, P 162

c. Sept. To Edwin M. Stanton, NE, mentioned, William E. Morgan to Lincoln, Mar. 8, 1863, DLC-RTL

Sept. 2. Rough draft of Emancipation Proclamation, listed, Chicago Book and Art Auctions Catalog, Dec., 1931

Sept. 2. To George G. Meade, concerning execution of Charles Williams, forgery, ALS, NN

Sept. 2. To Edwin M. Stanton, pass for woman to Culpeper Co., Va., forgery, ALS-P, ISLA

Sept. 2. To Edwin M. Stanton, requesting pass for woman with note for Gen. Meade, forgery, ALS-P, ISLA

Sept. 2. To Edwin M. Stanton, concerning James Collins, forgery, ALS-P, ISLA

Sept. 2. To Edwin M. Stanton, concerning soldier sentenced to death, forgery, ALS, NN

Sept. 2. To Edwin M. Stanton, referring letter from George H. Stuart offering to provide chaplains, missing from DNA WR RG 107, Sec. of War Letters Received, P 172

Sept. 3. To Edward Bates, on request from Roland D. Noble to Lincoln, Aug. 27, 1862, for pardon of George F. Rehn, "Respectfully submitted to the Attorney General. A. LINCOLN," AES, DNA RG 204, U.S. Pardon Atty., A 441

Sept. 3. To Edwin M. Stanton, clipped endorsement, "Submitted to the War Department. A. LINCOLN," AES, RPB

Sept. 3. To Edwin M. Stanton, referring offer of "Adams Guards" of Sixth Auditor's Office and request for arms, missing from DNA WR RG 107, Sec. of War Letters Received, P 168

Sept. 4. To Edwin M. Stanton, on forged letter from Stanton instructing Gen. Meade concerning Charles Miller, forgery, ALS, NN

Sept. 4. To Edwin M. Stanton, referring letter from Timothy O. Howe requesting appointment of Mrs. Lewis P. Harvey as "Embassadress" to Wisconsin soldiers, missing from DNA WR RG 107, Sec. of War Letters Received, P 171

Sept. 4. To Edwin M. Stanton, referring letter from Frederick A. Conkling introducing G. Schoen, missing from *ibid.*, P 175

Sept. 4. To Edwin M. Stanton, on letter from Henry E. Dummer and others to Lincoln, Aug. 13, 1862, recommending Rufus C. Crampton, "Submitted to the Sec. of War. A. LINCOLN," AES, IHi

Sept. 5. To Edwin M. Stanton, Hay for Lincoln, referring letter from James N. Brown to Lincoln, Aug. 24, 1862, concerning recruitment of men over forty-five, DNA WR RG 107, Sec. of War Letters Received, P 177

Sept. 6. To Salmon P. Chase, concerning B. C. Miller, ALS, forgery, NN

Sept. 6. To Edwin M. Stanton, secretary for Lincoln, referring letter from S. N. Cohez to Lincoln, Aug. 25, 1862, on raising a regiment, DNA WR RG 107, Sec. of War Letters Received, P 166

Sept. 8. To Edward Bates, on envelope of application for pardon of Joseph S. Hewins, "Respectfully submitted to the Attorney General. A. LINCOLN," AES, DNA RG 204, U.S. Pardon Atty., A 442

Sept. 8. To Henry W. Halleck, concerning promotion of Col. James Naglee, AES, Parke-Bernet Catalog 672, May 7-8, 1945, No. 353

c. Sept. 8. To Edwin M. Stanton, on petition of Ira Harris and others, Sept. 8, 1862, for appointment of S. D. Lewis, "Respectfully submitted to the Sec. of War. A. LINCOLN," AES, IHi

Sept. 9. To Henry W. Halleck, on envelope of letter from Franklin A. Dick to Edward Bates, Sept. 4, 1862, concerning lack of discipline in army, "Submitted to Gen. Halleck. A. LINCOLN," AES, DNA WR RG 108, H.Q.A., D 253, Box 57

Sept. 11. To Edwin M. Stanton, referring petition of Edward M. Samuel and others to Lincoln, Sept. 8, 1862, for disbanding Negro regiments in Clay and Jackson counties, Mo., missing from DNA WR RG 107, Sec. of War Letters Received, P 197

Sept. 12. To Montgomery C. Meigs, referring account of Heslope, missing from DNA WR RG 92, Q.M. Gen., P 2

Sept. 15. Endorsement on letter from Samuel C. Pomeroy concerning Chiriqui project, "Above approved. A. LINCOLN," AES, ORB

Sept. 15. To Joseph P. Taylor, referring letter from Samuel T. Glover recommending J. N. Straat, missing from DNA WR RG 92, Comm. Gen. of Subsistence, L 4

Sept. 15. To Edwin M. Stanton, Hay for Lincoln, referring letter from Alexander Ramsey to Lincoln, Sept. 8, 1862, urging appointment of Levi Nutting as provost marshal, DNA WR RG 107, Sec. of War Letters Received, P 181

c. Sept. 15. To Edwin M. Stanton, Hay for Lincoln, referring letter from William C. Wood to Lincoln, Sept. 15, 1862, applying for appointment, *ibid.*, Personnel Appts., Box 20

Sept. 15. To Edwin M. Stanton, on request of Gen. William R. Leslie that Lieut. Guy V. Henry be ordered to Maj. Gilbert in Kentucky, "Submitted to the Sec. of War. A. LINCOLN," AES, IHi

c. Sept. 16. To Edwin M. Stanton, concerning appointment of Thomas H. W. Monroe as chaplain, NE, mentioned, Peter H. Watson to Lincoln, Sept. 16, 1862, DLC-RTL

Sept. 17. To Edward Bates, on letter of James S. Wadsworth to Lincoln, Sept. 16, 1862, asking pardon of George W. Marples, 4th Pa. Vols., convicted for shooting a comrade, "Let the pardon be granted as within requested. A. LINCOLN," AES, DNA RG 204, U.S. Pardon Atty., A 442

c. Sept. 17. To James W. Ripley, "Give Major McKellup the arms he needs for his troops," newspaper clipping marked "St. Louis *Republic,* 1892," copy, ISLA

Sept. 17. To Edwin M. Stanton, submitting claims and vouchers of Henry L. Jones and Joseph W. Currier, missing from DNA WR RG 107, Sec. of War Letters Received, P 187

Sept. 17. To Edwin M. Stanton, referring letter from G. W. Griggs for permission to ship goods from Norfolk to Baltimore, missing from *ibid.*, P 180

Sept. 19. To Isaac Harvey, purported letter in N. B. Eyster, "Mr. Lincoln and the 'Crazy' Quaker," *The New Voice,* XVI (Aug. 12, 1899), 2. *See* similar item to Samuel Haddam, Sept. 20, 1862, *infra.*

Sept. 19. To William H. Seward, Nicolay for Lincoln, referring letter of George Blakey to Lincoln, Sept. 13, 1862, recommending Archer C. Dickerson, DNA FS RG 159, Appointments, Box 272

Sept. 20. To Army Headquarters, Hay for Lincoln, referring letters of George R. Patterson to Andrew G. Curtin and Curtin to Lincoln, Sept. 17, 1862, offering Patterson's services, DNA WR RG 108, H.Q.A., L 577, Box 50

Sept. 20. To Samuel Haddam, purported in N. B. Eyster, "A Day Among the Quakers," *Harper's New Monthly Magazine,* XLI (Sept. 1870), 541 (unreliable source). The same letter as that one purported to Isaac Harvey, Sept. 19, 1862, *supra.*

Sept. 20. To Edwin M. Stanton, secretary for Lincoln, referring letter of Thomas Ewing to Lincoln, Sept. 10, 1862, recommending Philomen Ewing, DNA WR RG 107, Sec. of War Letters Received Personnel Appts., Box 10

c. Sept. 20. To Gideon Welles, concerning Lieut. Egbert Thompson, NE, mentioned, J. H. Clay Mudd to Lincoln, Sept. 22, 1862, DLC-RTL

c. Sept. 22. To Edwin M. Stanton, referring "statement of Cyrus W. Blakeman in relation to the destruction of Government property at Aquia Creek," OR, I, XII, III, 814

Sept. 24. To Edwin M. Stanton, Hay for Lincoln, referring petition of William B. Mann and others to Gov. Curtin, Sept. 9, 1862, that enlistments for nine months be permitted, DNA WR RG 107, Sec. of War Letters Received, P 186

Sept. 24. To Edwin M. Stanton, referring letter from S. B. Welsbank and others enclosing petition of William B. Mann and others concerning organizing of subsistence troops in Pennsylvania, missing from *ibid.*, P 186

Sept. 25. To Joseph G. Totten, Hay for Lincoln, referring papers of William A. Cunningham of N.Y. for West Point, ALS, DNA WR RG 94, U.S. Mil. Acad., 1863, No. 41

Sept. 26. To Pope Pius IX, appointment of Richard M. Blatchford as minister, copy, DNA FS RG 59, Credences, IV, 399

Sept. 27. Endorsement on telegram received Sept. 10, 1862, "Overlooked till now. A. LINCOLN," F. H. Sweet List 58, No. 105

Sept. 27. To Henry W. Halleck, on letter from William H. Seward recommending Gen. Robert H. Milroy and Col. Gustave P. Cluseret for promotion, asking Halleck to examine records, Am. Art Assn. Anderson Galleries Catalog 3995, Nov. 10, 1932, No. 64

Sept. 27. To Edwin M. Stanton, referring telegram from Col. Arthur H. Grimshaw urging acceptance of 4th Delaware Vols., missing from DNA WR RG 107, Sec. of War Letters Received, P 190

Sept. 29. To West New Jersey Baptists, Seward for Lincoln, McPherson, *The Political History of the United States*, 476

Sept. 29. To John A. Dahlgren, endorsement on envelope, "Submitted to Capt. Dahlgren. A. LINCOLN," AES, City Book Auction Catalog, Mar. 1942, No. 200

Sept. 30. To Edwin M. Stanton, referring letter from Col. Henry J. Hunt asking appointment of John N. Craig to his staff, AES, Parke-Bernet Catalog 672, May 7-8, 1945, No. 351

Sept. 30. To Edward Wallace, NE, mentioned, Wallace to Lincoln, Oct. 1, 1862, DLC-RTL

Oct. 6. To Welsh Congregationalists of Pennsylvania, Seward for Lincoln, McPherson, *The Political History of the U.S.*, 481

Oct. 6. To William H. Seward, on letter from Edwin Croswell to Lincoln, Oct. 1, 1862, recommending Caleb Croswell, "Respectfully submitted to the Secretary of State. A. LINCOLN," AES, DNA FS RG 59, Appointments, Box 264

Oct. 8. To Edwin M. Stanton, endorsement recommending restoration of Capt. Leland, AES, Parke-Bernet Catalog 672, May 7-8, 1945, No. 351

Oct. 9. To Edwin M. Stanton, referring letter from G. J. F. Robinson on claim of Capt. E. Jones for back pay, missing from DNA WR RG 107, Sec. of War Letters Received, P 201

Oct. 9. To Edwin M. Stanton, referring letter of Schuyler Colfax, asking reconsideration of Capt. Benjamin P. Walker, dismissed, missing from *ibid.*, P 198

Oct. 9. To Lorenzo Thomas, concerning Calvin E. Pratt, missing from DNA WR RG 94, Adj. Gen. Letters Received, P 945 and P 133

Oct. 10. To Edwin M. Stanton, on letter of John S. Tarkington to John P. Usher, Aug. 13, 1862, asking appointment as judge advocate, "Submitted to the Secretary of War. A. LINCOLN," AES, IHi

Oct. 10. To Lorenzo Thomas, directing reservation of land in Benicia, California, missing from DNA WR RG 94, Adj. Gen. Letters Received, P 1331

Oct. 11. To Edwin M. Stanton, on petition of citizens of Hartford, Conn., Aug. 11, 1862, recommending Wait N. Hawley, "Submitted to the Secretary of War. A. LINCOLN," AES, DNA WR RG 107, Sec. of War Personnel Appts., Box 12

Oct. 11. To Edwin M. Stanton and Henry W. Halleck, on letter from Andrew G. Curtin, Sept. 30, 1862, "Submitted to the consideration of the Secretary of War and of General Halleck," OR, III, II, 624; missing from DNA WR RG 107, Sec. of War Letters Received, P 212

Oct. 11. To Edwin M. Stanton, on letter from Thomas H. Bradley to Lincoln, Sept. 7, 1862, recommending Joshua T. Bradley for paymaster, "Respectfully submitted to the Sec. of War. A. LINCOLN," AES, IHi

Oct. 13. To Fred A. Payne, sending autograph, ALS, ORB

Oct. 13. To Edwin M. Stanton, referring letter from Alexander Ramsey concerning appointment of commission to ascertain names of those killed and amount of property destroyed by Indians, missing from DNA WR RG 107, Sec. of War Letters Received, P 210

Oct. 14. To Edwin M. Stanton, referring letter from Mrs. A. S. Diven to Lincoln, Oct. 14, 1862, concerning paymastership for her son, AES, IHi

c. Oct. 15. To George B. McClellan, NE, mentioned, Lincoln to Lorenzo Thomas, Oct. 15, 1862

Oct. 15. To Edwin M. Stanton, on letter from F. A. Jennings asking a commission for his son, "Submitted to the War Department. A. LINCOLN," AES, DNA WR RG 107, Sec. of War Letters Received, P 208

Oct. 16. To Edwin M. Stanton, referring application of A. C. Barry to recruit a battalion of riflemen, missing from *ibid.*, P 206

Oct. 18. To Montgomery C. Meigs, endorsement on letter of A. Ely recommending James T. Pritchard, missing from DNA WR RG 92, Q.M. Gen., P 148

Oct. 19. To Don C. Buell, Halleck for Lincoln, OR, I, XVI, II, 626-67

Oct. 20. To Edwin M. Stanton, referring letter of Col. Gustave Wagner to Samuel C. Pomeroy concerning his dismissal, missing from DNA WR RG 107, Sec. of War Letters Received, P 213

Oct. 20. To Edwin M. Stanton, referring application of Jane Mangen for money, her husband Sergt. Michael Mangen not having received his pay for four months, missing from *ibid.*, P 211

Oct. 21. To George B. McClellan, Halleck for Lincoln, OR, I, XIX, I, 81

Oct. 23. To John Potts, Nicolay for Lincoln, transmitting to the chief clerk several cases of application for pardon, ALS, DNA WR RG 153, Judge Adv. Gen. Letters Received, No. 223

Oct. 23. To Edwin M. Stanton, on letter of Theodore J. Widney to Thomas J. Hood, Oct. 19, 1862, applying for appointment, "Submitted to the Sec. of War. A. LINCOLN," AES, DNA WR RG 107, Personnel Appts., Box 20

Oct. 24. To Henry W. Halleck, on letter from Andrew G. Curtin concerning promotion of Col. David M. Gregg, "Submitted to Gen. Halleck. A. LINCOLN," AES, RPB

Oct. 24. To Joseph Holt, on petition of H. Kallman and others on behalf of Justus Fay endorsed by Holt with suggestion that goods stolen by Fay be restored as condition of clemency, "Suggestion of Judge Advocate General approved. A. LINCOLN," AES, IHi

Oct. 24. To Edwin M. Stanton, Nicolay for Lincoln, referring letter from William D. Kelley and others tendering use of a hospital free, DNA WR RG 107, Sec. of War Letters Received, P 214

Oct. 25. To Edwin M. Stanton, on letter from S. F. Streeter to Lincoln, Oct. 23, 1862, concerning work done by the Union Relief Assn. for destitute families of Maryland Volunteers, "Respectfully submitted to the Secretary of War. A. LINCOLN," AES, DNA WR RG 107, Sec. of War Letters Received, P 216

Oct. 27. To Edward Bates, Nicolay for Lincoln, referring petition for pardon of John A. Miller, DNA RG 204, U.S. Pardon Atty., A 446

Oct. 28. Endorsement concerning S. Lockwood Brown, missing from DNA WR RG 92, Q.M. Gen., P 173, A 245

c. Oct. 28. To Edwin M. Stanton, referring request of Richard Yates for authority to appoint officers for battery raised by Capt. Edward C. Henshaw of Ottawa, Ill., missing from DNA WR RG 107, Sec. of War Letters Received, P 219

Oct. 29. To Edward Bates, Nicolay for Lincoln, referring letter from John F. Kinney to Lincoln, Oct. 22, 1862, DNA RG 60, Papers of Atty. Gen., Box 107

Oct. 29. To Montgomery C. Meigs, referring letter of J. B. Henderson introducing Capt. O. N. Cutler, missing from DNA WR RG 92, Q.M. Gen., P 175, S 542

Oct. 29. To Edwin M. Stanton, referring complaint of Jonathan Todd showing 97th Pa. Reg. had not been paid for nine months, missing from DNA WR RG 107, Sec. of War Letters Received, P 1

Oct. 30. To Joseph Holt, secretary for Lincoln, referring petition of late Capt. George D. H. Watts of 61st N.Y. Vols. for reinstatement, *ibid.*, P 94

Oct. 31. To Montgomery C. Meigs, concerning Sioux War claims of Minnesota, missing from DNA WR RG 92, Q.M. Gen., P 187, S 570

Oct. 31. To Edwin M. Stanton, referring application of M. Y. Johnson for trial or discharge, missing from DNA WR RG 107, Sec. of War Letters Received, P 221

c. Nov. 1. To James Speed, NE, mentioned, Speed to Lincoln, Nov. 8, 1862, DLC-RTL

Nov. 1. To Edwin M. Stanton, referring letter from Edwin D. Morgan introducing Benjamin Gates who is concerned with draft exemption for Quakers in Ohio, missing from DNA WR RG 107, Sec. of War Letters Received, P 220

Nov. 3. To Montgomery C. Meigs, directing free transportation for allotment commissioners, missing from DNA WR RG 92, Q.M. Gen., P 201

Nov. 3. To Edwin M. Stanton, on letter from Noah H. Swayne recommending John P. Gould for paymaster, "Respectfully submitted to the Sec. of War." AES, RPB

Nov. 6. Endorsement, "Within named goods received," Parke-Bernet Catalog 82, Jan. 18, 1939, No. 72

Nov. 6. To Samuel R. Curtis, NE, mentioned, Curtis to Lincoln, Nov. 9, 1862, DLC-RTL

Nov. 6. To Henry W. Halleck, Gustavus V. Fox for Lincoln, directing a meeting of Stanton, Welles, and Halleck, DNA WR RG 108, H.Q.A., F 286, Box 57

Nov. 6. To Montgomery C. Meigs, referring letter of recommendation for promotion of Capt. S. A. Potter, missing from DNA WR RG 92, Q.M. Gen., P 219, H 344

Nov. 7. To Edwin M. Stanton, on letter of John A. Andrew to Lincoln, Nov. 4, 1862, objecting to enlistment from Volunteers to Regular Army, "Submitted to the War Department. A. LINCOLN," AES, DNA WR RG 107, Sec. of War Letters Received, P 230

Nov. 7. To Edwin M. Stanton, on papers in case of Lieut. Frank C. Goodrich suggesting mitigation of sentence to six months' loss of command and pay, "Suggestion approved A. LINCOLN," AES, IHi

Nov. 10. To Montgomery C. Meigs, concerning forts on Red River and Lake Superior, missing from DNA WR RG 92, Q.M. Gen., P 233, S 698-99

Nov. 10. To John Potts, Nicolay for Lincoln, transmitting petition for release of 44 prisoners of German birth confined on Dry Tortugas, ALS, DNA WR RG 107, Sec. of War Letters Received, P 226

Nov. 10. To Edwin M. Stanton, referring letter from Julia A. Wilbur concerning sufferings among contrabands in Alexandria, Va., missing from *ibid.*, P 228

Nov. 11. To Edwin M. Stanton, on telegram from Alexander Ramsey to Lincoln, Nov. 10, 1862, recommending execution of Sioux Indians, "Respectfully referred to Secretary of War. A. LINCOLN." OR, I, XIII, 787; missing from DNA WR RG 107, Sec. of War Letters Received, P 227

Nov. 11. To Edwin M. Stanton, on letter from Ingham Coryell to Lincoln, Nov. 7, 1862, recommending promotion of Brig. Gen. J. M. Brannan, "Submitted to the War Department. A. LINCOLN," AES, *ibid.*, P 232

Nov. 13. To Edward Bates, Nicolay for Lincoln, referring petition of W. I. Skinner and others to Lincoln, Oct. 25, 1862, for pardon of Delos W. Crossman, DNA RG 204, U.S. Pardon Atty., A 448

Nov. 15. To Samuel F. B. Morse, Nicolay for Lincoln, concerning sale of Beaufort, N.C., libraries, ALS, DLC-Morse Papers

Nov. 15. Endorsement on letter of Gen. Naglee concerning Lieut. Palmer, "Approved. A. LINCOLN," forgery, AES, NN

Nov. 15. To the President of Nicaragua, appointment of Thomas H. Clay as minister, copy, DNA FS RG 59, Credences, IV, 405

Nov. 15. To Caleb B. Smith, Nicolay for Lincoln, forwarding applications for surveyor general, DNA NR RG 48, Applications, Surv. Gen., Iowa & Wis., Box 1263

Nov. 16. To Montgomery C. Meigs, introducing de Stackpole concerning steamboats, missing from DNA WR RG 92, Q.M. Gen., P 283

Nov. 19. To Henry W. Halleck, on letter of John Covode to Nathaniel P. Banks, Oct. 31, 1862, concerning promotion of Col. Joseph A. Haskin, "Submitted to Gen. Halleck. A. LINCOLN," AES, RPB

Nov. 20. To Edwin M. Stanton, referring letter from John W. Price enclosing resolutions of Florida citizens to Lincoln, Sept. 19, 1862, asking appointment of a military governor, missing from DNA WR RG 107, Sec. of War Letters Received, P 231

Nov. 21. To Mrs. Hagerthy, forgery, ALS, ICHi

Nov. 21. To Edwin M. Stanton, referring letter from Montgomery Blair asking that Francis P. Blair, Jr., be sent to join Gen. John A. McClernand or to Texas, missing from DNA WR RG 107, Sec. of War Letters Received, P 233

c. Nov. 22. To Charles P. McIlvaine, Seward for Lincoln, acknowledging receipt of the pastoral letter of the House of Bishops of the Protestant Episcopal Church, *Ill. State Journal*, Nov. 22, 1862

Nov. 23. Endorsement on remonstrance of Gen. Naglee, "Allow Mrs. Patrick to pass with her goods," forgery, NN

Nov. 24. To Montgomery C. Meigs, referring letter from John C. White, missing from DNA WR RG 92, Q.M. Gen. Letters Received, P 274

Nov. 27. To Lucius E. Chittenden, Nicolay for Lincoln, concerning expenses of executive office, ALS, DLC-Nicolay Papers

Nov. 27. To Lorenzo Thomas, transmitting recommendations of various officers, missing from DNA WR RG 94, Adj. Gen. Letters Received, P 1089

c. Nov. 30. Endorsement, "Treat him with mercy as he is a sincerely religious man," forgery, NN

Nov. 30. To Mrs. Lippincott, forgery, ALS, Scheide Library, Titusville, Pa.

Dec. 5. To Edwin M. Stanton, requesting answer to Senate resolution concerning citizens of Ky. arrested, missing from DNA WR RG 107, Sec. of War Letters Received, P 247

Dec. 6. Approval on 4th Army Corps *General Orders No. 120*, "Approved. A. LINCOLN," forgery, AES, NN

Dec. 9. To Hannibal Hamlin, draft of reply to Senate resolution concerning arrested citizens of Ky., not composed or signed by Lincoln, DLC-RTL

Dec. 9. To A. C. Richards, Hay for Lincoln, acknowledging Richards' letter of Dec. 4, 1862, conveying resolutions adopted by the N.Y. Chamber of Commerce, New York *Tribune*, Jan. 3, 1863

Dec. 9. To Edwin M. Stanton, on envelope, "Submitted to the Sec. of War. A. LINCOLN," AES, owned by John W. Haines, Norton, Mass.

Dec. 10. To Edwin M. Stanton, referring letters from Timothy O. Howe and Maj. A. E. Boray concerning Gen. Egbert L. Viele's government at Norfolk, Va., missing from DNA WR RG 107, Sec. of War Letters Received, P 239

Dec. 10. To Edwin M. Stanton, on letter from John F. Farnsworth to Lincoln, Dec. 7, 1862, recommending Mr. Gifford, "Submitted to the Sec. of War. A. LINCOLN," AES, *ibid.*, Personnel Appts., Box 11

Dec. 11. To R. Shelton Mackenzie, sending autograph "for your good lady," ALS, CSmH

Dec. 11. To Montgomery C. Meigs, recommending Charles H. Rockwell, missing from DNA WR RG 92, Q.M. Gen., P 351, R 453

Dec. 11. To William H. Seward, on letter from William A. Buckingham to Lincoln, Dec. 3, 1862, recommending Samuel G. Pond, "Respectfully submitted to the Sec. of State. A. LINCOLN," AES, DNA FS RG 59, Appointments, Box 364

Dec. 11. To Edwin M. Stanton, concerning Col. W. Harren (Warren?), "Submitted to the Secretary of War. The same officer I spoke of to-day. A. LINCOLN," AES, owned by Herman Blum, Blumhaven Library, Philadelphia

Dec. 11. To Edwin M. Stanton, referring letter from William A. Todd, late lieut. in 71st Pa. Vols., asking that his dismissal be revoked, missing from DNA WR RG 107, Sec. of War Letters Received, P 240

Dec. 12. To Edwin M. Stanton, referring letter from Lesley White, Nov. 25, 1862, concerning exercises for soldiers in loading arms, missing from *ibid.*, P 237

Dec. 13. To Henry W. Halleck, on letter of Jackson Grimshaw to Orville H. Browning, Dec. 8, 1862, concerning promotion of Brig. Gen. Benjamin M. Prentiss, "Submitted to Gen. Halleck. A. LINCOLN," AES, IHi

Dec. 13. To Henry W. Halleck, on copies of letters recommending promotion of Col. Michael K. Lawler, "Submitted to Gen. Halleck. A. LINCOLN," AES, IHi

Dec. 17. To Edwin M. Stanton, on letter of Mark W. Delahay to Lincoln, Dec. 12, 1862, recommending promotion of Gen. James G. Blunt, "Respectfully submitted to the Sec. of War and Gen. Halleck. A. LINCOLN," AES, RPB

c. Dec. 21. Endorsement on envelope of letter from John B. Henderson concerning John F. Long, "Duplicate sent to Navy Dept." AE, DNA WR RG 94, U.S. Mil. Acad., 1862, No. 168

Dec. 24. To Edwin M. Stanton, referring letter from James K. Moorhead with enclosures on restoration of Col. Campbell, missing from DNA WR RG 107, Sec. of War Letters Received, P 244

Dec. 24. To Edwin M. Stanton, referring petition of T. F. Shoemaker and others for reinstatement of Lieut. G. A. Parker, 86th N.Y. Vols., missing from *ibid.*, P 245

Dec. 26. To Edward Bates, Nicolay for Lincoln, referring petition for pardon of Ada Allen, DNA RG 204, U.S. Pardon Atty., A 454

Dec. 27. To Michael Hahn and Benjamin F. Flanders, NE, mentioned, Hahn to Lincoln, Dec. 29, 1862, DLC-RTL

Dec. 28. To Gen. W. W. Davis, forgery, ALS, NN

c. Dec. 28. Endorsement on letter from Charles Sumner to Lincoln, Dec. 28, 1862, enclosing letter from George Livermore, Dec. 25, 1862, asking for pen with which Emancipation Proclamation is to be signed, "The pen it is to be signed with," AE, DLC-RTL

Dec. 29. To Montgomery C. Meigs, recommending George F. Savitz for clerk, missing from DNA WR RG 92, Q.M. Gen., P 28, S 80

Dec. 29. To Edwin M. Stanton, referring letter of Collins & Hughes of N.Y., transmitting petition of wounded soldiers for $100 bounty on being discharged, missing from DNA WR RG No. 107, Sec. of War Letters Received, P 243

Dec. 29. To Gideon Welles, Nicolay for Lincoln, to notify naval officers of president's reception on New Year's Day, DNA WR NB RG 45, Exec. Letters, No. 161

Dec. 30. To Joseph Holt, Nicolay for Lincoln, concerning Col. Ford, DNA WR RG 153, Judge Adv. Gen. Letters Received, No. 266

Dec. 31. To Horace Greeley, Nicolay for Lincoln, concerning release of Emancipation Proclamation to newspapers, ALS, RPB

Dec. 31. To Henry J. Raymond, Nicolay for Lincoln, same as to Greeley, ALS, RPB

c. Dec. 31. To Edwin M. Stanton, Hay for Lincoln, referring letter from Edwin D. Morgan to Lincoln, Nov. 26, 1862, enclosing petition of N.Y. citizens for James Bowen to be placed in command at N.Y., DNA WR RG 108, H.Q.A., M 2303, Box 58

1863

c. 1863. To Charles H. Foster, NE, mentioned, Foster to Samuel C. Pomeroy, Apr. 11, 1863, DLC-RTL

c. 1863. Endorsement on envelope containing recommendations of Ira Root, "File & preserve. A. L.," AES, DNA FS RG 59, Appointments, Box 373

1863. To Edwin M. Stanton, introducing "these gentlemen," forgery, ALS, NN

1863. Order for discharge of Francis M. Wolf, *The Collector*, May, 1936

Jan. To Lorenzo Thomas, referring request of Missourians that Gen. John M. Schofield replace Gen. Samuel R. Curtis in command at St. Louis, missing from DNA WR RG 94, Adj. Gen. Letters Received, P 286

Jan. 1. Endorsement, "I cannot interfere in this case, A. LINCOLN," *Century Magazine*, Dec., 1895, p. 255

Jan. 5. To Edwin M. Stanton, asking him to see Capt. Watson "who wishes to bring a new battery into the service." Metropolitan Art Assn. Catalog, Jan. 14, 1914, No. 500

Jan. 6. To Edward Bates, Nicolay for Lincoln, requesting an opinion on a deed requiring president's signature, ALS, DNA RG 60, Papers of Atty. Gen., Box 112

Jan. 6. To William Hunter, Nicolay for Lincoln, concerning act to facilitate the discharge of disabled soldiers, ALS, DNA FS RG 59, Misc. Letters

Jan. 9. To Edwin M. Stanton, ordering him to lighten parole of two prisoners of war, ALS, Samuel T. Freeman Catalog, July 13-14, 1942, No. 550

c. Jan. 10. Endorsement on letter of W. H. Doherty to Salmon P. Chase, Jan. 10, 1863, "W. H. Doherty—to be Judge in N.C." AE, CSmH

Jan. 12. To Edward Bates, on petition of Margaret Buschrae for pardon of her son, "I think a pardon may be granted in this case. A. LINCOLN," AES, DNA RG 204, U.S. Pardon Atty., A 330

Jan. 12. To Chief Clerk of Interior Dept., Nicolay for Lincoln, transmitting papers for file, ALS, DNA NR RG 48, Indian Agencies, Misc., Box 1269

Jan. 12. To Edwin M. Stanton, referring report of Provost Marshal Gen. on Philip Loewenthal, missing from DNA WR RG 107, Sec. of War Letters Received, P 7

c. Jan. 13. Order for reappointment of Robert Bushnell to Naval Academy, NE, mentioned Browning's *Diary*, Jan. 13, 1863

Jan. 14. To Edward Bates, on letter from Benjamin F. Wade and others to Lincoln, Jan. 14, 1863, recommending Richard Field, "To be filed." AE, DNA RG 60, Papers of Atty. Gen., Appts., New Jersey, Box 643

Jan. 14. To Edward Bates, Nicolay for Lincoln (misdated 1862), requesting nomination of Richard Field for judge in N.J., ALS, DNA RG 60, Papers of Atty. Gen., Box 112

Jan. 14. To Samuel R. Curtis, Stanton for Lincoln, OR, I, XXII, II, 41

Jan. 14. To Edwin M. Stanton, transmitting letter from George S. Nutting to Lincoln, Dec. 15, 1862, concerning petition for recognition of his services as captain of Vols., DNA WR RG 107, Sec. of War Letters Received, P 6

Jan. 16. To Montgomery Blair, referring letter from Edward Bates to Lincoln, Jan. 15, 1863, transmitting request for pardon, "Submitted to the Post-Master-General. A. LINCOLN," AES, DLC-RTL

Jan. 16. To Samuel R. Curtis, on letter from John W. Noell to Lincoln, Jan. 16, 1863, presenting petition of U. P. Carney, "Respectfully submitted to Majr. Gen. Curtis. A. LINCOLN," AES, *ibid.*

Jan. 17. To Andrew J. Green, inscription on *General War Orders No. 1*, forgery, Parke-Bernet Catalog 1164, May 15-16, 1950

Jan. 19. To William H. Seward, on envelope of letter from William Marsh, "Submitted to the Sec. of State. A. LINCOLN," AES, DNA FS RG 59, Appointments, Box 341

c. Jan. 19. To Edwin M. Stanton, on recommendations of Duane M. Greene, "Submitted to the Secretary of War A. LINCOLN," AES, DNA WR RG 107, Sec. of War Personnel Appts., Box 22

Jan. 20. Approval on 18th Army Corps *General Orders No. 28*, forgery, AES, NN

Jan. 21. To Ulysses S. Grant, Halleck for Lincoln, NH, VIII, 199-200 (not in OR, but see similar communication to Gen. Samuel R. Curtis, OR, I, XXII, II, 65)

Jan. 21. To Edwin M. Stanton, on recommendation of Dr. Frank H. Hamilton as medical inspector, "Submitted to the Sec. of War. A. LINCOLN," AES, owned by Charles W. Olsen, Chicago Ill.

Jan. 21. To Lorenzo Thomas, referring letters from George S. Bergen and David Clark seeking release of their sons, missing from DNA WR RG 94, Adj. Gen. Letters Received, P 28

Jan. 23. Endorsement on application for pardon, "In consideration of the circumstances, and particularly the non-age, of George B. Smith, and that he has already suffered a considerable part of the punishment under the sentence, I do hereby pardon him, and remit so much of the punishment as has not already been inflicted. A. LINCOLN," AES, IHi

Jan. 23. To Edwin M. Stanton, on letter from James George to Lincoln, Jan. 12, 1863, concerning William A. Bennett, "Submitted to the Sec. of War. A. LINCOLN," AES, owned by Alvin R. Witt, Minneapolis, Minn.

Jan. 25. Order relieving Ambrose E. Burnside, Edward D. Townsend for Lincoln, OR, I, XXI, 1004-1005

Jan. 26. To Edwin M. Stanton, secretary for Lincoln, referring letter from Charles H. Upton to Lincoln, Jan. 20, 1863, concerning Rev.

W. C. Lipscomb, DNA WR RG 107, Sec. of War Letters Received, P 15

Jan. 28. To Joseph Holt, Nicolay for Lincoln, returning record in case of Col. Ford of Ohio, ALS, DLC-Holt Papers

Jan. 29. To Edwin M. Stanton, endorsement on envelope, "Submitted to the Secretary of War, A. LINCOLN," Freeman & Co. Catalog, Feb. 19, 1948, No. 751

Jan. 30. To Montgomery C. Meigs, referring letter from T. Stevens recommending Col. Jacob A. Schindel for a clerkship, missing from DNA WR RG 92, Q.M. Gen., P 171, S 507

Feb. Endorsement on application for West Point, "Jonathan Dayton Wood, was 17 last October—West Point," AE, DNA WR RG 94, U.S. Mil. Acad., 1861, No. 962

Feb. 1. To Ethan A. Hitchcock, Hay for Lincoln, granting permission to copy a letter, ALS, DLC-Hitchcock Papers

Feb. 2. To Edward Bates, on letter from Francis S. Corkran to Lincoln, Jan. 26, 1863, recommending William Thompson, "Submitted to the Attorney General. A. LINCOLN," AES, DNA GE RG 60, Papers of Atty. Gen., Segregated Lincoln Material

Feb. 2. To the President of Paraguay, appointment of Charles A. Washburn as minister, copy, DNA FS RG 59, Credences, IV, 406

Feb. 2. Receipt on a card, "Box accompanying this received. A. LINCOLN," copy, ISLA.

Feb. 2. To Edwin M. Stanton, on envelope of recommendations for Francis Nicholson, "Submitted to the Secretary of War A. LINCOLN," AES, DNA WR RG 107, Sec. of War Personnel Appts., Box 23

Feb. 2. To Edwin M. Stanton, referring letter of Mathew Somers requesting investigation of court-martial findings in his case, missing from *ibid.*, Letters Received, P 20

Feb. 2. To Edwin M. Stanton, referring letter from George A. Coffey asking release of Albert D. Boileau, missing from *ibid.*, P 23

Feb. 3. To Edwin M. Stanton, secretary for Lincoln, referring letter from A. Ladico Gajerski, London, Jan. 12, 1863, asking transportation for himself and twelve other Poles to fight for liberty, *ibid.*, P 19

Feb. 6. To Edwin M. Stanton on letter from Stephen A. Hurlbut to Lincoln, Feb. 1, 1863, asking commission in Regular Army for Jacob D. Lansing, 15th Ill. Vols., "Submitted to the Secretary of War. A. LINCOLN," AES, IHi

Feb. 9. To William A. Hammond, referring letter from Helen G. LeConte to Lincoln, Feb. 7, 1863, asking that her husband John L. LeConte be made a medical inspector, "Respectfully submitted to the Surgeon General. A. LINCOLN," AES, IHi

c. Feb. 10. List of persons who have candidates for West Point, written on letter from Galusha A. Grow to Lincoln, Feb. 10, 1863, DLC-RTL

Feb. 11. To Edwin M. Stanton, on letter of Benjamin N. Martin to Charles White concerning Gen. Henry W. Benham, "Submitted to the Sec. of War. A. LINCOLN," Estate of Gabriel Wells Catalog 4, May, 1950, No. 121

Feb. 13. To Benjamin F. Butler, Hay for Lincoln, transmitting letter from Foreign Affairs Committee, Sheffield, England, Jan. 24, 1863, approving Butler's course in New Orleans, ALS, DLC-Butler Papers

c. Feb. 13. To William A. Hammond, concerning Dr. S. W. Forsha, NE, mentioned, Hammond to Lincoln, Feb. 13, 1863, DLC-RTL

Feb. 15. To Benjamin F. Butler, Mrs. Lincoln for Lincoln, invitation to dinner this date, DLC-Butler Papers

Feb. 16. To Edward Bates, Nicolay for Lincoln, concerning letter of Mr. Brady, ALS, DNA RG 60, Papers of Atty. Gen., Box 111

c. Feb. 16. To Horace Greeley, NE, mentioned, Edward Yates to Lincoln, Feb. 16, 1863, DLC-RTL

Feb. 17. To Montgomery C. Meigs, referring letter from I. N. Harris recommending Miss Bull and Luther Bull for copyist and messenger, missing from DNA WR RG 92, Q.M. Gen., P 260

Feb. 17. To Edwin M. Stanton, referring telegram from William S. Rosecrans to Lincoln, Feb. 14, 1863, recommending list of promotions, "Submitted to the Sec. of War. A. LINCOLN," AES, NHi

Feb. 17. To Peter H. Watson, Nicolay for Lincoln, transmitting letter from Samuel J. Kirkwood, Feb. 2, 1863, asking investigation of acts of Gen. Willis A. Gorman and Amos F. Eno, DNA WR RG 107, Sec. of War Letters Received, P 32

Feb. 19. To Edwin M. Stanton, secretary for Lincoln, referring letter from Capt. Timothy C. Moore to Lincoln, Feb. 6, 1863, asking to be appointed recruiting captain, *ibid.*, P 29

Feb. 19. To Joseph Hooker, Stanton for Lincoln, OR, I, XXV, II, 71

Feb. 20. To Edwin M. Stanton, referring letter of Isaac J. Wistar to William D. Kelley proposing use of Negroes, missing from DNA WR RG 107, Sec. of War Letters Received, P 34

Feb. 21. To Anson G. Henry, Mrs. Lincoln for Lincoln, inviting Henry to dinner this date, ALS-P, ISLA

c. Feb. 21. Endorsement on letter of John B. S. Todd and P. Bliss, "George P. Waldron, of Dakota. to Assess Indian Damage in Minn.," AE, DNA NR RG 48, Applications, Indian Agencies, Box 1274

c. Feb. 24. To John T. Nixon, NE, mentioned, Nixon to Lincoln, Feb. 24, 1863, DLC-RTL

Feb. 24. To John A. Stevens, Jr., Hay for Lincoln, acknowledging resolutions of N.Y. Chamber of Commerce concerning Rio Grande frontier, N.Y. *Tribune*, Mar. 6, 1863

Feb. 26. To William H. Seward, Nicolay for Lincoln, granting permission to publish certain documents, ALS, NAuE

c. Feb. 26. To Edwin M. Stanton, referring application of Quartermaster James A. Ekin to transfer from Indianapolis to Philadelphia, missing from DNA WR RG 107, Sec. of War Letters Received, P 39

Feb. 28. To William H. Seward, Hay for Lincoln, referring recommendations of E. George Squier, by R. J. Walker and Louis Agassiz, ALS, DNA FS RG 59, Appointments, Box 385

Mar. 2. Endorsement on petition, Mar. 2, 1863, "New York Delegation in behalf of Hon. John T. Nixon," asking appointment in U.S. Court of Claims, Anderson Auction Co. Catalog 1025, Apr. 16, 1914, No. 412

c. Mar. 2. Endorsement on letter from Thomas Richmond to Lincoln, Mar. 2, 1863, "Good advice." AE, DLC-RTL

Mar. 2. To Edwin M. Stanton, concerning Mrs. Becker, forgery, ALS-P, ISLA

Mar. 4. To Edwin M. Stanton, referring letter of Joseph C. Jackson to John C. Ten Eyck, Feb. 28, 1863, concerning appointment as staff officer to Gen. George G. Meade, "Submitted to the Secretary of War. A. LINCOLN," AES, owned by Harry E. Pratt, Springfield, Ill.

Mar. 5. To Edward Bates, Nicolay for Lincoln, referring petition for pardon of George Becker, DNA RG 204, U.S. Pardon Atty., A 466

Mar. 6. To Edwin M. Stanton, Nicolay for Lincoln, instructing to remove name of Gen. Samuel D. Sturgis from list, LS, DLC-Stanton Papers

Mar. 7. To Edward Bates, endorsement clipped from attendant papers, "Submitted to the Attorney General. A. LINCOLN," AES, MB

c. Mar. 7. To Edwin M. Stanton and Gideon Welles, on envelope of letter from John A. Dix to Lincoln, Mar. 7, 1863, reporting conflict between Army and Navy authorities, "Submitted to Mars & Neptune." AE, DLC-RTL

Mar. 9. To Peter H. Watson, Nicolay for Lincoln, returning message for file, ALS, DNA WR RG 107, Sec. of War Letters Received, P 164

c. Mar. 11. To Joseph Holt, on papers in case of John T. Brady with Holt's recommendation for mitigation of sentence, Hay for Lincoln, "Approve recommendation of Judge Advocate General" (Lincoln's signature and date clipped), ES, DNA WR RG 153, Judge Adv. Gen., MM 335

Mar. 11. To Edwin M. Stanton, referring letter from Luther B. Hunt, Jr., to Lincoln, Mar. 1, 1863, concerning hospital at Fairfax C.H., Va., missing from DNA WR RG 107, Sec. of War Letters Received, P 47

Mar. 11. To Edwin M. Stanton, referring letter from Capt. Piazza, Belle Ile, France, to Lincoln, Jan. 30, 1863, offering services, missing from *ibid.*, P 46

Mar. 13. To Edward Bates, Nicolay for Lincoln, referring requests from Senate for return of resolutions rejecting Hillary C. Spalding, Thomas I. Williams, and James Cull, DNA RG 60, Papers of Atty. Gen., Box 111

Mar. 13. To George Harrington, appointment as acting secretary of the Treasury, DS, Stan. V. Henkels Catalog, Nov. 2, 1917, No. 56

Mar. 15. To Edwin M. Stanton, referring letter from Edward Salomon to Lincoln, Feb. 25, 1863, recommending establishment of hospital at Prairie du Chien, Wis., missing from DNA WR RG 107, Sec. of War Letters Received, P 52

c. Mar. 16. To Joseph Holt, on court-martial record of James H. Cain, "Sentence commuted to forfeiture of one months pay, and a reprimand by the prisoner's Division Commander. A. LINCOLN," ES, DNA WR RG 153, Judge Adv. Gen., MM 351

Mar. 16. To Kamehameha IV, appointment of James McBride as minister, DS, Archives of Hawaii; copy, DNA FS RG 59, Credences, IV, 408

Mar. 17. To William A. Hammond, referring letter from E. Harmon to Lincoln, Jan. 19, 1863, concerning a sandal for sore feet, "Submitted to the Surgeon General for his report. A. LINCOLN," AES, DLC-RTL

Mar. 18. To Edwin M. Stanton, NE, mentioned in endorsement by War Dept., Apr. 8, 1863, on letter of Joseph Holt to Lincoln, Mar. 20, 1863, concerning Lieut. J. Benson Williams, IHi

c. Mar. 18. To Edwin M. Stanton, referring letter from Gustave Koerner and Horatio J. Perry concerning purchase of muskets in Spain, missing from DNA WR RG 107, Sec. of War Letters Received, P 55; also missing from DNA WR RG 156, Office of Chief of Ordnance, WD 416 (see Z)

Mar. 19. To Edward Bates, Nicolay for Lincoln, referring letter from Robert Williams to Lincoln, Feb. 10, 1863, asking pardon for his wife, DNA RG 204, U.S. Pardon Atty., A 467

c. Mar. 21. Copy in Lincoln's autograph of letter from John P. Kennedy to Lincoln, Mar. 21, 1863, concerning George C. Neilson, DNA WR RG 94, U.S. Mil. Acad., 1862, No. 219

Mar. 21. To Edwin M. Stanton, on envelope of letter concerning John S. Phelps, "Submitted to the Secretary of War. A. LINCOLN," AES-P, DLC-Stanton Papers

Mar. 21. To Edwin M. Stanton, requesting leave for Gen. Fitz-Henry Warren to visit Washington, missing from DNA WR RG 107, Sec. of War Letters Received, P 178

Mar. 21. To George H. Stuart, Hay for Lincoln, referring letter from Mary T. Sorby of Derbyshire, England, enclosing money to buy Bibles for soldiers, ALS, DLC-Stuart Papers

Mar. 23. To Gideon Welles, Nicolay for Lincoln, requesting letter written by Capt. J. P. Gillis to Lincoln, ALS, DNA WR NB RG 45, Exec. Letters, No. 61

Mar. 24. Endorsement clipped from attendant papers, "Submitted to the Commissioner of Agriculture. A. LINCOLN," AES, CSmH

Mar. 26. To Edwin M. Stanton, referring letter from Gen. Robert H. Milroy concerning repairs of railroad between Winchester and Harper's Ferry, Va., missing from DNA WR RG 107, Sec. of War Letters Received, P 38, Irregular Book 5

Mar. 27. To Edwin M. Stanton, on petition for establishment of factory for army clothing at Hannibal, Mo., missing from ibid., P 69

Mar. 30. To William B. Thomas, NE, mentioned, Thomas to Lincoln, Mar. 31, 1863, concerning "Solidified Greek Fire," DLC-RTL

c. Mar. 31. Fifty-five endorsements, "Pardoned   A. LINCOLN," on court-martial sentences to be shot for desertion, cases forwarded by Gen. Joseph Hooker, with recommendation of pardon in view of the proclamation of Mar. 10, 1863, pardoning all deserters who returned before Apr. 1, 1863, ES, DNA WR RG 153, Judge Adv. Gen., MM 527-39, 541, 547-53, 555, 561, 563-64, 566, 568-70, 572-73

Apr. 2. Endorsement on petition for appointment of Fitzhugh Smith, forgery, AES-P, ISLA

Apr. 2. To Edwin M. Stanton, referring letter from Charles Jones concerning slaves, missing from DNA WR RG 107, Sec. of War, Letters Received, P 64

Apr. 3. To Andrew G. Curtin, Nicolay for Lincoln, concerning Lincoln's absence from Washington, ALS, RPB

Apr. 3. To Edwin M. Stanton, on letter from Capt. G. W. Smith asking commission, "Submitted to the War Department A. LINCOLN," AES, DNA WR RG 107, Sec. of War Personnel Appts., Box 24

Apr. 7. Endorsement, "Memorial & petition on Judgeship of N.C. W. H. Doherty, New Bern, N.C.," Chicago Book and Art Auctions Catalog 34, June 14-15, 1933, No. 494

Apr. 8. To George G. Meade, NE, mentioned in telegram from Meade to Lincoln, Aug. 12, 1863, concerning Col. Martin D. Hardin, DLC-RTL

Apr. 11. To John Pope, Halleck for Lincoln, OR, I, XXII, II, 211

Apr. 11. To Lorenzo Thomas, referring letter from Capt. Richard F. O'Beirne on his failure to send accounts, missing from DNA WR RG 94, Adj. Gen. Letters Received, P 266

Apr. 12. To Marshall Lefferts, forgery, ALS, NN

c. Apr. 13. To Salmon P. Chase, Nicolay for Lincoln, referring letter from John B. Henderson to Lincoln, Apr. 13, 1863, DNA FI RG 56, Letters from Exec. Officers, Series AB, I, 3

Apr. 14. To Edwin M. Stanton, on letter recommending Dr. Richard A. Wells for examining surgeon, "Submitted to the Sec. of War. A. LINCOLN," AES-P, ISLA

c. Apr. 16. To John E. Bouligny, NE, mentioned, Bouligny to Lincoln, Apr. 23, 1863, DLC-RTL

Apr. 16. To Joseph Holt, Nicolay for Lincoln, concerning papers of Capt. Shafer of 19th Ind. Vols., DNA WR RG 153, Judge Adv. Gen. Letters Received, No. 183

c. Apr. 16. To Joseph Holt, favoring reappointment of Capt. Shafer, missing from *ibid.*

Apr. 16. To Joseph Hooker, concerning promotion of Col. Hiram Berdan, NE, mentioned, Hooker to Lincoln, Apr. 21, 1863, DLC-RTL

Apr. 16. To the President of Nicaragua, withdrawal of Thomas H. Clay as minister, copy, DNA FS RG 59, Communications to Foreign Sovereigns and States, III, 205-206

Apr. 18. To Joseph Holt, Nicolay for Lincoln, referring papers in case of Thomas M. Griffith, DNA WR RG 153, Judge Adv. Gen., MM 189

Apr. 18. To the President of Honduras, withdrawal of James R. Partridge as minister, copy, DNA FS RG 59, Communications to Foreign Sovereigns and States, III, 206-207

Apr. 18. To the President of Honduras, appointment of Thomas H. Clay as minister, copy, *ibid.*, Credences, IV, 410

Apr. 18. To the President of Nicaragua, appointment of Andrew B. Dickinson as minister, copy, *ibid.*, 409

Apr. 18. To the President of Salvador, appointment of James R. Partridge as minister, copy, *ibid.*, 411

Apr. 18. To Lorenzo Thomas, reporting an interview with Edward Salomon, missing from DNA WR RG 94, Adj. Gen. Letters Received, P 1064

Apr. 20. To James W. Ripley, referring testimonials in favor of

Rafael gun, missing from DNA WR RG 156, Office of Chief of Ordnance, WD 413 (*see* Z)

Apr. 20. To William H. Seward, on envelope of recommendations for James Silvey, "Submitted to the Sec. of State. A. LINCOLN," AES, DNA FS RG 59, Appointments, Box 380

Apr. 23. To Adeline Marchant, sending autograph, Stan. V. Henkels Catalog 1347, Mar. 14, 1924, No. 178

c. Apr. 24. To William W. H. Davis, on letter of Capt. Stuart M. Taylor concerning maltreatment of Negroes, probably spurious, Argosy Book Shop Catalog, Apr., 1942

Apr. 24. Check to John Saunie for $4, DS-P, ISLA

Apr. 27. To the President of Bolivia, appointment of Allen A. Hall as minister, copy, DNA FS RG 59, Credences, IV, 412

Apr. 28. To Edwin M. Stanton, referring letter from Franklin Bound to Lincoln, Mar. 14, 1863, missing from DNA WR RG 107, Sec. of War Letters Received, P 86

Apr. 28. To Edwin M. Stanton, referring letter from Willson G. Smith to Lincoln, Apr. 21, 1863, concerning manufacture of guns, missing from *ibid.*, P 88

Apr. 28. To Edwin M. Stanton, referring letter from B. M. Hawkins to Lincoln, Apr. 11, 1863, concerning his loyalty, missing, from *ibid.*, P 89

Apr. 28. To Edwin M. Stanton, referring letter from John B. Rodgers charging disloyalty of Joseph H. Hilton, missing from *ibid.*, P 87

c. Apr. 28. To Edwin M. Stanton, referring letter from William Armand asking to be sent South, missing from *ibid.*, P 90

Apr. 29. To Ambrose E. Burnside, Stanton for Lincoln, OR, I, XXIII, II, 291

Apr. 29. Endorsement on appointment of Fitzhugh Smith, forgery, AES-F, ISLA

May 3. To Daniel Butterfield, Stanton for Lincoln, OR, I, XXV, II, 378

May 4. To Edward Bates, on letter from William S. Tuckerman and others to Lincoln, Apr. 21, 1863, asking pardon "Submitted to the Attorney General. A. LINCOLN," AES, DNA RG 204, U.S. Pardon Atty., A 371

May 8. Inscription in Bible, "For Charles W. Merrill of 19th Massachusetts. A. LINCOLN," AES, Essex Institute, Salem, Mass.

May 8. To Edwin M. Stanton, on telegram from Francis H. Peirpoint to Lincoln, May 7, 1863, "Submitted to the War Department A. LINCOLN," AES, NHi

May 8. To Edwin M. Stanton, on telegram from Oliver P. Morton to Lincoln, May 7, 1863, concerning conscription, "Submitted to the War Department. A. LINCOLN," AES, NHi

c. May 9. To Edwin M. Stanton, referring request of Miss E. E. Stephens concerning case of Mrs. Buchrach, missing from DNA WR RG 107, Sec. of War Letters Received, P 97

May 11. To Joseph Holt, concerning John E. Wilbur, "Sentence approved in this case A. LINCOLN," ES, DNA WR RG 153, Judge Adv. Gen., MM 87

May 11. To Gideon Welles, NE, mentioned in Welles' *Diary*, 296

May 13. To Edwin M. Stanton, Nicolay for Lincoln, concerning commissions, DNA WR RG 107, Sec. of War Letters Received, P 106

May 13. To Edwin M. Stanton, on petition of loyal citizens of Paducah, Ky., to Lincoln, Apr. 24, 1863, missing from *ibid.*, P 106½

May 14. To John A. Dahlgren, Nicolay for Lincoln, asking formal order for $2,000 to Isaac R. Diller, DNA WR RG 74, Navy Branch, Bur. of Ord., Diller's Powder, Letters Received

May 14. To Lorenzo Thomas, granting leave to Lt. Asher R. Eddy, missing from DNA WR RG 94, Adj. Gen. Letters Received, P 1077

c. May 16. To Edwin M. Stanton, referring letter from T. Harry Becktel concerning George P. Barnes, Jr., and Joseph A. Slipper, missing from DNA WR RG 107, Sec. of War Letters Received, P 99

May 17. To Francis J. Herron, Stanton for Lincoln, OR, I, XXII, II, 285

May 19. To Ambrose E. Burnside, Stanton for Lincoln, deporting Clement L. Vallandigham, OR, II, V, 657

May 19. To Montgomery C. Meigs, referring letter from Capt. Granville E. Johnson recommending P. Turner, missing from DNA WR RG 92, Q.M. Gen., P 322

May 20. To Ambrose E. Burnside, Canby for Lincoln, OR, II, V, 667

May 20. To Joseph Holt, on court-martial record of Michael McKew, "Sentence commuted to imprisonment for one year. A. LINCOLN," AES, DNA WR RG 153, Judge Adv. Gen., MM 141

May 20. To Montgomery C. Meigs, referring application of Lieut. A. Annon, missing from DNA WR RG 92, Q.M. Gen., P 248, A 432

May 20. To William S. Rosecrans, Stanton for Lincoln, OR, I, XXIII, II, 342

May 21. To James W. Ripley, directing payment of $1,500 to Isaac R. Diller, missing from DNA WR RG 156, Office of Chief of Ordnance, WD 566, see WD 470 (*see* Z)

May 22. To Quincy A. Gillmore, asking him to come to Washington, Nicolay for Lincoln, ALS, RPB

May 22. To Edwin M. Stanton, on letter of Col. James C. Rice to Henry Wilson, May 20, 1863, "Submitted to the Secretary of War A. LINCOLN," AES, IHi

c. May 23. Endorsement concerning John W. Wetherill, NE, mentioned, Lincoln to Stanton, May 23, 1863

May 25. To Joseph Holt, Nicolay for Lincoln, that president will take no action in case of George M. Fillmore, missing from DNA WR RG 153, Judge Adv. Gen. Letters Received, No. 410

May 27. Note concerning employment for Sergt. A. L. Fleming, a disabled soldier, Rains Gallery Catalog, May 14-15, 1936, No. 229

May 28. To Edwin M. Stanton, Nicolay for Lincoln, referring letter of William Alexander to Montgomery Blair, May 2, 1863, concerning pay of Texas officers, DNA WR RG 107, Sec. of War Letters Received, P 105

June. To Edwin M. Stanton, referring letter from Winn Gunn opposing pardon of William Stephens, missing from *ibid.*, P 28, Irregular Book 5

June 1. To Joseph Holt, Nicolay for Lincoln, asking Holt to a conference on court-martial cases, ALS, DLC-Holt Papers

June 1. To Edwin M. Stanton, referring letter from Horace S. Crofut to Lincoln, May 29, 1863, asking pay or discharge, missing from DNA WR RG 107, Sec. of War Letters Received, P 108

c. June 2. To Joseph Holt, on court-martial sentence of Henry H. Wiley commuted to apology and loss of three months' pay, "Gen. Rosecrans recommendation approved. A. LINCOLN," AES, DNA WR RG 153, Judge Adv. Gen., MM 382

June 9. To Montgomery C. Meigs, requesting appointment of G. H. Kellor as forage master, missing from DNA WR RG 92, Q.M. Gen., P 124

June 9. To Edwin M. Stanton, referring letter from W. H. Farrar on case of Capt. James H. Hunt, missing from DNA WR RG 107, Sec. of War Letters Received, P 70

June 11. To Edwin M. Stanton, on letter from Boniface Wimmer to Lincoln, June 10, 1863, "Submitted to the Secretary of War. A. LINCOLN," OR, III, III, 336

June 12. To Gustave Koerner, Hay for Lincoln, Tracy, 227

June 12. To Edwin M. Stanton, Hay for Lincoln, referring letter from James A. Garfield to Lincoln, June 6, 1863, recommending F. H. Nelson, DNA WR RG 96, Adj. Gen., 311 M, CB 1863

June 15. To Julian R. Campbell, Hay for Lincoln, acknowledging receipt of resolutions, copy, Nicolay and Hay Papers, IHi

June 19. To Park Benjamin, forgery, ALS-P, ISLA

June 22. To Joseph Holt, Nicolay for Lincoln, concerning case of Adelbert S. Eddy, DNA WR RG 153, Judge Adv. Gen., MM 187

June 22. To Edwin M. Stanton, referring papers in case of Col. R. C. Murphy, 8th Wis., missing from DNA WR RG 107, Sec. of War Letters Received, P 181

June 23. To Joseph Holt, endorsements on court-martial cases of Martin Finley, Warren McMullen, and Amos Taylor, "The sentence in this case is remitted. A. LINCOLN," AES, DNA WR RG 153, Judge Adv. Gen., MM 188, 422, 279

June 23. To Edwin M. Stanton, on petition of George D. H. Watts, late capt. 61st N.Y. Vols., "Petition refused. A. LINCOLN," AES, DNA WR RG 107, Sec. of War Letters Received, P 94

June 24. To Joseph Holt, on court-martial records of John H. Behan and William L. Colerick, "Sentence approved. A. LINCOLN," AES, DNA WR RG 153, Judge Adv. Gen., MM 421 and 267

June 25. Check to "Rev. Dr. [Phineas D.] Gurley (for church)," for $25, DS-F, ISLA

c. June 25. Endorsement on letter of Mrs. Robert K. Stone to Mrs. Lincoln, NE, mentioned, Lincoln to Stone, June 25, 1863

June 26. To John Hancock, forgery, ALS, ICHi-Logan Collection

June 26. To Joseph Holt, on court-martial record of Rodney B. Newkirk, "Sentence remitted A. LINCOLN," ES, DNA WR RG 153, Judge Adv. Gen., MM 352

June 28. To Edwin M. Stanton, on telegram from James Y. Smith to Lincoln, June 27, 1863, "Submitted to the Sec. of War, A. LINCOLN," AES, NHi

June 28. To Gideon Welles, Frederick W. Seward for Lincoln, signed printed form letter calling cabinet meeting, DLC-Welles Papers

July. To James E. Hardie, Hay for Lincoln, asking for Archbishop

John Hughes' letter recommending Eugene P. Murphy, DNA WR RG 94, U.S. Mil. Acad., 1862, No. 214

July. To Joseph Holt, on court-martial record of Geacomo Antonali, "Sentence approved A. LINCOLN," AES, DNA WR RG 153, Judge Adv. Gen., MM 463

July 1. To the President of Colombia, appointment of Allen A. Burton as minister, DNA FS RG 59, Credences, IV, 415

July 3. To Edwin M. Stanton, referring request from David L. Phillips for authority to employ counsel, DNA WR RG 107, Sec. of War Letters Received, P 48, Irregular Book 5

July 5. To William A. Hammond, asking facilities for Mrs. Ames "to go any where she can, to minister to our wounded soldiers," Libbie & Co. Catalog, Nov. 17, 1904, No. 659

July 8. To Joseph Holt, on court-martial record of Samuel Slingluff, "Report approved. A. LINCOLN," ES, DNA WR RG 153, Judge Adv. Gen., MM 365

July 8. To George G. Meade, Halleck for Lincoln, OR, I, XXVII, I, 84

July 9. To Joseph Holt, on court-martial record of William D. Stewart, order for reinstatement, DNA RG 130, White House Office, Army Court-Martial Cases

July 12. To Joseph Holt, on court-martial record of Austin Ripley sentenced to be shot, recommended commutation to two years' imprisonment, "Let the sentence be commuted as recommended A. LINCOLN," AES, DNA WR RG 153, Judge Adv. Gen., MM 509

July 13. To Edwin M. Stanton, concerning appointment of Col. Henry E. Davies, Jr., as brigadier general, ALS, *The Collector*, July, 1952

July 15. To Joseph G. Totten, Hay for Lincoln, concerning appointment of George S. Jenkins, ALS, DNA WR RG 94, U.S. Mil. Acad., 1863, No. 94

July 17. To Ulysses S. Grant, forgery, ALS, ICHi

July 18. To Joseph Holt, court-martial records endorsed by Lincoln approving sentence (15), disapproving, commuting, or remitting sentence (9), DNA WR RG 153, Judge Adv. Gen., MM 227, 271, 276, 278, 298, 302, 303, 307, 315, 347, 353, 374, 385, 402, 407, 450, 460, 517-20, 546, 557, 562

July 19. Doggerel, NE, mentioned in Hay's *Diary* as written on this day

c. July 20. Endorsement, Hay for Lincoln, on letter of Charles Sumner to Lincoln, July 20, 1863, recommending Chapman Dwight, AES, DNA WR RG 94, U.S. Mil. Acad., 1864, No. 242

July 21. To Joseph Holt, on court-martial record of James Ryan, recommendation for mitigation of death sentence to imprisonment at hard labor, "Recommendation of Genl. Heintzleman approved. A. LINCOLN," AES, DNA WR RG 153, Judge Adv. Gen., MM 487

July 22. To Joseph Holt, on court-martial record of Samuel Hall, commutation of death sentence to imprisonment at hard labor, "Sentence commuted in accordance with recommendation of Gen. Rosecrans. A. LINCOLN," ES, DNA WR RG 153, Judge Adv. Gen., MM 500

July 22. To Joseph Holt, on court-martial record of Hugh Haskins sentenced to be dismissed, "Sentence approved A. LINCOLN," AES, *ibid.*, MM 496

July 22. To Joseph Holt, on court-martial record of Thomas Johnson, death sentence commuted to imprisonment at hard labor, "Sentence commuted according to recommendation of the Judge Advocate General A. LINCOLN," ES, *ibid.*, MM 498

July 22. To Joseph Holt, on court-martial record of Lawrence Toney, death sentence remitted, "Recommendation of General [Israel] Vogdes approved. A. LINCOLN," ES, *ibid.*, MM 497

July 22. To Robert Dale Owen and James McKaye, introducing John Eaton, Jr., on dealer's list

July 22. To Edwin M. Stanton, requesting transfer of Albert Houston to another regiment, ALS, William D. Morley Catalog, Oct. 22, 1943, No. 311

July 23. To Montgomery Blair, two endorsements (one in case of Mrs. Melancthon Smith, Postmaster at Rockford, Ill.), NE, mentioned in Lincoln to Blair, July 24, 1863

July 23. To Joseph Holt, on court-martial record of Michael Meehan, death sentence commuted to two years' imprisonment at hard labor, "Sentence commuted in accordance with the recommendation A. LINCOLN," ES, DNA WR RG 153, Judge Adv. Gen., MM 510

July 23. To Montgomery C. Meigs, referring letters from Jesse K. Dubois and Ozias M. Hatch recommending James Campbell, missing from DNA WR RG 92, Q.M. Gen., P 74

July 24. To Edward Bates on letter from E. Delafield Smith to Lincoln, July 22, 1863, requesting a pardon to be made out for Rudolph Blumenberg, DNA RG 204, U.S. Pardon Atty., A 416

July 24. To Joseph Holt, on court-martial record of Edward Carter reporting sentence as inoperative, "Report of Judge Advocate General approved A. LINCOLN," ES, DNA WR RG 153, Judge Adv. Gen., MM 546

July 24. To Joseph Holt, on court-martial record of Edward M. Grant recommended by Holt for dishonorable discharge, "The recommendation of the Judge Advocate General is approved. A. LINCOLN," ES, *ibid.*, MM 516

July 31. To John W. Forney, asking him to confer about a new printing shop, offered for sale by dealer in 1949

July 31. To Montgomery C. Meigs, requesting payment of $1,000 to B. J. Britton, missing from DNA WR RG 92, Q.M. Gen., P 108, S 246, C 209

Aug. 1. To Edwin M. Stanton, on petition to Lincoln, July 30, 1863, for restoration of Gen. Robert H. Milroy to command, "Submitted to the Secretary of War. A. LINCOLN," AES, RPB

Aug. 1. To Edwin M. Stanton, referring letter from Mrs. Delphy Carlin, missing from DNA WR RG 107, Sec. of War Letters Received, P 141

Aug. 1. To Edwin M. Stanton, referring request for release of a prisoner in Old Capitol prison, Am. Art Assn. Anderson Galleries Catalog 3854, Oct. 20, 1930, No. 150

Aug. 3. To Edward Bates, referring petition, "Submitted to the Attorney General. A. LINCOLN," ES, Walpole Galleries Catalog 134, 1919, No. 105

Aug. 3. To William A. Hammond, on letter from Sgt. Benjamin Mc-Fadden requesting discharge as unfit for duty, "Submitted to the Surgeon General. A. LINCOLN," AES, DNA WR RG 107, Sec. of War Letters Received, P 165

Aug. 3. Order concerning Capt. Bricer (?), NE, mentioned in letter from Ira Harris to Lincoln, Aug. 14, 1863, DLC-RTL

Aug. 3. To Edwin M. Stanton and Henry W. Halleck, on letter from Generals Benjamin M. Prentiss, Frederick Salomon and Leonard F. Ross to Lincoln, July 11, 1863, recommending Col. W. E. McLean, "Submitted to the Sec. of War & Genl-in-Chief A. LINCOLN," AES, RPB

Aug. 5. To Edwin M. Stanton, referring request of John von Horn to Lincoln, July, 1863, missing from DNA WR RG 107, Sec. of War Letters Received, P 122

Aug. 5. To Lorenzo Thomas, Hay for Lincoln, concerning appointment of William H. Hodges, DNA WR RG 94, U.S. Mil. Acad., 1863, No. 91

Aug. 6. To Thomas J. Durant, NE, same as Lincoln to Flanders, this date

Aug. 6. To Michael Hahn, NE, same as Lincoln to Flanders, this date

Aug. 7. To Edwin M. Stanton, Hay for Lincoln, referring recommendation of Edmund Wolf by William L. Price and John V. L. Findlay to Lincoln, Aug. 7, 1863, DNA WR RG 107, Sec. of War Personnel Appts., Box 24

c. Aug. 7. To Edwin M. Stanton, referring letter of B. F. Camp concerning his son: "Please make the appointment, and if the young man shall not do well, remove him again." Copy of partial text in Register, but missing from DNA WR RG 107, Sec. of War Letters Received, P 121

Aug. 7. To Edwin M. Stanton, referring letter of F. C. Adams concerning Capt. Dan. Harkins, missing from *ibid.*, P 123

Aug. 7. To Edwin M. Stanton, referring communications from Col. Elias M. Greene, missing from *ibid.*, P 120

Aug. 8. To Edwin M. Stanton, referring telegram from James R. Doolittle to Lincoln, Aug. 7, 1863, concerning Capt. Trowbridge "Submitted to the Secretary of War. A. LINCOLN," AES, NHi

c. Aug. 10. To Edwin M. Stanton, concerning appointment of Thomas K. McCann, NE, mentioned, K. V. Whaley to Lincoln, Aug. 10, 1863, DLC-RTL

Aug. 11. To Edwin M. Stanton, "About Gen. Hooker, Sec. of War please forward for me. A. LINCOLN," AES, Metropolitan Art Assn. Catalog, Mar. 9, 1914, No. 641

Aug. 12. To Edwin M. Stanton and Henry W. Halleck, on letter of Richard Yates to Lincoln, Aug. 5, 1863, concerning construction of arsenal at Rock Island, Ill., "Respectfully referred to the Secretary of War. A. LINCOLN," ES, IHi

Aug. 12. To Edwin M. Stanton, on letter of E. B. French and 31 others, on treatment of Gen. Neal Dow by rebels, "Submitted to the Secretary of War and General-in-Chief. A. LINCOLN," OR, II, VI, 192; missing from DNA WR RG 107, Sec. of War Letters Received, P 125

Aug. 12. To Edwin M. Stanton, referring case of James O'Grady, missing from *ibid.*, P 128

Aug. 14. To Edwin M. Stanton and Henry W. Halleck, on letter from Carl Schurz concerning Col. Wladimir Krzyzanowski, "Submitted to the Sec. of War & General-in-chief. A LINCOLN," John Heise Catalog 2464, No. 76

Aug. 16. To Edwin M. Stanton, concerning "Quartermaster Meiggs," forgery, ALS, NN

Aug. 17. To Edwin M. Stanton, on letter of James O'Grady to Lincoln, Aug. 11, 1863, "Respectfully referred to the Hon. Secretary of War. A. LINCOLN," ES, IHi

Aug. 18. To Edwin M. Stanton, Hay for Lincoln, referring letter from Hugh McCulloch to Lincoln, Aug. 17, 1863, recommending release of G. Shick, DNA WR RG 107, Sec. of War Letters Received, P 133

Aug. 20. To Edwin M. Stanton, referring application of Mrs. Ann Hunter and Lavinia H. Jackson, Granville Co., N.C., to come North, "Old Lady might come but not the daughter," copy in Register; missing from *ibid.*, P 135

Aug. 20. To Edwin M. Stanton, on communication from Ira O. Wilkinson and Thomas J. Buford to Lincoln, Aug. 19, 1863, concerning Rock Island Arsenal, "Submitted to the Sec. of War A. LINCOLN," AES, IHi

Aug. 21. To Edwin M. Stanton, on telegram from Richard Yates to Lincoln, Aug. 20, 1863, concerning Col. Indis, "Submitted to the Sec. of War. A. LINCOLN," AES, NHi

Aug. 21. To Edwin M. Stanton, referring letter of John P. Hart to Lincoln, Aug. 11, 1863, concerning Gen. Napoleon B. Buford and Col. Lewis B. Parsons (referred by Stanton to Meigs), missing from DNA WR RG 92, Q.M. Gen., P 259, S 553

Aug. 29. To Edwin M. Stanton, on letter from William R. Strachan to Stanton, Aug. 28, 1863, requesting commission, "Submitted to the Secretary of War. A. LINCOLN," AES, DNA WR RG 107, Sec. of War Letters Received, P 144

Aug. 29. To Edwin M. Stanton, referring letter from John A. Logan requesting authority for Dr. Joseph G. Stuart to raise a cavalry regiment in Miss., missing from *ibid.*, P 145

Aug. 29. To Edwin M. Stanton, referring letter from James B. Pickett requesting pass to Red River, missing from *ibid.*, P 142

Aug. 31. To Edwin M. Stanton, "If you have any new dispatches, please send them over," copy, ISLA

Aug. 31. To Edwin M. Stanton, on letter of Thornton A. Jenkins, Jr., to Salmon P. Chase, Aug. 27, 1863, "Submitted to the Sec. of War. A. LINCOLN," AES, DNA WR RG 94, U.S. Mil. Acad., 1864, No. 309

c. Sept. 1. Order for suspension of trial of Robert H. Milroy, purported but not authentic, Rice, ed., *Reminiscences of Abraham Lincoln*, 492

c. Sept. 2. To John P. Usher, concerning John M. Allen, referring letter from William Jayne to Lincoln, Aug. 26, 1863, NE, mentioned in letter from William T. Otto to Lincoln, Sept. 2, 1863, DLC-RTL

Sept. 3. To Edward Bates, clipped endorsement, "Submitted to the Attorney General. A. LINCOLN," Anderson Galleries Catalog 1786, Dec. 17, 1923, No. 52

Sept. 3. To Stephen A. Hurlbut, referring claim of J. R. Syphus, missing from DNA WR RG 94, Adj. Gen. Letters Received, P 635

Sept. 4. To Edwin M. Stanton, referring petition for release of prisoner in Old Capitol prison, missing from DNA WR RG 107, Sec. of War Letters Received, P 158

Sept. 6. To Edwin M. Stanton, on letter from James R. Doolittle to Lincoln, Sept. 6, 1863, recommending James Sawyer, "Submitted to the Sec. of War. A. LINCOLN," AES, DNA WR RG 94, U.S. Mil. Acad., 1861, No. 741

Sept. 7. To Edwin M. Stanton, referring letter from B. S. Bailey requesting discharge of Frank W. Sloan, missing from DNA WR RG 107, Sec. of War Letters Received, P 151

Sept. 10. To Joseph Holt, on court-martial record of John C. Nicholas sentenced to be shot for being a guerrilla, "Sentence approved. A. LINCOLN," AES, DNA WR RG 153, Judge Adv. Gen., MM 746

Sept. 10. To Edwin M. Stanton, on recommendations of Horatio M. Jones, "Submitted to the Sec. of War. Quite a good case. A. LINCOLN," AES, DNA WR RG 94, U.S. Mil. Acad., 1863, No. 95

Sept. 10. To Edwin M. Stanton, on letter from Thomas H. Hicks to Lincoln, Sept. 3, 1863, recommending Grayson W. Sharretts, "Submitted to the Sec. of War. A. LINCOLN," AES, *ibid.*, 1862, No. 263

Sept. 10. To Edwin M. Stanton, Hay for Lincoln, requesting audience for G. Rush Smith, owned by W. Easton Louttit, Jr., Providence, R.I.

Sept. 11. To Lorenzo Thomas, directing that Thomas J. Killinger, deserter from 5th N.Y. Vols., be sent to Navy if permitted, missing from DNA WR RG 94, Adj. Gen. Letters Received, P 661

Sept. 12. To Murray Forbes, Hay for Lincoln, *Letters . . . of John Murray Forbes*, II, 76

Sept. 14. To Edwin M. Stanton, referring claim of Robert H. Allen of Louisiana, missing from DNA WR RG 107, Sec. of War Letters Received, P 169

c. Sept. 14. To Edwin M. Stanton, referring letter of George D. Blakey to Salmon P. Chase requesting pardon of two men sentenced to be shot, missing from *ibid.*, P 154

Sept. 15. To William A. Hammond, asking a report on case of Jason P. Risley, missing, but recorded DNA RG 130, White House Office, U.S. Army Court Martial Cases

Sept. 18. To Edward Bates, ordering pardon of Jacob Jacoby, ALS, Anderson Galleries Catalog, Feb. 26, 1917, No. 885

Sept. 18. To Edwin M. Stanton, on letter from Edmund T. Ryan and others to Lincoln, Sept. 7, 1863, "Submitted to the Sec. of War. A. LINCOLN," AES, DNA WR RG 94, U.S. Mil. Acad., 1864, No. 404

Sept. 23. To Edwin M. Stanton, on letter of Josiah H. Drummond to Lincoln, Sept. 19, 1863, recommending John M. Stevens, "Submitted to the Sec. of War. A. LINCOLN," AES, *ibid.*, No. 420

Sept. 24. To Edwin M. Stanton, Hay for Lincoln, referring telegram from R. Fisher to Lincoln, received Sept. 23, 1863, DNA WR RG 107, Sec. of War Letters Received, P 162

Sept. 25. To Edwin M. Stanton and Henry W. Halleck, on letter from Gen. Michael Corcoran to Lincoln, Aug. 17, 1863, asking transfer, "Submitted to the Sec. of War & Genl. in Chief A. LINCOLN," AES, DNA WR RG 153, Judge Adv. Gen., MM 682

Sept. 25. To William H. Seward, on letter from Oliver D. Filley to Lincoln, Aug. 24, 1863, recommending Julius Rapp, "Submitted to the Sec. of State. A. LINCOLN," AES, DNA FS RG 59, Appointments, Box 368

Sept. 25. To Edwin M. Stanton, referring letter of Stephen A. Hurlbut, introducing Henry T. Hurlbut, on dealer's list

Sept. 25. To Edwin M. Stanton on letter of Benjamin F. Hickman asking release of his son, a prisoner of war, July 15, 1863, "Submitted to the Sec. of War. A. LINCOLN," AES, IHi

Sept. 25. To Edwin M. Stanton, on letter of Augustus W. Bradford to Montgomery Blair, Sept. 11, 1863, protesting enlistment of Negroes, "Submitted to the Sec. of War. A. LINCOLN," AES, DNA WR RG 107, Sec. of War Letters Received, P 164

Sept. 25. To Edwin M. Stanton, referring letter from Charles B. Calvert concerning Col. Edward D. Baker, missing from *ibid.*, P 40, Irregular Book 5

Sept. 25. To Edwin M. Stanton and Henry W. Halleck, on letter of James H. Bristow to Lincoln, Sept. 22, 1863, concerning promotion of Col. Marc Mundy, "Submitted to the Sec. of War & General-in-Chief. A. LINCOLN," AES, IHi

Sept. 25. To Edwin M. Stanton and Henry W. Halleck, on letter of Benjamin F. Wade to Stanton, July 6, 1863, asking promotion of Col. William Wallace, "Submitted to Sec. of War & General in Chief. A. LINCOLN," AES, IHi

Sept. 26. To James Morton, "For Mr. James Morton. A. LINCOLN," copy, ISLA

c. Sept. 28. To Edwin M. Stanton, on letter of H. M. Johnson to Edward Bates, Sept. 28, 1863, recommending A. D. Bache Smead, "Submitted to the Sec. of War. A. LINCOLN," AES, DNA WR RG 94, U.S. Mil. Acad., 1864, No. 415

c. Oct. To Edwin M. Stanton, concerning Col. Eli F. Jennings, NE, mentioned, Samuel Galloway to Lincoln, Mar. 17, 1864, DLC-RTL

c. Oct. 1. To Ethan A. Hitchcock, Hay for Lincoln, ALS, DLC-Hitchcock Papers

c. Oct. 1. To Norman B. Judd, NE, concerning his son Frank R. Judd, mentioned, Judd to Lincoln, Oct. 17, 1863, DLC-RTL

Oct. 1. To George G. Meade, forgery, purportedly in Hay's handwriting signed by Lincoln, same text as genuine telegram printed under this date but without endorsement to Eckert, LS-P, ISLA

Oct. 1. To Edwin M. Stanton, on letter of Augustus W. Bradford to Lincoln, Sept. 28, 1863, about Negro enlistments, "Submitted to the Secretary of War. A. LINCOLN," AES, DLC-RTL

Oct. 1. To A. H. Terry, forgery, ALS, NN

Oct. 3. To Edward Bates, Stoddard for Lincoln, referring appeal from decision of Gen. Land Office and claim of Lewis Bollman, ALS, DNA RG 60, Papers of Atty. Gen., Box 112

c. Oct. 4. To John Brough, NE, mentioned, John Hay to Lincoln, Oct. 4, 1863, DLC-RTL

Oct. 6. To Gideon Welles, N. S. Howe for Lincoln, DNA WR NB RG 45, Exec. Letters, No. 7

Oct. 9. To Edwin M. Stanton, referring application of George H. Stuart for transportation to New Orleans for Mrs. Sarah A. Fulton, missing from DNA WR RG 107, Sec. of War Letters Received, P 170

Oct. 12. To Caleb Cushing, N. S. Howe for Lincoln, confirming interview, DLC-Cushing Papers

Oct. 13. To Edward Bates, on letter from A. Chester to Lincoln, Oct. 13, 1863, recommending Elisha W. Chester, "Submitted to the Attorney General. A. LINCOLN," AES, DNA RG 60, Appts., Georgia

Oct. 13. To John Brough, three purported telegrams not authenticated, Hertz, II, 914

Oct. 13. To Fred A. Payne, autograph (also Mrs. Lincoln's), ORB

Oct. 13. To Edwin M. Stanton, referring letters from George Opdyke and James A. Hamilton to Lincoln, Aug. 11, 1863, concerning release of William Aiken, missing from DNA WR RG 107, Sec. of War Letters Received, P 175

Oct. 14. To Edwin M. Stanton, concerning shipping horses to Cuba, "Submitted to the Secretary of War to go with the papers of Mr. Gordon [Codwin?] submitted recently by Hon. Truman Smith," *Hobbies*, Nov., 1938 (missing from DNA WR RG 107, Sec. of War Letters Received, P 173)

Oct. 14. To Edwin M. Stanton, referring order for dismissal of Charles H. Gaubert, missing from DNA WR RG 107, Sec. of War Letters Received, P 186

Oct. 16. To James O. Brown, LS, Am. Art Assn. Anderson Galleries Catalog 4190, Oct. 15-16, 1935, No. 282

Oct. 19. To Montgomery C. Meigs, referring recommendations of Lt. A. T. Drake, missing from DNA WR RG 92, Q.M. Gen., P 311, S 604

Oct. 19. To Edwin M. Stanton, referring testimonials concerning Capt. Dan. H. Harkins, missing from DNA WR RG 107, Sec. of War Letters Received, P 176

Oct. 19. To Edwin M. Stanton, on letter of Thomas E. Bramlette to Green Adams, Sept. 9, 1863, asking that Gen. W. E. Woodruff be placed in active service, "Submitted to the Sec. of War. A. LINCOLN," AES, IHi

Oct. 20. Memorandum of strength of Gen. Burnside's forces, compiled from his reports to Lincoln and Stanton, AD, Madigan, *A Catalogue of Lincolniana*, No. 48

Oct. 20. To Col. Rowland, NE, mentioned in Hay's *Diary*, Oct. 20, 1863

Oct. 22. To Miles O'Reilly, hoax telegram, N.Y. *Herald*, Oct. 23, 1863

Oct. 22. To Edwin M. Stanton, asking pass to Williamsburg, Va., for Mrs. Cavanaugh, missing from DNA WR RG 107, Sec. of War Letters Received, P 179

Oct. 22. To Edwin M. Stanton, on letter of Medical Inspector Dr. George W. Stipp to Col. John M. Cuyler asking to be assigned to the

Dept. of the Ohio, "Submitted to the Sec. of War. A. LINCOLN," AES, IHi

Oct. 24. To Ambrose E. Burnside, concerning Lee W. Long, forgery, ALS, NN

Oct. 24. Speech at Government Printing Office, mentioned, Washington *Morning Chronicle*, Oct. 25, 1863

Oct. 25. To Edwin M. Stanton, referring request for investigation of charges against Capt. Dennis McGee, missing from DNA WR RG 107, Sec. of War Letters Received, P 183

Oct. 26. To Commissioner of Internal Revenue, ALS, Bangs and Co. Catalog, Nov. 22, 1900, No. 286

Oct. 26. To George G. Meade, concerning Rhett Bannister, spurious, Hertz, II, 914

Oct. 27. To Edwin M. Stanton, on petition for appointment of Gen. Erastus B. Tyler, to command at Baltimore, "Submitted to the Sec. of War. A. LINCOLN," AES, DNA WR RG 107, Sec. of War Letters Received, P 193

Oct. 28. To Edwin M. Stanton, on card, "Submitted to the Secretary of War, A. LINCOLN," Parke-Bernet Catalog, Jan. 18, 1938, No. 245A

Oct. 28. To Edwin M. Stanton, on envelope of letter from William F. Barrett to Lincoln, Oct. 19, 1863, submitting petition for pardon of Malcom H. Branaugh, "Submitted to the War Department. A. LINCOLN," AES, DNA WR RG 107, Sec. of War Letters Received, P 191

Oct. 29. To Benson J. Lossing, Hay for Lincoln, forwarding photograph of Emancipation Proclamation, ALS, RPB

Oct. 29. To Edwin M. Stanton, on memo of Edward S. Moffat, "West-Point. Submitted to Sec. of War. A. LINCOLN," AES, DNA RG 94, U.S. Mil. Acad., 1864, No. 349

c. Oct. 31. To James Dixon, regarding credentials for H.R. members, NE, mentioned, Dixon to Lincoln, Nov. 14, 1863, DLC-RTL

c. Oct. 31. To John P. Hale, regarding credentials for H.R. members, NE, mentioned, Hale to Lincoln, Nov. 4, 1863, *ibid.*

Oct. 31. To Abram Wakeman, Hay for Lincoln, Tarbell (Appendix), 397

Nov. 3. To Edwin M. Stanton, Hay for Lincoln, referring letter from Harrison Leib to Lincoln, Nov. 2, 1863, DNA WR RG 107, Sec. of War Letters Received, P 196

Nov. 5. To James Mitchell, Nicolay for Lincoln, granting interview for this date, DLC-Nicolay Papers

Nov. 6. Appointment of George Harrington as acting secretary of Treasury, DS, Parke-Bernet Catalog, Jan. 22-24, 1941, No. 428

Nov. 7. To Joseph Holt, routine endorsements pardoning, approving, commuting, or remitting sentences imposed by courts-martial, DNA WR RG 153, Judge Advocate General, MM 280, 492, 681, 765, 793, 822, 834, 837, 901, 944, 949, 961, 993, 995, 996, 997, 1025

Nov. 7. To Major Rogers, spurious, Argosy Book Shop Catalog, Apr. 1942

Nov. 10. To Joseph Holt, Nicolay for Lincoln, referring papers in case of Michael Nash, DNA WR RG 153, Judge Adv. Gen., LL 506

Nov. 11. To Theodore T. S. Laidley, concerning "Wurtz Accelerator," NE, mentioned, Laidley to George D. Ramsay, Dec. 15, 1863, DLC-RTL

Nov. 14. To Edwin M. Stanton, on letter from Frank P. Blair, Jr., to "Dear Judge" (Montgomery Blair?) concerning appointment of Rufus K. Sanders, AES, on dealer's list, 1952

Nov. 17. To Gideon Welles, on blank paper, "Submitted to the Secretary of the Navy. A. LINCOLN," AES, NHi

c. Nov. 18. Note that William H. Johnson will accompany him to Gettysburg, Madigan Catalog, 1937, No. 146

c. Nov. 21. To Edward Bates, Hay for Lincoln, referring letter of John Dougherty to Lincoln, Nov. 3, 1863, asking pardon of Newton F. Jones, AES, DNA RG 204, U.S. Pardon Atty., A 428

c. Dec. Endorsement concerning A. Chester, NE, mentioned, Chester to Lincoln, Dec. 8, 1864, DLC-RTL

Dec. 1. To John A. Dix, Hay for Lincoln, in reply to Gen. John A. Dix to Lincoln, Nov. 23, 1863, expressing regrets that illness prevents his writing a communication to be read at the breaking of ground for the Union Pacific Railroad on Dec. 1 or 2, 1863, ALS, RPB

Dec. 1. To Edwin M. Stanton, referring letter of Curtin to Lincoln enclosing request of Capt. W. H. Weaver that proceedings against him be suspended, missing from DNA WR RG 107, Sec. of War Letters Received, P 212

c. Dec. 1. To Edwin M. Stanton, referring petition of Richard M. Corwine for reconsideration of case of E. A. Smith, missing from ibid., P 208

Dec. 9. To Joseph Holt, Hay for Lincoln, asking suspension of sentence in court-martial cases, Tarbell (Appendix), 403

Dec. 11. To Edward Bates, Hay for Lincoln, ordering pardon of Josiah M. Sargent, DNA RG 204, U.S. Pardon Atty., A 495

Dec. 11. Endorsement on medical report of Dr. Andrew Thompson, Nov. 16, 1863, "Let George O. Hale, Sergt. in 8th N.Y. Cavalry be discharged. A. LINCOLN," copy, ISLA

Dec. 12. To Edwin M. Stanton, referring letter of Brutus J. Clay for release of David J. Pendleton, missing from DNA WR RG 107, Sec. of War Letters Received, P 216

Dec. 14. To Joseph Holt, Hay for Lincoln, suspending execution of Private William Gibson, DNA WR RG 153, Judge Adv. Gen., MM 1199

c. Dec. 14. To Edwin M. Stanton, referring letter of Brutus J. Clay that Mrs. Robertson be allowed to go South, missing from DNA WR RG 107, Sec. of War Letters Received, P 218

c. Dec. 14. To Edwin M. Stanton, referring request of David A. Sayel for pass for Mrs. Webb, missing from ibid., P 219

Dec. 15. To Edwin M. Stanton, on recommendations of Nelson L. Brakeman for chaplain, "Submitted to the Sec. of War. A. LINCOLN," AES, IHi

c. Dec. 15. To Edwin M. Stanton, secretary for Lincoln, referring request of LaFayette S. Foster that Surg. Gen. William A. Hammond be heard before removal from office, DNA WR RG 107, Sec. of War Letters Received, P 222

Dec. 15. To Edwin M. Stanton and Henry W. Halleck, on letter of Gen. Nathan Kimball to John P. Usher, Nov. 19, 1863, concerning promotion. "Submitted to the Sec. of War & General-in-chief. A. LINCOLN," AES, IHi

Dec. 15. To Edwin M. Stanton and Henry W. Halleck, referring papers, "Col. Isaac C. Pugh Submitted to the Sec. of War & General-in-Chief. A. LINCOLN," AES, IHi

Dec. 16. Endorsement on order postponing execution of Private John Kendall, forgery, AES, NN

Dec. 17. To Edward Bates, on envelope of case of D. Henry Burtinett (Burtnete) "Submitted to the Attorney General for report, A. LINCOLN," AES, DNA RG 204, U.S. Pardon Atty., A 496

Dec. 17. To Quincy A. Gillmore, concerning trunk for Mrs. John H. Kinsey, NE, mentioned, Gillmore to Lincoln, Dec. 26, 1863, DLC-RTL

Dec. 17. To William H. Seward, on letter from William H. Russell to Lincoln, Nov. 12, 1863, recommending Henry C. Hall, "Submitted to the Sec. of State. A. LINCOLN," AES, DNA FS RG 59, Appointments, Box 300

Dec. 17. To Edwin M. Stanton, referring case of George H. Hill, missing from DNA WR RG 107, Sec. of War Letters Received, P 230

Dec. 17. To Edwin M. Stanton, referring papers for discharge of John Baker, 138th Pa. Vols., missing from *ibid.*, P 231

Dec. 17. To Edwin M. Stanton, Nicolay for Lincoln, referring request of Mrs. Eliza Rompe to bring money out of Virginia, reply to be addressed to Sen. Lazarus W. Powell, ALS, *ibid.*, P 236

Dec. 17. To Edwin M. Stanton, NE, mentioned, Benjamin P. Moore, Jr., to Lincoln, Dec. 18, 1863, DLC-RTL

c. Dec. 18. Pass for Mr. and Mrs. Young, NE, mentioned in letter of John T. Stuart to wife, Dec. 20, 1863, IHi

Dec. 19. Invitation, printed, Mr. and Mrs. Lincoln at home, DLC-Lincoln, Personal

Dec. 20. To Edward Bates, Hay for Lincoln, asking return of letter from Philo F. Barnum, DNA RG 60, Papers of Atty. Gen., Appts., Connecticut

Dec. 22. Endorsement on letter from Gen. John A. Logan to Stanton, Oct. 29, 1863, concerning promotion of Col. M. M. Bane, Anderson Auction Co. Catalog 451, Apr. 17, 1906, No. 789

Dec. 22. Memorandum concerning request from members of Washington Territory Senate that "Gen. Alvord's place be given to Maj. Whittlesey," on dealer's list

Dec. 22. To Edwin M. Stanton, on letter of Clifford Nathan to William Whiting, asking commission for Samuel Gilman, Jr., "Submitted to the Sec. of War A. LINCOLN." AES, DLC-RTL

Dec. 22. To Edwin M. Stanton and Henry W. Halleck, on letter from Col. Joseph E. Hamblin to Lincoln, Nov. 15, 1863, asking appointment of Capt. William W. Tracy in the Regular Army, "Submitted to the Sec. of War & Genl-in-Chief. A. LINCOLN," AES, IHi

Dec. 24. To Edwin M. Stanton, on letter from James K. Thompson to John H. Rice, Dec. 18, 1863, "Submitted to the Secretary of War. A. LINCOLN," AES, DLC-Hitchcock Papers

Dec. 24. To Edwin M. Stanton and Henry W. Halleck, on envelope of recommendations for renomination of Gen. Edwin H. Stoughton: "Gov. Holbrook/W. M. Evarts/Hon. F. E. Woodbridge/Sen. Harris/ Sen. Dixon/Sen. Hale/Sen. Collamer/Sen. Foote/Gen. Heintzel-

man./Submitted to the Sec. of War & General in Chief. A. LINCOLN,"
AES, owned by Dale Carnegie, New York City

c. Dec. 26. To Edwin M. Stanton, Hay for Lincoln, referring petitions
from Indiana that soldiers be allowed to convalesce at home, missing
from DNA WR RG 107, Sec. of War Letters Received, P 245

Dec. 29. To Edward Bates, Nicolay for Lincoln, referring petition to
Lincoln from Henry Schuyler and others, Nov. 30, 1863, for pardon
of Erhart Hagen, DNA RG 204, U.S. Pardon Atty., A 502

Dec. 29. To Edwin M. Stanton and Henry W. Halleck, on letter of
Andrew G. Curtin to Lincoln, Nov. 21, 1863, asking promotion of
Col. John R. Brooke, "Submitted to the Sec of War and General in
Chief. A LINCOLN," AES, owned by Gordon A. Block, Philadelphia

Dec. 29. To Edwin M. Stanton, Nicolay for Lincoln, asking usual notice to officers that president will receive them on New Year's Day,
DNA WR RG 94, Adj. Gen. Letters Received, P 1020

Dec. 30. To Edwin M. Stanton, NE, mentioned, Stanton to Lincoln,
Dec. 30, 1863, concerning John N. King, DLC-RTL

Dec. 31. To Joseph K. Barnes, concerning vacancy for hospital chaplain, Anderson Galleries Catalog 2167, May 3, 1927, No. 213

Dec. 31. To Edwin M. Stanton, referring resolutions of legislature of
New Mexico, Jan. 26 and 29, 1863, thanking California and Colorado
troops and Gen. James H. Carleton, and asking authority to raise
their own troops, missing from DNA WR RG 107, Sec. of War Letters
Received, P 257-58

Dec. 31. Remarks to Minister from Sweden and Norway, mentioned,
Washington *Daily Morning Chronicle*, Jan. 1, 1864

1864

c. ——. Note stating that Mrs. Emily Todd Helm was probably at Lexington, Ky., Anderson Galleries Catalog 2065, Apr. 26, 1926, No. 205

——?. Pass for Olivia S. Edmunds, NE, mentioned, Joseph A. Gilmore
to Lincoln, Jan. 24, 1865, DLC-RTL

——. To William P. Fessenden, concerning appointment of Lewis C.
Gunn and Frank Soulé, purported by John Conness in Rice, ed.,
Reminiscences, 570

c. ——. Business card announcing return to law practice, forgery, PHi

c. ——. To Gideon Welles, concerning T. T. Woods, NE, mentioned,
Augustus Brandegee to Lincoln, July 20, 1864

Jan. 1. To "Mr. Groceryman," spurious, N.Y. [*Journal of*] *Commerce*,
July 20, 1895

Jan. 2. To Salmon P. Chase, Nicolay for Lincoln, requesting report on
investigation of Branch Mint at San Francisco, DNA FI RG 56, Letters from Exec. Officers, Series AB, I, 1

Jan. 5. To Horace G. Babcock, sending autograph, LS, Stan. V. Henkels
Catalog 1430, Apr. 24, 1929, No. 15

Jan. 5. Endorsement on letter, "Let John L. Harlo, now a prisoner at
Camp Douglas, take the oath of allegiance, be discharged and go to
California with his brother. A. LINCOLN," copy, ISLA

Jan. 7. To Edwin M. Stanton and Joseph G. Totten, on recommendation
for appointment of William J. Volkmar, "Submitted to Sec. of War

& Chief of Engineer Bureau. A. LINCOLN," AES, DNA WR RG 94, U.S. Mil. Acad., 1864, No. 175

Jan. 8. To James A. Hardie (?), Hay for Lincoln, concerning Lieut. Edward King, DNA WR RG 153, Judge Adv. Gen., MM 1182

Jan. 9. To Edwin M. Stanton, referring telegram from Thomas Carney on raising a cavalry regiment, missing from DNA WR RG 107, Sec. of War Letters Received, P 11

Jan. 9. To Edwin M. Stanton, referring letter of Silas E. Burrows to Lincoln, Dec. 31, 1863, "Respectfully referred by the President to the Honorable Secretary of War. A. LINCOLN," OR, II, VI, 801

Jan. 10. To Edwin M. Stanton, Nicolay for Lincoln, referring letter of Franklin Kasmire to Lincoln, Jan. 7, 1864, DNA WR RG 107, Personnel Appts., Box 35

c. Jan. 11. To Joseph Holt, copied in court-martial record of Edgar Burroughs, "This case is obsolete by the death of the Convict," missing from DNA WR RG 153, Judge Adv. Gen., MM 1200

Jan. 11. To Edwin M. Stanton, on letter of John T. Flynn to Lincoln, requesting pass to City Point, "Submitted to Sec. of War. A. LINCOLN," AES, NHi

Jan. 12. To Edwin M. Stanton, referring letter of C. Ballance, missing from DNA WR RG 107, Sec. of War Letters Received, P 978

Jan. 12. To Edwin M. Stanton and Henry W. Halleck, on recommendation of Julian M. Sturtevant and others to Lincoln, Dec. 29, 1863, that Charles E. Lippincott be made a brigadier general, "Submitted to the Sec. of War & General-in-chief. A. LINCOLN," AES, RPB

Jan. 12. To Edwin M. Stanton and Henry W. Halleck, on request of Mrs. A. H. Hoge to Lyman Trumbull, Jan. 4, 1864, for promotion of son George B. Hoge, "Submitted to the Sec. of War & Genl.-in-Chief. A. LINCOLN," AES, IHi

Jan. 13. To Edwin M. Stanton, referring letter concerning Kent Weems, missing from DNA WR RG 107, Sec. of War Letters Received, P 22

Jan. 15. To Edward Bates, Nicolay for Lincoln, requesting "nomination of Mr. Kerr to be Deputy Solicitor of the Court of Claims," ALS, DNA RG 60, Papers of Atty. Gen., Box 116

Jan. 15. To James W. Grimes, mentioned, Grimes to Lincoln, Jan. 20, 1864, and referred to Stanton by Lincoln, Jan. 21, 1864

Jan. 15. To Edwin M. Stanton and Henry W. Halleck, on recommendation for promotion of Colonels Joseph Snider and Thomas M. Harris, "Submitted to the Sec. of War & Gen-in-Chief. A. LINCOLN," AES, RPB

Jan. 15. To Edwin M. Stanton, on application of Arthur Bryant, "Submitted to Sec. of War. A. LINCOLN," AES, DNA WR RG 94, U.S. Mil. Acad., 1864, No. 475

Jan. 16. To W. R. Powell, LS, Anderson Galleries Catalog 1786, Dec. 17, 1923, No. 55

Jan. 17. To Mrs. James L. Hirsch, probably spurious, Union Art Galleries Catalog 25, May 9, 1934, No. 148

Jan. 18. To Edwin M. Stanton, referring request of Green C. Smith that Mrs. Blanton Duncan be permitted to join her father-in-law in England, missing from DNA WR RG 107, Sec. of War Letters Received, P 26

Jan. 19. To John A. Dix, ordering arrest of persons "concerned in defrauding recruits of their bounty or doing any other act or thing contrary to the rules of service or the laws of war," Samuel T. Freeman & Co. Catalog, July 13-14, 1942, No. 551

Jan. 20. To H. J. Alvord, Nicolay for Lincoln, expressing "thanks to Mr. Clark and yourself for the present of White fish," *Lincoln Herald*, June, 1946, p. 37

Jan. 20. To Edward Bates, Nicolay for Lincoln, returning a paper on the Western Branch of the Union Pacific Railroad, ALS, DNA RG 60, Papers of Atty. Gen., Box 116

Jan. 20. To William H. Seward, on recommendation of J. P. M. Epping, "Submitted to the Sec. of State. A. LINCOLN," AES, DNA FS RG 59, Appointments, Box 280

Jan. 21. To Salmon P. Chase, Nicolay for Lincoln, enclosing recommendations of E. A. Rollins, DNA FI RG 56, Letters from Exec. Officers, Series AB, I, 3

Jan. 21. To Joseph Holt, on court-martial record of William Grantsyn "Sentence of the court commuted to forfeiture of pay proper for a period of six months from Sept. 1st 1863. A. LINCOLN," ES, DNA WR RG 153, Judge Adv. Gen., MM 782

Jan. 21. To Edwin M. Stanton, on letter of James W. Grimes, Jan. 20, 1864, concerning military promotions, "Submitted to the Sec. of War for further information. A. LINCOLN," AES, NHi

Jan. 21. To Edwin M. Stanton and Henry W. Halleck, on recommendation for promotion of Col. William H. Graves by Gen. Nathan Kimball, Nov. 19, 1863, "Submitted to the Sec. of War & Genl. in-chief. A. LINCOLN," AES, IHi

c. Jan. 25. To John L. Pendleton, requesting pass, NE, mentioned, Pendleton to Lincoln, Jan. 25, 1865, DLC-RTL

Jan. 25. Endorsement refusing release of a prisoner, without more information, ES, Am. Art Assn. Anderson Galleries Catalog 3854, Oct. 20, 1930, No. 155

Jan. 27. To Salmon P. Chase, suggesting that proof sheets of new rules be looked over carefully, ALS, Anderson Galleries Catalog 2086, Oct. 19-20, 1926, No. 513

Jan. 28. To Edwin M. Stanton, referring letter of William M. Fishback concerning G. T. Epperson and Arnold, late officers in rebel army, missing from DNA WR RG 107, Sec. of War Letters Received, P 102

Jan. 30. To J. Connors (Conness?), Anderson Auction Co. Catalog, Dec. 7, 1904, No. 292

Jan. 30. To Joseph Holt, Nicolay for Lincoln, referring petition on behalf of John S. Lounsberry, DNA WR RG 153, Judge Adv. Gen., LL 334

Feb. —. To Hiram Barney, NE, mentioned, John Dolan to Lincoln, Sept. 25, 1864, DLC-RTL

c. Feb. Passes for Mrs. Emily H. Tubman and Miss Cornelia B. Polk, NE, mentioned, A. G. Hodges to Lincoln, July 19, 1864, DLC-RTL

c. Feb. Pass for Mrs. E. W. Easby Smith, NE, mentioned, Mrs. Smith to Lincoln, Dec. 8, 1864

Feb. 3. To Edwin M. Stanton, concerning case of Col. George P. Ihrie, Nicolay for Lincoln, referring letter of J. Richard Barret to Lincoln, Jan. 30, 1864, DNA WR RG 107, Sec. of War Letters Received, P 333

c. Feb. 4. To Mrs. Goddard, Mrs. Lincoln for "The President & Mrs. Lincoln," invitation to dinner on Feb. 4, 1864, ORB

Feb. 4. To Edwin M. Stanton, referring requests of Rev. Mr. Bitting and Andrew Jamisson of Alexandria, Va., for restoration of Baptist church used as hospital, missing from DNA WR RG 107, Sec. of War Letters Received, P 79 and 98

Feb. 4. To Edwin M. Stanton, referring request of Francis W. Kellogg for release of Henry J. Weit at Rock Island, Ill., missing from *ibid.*, P 51

Feb. 5. To Edward Bates, Nicolay for Lincoln, forwarding nomination of Edward H. Durell, returned by Senate, Feb. 3, 1864, DNA RG 60, Papers of Atty. Gen., Box 122

Feb. 5. To Edwin M. Stanton and Henry W. Halleck, on envelope, "Capt. James Thompson/Submitted to the Sec. of War and General-in-Chief. A. LINCOLN," AES, IHi

Feb. 5. To Benjamin F. Wade, NE, mentioned, Wade to Lincoln, Feb. 6, 1864, concerning time of committee meeting, DLC-RTL

Feb. 6. To Benjamin F. Butler, telegram ordering suspension of execution of George M. Sullivan alias Michael Gardiner, missing from DNA WR RG 153, Judge Adv. Gen., MM 1223

Feb. 7. To Edwin M. Stanton, referring papers in claim of Mrs. J. M. Williamson, Helena, Ark., missing from DNA WR RG 107, Sec. of War Letters Received, P 1252

Feb. 8. To Joseph Holt, on court-martial record of John Carter, "Sentence commuted in this case to confinement during the war. A. LINCOLN," AES, DNA WR RG 153, Judge Adv. Gen., MM 961

Feb. 8. To John P. Usher, NE, Nicolay for Lincoln, mentioned, Usher to Lincoln, Feb. 9, 1864, DLC-RTL

Feb. 8. To Edwin M. Stanton, ordering transportation to Cincinnati for Sophia Johnson, LS, Parke-Bernet Catalog 63, Nov. 16-17, 1938, No. 185

Feb. 8. To Edwin M. Stanton, referring application of Mrs. Payne, Alexandria, Va., for release of her son, missing from DNA WR RG 107, Sec. of War Letters Received, P 57

Feb. 9. To Edward Bates, on letter of George S. Gideon to John P. Usher, Feb. 6, 1864, "Submitted to the Attorney General. A. LINCOLN," AES, DNA GE RG 60, Papers of Atty. Gen., Segregated Lincoln Material

Feb. 9. To Joseph Holt, of sixty-two court-martial cases reviewed this date, fifty endorsed by Lincoln pardoning, approving, remitting, or commuting sentences, DNA WR RG 153, Judge Adv. Gen., LL 296, 832, 866; MM 298, 668, 775, 777, 797, 818, 832, 841, 856, 860, 918, 933, 937, 939, 952, 1001, 1006, 1009, 1013, 1026, 1029, 1030, 1032, 1043, 1058, 1067 (2 cases), 1132, 1136, 1148, 1151, 1173, 1174, 1183, 1198, 1203, 1204 (*see also* 1206), 1205, 1215, 1237; NN 895, 901, 909, 1003, 1006, 1029; and DNA RG 130, White House Office, Army Court-Martial Cases (Luther Dart)

Feb. 10. To Edward Bates, Nicolay for Lincoln, referring petition for pardon of Amos Burton, DNA RG 204, U.S. Pardon Atty., A 510

Feb. 10. Endorsement, clipped from attendant papers, "Recom. of Gen. Burnside approved & ordered. A. LINCOLN," AES, InFtwL

Feb. 10. To Joseph Holt, in addition to three items printed under this date, thirty-two court-martial cases endorsed by Lincoln, pardoning, approving, commuting, or remitting sentences, DNA WR RG 153, Judge Adv. Gen., MM 219 (see also 991), 667, 672, 741, 742, 767, 802, 803, 825, 833, 881, 919, 924, 951, 989, 1000, 1020, 1021, 1035, 1056, 1062, 1128, 1138, 1208, 1215, 1219, 1228, 1232; NN 975, 993, 1008, 1009

Feb. 10. To Edwin M. Stanton, referring application of George H. Yeaman for pass for Mrs. Sarah Moorman, missing from DNA WR RG 107, Sec. of War Letters Received, P 100

Feb. 11. Reply to Committee of Reformed Presbyterian Synod on the subject "of amending the Constitution in favor of freedom. . . . The President promised to give the matter his earnest consideration." Washington Evening Star, Feb. 12, 1864

c. Feb. 13. Endorsement, on card from John Hogan thanking Lincoln for order concerning Methodist churches in Missouri, "To Rev. John Hogan, about Methodist Order," AE, DLC-RTL

Feb. 13. To Joseph Holt, Nicolay for Lincoln, setting conference on court-martial cases "on Monday morning," ALS, DLC-Holt Papers

Feb. 13. To Edwin M. Stanton and Henry W. Halleck, Nicolay for Lincoln, referring resolution of Kansas legislature that western counties in Missouri south of the Kansas River be attached to department of Gen. Samuel R. Curtis, DNA WR RG 107, Sec. of War Letters Received, P 74

Feb. 13. To Edwin M. Stanton and Henry W. Halleck, on letter of B. J. Bettelheim to Lincoln, Feb. 8, 1864, asking appointment as surgeon, "Submitted to the Sec. of War & General-in-Chief A. LINCOLN," AES, IHi

Feb. 15. To Joseph Holt, forty-eight court-martial cases endorsed by Lincoln on this date, pardoning, commuting, remitting, or approving sentences, DNA WR RG 153, Judge Adv. Gen., KK 142; LL 322; MM 189 (8 cases), 396, 397, 398, 486, 735, 762, 794, 888, 904, 921, 941, 978, 998, 1002, 1008, 1012, 1017, 1023, 1024, 1036, 1054, 1065, 1076, 1086, 1131, 1185 (2 cases), 1197, 1213, 1234; NN 111, 547, 840, 841 (2 cases), 989, 1082; OO 42

Feb. 15. To James E. Murdoch, Nicolay for Lincoln, requesting enclosed poem, "Am I For Peace? Yes!" to be read by Murdoch at benefit for U.S. Sanitary Commission that evening. Patriotism in Poetry and Prose . . . from Lectures and Patriotic Readings by James E. Murdoch. . . . (1865), 34-35

Feb. 17. To Joseph Holt, on court-martial record of C. J. Ham, "Sentenced commuted to imprisonment during the war, as recommended by Gen. Schofield. A. LINCOLN," AES, ibid., MM 1216

Feb. 17. Endorsement, concerning A. M. Hughes, Jr., "As a boon to Governor [Andrew] Johnson, let this young man take the oath of December 8, and be discharged. A. LINCOLN," Century Magazine, Dec. 1895, p. 255

Feb. 17. To Edwin M. Stanton and Henry W. Halleck, on letter of Samuel R. Mott to Gordon N. Mott, asking promotion to brigadier general, "Submitted to the Sec. of War & Genl.-in-Chief. A. LINCOLN," AES, IHi

Feb. 18. To Edward Bates, Nicolay for Lincoln, referring request of E. C. Larned and Thomas Drummond to Lincoln, Feb. 8, 1864, for pardon of Michael Quinlin, DNA RG 204, U.S. Pardon Atty., A 517

Feb. 18. To Edward Bates, Nicolay for Lincoln, referring request of Ira Harris to Lincoln, Feb. 10, 1864, for pardon of Robert Little, *ibid.*, A 515

Feb. 18. To Joseph Holt, on court-martial record of Thornton Smith revoking order of dismissal, DNA RG 130, White House Office, Army Court-Martial Cases

Feb. 19. To Joseph Holt, on court martial record of Floyd Jackson sentenced to be shot, "Sentence disapproved A LINCOLN," AES, DNA WR RG 153, Judge Adv. Gen., MM 791

Feb. 19. To Edwin M. Stanton, referring letter of R. Johnson and petition of Mrs. Henkle and daughter to accompany Rev. Dr. Henkle to the South, missing from DNA WR RG 107, Sec. of War Letters Received, P 87

Feb. 20. Endorsement, on telegram of Robert T. Lincoln to Larz Anderson, "Let this go by Telegraph. A. LINCOLN," AES, RPB

Feb. 22. Endorsement on letter of John A. Andrew concerning raising a regiment of colored troops, William D. Morley Catalog, Oct. 13, 1944, No. 280

Feb. 22. To Edward R. S. Canby, Nicolay for Lincoln, transmitting papers of Priv. Robert Babbett, LS, DNA WR RG 107, Sec. of War Letters Received, P 96

c. Feb. 22. To George G. Meade, NE, mentioned in telegram from Meade, Feb. 22, 1864, concerning parole of Benjamin Van Horn, DNA WR RG 153, Judge Adv. Gen., NN 1103

Feb. 22. To Edwin M. Stanton, on letter of Thomas L. Price asking release of nephew, "Submitted to the Sec. of War. A. LINCOLN," Estate of Gabriel Wells Catalog 4, No. 123

Feb. 22. To Edwin M. Stanton, on recommendation by Richard Yates and others to Lincoln, Feb. 11, 1864, that William O. Jones be appointed paymaster, "Submitted to the Sec. of War. A. LINCOLN." AES, IHi

Feb. 22. To Edwin M. Stanton, Nicolay for Lincoln, referring letter of John Brough to Lincoln, Feb. 6, 1864, protesting promotion of Col. Fuller, DNA WR RG 107, Sec. of War Letters Received, P 105

Feb. 22. To Edwin M. Stanton and Henry W. Halleck, on letter of John A. Andrew concerning promotion of Gen. George L. Andrews, "Submitted to the Sec. of War & General-in-Chief. A. LINCOLN," AES, owned by Frederick M. Dearborn, New York City

Feb. 23. To Joseph Holt, Nicolay for Lincoln, referring papers of George C. Odell for report, DNA WR RG 153, Judge Adv. Gen., LL 855

Feb. 24. To Edwin M. Stanton, referring letter of Gen. Henry W. Slocum, Dec. 26, 1863, AES, Carnegie Book Shop Catalog 142, No. 252

c. Feb. 24. To John P. Usher, on application of Henry DePuy to Lincoln, Feb. 24, 1864, "Submitted to the Sec. of Interior. A. LINCOLN," AES, DNA NR RG 48, Applications, Surveyor General, Idaho, Box 1264

Feb. 26. To Edwin M. Stanton, returning War Dept. letter of Feb. 19, 1864, concerning Capt. G. T. Epperson, rebel deserter, and Arnold, who desires his company mustered, missing from DNA WR RG 107, Sec. of War Letters Received, P 103

Feb. 26. To Edwin M. Stanton, referring application of Gen. Benjamin S. Roberts to go on active duty, missing from *ibid.*, P 121

Feb. 29. To Joseph Holt, setting aside order dismissing Surgeon William H. Thayer, missing from DNA WR RG 153, Judge Adv. Gen., MM 1128, and from *ibid.*, RG 107, Sec. of War Letters Received, P 104

c. Mar. To Salmon P. Chase, NE, mentioned, J. P. M. Epping to Lincoln, Mar. 17, 1864, DLC-RTL

Mar. 1. Endorsement on letter from Chase introducing "Mr. Metcalf" who wishes to paint Lincoln's portrait, "Nix," AE, DLC-RTL

Mar. 1. To Edwin M. Stanton, Nicolay for Lincoln, referring letter from Gen. Edward O. C. Ord to Lincoln, Feb. 19, 1864, asking to be transferred from New Orleans, DNA WR RG 107, Sec. of War Letters Received, P 161

Mar. 2. To Edwin M. Stanton, Nicolay for Lincoln, concerning insurrection in Edgar Co., Ill., DLC-RTL

Mar. 2. To Edwin M. Stanton and Henry W. Halleck, on letter from Mrs. A. H. Hoge asking appointment of her son as brigadier, "Submitted to the Sec. of War & Genl.-in-Chief. A. LINCOLN," AES, owned by Katharine Matthies, Seymour, Conn.

Mar. 2. To Gideon Welles, "Submitted to the Secretary of the Navy. A. LINCOLN," AES, C. F. Libbie & Co. Catalog, May 12, 1909, No. 148

Mar. 3. To Edward Bates, Nicolay for Lincoln, referring petition of Charles A. Eldridge to Lincoln, Feb. 26, 1864, for pardon of David K. Staples, DNA RG 204, U.S. Pardon Atty., A 520

Mar. 3. To Edward Bates, Nicolay for Lincoln, referring request of James Grant and others to Lincoln, Feb. 22, 1864, for pardon of John Morris alias Calahan, *ibid.*, A 521

Mar. 3. To Edwin M. Stanton, Nicolay for Lincoln, referring letter from Joel Parker to Lincoln, Feb. 23, 1864, DNA WR RG 107, Sec. of War Letters Received, P 252

c. Mar. 4. Proclamation concerning Texas elections, spurious, Hertz, II, 920

Mar. 4. To Edwin M. Stanton, referring offer of John C. Swift and John H. Shoemaker of $200 per month for castoff clothing from Army of Potomac, missing from DNA WR RG 107, Sec. of War Letters Received, P 311

Mar. 5. To Edward Bates, Nicolay for Lincoln, referring petition of Joseph W. White to Lincoln, Mar. 4, 1864, on behalf of John Racey, Andrew Coyle and Samuel McFarren, DNA RG 204, U.S. Pardon Atty., A 552

Mar. 7. To Gideon Welles, on letter from Reverdy Johnson concerning promotion of A. G. Stembel, "Submitted to the Sec. of the Navy. A. LINCOLN," Stan. V. Henkels Catalog 1328, May 25, 1923, No. 269

Mar. 7. To Gideon Welles, endorsement clipped, "Submitted to the Sec. of Navy. A. LINCOLN," AES, on dealer's list.

Mar. 8. To Salmon P. Chase, Nicolay for Lincoln, requesting return of confirmation of Henry Denlinger as collector of internal revenue for Oregon, LS, DNA Fl RG 56, Letters from Exec. Officers, Series AB, I, 8

Mar. 9 To Edwin M. Stanton, Nicolay for Lincoln, referring resolutions of Calif. legislature asking exemption from order prohibiting export of munitions, to permit blasting, DNA WR RG 107, Sec. of War Letters Received, P 128

Mar. 9. To Edwin M. Stanton, referring offer of John C. Swift and H. C. Moore for $200 per month for castoff clothing of Grant's army, missing from *ibid.*, P 134

Mar. 10. To Edward Bates, Nicolay for Lincoln, concerning nomination of Charles Gilpin as U.S. district attorney, ALS, DNA RG 60, Papers of Atty. Gen., Box 120

Mar. 10. To Edward Bates, Nicolay for Lincoln, referring letter of E. A. Layton to Lincoln, Mar. 4, 1864, asking pardon of Charles Eddy and C. W. French alias J. W. Manning. DNA WR RG 204, U.S. Pardon Atty., A 524

Mar. 10. To Edward Bates, on petition for pardon of James B. Shehan, "Submitted to the Attorney General. A. LINCOLN," AES, *ibid.*, A 523

Mar. 10. To Edwin M. Stanton, asking return of Senate resolution confirming Capt. Granville E. Johnson as major and aide-de-camp, with enclosure, missing from DNA WR RG 107, Sec. of War Letters Received, P 62, Irregular Book

Mar. 10. To Edwin M. Stanton, Nicolay for Lincoln, requesting papers of Lt. Henry A. Sargent, ALS, *ibid.*, P 173

Mar. 11. To William H. Seward, Nicolay for Lincoln, referring letter of Joseph L. Stiger to Lincoln, concerning his pamphlet on slavery, DNA FS RG 59, Appointments, Box 388

Mar. 11. To Edwin M. Stanton, referring letter of Silas Cargon concerning pay lost by court-martial, missing from DNA WR RG 107, Sec. of War Letters Received, P 158

Mar. 11. To Edwin M. Stanton, Nicolay for Lincoln, referring letter of Granville Moody to Lincoln, requesting field assignment for Gen. James S. Negley, *ibid.*, P 478

Mar. 11. To John P. Usher, Nicolay for Lincoln, requesting nomination for reappointment of Benjamin M. Trumbull, DNA NR RG 48, Appts., Land Office, Natitoches, La., Box 35

Mar. 12. To Edwin M. Stanton, Nicolay for Lincoln, referring St. Louis citizens' petition for appointment of John T. Witham to board of awarders of compensation for slaves enlisted in U.S. forces, DNA WR RG 107, Sec. of War Letters Received, P 979

Mar. 13. To Edwin M. Stanton, Nicolay for Lincoln, referring Pittsburgh citizens' petition for assignment of Gen. James S. Negley to field command, *ibid.*, P 478

Mar. 16. To Henry T. Blow, sending autograph "requested for Mr Dreer," ALS, CSmH

Mar. 16. Endorsement on letter from Gov. Andrew G. Curtin concerning "Captain Thomas," AES, Morley's Catalog, Apr. 28, 1944, No. 212

Mar. 17. Endorsement, on letter of Gen. William T. Sherman to Stanton, Jan. 26, 1864, recommending Col. J. D. Brum, "Excellent recommendations. A. LINCOLN," copy, ISLA

Mar. 17. To Edwin M. Stanton, on recommendation that Patrick H. Jones be appointed brigadier general, "Submitted to Sec. of War. A. LINCOLN," AES, RPB

Mar.' 18. To William H. Seward, on recommendation of Joseph A. Wright to Lincoln, Mar. 16, 1864, that William A. Patton be made bearer of dispatches to Europe, "Submitted to the Sec. of State. A. LINCOLN," copy, DLC-RTL

Mar. 19. To Edward Bates, Nicolay for Lincoln, referring papers transmitted by Gov. John Brough to Lincoln, Mar. 15, 1864, asking pardon for Louis (Lewis) Kirkman, DNA RG 204, U.S. Pardon Atty., A 525

Mar. 19. To Edwin M. Stanton, referring resignation of Capt. George W. Ford, missing from DNA WR RG 107, Sec. of War Letters Received, P 154

Mar. 19. To William B. Thomas, sending autograph "for the Sanitary Fair," ALS, Anderson Galleries Catalog 2193, Nov. 15, 1927, No. 277

Mar. 19. To O. B. Yoder, sending autograph, ALS, owned by George A. Ball, Muncie, Ind.

Mar. 21. To Edwin M. Stanton, Nicolay for Lincoln, referring letter of Andrew G. Curtin to Lincoln, Mar. 18, 1864, concerning promotions, DNA WR RG 107, Sec. of War Letters Received, P 251

Mar. 21. To Edwin M. Stanton, Nicolay for Lincoln, referring letter of R. Clay Crawford to Lincoln, Mar. 18, 1864, reporting conspiracy in Kentucky, *ibid.*, P 498½

Mar. 21. To Edwin M. Stanton, Nicolay for Lincoln, referring recommendations by citizens of Delaware Co., Ind., Mar. 7, 1864, of Thomas J. Brady, *ibid.*, Personnel Appts., Box 25

Mar. 22. To John Evans, Nicolay for Lincoln, that Colorado enabling act was signed Mar. 21, 1864, DNA WR RG 107, Presidential Telegrams, I, 14

Mar. 22. Pass for Mrs. Smith, Madigan, *The Autograph Album*, Dec., 1933, No. 177

Mar. 24. To Edward Bates, on letter of Lucian Anderson and others recommending R. K. Williams for judge, "Submitted to the Attorney General. A. LINCOLN," AES, F. H. Sweet Catalog 49, No. 88

Mar. 24. To Edwin M. Stanton, on envelope franked by Samuel G. Daily, "Submitted to the Sec. of War. A. LINCOLN," AES, owned by Mrs. Victor Jacobs, Dayton, Ohio

Mar. 24. To Edwin M. Stanton, on envelope marked "Hon. Daniel Morris," "Submitted to the Sec. of War. A. LINCOLN," AES, IHi

Mar. 25. To Joseph Holt, on report of case of Lieut. Henry M. Day to Lincoln, Mar. 4, 1864, "Recommendation of Judge Advocate General approved and ordered." ES, DNA RG 94, Colored Troops Division, AGO

Mar. 25. To Edwin M. Stanton, referring case of Enoch Hayner and others at Camp Chase with request for further papers, missing from DNA WR RG 107, Sec. of War Letters Received, P 182

Mar. 26. To Edwin M. Stanton, on letter of Andrew G. Curtin to Lincoln, Mar. 5, 1864, concerning promotion of Capt. C. M. Thomas and Thomas C. Sullivan, "Submitted to the Sec. of War. A. LINCOLN," AES, owned by Frederick M. Dearborn, New York City

Mar. 26. To Edwin M. Stanton, Hay for Lincoln, referring letter of Henry Connelly to Lincoln, Feb. 29, 1864, recommending Gen. James H. Carleton, DNA WR RG 108, H.Q.A., C 451

Mar. 26. To Edwin M. Stanton, Hay for Lincoln, referring letter of Mrs. J. M. McCombs to Lincoln, Mar. 16, 1864, protesting order prohibiting Rev. J. O. Stedman from preaching in Memphis, Tenn., DNA WR RG 107, Sec. of War Letters Received, P 170

Mar. 26. To John P. Usher, Hay for Lincoln, transmitting Senate resolution asking report of Committee of Emigration for 1863, ALS, DNA NR RG 48, Sec. of Interior, Patents & Misc., Box 57

Mar. 28. To James B. Fry, on letters of James M. Scovel and others concerning the "Johnson-Fry incident," Am. Autograph Shop Catalog, 1938, No. 143

Mar. 28. To Edwin M. Stanton, secretary for Lincoln, referring letter of Mrs. Joseph R. Hawley, requesting pass, DNA WR RG 107, Sec. of War Letters Received, P 202

Mar. 28. To Edwin M. Stanton, Nicolay for Lincoln, referring letter of Erastus B. Tyler to Lincoln, Mar. 20, 1864, transmitting report of Capt. Louis D. Watkins concerning depredations by colored troops, *ibid.*, P 297

Mar. 28. To Edwin M. Stanton, referring letter of Jesse K. Dubois concerning prisoners in Libby Prison, missing from *ibid.*, P 178

Mar. 28. To Edwin M. Stanton, referring letter from William H. Randall on behalf of William H. Pierce, prisoner in Richmond, missing from *ibid.*, P 179

Mar. 30. To Edwin M. Stanton, asking transfer of Asst. Surg. Charles C. Bombaugh, missing from *ibid.*, P 198

c. Mar. 31. Check to Dennis F. Hanks for $50, NE, mentioned, Hanks to Lincoln, Apr. 5, 1864, DLC-RTL

Apr. 1. To Edward Bates, Hay for Lincoln, referring letter from William Johnston to Lincoln, Mar. 18, 1864, recommending Robert Martin, DNA RG 60, Papers of Atty. Gen., Appts., Montana, Box 620

Apr. 1. To Edwin M. Stanton, on letter of Joseph Segar to Lincoln, Mar. 29, 1864, concerning Col. James T. Close, "Submitted to the Sec. of War. A. LINCOLN," AES, owned by Charles W. Olsen, Chicago, Ill.

Apr. 1. To Joseph Holt, on court-martial record of John S. Walter sentenced to five years at hard labor with pay to be sent to family, Gen. George G. Meade disapproving of pay being sent to family, "Sentence as modified by Gen. Meade approved. A. LINCOLN," AES, DNA WR RG 153, Judge Adv. Gen, MM 1333

Apr. 2. To Edward Bates, Hay for Lincoln, referring petition for pardon of Eli Burk, DNA RG 204, U.S. Pardon Atty., A 527

Apr. 3. Order for release of Ludwell Y. Browning, NE, mentioned in Orville H. Browning's *Diary*, Apr. 3, 1864

Apr. 4. To Edwin M. Stanton, Hay for Lincoln, referring application of Wells W. Leggett to Lincoln, Apr. 1, 1864, DNA WR RG 94, U.S. Mil. Acad., 1863, No. 105

Apr. 4. To Edwin M. Stanton, Nicolay for Lincoln, referring petition of Maryland Vols. to Lincoln, Mar. 31, 1864, to go home and vote, DNA WR RG 107, Sec. of War Letters Received, P 219

c. Apr. 4. To Edwin M. Stanton, referring request of E. M. Bruce for his wife to join him in Richmond, Va., missing from *ibid.*, P 866

Apr. 5. To John Brough, Hay for Lincoln, ordering pardon of soldiers in 12th Ohio, ALS, DNA WR RG 107, Pres. Telegrams, I, 19

Apr. 5. To William H. Seward, on letter from Zachariah Chandler to Lincoln, Apr. 4, 1864, recommending Albert J. Dezeyk, "Submitted to the Sec. of State. A. LINCOLN," AES, DNA FS RG 59, Appointments, Box 269

Apr. 7. To William Dennison, Nicolay for Lincoln, "The President thinks he cannot safely write that class of letters," DNA WR RG 107, Pres. Telegrams, I, 23

Apr. 8. Appointment of Ferdinand Andrews as Second Auditor during sickness of E. B. French, Stan. V. Henkels Catalog 1348, Mar. 14, 1924, No. 176

Apr. 8. To Salmon P. Chase, Nicolay for Lincoln, concerning order prohibiting export of salted provisions, copy, DNA FI RG 56, Letters from Exec. Officers, Series AB, I, 10

Apr. 9. To Edward R. S. Canby, Nicolay for Lincoln, asking for papers in case of Capt. George A. Wallace, DNA WR RG 107, Sec. of War Letters Received, P 240

Apr. 9. To Edwin M. Stanton, Nicolay for Lincoln, referring letter of Robert Y. Morris, Jr., to Lincoln, Apr. 8, 1864, offering to destroy railroad bridges in Virginia, DNA WR RG 108, H.Q.A., M 415, Box 69

Apr. 9. To Edwin M. Stanton, Nicolay for Lincoln, referring letter of Casado, Galwey & Teller to Lincoln, Apr. 6, 1864, asking permission to ship horses to Mexico, DNA WR RG 107, Sec. of War Letters Received, P 243

Apr. 11. To Joseph Holt, Hay for Lincoln, requesting papers in case of Lt. Jason D. Snell, DNA WR RG 153, Judge Adv. Gen., MM 129

Apr. 11. To Edwin M. Stanton, on telegram of Richard Yates to Col. J. S. Loomis requesting arms for Ill. Militia, "Submitted to the Sec. of War. A. LINCOLN," AES, NHi

Apr. 12. To Edward Bates, Nicolay for Lincoln, referring communication from Kirby Benedict to Lincoln, Jan. 10, 1864, protesting his rumored removal as judge in New Mexico, DNA RG 60, Papers of Atty. Gen., Box 116

Apr. 12. To Edwin M. Stanton, Nicolay for Lincoln, referring letters from George C. Carson & Co. to Lincoln, Mar. 30 and Apr. 7, 1864, requesting permission to ship coal to Cuba, DNA WR RG 107, Sec. of War Letters Received, P 242

Apr. 13. To Joseph Holt, Hay for Lincoln, making appointment to take up court-martial cases on Apr. 14, 1864, LS, DLC-Holt Papers

Apr. 13. To Lorenzo Thomas, Hay for Lincoln, concerning Alpheus Lewis, DLC-RTL

Apr. 14. To Ulysses S. Grant, forgery, ALS, NN

Apr. 14. To Joseph Holt. Of sixty-four court-martial cases reviewed by Lincoln in addition to the three printed under this date, thirty-seven bear routine endorsements in Lincoln's autograph approving, disapproving, mitigating, commuting, or pardoning, DNA WR RG 153, Judge Adv. Gen., MM 222, 269, 672, 680, 716, 864, 923, 940, 969, 970, 973, 982, 983, 1010, 1031, 1067, 1092, 1133, 1137, 1152, 1168, 1176, 1222, 1227, 1254, 1261, 1296, 1302, 1303, 1307, 1309, 1322; NN 1153, 1172, 1202, 1226, 3848 (formerly MM 1299)

Apr. 14. To Edwin M. Stanton, Nicolay for Lincoln, referring letter from John H. Morse to Lincoln, Mar. 31, 1864, enclosing Gen. Napoleon B. Buford's General Order, DNA WR RG 107, Sec. of War Letters Received, P 237

Apr. 14. To Edwin M. Stanton, on letter of "Miss C. N." asking discharge of "would be husband," "Hon. Sec. of War Send him to her, by all means," purported copy, InFtwL

Apr. 15. To Edwin M. Stanton, secretary for Lincoln, referring letter of L. H. Chandler to Lincoln, Apr. 15, 1864, stating that Mrs. E. B. Fitchett wishes her husband allowed to come home from South, DNA WR RG 107, Sec. of War Letters Received, P 238

Apr. 18. To Joseph Holt, on court-martial record of Capt. G. L. Turner dismissed for conduct unbecoming an officer, "Sentence remitted A. LINCOLN," AES, DNA WR RG 153, Judge Adv. Gen., MM 1338

Apr. 18. To Edwin M. Stanton, Nicolay for Lincoln, referring letters of George C. Carson & Co. to Lincoln, Apr. 16, 1864, about shipping coal to Cuba, DNA WR RG 107, Sec. of War Letters Received, P 244

Apr. 18. To Lorenzo Thomas, concerning release of James Cremin, missing from DNA WR RG 94, Adj. Gen. Letters Received, P 445

Apr. 18. To John P. Usher, Nicolay for Lincoln, requesting a new nomination for Josiah C. Redfield as receiver for Land Office, Humboldt, Kansas, LS, DNA NR RG 48, Applications, Gen. Land Office, Registers and Receivers, Kansas, Box 1279

Apr. 20. To Edwin M. Stanton, concerning appointment of John M. Wallace as paymaster, missing from DNA WR RG 107, Sec. of War Letters Received, P 288

Apr. 20. To Edwin M. Stanton, Nicolay for Lincoln, referring letter from Andrew G. Curtin to Lincoln, Apr. 13, 1864, transmitting Pennsylvania claims for damages, *ibid.*, P 290

Apr. 21. To Joseph Holt, among seventy-one court-martial cases reviewed by Lincoln this day, thirty-nine bear routine endorsements in Lincoln's autograph, remitting, commuting, approving, disapproving, or pardoning, DNA WR RG 153, Judge Adv. Gen., MM 219, 759, 766, 769, 890, 1024, 1028, 1212, 1253, 1274, 1300, 1319, 1326, 1331, 1332, 1340, 1347, 1352, 1357, 1375; NN 423, 626 (in IHi), 911, 1005, 1099, 1207, 1215, 1231, 1368 (4 cases), 1374, 1391, 1392, 1396, 1415, 1416, 1442

Apr. 21. To Lorenzo Thomas, suspending execution of Lorenzo Stewart and directing an examination by Dr. John P. Gray for sanity, missing from DNA WR RG 94, Adj. Gen. Letters Received, P 451

Apr. 22. Endorsement on letter from Franz Sigel, AES, Morley Catalog, Apr. 28, 1944, No. 213

Apr. 22. To Edwin M. Stanton, Nicolay for Lincoln, asking return of confirmation of Capt. Elisha H. Ludington, LS, DNA WR RG 107, Sec. of War Letters Received, P 255

Apr. 23. To Edwin M. Stanton, secretary for Lincoln, referring letter of Augustus L. Chetlain to Elihu B. Washburne, Apr. 14, 1864, reporting massacre at Fort Pillow, *ibid.*, P 259

Apr. 23. To Edwin M. Stanton, referring statement of damages to property of William Spence, missing from *ibid.*, P 254 with P 2420 EB 12

Apr. 25. To Joseph Holt, Nicolay for Lincoln, concerning impossibility of taking up court-martial cases on this day, ALS, DLC-Holt Papers

Apr. 26. To Joseph Holt, among fifty-one court-martial cases reviewed by Lincoln on this day, appear twenty-nine routine endorsements in Lincoln's autograph, commuting, remitting, approving, disapproving, or pardoning, DNA WR RG 153, Judge Adv. Gen., LL 1035; MM 744, 852, 943, 957, 971, 1014, 1019, 1038, 1289, 1301, 1324; NN 523, 1126, 1180, 1208, 1234, 1236, 1282, 1293, 1362, 1379, 1418, 1452, 1462, 1474, 1475, 1476, 1477

Apr. 26. To Edwin M. Stanton, referring letter from John W. Parker to Lincoln asking discharge of son Thomas M. Parker, missing from DNA WR RG 107, Sec. of War Letters Received, P 256

Apr. 26. To Lorenzo Thomas, Nicolay for Lincoln, ordering suspension of execution of James Gray, ALS, DNA WR RG 94, Adj. Gen. Letters Received, P 496

Apr. 27. To Joseph Holt, among thirty-six court-martial cases reviewed by Lincoln on this date, twenty routine endorsements in Lincoln's autograph, commuting, remitting, approving, disapproving, or pardoning, DNA WR RG 153, Judge Adv. Gen., LL 717, 1670; MM 219, 773, 959, 962, 977, 990, 1042, 1083, 1109, 1130, 1201, 1221, 1258, 1267, 1270; NN 1411, 1434, 1441

Apr. 27. To Edwin M. Stanton, referring application for reinstatement of Lieut. T. C. Owen, missing from DNA WR RG 107, Sec. of War Letters Received, P 275

Apr. 28. To Calvin Bates, spurious, Ralph O. Bates, *Billy and Dick from Andersonville . . . to the White House* (1910), 88

Apr. 28. To Edward Bates, Nicolay for Lincoln, referring petition for pardon of George W. McGill, DNA RG 204, U.S. Pardon Atty., A 533

Apr. 28. To Joseph P. Taylor, referring letter of Thomas O. Wallis concerning his losses, Apr. 18, 1864, missing from DNA WR RG 192, Comm. Gen. of Subsistence, L 8

Apr. 29. To Lorenzo Thomas, Nicolay for Lincoln, postponing execution of Thomas Cusick and James Gray, ALS, DNA WR RG 94, Adj. Gen. Letters Received, P 496

Apr. 29. To Lorenzo Thomas, Nicolay for Lincoln, referring letters of H. A. Brewster and George W. Ashburn on rebel activity in Union Place Hotel, N.Y., missing from *ibid.*, P 499

Apr. 30. To Edwin M. Stanton, referring letter of Mrs. Helen Revel to Lincoln, July 23, 1863, on kidnaping of her son Emile, missing from DNA WR RG 107, Sec. of War Letters Received, P 267

Apr. 30. To Edwin M. Stanton, referring letter of William H. Cole, missing from *ibid.*, P 266

May ?. Purported endorsement in J. L. Campbell's *Idaho: Six Months in the New Gold Diggings* (1864), "Mr. Campbell tells me personally he has done more for this country than any other man," owned by Thomas W. Streeter, Morristown, N.J.

May —. Endorsement, on recommendations of LaFayette Landon, "West Point—a good case," AE, DNA WR RG 94, U.S. Mil. Acad., 1864, No. 236

May 2. To Edward Bates, Nicolay for Lincoln, referring petition of citizens of Rochester, N.Y., Mar. 30, 1864, for restoration of citizenship to William Westcott, DNA RG 204, U.S. Pardon Atty., A 534

May 2. To Edwin M. Stanton, Nicolay for Lincoln, referring letter of C. B. Dungan to Lincoln, Apr. 29, 1864, DNA WR RG 108, H.Q. A., Box 67, D 186

May 3. To Edward Bates, on Senate resolution requesting copies of his opinions on rights of colored persons in U.S. service, "Submitted to the Attorney-General. A. LINCOLN," AES, DLC-RTL

May 3. To Edwin M. Stanton, Nicolay for Lincoln, referring case of Mrs. A. S. Hebron, DNA WR RG 107, Sec. of War Letters Received, P 269

May 3. To Edwin M. Stanton, Nicolay for Lincoln, referring request of Henry C. Jenks, for pass for wife and child to come from Virginia, *ibid.*, P 282

May 3. To Edwin M. Stanton, referring letter of Thomas M. Finney to Lincoln, Apr. 22, 1864, enclosing resolutions of Methodist Episcopal ministers protesting Bishop Edward R. Ames' order, missing from *ibid.*, P 283

May 4. Check to Franklin & Co., for $2.50, DS-P, ISLA

May 4. To Edwin M. Stanton, asking transportation for bearer to Tennessee and return, Am. Art Assn. Anderson Galleries Catalog 4180, May 8-9, 1935, No. 211

May 5. To William S. Rosecrans, Hay for Lincoln, telegram concerning day set for execution of Robert Louden, ALS, DNA WR RG 107, Pres. Telegrams, I, 46

May 5. To Lorenzo Thomas, Nicolay for Lincoln, requesting order issued to suspend execution of Thomas Cusick and James Gray, ALS, DNA WR RG 94, Adj. Gen. Letters Received, P 496

May 9. To William H. Seward, Nicolay for Lincoln, referring application of Francis G. Young to Lincoln, May 5, 1864, for consulship, DNA FS RG 59, Appointments, Box 407

May 10. To Albert G. Riddle, Nicolay for Lincoln, replying to Riddle's letter to Lincoln, Apr. 7, 1864, DLC-Nicolay Papers

May 10. To J. M. Wright, Nicolay for Lincoln, referring Wright to Joseph Holt concerning case of Priv. William H. Blake, ALS, DNA WR RG 153, Judge Adv. Gen., MM 1201

May 11. To Samuel Burnham, Nicolay for Lincoln, enclosing copy of reply of Joseph Henry, DLC-Nicolay Papers

May 11. To Joseph Holt, on court-martial record of Frank Gurley sentenced to death but recommended for commutation to five years in prison, "Recom. of Genl. Thomas approved & ordered April 21. 1864 A. LINCOLN." "Sentence Approved. May 11. 1864 A. LINCOLN This entry negated because made by mistake." AES, DNA WR RG 153, Judge Adv. Gen., MM 1326

May 13. To Edward Bates, on letter of Lyman Trumbull to Lincoln, May 11, 1864, asking about supposed vacancy to which Henry C. Caldwell was appointed, "Submitted to the Attorney General. A. LINCOLN," AES, DNA GE RG 60, Papers of Atty. Gen., Segregated Lincoln Material

May 13. To Joseph Holt, Nicolay for Lincoln, transmitting papers in case of Lt. Edward King, ALS, DNA WR RG 153, Judge Adv. Gen., MM 1182

c. May 18. Endorsement, on letter of Alexander Hamilton to Seward, May 18, 1864, protesting keeping Generals Ambrose E. Burnside and Franz Sigel in command, "Wisdom of Hamilton," AE, DLC-RTL

May 19. To Annie L. Ash, NE, mentioned, Miss Ash to Lincoln, Dec. 14, 1864, concerning brother, the late Capt. Joseph P. Ash, DLC-RTL

c. May 20. Endorsement, on envelope of recommendations for John H. Collamore, "West-Point To go with the papers of J. H. Collamore," AE, DNA WR RG 94, U.S. Mil. Acad., 1863, No. 225

May 20. To Edwin M. Stanton, requesting that he "ask Mr. Dana to call and see me before he starts to the front," The Collector, July, 1951

May 21. To Thomas T. Eckert, NE, mentioned in Nicolay and Hay MS. list: "Scott's Index: Lincoln to Eckert, May 21, 1864," IHi-Nicolay and Hay Papers

May 21. To Edwin M. Stanton, referring letter of E. C. Stanelsfield asking discharge of John H. Rice, missing from DNA WR RG 107, Sec. of War Letters Received, P 357

May 23. Order for release of Capt. Samuel Black, NE, mentioned in Orville H. Browning's Diary, May 23, 1864

May 23. To the Pacha of Egypt, appointment of Charles Hale as consul, copy, DNA FS RG 59, Credences, IV, 419

May 23. To Edwin M. Stanton, ordering release of Capt. W. White, NE, mentioned, Stanton to Lincoln, May 23, 1864, DLC-RTL

May 23. To Joshua Whitney, Hay for Lincoln, acknowledging receipt of a letter and enclosing Lincoln's photograph, ALS, RPB

May 24. To Edwin M. Stanton, on application of Francis D. Clark to Lincoln, May 18, 1864, "Submitted to the Secretary of War. A. LINCOLN," AES, IHi

May 25. Endorsement on a letter to Sen. James Harlan, AES, Morley Catalog, Oct. 13, 1944, No. 283

May 25. To Edwin M. Stanton, referring petition of J. R. Sypher concerning a claim, missing from DNA WR RG 107, Sec. of War Letters Received, P 313 with S 933, Mar. 1865

May 25. To Edwin M. Stanton, referring letter of Maj. Alexander Montgomery asking to be restored to duty, missing from ibid., P 355 with C 574, Nov. 1868

May 26. Pass for Mr. Nash to Norfolk, Va., Parke-Bernet Catalog 239, Dec. 12, 1940, No. 143

May 27. To Edwin M. Stanton, referring complaint of Leander Teasa for false imprisonment, missing from DNA WR RG 107, Sec. of War Letters Received, P 316

May 31. To Edwin M. Stanton, Nicolay for Lincoln, referring letter of Dr. Henry Isham to Lincoln, May 28, 1864, concerning Fred B. Ward, *ibid.*, P 328

June —. To Gideon Welles, NE, mentioned, Augustus Brandegee to Lincoln, July 20, 1864, concerning appointment of nephew T. T. Wood to the Naval Academy, DLC-RTL

June 1. To Edwin M. Stanton, referring application for release of Franklin Thomas, missing from DNA WR RG 107, Sec. of War Letters Received, P 325 with P 888

June 2. Order, on affidavit for discharge of James G. Henderson, "Let this boy be discharged, upon refunding any bounty received. A. LINCOLN," AES, owned by Dale Carnegie, New York City

June 2. To Edwin M. Stanton, authorizing the Rev. Dr. Wilson to make an exchange of hospital chaplains, Am. Art Assn. Anderson Galleries Catalog 4104, Apr. 18-19, 1934, No. 503

June 2. To Edwin M. Stanton and Henry W. Halleck, on letter of Alfred H. Terry to William Faxon, May 29, 1864, recommending promotion of Joseph Hawley, "Submitted to the Sec. of War & Gen. Halleck. A. LINCOLN," AES, RPB

June 3. To Salmon P. Chase, requesting nomination for Thomas Steinburgh, NE (?), mentioned, Maunsell B. Field to Lincoln, June 4, 1864, copy, DNA FI RG 56, Misc. Letters to Pres., p. 521

June 3. To Joseph Holt, asking information concerning conviction and pardon of a man who had taken the oath of Dec. 8, 1863, ALS, Am. Art Assn. Anderson Galleries Catalog 4020, Feb. 21, 1933, No. 157

June 3. To Edwin M. Stanton and Henry W. Halleck, on letter of James H. Lane and others to Lincoln, May 31, 1864, asking promotion of Col. Thomas M. Bowen, "Submitted to the Sec. of War & Gen. Halleck. A. LINCOLN," AES, RPB

June 3 To Edwin M. Stanton and Henry W. Halleck, on petition of Abel C. Wilder and others to Lincoln, June 21, 1864, that Gen. James Blunt be ordered to report to Gen. Edward R. S. Canby, "Submitted to the Sec. of War & Gen. Halleck. A. LINCOLN," AES, DNA WR RG 108, H.Q.A., Q 391, Box 71

June 4. To Edwin M. Stanton, referring letter of Maj. George W. Todd enclosing letter from Capt. F. B. Gilbert concerning Corp. Gordon, missing from DNA WR RG 107, Sec. of War Letters Received, P 67

June 6. To Joseph Henry, NE, mentioned, Stephen Massett to Lincoln, June 6, 1864, DLC-RTL

June 6. To Edwin M. Stanton, referring letter of Lieut. N. M. Hoffman on appointment of Dr. Boughner as paymaster, missing from DNA WR RG 107, Sec. of War Letters Received, P 345

June 6. To Edwin M. Stanton, referring application of Mrs. Margaret Smith for release of her son Daniel, missing from *ibid.*, P 343

June 7. To Edward Bates, Hay for Lincoln, referring letter of A. Chester to Lincoln, June 2, 1864, recommending Elisha W. Chester, DNA RG 60, Papers of Atty. Gen., Appts., Georgia

June 7. To Edwin M. Stanton, Hay for Lincoln, referring letter of Mortimer D. Leggett recommending son Wells W. Leggett, DNA WR RG 94, U.S. Mil. Acad., 1863, No. 105

June 7. To Edwin M. Stanton, referring letter of Col. Washington C. Tevis to Mrs. Moore concerning case of Capt. Moore, 3d Md. Cav., from DNA WR RG 107, Sec. of War Letters Received, P 359

June 8. To Edwin M. Stanton, referring letter of Otto Young in Central Guard House, Washington, D.C., as deserter, "not unlikely this is a good soldier unnecessarily tied up," (from Register), missing from *ibid.*, P 353

c. June 9. Endorsement, on letter of Augustus W. Bradford to Lincoln, June 9, 1864, concerning case of Dr. Thomas A. Lynch, held for trial in death of Negro woman, "Gov. Bradford—about whipping a woman to death," AE, NHi

June 13. To Edwin M. Stanton, on letter of Irad Kelley to Lincoln, June 11, 1864, concerning defense of Kelley's Island, "Submitted to the Sec. of War. A. LINCOLN," AES, DNA WR RG 107, Sec. of War Letters Received, P 365

June 14. To Edward Bates, NE, mentioned, Bates to Lincoln, June 14, 1864, stating no vacancy in office of U.S. district attorney for Utah, DLC-RTL

June 14. To Edward Bates, on envelope of applications for pardon of Harvey Walker convicted of forgery, "Submitted to the Attorney General. A. LINCOLN," AES, DNA RG 204, U.S. Pardon Atty., A 539

June 14. To Edwin M. Stanton, referring letter of John B. Allen concerning minor named "Wilson" held as a deserter, missing from DNA WR RG 107, Sec. of War Letters Received, P 361

June 14. To Edwin M. Stanton, forgery on torn flyleaf containing purported signature of John Quincy Adams, ALS-P, ISLA

June 15. To Joseph Holt, on court-martial record of Robert H. Hughes sentenced to death for assault with intent to rape, "Sentence approved A. LINCOLN," AES, DNA WR RG 153, Judge Adv. Gen., MM 1470

June 15. To Gen. Daniel Tyler, forgery, ALS-P, ISLA

June 16. Speech to Ladies of New Jersey at Philadelphia Fair on presentation of a staff from the Washington arch at Trenton, mentioned, Philadelphia *Press*, June 17, 1864

June 18. To Edwin M. Stanton, referring application for discharge of Florin S. Howe, missing from DNA WR RG 107, Sec. of War Letters Received, P 370

June 20. To Edwin M. Stanton, referring letter of Richard Yates, concerning necessity for a District Committee for Illinois, missing from *ibid.*, P 389

June 21. To Edward Bates, Hay for Lincoln, referring request of Fernando C. Beaman to Lincoln, June 12, 1864, for pardon of Thomas Lean convicted of mail robbery, DNA RG 204, U.S. Pardon Atty., A 353

June 21. To William H. Seward, Hay for Lincoln, referring letter of

John Conness to Lincoln, June 16, 1864, with application of Silas D. Cochran, DNA FS RG 59, Appointments, Box 257

June 22. To Edwin M. Stanton, referring court-martial cases of Theodore Rogers and Patrick Lawless, missing from DNA WR RG 107, Sec. of War Letters Received, P 373

June 22. To Edwin M. Stanton, referring letter of George F. Dunning asking pardon for Patrick Lawless, missing from *ibid.*, P 374

June 22. To Edwin M. Stanton, referring letter of William H. Gibney asking for release, missing from *ibid.*, P 375

June 22. To Edwin M. Stanton, referring claim of J. A. Richardson, missing from *ibid.*, P 376 with 2716/B WD 1882

June 24. To Edwin M. Stanton, Hay for Lincoln, referring telegram of George W. Deitzler to Lincoln, June 21, 1864, asking militia to protect Kansas, DNA WR RG 108, H.Q.A., D 176, Box 67

June 24. To Edwin M. Stanton, secretary for Lincoln, referring letter of G. H. Briggs to Lincoln, June 20, 1864, confessing that Winthrop E. Hilton was imprisoned on false charges, DNA WR RG 107, Sec. of War Letters Received, P 379

June 25. To Mrs. Louisa Drew, thanking her for theatre tickets, NE (destroyed in fire?), formerly in possession of the late John Barrymore, Hollywood, Calif.

June 25. To William H. Seward, Hay for Lincoln, referring letter of C. M. Vandervoort to Lincoln, June 24, 1864, applying for consulship, DNA FS RG 59, Appointments, Box 396

June 25. To Edwin M. Stanton, referring petition in favor of Private Harmon Bierlien, missing from DNA WR RG 107, Sec. of War Letters Received, P 385

June 27. To Edwin M. Stanton, referring application for discharge of Nelson Kelly alias Henry Mapes, missing from DNA WR RG 107, Sec. of War Letters Received, P 403

June 28. To Joseph Holt, on court-martial record of Charles Langenbein, "Judge Advocate General please examine & report on this case. A. LINCOLN," AES, DNA WR RG 153, Judge Adv. Gen., NN 1787

c. June 29. Endorsements on *Special Orders No. 256*, Dept. of the South, concerning deserters restored to duty, spurious, Argosy Book Shop Catalog, Apr. 1942, No. 17

June 29. To Lorenzo Thomas, ordering discharge of Morris Finks alias David Stocionski as recommended by Ebon C. Ingersoll, missing from DNA WR RG 94, Adj. Gen. Letters Received, P 693

June 30. To Edward Bates, Hay for Lincoln, referring letter of S. C. Browne to Lincoln, June 7, 1864, protesting pardons of Isaac Baker and Robert Ford, DNA RG 204, U.S. Pardon Atty., A 935

June 30. To William H. Seward, Hay for Lincoln, referring letter of B. C. Champney recommending P. Frazer Smith, DNA FS RG 59, Appointments, Box 383

June 30. To William H. Seward, Hay for Lincoln, referring application of C. Lee Moses, *ibid.*, Box 349

June 30. To William H. Seward and Edwin M. Stanton, on letter of Lucian Anderson, William H. Randall and Green C. Smith to Lincoln, June 29, 1864, asking martial law in Kentucky, "Submitted to Sec. of State and Sec. of War. A. LINCOLN," AES, IHi

June 30. To Edwin M. Stanton, referring letter of Richard Yates asking discharge of John Purkapile, missing from DNA WR RG 107, Sec. of War Letters Received, P 393

June 30. To Edwin M. Stanton, Hay for Lincoln, referring letter of Lorenzo Sherwood enclosing letter of Alexander Rossy of Texas for damages by U.S. troops, *ibid.*, P 394

June 30. To Edwin M. Stanton, referring application of Lawrence V. Houghton, missing from *ibid.*, P 405

c. July 1. Endorsement, ordering discharge of James M. Philips, NE, mentioned, Lincoln to Stanton, July 5, 1864

July 4. Endorsement, on letter of Capt. Dennis to Amasa Cobb, concerning an appointment desired by the Wisconsin delegation, AES, William D. Morley Catalog, Oct. 13, 1944, No. 284

July 4. To Edwin M. Stanton, referring petition of Horace Greeley and others for trial or release of Winthrop E. Hilton, missing from DNA WR RG 107, Sec. of War Letters Received, P 415

July 5. To Horatio Seymour, Stanton for Lincoln, calling for 12,000 militia, OR, I, XXXVII, II, 77 (same to Andrew G. Curtin, *ibid.*, 74)

July 5. To Edwin M. Stanton, referring application of Mrs. Nancy Kelly for discharge of son Thomas, missing from DNA WR RG 107, Sec. of War Letters Received, P 413

July 5. To Edwin M. Stanton, referring petition for discharge of Steward Saylor, a minor, missing from *ibid.*, P 414

July 6. To Edwin M. Stanton, requesting papers in case of John Steele, banished to Canada, missing from *ibid.*, P 419

c. July 7. Endorsement by Hay for Lincoln, on letter from John Owen to Lincoln, July 7, 1864, DLC-RTL

July 7. To Edwin M. Stanton, Hay for Lincoln, referring letter of Oliver P. Wharton to Lincoln, July 2, 1864, DNA WR RG 108, H.Q.A., W 405, Box 71

July 7. To Edwin M. Stanton, referring letter of D. S. Gregory requesting reinstatement of William B. Dunning, missing from DNA WR RG 107, Sec. of War Letters Received, P 427

July 8. To Joseph Holt, among thirty-five court-martial cases reviewed by Lincoln this day, twenty-two routine endorsements in Lincoln's autograph approving, disapproving, commuting, or remitting sentence, DNA WR RG 153, Judge Adv. Gen., LL 2050; MM 1072 (2 cases), 1271, 1346, 1389, 1457, 1481 (2 cases); NN 1478 (2 cases), 1501, 1528, 1692, 1754, 1796, 1800, 1820, 1822, 1823, 1828, 1954 and 1958 (1 case)

July 8. To Edwin M. Stanton, referring letter of Mrs. George Rice protesting transfer of husband, missing from DNA WR RG 107, Sec. of War Letters Received, P 430

July 9. To Joseph Holt, among thirty-one court-martial cases reviewed by Lincoln this day, ten routine endorsements in his autograph, approving, disapproving, remitting, commuting, or pardoning, DNA WR RG 153, Judge Adv. Gen., MM 1381, 1406, 1408, 1424, 1428, 1442; NN 1145, 1858, 1882; DNA RG 130 White House Office, Army Court-Martial Cases (James Bullard)

July 10. To Ulysses S. Grant, concerning "Corporal Hardy," forgery, Hertz, II, 936

July 13. To Edwin M. Stanton, referring request of Col. Joseph J. Morrison for investigation of case of himself and other officers, missing from DNA WR RG 107, Sec. of War Letters Received, P 669

July 14. To Edwin M. Stanton, referring letter of Franklin Brooks and requesting papers in case of Albert Brooks, missing from *ibid.*, P 437

July 14. To John B. S. Todd, inscription on flyleaf of Herman Haupt, *Military Bridges* (1864), "Presented to Gen. J. B. S. Todd by A. Lincoln, July 14, 1864." Parke-Bernet Catalog 223, Oct. 30–Nov. 1, 1940, No. 433

c. July 15. To Edwin M. Stanton, referring case of Col. Augustus Raybold, missing from DNA WR RG 107, Sec. of War Letters Received, P 440

July 16. Endorsement, on document signed by Gen. John Gibbon preferring charges against Gen. Joshua T. Owen, "Recommendation of Gen. Grant approved." AES, Am. Art Assn. Anderson Galleries Catalog 4325, Apr. 29-30, 1937, No. 324

July 16. To Joseph Holt, on court-martial record of James Enright, application for clemency, "Application denied. A. LINCOLN," AES, DNA WR RG 153, Judge Adv. Gen., MM 844

July 16. To Edwin M. Stanton, referring letter from Weldon E. Wright to Lincoln, July 8, 1864, concerning claim for damages, "Submitted to the Sec. of War. A. LINCOLN," AES, DNA WR RG 107, Sec. of War Letters Received, P 443

July 16. To Edwin M. Stanton referring letter of Gen. James W. McMillan to John P. Usher, June 21, 1864, concerning his transfer North, "Submitted to the Sec. of War. A. LINCOLN," AES, DNA WR RG 94, Adj. Gen. Letters Received, P 768 filed with 2415 ACP 1877

July 18. To Lorenzo Thomas, referring letter of Louise M. Mitchell asking exchange of Lieut. J. de W. Whiting, missing from DNA WR RG 94, Adj. Gen. Letters Received, P 776

July 19. To Edwin M. Stanton, Nicolay for Lincoln, referring letter of Anson Herrick to Lincoln, July 16, 1864, requesting pass for Mrs. Hoffmayer and child to come North, DNA WR RG 107, Sec. of War Letters Received, P 457

July 19. To Edwin M. Stanton, Edward D. Neill for Lincoln, referring letter of A. Conant, Jr., asking action on his case, *ibid.*, P 465

July 20. To Edwin M. Stanton, on letter of Dr. A. M. Ross to Lincoln, July 15, 1864, concerning rebel officers in Canada, "Submitted to Sec. of War. A. LINCOLN," AES, DNA WR RG 108, H.Q.A., R 168, Box 70

July 20. To Edwin M. Stanton, referring case of James H. Lane in regard to order of Gen. George G. Meade, missing from DNA WR RG 107, Sec. of War Letters Received, P 460

July 21. To Joseph Holt, on letter of attorney for Charles Langenbein, "Let Judge Advocate General report on the Langenbein case & send to me. A. LINCOLN," AES, DNA WR RG 153, Judge Adv. Gen., NN 1787

July 22. To Charles A. Dana, on letter of P. C. Wright to Edward Bates, July 15, 1864, asking investigation of his case, "Submitted to the Assistant Sec. of War—Dana. A. LINCOLN," AES, DNA WR RG 107, Sec. of War Letters Received, P 468

July 23. To Joseph Holt, on court-martial record of W. A. Warren, acquitted, but recommended by Gen. Lorenzo Thomas for dismissal, "Let the decision of the Court-Martial stand. A. LINCOLN," AES, DNA WR RG 153, Judge Adv. Gen., NN 1805

July 25. To Lorenzo Thomas, referring application of Robert G. Grindy for release, missing from DNA WR RG 94, Adj. Gen. Letters Received, P 794

July 27. To Miss McDowell, sending autograph, ALS, Public Library, Brookline, Mass.

July 27. Note, "Let this be done A. LINCOLN," ALS, RPB

July 27. To Edwin M. Stanton, referring telegram of Gov. James Y. Smith to revoke commission of John T. Pitman and appoint Henry M. Amesbury, missing from DNA WR RG 107, Sec. of War Letters Received, P 511

July 28-30. To Leland & Co., missing from DNA WR RG 107, Pres. Telegrams, I, 115

July 28. To Edwin M. Stanton, Hay for Lincoln, referring letter of David Heaton to Lincoln, July 16, 1864, on invading North Carolina, DNA WR RG 108, H.Q.A., H 656, Box 68

July 28. To Edwin M. Stanton, Hay for Lincoln, referring letter of Charles Duffy to Lincoln, July 25, 1864, alleging he is improperly confined, DNA WR RG 107, Sec. of War, Misc. Papers, Box 583 (formerly P 483)

July 28. To Edwin M. Stanton, Hay for Lincoln, referring letter of James H. Lane and Benjamin F. Loan to Lincoln, July 13, 1864, that requisition of Gen. William S. Rosecrans be paid, DNA WR RG 107, Sec. of War Letters Received, P 477

July 28. To Edwin M. Stanton, Hay for Lincoln, referring letter of George P. Ihrie to Lincoln, July 27, 1864, requesting authority to raise a volunteer regiment in California, *ibid.*, P 497

July 29. To Edward Bates, Hay for Lincoln, referring letter of Philip Fraser to Lincoln, July 9, 1864, recommending C. P. Chamberlin, DNA RG 60, Papers of Atty. Gen., Appts., Florida

July 29. To Samuel Cony, Hay for Lincoln, acknowledging Cony's letter to Lincoln, July 22, 1864, concerning congressional inspection tour to Northeastern frontier, DLC-RTL

c. July 29. Endorsement concerning H. W. Tuller, NE, mentioned, Tuller to Lincoln, July 29, 1864, DLC-RTL

July 29. To Edwin M. Stanton, Hay for Lincoln, transmitting copy of letter from Miles Pliny to Lincoln, July 4, 1864, enclosing letter from London *Times* urging capture of Wilmington, N.C., DNA WR RG 108, H.Q.A., L 191, Box 69

July 29. To Edwin M. Stanton, Hay for Lincoln, referring resolutions of Arkansas legislature for protection of loyal citizens, *ibid.*, L 193, Box 69

July 29. To Edwin M. Stanton, Hay for Lincoln, referring act of Arkansas legislature for defense of state, *ibid.*, L 192, Box 69

July 30. To Edwin M. Stanton, referring appeal of George W. Rae, missing from DNA WR RG 107, Sec. of War Letters Received, P 507

c. July 30. To Edwin M. Stanton, referring complaint of Mrs. Annette S. Ingham that her son James has been discharged, missing from *ibid.*, P 492

c. July 30. Endorsement on letter from Henry W. Bellows to Lincoln, July 30, 1864, concerning Frederick A. Walton, "This boy was born Oct. 1–1846," AE, DNA WR RG 94, U.S. Mil. Acad., 1864, No. 419

Aug. 1. To Joseph Holt, Hay for Lincoln, referring petitions on behalf of Andrew J. Smith, DNA WR RG 153, Judge Adv. Gen., MM 847

Aug. 1. To Edwin M. Stanton on telegram from Simon Cameron advocating replacement of Gen. Darius N. Couch by Gen. George Cadwalader, "Submitted to the respectful consideration of the Sec. of War. A. LINCOLN," AES, Am. Art Assn. Anderson Galleries Catalog 3854, Oct. 20, 1930, No. 158

Aug. 1. To Edwin M. Stanton, referring telegram from Alexander K. McClure for retention of Gen. Darius N. Couch, missing from DNA WR RG 107, Sec. of War Letters Received, P 871

c. Aug. 1. To Edwin M. Stanton, referring application of John Hayes for release, missing from *ibid.*, P 514

Aug. 1. To John P. Usher, Hay for Lincoln, referring letter of John B. S. Todd to Lincoln, July 27, 1864, recommending Joel A. Potter, AES, DNA NR RG 48, Applications, Indian Agencies, Ponca, Box 1271

Aug. 2. To Edwin M. Stanton, Hay for Lincoln (misdated July 2), referring request of Rev. John O'Kane to Lincoln, July 27, 1864, to visit son at Johnson's Island, DNA WR RG 107, Sec. of War Letters Received, P 516

Aug. 3. To Edwin M. Stanton, referring letter of Gen. Innis N. Palmer and others protesting evacuation of New Bern, N.C., missing from *ibid.*, P 518

Aug. 5. To Edwin M. Stanton, referring petition for pardon of Maj. McLaskey, missing from *ibid.*, P 525

Aug. 5. To Edwin M. Stanton, Nicolay for Lincoln, referring letter of Lawson Black to Lincoln, July 24, 1864, asking permission for son Alfred to visit, *ibid.*, P 545

Aug. 5. To Edwin M. Stanton, referring petition of Leopold Feuerstein for exemption from military duty, missing from *ibid.*, P 664

Aug. 6. To Edwin M. Stanton, referring case of Col. Jacob Higgins, missing from *ibid.*, P 529

Aug. 6. To Edwin M. Stanton, Nicolay for Lincoln, referring request of Mrs. Louise W. Dickerson to Lincoln, Aug. 2, 1864, for pass to join her husband, a prisoner of war, *ibid.*, P 542

Aug. 6. To Edwin M. Stanton, referring application of James F. Pierce for pass to recover body of Thornton S. Pierce, missing from *ibid.*, P 637

Aug. 9. To David G. Farragut, order concerning Andrew J. Hamilton's shipment of cotton, NE, *see* order to Edward R. S. Canby this date

Aug. 9. To Joseph Holt, ten routine autograph endorsements on court-martial records, commuting, remitting, and approving sentences, DNA WR RG 153, Judge Adv. Gen., MM 1003, 1005, 1016, 1375, 1407; NN 1660, 1707 (2 cases), 1712, 2085

Aug. 9. To Carl Schurz, Hay for Lincoln, acknowledging his letter to Lincoln, Aug. 8, 1864, ALS, DLC-Schurz Papers

Aug. 10. To Edwin M. Stanton, Nicolay for Lincoln, referring letter of W. Davenport to Lincoln, July 31, 1864, asking pass for Joseph Dixon, DNA WR RG 107, Sec. of War Letters Received, P 547

Aug. 11. To Joseph Holt, on court-martial record of Richard W. Thompson, Jr., "Unexecuted portion of sentence remitted. A. LINCOLN," AES, DNA WR RG 153, Judge Adv. Gen., LL 2161

Aug. 11. To Carl Schurz, Hay for Lincoln, asking him to come to Washington, DNA WR RG 107, Pres. Telegrams, I, 130

Aug. 11. To William H. Seward, Nicolay for Lincoln, referring application of Frederick L. P. Fogg to Lincoln, Aug. 8, 1864, DNA FS RG 59, Appointments, Box 286

Aug. 11. To Edwin M. Stanton, Nicolay for Lincoln, referring letter of A. Wolcott to Lincoln, July 27, 1864, protesting order of Gen. Mason Brayman expelling Roman Catholic Bishop William H. Elder, DNA WR RG 107, Sec. of War Letters Received, P 562 with D 1141

Aug. 12. To Edwin M. Stanton, Nicolay for Lincoln, referring letter of Jason O. Deanes to Lincoln, Aug. 9, 1864, asking that Gen. George B. McClellan be authorized to raise 100,000 men, DNA WR RG 107, Sec. of War Letters Received, P 561

Aug. 12, To Edwin M. Stanton, Nicolay for Lincoln, referring letter of R. Cromelien to Lincoln, Aug. 10, 1864, urging protection of Niagara suspension bridge, *ibid.*, P 573

Aug. 12. To Edwin M. Stanton, referring letter of Daniel E. Sickles to Lincoln, Aug. 10, 1864, with suggestions for prisoners of war in rebel states, missing from *ibid.*, P 594

Aug. 12. To Edwin M. Stanton, Nicolay for Lincoln, referring letter of William H. Conkle to Lincoln, Aug. 9, 1864, reporting organization of 250,000 in Philadelphia prepared to oppose administration with force, *ibid* , P 602

Aug. 12. To Lorenzo Thomas, directing Maj. John Hay to proceed to Keokuk, Iowa, execute verbal orders and return, missing from *ibid.*, P 1056

c. Aug. 13. To Robert Anderson, Hay for "The President & Mrs. Lincoln," invitation to dinner on Aug. 13, 1864, DLC-Anderson Papers

Aug. 13. To William H. Seward, Nicolay for Lincoln, referring application of William B. Parker to Lincoln, Aug. 10, 1864, DNA FS RG 59, Appointments, Box 359

c. Aug. 13. To Edwin M. Stanton, referring case of Capt. S. Stevens, not confirmed by Senate, missing from DNA WR RG 107, Sec. of War Letters Received, P 544

Aug. 13. To Edwin M. Stanton, Nicolay for Lincoln, referring letter of D. Weisel to Lincoln, Aug. 10, 1864, asking release of prisoners, *ibid.*, P 548

Aug. 13. To Edwin M. Stanton, referring application of Frank Arthur for release from prison, missing from *ibid.*, P 585

Aug. 13. To Edwin M. Stanton, referring application of W. H. Walford to ship rifles to Cuba, missing from *ibid.*, P 636

Aug. 15. To Edward Bates, Nicolay for Lincoln, asking for recommendations of C. P. Leslie for attorney for Montana, LS, DNA RG 60, Papers of Atty. Gen., Box 122

c. Aug. 15. To Ethan A. Hitchcock, referring letter of Mrs. H. E. Weaver to Lincoln, Aug. 15, 1864, asking exchange of brother Henry K. Steever, missing from DLC-Hitchcock Papers, Box 6

c. Aug. 15. To Edwin M. Stanton, referring application for discharge of William H. Harper, missing from DNA WR RG 107, Sec. of War Letters Received, P 564

c. Aug. 15. To Edwin M. Stanton, referring letters of Mrs. Hestor Skinner on behalf of her brother Thomas Skinner, missing from *ibid.*, P 506

c. Aug. 15. To Edwin M. Stanton, referring application of William Little for discharge, missing from *ibid.*, P 572

c. Aug. 15. To Edwin M. Stanton, referring application of Preston Stone for discharge, missing from *ibid.*, P 579

Aug. 15. To Edwin M. Stanton, Nicolay for Lincoln, referring letter of Mrs. C. M. Liborius to Lincoln, Aug. 13, 1864, asking pass for George W. Frost to recover remains of Ernest Liborius, *ibid.*, P 598

Aug. 15. To John P. Usher, on letter of John Beeson to Lincoln, Aug. 12, 1864, concerning control of Indians, "Submitted to the Sec. of the Interior. A. LINCOLN," AES, DNA NR RG 75, Office of Indian Affairs, Letters Received, Misc., p. 231

Aug. 16. To Joseph Holt, among court-martial cases reviewed by Lincoln seven routine endorsements in Lincoln's autograph, approving sentence, DNA WR RG 153, Judge Adv. Gen., MM 917, 1384, 1386, 1390, 1395, 1480; NN 1373

c. Aug. 16. To Edwin M. Stanton, referring letter of Barker Gummere and Jacob R. Freese to Lincoln, June 22, 1864, with resolution asking removal of Col. Robert C. Buchanan, Maj. L. Jones, Capt. John Whipple, and E. I. Grant, missing from DNA WR RG 107, Sec. of War Letters Received, P 599

c. Aug. 16. To Lorenzo Thomas, referring letter of John Howard enclosing letter of L. S. Wood concerning American Knights, missing from DNA WR RG 94, Adj. Gen. Letters Received, P 885

Aug. 17. To Thomas E. Bramlette, spurious, copy, CSmH

Aug. 17. To Joseph Holt, among court-martial cases reviewed by Lincoln fifteen routine endorsements in Lincoln's autograph, DNA WR RG 153, Judge Adv. Gen., LL 1715; MM 948, 1317, 1387, 1401, 1479; NN 373, 1733, 1837, 1961, 2090, 2128, 2150, 2168, 2327

Aug. 17. To Edwin M. Stanton, Nicolay for Lincoln, referring letter of Alfred Clapp to Lincoln, Aug. 12, 1864, on Copperhead policy of Gen. Frederick Steele, DNA WR RG 108, H.Q.A., C 550, Box 67

Aug. 17. To Edwin M. Stanton, referring letter of A. D. Desher requesting transfer of New Jersey soldiers in hospital at Louisville, Ky., missing from DNA WR RG 107, Sec. of War Letters Received, P 623

Aug. 17. To Edwin M. Stanton, requesting him to hear evidence on arrest of Dr. P. A. Dougherty, missing from *ibid.*, P 686

Aug. 18. To Joseph Holt, in court-martial record of Robert Hopkins alias Chaskedan, petition on his behalf by other Sioux Indians, endorsed, "Pardons. A. LINCOLN," AES, DNA WR RG 153, Judge Adv. Gen., NN 2323

Aug. 18. To Edwin M. Stanton, Nicolay for Lincoln, referring letter of Hallin & Sander to Lincoln, Aug. 11, 1864, asking permission to export arms to Japan, DNA WR RG 107, Sec. of War Letters Received, P 611

Aug. 19. To D. S. D. Baldwin, Nicolay for Lincoln, returning Baldwin's application of Aug. 17, 1864, and Daniel Dickinson's recommendation, DLC-RTL

Aug. 19. To Benjamin F. Butler, Nicolay for Lincoln, referring letter of Oliver Williamson to Lincoln, Aug. 15, 1864, ES, DLC-Butler Papers

Aug. 19. To Joseph Holt, on court-martial record of John Carroll sentenced to be shot, "Sentence approved A. LINCOLN," AES, DNA WR RG 153, Judge Adv. Gen., MM 1372

Aug. 19. To Edwin M. Stanton, Nicolay for Lincoln, referring letter of Lizzie B. Bruce to Lincoln, Aug. 10, 1864, appealing from order that wives of men in rebel service report to provost marshal, DNA WR RG 107, Sec. of War Letters Received, P 595

Aug. 19. To Edwin M. Stanton, referring letter of Gen. John A. Logan concerning assignment of Lt. Col. Charles Ewing and Capt. Louis E. Yorke, missing from *ibid.*, P 625

Aug. 19. To Mrs. John Tyler, Nicolay for Lincoln, that her letter to Lincoln, Aug. 15, 1864, concerning restoration of her estate, is referred to Gen. Benjamin F. Butler, DLC-Butler Papers

Aug. 20. To Joseph Holt, Nicolay for Lincoln, referring letter of Charles Naylor to Lincoln, asking clemency for William Bockman, DNA WR RG 153, Judge Adv. Gen., LL 2048

c. Aug. 20. To Edwin M. Stanton, referring letter of Amos McDonald, secretary of Working Woman's Relief Assn., concerning an investigating committee, missing from DNA WR RG 107, Sec. of War Letters Received, P 626

c. Aug. 20. To Edwin M. Stanton, referring petition of Sachem chiefs, Tuscarora reservation, for furlough of Sam Barefoot alias Eli Patterson, missing from *ibid.*, P 629

c. Aug. 20. To Edwin M. Stanton, referring appeal of Mrs. Mary Sapper that her husband under arrest since Feb. 1863, be tried or she be supported, missing from *ibid.*, P 631

c. Aug. 20. To Edwin M. Stanton, referring application from recruiting officers that Gen. Benjamin F. Butler's recruiting order be revised, missing from *ibid.*, P 633

Aug. 20. To President of Venezuela, appointing of Erastus D. Culver as minister, DNA FS RG 59, Credences, IV, 423

Aug. 22. To Edward Bates, Nicolay for Lincoln, referring letter of S. E. Browers to Lincoln, Aug. 5, 1864, asking pardon for Michael D. Curran, DNA RG 204, U.S. Pardon Atty., A 546

Aug. 22. To Edward Bates, Nicolay for Lincoln, referring letter of John Lintner to Thaddeus Stevens, Aug. 16, 1864, concerning pardon of his son Amos, *ibid.*, A 543

Aug. 22. To William T. Otto, Nicolay for Lincoln, to make appointments of Edward D. Neill as secretary to the president, to sign land patents, and Charles H. Philbrick to replace Neill. DLC-Nicolay Papers

Aug. 22. To Edwin M. Stanton, referring memorial of officers of N.Y. Workingmen's Union, concerning an order of Gen. William S. Rosecrans and Gen. Stephen G. Burbridge, missing from DNA WR RG 107, Sec. of War Letters Received, P 639

Aug. 22. To Edwin M. Stanton, referring letter of F. A. Richardson asking release, missing from *ibid.*, P 645

Aug. 22. To Edwin M. Stanton, referring application for discharge of Daniel Fender and Jesse Decar, missing from *ibid.*, P 647

Aug. 22. To Edwin M. Stanton, referring letter of John Manly enclosing letter from Treas. Dept. concerning bringing of livestock from Canada for N.Y. Agric. Soc. Fair, missing from *ibid.*, P 684

Aug. 23. To William P. Fessenden, on petition of Mr. Swenson to be paid Texas coupons, "Submitted to the Secretary of the Treasury. A. LINCOLN," AES, OClWHi

Aug. 23. To Edwin M. Stanton, referring letter of James C. Hennessey desiring a fair trial, missing from DNA WR RG 107, Sec. of War Letters Received, P 677

Aug. 23. Thanks to 147th Ohio Regiment, mentioned, New York *Times*, Aug. 25, 1864

Aug. 24. To Simon Cameron, Nicolay for Lincoln, acknowledging letter of Cameron to Lincoln, Aug. 22, 1864, LS, DLC-Cameron Papers

Aug. 24. To William S. Rosecrans, Nicolay for Lincoln, requesting examination of case of David D. Mills sentenced to hang, LS, DNA WR RG 107, Pres. Telegrams, I, 140

Aug. 24. To Edwin M. Stanton, Nicolay for Lincoln, referring letter of James Smith asking for interview, DNA WR RG 108, H.Q.A., S 732, Box 70

c. Aug. 24. To Edwin M. Stanton, referring letter of William Bottles, arrested as deserter, missing from DNA WR RG 107, Sec. of War Letters Received, P 653

Aug. 24. To Edwin M. Stanton, referring letter of Gov. James T. Lewis requesting assignment of Rev. Alfred C. Barry to Harvey Hospital at Madison, Wis., missing from *ibid.*, P 655

Aug. 24. To Edwin M. Stanton, referring letter of Samuel A. Purviance, missing from *ibid.*, P 1111

Aug. 24. To Edwin M. Stanton, on note concerning Judge John C. Underwood, "Submitted to Sec. of War for Gen. Hitchcock. A. LINCOLN," AES, owned by Dale Carnegie, New York City

Aug. 25. To Edwin M. Stanton, referring request of John Brough for exchange of John David, clerk of Ohio Senate, for J. M. Vernon, rebel prisoner, missing from DNA WR RG 107, Sec. of War Letters Received, P 667

Aug. 26. To Edward Bates, Nicolay for Lincoln, referring letter of John Lintner to Lincoln, Aug. 22, 1864, asking pardon for son Amos, DNA RG 204, U.S. Pardon Atty., A 543

Aug. 26. To Edward Bates, Nicolay for Lincoln, referring letter of Amasa Cobb to Lincoln, Aug. 20, 1864, recommending Stephen S. Barlow, DNA RG 60, Papers of Atty. Gen., Appts., Florida

Aug. 26. To Joseph Holt, on certificate of Hugh McCulloch that William G. Gilbert is a monomaniac, "Let Wm. Gates Gilbert named within be pardoned for his desertion, and discharged from the service of the U.S," copy, DNA RG 130, White House Office, Army Court-Martial Cases

Aug. 26. To Edwin M. Stanton, on telegram from John A. Dix to Lincoln, Aug. 25, 1864, asking that Francis A. Mallison be released, "Submitted to the Sec. of War. A. LINCOLN," AES, NHi

Aug. 27. To William Dorsheimer, Nicolay for Lincoln, acknowledging Dorsheimer's letter to Lincoln, Aug. 24, 1864, concerning Niagara Falls conference, DLC-Nicolay Papers

Aug. 27. To Joseph Holt. Same endorsement on cases of John R. H. Emberet, Samuel B. Hearn, Branton Lyons, and William H. Rodgers, "The sentence in this case is commuted to confinement at hard labor in the penitentiary during the war. A. LINCOLN," ES, DNA WR RG 153, Judge Adv. Gen., LL 2297

Aug. 27. To Edwin M. Stanton, referring request of Miss Bina Crump for pass to visit brother William D. Crump at Camp Douglas, missing from DNA WR RG 107, Sec. of War Letters Received, P 689

Aug. 28. To Reverdy Johnson, Nicolay for Lincoln, advising telegram was sent to Gen. Lewis Wallace, DNA WR RG 107, Pres. Telegrams, I, 146

Aug. 28. To Charles J. M. Gwinn, Nicolay for Lincoln, advising telegram was sent to Gen. Lewis Wallace, *ibid.*, 147

Aug. 29. To William W. Morris, NE, mentioned in telegram from Morris to Lincoln, Aug. 29, 1864, concerning Gen. Lewis Wallace's order, DLC-RTL

Aug. 30. To Edward R. S. Canby, NE, mentioned, Canby to Lincoln, Oct. 25, 1864, concerning Gen. Napoleon J. T. Dana's report on "O. M. Burbridge and Col. Starling," DLC-RTL

Aug. 30. To Edwin M. Stanton, introducing Thomas C. Kelly, missing from DNA WR RG 107, Sec. of War Letters Received, P 836

Aug. 31. To Andrew Johnson, NE, mentioned, Johnson to Lincoln, Jan. 24, 1865, concerning the "McKindree Church" case, DLC-RTL

Sept. 1. Order concerning Monroe Conner, on letter of W. W. Conner to Lincoln, Aug. 30, 1864, asking discharge of son Monroe for disability, "Let this man be discharged. A. LINCOLN," AES, owned by Dale Carnegie, New York City

Sept. 1. To Joseph Holt, Neill for Lincoln, referring file of Jourdan Moseley, DNA WR RG 153, Judge Adv. Gen., NN 1820

Sept. 1. To Edwin M. Stanton, clipped endorsement, ". . . see and hear the bearers of this from Chambersburg," AES, owned by Dale Carnegie, New York City

Sept. 1. To Edwin M. Stanton, on letter from Morgan Morgan to Lincoln, Aug. 30, 1864, introducing Berry Fitch of Darien County, Conn., concerning an officer to take charge of Fitch Home for disabled soldiers and their orphans, "Hon. Secretary of War, please see & oblige Mr. Fitch, who presents this. A. LINCOLN," AES, copy, ISLA

Sept. 1. To Lorenzo Thomas, on application from E. McPherson for detailing Capt. A. W. Scott to special detective service, "Let the detail be made," copy in Register, but missing from DNA WR RG 94, Adj. Gen. Letters Received, P 1349

Sept. 2. To Joseph Holt, on petition of wife for pardon of Matthias Garlitztorf, "Submitted to J.A.G. A. LINCOLN," AES, IHi

c. Sept. 2. Endorsement on *General Orders No. 36*, Dist. of Vicksburg, closing all stores except those licensed by government on Sept. 3, 1864, "Rather short notice," AE, DLC-RTL

Sept. 2. To Edwin M. Stanton, on letter of Charles W. Sandford to Lincoln, Aug. 30, 1864, against enforcing a draft in N.Y. "Sec. of War. A.L.," AES, DLC-Stanton Papers

Sept. 3. To Edward Bates, Nicolay for Lincoln, referring letter of John F. Potter to Lincoln, Aug. 30, 1864, asking pardon of Harvey D. Winson, DNA RG 204, U.S. Pardon Atty., A 539

Sept. 3. To Edwin M. Stanton, Nicolay for Lincoln, referring letter of Edward M. Samuel to Lincoln, Aug. 24, 1864, suggesting formation of a new military dept. for Missouri, DNA WR RG 108, H.Q.A., S 737, Box 70

Sept. 3. To Edwin M. Stanton, on letter of Schuyler Colfax to Lincoln, Aug. 29, 1864, "Submitted to the Sec. of War. A. LINCOLN," AES, DLC-Stanton Papers

Sept. 3. To Edwin M. Stanton, referring letter of Mrs. William P. Rucker concerning claim of her husband for services as secret agent to Gen. John C. Frémont, missing from DNA WR RG 107, Sec. of War Letters Received, P 693

Sept. 3. To Edwin M. Stanton, referring letter of Herman Schaase von Lex Ramp tendering services, missing from *ibid.*, P 710

Sept. 3. To Edwin M. Stanton, referring request of Edward Atkinson for free transportation for teachers of Freedmen's Aid Society to South Carolina, missing from *ibid.*, P 723

Sept. 3. To Edwin M. Stanton, referring request of Mrs. L. J. Price to visit Ft. Delaware, missing from *ibid.*, P 739

c. Sept. 5. To Edwin M. Stanton, referring letter of Mrs. T. A. Fox, near Vicksburg, Miss., asking rations for herself and children, missing from *ibid.*, P 699

Sept. 6. To Edward Bates, on letter of Robert Martin to Lincoln, Sept. 5, 1864, asking pardon for John Sutcliffe, "Submitted to the Attorney General. A. LINCOLN," AES, DNA RG 204, U.S. Pardon Atty., A 547

Sept. 7. To Joseph Holt, Nicolay for Lincoln, declining to interfere in case of Jourdan Moseley, DNA WR RG 153, Judge Adv. Gen., NN 1820

c. Sept. 7. To Edwin M. Stanton, referring letter of Julius Friedberger concerning brother Alfred imprisoned in Old Capitol Prison, missing from DNA WR RG 107, Sec. of War Letters Received, P 717

c. Sept. 7. To Edwin M. Stanton, referring application of A. H. Shockey for release, missing from *ibid.*, P 720

Sept. 8. To Joseph Holt, concerning Col. William S. Truex, "Order of dismissal revoked and whether there shall be a trial by court martial left to the discretion of Gen. Sheridan," copy in Ledger, but missing from DNA WR RG 153, Judge Adv. Gen., NN 2930

Sept. 8. To Edwin M. Stanton, referring petition of 215 privates in 187th Pa. Vols. for redress of grievances, missing from DNA WR RG 107, Sec. of War Letters Received, P 733

c. Sept. 8. To Edwin M. Stanton, referring application of John B. Henderson for release of W. H. Thurber, a prisoner at Rock Island, Ill., missing from *ibid.*, P 727

Sept. 8. To Edwin M. Stanton, referring request of Rev. W. G. E. Cunnyngham for pass to Abingdon, Va., missing from *ibid.*, P 740

Sept. 9. To John Bright, purported copy of letter thanking him for a photograph (text questionable), copy, ISLA

c. Sept. 9. To Edwin M. Stanton, referring request for parole of Samuel Murrell, prisoner at Camp Douglas, missing from DNA WR RG 107, Sec. of War Letters Received, P 730

c. Sept. 10. To Green Adams, NE, mentioned, Lucian Anderson to Adams, Sept. 10, 1864, DLC-RTL

Sept. 10. To Edward Bates, Nicolay for Lincoln, referring petition of citizens of Bedford County, Pa., for pardon of Alexander McGregor, DNA RG 204, U.S. Pardon Atty., A 548

Sept. 12. To James C. Conkling, Nicolay for Lincoln, replying to letters of Sept. 5 and 6, 1864, concerning Cincinnati convention, DLC-Nicolay Papers

Sept. 12. To William H. Seward, referring documents from Gov. Thomas E. Bramlette on state affairs in Kentucky, missing from DNA WR RG 107, Sec. of War Letters Received, P 61, Irregular Book 5

Sept. 12. To Edwin M. Stanton, referring request of Andrew Johnson for release of Josiah V. Rainey, missing from *ibid.*, P 742

Sept. 13. To Joseph Holt, Nicolay for Lincoln, referring request of L. R. Critchfield to Lincoln, Sept. 8, 1864, for release of Laurent Blanchet, DNA RG 204, U.S. Pardon Atty., A 547

Sept. 13. To Edwin M. Stanton, referring application for discharge of Shadrach H. Pitcher, missing from DNA WR RG 107, Sec. of War Letters Received, P 743

Sept. 13. To Edwin M. Stanton, referring petition for release of Austin B. Price and Samuel R. Holland, missing from *ibid.*, P 746 with P 922

Sept. 13. To Edwin M. Stanton, referring letter of John Campbell, Little Rock, Ark., complaining of lack of military vigilance, missing from *ibid.*, P 790

Sept. 13. To Edwin M. Stanton, referring letter of James W. Hewlett asking pass for two aunts to come North, missing from *ibid.*, P 799

Sept. 13. To John P. Usher, NE, mentioned, William T. Otto to Lincoln, Sept. 14, 1864, concerning William B. Allison, DLC-RTL

Sept. 15. To Edward Bates, on envelope of case of Robert D. Eggleston, "Pardon for unexecuted part of sentence. A. LINCOLN," AES, DNA RG 204, U.S. Pardon Atty., A 550

Sept. 15. To Edwin M. Stanton, Nicolay for Lincoln, referring letter from James F. Babcock to Lincoln, Sept. 15, 1864, recommending Wilbur R. Bacon, DNA WR RG 94, U.S. Mil. Acad., 1863, No. 185

Sept. 15. To Edwin M. Stanton, referring request of John Q. A. King of Paducah, Ky., for protection of his dwelling, missing from DNA WR RG 107, Sec. of War Letters Received, P 767

Sept. 15. To Edwin M. Stanton, referring request of Abraham W. McKee for payment for forage, missing from *ibid.*, P 769

Sept. 15. To Edwin M. Stanton, Nicolay for Lincoln, forwarding letters based on political requests, LS, *ibid.*, P 1253

Sept. 15. To Edwin M. Stanton, referring letter of J. R. Whiting on seizure of arms en route to Canada, missing from *ibid.*, P 753

Sept. 16. To Mrs. Samuel H. Melvin, "For Mrs. S. H. Melvin A. LINCOLN," on card, ALS-F, ISLA

c. Sept. 16. To Edwin M. Stanton, referring request of Rev. F. C. Goebel for pay, missing from DNA WR RG 107, Sec. of War Letters Received, P 757

Sept. 17. To Edwin M. Stanton, referring letter of Robert Haysleys complaining of citizens going South who ought to be in the Army, missing from *ibid.*, P 774

Sept. 17. To Edwin M. Stanton, referring letter of Angelo Durand claiming pay, missing from *ibid.*, P 780

Sept. 17. To Edwin M. Stanton, referring claim of James Stewart for bounty, missing from *ibid.*, P 783

Sept. 17. To Edwin M. Stanton, Nicolay for Lincoln, forwarding letters based on political requests, LS, *ibid.*, P 1253

Sept. 17. To Lorenzo Thomas, directing suspension of order for release of Quartermaster Henry C. Hodges at Leavenworth, Kans., by Col. John McFerran, missing from DNA WR RG 94, Adj. Gen. Letters Received, P 1047

Sept. 19. To Edward Bates, Nicolay for Lincoln, referring letter of G. T. Cobb to Lincoln, Sept. 16, 1864, asking pardon for two boys, Edward Leber and John Gilorley, DNA RG 204, U.S. Pardon Atty., A 550

Sept. 19. To Ethan A. Hitchcock, Nicolay for Lincoln, concerning brother of Frederick Hassaurek, ALS, Am. Autograph Shop Catalog, Dec., 1938

Sept. 19. Order for transportation for Hon. William Mitchell and friend to Gen. William T. Sherman's headquarters and return, Am. Art Assn. Anderson Galleries Catalog 4231, Feb. 5-6, 1936

Sept. 19. To Edwin M. Stanton, referring letter of A. Sterling enclosing claim of Severn Eyre concerning lighthouse on Smith's Island, missing from DNA WR RG 107, Sec. of War Letters Received, P 789

Sept. 19. To Edwin M. Stanton, referring application of F. C. Adams and J. R. Young to work mines on government property at West Point, N.Y., missing from *ibid.*, P 891

Sept. 19. To Edwin M. Stanton, referring letter of Joseph Sweeney asking employment as a scout, missing from *ibid.*, P 793

Sept. 19. To Edwin M. Stanton, referring letter of John B. Henderson asking release of W. H. Thurber and Young Nelson, missing from *ibid.*, P 798

Sept. 19. To Edwin M. Stanton, Nicolay for Lincoln, forwarding letters of request based on political reasons, LS, *ibid.*, P 1253

Sept. 19. To Gideon Welles, concerning Mrs. Bushnell's son, Stan. V. Henkels Catalog 1342, Jan. 4, 1924, No. 48H

c. Sept. 20. To Edward Bates, Hay for Lincoln, referring letter of Oliver P. Morton to Lincoln, Sept. 20, 1864, recommending John D. Howland, DNA RG 60, Papers of Atty. Gen., Appts., Indiana, Box 406

Sept. 20. To Edward Bates, Hay for Lincoln, referring case of Laurent Blanchet, DNA RG 204, U.S. Pardon Atty., A 547

Sept. 20. To Edwin M. Stanton, Hay for Lincoln, forwarding letters of request for political reasons, LS, DNA WR RG 107, Sec. of War Letters Received, P 1253

Sept. 20. To Edwin M. Stanton, referring application of Malcolm Campbell for release of George H. Elwell, missing from *ibid.*, P 810

Sept. 21. To Edward Bates, Hay for Lincoln, referring letter of Noah H. Swayne to Lincoln, Sept. 16, 1864, recommending David McDonald, DNA RG 60, Papers of Atty. Gen., Appts., Indiana, Box 406

Sept. 21. To Edwin M. Stanton, Hay for Lincoln, referring letter of LaFayette S. Foster asking clemency for John H. Lester, DNA WR RG 153, Judge Adv. Gen., NN 1785

Sept. 21. To Edwin M. Stanton, Hay for Lincoln, forwarding letters of request for political reasons, DNA WR RG 107, Sec. of War Letters Received, P 1253

Sept. 21. To Lorenzo Thomas, Hay for Lincoln, referring letter of "A Virginia Republican" protesting selling of liquor in Portsmouth, Va., missing from DNA WR RG 94, Adj. Gen. Letters Received, P 1069

Sept. 22. To Edward Bates, Hay for Lincoln, referring letter of John L. Ketcham to Lincoln, Sept. 17, 1864, recommending John H. Bradley, DNA RG 60, Papers of Atty. Gen., Appts., Indiana, Box 406

Sept. 22. To Edward Bates, Hay for Lincoln, referring letter of John F. Starr to Lincoln, Sept. 20, 1864, asking pardon for Peter A. Bleyler, DNA RG 204, U.S. Pardon Atty., A 551

Sept. 22. To Edwin M. Stanton, referring request of M. K. Mackenzie to write concerning exchange to James Murdock, prisoner of war, missing from DNA WR RG 107, Sec. of War Letters Received, P 826

Sept. 23. Order, endorsed on letter of G. W. Schofield, "I do not remember this promise, but doubtless Mr Schofield does. Let the man be discharged on taking the oath of Dec 8, 1863 A LINCOLN," Stan. V. Henkels Catalog 1373, May 19, 1925, No. 141

c. Sept. 23. To Edwin M. Stanton, referring petition of James King for release of U.S. prisoners of war in Georgia, missing from DNA WR RG 107, Sec. of War Letters Received, P 814

c. Sept. 23. To Edwin M. Stanton, referring letter of Mrs. Fannie Donnelly, Crab Orchard, Ky., concerning loss of property, missing from *ibid.*, P 823

Sept. 24. To Edward Bates, Hay for Lincoln, requesting appointments for William O. Stoddard and Charles P. Redmond, ALS, DNA RG 60, Papers of Atty. Gen., Box 121

c. Sept. 24. To James B. Fry, NE, mentioned, Fry to Lincoln, Sept. 24, 1864, concerning Tom Crow, DLC-RTL

Sept. 24. To Edwin M. Stanton, referring letter of A. P. Stringer asking for pay, missing from DNA WR RG 107, Sec. of War Letters Received, P 833

c. Sept. 24. To Edwin M. Stanton, referring letter of S. R. B. Walton, Jefferson Co., Ark., complaining of property taken, missing from *ibid.*, P 831

c. Sept. 26. Endorsement, on letter of Hamilton G. Fant to Leonard Swett, Sept. 26, 1864, asking Swett to report to Lincoln the Fant Bank's actions on unpaid requisitions, "Read and return," AE, DLC-RTL

Sept. 26. To Montgomery C. Meigs, NE, mentioned, Meigs to Lincoln, Sept. 27, 1864, concerning Capt. James C. Slaght, DLC-RTL

Sept. 26. To Edwin M. Stanton, referring petition of Thomas Roaney, prisoner at Camp Morton, missing from DNA WR RG 107, Sec. of War Letters Received, P 838

c. Sept. 26. To Edwin M. Stanton, referring letter of James A. Garfield with enclosures asking revocation of order dismissing Lieut. Thornton Owens, missing from *ibid.*, P 842

Sept. 26. To Edwin M. Stanton, Nicolay for Lincoln, referring letters of request for political reasons, LS, *ibid.*, P 1253

Sept. 27. To Edwin M. Stanton, Nicolay for Lincoln, referring letter of James R. Doolittle to Nicolay, Sept. 22, 1864, recommending J.

E. Reece, DNA WR RG 107, Sec. of War Personnel Appts., Box 30

Sept. 27. To Edwin M. Stanton, referring petition of James Speed and others for pardon for John Q. Grable, missing from DNA WR RG 107, Sec. of War Letters Received, P 848

Sept. 27. To Edwin M. Stanton, referring request of Henry Janney that his son Joseph J. be ordered to Washington for special duty, missing from *ibid.*, P 853

Sept. 27. To Edwin M. Stanton, Hay for Lincoln, referring letter of John C. Ten Eyck to Lincoln, Sept. 24, 1864, asking pass for Mrs. J. K. Hora to come North, *ibid.*, P 934

Sept. 27. To Edwin M. Stanton, Nicolay for Lincoln, referring letter of James A. Price based on political reasons, *ibid.*, P 1253

Sept. 28. To Edward Bates, Nicolay for Lincoln, referring letter of P. Avandano, complaining of unjust treatment of Judge W. W. Handlin at New Orleans, DLC-RTL

Sept. 28. To Edward Bates, Hay for Lincoln, referring letter of David Davis to Lincoln, Sept. 6, 1864, recommending David McDonald, DNA RG 60, Papers of Atty. Gen., Appts., Indiana, Box 406

Sept. 28. To Edward Bates, Nicolay for Lincoln, referring letter from J. W. North to Lincoln, Aug. 22, 1864, resigning as associate justice of Nevada Territory, DNA RG 60, Papers of Atty. Gen., Box 119

Sept. 28. To Edward Bates, Nicolay for Lincoln, referring letter of Anson G. Henry to Lincoln, Aug. 15, 1864, concerning attempt to remove Judge Ethelbert P. Oliphant, *ibid.*, Box 122

Sept. 28. To Edward Bates, Nicolay for Lincoln, referring resignation and letter of George Turner resigning as chief justice of Nevada Territory, *ibid.*, Box 116 and 119

Sept. 28. To William P. Fessenden, Hay for Lincoln, referring letter of Cuthbert Bullitt to Lincoln, Sept. 12, 1864, DLC-RTL

Sept. 28. To Edwin M. Stanton, Nicolay for Lincoln, referring letter of J. S. Gearhart asking exchange of his son, DNA WR RG 107, Sec. of War Letters Received, P 861

Sept. 28. To Edwin M. Stanton, referring request of Gov. Richard Yates for court of inquiry for Gen. Stephen A. Hurlbut, missing from *ibid.*, P 867

Sept. 28. To Edwin M. Stanton, asking investigation of failure to muster Col. John H. Stover, missing from *ibid.*, P 899

Sept. 28. To Lorenzo Thomas, Nicolay for Lincoln, referring letter of Mrs. John Tyler asking restoration of her property at City Point, Va., missing from DNA WR RG 94, Adj. Gen. Letters Received, P 1096

Sept. 29. To Edward Bates, Hay for Lincoln, referring letter of James Hughes to Lincoln, Sept. 29, 1864, recommending David McDonald, DNA RG 60, Papers of Atty. Gen., Appts., Indiana, Box 406

Sept. 29. To Joseph Holt, Nicolay for Lincoln, referring letter of Eliza Hogue on behalf of husband Louis D. Hogue, DNA WR RG 153, Judge Adv. Gen., NN 1156

c. Sept. 29. To Edwin M. Stanton, referring letter of I. N. Henry protesting Gov. Hamilton R. Gamble's refusal to appoint him captain of company he raised, missing from DNA WR RG 107, Sec. of War Letters Received, P 856

c. Sept. 29. To Edwin M. Stanton, referring complaint of Joseph C. Clark that his son Joseph C. Jr., an assistant professor at West Point, has not been promoted, missing from *ibid.*, P 860

Sept. 29. To Edwin M. Stanton, referring anonymous letter with printed copy of *General Orders No. 4*, H.Q. of Gen. Joseph Hooker's Division, Feb. 28, 1862, and report on Silas Seymour, sutler, missing from *ibid.*, P 948

Sept. 29. To Edwin M. Stanton, Nicolay for Lincoln, forwarding letters of request for political reasons, LS, *ibid.*, P 1253

Sept. 30. To Edward Bates, Nicolay for Lincoln, referring letter of Samuel Walker to Lincoln, Sept. 21, 1864, asking appointment, DNA RG 60, Papers of Atty. Gen., Appts., Florida

Sept. 30. To Edwin M. Stanton, Nicolay for Lincoln, forwarding letters of request based on political reasons, LS, DNA WR RG 107, Sec. of War Letters Received, P 1253

c. Sept. 30. To Edwin M. Stanton, referring letter of David L. Phillips that civil and military authorities in Missouri are enemies of the administration, missing from *ibid.*, P 869

Oct. 1. To Edward Bates, Nicolay for Lincoln, referring letter of Willard P. Hall recommending Mordecai Oliver, DLC-RTL

Oct. 2. To Thomas Allcock, forgery, ALS, NN

Oct. 2. To Charles A. Dana, forgery, ALS, NN

Oct. 3. To Edwin M. Stanton, Nicolay for Lincoln, referring letters of request based on political reasons, LS, DNA WR RG 107, Sec. of War Letters Received, P 1253

Oct. 3. To Edwin M. Stanton, Nicolay for Lincoln, referring letter of Joshua H. Rodgers to Lincoln, Sept. 28, 1864, asking furlough to vote at home, ES, *ibid.*

Oct. 3. To Lorenzo Thomas, referring letter of John Peacher, Jr., concerning injustice in assessing damages to his property, DNA WR RG 94, Adj. Gen. Letters Received, P 1117

Oct. 4. To Edward Bates, Nicolay for Lincoln, referring petition of Peter Strobeck to Lincoln, Sept. 29, 1864, for return of citizenship, DNA WR RG 204, U.S. Pardon Atty., A 554

c. Oct. 4. To William S. Rosecrans, NE, mentioned, Rosecrans to Lincoln, Oct. 4, 1864, concerning Oliver D. Greene, John V. DuBois and Col. Myers, DLC-RTL

c. Oct. 4. To Edwin M. Stanton, referring application of H. G. Fitzhugh for release of George Brown at Ft. Delaware, missing from DNA WR RG 107, Sec. of War Letters Received, P 883

c. Oct. 4. To Edwin M. Stanton, referring application for discharge of Aaron P. Smith, missing from *ibid.*, 884

c. Oct. 4. To Edwin M. Stanton, referring letter of Mrs. Mary Barton complaining that Gen. Gordon Granger has turned her out of her house in Nashville, Tenn., missing from *ibid.*, P 886

c. Oct. 4. To Edwin M. Stanton, referring letter of Franklin Thomas a prisoner at Camp Chase who insists he is loyal, missing from *ibid.*, P 888

Oct. 4. To Edwin M. Stanton, referring application of John Sharpe, arrested as a deserter after having been discharged while a paroled prisoner, missing from *ibid.*, P 893

ОCTOBER 8, 1864

Oct. 4. To Edwin M. Stanton, referring application of William T. Norville for release, missing from *ibid.*, P 895

Oct. 5. To Edward Bates, Hay for Lincoln, referring letter of George Turner to Lincoln, Aug. 4, 1864 (duplicate), resigning as chief justice of Nevada Territory, DNA RG 60, Papers of Atty. Gen., Box 122

Oct. 5. To Edwin M. Stanton, Hay for Lincoln, referring requests based on political reasons, LS, DNA WR RG 94, Adj Gen. Letters Received, P 1112

Oct. 5. To Edwin M. Stanton, referring application of G. Kammerling for investigation of his dismissal, missing from DNA WR RG 107, Sec. of War Letters Received, P 896

Oct. 5. To Edwin M. Stanton, referring application of Fleetwood C. Toplis for discharge, missing from *ibid.*, P 900

Oct. 6. To Edwin M. Stanton, Hay for Lincoln, referring requests based upon political reasons, LS, *ibid.*, P 1253

Oct. 6. To Edwin M. Stanton, referring application for release of Andrew J. Sommers from Camp Douglas, missing from *ibid.*, P 897

Oct. 7. To Edward Bates, Hay for Lincoln, referring letter of J. Whitehead to Lincoln, Oct. 4, 1864, for release of Edward Leber and John Gilorley, DNA RG 204, U.S. Pardon Atty., A 550

Oct. 7. To Edward Bates, Hay for Lincoln, referring letter of Silas Woodson to Lincoln, Aug. 16, 1864, refusing appointment as chief justice of Idaho Territory, DNA RG 60, Papers of Atty. Gen., Box 120

Oct. 7. To George J. Holyoake, Hay for Lincoln, acknowledging letter of Sept. 4, 1864, ADf, DLC-RTL

c. Oct. 7. To Edwin M. Stanton, referring appeal for clemency for William T. Higgins, missing from DNA WR RG 107, Sec. of War Letters Received, P 902

Oct. 7. To Edwin M. Stanton, Hay for Lincoln, referring requests based upon political reasons, LS, *ibid.*, P 1253

c. Oct. 8. To Edwin M. Stanton, referring petition of Maggie Porter on behalf of her brother Joseph K., missing from *ibid.*, P 903

c. Oct. 8. To Edwin M. Stanton, referring application for exchange of Maj. W. II. Williamson, CSA, missing from *ibid.*, P 904

c. Oct. 8. To Edwin M. Stanton, referring application for release of Berryman Henwood, missing from *ibid.*, P 905

c. Oct. 8. To Edwin M. Stanton, referring claim of Peter Wise for a horse, missing from *ibid.*, P 911

c. Oct. 8. To Edwin M. Stanton, referring application for release of Daniel M. Staton, missing from *ibid.*, P 912

Oct. 8. To Edwin M. Stanton, Hay for Lincoln, referring petition by Curtis Stevens and others to Lincoln, Aug. 18, 1864, for release of N. W. Hammond, *ibid.*, P 916

Oct. 8. To Edwin M. Stanton, Hay for Lincoln, referring letter of Andrew Stewart to Lincoln, Oct. 5, 1864, asking exchange of son Andrew, Jr., *ibid.*, P 917

Oct. 8. To Edwin M. Stanton, Hay for Lincoln, referring letter of James A. Price to Lincoln, Sept. 29, 1864, concerning Copperhead activities in Missouri, *ibid.*, P 919

[561]

Oct. 8. To Edwin M. Stanton, Hay for Lincoln, referring letter from Zack White to Lincoln, Oct. 1, 1864, asking government to repair damages to his plantation near Vicksburg, *ibid.*, P 920

Oct. 11. To Edward Bates, Nicolay for Lincoln, referring petition of Joseph Brantenburg and Franklin Edmiston to Lincoln, Oct. 10, 1864, for pardon, DNA RG 204, U.S. Pardon Atty., A 558

Oct. 11. To Edward Bates, Hay for Lincoln, referring letter of Charles A. Rogers to Lincoln, Oct. 6, 1864, asking whether an alien who has served in Army is entitled to citizenship, DNA RG 60, Papers of Atty. Gen., Box 122

Oct. 11. To Edwin M. Stanton, referring application of Gov. Thomas E. Bramlette for release of Austin B. Price, missing from DNA WR RG 107, Sec. of War Letters Received, P 922

Oct. 11. To Edwin M. Stanton, Hay for Lincoln, referring request of Annie Spaulding to Lincoln, Oct. 2, 1864, for exchange of brother Lieut. Edward J. Spaulding, *ibid.*, P 923

Oct. 11. To Edwin M. Stanton, Hay for Lincoln, referring letter of Lawrence V. Houghton to Lincoln, Sept. 28, 1864, protesting order of Gen. Napoleon J. T. Dana closing probate court at Vicksburg, *ibid.*, P 928

c. Oct. 11. To Edwin M. Stanton, referring application of Jesse O. Norton for release of George Keel, missing from *ibid.*, P 929

c. Oct. 11. To Edwin M. Stanton, referring letter of Charles E. Sherman on injustice to 15th N.Y. Engineers, missing from *ibid.*, P 930

Oct. 12. To Edward Bates, on petition of Gideon Haynes and others to Lincoln, Aug. 15, 1864, for pardon for William Herbert, Charles C. Stanley, and Richard Carther, "Submitted to the Attorney General. A. LINCOLN," AES, DNA RG 204, U.S. Pardon Atty., A 559

Oct. 12. To Charles A. Dana, on envelope of letters on behalf of Samuel Sterett imprisoned for violation of 57th Art. of War, "Submitted to Mr. Dana. A.L.," AES, DNA WR RG 153, Judge Adv. Gen., MM 1106

Oct. 12. To Joseph Holt, on court-martial record of Frederick Wittig, sentenced to two years, "Application denied A. LINCOLN," *ibid.*, NN 1959

Oct. 12. To Edwin M. Stanton, on envelope in court-martial record of Samuel Sterett, "Submitted to the Sec. of War. A. LINCOLN," AES, *ibid.*, MM 1106

c. Oct. 12. To Edwin M. Stanton, referring application for release of James Farrell, missing from DNA WR RG 107, Sec. of War Letters Received, P 936

c. Oct. 12. To Edwin M. Stanton, referring letter of R. B. Smith complaining of his unjust imprisonment at Gratiot St. Prison, St. Louis, missing from *ibid.*, P 937

Oct. 12. To Lorenzo Thomas, referring letter of W. Willoughby, attorney for Alexandria, Va., on illegal manner of trying persons charged with violating military laws, "What does this mean," copy in Register, but missing from DNA WR RG 94, Adj. Gen. Letters Received, P 1167; also missing from DNA WR RG 107, Sec. of War Letters Received, P 952

Oct. 12. Endorsement, on letter of John L. Wilderman to Lincoln, Oct. 3, 1864, "What is this about? A. LINCOLN," copy, ISLA

Oct. 13. To Andrew G. Curtin, Hay for Lincoln, acknowledging receipt of communication from Erie, Pa., LS, DNA WR RG 107, Pres. Telegrams, I, 202

Oct. 13. To Joseph Holt, on court-martial record of Jesse A. Broadway, "Sentence in this case commuted to imprisonment in the penitentiary at hard labor for three years. A. LINCOLN," AES, DNA WR RG 153, Judge Adv. Gen., NN 1822

c. Oct. 13. To Edwin M. Stanton, referring letter of R. H. Duell asking exchange of certain members of 15th N.Y. Engineers, missing from DNA WR RG 107, Sec. of War Letters Received, P 940

Oct. 15. To Edwin M. Stanton, Hay for Lincoln, referring letter of Richard Yates to Lincoln, Oct. 11, 1864, asking exchange of Edward P. Strickland, 114th Ill. Vols., ibid., P 951

Oct. 15. To Edwin M. Stanton, Hay for Lincoln, referring letter of James L. Meigs to Lincoln, Oct. 10, 1864, asking permission for Mrs. Thomas Smith to visit her son Felix at Johnson's Island, ibid., P 963

Oct. 17. To Edwin M. Stanton, Hay for Lincoln, referring letter of George L. Ashmead to Lincoln, Oct. 15, 1864, asking permission to visit his son George, Jr., at Camp Lookout, Md., ibid., P 956

Oct. 17. To Edwin M. Stanton, Hay for Lincoln, referring letter of P. Hammond to Lincoln, Oct. 15, 1864, asking special exchange of captain and crew of Emily, ibid., P 958

Oct. 17. To Edwin M. Stanton, on letter of J. C. Starkweather to Oliver P. Morton, Nov. 7, 1863, recommending John P. Dunn, "Submitted to the Secretary of War. A. LINCOLN," AES, ibid., Personnel Appts., Box 26

c. Oct. 17. Endorsement, on envelope of Elihu Washburne's letter to Lincoln, Oct. 17, 1864, giving gloomy predictions on the election, "Stampeded," AE, DLC-RTL

Oct. 18. To Edward Bates, Hay for Lincoln, referring resignation of Joseph G. Easton to Lincoln, Oct. 10, 1864, as U.S. Marshal at St. Louis, DNA RG 60, Papers of Atty. Gen., Box 122

c. Oct. 18. To Edwin M. Stanton, referring application of Lieut. W. Alexander, for release from Ft. Delaware, missing from DNA WR RG 107, Sec. of War Letters Received, P 957

Oct. 19. To Edward Bates, referring petition for pardon of William Ward, DNA RG 204, U.S. Pardon Atty., A 560

Oct. 19. To John Hay, check for $5.50, DS, RPB

Oct. 19. To Ethan A. Hitchcock, on petition for exchange of Lieut. Thomas J. Crossley, 57th Pa. Vols., and Joseph L. Leslie, 18th Pa. Cav., "Respectfully submitted to Gen. Hitchcock A. LINCOLN," AES, DNA WR RG 107, Sec. of War Letters Received, P 1036

Oct. 19. To Joseph Holt, on court-martial record of Victor Jaeger, 15th Ill. Cav., "Pardon. A. LINCOLN," AES, DNA WR RG 153, Judge Adv. Gen., MM 1371

c. Oct. 19. To Edwin M. Stanton, referring letter of Mrs. C. J. Foote asking trial of Edward M. Grant at Camp Chase, missing from DNA WR RG 107, Sec. of War Letters Received, P 959

c. Oct. 19. To Edwin M. Stanton, referring application of A. A. Kyle to visit prisoners at Ft. Delaware, missing from *ibid.*, P 965

Oct. 20. To Edwin M. Stanton, referring petition for release of Henry Loser, missing from *ibid.*, P 966

c. Oct. 20. To Edwin M. Stanton, referring letter of J. R. Fairlamb, consul at Zurich, enclosing letter of Baron von Apel asking exchange of his son Philip, 16th N.Y. Cav., missing from *ibid.*, P 967

Oct. 20. To Edwin M. Stanton, referring application for release of Francis Burke, missing from *ibid.*, P 968

c. Oct. 20. To Edwin M. Stanton, Hay for Lincoln, referring letter of John L. N. Stratton to Lincoln, Oct. 20, 1864, and petition of Mrs. Mary Slaughter and son to return to Lynchburg, Va., *ibid.*, P 982

c. Oct. 21. To Edwin M. Stanton, referring claim of Capt. Joseph Indest for back pay, missing from *ibid.*, P 973

Oct. 22. To Edward Bates, Hay for Lincoln, referring letter of Henry S. Lane to Lincoln, Oct. 15, 1864, recommending Richard W. Thompson, DNA RG 60, Papers of Atty. Gen., Appts., Indiana, Box 406

Oct. 22. To Edward Bates, Hay for Lincoln, referring letter of John D. Defrees to Lincoln, Oct. 15, 1864, recommending John H. Bradley, *ibid.*

Oct. 22. To Edward Bates, Hay for Lincoln, referring letter of Schuyler Colfax to Lincoln, Oct. 15, 1864, recommending Andrew L. Osborne, *ibid.*

Oct. 22. Endorsement on letter from James Speed requesting release of Granville Garnett, AES, Metropolitan Art Assn. Catalog, Apr. 1, 1914, No. 573

Oct. 24. To Edward Bates, Hay for Lincoln, referring letter of Archibald Dixon to Lincoln, Oct. 11, 1864, recommending James G. Jones, DNA RG 60, Papers of Atty. Gen., Appts., Indiana, Box 406

Oct. 24. To Edward Bates, Hay for Lincoln, referring letter of Ralph Hill to Lincoln, Oct. 18, 1864, recommending Simeon Stanifer, *ibid.*

Oct. 24. To Edward Bates, Hay for Lincoln, referring letter of John Hanna to Lincoln, Oct. 20, 1864, urging appointment of successor to "Judge Waite," *ibid.* (1864), Box 122

Oct. 24. Endorsement on letter of Edwin H. Webster to Lincoln, Oct. 20, 1864, "Wm. Penn Duvall born Jan. 13, 1847. Applies for West Point. A. LINCOLN," AES, DNA WR RG 94, U.S. Mil. Acad., 1864, No. 318

c. Oct. 24. To Edwin M. Stanton, referring letter on dismissal of Lieut. Truman A. Post, missing from DNA WR RG 107, Sec. of War Letters Received, P 976

c. Oct. 24. To Edwin M. Stanton, referring application of Joseph Holt for release from draft of son of Mrs. Rhoda Wickliffe of Ky., missing from *ibid.*, P 977

c. Oct. 24. To Edwin M. Stanton, referring letter of John L. Scripps enclosing letter of Col. William A. Phillips complaining of his removal from command of Indian Dept. and of frauds at Ft. Smith, missing from *ibid.*, P 989

Oct. 25. To Joseph Holt, Hay for Lincoln, referring letter of Rev. Phineas D. Gurley to Lincoln, Oct. 12, 1864, respecting case of Rev Dr. Handy confined at Ft. Delaware, DLC-RTL

Oct. 25. To Edwin M. Stanton, Hay for Lincoln, referring letter of J. M. Christopher requesting special exchange of his son John in Charleston Prison, DNA WR RG 107, Sec. of War Letters Received, P 986

Oct. 25. To Edward D. Townsend, Hay for Lincoln, referring telegram from Gustave P. Koerner to Lincoln, Oct. 25, 1864, asking 300 drafted men assigned to 43rd Ill. Vols., DLC-RTL

Oct. 26. To Joseph K. Barnes, on petition of dismissed hospital chaplain, "Surgeon General, please report, A. LINCOLN," AES, Parke-Bernet Catalog 82, Jan. 18, 1939, No. 88

Oct. 26. To Edwin M. Stanton, requesting report on case of Samuel Sterett, missing from DNA WR RG 107, Sec. of War Letters Received, P 999-Pres. 15

c. Oct. 27. To Edwin M. Stanton, referring application of John Gampher for discharge of his son in Chestnut Hill Hospital, missing from *ibid.*, P 988

Oct. 28. To Edward Bates, Hay for Lincoln, referring letter of W. Y. Fendall to Lincoln, Oct. 25, 1864, asking pardon for Franklin Edmiston, DNA RG 204, U.S. Pardon Atty., A 558

Oct. 28. To Edwin M. Stanton, on letter of Gov. Joel Parker to Lincoln, Oct. 26, 1864, concerning resolution of N.J. legislature on soldier voting, "Submitted to the Secretary of War. A LINCOLN," AES, NN

Oct. 28. To Edwin M. Stanton, referring application of Jesse O. Norton for discharge of Ashbury C. Jewett, 88th Ill. Inf., missing from DNA WR RG 107, Sec. of War Letters Received, P 992

Oct. 29. To Edward Bates, Hay for Lincoln, referring letter of John Lintner to Lincoln, Oct. 25, 1864, asking pardon of son Amos, DNA RG 204, U.S. Pardon Atty., A 543

Oct. 29. To Edwin M. Stanton, referring application of W. P. Jones for release of nephew at Johnson's Island, missing from DNA WR RG 107, Sec. of War Letters Received, P 994

c. Oct. 29. To Edwin M. Stanton, referring application for release of Spurlock, prisoner of war at Rock Island, Ill., missing from *ibid.*, P 996

Oct. 31. To Joseph Holt, mitigating sentence of George H. Farnsworth, missing from DNA WR RG 153, Judge Adv. Gen., LL 2212

Oct. 31. To Ethan A. Hitchcock, on letter of John L. Hancock and "Jno. F. Beaty," "Submitted to General Hitchcock. A. LINCOLN," OR, II, VII, 1015

Oct. 31. To Edwin M. Stanton, referring application of John R. Woods to take over government building for Sanitary Commission at Springfield, Ill., missing from DNA WR RG 107, Sec. of War Letters Received, P 1001

Nov. 1. To Edward Bates, Hay for Lincoln, referring telegram from James Y. Smith to Lincoln, received Nov. 1, 1864, asking pardon for William A. Harlow, DNA RG 204, U.S. Pardon Atty., A 557

Nov. 1. To Joseph Holt, on court-martial record of Joseph M. Marsh, "Pardon for unexecuted part of punishment A. LINCOLN," AES, DNA WR RG 153, Judge Adv. Gen., NN 1844

Nov. 1. To Meyer S. Isaacs, Hay for Lincoln, acknowledging receipt of Isaacs' letter to Lincoln, Oct. 25, 1864, concerning an interview Lincoln had with "certain gentlemen of the Hebrew faith," DLC-RTL

c. Nov. 1. To Edwin M. Stanton, on petition of Cincinnati citizens for appointment of James A. Crawford as assistant quartermaster general, Nov. 1, 1864, "[Sub]mitted [to the Sec. of] War A. LINCOLN," AES-P, ISLA

Nov. 1. To Edwin M. Stanton, Hay for Lincoln, referring letter of J. M. Christopher for exchange of son John in Charleston Prison, DNA WR RG 107, Sec. of War Letters Received, P 986

Nov. 2. To G. H. Blakeslee, sending autograph, ALS-F, Francis D. Blakeslee, *How My Father Secured Lincoln's Autograph* (1927)

Nov. 3. To Edward Bates, Hay for Lincoln, referring letter of George W. Hull to Lincoln, Oct. 31, 1864, concerning right to vote, DNA RG 60, Papers of Atty. Gen., Box 122

Nov. 3. To Edwin M. Stanton, referring application of Lieut. W. J. Keys, 16th N.Y. Cav., for restoration of pay, missing from DNA WR RG 107, Sec. of War Letters Received, P 1008

Nov. 3. To Edwin M. Stanton, Hay for Lincoln, referring letter from H. Wilber to Lincoln, Oct. 8, 1864, asking permission to ship pistols abroad, *ibid.*, P 1025

Nov. 4. To Edward Bates, Hay for Lincoln, referring letter of E. S. Terry recommending David McDonald, DNA RG 60, Papers of Atty. Gen., Appts., Indiana, Box 406

Nov. 4. To Montgomery C. Meigs, mentioned, Lebanon, Pa. *Reporter*, Feb. 10, 1909

Nov. 4. To Edwin M. Stanton, referring application for remission of sentence in case of Bartholomew Hileman, missing from DNA WR RG 107, Sec. of War Letters Received, P 1091

Nov. 5. To Edwin M. Stanton, Hay for Lincoln, referring letter of Thomas L. Kane to Lincoln, Oct. 31, 1864, asking release of nephew, prisoner at Ft. Delaware, *ibid.*, P 1036

Nov. 9. To Edward Bates, Hay for Lincoln, referring attested copy of petition from Union League of Terre Haute, Ind., to Lincoln, Oct. 31, 1864, for appointment of Richard W. Thompson, DNA RG 60, Papers of Atty. Gen., Appts., Indiana, Box 406

Nov. 10. To D. A. Harsha, NE, mentioned, Harsha to Lincoln, Nov. 23, 1864, concerning gift copy of "Sumner's Life," DLC-RTL

c. Nov. 11. To Anson G. Henry, NE, mentioned in Noah Brooks, "Lincoln's Reelection," *Century Magazine*, XLIX (April, 1895), 866

Nov. 11. To Edwin M. Stanton, referring petition for discharge of George B. Lucas, missing from DNA WR RG 107, Sec. of War Letters Received, P 1020

Nov. 11. To Edwin M. Stanton, Hay for Lincoln, referring letter of Sallie A. Barrett to Lincoln, Nov. 4, 1864, asking exchange of husband in Charleston Prison, *ibid.*, P 1021

Nov. 11. To Edwin M. Stanton, Hay for Lincoln, referring petition of Charles L. Shepherd, Lyman Trumbull and John L. Scripps to Lincoln, Nov. 3, 1864, for exchange of Frank P. Shepherd, *ibid.*, P 1023

Nov. 12. To Joseph Holt, on letter of John P. Glass asking clemency for Thomas Dain, "Pardon A. Lincoln," AES, DNA WR RG 153, Judge Adv. Gen., NN 2090

Nov. 12. To Edwin M. Stanton, referring petition for discharge of Agnew Sellers, missing from DNA WR RG 107, Sec. of War Letters Received, P 1024

Nov. 14. To Edward Bates, Hay for Lincoln, referring petition of C. Van Allen and others to Lincoln, Oct. 28, 1864, for pardon of William H. McIntosh, DNA RG 204, U.S. Pardon Atty., A 569

Nov. 14. To Edwin M. Stanton, on letter of Bellamy Storer to Lincoln, Nov. 1, 1864, enclosing a petition by citizens of Cincinnati, "Respectfully submitted to the Sec. of War A. Lincoln," AES, IHi

Nov. 15. To Edward Bates, Hay for Lincoln, referring letter of Solomon Meredith to Lincoln, Nov. 4, 1864, recommending George Holland, DNA RG 60, Papers of Atty. Gen., Appts., Indiana, Box 406

Nov. 15. To Edward Bates, Hay for Lincoln, referring request for pardon of Charles Hellerson, DNA RG 204, U.S. Pardon Atty., B 10

Nov. 15. To Edwin M. Stanton, Hay for Lincoln, referring letter of William H. Schwindler to Lincoln, c. Nov. 1864, DNA WR RG 107, Sec. of War Letters Received, P 1027

Nov. 15. To Edwin M. Stanton, referring letter of Jean Barbier complaining of mistreatment in the Alexandria, Va., jail, missing from *ibid.*, P 1028

Nov. 15. To Edwin M. Stanton, referring petition of Edwin Maxwell and others, for discharge of A. Werninger, Jr., missing from *ibid.*, P 1031

Nov. 15. To Edwin M. Stanton, referring petition for release of Samuel R. Ridlen, missing from *ibid.*, P 1032

Nov. 15. To Edwin M. Stanton, referring petition for pardon of James D. Maloney, missing from *ibid.*, P 1034

Nov. 16. To Edwin M. Stanton, on copy of letter of Gen. Frederick Steele to Stanton, Sept. 16, 1864, recommending Col. Thomas H. Benton, Jr., "Submitted to the Sec. of War. A. Lincoln," AES, RPB

Nov. 17. To Joseph Holt, Hay for Lincoln, referring petition for executive clemency for Benjamin Jones, DNA WR RG 153, Judge Adv. Gen., LL 2393

Nov. 17. To Edwin M. Stanton, Hay for Lincoln, referring letter of Samuel Howard to Gov. Thomas E. Bramlette, Nov. 2, 1864, protesting unjust imprisonment, DNA WR RG 107, Sec. of War Letters Received, P 1040

Nov. 17. To Edwin M. Stanton, Hay for Lincoln, referring letter of Bettie F. Harkness asking exchange of husband Capt. Robert Harkness, *ibid.*, P 1041

Nov. 17. To Edwin M. Stanton, referring letter of John Conley, rebel deserter, asking release from Ft. McHenry, missing from *ibid.*, P 1051

c. Nov. 18. To Rev. and Mrs. Phineas D. Gurley, form invitation to dinner, Nov. 18, 1864, Parke-Bernet Catalog 1352, May 27, 1952, No. 182

c. Nov. 18. To Edwin M. Stanton, referring letter of John P. Vance on behalf of A. T. Doty arrested for violating oath of allegiance, missing from DNA WR RG 107, Sec. of War Letters Received, P 1043

Nov. 18. To Edwin M. Stanton, Hay for Lincoln, referring letter of Mr. Hooper of Meigsville, Ohio, to Lincoln, Nov. 10, 1864, asking that body of his son John be shipped to him, *ibid.*, P 1055

Nov. 18. To Edwin M. Stanton, Hay for Lincoln, referring letter of Ella C. McCarty to Lincoln, Nov. 13, 1864, asking exchange of father, Capt. William W. McCarty, *ibid.*, P 1057

Nov. 18. To Edwin M. Stanton, Hay for Lincoln, referring letter of Mrs. Henry C. Davis, Nov. 18, 1864, asking exchange of husband, *ibid.*, P 1058

Nov. 18. To Edwin M. Stanton, referring letter of J. T. Fulton concerning contract for hats, missing from *ibid.*, P 1090

Nov. 19. To Edward Bates, Hay for Lincoln, referring letter of J. A. Matson to Gov. William Dennison, Nov. 7, 1864, asking appointment, DNA RG 60, Papers of Atty. Gen., Appts., Indiana, Box 406

c. Nov. 19. To Edwin M. Stanton, referring letter of John Devite, rebel deserter at Ft. McHenry, missing from DNA WR RG 107, Sec. of War Letters Received, P 1052

Nov. 19. To Edwin M. Stanton, Hay for Lincoln, referring letter of Mrs. Ninian E. Primm to Lincoln, Nov. 13, 1864, asking relief, *ibid.*, P 1064

Nov. 19. To Edwin M. Stanton, Hay for Lincoln, referring letter of A. Galbraith to Lincoln, Nov. 13, 1864, asking exchange of Capt. S. G. Galbraith, *ibid.*, P 1065

Nov. 19. To Lorenzo Thomas, Hay for Lincoln, referring request for appointment of Rev. S. W. Madden as chaplain of Freedmen's Hospital, Washington, missing from DNA WR RG 94, Adj. Gen. Letters Received, P 1337

Nov. 20. To Charles A. Dana, asking him to see Mr. Stokes, Metropolitan Art Assn. Catalog, Apr. 1, 1914, No. 574

Nov. 21. To Edward Bates, Hay for Lincoln, referring petition on behalf of David S. Everett, DNA RG 204, U.S. Pardon Atty., A 572

Nov. 21. To William H. Seward, Hay for Lincoln, referring application of Otis O. Ordway to Lincoln, Nov. 15, 1864, DNA FS RG 59, Appointments, Box 356

c. Nov. 21. To Edwin M. Stanton, referring letter of W. T. Love concerning sale of arms to Indiana conspirators, missing from DNA WR RG 107, Sec. of War Letters Received, P 1059

c. Nov. 21. To Edwin M. Stanton, referring application for release of Alfred Barrey, prisoner at Ft. Delaware, missing from *ibid.*, P 1063

Nov. 21. To Edwin M. Stanton, referring petition of members of 42nd Ohio Vols. unjustly held beyond their term, missing from *ibid.*, P 1068

Nov. 21. To Edwin M. Stanton, Hay for Lincoln, referring Lawrence V. Houghton to Lincoln, Nov. 10, 1864, complaining of Gen. Napoleon J. T. Dana's administration in Vicksburg, *ibid.*, P 1070

Nov. 21. To Edwin M. Stanton, Hay for Lincoln, referring letter of Mrs. Barbara Hester to Lincoln, Nov. 18, 1864, asking pass to Georgia to get remains of son, H. L. Breneman, *ibid.*, P 1076

Nov. 21. To Edwin M. Stanton, Hay for Lincoln, referring letter of Thomas Osborne to Lincoln, Nov. 18, 1864, asking release from Washington jail, *ibid.*, P 1081

Nov. 23. To Edward Bates, Hay for Lincoln, referring letter of Ebon C. Ingersoll to Lincoln, Nov. 17, 1864, asking that brother Robert G. be appointed U.S. attorney for Northern Illinois, DNA RG 60, Papers of Atty. Gen., Appts., Illinois, Box 373

Nov. 23. To Edwin M. Stanton, Hay for Lincoln, referring letter of James Speed to Lincoln, Oct. 21, 1864, introducing Mrs. Lucy M. Forde who wishes to go to Richmond, DNA WR RG 107, Sec. of War Letters Received, P 1087

Nov. 23. To Edwin M. Stanton, referring request of R. H. Duell that some men of 8th N.Y. Cav. be discharged, missing from *ibid.*, P 1094

Nov. 23. To Edwin M. Stanton, referring letter of Moses F. Odell to Lincoln, asking information on case of John O'Brien, missing from *ibid.*, P 1096

c. Nov. 23. To Lorenzo Thomas, referring letter of Alexander K. Mc-Clure recommending the uniforming of the militia of Franklin Co., Pa., missing from DNA WR RG 94, Adj. Gen. Letters Received, P 1329

c. Nov. 24. To Edwin M. Stanton, Nicolay for Lincoln, referring letter of Virginia C. Wickliffe, Lexington, Ky., to Lincoln, Nov. 21, 1864, asking permission for husband D. C. Wickliffe to return from South, DNA WR RG 107, Sec. of War Letters Received, P 1116

Nov. 25. To George B. Smith, Hay for Lincoln, acknowledging present of piece of beef, DLC-RTL

Nov. 25. To Edwin M. Stanton, referring letter of John A. Andrew asking reconsideration of dismissal of Capt. Henry S. Burrage, missing from DNA WR RG 107, Sec. of War Letters Received, P 1164

Nov. 25. To Edwin M. Stanton, on letter of Gen. David Hunter to Lincoln, Nov. 24, 1864, recommending Lieut. William Alexander, "Respectfully commended to the favorable consideration of the Secretary of War   A. LINCOLN," ES, IHi

Nov. 27. To Edwin M. Stanton, Hay for Lincoln, referring letter of L. B. Wynne to John Hay, Nov. 23, 1864, enclosing petition from Menard County, Ill., for exchange of Marion D. Gadsby, DNA WR RG 107, Sec. of War Letters Received, P 1097

Nov. 28. To Edward Bates, concerning appointment of Richard W. Thompson, missing from DNA RG 60, Papers of Atty. Gen., Appts., Indiana, Box 406

c. Nov. 28. To Edward Bates, Nicolay for Lincoln, referring letter of William A. Dart to Lincoln, Nov. 28, 1864, asking pardon for Alexander Powell, DNA RG 204, U.S. Pardon Atty., A 571

c. Nov. 28. Endorsement, on letter of Henry Upton and Horatio Wright to Stanton, Nov. 28, 1864, recommending Robert L. Wright, "West-Point—good Vouchers," AE, DNA WR RG 94, U.S. Mil. Acad., 1864, No. 427

c. Nov. 28. To Edwin M. Stanton, referring request of P. S. Jones for aid in repairing First Baptist Church in Memphis, missing from DNA WR RG 107, Sec. of War Letters Received, P 1098

c. Nov. 28. To Edwin M. Stanton, referring letter of August P. Reitscher asking trial by court-martial, missing from *ibid.*, P 1099

Nov. 28. To Edwin M. Stanton, Hay for Lincoln, referring letter of Mrs. Daniel S. Wilder asking exchange of husband, *ibid.*, P 1102

Nov. 28. To Edwin M. Stanton, referring letter of Prof. H. B. Hackett endorsed by Charles Sumner on behalf of Henry S. Burrage, missing from *ibid.*, P 1103 with Pres. 1164 EB 8

Nov. 28. To Edwin M. Stanton, Hay for Lincoln, referring letter of Henry W. Davis to Lincoln, Nov. 26, 1864, enclosing papers on case of Hamilton Easter, *ibid.*, P 1117

Nov. 28. To Edwin M. Stanton, referring letter of T. C. Bailey and John Lindsey charging Capt. Nathan Willard with fraud, missing from *ibid.*, P 1121

c. Nov. 29. To Edwin M. Stanton, referring application of William H. Herndon for discharge of William Zane, missing from *ibid.*, P 1104

c. Nov. 29. To Edwin M. Stanton, referring application of Peter Tatro, Jr., for discharge of son Talmer, missing from *ibid.*, P 1105

Dec. —. To Edmund D. Taylor, concerning greenbacks, spurious, Hertz, II, 957

c. Dec. 1. To Edwin M. Stanton, ordering release of Alfred Simpson, prisoner at Camp Morton, missing from DNA WR RG 107, Sec. of War, Misc. Papers, Box 583, D 333

Dec. 1. To Edwin M. Stanton, referring application of Alexander Davidson for release of R. B. Hook, rebel deserter in Old Capitol Prison, missing from *ibid.*, Letters Received, P 1118

Dec. 3. To Edwin M. Stanton, referring letter of Col. Alexander Cummings requesting appointment of Lieut. A. P. King, Jr., to detail of inspecting barracks and draft rendezvous at Phila., missing from *ibid.*, P 446

c. Dec. 3. To Edwin M. Stanton, Nicolay for Lincoln, referring letter of Gideon Bautz to Lincoln, Dec. 3, 1864, with request of B. Ebert & Sons to ship firearms, missing from *ibid.*, P 1123

Dec. 5. To James Speed, Nicolay for Lincoln, referring letter of James M. Ellis to Lincoln, Nov. 28, 1864, asking appointment, DNA RG 60, Papers of Atty. Gen., Appts., Territories, General, Box 1111

Dec. 6. To James Speed, John P. Usher for Lincoln, on letter of George C. Whiting to Usher, Dec. 6, 1864, asking pardon for George Simms, "Let a pardon issue in this case." DNA RG 204, U.S. Pardon Atty., A 376

Dec. 7. To Edwin M. Stanton, referring letter of R. Stockett Mathews concerning case of James and Charles Sears, missing from DNA WR RG 107, Sec. of War Letters Received, P 284

Dec. 7. To Edwin M. Stanton, referring claim of William Edwards that he was wrongfully arrested as a deserter, missing from *ibid.*, P 1128

Dec. 8. Endorsement, clipped from document, "I suppose there is some charge against this man; but if there is none, let him be discharged. A. LINCOLN," AES, owned by Mrs. Charles M. Kindel, Grand Rapids, Mich.

c. Dec. 8. To Edwin M. Stanton, referring application for mustering out James H. Terwiliger and Samuel Howry, missing from DNA WR RG 107, Sec. of War Letters Received, P 1125

Dec. 8. To Edwin M. Stanton, on envelope containing letters of Gen. Solomon Meredith asking assignment of Col. J. J. Guppey and Gen.

Alexander Shaler to his command, "Submitted to the Sec. of War. A. LINCOLN," AES, DNA WR RG 94, Adj. Gen. Letters Received, P 1472 (formerly P 1185)

Dec. 9. To Edwin M. Stanton, referring letter of Evan Davis, deserter, 2nd U.S. Dragoons, asking to be returned to his company, missing from DNA WR RG 107, Sec. of War Letters Received, P 1138

Dec. 9. To Edwin M. Stanton, referring letter of Mrs. Allie de Frate asking to join husband in 16th Vet. Res. Corps, missing from *ibid.*, P 1151

c. Dec. 9. To John P. Usher, on letter of James H. Lane to Lincoln, Dec. 9, 1864, recommending D. W. Stormant as receiver at Topeka, Kansas, "No controversy," AE, DNA NR RG 48, Appts., Land Offices, Topeka, Box 46

c. Dec. 9. To John P. Usher, on letter of James H. Lane to Lincoln, Dec. 9, 1864, recommending Dr. George W. Martin as register at Junction City, Kansas, "No controversy," AE, *ibid.*, Junction City, Box 28

Dec. 10. To Edwin M. Stanton, referring letter of Mrs. M. Fourbe for information concerning son William in 28th N.Y. Vols., missing from DNA WR RG 107, Sec. of War Letters Received, P 563

Dec. 10. To Edwin M. Stanton, referring letter of Woolman Hunt charging Dr. M. Goldsmith, surgeon U.S. Hospital, Jeffersonville, Ind., with stealing hogs, missing from *ibid.*, P 1141

Dec. 10. To Edwin M. Stanton, Nicolay for Lincoln, referring letter of A. Stirling and John L. Thomas to Lincoln, Dec. 8, 1864, concerning case of Moses Weisenfeldt & Co., *ibid.*, P 1143

Dec. 12. Endorsement, on letter of Robert Lincoln asking release of seventeen-year-old boy, "Let this boy be discharged on refunding any bounty received, A. LINCOLN," AES, William D. Morley Catalog, Jan. 28, 1944, No. 87

Dec. 12. To Ethan A. Hitchcock, on request of John T. and W. A. Gunn to W. C. Goodloe for discharge of Lieut. Thomas M. Gunn, "Submitted to Gen. Hitchcock," AES, Stan. V. Henkels Catalog 1401, Apr. 21, 1927, No. 166

Dec. 12. To Joseph Holt, on court-martial record of George H. Farnsworth, "Pardon for unexecuted part of sentence. A. LINCOLN," AES, DNA WR RG 153, Judge Adv. Gen., LL 2212

Dec. 12. To Joseph Holt, on petition for pardon of James C. Lessig, "Pardon, for unexecuted part of sentence. A. LINCOLN," AES, IHi

Dec. 12. To Joseph Holt, on court-martial record of Col. H. L. Potter, "Pardon and disability removed A. LINCOLN," AES, DNA WR RG 153, Judge Adv. Gen., NN 1929 and 2044

Dec. 12. To William H. Seward, Nicolay for Lincoln, referring letter of James K. Moorhead to Lincoln, Dec. 8, 1864, recommending William W. Ketchum, DNA FS RG 59, Appointments, Box 323

Dec. 12. To James Speed, Hay for Lincoln, referring letter of Oliver P. Morton to Lincoln, Nov. 14, 1864, recommending Andrew L. Osborne, DNA RG 60, Papers of Atty. Gen., Appts., Indiana, Box 406

Dec. 12. To Edwin M. Stanton, referring application of Samuel Waller for discharge of son George, missing from DNA WR RG 107, Sec. of War Letters Received, P 1148

Dec. 12. To Edwin M. Stanton, referring application of Capt. C. H. Goebel for revocation of his discharge, missing from *ibid.*, P 1196

Dec. 13. To William H. Seward, Nicolay for Lincoln, referring letter of Benjamin H. Brewster to Lincoln, c. Dec. 1864, recommending Wilson Eyre, DNA FS RG 59, Appointments, Box 282

c. Dec. 13. To Edwin M. Stanton, referring letter of John Stransky asking release from military prison in Cincinnati, DNA WR RG 107, Sec. of War Letters Received, P 1149

Dec. 15. To Governors and Lieutenant Governors, introducing Maurice H. Burr, forgery, ALS, DLC-Nicolay Papers

Dec. 15. To James Speed, on petition signed by members of Congress to Lincoln, c. Dec. 1864, "Attorney General please make out a pardon in this case. A. LINCOLN," AES, DNA RG 204, U.S. Pardon Atty., A 371

Dec. 15. To Edwin M. Stanton, Nicolay for Lincoln, referring letter of A. Callahan in Charleston Prison asking speedy exchange, DNA WR RG 107, Sec. of War Letters Received, P 1163

Dec. 15. To Edwin M. Stanton, referring application for release of Robert E. Dovan, prisoner at Camp Morton, missing from *ibid.*, P 1166

Dec. 17. To James Speed, Nicolay for Lincoln, referring letter of Benjamin F. Loan to Lincoln, Dec. 14, 1864, concerning appointment of P. Bliss as judge of the Western district of Missouri, RPB

Dec. 19. To Joseph Holt, on court-martial record of William S. Fish, "Pardon for unexecuted part of sentence. A. LINCOLN," AES, DNA WR RG 153, Judge Adv. Gen., MM 1356

Dec. 20. To James Speed, Nicolay for Lincoln, referring letter of William N. Grover to Lincoln, Dec. 15, 1864, recommending John Maguire, DNA RG 60, Papers of Atty. Gen., Appts., Missouri, Box 588

Dec. 20. To Edwin M. Stanton, referring application of Phineas C. Branch for discharge, missing from DNA WR RG 107, Sec. of War Letters Received, P 1188

Dec. 20. To Edwin M. Stanton, referring letter of Frank P. Blair, Jr. to George K. McGunnegle, June 2, 1862, concerning appointment of McGunnegle's son, "Submitted to the Sec. of War. A. LINCOLN," copy, ISLA

Dec. 20. To Edward D. Townsend, Nicolay for Lincoln, asking recommendations for promotion of Col. P. Sidney Post, DNA WR RG 94, Adj. Gen. Letters Received, P 1470

Dec. 21. To Joseph K. Barnes, Nicolay for Lincoln, referring letter of Edward D. Neill asking recognition for services of women volunteers in hospitals, DLC-RTL

Dec. 21. To Edwin M. Stanton, referring letter of Mrs. J. W. Cook whose husband in Canada wants a pardon, missing from DNA WR RG 107, Sec. of War Letters Received, P 1193

Dec. 21. To Edwin M. Stanton, referring application of Daniel L. Bordan and others for release of Henson Pool, missing from *ibid.*, P 1197

Dec. 22. To Joseph Holt, on court-martial record of Joshua H. Shipley, "Unexecuted part of sentence remitted. A. LINCOLN," AES, DNA WR RG 153, Judge Adv. Gen., LL 2354

Dec. 22. To Edwin M. Stanton, referring application of Benjamin F. James for release of George Brown from Ft. Delaware, missing from DNA WR RG 107, Sec. of War Letters Received, P 1201

Dec. 23. To Joseph Holt, on court-martial record of William B. Belch, "Pardon for unexecuted part of sentence A. LINCOLN," AES, DNA WR RG 153, Judge Adv. Gen., NN 1728

Dec. 23. To Edwin M. Stanton, on telegram of Maj. Gen. Andrew J. Smith to Lincoln, Dec. 18, 1864, recommending appointment of Col. William L. McMillen as brigadier general, "Submitted to the Sec. of War. A. LINCOLN," AES, RPB

Dec. 24. To William H. Seward, Nicolay for Lincoln, referring letter of Helen H. Patterson to Lincoln, Dec. 22, 1864, recommending John A. Dix, DNA FS RG 59, Appointments, Box 273

Dec. 24. To James Speed, Nicolay for Lincoln, referring petition of citizens of Maine to Lincoln, July 4, 1864, for pardon of Charles H. Allen, DNA RG 204, U.S. Pardon Atty., A 519

Dec. 24. To James Speed, Nicolay for Lincoln, referring letter of Nathaniel B. Smithers to Lincoln, Dec. 22, 1864, transmitting memorial on behalf of Charles H. Wooster, ibid., A 575

Dec. 24. To Edwin M. Stanton, referring application of Augustus Pleasonton for reappointment in U.S. Cavalry, missing from DNA WR RG 107, Sec. of War Letters Received, P 20

Dec. 24. To Edwin M. Stanton, Nicolay for Lincoln, referring letter of H. G. Tuthill to Lincoln, Dec. 22, 1864, asking pass for sister Anna to come from Columbia, S.C., ibid., P 1203

Dec. 24. To Edwin M. Stanton, referring application for discharge of Benjamin F. Swangel, missing from ibid., P 1204

c. Dec. 24. To Edwin M. Stanton, referring application of Mrs. R. Kellogg for discharge of son Charles, missing from ibid., P 1205

c. Dec. 24. To Edwin M. Stanton, referring application of Ransom Sloat for discharge of George F. Fuller, missing from ibid., P 1208

c. Dec. 24. To Edwin M. Stanton, referring application of Alexander Randall and others for release of Rev. R. H. Phillips, prisoner at Camp Chase, missing from ibid., P 1210 with M 3457

Dec. 24. To Edwin M. Stanton, referring letter of Gov. Joseph A. Gilmore requesting payment of $500,000 due New Hampshire, missing from ibid., P 1215

Dec. 24. To John P. Usher, Nicolay for Lincoln, referring letter of Thomas Ewing to Lincoln, Dec. 14, 1864, recommending Rev. J. W. Ricks, DNA NR RG 48, Supt. of Indian Affairs, Calif., Box 85

Dec. 26. To Richard Delafield, Nicolay for Lincoln, acknowledging receipt of army maps, DNA WR RG 77, Office of Chief of Engineers, P 2032

Dec. 27. To William P. Fessenden, "Hon. Secretary of the Treasury, & oblige him if you consistently can. A. LINCOLN," as printed in Stan. V. Henkels Catalog 1477, Oct. 16, 1930, No. 86a

Dec. 27. To Edwin M. Stanton, requesting papers in case of Lieut. Abraham C. Merritt, missing from DNA WR RG 107, Sec. of War Letters Received, P 1216

c. Dec. 28. To James Speed, Hay for Lincoln, referring letter of Charles Sumner to Lincoln, Dec. 28, 1864, concerning pardon for

William Herbert, Charles C. Stanley and Richard Carther, DNA RG 204, U.S. Pardon Atty., A 559

Dec. 29. To William P. Fessenden, Nicolay for Lincoln, invitation to New Year's Day reception, LS, RPB

Dec. 29. To Edwin M. Stanton, invitation to officers of the Army to New Year's Day reception, DNA WR RG 94, Adj. Gen. Letters Received, P 1502

Dec. 29. To Edwin M. Stanton, referring letter of H. B. Coskery and Arabella Spillman for release of B. H. Richardson, missing from DNA WR RG 107, Sec. of War Letters Received, P 1238

Dec. 30. To John M. Palmer, Nicolay for Lincoln, answering Palmer's letter to Nicolay, Dec. 22, 1864, outlining course satisfactory to Lincoln, DLC-Nicolay Papers

Dec. 30. To William H. Seward, Nicolay for Lincoln, referring petition of John B. Henderson and others to Lincoln, c. Dec. 1864, recommending Benjamin Farrar, DNA FS RG 59, Appointments, Box 283

Dec. 30. To William H. Seward, Nicolay for Lincoln, referring letter of Charles W. Carrigan to Lincoln, Dec. 27, 1864, recommending John McClintock, *ibid.*, Box 335

Dec. 30. To James Speed, Nicolay for Lincoln, referring letter of E. C. Bailey to Nicolay, Dec. 22, 1864, recommending Col. Patrick R. Guiney, DNA RG 60, Papers of Atty. Gen., Appts., New Mexico, Box 660

c. Dec. 30. To Edwin M. Stanton, referring letter of J. A. Stewart asking adjustment of claim for mill burned in Georgia, missing from DNA WR RG 107, Sec. of War Letters Received, P 1243

Dec. 30. To Edwin M. Stanton, Nicolay for Lincoln, referring letter of Mrs. Sarah Anne M. Harding to Lincoln, Dec. 28, 1864, asking release of son Samuel (husband of Belle Boyd), *ibid.*, P 1244

Dec. 30. To Edwin M. Stanton, referring papers of Robert C. Schenck dealing with secret service, missing from *ibid.*, P 1248

c. Dec. 31. To Mrs. Ann Fox, NE, mentioned, Mrs. Fox to Lincoln, Dec. 31, 1864, DLC-RTL

Dec. 31. To William H. Seward, Nicolay for Lincoln, referring letter of William March to Lincoln, Nov. 26, 1864, asking more lucrative consulate, DNA FS RG 59, Appointments, Box 341

c. Dec. 31. To Edwin M. Stanton, referring petition of Executive Committee of Union League of America, for investigation of case of Col. North, missing from DNA WR RG 107, Sec. of War Letters Received, P 1254

Dec. 31. To Edwin M. Stanton, referring affidavits and petitions of T. R. Westbrook to Lincoln, for release of Daniel D. Bell from Ft. Lafayette, missing from *ibid.*, P 1255

Dec. 31. To Edwin M. Stanton, referring letter of Thomas Corwin enclosing papers relative to Levin L. Waters, missing from *ibid.*, P 1256

1865

Jan. 3. To William H. Seward, Nicolay for Lincoln, referring letter of Benjamin F. Loan to Lincoln, Dec. 30, 1864, recommending Benjamin Farrar, DNA FS RG 59, Appointments, Box 283

Jan. 3. To James Speed, Hay for Lincoln, referring letter of Allen A.

Bradford to Lincoln, Dec. 17, 1864, asking pardon for Lorenzo Mais, DNA RG 204, U.S. Pardon Atty., A 579

Jan. 3. To Edwin M. Stanton, Nicolay for Lincoln, referring letter of Mrs. H. C. Hill to Lincoln, Dec. 16, 1864, asking exchange of Capt. William Allabaugh, DNA WR RG 107, Sec. of War Letters Received, P 5

Jan. 4. To James Speed, Nicolay for Lincoln, referring letter of Luther Haven to Lincoln, Dec. 23, 1864, recommending William A. Porter, DNA RG 60, Papers of Atty. Gen., Appts., Illinois, Box 373

Jan. 4. To Edwin M. Stanton, referring letter of R. P. Lowe asking parole of L. Rogan and Thomas A. Hunt, missing from DNA WR RG 107, Sec. of War Letters Received, P 18

c. Jan. 4. Order for pardon of Will A. Winters, NE, mentioned, Winters to Lincoln, Jan. 4, 1865

Jan. 5. Appointment of Charles A. Dana as acting secretary of war, missing from DNA WR RG 107, Sec. of War Letters Received, P 9

Jan. 6. Check to self for $725, DS-P, ISLA

Jan. 7. To Edwin M. Stanton, referring letter of C. G. Hutchinson complaining of swindling by Col. Jones, assistant provost marshal general, missing from DNA WR RG 107, Sec. of War Letters Received, P 40

Jan. 7. To Edwin M. Stanton, Nicolay for Lincoln, referring letter from John P. Franklin to Lincoln, Jan. 5, 1865, for permission to correspond with brother in Texas, *ibid.*, P 41

Jan. 9. To Edwin M. Stanton, referring affidavit of Edward Herbert and Daniel Clark concerning statement of Gov. Thomas G. Pratt of Md., missing from *ibid.*, P 1249

Jan. 10. To Joseph Holt, on court-martial record of Spencer Collinsgrove, "Pardon on condition of re-enlisting for three years. A. LINCOLN," AES, DNA WR RG 153, Judge Adv. Gen., LL 2048

Jan. 10. To James Speed, Nicolay for Lincoln, referring letter of Joseph W. McClurg to Lincoln, Jan. 9, 1865, asking pardon for Harvey Walker, DNA RG 204, U.S. Pardon Atty., A 539

Jan. 11. Permit for Mrs. Burt to visit husband once a week at Rock Island Prison, Anderson Galleries Catalog 2193, Nov. 15, 1927, No. 347

c. Jan. 11. Permit for Maria L. Thompson, NE, mentioned in letter from her to Lincoln, Jan. 11, 1865, DLC-RTL

Jan. 11. To Edwin M. Stanton, Nicolay for Lincoln, referring letter of Lucy A. Barker to Lincoln, Jan. 4, 1865, that government occupies her house in Louisville, Ky., without paying rent, DNA WR RG 107, Sec. of War Letters Received, P 49

c. Jan. 12. To Mrs. Julia A. Chapman, NE, mentioned, Mrs. Chapman to Lincoln, Jan. 12, 1865, concerning her son, Jan. 12, 1865, DLC-RTL

Jan. 12. To Joseph Holt, Nicolay for Lincoln, referring papers in case of John H. Lester, DNA WR RG 153, Judge Adv. Gen., NN 1785

Jan. 12. To Edwin M. Stanton, requesting papers in case of Thomas Clume, missing from DNA WR RG 107, Sec. of War Letters Received, P 75

Jan. 12. To H. A. Swift, Nicolay for Lincoln, concerning petition of Gen. H. Barnes, LS, DNA WR RG 107, Pres. Telegrams, I, 286

Jan. 12. Order for discharge of Harry B. French, on letter from French to Lincoln, Jan. 11, 1865, forgery, AES-P, ISLA

Jan. 13. To James Speed, Nicolay for Lincoln, requesting nominations for Senate, LS, DNA RG 60, Papers of Atty. Gen., Box 137

Jan. 13. To Edwin M. Stanton, referring petition endorsed by John A. Griswold on behalf of Barney Rourke, missing from DNA WR RG 107, Sec. of War Letters Received, P 69

c. Jan. 14. To Edwin M. Stanton, referring petition of R. S. Mathews for pardon of William Reiside, missing from *ibid.*, P 70

Jan. 15. Announcement of death of Edward Everett, Seward for Lincoln, N.Y. *Tribune*, Jan. 16, 1865

Jan. 16. Endorsement pardoning a deserter, AES, Am. Art Assn. Anderson Galleries Catalog, Jan. 20-21, 1937, No. 281

Jan. 16. To James Speed, Nicolay for Lincoln, referring letter of J. Young Scammon to Lincoln, Dec. 30, 1864, recommending William A. Porter, DNA RG 60, Papers of Atty. Gen., Appts., Illinois, Box 373

c. Jan. 16. To Edwin M. Stanton, referring application of Col. R. F. Taylor, missing from DNA WR RG 107, Sec. of War Letters Received, P 80

Jan. 16. To Edwin M. Stanton, referring application for release of Jacob Garrison, missing from *ibid.*, P 92

Jan. 17. To William H. Seward, Hay for Lincoln, referring recommendations of Anthony Ruppaner by Henry Wilson and others to Lincoln, Jan. 1865, DNA FS RG 59, Appointments, Box 375

Jan. 18. To William H. Seward, Nicolay for Lincoln, referring letter of Robert L. Wintersmith to Lincoln, Jan. 12, 1865, recommending son Robert, *ibid.*, Box 405

Jan. 19. To Edwin M. Stanton, referring letter of Rev. Samuel F. Colt recommending camps and schools for Freedmen and Negro soldiers, missing from DNA WR RG 107, Sec. of War Letters Received, P 187

Jan. 19. To Edwin M. Stanton, Nicolay for Lincoln, referring letter of P. V. Merrick to Lincoln, Jan. 12, 1865, concerning relief of distressed in Savannah, Ga., *ibid.*, P 437

c. Jan. 20. To Benjamin W. Brice, NE, mentioned, Brice to Lincoln, Jan. 20, 1865, concerning paymastership for "Mr. Abel," DLC-RTL

Jan. 20. Endorsement on petition signed by Sen. John C. Ten Eyck and citizens of Bloomfield, N.J., "Pardon for unexecuted part of sentence. A. LINCOLN," Chas. F. Heartman Catalog 210, Dec. 7, 1929, No. 109

Jan. 20. To Edwin M. Stanton, Nicolay for Lincoln, referring request of Albert Clark to Lincoln, Jan. 16, 1865, for exchange of brother, Capt. M. S. Clark, DNA WR RG 107, Sec. of War, Misc. Papers, Box 583

Jan. 20. To Edwin M. Stanton, Nicolay for Lincoln, referring letter of W. H. Harding to Lincoln, Jan. 19, 1865, for pass to visit parents in Virginia, *ibid.*, Letters Received, P 134

Jan. 21. To James Speed, Nicolay for Lincoln, referring petition from Pa. legislature to Lincoln, Jan. 19, 1865, for reappointment of Alex Murdoch, DNA RG 60, Papers of Atty. Gen., Appts., Pennsylvania, Box 828

Jan. 21. To Edwin M. Stanton, referring application of Mrs. S. A. Whittier for self and others to come North from Georgia, missing from DNA WR RG 107, Sec. of War Letters Received, P 133

Jan. 21. To Edwin M. Stanton, Nicolay for Lincoln, referring letter of Mrs. Sallie H. Hays to Lincoln, Jan. 15, 1865, for pass to Richmond, Va., *ibid.*, P 140

Jan. 21. To Edwin M. Stanton, Nicolay for Lincoln, referring letter of Phebe W. Woodhull to Lincoln, Oct. 29, 1864, asking pass for mother from S.C. to N.Y., *ibid.*, P 141

Jan. 21. To Edwin M. Stanton, on letter of W. B. Hazen to William Dennison, Nov. 2, 1864, asking help for promotion to major general, "Submitted to the Sec. of War. A. LINCOLN," AES, IHi

c. Jan. 22. To D. M. Leatherman, NE, mentioned, Leatherman to Lincoln, Jan. 28, 1865, DLC-RTL

Jan. 22. To Edwin M. Stanton, referring letter of W. G. Coffin to William P. Dole, Jan. 16, 1865, protesting evacuation of Ft. Smith, and Dole to Usher, Jan. 16, 1865, missing from DNA WR RG 107, Sec. of War Letters Received, P 217

Jan. 23. To Joseph Holt. In addition to the two items printed under this date, fourteen routine endorsements, pardoning, remitting sentence, or denying applications, appear among forty-five court-martial cases reviewed this day, DNA WR RG 153, Judge Adv. Gen., LL 1501, 2175, 2393; MM 1478; NN 98, 1156, 1187, 1191, 1308, 1538, 2260, 2361, 2576, 2627

Jan. 23. To Edwin M. Stanton, Nicolay for Lincoln, referring letter of Thomas W. Dresser to Lincoln, Jan. 16, 1865, asking permission for mother to visit Petersburg, Va., DNA WR RG 107, Sec. of War Letters Received, P 211

Jan. 24. To Joseph Holt, Hay for Lincoln, asking report on case of Cornelius E. Peacher, DNA WR RG 153, Judge Adv. Gen., OO 1188

Jan. 24. To William H. Seward, Nicolay for Lincoln, referring letter of Charles Eliot to Lincoln, Jan. 17, 1865, applying for consulship, DNA FS RG 59, Appointments, Box 280

Jan. 24. To William H. Seward, Nicolay for Lincoln, referring letter of Reuben E. Fenton to Lincoln, Jan. 19, 1865, recommending G. H. Colton Salter, *ibid.*, Box 376

Jan. 24. To James Speed, Nicolay for Lincoln, referring letter of William Thomas to Lincoln, Dec. 13, 1864, recommending Isaac L. Morrison, DNA RG 60, Papers of Atty. Gen., Appts., Illinois, Box 372

Jan. 24. To James Speed, Nicolay for Lincoln, referring application of John Maguire to Lincoln, Nov. 26, 1864, *ibid.*, Appts., Missouri, Box 588

Jan. 24. To James Speed, Nicolay for Lincoln, referring letter of Sec. of the Senate John W. Forney to Lincoln, Jan. 23, 1865, returning nominations and asking whether said offices are vacant, *ibid.*, Box 125

Jan. 24. To Edwin M. Stanton, Nicolay for Lincoln, referring letter of Betsy Tolson to Lincoln, Jan. 8, 1865, asking pass for self and family to return to Texas, DNA WR RG 107, Sec. of War Letters Received, P 173

Jan. 24. To Edwin M. Stanton, referring request of Mrs. A. M. Richards for pay as teacher in school for Negroes in New Orleans, missing from *ibid.*, P 176

Jan. 24. To Edwin M. Stanton, Nicolay for Lincoln, referring letter of Mrs. V. E. Venable to Lincoln, Jan. 15, 1865, *ibid.*, P 210

Jan. 25. To Joseph Holt, thirteen routine endorsements commuting, pardoning, denying application, etc., among thirty court-martial cases reviewed this day, DNA WR RG 153, Judge Adv. Gen., LL 1431, 2626; NN 1362, 1774, 1787, 1887, 2248, 2357, 2427, 2474, 2603, 2677, 3237

Jan. 25. To Edwin M. Stanton, referring application of James M. Suelson (Luelson?) for release from prison at Rock Island, Ill., missing from DNA WR RG 107, Sec. of War Letters Received, P 180

Jan. 25. To Edwin M. Stanton, referring letter of Mrs. A. H. Kincheloe asking return of colored servant, Burt Kincheloe, pressed into service, missing from *ibid.*, P 193

Jan. 25. To Edwin M. Stanton, Nicolay for Lincoln, referring letter of Mrs. Elvira Fisher to Lincoln, Jan. 11, 1865, asking permission to go from Lynchburg, Va. to Kentucky, *ibid.*, P 208

Jan. 25. To Edwin M. Stanton, Nicolay for Lincoln, referring request of Mrs. S. C. Arthurs to Lincoln, Jan. 22, 1865, for exchange of husband, *ibid.*, Misc. Papers, Box 583

Jan. 26. To James R. Gilmore, NE, mentioned, Gilmore to Lincoln, Feb. 2, 1865, DLC-Nicolay Papers

Jan. 26. To William H. Seward, Nicolay for Lincoln, referring letter of William D'Oench to Lincoln, Jan. 20, 1865, applying for consulship, DNA WR RG 59, Appointments, Box 274

Jan. 26. To Edwin M. Stanton, Nicolay for Lincoln, referring protest of John B. Wilgus to Lincoln, Jan. 17, 1865, on change of military policy in Kentucky, DNA WR RG 157, Sec. of War Letters Received, P 235

Jan. 27. To James Speed, Nicolay for Lincoln, requesting Senate resolution concerning vacancies, ALS, DNA RG 60, Papers of Atty. Gen., Box 125

c. Jan. 27. To Edwin M. Stanton, referring petition for discharge of Tobias M. Elliott, missing from DNA WR RG 107, Sec. of War Letters Received, P 207

Jan. 28. To Joseph Holt, on court-martial records of Caleb Mock and William H. Wigginton, "Pardon, for unexecuted part of sentence. A. LINCOLN," AES, DNA WR RG 153, Judge Adv. Gen., NN 1416 and MM 1083

Jan. 30. To James Speed, Nicolay for Lincoln, referring application of James G. Jones to Lincoln, Jan. 21, 1865, DNA RG 60, Papers of Atty. Gen., Appts., Indiana, Box 406

Jan. 30. To James Speed, Nicolay for Lincoln, referring letter of Mrs. George W. Hood asking pardon for husband, DNA RG 204, U.S. Pardon Atty., A 350

Jan. 31. To Edwin M. Stanton, Nicolay for Lincoln, referring letter of George W. Allen to Lincoln, Jan. 20, 1865, asking exchange of Capt. Pace and Lieuts. Pavey and Randall, DNA WR RG 107, Sec. of War Letters Received, P 279

c. Jan. 31. To Edwin M. Stanton, referring letter of Eugene Maring complaining of bounty received for enlistment, missing from *ibid.*, P 251

c. Feb. Permit to Mrs. Elizabeth Gaugan and daughter to come to Maryland, NE, mentioned in letter from her sister Marion Price to Lincoln, Feb. 9, 1865, DLC-RTL

Feb. 1. To John A. Andrew, Nicolay for Lincoln, concerning Thirteenth Amendment, DNA WR RG 107, ALS, Pres. Telegrams, I, 315

Feb. 1. To Richard J. Oglesby, Nicolay for Lincoln, concerning Thirteenth Amendment, ALS, *ibid.*, 317

Feb. 2. Check to John G. Nicolay for $20, DS, owned by Richard F. Lufkin, Boston, Mass.

Feb. 2. To James Speed, Nicolay for Lincoln, referring application of John A. J. Creswell to Lincoln, Jan. 31, 1865, DNA RG 60, Papers of Atty. Gen., Appts., Maryland, Box 528

Feb. 2. To Lorenzo Thomas, Nicolay for Lincoln, referring letter of Gen. Egbert B. Brown concerning false charges against him, DNA WR RG 94, Adj. Gen. Letters Received, P 150

Feb. 5. To Gideon Welles, Frederick W. Seward for Lincoln, form letter calling cabinet meeting for 7 P.M., DLC-Welles Papers

Feb. 6. To James Speed, Nicolay for Lincoln, referring letter of William Thomas to Lincoln, Jan. 24, 1865, recommending Alexander Simpson, DNA RG 60, Papers of Atty. Gen., Appts., Illinois, Box 373

Feb. 6. To James Speed, Nicolay for Lincoln, referring petition of D. J. Morrell and H. A. Boggs to Lincoln, Jan. 31, 1865, for pardon of William Ward, DNA RG 204, U.S. Pardon Atty., A 560

Feb. 6. To James Speed, Nicolay for Lincoln, referring letter of Abram Baldwin Olin to Lincoln, Feb. 1, 1865, asking pardon for Eliza Banks, *ibid.*, A 582

Feb. 7. To James Speed, Nicolay for Lincoln, referring letter of Wilkins Ross to Fernando C. Beaman, Feb. 3, 1865, asking pardon for Thomas Lean, *ibid.*, A 353

Feb. 8. To Mark Hoyt, Nicolay for Lincoln, granting request for interview, DNA WR RG 107, Pres. Telegrams, I, 330

Feb. 8. To James Speed, Nicolay for Lincoln, referring petition for pardon of Isaac Shockley, DNA RG 204, U.S. Pardon Atty., A 447

Feb. 8. To James Speed, Nicolay for Lincoln, referring letter of William Sprague and others recommending Jonathan R. Bullock, DNA RG 60, Papers of Atty. Gen., Box 124

Feb. 8. To Edwin M. Stanton, Nicolay for Lincoln, referring letter of Thomas J. Henderson to Lincoln, Jan. 30, 1865, asking exchange of Lieut. James Griffin, DNA WR RG 107, Sec. of War Letters Received, P 356

Feb. 9. To John A. Andrew, Nicolay for Lincoln, concerning Hugh F. Riley, DNA WR RG 107, Pres. Telegrams, I, 335

Feb. 9. To William H. Seward, Nicolay for Lincoln, referring recommendations of Samuel J. Davis for consul at Cardiff, DNA FS RG 59, Appointments

Feb. 9. To Edwin M. Stanton, Nicolay for Lincoln, referring petition of citizens of Racine, Wis., to Lincoln, Jan. 20, 1865, that rebel prisoners be put under former Union prisoners, etc., DNA WR RG 107, Sec. of War Letters Received, P 330

Feb. 10. To Edwin M. Stanton, referring letter of John P. Birch that brother Joseph C. Birch is illegally held in service, missing from *ibid.*, P 331

Feb. 11. Memorandum attached to petition signed by Baltimore merchants and letter of transmittal by James W. Garrett concerning T. W. Johnson and R. M. Sutton, Chicago Book & Art Auctions Catalog 45, Nov. 27, 1934, No. 134

Feb. 12. To Edwin M. Stanton, on letter of Atwood G. Hobson to Henry Grider, Jan. 27, 1865, asking promotion of Col. William E. Hobson, "Submitted to the Secretary of War. A. LINCOLN," AES, IHi

c. Feb. 13. To Zachariah Chandler, printed invitation from "The President & Mrs. Lincoln," for dinner on Feb. 13, 1865, DLC-Chandler Papers

Feb. 13. To Joseph Holt, Nicolay for Lincoln, referring letter of William Dennison to Lincoln, Feb. 9, 1865, on behalf of Samuel Sterett, DNA WR RG 153, Judge Adv. Gen., MM 1106

Feb. 13. To James Speed, on letter of William A. Buckingham to Lincoln, Jan. 26, 1865, "Col. Nelson L. White, for territorial Judgeship. File—A.L.," AES, RPB

Feb. 13. To Edwin M. Stanton, referring petition of Lieut. John Elliott retired to be placed on active duty, missing from DNA WR RG 107, Sec. of War Letters Received, P 369

Feb. 13. To Edwin M. Stanton, referring application of Andrew Vrooman for discharge of son, missing from *ibid.*, P 371

Feb. 13. To Edwin M. Stanton, referring application of Joseph Hines for draft exemption for son, missing from *ibid.*, P 378

Feb. 13. To Edwin M. Stanton, Nicolay for Lincoln, referring letter of Bridget Lawton to Lincoln, Feb. 4, 1865, asking permission to recover remains of brother William in Georgia, *ibid.*, P 385

Feb. 13. To Edwin M. Stanton, Nicolay for Lincoln, referring letter of Gardiner Tufts to Lincoln, Feb. 11, 1865, asking transportation for discharged men, *ibid.*, P 387

Feb. 13. To Edwin M. Stanton, Nicolay for Lincoln, referring letter of Benjamin E. Grey to Lincoln, Dec. 26, 1864, asking pass for wife and daughter to Kentucky, *ibid.*, P 388

Feb. 13. To Edwin M. Stanton, referring letter of John B. Henderson asking correction of quota for Missouri troops, missing from *ibid.*, P 390

Feb. 14. To James Speed, Nicolay for Lincoln, referring petition of Albert G. Riddle to Lincoln, Feb. 1865, for appointment as district attorney, DNA RG 60, Papers of Atty. Gen., Appts., Dist. of Columbia

Feb. 14. To James Speed, Nicolay for Lincoln, forwarding papers for file, ALS, *ibid.*, Box 125

Feb. 15. To William H. Seward, Nicolay for Lincoln, referring letter of Francis A. Hoffman to Lincoln, Jan. 7, 1865, recommending Emil Ulrici, DNA FS RG 59, Appointments, Box 395

Feb. 15. To Edwin M. Stanton, referring application of Sergt. J. S. Webster for discharge, missing from DNA WR RG 107, Sec. of War Letters Received, P 399

Feb. 15. To Edwin M. Stanton, Nicolay for Lincoln, referring letter of Reuben E. Fenton to Lincoln, Jan. 20, 1865, asking pass for G. W. Yerby to Richmond, *ibid.*, P 496

Feb. 16. Check to Robert Lincoln for $100, DS, owned by Edward Stern, New York City

c. Feb. 17. To Martin Burke, ordering release of Roger A. Pryor, NE, mentioned in Mrs. Roger A. Pryor, *Reminiscences of Peace and War*, 340

c. Feb. 17. To John A. Dix, ordering respite for John Y. Beall, NE, mentioned in Browning's *Diary*, Feb. 17, 1865

Feb. 17. To James Speed, on letter of David Risley to Speed, Feb. 16, 1865, concerning $10,000 draft on S.C. bank attached by government, "Submitted to the Attorney General. A. LINCOLN," AES, DLC-RTL

Feb. 18. Check to "Self" for $761, DS, owned by Richard M. Lederer (Reredel Corp.), New York City

Feb. 20. To Joseph Holt, on court-martial record of Albert E. Griswold, "Pardon. A. LINCOLN," AES, DNA WR RG 153, Judge Adv. Gen., LL 2744

c. Feb. 20. To Edwin M. Stanton, referring petition recommending Brig. Gen. Solomon Meredith for post in Kentucky, missing from DNA WR RG 107, Sec. of War Letters Received, P 449

Feb. 20. To Lorenzo Thomas, referring letter of Maj. A. G. Usher, Feb. 18, 1865, concerning pay of Maj. Joseph M. Bell, missing from DNA WR RG 94, Adj. Gen. Letters Received, P 260

c. Feb. 22. To Edwin M. Stanton, referring letter of Mrs. Julia Stinbach (Steinbach?) asking payment for property taken, missing from DNA WR RG 107, Sec. of War Letters Received, P 467, P 516 (Feb. 24, 1865)

Feb. 23. To "Mr. Diver's soldier friend," sending autograph (also of Mrs. Lincoln), copy, ISLA

Feb. 23. To William H. Seward, Nicolay for Lincoln, referring letter of James Lesley, Jr. to Lincoln, Jan. 28, 1865, applying for position in Paris legation, DNA FS RG 59, Appointments, Box 330

Feb. 23. To James Speed, Nicolay for Lincoln, referring letter of Cyrus M. Allen to Lincoln, Feb. 14, 1865, recommending James G. Jones, DNA RG 60, Papers of Atty. Gen., Appts., Indiana, Box 406

Feb. 23. To James Speed, Nicolay for Lincoln, referring petition of New Mexico citizens to Lincoln, Jan. 2, 1865, protesting appointment of George W. Bowie, *ibid.*, New Mexico, Box 660

Feb. 23. To Edwin M. Stanton, Nicolay for Lincoln, referring letter of John Hogan to Lincoln, Feb. 20, 1865, asking trial or release of Riley Whiting, DNA WR RG 107, Sec. of War Letters Received, P 525

Feb. 23. To Edwin M. Stanton, referring letter of Simon Cameron to Stanton, Feb. 5, 1865, enclosing petition dated Dec. 20, 1864, of Union soldiers in Columbia, S.C., Prison for exchange, missing from *ibid.*, P 527

Feb. 24. To Gustavus V. Fox, Nicolay for Lincoln, replying to request for record of papers relative to David D. Porter's mission to Pensacola, DLC-Nicolay Papers

Feb. 24. To James Speed, Nicolay for Lincoln, referring letter of Hiram P. Bennet to Lincoln, Feb. 22, 1865, recommending Charles L. Armour, DNA RG 60, Papers of Atty. Gen., Appointments, Colorado Territory

c. Feb. 25. To Edwin M. Stanton, referring application of Mrs. E. A. Van Dyke for release of husband, missing from DNA WR RG 107, Sec. of War Letters Received, P 518

Feb. 27. To Mrs. T. Balch, sending autograph, forgery, DS, NN

Feb. 27. To William H. Seward, Nicolay for Lincoln, referring letter of Moses H. Sydenham to Lincoln, Feb. 12, 1865, recommending Alvin Saunders, DNA FS RG 59, Appointments, Box 376

Feb. 27. To James Speed, Nicolay for Lincoln, referring letter of Jacob M. Howard to Lincoln, Feb. 1, 1865, asking pardon for John W. Gibbs, DNA RG 204, U.S. Pardon Atty., A 572

Feb. 27. To Edwin M. Stanton, Nicolay for Lincoln, referring letter of Oliver P. Morton to Lincoln, Jan. 30, 1865, asking pass for Mrs. R. B. Halderman to Shelby Springs, DNA WR RG 107, Sec. of War Letters Received, P 319

Feb. 27. To Edwin M. Stanton, Nicolay for Lincoln, referring letter of Mrs. A. C. James to Lincoln, Jan. 30, 1865, asking permission for daughters to come from Georgia, *ibid.*, P 358

Feb. 27. To Edwin M. Stanton, Nicolay for Lincoln, referring petition of citizens of Albion, N.Y., that Benjamin F. Butler be appointed provost marshal general for South Carolina, *ibid.*, P 562

Feb. 28. To Edwin M. Stanton, referring letter of Capt. John F. Loudon asking relief for people near Ft. Smith, Ark., missing from *ibid.*, P 598

Mar. —. To Mrs. Royston, purported letter, "In the midst of strife it is a comfort to find hearts like yours. I thank you for meeting a brave deed with another. A. LINCOLN." Kansas City, Mo., *Times*, Feb. 12, 1926

c. Mar. To Alfred Onghetten, NE, mentioned, Onghetten to Lincoln, Mar. 11, 1865, concerning exemption of drafted son, DLC-RTL

Mar. 1. To James Speed, Nicolay for Lincoln, referring request of congressmen from Arkansas to Lincoln, Feb. 28, 1865, for appointment of Orville Jennings as U.S. district attorney, DNA RG 60, Papers of Atty. Gen., Box 124

Mar. 1. To James Speed, Nicolay for Lincoln, referring letter of Chilton A. White to Lincoln, Feb. 27, 1865, asking pardon for Henry M. Pickering, DNA RG 204, U.S. Pardon Atty., A 586

Mar. 1. To James Speed, Nicolay for Lincoln, referring request of Abraham McCauley to Lincoln, Feb. 23, 1865, for pardon, *ibid.*, A 555

Mar. 1. To James Speed, Nicolay for Lincoln, introducing Mrs. William Wagener whose husband has been convicted of counterfeiting, ALS, *ibid.*, A 587

Mar. 1. To Edwin M. Stanton, referring request of Henry B. Reese for transfer to Regular Army, missing from DNA WR RG 107, Sec. of War Letters Received, P 589

c. Mar. 1. To Edwin M. Stanton, referring petition of citizens of Frederick Co., Md., levied upon to indemnify Thomas Harris, missing from *ibid.*, P 590

c. Mar. 1. To Edwin M. Stanton, referring statement of Capt. Lewis Todhunter on his examination by board of officers, missing from *ibid.*, P 593

Mar. 1. To Edwin M. Stanton, referring request of Bishop John Mc-Gill to come from Richmond, Va., missing from *ibid.*, P 594

Mar. 1. To Edwin M. Stanton, referring request of Mrs. Mary D. Rogers for discharge of son, missing from *ibid.*, P 599

Mar. 2. To Joseph Holt, Nicolay for Lincoln, referring letter of H. C. Hain to Lincoln, Feb. 27, 1865, asking release of Samuel Williams, DNA WR RG 107, Judge Adv. Gen. Letters Received, A 1109

c. Mar. 2. To Edwin M. Stanton, referring letter of Benjamin Noyes in regard to shipping Canadian horses to Barbados, missing from DNA WR RG 107, Sec. of War Letters Received, P 600

Mar. 2. To Edwin M. Stanton, referring applications of M. Russell Thayer and Robert C. Schenck for reinstatement of William H. D. Hatton as hospital chaplain, missing from *ibid.*, P 605

Mar. 2. To Edwin M. Stanton, referring letter of Peter Pelisan who shot Gen. Benjamin McCulloch, and wants to keep McCulloch's watch, missing from *ibid.*, P 632

Mar. 2. To Edwin M. Stanton, referring application of Newton Crawford for discharge of Eli W. Row, missing from *ibid.*, P 636

Mar. 2. To Edwin M. Stanton, referring request of Mrs. Abram Buford to visit wounded husband, a rebel general, missing from *ibid.*, P 643

Mar. 3. To James Speed, Nicolay for Lincoln, referring recommendations of Francisco Perea and others to Lincoln, Feb. 20, 1865, for Perry C. Brocchus, DNA RG 60, Papers of Atty. Gen., Appts., Colorado Territory

Mar. 3. To Edwin M. Stanton, referring letter of Richard Oglesby introducing William L. Mayo, missing from DNA WR RG 107, Sec. of War Letters Received, P 631

Mar. 3. To Edwin M. Stanton, referring letter of E. M. Young asking permission to take possession of Sheppard House in Nashville, Tenn., missing from *ibid.*, P 638

Mar. 3. To Edwin M. Stanton, referring letter of John M. Broomall for discharge of David M. Roberts, missing from *ibid.*, P 667

Mar. 3. To Silas H. Stringham, NE, mentioned, Stringham to Lincoln, Mar. 6, 1865, acknowledging receipt of congressional resolution, DLC-RTL

Mar. 4. To Joseph Holt, Nicolay for Lincoln, returning report concerning George Maynard, DNA WR RG 153, Judge Adv. Gen., NN 3617

Mar. 6. To Bureau of Engineers, Nicolay for Lincoln, referring letter of Grant to Stanton, Feb. 17, 1865, recommending Reade M. Washington, DNA WR RG 94, U.S. Mil. Acad., 1864, No. 260

Mar. 6. To James Speed, Nicolay for Lincoln, referring letter of William Thomas to Lincoln, Feb. 20, 1865, recommending John Logan, DNA RG 60, Papers of Atty. Gen., Appts., Illinois

Mar. 6. To James Speed, Nicolay for Lincoln, referring petition of citizens of East Tennessee to Lincoln, for appointment of James M. Meek, *ibid.*, Appts., Tennessee

Mar. 6. To Edwin M. Stanton, referring request of W. C. and I. B. Langston for pass to Nashville, Tenn., to recover remains of J. W. Langston, missing from DNA WR RG 107, Sec. of War Letters Received, P 639

Mar. 6. To Edwin M. Stanton, referring letter of George H. Yeaman and Henry Grider that Baptist Church in Bowling Green, Ky., be protected from Army use, missing from *ibid.*, P 644

Mar. 7. Order concerning David A. Newman for trade, DS, Anderson Auction Co. Catalog 518, Feb. 18, 1907, No. 170

Mar. 7. Order concerning Charles M. Simpson for trade, DS, for sale by dealer, 1949

Mar. 7. To John P. Usher, Nicolay for Lincoln, referring petition of F. Hancock and others to Lincoln, for removal of Indian Agent John Loree, DNA NR RG 48, Appts., Indian Agents, Box 72

Mar. 8. To William H. Seward, for sale by dealer, 1949

Mar. 8. To James Speed, Nicolay for Lincoln, withdrawing papers of William E. Robinson, DNA RG 60, Papers of Atty. Gen., Appts., New York-North, Box 690

Mar. 8. To James Speed, Nicolay for Lincoln, referring letter of John W. Forney returning nominations not acted on by Senate, *ibid.*, Box 131

Mar. 8. To Edwin M. Stanton, Nicolay for Lincoln, referring letter of Jeremiah C. Sullivan to Henry S. Lane, Feb. 28, 1865, asking if he is to be mustered out, DNA WR RG 108, H.Q.A., P 353, Box 78

Mar. 8. To Edwin M. Stanton, referring letter of Gen. William Vandever, Feb. 3, 1865, asking promotion of Lt. James S. King, 16th Ill., AES, Carnegie Book Shop Catalog 129, No. 164

Mar. 8. To John P. Usher, Nicolay for Lincoln, referring recommendations of John R. McBride and others to Lincoln, Feb. 1865, for Anson G. Henry, DNA NR RG 48, Appts., Indian Commissioners, Box 53

Mar. 8. To Gideon Welles, Nicolay for Lincoln, referring letter of William Jones to Lincoln, Feb. 27, 1865, protesting injustice done him by Navy Dept., DNA WR NB RG 45, Naval Records, Exec. Letters, No. 173

Mar. 9. To James Harlan, Nicolay for Lincoln, referring letter of Walter D. McIndoe to Lincoln, Mar. 4, 1865, asking appointment of L. E. Webb, DNA NR RG 48, Appts., Indian Agencies, Box 58

Mar. 9. To James Speed, Nicolay for Lincoln, requesting nominations of Henry T. Backus, Alexander W. Baldwin, Edward Irwin and Robert M. Clark, DNA RG 60, Papers of Atty. Gen., Box 124

Mar. 9. To Edwin M. Stanton, referring request of Thomas Troy for pay and discharge, missing from DNA WR RG 107, Sec. of War Letters Received, P 701

Mar. 9. To Edwin M. Stanton, referring letter of J. M. Best on behalf of Gen. Paine, missing from *ibid.*, P 722

c. Mar. 9. To Edwin M. Stanton, referring petition of citizens of Benzinger Township, Pa., for discharge of four drafted men, missing from *ibid.*, P 676

Mar. 9. To John P. Usher, Nicolay for Lincoln, requesting nominations of William T. Howell and DeWitt C. Leach, LS, DNA NR RG 48, Appts., Indian Agencies, Box 64

Mar. 10. To James Speed, Nicolay for Lincoln, referring application of Earl Bill, Mar. 7, 1865, DNA RG 60, Papers of Atty. Gen., Appts., Ohio-North, Box 756

Mar. 10. To Edwin M. Stanton, referring letter of John P. Wilson concerning bond for substitute, missing from DNA WR RG 107, Sec. of War Letters Received, P 704

Mar. 10. To Edwin M. Stanton, referring request of Mrs. M. P. Grinley for pass to Savannah, Ga., missing from *ibid.*, P 711

Mar. 11. To John Sherman, Robert Morrow for Lincoln, regarding interview on Mar. 12, 1865, DLC-Sherman Papers

c. Mar. 11. To Edwin M. Stanton, referring letter of H. Malin Afflick claiming false arrest, missing from DNA WR RG 107, Sec. of War Letters Received, P 693

c. Mar. 11. To Edwin M. Stanton, referring letter of Reuben E. Fenton for discharge of Joseph B. Boyce, missing from *ibid.*, P 705

Mar. 11. To Edwin M. Stanton, referring application of James Selden for exemption from draft, missing from *ibid.*, P 720

Mar. 11. To John P. Usher, Nicolay for Lincoln, requesting nomination reappointing Benjamin M. Trumbull, ALS, DNA NR RG 48, Appts., Land Office, Louisiana, Box 35

Mar. 13. To William H. Seward, Nicolay for Lincoln, referring letter of Edwin D. Morgan recommending Algernon S. Paddock, DNA FS RG 59, Appointments, Box 357

Mar. 13. To Edwin M. Stanton, referring letter of Mrs. Eliza Fryman complaining that her husband (Smith) was drafted without medical examination, missing from DNA WR RG 107, Sec. of War Letters Received, P 721

Mar. 14. To James Speed, Nicolay for Lincoln, referring petition of citizens of Pennsylvania and New Jersey, Mar. 1865, for pardon of Francis Bauer, DNA RG 204, U.S. Pardon Atty., B 2

Mar. 14. To James Speed, Nicolay for Lincoln, referring letter of J. J. Pennal to Lincoln, Mar. 10, 1865, asking pardon for Frank Bowen, *ibid.*

Mar. 14. To Edwin M. Stanton, referring petition for discharge of James A. Waugh, missing from DNA WR RG 107, Sec. of War Letters Received, P 723

Mar. 14. To Edwin M. Stanton, referring petition of Mrs. Catharine Mylacrain for discharge of son William, missing from *ibid.*, P 725

c. Mar. 14. To Edwin M. Stanton, referring application of William Brown at Ft. Delaware, for pardon and permission to enlist, missing from *ibid.*, P 726

Mar. 14. To Edwin M. Stanton, referring application for discharge of Claudius B. Somers, missing from *ibid.*, P 734

Mar. 15. Order for furlough, "Allow this man thirty days time," AES, Am. Art Assn. Anderson Galleries Catalog 4292, Jan. 20-21, 1937, No. 282

Mar. 15. To William H. Seward, on letter of Samuel Shellabarger to Lincoln, Feb. 26, 1865, recommending John C. Miller, "Submitted to the Secretary of State. A.L.," AES, DNA FS RG 59, Appointments, Box 345

Mar. 16. To Joseph Holt, on court-martial record of Wilson B. Kearns (Kerns), "Pardon for unexecuted part of sentence. A. LINCOLN," AES, DNA WR RG 153, Judge Adv. Gen., NN 964

Mar. 16. To Edwin M. Stanton, referring letter of H. G. Jones thanking William D. Kelley for presenting name to President, missing from DNA WR RG 107, Sec. of War Letters Received, P 770

Mar. 17. To James Speed, Nicolay for Lincoln, referring letter of B. M. Dannel to Lincoln, Mar. 4, 1865, asking to be retained in office, DNA RG 60, Papers of Atty. Gen., Appts., Tennessee, Box 886

Mar. 17. To James Speed, Nicolay for Lincoln, referring letter of Richard Yates and others to Lincoln, Feb. 14, 1865, recommending Jesse Bishop, *ibid.*, Territories, General, Box 1111

Mar. 17. To James Speed, Nicolay for Lincoln, referring letter of W. Jones of St. Joseph, Mo., to Lincoln, Mar. 9, 1865, for pardon of William D. Donaldson, DNA RG 204, U.S. Pardon Atty., B 3

Mar. 17. To James Speed, Nicolay for Lincoln, referring letter of Samuel Treat to Lincoln, Mar. 9, 1865, for pardon of Wyman Parker, *ibid.*, B 4

c. Mar. 17. To Edwin M. Stanton, referring application of Martin D. Bates for bounty money, missing from DNA WR RG 107, Sec. of War Letters Received, P 767

Mar. 17. To Edwin M. Stanton, referring request of John N. Williams to visit Culpeper, missing from *ibid.*, P 776

Mar. 18. To Napoleon III, appointment of John Bigelow as minister, copy, DNA FS RG 59, Credences, IV, 426

c. Mar. 18. To Edwin M. Stanton, referring letter of Mrs. C. Farquhar asking refund of fine collected from her husband in Alexandria, Va., missing from DNA WR RG 107, Sec. of War Letters Received, P 769

c. Mar. 18. To Edwin M. Stanton, referring letter of Marcus L. Ward enclosing application for discharge of Thomas Burtchill, missing from *ibid.*, P 774

Mar. 20. To James Harlan, Nicolay for Lincoln, referring letter of James H. Lane to Lincoln, Mar. 11, 1865, concerning nomination of George W. Martin, DNA RG 48, Appts., Land Offices, Junction City, Kans., Box 28

c. Mar. 20. To Edwin M. Stanton, referring request of H. Barnstoff & Co. to ship horses to Santiago, Cuba, missing from DNA WR RG 107, Sec. of War Letters Received, P 770

c. Mar. 20. To Edwin M. Stanton, referring request of Charles Thayer to ship hay to Havana, Cuba, missing from *ibid.*

Mar. 20. To Edwin M. Stanton, referring request of Dr. E. S. Hawkes for expenses to Wilderness battlefield to care for wounded, missing from *ibid.*, P 784

Mar. 21. To James Speed, Hay for Lincoln, referring letter of Hezekiah S. Bundy to Lincoln, Mar. 29, 1865, for pardon of "Barrett" of Pa., convicted of mail robbery, DNA RG 204, U.S. Pardon Atty., B 8

Mar. 21. To John P. Usher, Hay for Lincoln, referring petition of Dakota Territory Republicans to Lincoln, Mar. 20, 1865, recommending James M. Stone, DNA NR RG 48, Applications, Indian Agencies, Misc., Box 1269

Mar. 22. To Joseph Holt, on court-martial record of F. A. Hanford, citizen of Missouri, "Pardon for unexecuted part of sentence. A. LINCOLN," AES, DNA WR RG 153, Judge Adv. Gen., NN 3275

Mar. 22. To William H. Seward, Nicolay for Lincoln, referring letter of Paul Petrément Van de Leuf, Mexico, to Lincoln, Feb. 7, 1865, reporting scheme of ex-Senator William Gwin for emigration from Confederacy, DNA FS RG 59, Appointments, Box 396

c. Mar. 22. To Edwin M. Stanton, referring application of Fred P. Stanton for discharge of two prisoners, missing from DNA WR RG 107, Sec. of War Letters Received, P 804

Mar. 22. To Edwin M. Stanton, referring request of John M. Clay to bring horses from Kentucky, missing from *ibid.*, P 820

c. Mar. 22. To John P. Usher, directing appointment of Arthur A. Denny and Joseph Cushman, missing from DNA NR RG 48, Appts., Land Offices, Olympia, Wash., and Redwood Falls, Minn., Box 37

Mar. 23. To William H. Seward, Nicolay for Lincoln, referring application of John W. Williams to Lincoln, Feb. 7, 1865, DNA FS RG 59, Appointments, Box 403

Mar. 23. To James Speed, Nicolay for Lincoln, referring letter of James Lopinto to Lincoln, Mar. 10, 1865, asking pardon, DNA RG 204, U.S. Pardon Atty., B 5

Mar. 23. To Edwin M. Stanton, Nicolay for Lincoln, referring letter of J. Madison Wells, Mar. 6, 1865, stating as governor of Louisiana he needed military as well as civil power, DLC-Andrew Johnson Papers

Mar. 23. To Edwin M. Stanton, referring request of Philip L. Watson asking return of papers filed with application for appointment, missing from DNA WR RG 107, Sec. of War Letters Received, P 816

c. Mar. 25. To Augustus H. Chapman, NE, mentioned, Chapman to Lincoln, Mar. 25, 1865, concerning acceptance of his resignation, DLC-RTL

Mar. 25. To Joseph Holt, Nicolay for Lincoln, referring letter from Lucinda Maxwell to Lincoln, Mar. 9, 1865, with attached petition for pardon of William Maxwell, DNA RG 204, U.S. Pardon Atty., B 11

Mar. 25. To James Speed, Nicolay for Lincoln, referring petition of citizens of St. Clair County, Mich., to Lincoln, c. Mar. 1865, for pardon of George Curry, *ibid.*, B 7

Mar. 25. To James Speed, Nicolay for Lincoln, referring letter of Thomas N. Stillwell to Lincoln, Mar. 5, 1865, recommending David G. Rose, DNA RG 60, Papers of Atty. Gen., Appts., Indiana, Box 406

c. Mar. 25. To Edwin M. Stanton, referring letter of W. H. DeMott, Indian military agent, enclosing application for discharge of Jonathan Mow, missing from DNA WR RG 107, Sec. of War Letters Received, P 803

c. Mar. 25. To Edwin M. Stanton, referring request of John C. Breckinridge and Salmon P. Chase for exchange of Robert J. Breckinridge, missing from *ibid.*, P 850

c. Mar. 25. To Edwin M. Stanton, referring letter of John Wentworth enclosing application of Nellie K. Gordon to take cotton from Savannah, Ga., missing from *ibid.*, P 851

Mar. 25. To Edwin M. Stanton, referring letter of Baptiste Peoria endorsed by Samuel C. Pomeroy, asking discharge of Jim Wasp, missing from *ibid.*, P 854

Mar. 25. To Edwin M. Stanton, referring letter of J. H. Hickman asking permission to remove remains of Rev. Vincent Hall to Anderson Co., Ky., missing from *ibid.*, P 862

c. Mar. 27. To Edwin M. Stanton, referring letter of Spencer H. C. Dunshee on organizing a bureau for hiring freedmen, missing from *ibid.*, P 856

c. Mar. 27. To Edwin M. Stanton, referring request of J. M. Hubbell, late lieutenant, 5th Ohio, for back pay, missing from *ibid.*, P 859

c. Mar. 28. To Edwin M. Stanton, referring letter of Mrs. Susan S. Grigsby asking permission to go South, missing from *ibid.*, P 860

Mar. 31. To James Speed, Hay for Lincoln, referring petition of citizens of Clayton, Ill., for pardon of William D. Donaldson, DNA RG 204, U.S. Pardon Atty., B 3

Apr. 1. To Alfonso Donn, instruction to bring carriage to arsenal wharf at 8 A.M., Apr. 2, 1865, and remain until Mrs. Lincoln's arrival, Stan. V. Henkels Catalog 1345, Feb. 19, 1924, No. 153

Apr. 1. To Horatio G. Wright, NE, mentioned, Wright to Lincoln, Apr. 1, 1865, concerning military situation, DLC-RTL

Apr. 4. Remarks to Colored People at Richmond Va., purported, Hertz, II, 964, partially excerpted from reminiscence by David D. Porter, "President Lincoln's Entry into Richmond. . . ." *Belford's Magazine*, V (Sept. 1890), 590

Apr. 5. To James Speed, Hay for Lincoln, referring letter of S. H. Johnson to Lincoln, Mar. 31, 1865, asking remission of fine on Thomas Duffy, DNA RG 204, U.S. Pardon Atty., A 576

c. Apr. 5. To Edwin M. Stanton, referring request of Thomas Smelt for discharge of son Stephen, missing from DNA WR RG 107, Sec. of War Letters Received, P 868

Apr. 6. To Edwin M. Stanton, referring letter of Emily Wiltberger asking restoration of property in Savannah, Ga., missing from *ibid.*, P 870

Apr. 7. To John P. Usher, Hay for Lincoln, referring letter of John T. Knox to Lincoln, Dec. 20, 1864, applying for Indian agency for Washington Territory, endorsed by John A. Logan, DNA NR RG 48, Appts., Indian Supts., Box 77

Apr. 10. To Benjamin F. Butler, Hay for Lincoln, making appointment for "tomorrow," ALS, DLC-Butler Papers

Apr. 10. To George P. Floyd, requesting him to attend to a matter concerning Mrs. Lincoln and her brother, purported, Rufus Rockwell Wilson, *Lincoln Among His Friends*, 182

Apr. 10. To John P. Usher, Hay for Lincoln, referring letter of Samuel C. Pomeroy to Lincoln, Mar. 18, 1865, recommending that William P. Dole be continued as Commissioner of Indian Affairs, DNA NR RG 48, Appts., Commissioners of Indian Affairs, Box 53

Apr. 11. To Ulysses S. Grant, Mrs. Lincoln for Lincoln (n.d.), reporting Lincoln ill, but "would be very much pleased to see you this . . . evening . . . & *I* want you to drive . . . with us to see the illumination." ALS, Berkshire Museum, Pittsfield, Mass.

Apr. 11. To James Speed, Hay for Lincoln, referring letter of Schuyler Colfax to Lincoln, Mar. 14, 1864 (1865?), recommending David G. Rose, DNA RG 60, Papers of Atty. Gen., Appts., Indiana, Box 406

Apr. 11. To James Speed, Hay for Lincoln, referring letter of Walter B. Scates to Lincoln, Mar. 25, 1865, declining appointment as chief justice of New Mexico, *ibid.*, New Mexico, Box 660

c. Apr. 12. To Edwin M. Stanton, referring petition for discharge of William G. Zimmer, missing from DNA WR RG 107, Sec. of War Letters Received, P 881

c. Apr. 12. To Edwin M. Stanton, referring application of Elihu B. Washburne for release of Louis Kleine, missing from *ibid.*, P 906

Apr. 13. To Grenville M. Dodge, purported, Dodge, *Personal Recollections,* 27

Apr. 13. Check to "Self" for $800, DS, owned by Union Bank of Commerce, Cleveland

Apr. 13. To James Speed, Hay for Lincoln, referring petition of citizens of New York to Lincoln, c. Apr. 1865, on behalf of Charles Hellerson, DNA RG 204, U.S. Pardon Atty., B 10

c. Apr. 13. To Edwin M. Stanton, referring petition for release of J. W. Thomas and others at Ft. Delaware, missing from DNA WR RG 107, Sec. of War Letters Received, P 936

Apr. 14. Remarks to Sir Frederick A. W. Bruce, purported, Hertz, II, 969-70, with no evidence of Lincoln's composition

Apr. 14. To Schuyler Colfax, concerning message to Western miners, purported, Hertz, II, 967-68

Apr. 14. To William M. Stewart, purported, *Reminiscences of Senator William M. Stewart of Nevada,* 190

UNDATED

Advertisement, "Goods, wares, merchandize . . . ," spurious, AD-P, ISLA

Article XIII, written at end of chapter on Amendments in Furman Sheppard, *The Constitutional Text-Book,* spurious, Hertz, II, 916-17

To the Attorney General, endorsement on petition of N.Y. legislature, Anderson Galleries Catalog 1709, Feb. 13-14, 1923, No. 464

Certification of Reuben M. Benjamin for admission to the bar, NE, mentioned in Elmo Scott Watson, *Illinois Wesleyan Story,* 238n.

To John A. Bingham, "Respy. submitted to Mr. Bingham. A. LINCOLN. March 14, ——," Am. Art Assn. Catalog, May 16, 1915, No. 317

To Simon Cameron, concerning Lieut. Hall, purported, Loyal Legion, D.C., *War Papers 71, a Non Commissioned Officer's Interview with President Lincoln,* 18

Corporations Enthroned, spurious, Hertz, II, 954-55

To George M. Davis, endorsement on Davis to Lincoln, AES, Morley Catalog, May 29, 1942, No. 180

To "Dear Colonel: Let John go home and marry Mary," spurious, Hertz, II, 950

To "Dear Madam," enclose stamp when requesting favor of a reply, purported, *ibid.,* 858

Concerning Betsy Ann Dougherty, purported, Lamon, *Recollections*, 84

Credit report on resident of Springfield, Ill. to New York firm (Dun & Bradstreet?), ". . . rat-hole, which will bear looking into," spurious, Hertz, II, 767

Endorsement, "This I think is a very meritorious case, and especially wish it brought to my attention when the time for action comes. A. LINCOLN," Anderson Galleries Catalog 1583, May 9, 1921, No. 448

Endorsement, on back of letter of Henry J. Raymond recommending Thomas B. Thorpe, *The Collector*, May, 1911, p. 81

To Col. Fielding, purported, Gross, *Lincoln's Own Stories*, 197

To George Glasscock, mentioning purported partnership "on the Sangamon River," probably spurious, Hertz, II, 953-54

To Henry W. Halleck, "Submitted to Gen. Halleck," Am. Art Assn. Anderson Galleries Catalog 3955, Mar. 4, 1932, No. 119

"I hold if the Almighty had ever made a set of men that should do all the eating and none of the work. . .," probably spurious text, copy, ISLA

Inscriptions in William Nielson, *Syntax of the Greek Language* (Deliberate slowly, etc.), purported, Sandburg, *Prairie Years*, I, 415, 419; II, 156

Subscription for repair of Ward H. Lamon's trousers ("I can contribute nothing to the end in view"), purported, *ibid.*, II, 80

To Robert T. Lincoln, concerning postmastership at Cambridge, Mass., purported, Henry S. Huidekoper, *Personal Notes*, 6

To Stephen T. Logan, regarding law examination of Jonathan Birch (". . . good deal smarter than he looks"), purported, Sandburg, *Prairie Years*, II, 72. See *Outlook*, Feb. 11, 1911, p. 311

To George B. McClellan, Anderson Auction Co. Catalog 285, Mar. 22, 1904, No. 91

To Montgomery C. Meigs, concerning Lieut. Hall, purported, Loyal Legion, D.C., *War Papers 71, A Non Commissioned Officer's Interview with President Lincoln*, 18

Notes on law written on flyleaf of *An Introduction to Algebra* by Jeremiah Day (1847), attributed to Lincoln in Barton, *Lincoln*, I, 305, but spurious; original, ICHi

Note, "If the services of this man can be made useful, let him be appointed. A. LINCOLN," Parke-Bernet Catalog 711, Nov. 19, 1945, No. 350

Order concerning Michael Lehman, purported, *Classmate*, Feb. 7, 1920

Order concerning Jesse Macy at request of David Morgan, purported, Oskaloosa, Iowa, *Saturday Globe*, Feb. 12, 1921

To Col. Mulligan, concerning shooting of Barney D——, purported, Allen C. Clark, *Abraham Lincoln in the National Capital*, 50

Order concerning executions, purported, Gross, *Lincoln's Own Stories*, 194

Pardon clipped from attendant papers: "Let this man be pardoned, and given to his parents. A. LINCOLN," AES, owned by Charles W. Olsen, Chicago, Ill.

Poem: copy in Lincoln's autograph of William Knox's "Mortality" (O why should the spirit of mortal be proud?), AD, ORB

Inscription concerning Ann Rutledge in *Kirkham's Grammar*, incorrectly attributed to Lincoln; original, DLC

To Secretary of War, "This will introduce to you James T. Cunningham, a friend of mine. If there is anything you can do for him, I will appreciate it. A. LINCOLN," quoted in Charles H. Coleman, "Lincoln in Coles County," MS (unpublished)

To Secretary of War, "It appears to me that the appointment within recommended would be proper but I refer it to the Secretary of War. A. LINCOLN," offered for sale by Charles Sessler

To Ben Smith, forgery, ALS-P, Manie Morgan, *The New Stars*, 224

Order concerning Job Smith, purported, Curtis, *True Abraham Lincoln*, 294

Speech at Springfield, Ill., "I don't object to being interrupted with sensible questions, but . . . my boisterous friend does not always make inquiries that properly come under that head. . . ," purported, Seitz, *Lincoln*, 42-43

To Edwin M. Stanton, concerning Lieut. Tappan, purported, Curtis, *True Abraham Lincoln*, 223

To Edwin M. Stanton, concerning appointment of a chaplain, purported (probably spurious), Hertz, II, 915-16

To Edwin M. Stanton, "Mrs. —— is a personal friend of mine, and if not very dangerous to the public welfare, I wish you would give her a permit to visit her husband. A. LINCOLN," clipping from *Commercial Gazette*, Jan. 9, 1887, quoting Chicago *Herald*

To Edwin M. Stanton, "Appoint my young friend [Caesar R.] May a captain," purported, clipping from an unidentified newspaper, copy, ISLA

To Edwin M. Stanton, "This woman, dear Stanton, is smarter than she looks to be," spurious, Curtis, *True Abraham Lincoln*, 290

Table of figures, probably of war losses, arranged by date (July 19 through Oct. 5 ——), on War Dept. stationery, and endorsed on verso, "War," AD, DLC-Nicolay Papers

Ten Things You Cannot Do, spurious quotations such as "You cannot bring about prosperity by discouraging thrift," *The Royle Forum* (Paterson, N.J.), Sept. 15, 1943, No. 24, p. 4 (widely copied by other journals). See *Abraham Lincoln Quarterly*, VI (June, 1950), 89-102

Thanksgiving, "the noblest holiday," spurious, *Delineator*, Nov. 1914

To Lorenzo Thomas, about assembling a regiment, City Book Auctions Catalog, Sept. 29, 1945, No. 800

Endorsement on letter of Israel Washburn, Jr. to Hannibal Hamlin about appointment of son as lieutenant, *ibid.*, Dec. 1914, No. 41

To Robert J. Walker, concerning interview with Walker and James R. Gilmore, purported, Sandburg, *War Years*, I, 402

To Gideon Welles, Nicolay for Lincoln, calling cabinet meeting for 8 P.M., Apr. 24, ——, Madigan, *Catalogue of Lincolniana*, 69

To Gideon Welles, "I thank you in the nations name. A. LINCOLN," forgery, AES-P, ISLA

ADDITIONS

Iᴛᴇᴍs received too late for inclusion in their proper chronological order or in Appendix I.

To Joseph Gillespie[1]

Springfield,
Dear Gillespie—   March 29. 1850

I suppose you are well acquainted at Greenville, and attend court there regularly. There are, at or near that place, two brothers, and a brother-in-law, by the names of Richard Briggs, Henry Briggs, and James Bradford. They have a niece here, a near neighbor of mine, by the name of Stout, formerly Huldah Briggs, who thinks they have wronged her in relation to the estates of her grand-father and grand-mother Briggs—and she is resolved to be righted if possible. I doubt not she confidently believes in the justice of her cause; and she has so far convinced me, that I strongly sympathise with her, and intend to not drop the case till I know more about it. She writes them, and they will not answer her— itself a suspicious circumstance. Now I desire you, as a favor to me, when next you are there, to see them, and tell them of this determination of hers, and notify them to do her justice, either by giving her, her own, or taking the small trouble of convincing her, that they have nothing of hers. Generally, find out all you can, in your own way, about the matter, and write the result to Ebenezer Stout, the lady's husband, at this place. Write *him*, because *I* shall be absent on the circuit. The grand-father died in Massachusetts; and the grand-mother in Bond county, whither it is thought she brought effects of her husband, and where she certainly drew a large pension for several years. Whether there was any administration in Bond, of the effects of either, you can readily see.

Please attend to this without failure; and I will do as much, with interest, for you, on demand. Yours as ever   A. Lincoln—

1 ALS, ICHi. See Lincoln's letter to John Tillson, February 15, 1850, *supra* (II, 73).

To Adam Adams[1]

Mr. Adam Adams   Springfield,
Dear Sir: Jany. 19. 1853.

The Judge this morning, decided our case against us. I paid the cost, and took a new trial. It will not be tried again until next summer term. Feeling more than an ordinary interest for you, in this case, it is my opinion, you should be on hand, with your witnesses next summer, so as to get a trial, the record of which, shall be in the best possible form to go to the Supreme court. In addition to what we proved before about possession, I want to get in such circumstances as shall make it almost, or quite certain, that you had no actual notice of Kemper's judgment, when you bought, and took possession of the land. I think it may be important to make this point of *"want of actual notice"* distinctly. When you receive this, let Mr. Bovey know of it. Yours truly　　　　A. LINCOLN—

¹ ALS, Newberry Library, Chicago. See Lincoln's letter to Adam Adams and John Bovey, August 2, 1852, *supra* (II, 133-34).

To A. McKim Dubois¹

A. McKim Dubois　　　　　　Springfield　Nov 13. 1854.

Dear Sir　Our court sets on the 20th Inst. and you will be wanted as a witness in the Illinois College case.² I merely write this to notify you will be wanted. When we fix a day we will give you more particular notice. Yours &c.　　　　A. LINCOLN.

¹ Copy, ISLA. Dubois was a land dealer in Carlinville, Illinois.
² Gilman *et al v.* Hamilton *et al*, involving a trust for Illinois College, Jacksonville, Illinois, appealed from Sangamon County to the Supreme Court of Illinois.

To Simon Cameron¹

Hon. Sec. of War　　　　　　Executive Mansion
My dear Sir:　　　　　　　　July 30. 1861

In addition to those named in my note of yesterday,² please send me nominations, as Brigadier Generals of Volunteers,³ for Ulysses S. Grant, John A. McClernand, and Benjamin M. Prentiss, of Illinois; B　　F. Kelly, and Frederick⁴ W. Lander, of Virginia;⁵ Joseph⁶ Hooker, of California; Edward D. Baker, of Oregon; Siegel, of Missouri; Rufus King, of Wisconsin,⁷ and Thomas W. Sherman, of the regular Army.

You perceive I have only the initials for Kelly & Lander; and no part of the christian names for Hooker & Siegel.⁸ Please fill these in, so far as you have the means, and leave spaces for me to find the rest, which I shall try to do.

And be sure to have the nominations reach me in time to be sent to the Senate to-day.⁹ Yours very truly　　　　A. LINCOLN

¹ ALS-F, ISLA.
² Lincoln had sent to the Senate the nominations of Nathaniel P. Banks, John

A. Dix and Benjamin F. Butler to be major generals as of May 16, 1861.

3 "Lt. Col. Thomas W. Sherman, 5 Art." has been inadvertently inserted (not in Lincoln's handwriting) at this point.

4 "Rederick" filled in (not in Lincoln's handwriting).

5 Lander was from Massachusetts.

6 "Joseph" filled in (not in Lincoln's handwriting).

7 "Rufus King, of Wisconsin" which Lincoln had inserted, has been crossed out.   8 "Siegel" has been crossed out.

9 Thomas W. Sherman, Ulysses S. Grant, John A. McClernand, Benjamin M. Prentiss, Benjamin F. Kelly, Frederick W. Lander, Joseph Hooker, Edward D. Baker, Franz Sigel and Rufus King were appointed brigadier generals of Volunteers as of May 17, 1861.

To Charles Sumner[1]

Hon. Charles Sumner   Executive Mansion,
My dear Sir: Washington, July 21, 1862.

Such representations are made to me as to make me feel that Mr. Holmes can not be permitted to remain as Secretary of New-Mexico. Please drop me a line. Yours very truly

A. LINCOLN.

1 ALS, MH. See John Hay (for Lincoln) to William H. Seward, concerning James H. Holmes, August 2, 1862, *supra*, p. 497.

To Edwin M. Stanton[1]

Submitted to the War Department.   A. LINCOLN
Sep. 2, 1862.

1 Copy, ISLA. Lincoln's endorsement appears on a letter from Isaac N. Arnold, August 29, 1862, concurred in by Elihu B. Washburne, recommending August H. Boyden, treasurer of Cook County, Illinois, for paymaster. Boyden received the appointment.

To Joseph Holt[1]

Executive Mansion
October 27, 1863

The report of the Judge Advocate is approved. Let Capt. C. L. Smith be paid the sum which is in equity due him.

A. LINCOLN.

1 Copy, ISLA. Lincoln's endorsement is on the back of a letter from Judge Advocate General Joseph Holt requesting reinstatement of Captain Charles L. Smith who had been erroneously dismissed from service.

To Samuel L. Casey[1]

Hon. Samuel L. Casey   Executive Mansion,
My dear Sir: Washington, Feb. 8, 1864..
    Please call on the Sec. of State, and Sec. of War, in turn, and
talk with them fully. I have told them you will. Yours truly
                                                            A. LINCOLN

    [1] ALS, owned by Samuel Stager, Cadmus Book Shop, Inc., New York City.
Casey replied: "I have Recd your letter of this date and and (*sic*) will do as you
direct." (DLC-RTL). With Lincoln's letter is an account by Casey's son, George
F. Casey of Greenville, Illinois, May 18, 1928, contending it was Lincoln's plan
to send his father to General E. Kirby Smith, CSA, at Shreveport on the Red
River "to negotiate for the disbanding of his troops, thus releasing . . . forces
under Banks from guard duty" and to purchase "three years' crops of cotton."
Successful in his mission, Casey left for Washington, but at Vicksburg learned
of Banks' expedition up the Red River, and the ultimate destruction of the cotton by the Confederates. See Fred H. Harrington, *Fighting Politician Major
General N. P. Banks* (1948), pp. 161-62; also Lincoln's order of December 14,
1863 and draft of order concerning Casey, February 29, 1864 (VII, 63 and 213-
14, *supra*).

Endorsement[1]

June 3, 1864.
    I shall be obliged if Bishop Simpson of the Methodist Episcopal
Church will perform my part in the above programme.
June 3. 1864   A. LINCOLN

    [1] AES-P, ISLA. Lincoln's endorsement appears below a tentative program for
the opening ceremonies of the Philadelphia Sanitary Fair, June 7, 1864.

Endorsement Concerning Daniel Coyle[1]

December 29, 1864.
If this man's Colonel will say in writing on this sheet that he is
willing to receive him back to his regiment, I will discharge &
send him.   A. LINCOLN
    Dec. 29. 1864.

    [1] Lincoln's endorsement appears on a letter from Daniel Coyle, Company K,
Fifth New York Heavy Artillery, December 26, 1864. Coyle was arrested for
desertion on June 6, 1864, returned to duty during July and August, and tried
by court-martial on November 21. Coyle's letter, written from Old Capitol
Prison, carries no endorsement by "this man's Colonel."

3

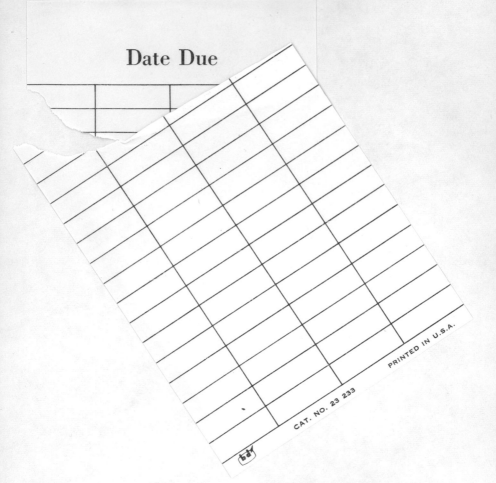

Date Due

CAT. NO. 23 233

PRINTED IN U.S.A.